MW01608847

# Army Detective

Life and Times of Dick Miller
Retired Special Agent US Army Criminal

Dick Miller

First published by Dog Ear Publishing
4011 Vincennes Rd
Indianapolis, IN 46268
www.dogearpublishing.net

ISBN: 978-1-4575-6158-0

This book is printed on acid-free paper.

Printed in the United States of America

To Elda, my lovely wife,
who is the most loyal and understanding
woman I have ever known and son, Chris,
who inspired me to do better.

# CONTENTS

# INTRODUCTION

At birth, I was named Dietzel Morris Miller (my friends, relatives, and professional colleagues call me *Dick* or *Dietz*). I obtained the first name of *Dick* from my mom, who named me after her favorite brother, Dietzel. Dick was my mom's brother's nickname, so I inherited it as well. *Dietz* came along much later in life, when people started referring to me by that name, which was obviously derived from my given first name of Dietzel.

I spent the first fifteen years of my life in Bicknell, Indiana, where I attended elementary school and the first two years of high school. In 1962, my family moved to Terre Haute, Indiana, where I finished high school in 1964. I entered the US Army in 1965 and spent a year in Vietnam. In 1967, after I left the US Army, I entered Indiana State University (ISU) and graduated in 1972 with a bachelor of science degree in criminology with the goal of working in civilian law enforcement. However, in the early '70s, even with a BS degree in criminology, the offers from city, county, and state police departments were few and far between. Thus, to circumvent the usual hiring snags associated with civilian law enforcement, I reentered the US Army in 1972 and became a special agent with the US Army Criminal Investigation Division (CID).

I never considered writing a book. However, after full retirement in August 2011 and almost twenty-five years after I left the US Army, I found that I needed something to do, so I started writing as a way of occupying my time. In late 2014, I began writing this book, which is based on my life and investigative career as a CID special agent. Investigating gruesome, offensive, revolting, and horribly shocking violent crimes can be captivating and stimulating but, not being convinced that a book about my personal and professional experiences would keep the attention of those who choose to read it, I had to create a story that was thought provoking, intriguing, and enjoyable.

The book had to tell a story not only about a career in investigations of felony crime in the US Army between the 1970s and 1990s but also include a detailed account of my personal life as well. The book's ultimate purpose is to tell a story to my son. The manuscript should serve as a historical reference about my early life and lifelong work so that my son can have a better understanding of me as an individual and father. The book should explain to him factors and dynamics that set-in motion events and circumstances surrounding my divorce from his mother and the reasons a US Army investigative career was chosen over civilian law enforcement.

I chose to use an autobiographical story format. The story details my early childhood, struggles through school, obstacles encountered in my first attempt to join the US Army, and the time and undertakings of my first enlistment, including details of a one-year tour in the Vietnam War. The book not only covers my early childhood and US Army career; it's the story of my college years and the circumstances ongoing at the time of my son's birth and our relationship, all the while recognizing that my marriage to his mother was a mistake. The book details my decision to re-enter the US Army after graduating from college to pursue a career as a criminal investigator—a move that ultimately provided me with a second chance at marriage that brought stability in my life.

The fundamentals of a long and productive career as a special agent with the US Army CID and the various types of crimes investigated are chronicled.

Although considered a success, my professional career carried with it some perpetual challenges and disappointments into retirement. It has led to everlasting feelings of irritability, difficulty with concentration, and withdrawing and disconnecting with others. I have insomnia, get startled easily, especially with loud noises, experience constant aches and pains, and have a sense of guilt that I cannot undo actions that affected others. These physical conditions are believed to have been gradually brought on by the constant stress of dealing with the ambiguity of people I dealt with on the job and the frequent exposure of human misery because of the many investigations involving death, rape, sexual assault, and other hideous crimes.

One who is knowledgeable of a US Army CID special agent's work may never consider how twenty-plus years of constant stress affects the special agent's personality. Being a CID special agent is unlike the transitional soldier; a CID special agent's role as a criminal investigator is constant and real in both peace and war. The work is difficult and tedious with moments of exciting, fast-paced activity mixed with relentless pressure to get the job done to the humdrum of boredom.

Promotions led me to advanced positions to supervisory special agent and special agent in charge. These positions brought with them increased responsibilities in leadership and management roles with greater challenges that added to the stress. The many operational decisions on investigative and administrative matters that affected the outcome of investigations along with personnel issues brought additional pressure when dealing with the investigative process and relationships with subordinates, supervisors, commanders, and the people supported.

Difficulties experienced in the performance of my duties and responsibilities triggered traumatic physical, emotional, and psychological feelings that continue to this day. Some of the factors producing these feelings are a result of a hearing loss that occurred during a live-fire training exercise with the M870 shotgun in the CID basic course. This condition often resulted in an inaccurate interpretation of guidance or understanding of what was said. Also, contributing to these feelings is an overwhelming anguish in the repeated handling of personnel issues, constant feelings of frustration in not adequately defending my positions in dealing with superiors, and mainly experiencing the ugliness and horrific nature of the many death investigations.

I experienced an evolving psychological stress brought on by the constant vision of many murdered victims, especially infants in their parents' care, and the feelings of helplessness of not knowing whom to see—or even think you could see—to talk about the way you feel, as well as the effects the images and memories the dead had on my emotions. I show how the job as a special agent with the US Army CID, combined with the demanding and grueling process, only intensified and compounded these concerns. As time went on, to cope, I merely desensitized my feelings, but I never forgot the images and visions stuck in my cognitive thinking of what I saw and felt through the years.

Some of the more memorable cases I either investigated or supervised are provided in an anecdotal history of my criminal investigations; murder, rape, aggravated sexual and physical assaults, thefts, forgeries, and undercover narcotics investigations are highlighted in narrative format. Explanations of the methods and procedures used in conducting these investigations and the management and leadership style used in supervision of subordinates and my dealings with supervisors and investigative managers are covered. Besides providing a historical account of my career and examining the relationships with family, professional colleagues, and others, I offer—in a unique and spirited way—my personal views and thoughts on events, individuals, and situations associated with my career. Sprinkled in the mix are my thoughts, feelings, and philosophies about the people associated with the investigative process. I reveal the true names of some people and discuss their unique personalities and characters. However, for privacy and discretionary reasons, pseudonyms were used for other individuals involved in criminal investigations, personal situations, and for those names that are lost to memory.

# 1

# The Early Years

Where It All Started

Growing Up in Indiana

*My character and values were shaped and influenced
by my upbringing in small-town America*

ased on family research, the beginnings of the Miller clan can be traced to the 1700s. Henry Miller, Dad's great-grandfather, was born in 1799 in the state of Württemberg, city of Baden-Baden, Germany, at the northern foothills of the Black Forest near the Oos River. Henry's wife, Marie, was also born in 1799. They had six boys and a girl. One son was Charles Henry Frederick Miller, born on August 18, 1823, Dad's grandfather. Sometime in the mid-1800s, the family, including Charles, immigrated to the United States and settled in Marion County, near Indianapolis, Indiana. Dad's grandfather Charles had a son named John William Rufus Miller, Dad's father and my grandfather, who was born on March 22, 1863, in Marion County, Indianapolis, Indiana.

Rachel Mariah Houser Hatfield, John's future wife, was born on February 13, 1868, in Greene County, Indiana, near the border of Sullivan County. Her parents were poor, and they had trouble making ends meet. So, as family history indicates, a person named Parke Rusher came into Rachel's life. Rusher and his wife, Jenny, took custody of Rachel when she was about six years old. Around 1878, when Rachel was ten years old, the Rushers, with Rachel in hand, moved to Kansas. In Kansas, Parke ran a ranch with a lot of cattle and horses. Running the ranch became too much for one man, so Parke hired a foreman named Arthur Houser. Rachel and Arthur were immediately smitten with each other, and after a romantic courtship, they were married in June 1885 in Neodesha, Kansas, where Arthur had a small farm. They had two children, Iida May Houser, born in 1886, and Jesse Sylvester Houser, born in 1888. In 1889, Arthur fell ill with typhoid fever and died; Rachel then went to work for a family named Miller in Coffey County, Kansas, taking her two small children with her.

One of the Miller's sons, John William Rufus Miller, was away on a cattle ranch near Kansas City when Rachel started working for the Miller family. John first met Rachel upon his return to the family after the summer roundup was completed. Rachel and John had an instant attraction to each other, which resulted in a romantic relationship. John eventually asked Rachel for her hand in marriage. Thinking the marriage would be good for her and the two young ones, she readily consented, and they were married in September 1889. John and Rachel had their first child, a daughter, Charlotte Matilda (Lottie), born on March 17, 1890, and a son, Albert Clarence, my father, came along on March 23, 1892. As family lore tells it, when Albert, who went by the nickname Bert, was about a year old, the Miller family left Kansas by wagon train and headed east to Sullivan, Indiana, where Rachel bore four more children: Bessie Fern, born November 9, 1894; Emma Louise, born June 5, 1900; Theodore Roosevelt (presumably named after Teddy Roosevelt, our twenty-sixth president of the United States), born June 11, 1902; and Bertha Gertrude, born December 19, 1904.

Dad, as I always called him, grew up in a time and culture where physical strength and hard work, not education, were the means to a job. If you had a paycheck at the end of the week, regardless of how much money you brought home, you were considered successful. Dad only made it to the third grade before dropping out of school. I remember Dad as a thin-haired, almost bald, slender, small-framed man of about five feet six or seven inches tall. He routinely dressed in a shirt, slacks, and a hat with a bill. He was a stubborn, cantankerous fellow that appeared older than his actual years. Some would call him mean spirited, but despite our age differences (he was fifty-four when I was born), we basically got along. I recall sitting for hours on end talking to Dad about everything I could think of. He could come up with an answer to almost every question, and at the time, I thought he was smart. However, in retrospect, a lot of Dad's answers were no more than made up to fit our conversation at the time. He had worked at odd, menial, unskilled jobs that earned low pay with trifling benefits his whole life. His longest stable job was as a coal miner.

On July 31, 1913, Dad married a woman named Bessie May Goodman, who gave birth on January 11, 1914, to a daughter, Hazel Pauline Miller, in Sullivan, Indiana. On January 26, 1914, Bessie May died from possible complications after giving birth to Hazel. Dad could not afford to raise Hazel, so she lived with her mother's relatives in Illinois. Dad remained single for three years, and then he met and married Anna Strahle on March 1, 1917; they had five children—two sons, (John, born on June 5, 1917; Roy, born on October 1, 1926) and three daughters (Nora Mae, born on May 25, 1919; Inez Ruth, born on July 4, 1928; and Rachel, born on June 21, 1930).

On April 30, 1931, tragedy struck the family when a house fire killed Ruth and Roy, and Anna, who was seriously injured, died the following day. The fire started when Anna supposedly threw gasoline into the kitchen stove to heat up an already burning fire, causing everyone in its path to be badly burned. During the fire, Nora grabbed Rachel in her arms, covering her with her chest, and ran from the burning house, essentially saving her life. Dad and John were away from the house at the time of the fire. After this awful unfortunate accident, Dad had to decide on what to do with Rachel.

Knowing he could not devote the time due to work or afford to raise a baby (Rachel was only eleven months old at the time) without a wife around, Dad allowed a family to adopt her. Since John was almost thirteen and Nora about eleven, they stayed with Dad. Despite an age difference of twenty-seven years, Nora and I became close over the years and visited each other quite often. John went on to have a career in the US Army and, after retirement, became a city fireman in Terre Haute, Indiana. John and I were not close. We never visited and did not actually get to know each other well. Rachel stayed close to several family members, primarily June, my biological sister, and she eventually became part of the family again after Dad died, although Rachel was raised in a loving, caring, and comfortable home by her adopted mother, Leora Crispin. I do not think that Rachel ever forgave Dad for letting her be adopted.

Dad quit his job as a coal miner in the early 1950s for health reasons. Because of an injury at work, he was experiencing paralysis in his legs, making it extremely difficult for him to walk. He eventually was confined to a wheelchair to get around. His health problems were compounded with a condition called pneumoconiosis (black lung disease). Pneumoconiosis was caused by breathing in coal dust over a long period. He was about fifty-eight at the time. He was paid a small pension of about $170 and social security disability benefits of $75, for a total of about $245 per month. Even back in the 1950s and early 1960s, $245 did not go far for a family of four.

In the 1950s, the exact dangers of black lung disease were not well understood by the public. However, under the stewardship of John L. Lewis, president of the miners' union, the United Mine Workers of America (UMWA), it was well known that the rapid mechanization of the mining equipment, such as drills, produced more coal dust. Knowing this, Lewis decided not to raise the black lung concern affecting the miners' health, because it might impede the mechanization that was producing greater productivity of coal and creating higher wages for coal miners. The main UMWA priorities at the time were supposedly the health and welfare of the miners and retirement fund of the miners and the higher output of coal. After Lewis died, this opposition was dropped, and the Federal Coal Mine Health and Safety Act (FCMHSA) of 1969 became law. This legislation directed that the coal dust be reduced in mines, and it set up the Black Lung Disability Trust.[1] Dad died before the FCMHSA was signed into law. It's ironic that before the FCMHSA became law, one of the UMWA's priorities was "welfare" of the miners, but it ignored the black lung illness because of the perceived assumption that by not addressing the disease unique to coal miners, it would not interfere with coal production, which increased the mine corporation profits. It is also ironic that after he left the UMWA presidency, Lewis headed the miners' retirement fund until his death in 1969, the year the FCMHSA became law. The black lung disease contributed to Dad's declining health, and just like many thousands like him at the time, their conditions were ignored by the UMWA.

I never felt that Dad's inability to walk played any role in my relationship with him. He smoked a lot and had (even in the 1950s and 1960s) the outdated habit of using Bull Durham tobacco to roll his own cigarettes. He liked to tell whoppers, thinking that people believed the stories he told were true. I accepted him as my father but did not look at him as a role model. In the evenings, I enjoyed sitting around the radio and talking with him while listening to the Saint Louis Cardinals baseball games on radio station KMOX (Saint Louis).

Dad had a strange sense of humor. I recall on one occasion when I was in elementary school, I brought home a report card that showed I was failing most of my classes. Dad said that good grades were not that important, because I did not need an education. After saying this, he told me he was proud of me. Dad never associated education with life employment opportunities. He thought a person did not need an education to succeed in life. Prior to Dad being confined to a wheelchair, he used to walk with a cane. It was not unusual for Dad to go out in the evenings to one of the local nightspots in downtown Bicknell to play poker. His good nights brought maybe ten dollars or so. June and I always knew when he'd had a good night, because he brought home a few candy bars for us. I got along with Dad and enjoyed his presence. His "strange" attitude and unusual, almost indifferent persona never seemed to bother me much. He was what he was!

My parents had few possessions and not much money. Until I was about ten years old, our family rented houses that were heated by potbellied stoves fueled by coal. It was one of my chores to go out to the coal shed located in the backyard to fill several coal buckets with coal and bring them into the house each night. We had no indoor bathroom, nor did we have "unnecessary items," as Dad called them, such as a television or a telephone. During the early years in Bicknell, Mom and Dad moved quite often. When I reached eleven years old, we had already lived in four houses. Of the four houses my parents rented in Bicknell, three have since been torn down, and the fourth is vacant and falling apart. Dad and Mom were never able to put enough money together to buy their own home.

There is only one memory that I had of our family experiencing a lack of comfort. This occurred when I was thirteen, when Dad and Mom rented a house on Bruceville Avenue in Bicknell—the first house we lived in that had an actual indoor bathroom with a shower. Dad, *brilliantly*, decided not to pay an extra few bucks a month for hot water, so we had to shower in cold water. Fortunately, our family only stayed in the house for about six months, mostly in the summer of 1960.

At the time, I did not realize the difficult predicament over money that Dad was placing on Mom. He gave Mom only about $170 per month for living expenses. She always made sure we had food, clothing, shoes, and, on occasion, something special for June and me. I remember that Dad kept about $75 each month in his shirt pocket so he could have personal spending money. This money was so desperately needed by Mom for living expenses. Money became an issue when Dad and Mom rented the last house where we lived in Bicknell, which cost them $120 per month. Since Mom had only about $170 to use, this left her with a whopping $50 each month for living expenses. Mom felt the pressure and was under a lot of stress trying to stretch each dollar to make it last until the next pay-day. Her health started to decline, and she spent a few days in the hospital for exhaustion. The lack of money eventually caused major changes in our family.

Mom, Mary Woodrow Knight, was born at the hospital in Hopkinsville, Kentucky, in 1915. She was the ninth and last child and only daughter to Anna and Guy Knight. My grandmother (Anna Knight) gave Mom her middle name of Woodrow in honor of Woodrow Wilson, who was president at the time of her birth. (What a dirty trick.) When I was born, five of Mom's eight brothers had already died. Those that survived were uncles Robert, Guy, and Ruby. Ruby died when I was about ten years old. Robert died in 1979, and Guy died in 1982. Ruby had been a police officer in Mortons Gap, Kentucky, a small town near Madisonville, where Mom lived until her early twenties. I was impressed that Uncle Ruby was a policeman, and I consistently thought about how exciting it would be to be a policeman. I did not know Ruby well, and I do not recall ever talking to him about police work. However, I guess it was around this time I started thinking about becoming a policeman when I grew up.

Mom was sickly most of her life and suffered from Migraine headaches. She also smoked way too much, but in those days, outside of someone occasionally saying it was a nasty habit, few people spoke or even knew of the ill effects cigarettes had on one's health. She spent her childhood and teen years in Mortons Gap, Kentucky. Mom, like Dad, had quit her education before she got to high school. In her later years, Mom managed to obtain her GED certificate. In her early twenties, she followed her father, Guy, and brother Bob to Bicknell, Indiana, where they had traveled to get work in the coal mines. Grandma Knight eventually joined Grandpa in Bicknell, where they and Uncle Bob lived for the rest of their lives. Mom was a kind, considerate, and thoughtful mother who was dedicated to Dad's welfare. When his condition deteriorated to the point where he was confined to a wheelchair, Mom spent her entire day providing for his personal needs. It became extremely difficult for her to lift him from his chair on the occasions he had to use the bathroom or when he went to bed. She also had to dress him in the morning and get him ready for bed in the evening. Dad suffered in this condition for many years, and the daily care given took a toll on Mom's physical and mental health. I had to assist Mom with the physical aspects of Dad's care, but Mom took it upon herself to do most of it. June was never expected to assist in his physical care.

In the 1950s, Bicknell was a small, thriving farming and coal mining town of about five thousand people. Bicknell hit its height in population in the 1930s, when it peaked at around eight thousand people. Bicknell was named after its founder, John Bicknell, who came to the area in the mid-1860s.[2] At one time, there were five fully operational coal mines in and around Bicknell. I can easily say that most Bicknell's working male population worked at one of the mines. The other men worked on farms. In my younger years, I recall saying to myself, *I never want to work in the coal mines.* The town is now gradually going downhill. As recently as 2013, I drove through the town and was sad to see that a lot of the downtown buildings were either leveled to the ground or boarded up with plywood.

In 1962, the year our family moved from Bicknell, there was a doctor's office, a bank, two grocery stores, two gas stations, a furniture store, a diner, a barbershop, a movie theater, a five-and-dime store, and many other small businesses, all located on Main Street. There was another movie theater, a second barbershop, and a doctor's office with other small businesses located on side streets in downtown Bicknell. Most businesses are gone now, and the population is down to about twenty-nine hundred people.[3]

Mom met Dad when she was waiting on tables at a hotel/restaurant in Bicknell, Indiana, called Pearls, sometime in about 1935. The hotel served as the town's train depot and eating place for travelers and locals as well. Train passengers going through Bicknell to other cities like Indianapolis, Evansville, and Muncie, Indiana, and Chicago in the 1920s, 1930s, and 1940s often stayed overnight before continuing their trip. Dad had moved to Bicknell, located about thirty miles south of Sullivan, a few years prior to meeting Mom. By chance, Dad and Mom's father and brother all worked in the same coal mine—number five—near Bicknell. The relationship between Mom and Dad blossomed, and they were married on February 8, 1939. At the time of their marriage, Dad was forty-seven and Mom was twenty-four. Mom and Dad had two children: my sister June, born on March 14, 1943, and I came along in 1946. Mom told me there was a third child, a boy, that was conceived before June and me, but he died.

I was born at 3:00 a.m. in Good Samaritan Hospital in Vincennes, Indiana, on October 25, 1946. My character and values were shaped and influenced by my upbringing in small-town America. I spent the first fifteen years of my life in

Bicknell, Indiana. My family initially resided at 812 Durbin Street on the south side of town, where I went to South Side Elementary School. When I was seven, our family moved to 409 West Second Street, where I attended West Side Elementary School. I have a memory of Mom bringing a pair of pants with a back pocket into my bedroom on my first day of school. It had been my wish that on my first day of school to wear pants with back pockets, and although the pants had only one back pocket, I was extremely proud of Mom for trying her best to make it happen. I was hardly what you could call a good student, but there were times when I did do well. This was a direct result of Mom helping me with homework. I rarely got promoted in school, but instead was "passed" from grade to grade. From 1960 to 1962, I attended my freshman and sophomore years at Central High School in Bicknell. During these years, we had little money, but our spirits were high. I recall that birthdays and Christmas were happy times. I have memories of having a very warm and excitable feeling at seeing presents under the Christmas tree. I don't know where Mom got the money, but she always made sure that we had a good Christmas with plenty of presents.

Mom was the backbone of the family who always made the house whole. She, more than Dad, had a warm and an accepting personality. Dad was not a bad parent, just indifferent. He never yelled, verbally abused June, Mom, or me, nor did he openly display any affection toward us. Mom and Dad did not use profanity, but there were times and situations when their true feelings for each other were evident. Dad had a habit of sitting on the front and back porches of our home on West Second Street. One day as Dad sat on the back porch in his wheelchair, a thunderstorm with heavy rain and wind suddenly appeared. Mom, without regard for her own safety, ran out to the back porch, grabbed Dad, and got him safely inside the house in the nick of time just before a large limb from a nearby tree fell on the very spot where he was sitting. If Dad had been struck by the tree limb, there was no doubt he would have been seriously hurt or even killed. On another occasion, Mom was working around the house, and Dad pushed his wheelchair up close to where she was standing and gave her a hug for no apparent reason other than to show affection. This was the only time I ever saw the two embracing.

My favorite aunt and uncle, Robert (Mom's brother) and Liza Knight, lived next door to us on West Second Street. Uncle Bob was a coal miner most of his life and a dyed-in-the-wool alcoholic. Uncle Bob had his usual hangovers each Saturday after getting drunk on Friday nights at local bars in Bicknell. Although he had a drinking problem, Uncle Bob was a friendly, easygoing fellow who always was kind to people, especially me. Since our family did not have a TV, I remember going next door to Uncle Bob's on Saturdays during the summers to watch baseball on CBS. We watched and listened to Dizzy Dean, a brash and colorful announcer in the 1960s, who was from Arkansas and himself a former major-league pitcher who won thirty games for the Saint Louis Cardinals in 1934.[4] The team most watched was the New York Yankees. Later, I found out that the reason we watched the Yankees more than other teams was that the Yankees had more money than most other teams in the majors, and they were also one of the most popular teams at the time. On the weekends when we lived next door to Uncle Bob and Aunt Liza, I spent a lot of time playing outside in the yard.

Routinely, when Aunt Liza would see me playing in the yard, she would ask me to run to the local grocery store a couple of blocks away to get milk and eggs for her breakfast. She would give me money for the groceries and usually a nickel or dime as a tip for doing her the favor. One Saturday morning after she had given me money, including my tip, instead of running directly to the store, I continued to play around the yard. She became very impatient and annoyed with me because I was not rushing to the store for her. She scolded me for taking my "sweet old time" and demanded her money back. As I reached out my hand to give her the money, she reminded me that she wanted the tip money as well. I learned a valuable lesson that day. From that day forward, I established this as one of my valuable rules. Rule One: *Focus and timeliness are the best components to success on a job.*

I was a typical kid growing up! I enjoyed playing sandlot baseball in a vacant field in our neighborhood on West Second Street. I ran with kids from the neighborhood. Bruce Lagneau, Ricky Carroll, the Hawkins twins, Robert and Roger, the Messer brothers, Floyd and Bill, and David Trowbridge, who lived down the street several blocks from the neighborhood, made up the main neighborhood gang. But my best friend is still Norman Roark; he did not play sports, was about four years younger than I, and was not a full-fledged member of the gang. In the evenings, you could always find me at Norman's house. His parents, Emily and Norman, sister, Linda, and brother, Aaron, were my surrogate family. I still see Norman and Aaron on occasions when I visit the town of Bicknell, and I have seen Bruce, who lives in Princeton, Indiana, one time since moving from Bicknell in 1962.

The use of the word *gang* to describe the group of neighborhood boys in the day did not mean we were troublemakers. Quite the contrary; we never got into any real trouble, but I could be rambunctious at times. There was one memory I have of Norman and me hiking down the railroad tracks outside of Bicknell one afternoon when we found a large black snake. I managed to pick it up without being bitten, and I recall Norman saying, "That is a big, unhappy snake." Holding the snake's head so it could not bite me, I carried it to Norman's house a couple of miles away. As I stood just outside their back door, he ran in and got his parents to look through the door's window. They did not want anything to do with the black creature and told me to get it out of their yard. I eventually let the snake go.

Norman and I have taken different paths in our lives. He stayed in the old hometown and worked in the residential construction business. He injured his back early in his career and is now on disability.

Between 1956 and 1960, Bruce Lagneau, another close friend, and I were avid baseball card collectors. We anxiously waited for the new series of Topps baseball cards to come out each year. If we only knew, then what we know now—that some of the baseball cards we possessed would be worth thousands of dollars. God only knows what we did with all those baseball cards.

Another activity that I liked in my childhood days was hiking down the railroad tracks outside Bicknell and finding a place to camp for a night or two. David Trowbridge and I built a small one-room cabin out of some old railroad ties we'd found stacked near the train tracks, where we would spend a lot of weekends. One Saturday morning, after David and I had spent Friday night at the cabin, two of our classmates from Bicknell High School were venturing down the train tracks, headed for a strawberry farm a few more miles from our cabin. Their plans were to get a job picking strawberries that day. When they ran into David and me, they decided it would be more fun to spend the day sitting around the cabin with us and doing nothing. We told the two that they were free to use the cabin anytime they wanted but to coordinate with either David or me before hiking out to the cabin.

One Friday evening about a month later, expecting to spend the weekend, David and I set out for the cabin, only to find it had been burn to the ground. We suspected the two classmates had committed the dastardly deed, but we confronted them at school the following Monday, and they both denied the crime. David, I, and, on occasions, Norman continued to hike down the tracks, camping out at various locations we found for another year or so, before I moved to Terre Haute. Those were the good old days. David and I never did found out for sure who had destroyed our cabin.

When I wasn't camping, playing sandlot baseball, or running with the neighborhood gang, I was always giving my older sister June a hard time. June was a pretty, young girl, who was very popular in school and with people in general, like our relatives. She was far more mature than her little brother. One year, June's picture made the front page of the local newspaper, *Bicknell Daily News* for being selected as the school's "Betty Crocker Homemaker" of the year. She had talent and excelled in school. Early in our lives, we used to play games on Saturday mornings, like Monopoly, Chinese checkers, or card games. Some of my fondest memories with June were when we played those games while sharing a bottle of Pepsi. It was a tradition in our family that every time Mom bought some pop, as we called soft drinks in those days, she always purchased one bottle of orange for Dad, two small Cokes for herself, and three bottles of Pepsi for June and me. We were allowed one Pepsi each and shared the third. June was a role model who helped me a lot when I was growing up. Although I am sure that she did not realize it, she encouraged me to do better. Her expectations of my abilities and chances for a successful future, however, were dim considering my immaturity and lack of focus in school as a young boy growing up.

Other than Uncle Bob and Aunt Liza, our relatives lived several miles away. Dad and Mom usually took time to see the Millers in Sullivan and the McAtees in Linton every few weeks. The Miller family consisted of Uncle Ted, Dad's brother, his wife, Aunt Louise, and their eight children: sons Bill, Ernie, Tom, and Roy; and daughters Marge, Evelyn, Midge, and Phyllis. In the McAtee family, there was Hubert and Nora (Dad's oldest daughter from his marriage to Anna Strahle) and their four children: daughters Merilee and Marsha; and sons Wes and John. Hubert was our family's hero from World War II. He originally went into the army as a cook and, in 1944, ended up in England. He often talked about his job in the bakery. "We baked over eight tons of bread every day for the army," Hubert said. In the fall of that year, he got tired of that job, so Hubert and a buddy volunteered for the infantry; they were accepted and attended an infantry school in England. In October 1944, while on his first patrol near Aachen, Germany, with the Eighth Infantry Division, he and his squad members were captured by a small German patrol. Hubert and his squad were temporarily held prisoners by the patrol in a small farmhouse for about an hour. When members of Hubert's unit showed up, the Germans immediately surrendered to the Americans, and Hubert and his squad members were liberated.[5] Soon afterward, he was on patrol when his squad ran into a German patrol supported by a panzer tank. The tank fired its gun and shattered the railcar he was hiding near. He received severe shrapnel wounds to his right shoulder. He spent a month in a Paris hospital before being returned to his unit to fight the rest of the war. The day that Hubert rejoined his unit, he was told that his buddy that volunteered for the infantry with him had been killed two weeks earlier.

We usually saw Dad's sisters and more distant relatives at the annual Miller, Bird, and Schrader family reunion held in either Terre Haute or Sullivan in June of every year. I was too young and immature at the time, so I did not realize that Dad's sisters did not get along with Mom. On rare occasions, aunts Bessie Bird, Lottie Wilmouth, and Dad's half-sister, Ida Brown, would visit, but his other sister, Gertrude Schrader, stayed away. It wasn't until years later that I recognized the animosity Dad's sisters felt for Mom was based on her and Dad's age difference Mom was a real trooper about the ordeal and never let on that their attitudes bothered her.

Aunt Bessie was the only aunt on Dad's side of the family that I ever visited. I stayed with her when she was living in a small house next to Tom Bird (her son) in Dunkirk, Indiana. I stayed two weeks during the summer of 1960. The visit was not a pleasurable one, to say the least. It was the first time I was away from Mom and Dad and was homesick most of the time. Tom's son (Tommy Lee), about a year older than I, spent a little time with me on the farm during that visit. We played in the barn when Tommy Lee was not working, but we never became close. I recall on the first day I was there, Tommy came to Aunt Bessie's house and sat down at the kitchen table to talk with me. About fifteen minutes later his father, Tom, came rushing through the back door to the kitchen and found him sitting at the table. Tom grabbed his son's arm and pulled him out the back door, yelling and screaming at him that he was supposed to be working and not sitting on his ass. Aunt Bessie usually only responded to me after I asked her a question during conversations, but she never talked about anything important. Although I did not particularly enjoy my stay at Aunt Bessie's for those two weeks, I do often think of that trip and how pleased I was with her for allowing me to visit.

In August 1962, the family faced a major crisis due to the lack of money. Mom continued to have problems stretching the money that she received from Dad. Mom decided not to pay the rent to the landlord, but instead used the money to buy food. Apparently, this practice went on for a couple of months until the landlord confronted Mom and Dad about the rent payments. Dad, in his typical style, decided the way to face the problem was to move. That month, we moved to Terre Haute, Indiana, about fifty miles north of Bicknell. The day Mom and Dad moved, I was on a camping trip for a few days at Shakamak State Park, near Jasonville, Indiana, with David Trowbridge. We were into day two of a four-day wildlife adventure when my dad, being driven by Tom Bird, showed up at our campsite and told me, "Get your things. We're moving to Terre Haute."

This caught me completely by surprise. I am glad I did not finish my camp outing and return home to Bicknell. If I had, I would have returned to an empty house.

Dad, Mom, and I moved in with Aunt Bessie, who had relocated back to Terre Haute at her house on Maple Avenue. We soon realized that the house was too small for all of us, so Aunt Bessie moved in with her daughter Mary Fulk and her children—sons, Jerry and Terry, and daughter, Missy—in a different part of the city. June did not initially move with us. Immediately after graduating from Bicknell High School in 1961, June moved to Gary, Indiana, to live with friends. She found a job working in a shoe store and did not move to Terre Haute until later in 1962. Eventually, June joined the family and found a job as a data processing clerk at Columbia Records (an affiliate of CBS) at their facility in Terre Haute. For our social and economic status, it was good employment for the times.

The summer of 1962 was spent getting to know the city of Terre Haute and my relatives who lived there. One of my fondest memories of that summer was hanging out with cousins Jerry and Terry Fulk. Jerry was an established local athletic who was a standout in both baseball and basketball. On one occasion, Jerry, thinking I would not figure it out, claimed that he made the all-star team and was not allowed to play a scheduled baseball game at Spencer Park in Terre Haute. Since I was with him to attend the game, he asked the coaching staff if I could take his place on the team for the game. They allowed me to play second base. I loved baseball and enjoyed playing the game, but I was a long way from becoming a major-league prospect. In four times at bat, I walked and scored a run. My effort in the game was the talk of the evening with Aunt Bessie and the Fulks. We won the game by one run.

In September 1962, I started attending classes at Gerstmeyer Technical High School in Terre Haute, Indiana. I found it extremely tough and challenging to fit in both academically and socially to the new school. I spent my entire junior year of 1962 and a good portion of 1963 at Gerstmeyer with no real friends. I wanted so desperately to go back to my hometown of Bicknell, where my heart wanted to be and friends were. Here I was, fifteen years old and barely passing my courses, having no social life or any real focus for the future. Throughout the entire school year, I struggled academically and socially.

June, who was the smart one in the family, saw my quandary. I know it appeared to her that I was one of those kids that was destined to go nowhere in life. She tried to intervene by buying me a new suit so I would look better on special occasions and tried to get me hooked up with the Indiana Job Corps (IJC). The IJC was an alternative to high school. The IJC was an organization that taught vocational trades to young people that eventually led to blue-collar-type jobs. The targeted group were youths from dysfunctional families, who had not done well academically and showed no promise of a productive life. The candidates frequently dropped out of school and usually got in trouble with the law. IJC students' families often had limited income. The IJC program was initiated on the premise that without organizations like IJC focusing on the troubled youth, the youth's bleak future was assured. I never considered our family being dysfunctional, but nevertheless, I was a good candidate for IJC. I did not want to get involved with the IJC program, however. Every time IJC was mentioned, I would change the subject. June and some other family members felt that since I did not do well in school and was somewhat socially awkward, I was headed down the long path to nowhere and destined for a life of uncertainties.

Not doing well in school, being socially inept, showing a lack of motivation, and having no confidence and a very low esteem were indicators that set the foundation for failure in life. I did not think that my life could get any more pointless, but I was wrong! Before I got on a track to success and developing a purpose in life, I had to overcome much more than social and academic obstacles. Some other family members noticed that I did not display much potential in life. Fern Schultz, Aunt Bessie's daughter, took me aside and had that "you need to grow up someday" talk with me. She wanted to know what my ambitions and goals in life were going to be. She had the notion that I would never graduate from high school. I tried to assure her that I wanted to graduate from high school and find a meaningful job one day. I am not sure she took me seriously, but I have often thought about the day she had that talk with me. I am not sure it had any influence or impact over my future or not, but I always appreciated her efforts. Fern had two sons and was married to a good man named Bill Schultz. Her life was tragically cut short when she died of a heart attack in her late forties.

In late 1962, I struck up a friendship with a Gerstmeyer classmate named Charles (Chuck) B. Holmes. Chuck and I became close friends and ran the streets of Terre Haute until he graduated from high school in June 1963. Neither of us was into drugs, drinking alcohol, or getting into trouble with the law; we were just two young boys that were more interested in instant gratification than initiating long-term commitments in our lives. I still looked up to him as a person who had a positive outlook on life, and I listened to what he had to say. A few months after graduation, Chuck enlisted in the US Army. I would see him when he returned home on leave. I asked him about army life and if he was going to make it a career. He indicated he did not like army life and would be getting out when his hitch was up.

On one of his home leaves before reporting to Germany, I had a conversation with Chuck about if I should go into the army. I told him my high school grades were deplorable and I often played hooky. I told him I was going nowhere fast and felt the army might be a positive change for me. He told me if I wanted to join the army, give it a try. Neither Chuck, who was in the US Army, nor I ever spoke of what was happening in Vietnam in 1963. Vietnam was not yet on the radar screen, not the lead story on nightly newscasts, and most citizens in the United States, outside of Washington, DC, still had not heard of Vietnam. Neither did they have any idea where the country was located on the map. In 1963, I was totally ignorant of the United States' gradual involvement in South Vietnam's conflict with North Vietnam. Although I am loyal to the United States, my desire to try the US Army was not based as much on patriotism as it was on the fact I needed to get a job. Chuck agreed to accompany me to the US Army recruiter at the federal building in downtown Terre Haute, Indiana.

At the recruiting office, the recruiter, a huge, robust individual whose belly hung over his belt, stood up from the chair and, with a stern, almost stoical look on his face, greeted me with a sturdy handshake. I told him I wanted to check out what the US Army had to offer. He started off by giving me his usual gung-ho speech about army life and how serving a tour in the US Army gave individuals a sense of self-respect and purpose in life. He told me that it would be a strong start to a career in almost any field. I thought for a moment and then thought, *wouldn't this be a great way to enter the field of law enforcement by becoming a military policeman!* I continued to listen to him for a few minutes about how good US Army life was for a young man. Back in the day, there were few women in the US Army, but later, that would change. The recruiter then asked me if I had graduated from high school, and I told him no. With his eyes avoiding contact with mine, he said they were recruiting non-high school grads, but it would be harder to pick a field in the US Army without a high school degree. Then he commented that soldiers could easily pick up a high school diploma while in the US Army.

After I had informed the recruiter that I had not graduated from high school, he became less cheerful and not so enthusiastic about selling me the idea of going into the US Army and became taut and direct about my choices about entering the US Army. The recruiter then told me he wanted to give me some tests to home in on the skills I was best suited for. I was given a series of multiple-choice questions about math, folding angles, squares, triangles, and rectangles back into blocks, word problems, and so on. Without understanding how these tests worked, I completed them as fast as I could. I spent the better part of an hour answering these questions, and when all was done, the recruiter told me that I had not done well on the test and could not be further processed for the US Army. What a disappointment it was to have "failed" the army's entrance examination. Chuck, who had waited on me to complete the tests, and I left the recruiter's office, and I was physically and emotionally exhausted. I was extremely depressed, and although I did not know it at the time, by me failing the US Army entrance examination, it was an omen in disguise. As I found out later, things have a way of working out for the best.

After the humiliation at the US Army recruiting office, things in my life pretty much settled into a dull routine. Not surprisingly, my grades never improved, and I still had not set goals and had no aspirations about the future. Things became somewhat worse when two significant events occurred in November and December of 1963 that would affect the rest of my life. On November 22, 1963, a "lone" gunman (per the Warren Commission) named Lee Harvey Oswald assassinated President John F. Kennedy in Dallas, Texas, throwing the country into a national turmoil that changed our country's political landscape for decades. In retrospect, I considered the assassination of Kennedy as a time when our country lost its innocence and was the beginning of the decline of our prestige around the world.

The second thing that happened that altered my direction in life occurred. About a month later, in December 1963, shortly before Christmas, Dad had a stroke, requiring him to have constant care. Mom had pushed the idea of putting him in a nursing home, but his sisters were against it. Eventually, Mom won that round, and we placed Dad in a nursing home near Linton, Indiana. We visited him a couple of times, and except for his activities being restricted to his room, a small lounge area where he could watch television with no privacy, and an occasional venture to the front lawn in his wheelchair to sit by a shade tree, he appeared to be somewhat content. His attitude changed on our second visit to see him. Almost immediately after arriving at the home and exchanging small conversation, he became very adamant when he told Mom, "I want to go home—now."

We took him home to Terre Haute, where his health continued to slowly decline, and he eventually became bedridden. I noticed that his mind was gradually fading and his memory was almost gone. He started talking about things that had happened years earlier as if they were happening in the present. He became confused about where he lived. His mind had him living in Bicknell, and he seemed to have no recollection of residing in Terre Haute. Around Christmastime 1963, the decision was made to place him into a full-service care facility, where he could be watched 24-7.

With most of the money from Dad's retirement going to the cost of the care facility, Mom had virtually none left over. June contributed money for food, but with my job as a dishwasher at Henry's Restaurant bringing in only $26 weekly, I could not match or give much to the family due to my own expenses. With the help of Hubert, my brother-in-law, who cosigned for the loan, I could purchase a 1955 Bel-Air Chevrolet. The payments were costing me about one and a half paychecks each month. With little money, we were very fortunate, however, in that Aunt Bessie allowed us to continue living in her home without paying rent.

The time I spent at my dishwashing job in the evenings, the issue with Dad's health, Mom's financial predicament, and my inability to contribute financially to the household played heavily on my mind. Because of the hours that I spent at my job, I had no time to study. I had no control over Dad's health and was in no way capable of improving the family's finances. These stressors were getting to me. I was giving no attention or time at all to school studies. On rare occasions, I robotically attended classes but was never prepared, and I lost all interest in school.

In early March 1964, my stress became more palpable when the dean of boys at Gerstmeyer, Mr. Fred Heine, called me into his office and counseled me about my poor attendance, failing grades, and lack of enthusiasm for school. Mr. Heine, an understanding and affable man, seemed to want to help students succeed. He was easy to talk to, and he listened intently to what I said. I explained to him that Dad was ill and not expected to live much longer and about the family's financial predicament and the hours that I spent on my job were causing me to put studying a side. Mr. Heine, in a very sympathetic but stern response, informed me that to graduate, I had to make drastic improvements in my grades. I tried to ensure him that I would do my best to improve my grades, but as I walked out of his office, I felt awfully downhearted and miserable. In my emotional state, I was unsure if I could handle my academic dilemma, let alone my personal, economic, and emotional concerns.

On March 21, 1964, a bright and sunny but cool Saturday afternoon, I came home and noticed Mom was getting ready to go somewhere. I asked her where she was going, and she said, "Your dad has taken a turn for the worse, and we [she and Dad's sisters] are going down to see him." As she straightened her dress with her hands and continued to put on her makeup, she turned directly to me, eyes puffy and swollen from crying, and said, "You need to prepare yourself, because your father has taken a turn for the worse." She gave me no time frame on how long she and Dad's sisters would be gone. Almost immediately after she stopped talking, we heard a car horn honking. I watched Mom walk to the waiting car without turning back to look at me, and speaking in a tone louder than normal, she said, "I will call with any news."

On Monday, March 23, 1964, I did not go to school. If the school called, I was prepared to use the excuse that I stayed home, because I was waiting for a call from Mom concerning Dad. However, about 10:00 a.m. that morning, the telephone did ring, but I did not pick up the receiver. Instead of thinking the call may have been from Mom, I assumed the school was calling to find out why I was not there, and I did not want to speak with them.

Around 3:00 p.m., I received another call; this time, I decided to answer it. It was Aunt Ida, who immediately began to scold me about not caring for my father. I told her that I did care about Dad and was very concerned about him. She then blurted out, "Well, are you going to his funeral?" This is how I found out that Dad had died the previous evening. Aunt Ida was having a hard time letting me know that Dad had died. Instead of being compassionate and sympathetic in telling me that he had passed, apparently feeling grief and sadness, she harshly and with a condescending tone in her voice told me that he was dead.

The funeral was on Friday of that week. Dad's sisters got together, without bringing Mom into the discussion, and collectively decided as a group that Dad would be buried next to his first wife, Anna, in a family cemetery outside of Linton, Indiana. This decision started a major rift between me and other family members, especially with Dad's sisters, that has lasted to this day. After the funeral, Mom, June, and I returned to Aunt Bessie's house, where we continued to live rent-free until late 1964.

A strange thing occurred to me on the night we came home from Dad's funeral. No one in the family came to see us that night, and there were no phone calls expressing any condolences; it was just the three of us—Mom, June, and me. We all went to bed early that night, Mom sleeping in her bedroom and June in the second bedroom in the back of the house; I was relegated to the living room couch. A short time after dozing off, something suddenly startled me out of my sleep. I was lying on my side facing the back of the couch, my body sweating profusely. I felt that someone or something was staring at me from behind. It was the most eerily intense feeling of anxiety I had ever experienced. I slowly turned and saw a ghostly figure standing near the door to the kitchen, the face obscured by a hood, with the rest of the body covered in a long white robe. The figure did not speak, but when my eyes locked onto the darkness of the face, it started moving toward me, not walking, but sort of floating in midair toward me, getting closer and closer.

"What do you want?" I shouted.

With nary a sound, the figure kept floating in my direction. Scared out of my wits, I threw a pillow at it, and the figure disappeared right before my eyes.

It took me a few seconds to catch my breath, but I got up and walked the maybe two to three feet to where the figure was before it disappeared. There on the floor was the pillow I had just thrown, but nothing else. I picked up the pillow, which felt damp, like it had just been rained upon. I stood in the place where I'd last seen the figure for a good bit, trying to comprehend what I had just seen, but I couldn't put it together. I felt the area where I'd seen the figure was chillier than the rest of the room. I then realized that it was not only the face I did not see, but as it was floating toward me, I saw no arms or feet—just a body moving slowly and quietly across the living room floor. It would be many years before I ever revealed to anyone what I had seen. I know for a fact that what I saw was not a dream, but real. It is just one of those things in life for which there will never be any resolution, at least in my earthly life. Could it have been my dad trying to tell me something before he passed to the other side? It is odd that I think of this occurrence quite frequently but have not yet made any sense of why it happened and for what reason.

When I went back to school the following Monday, I met with Mr. Heine in his office and informed him that I had been off the previous week due to the death of my father. After giving me his condolences, in a very emphatic manner, he recapped details of our conversation that occurred about two weeks earlier. I told him that since my dad died, that worry was behind me, and I was now in a better position to give my studies the highest priority over everything else. He smiled and offered any assistance I needed. I politely told him that my grades were my responsibility and I should be the one to correct them. Mr. Heine did indicate that he had talked to all my teachers, and they agreed to allow me to catch up on work. I am not sure how I did it, but I passed every class except English. I had enough points to graduate in June 1964 at the early age of seventeen. My ranking was not the best—259 out of 285—but I received my diploma.

On the evening of June 9, 1964, during the graduation ceremony in the auditorium at Indiana State University, as I was shaking his hand while receiving my high school diploma, I still remember the look of pure elation on Mr. Heine's face, and I sensed his satisfaction that one of his wayward students had made it.

Now I had to focus on what was next in my life. After high school, I became an expert at washing dishes in local restaurants. Since my high school grades were marginal at best, I did not have any great desire or motivation or even hope of pursuing college, and I had already tried the US Army without success. So, I spent the rest of 1964 working as a dishwasher at local restaurants like Henry's, Howard Johnson's, and at the cafeteria at Columbia Records, where June worked. All the time, I was contemplating what I was going to do. For a while, June had gotten a second job as a waitress at Howard Johnson's, and we worked well together. During this time, Mom was still grieving for Dad. I had made a couple of friends while working at Howard Johnson's, and we began the routine of riding home together after work.

One of those friends was a cook named Roscoe Jones, who was an orphan at the Glenn Home just a mile down the highway from where we worked at Howard Johnson's, located in the small enclave of East Glenn, Indiana. Roscoe also stayed a couple of nights a week with an aunt in Terre Haute. We would oblige him and take him wherever he wanted to go after work. In the fall of 1964, on one of our rides to his aunt's house in Terre Haute, Roscoe ask me for a personal loan of fifty dollars so he could put it down on a cherry-red 1957 Chrysler Imperial. I told him that I did not make as much money as he did, so how did he expect me to come up with that amount of money? I had seventy-five dollars in my bank account and was somewhat toying with him.

Roscoe told me that the reason he could not come up with the entire fifty dollars was that he had given his aunt fifteen dollars a week out of his paycheck as rent for staying with her a few nights a week. I thought that was admirable for him to do that. After a few minutes of pretending to question the rationality of giving him the money, I told him I would, but I first wanted to know from him what his payback arrangements would be. Roscoe said he would give me twenty dollars a week for two weeks and ten dollars the third week. Without ever considering any interest that should accompany his payback, I accepted. Having full confidence that he would meet the terms of our agreement, I gave him the money the next day. Mom instilled in me a trait that I should trust people based on their word until they proved you wrong. I had a good sense of trust with Roscoe and did not even consider the possibility that he would not repay the loan. Mom's advice proved to be correct in Roscoe's case, because he paid the money in full per our agreement. Although I have not seen Roscoe since our days at Howard Johnson's, I'll always remember him as an honest, trustworthy, and respectful person—the type of person the world should have more of. His actions instilled in me a lifelong rule. Rule Two: *Trust is the most valuable component in dealing with people.*

In November 1964, I quit Howard Johnson's and started to work at the cafeteria at Columbia Records, which provided me a whopping pay raise of eighty-five cents per hour. In early December 1964, just before the Christmas holidays, for no other reason than I just did not want to go to work, I quit my job at the Columbia Records cafeteria. I immediate landed a job working at the Terre Haute Eastside Drive-In Theater near the airport. My main duties were to hand out car heaters used during the winter months. One evening, after I had worked at the drive-in about two weeks, another worker and I were using a flame torch to start the heaters just before passing them to the drivers of cars entering the drive-in. The heaters were the type that hung on the driver-side window of the moviegoers and hopefully would heat the car during the entire playing of the movie, but often we had to replace them when they ran out of gas. We worked in an area inside a framed wooden structure directly behind the screen that showed the movies. On this evening, as the torch was being passed to me, it fell and rolled, with the flame still burning, underneath a wall that supported the movie screen, causing a fire that destroyed the entire movie screen. The wooden frame supporting the movie screen was old and very dry. Thus, the fire spread so fast that the flames consumed the entire structure within seconds. Although we told the manager of the drive-in theater what had happened, it was very strange that neither the coworker nor I were ever interviewed by responding firefighters or police officers at the scene. We also were never interviewed by any insurance company official that inspected the damaged structure. That job did not last very long, and the only job from which you could say I was fired.

During the period between December 1964 and March 1965, I drifted for days on end, where I did absolutely nothing positive with my life. I did not work, nor did I look for work. I slept late and lived on whatever money Mom and June gave me. I was your typical bum with no motivation or purpose in life. One bright note in my life during this period was that I had met and started dating Judy Deal, the daughter of one of my coworkers at Howard Johnson's. Since I did not have a car (the Bel-Air had terminal cancer and was not drivable, but I was still making monthly payments), we always had to use hers. She would pick me up and drive us to wherever we decided to go.

During this time, the Vietnam War was starting to hit the news almost nightly. In August 1964, there was an alleged incident that triggered the United States' direct combat involvement in Vietnam. This incident reportedly occurred when North Vietnamese PT boats allegedly attacked the USS *Maddox,* a United States naval destroyer that was patrolling about four miles off the coast in the Gulf of Tonkin, near Hon Me, North Vietnam. Hon Me was the site of a radar station and home port for North Vietnamese patrol torpedo (PT) boats. The incident has always been shrouded in controversy but did lead to the Gulf of Tonkin Incident Resolution. The Tonkin Resolution essentially gave President Johnson the authority to "take all necessary measures to repel an armed attack against the forces of the United States and to prevent further aggression."

The Tonkin Resolution was almost immediately used to start bombing North Vietnam. Then, on Christmas Eve in December 1964, a car bomb at the Brinks Hotel (Brink Bachelor Officers Quarters [BOQ]) in Saigon that killed two Americans and wounded sixty-five Americans and Vietnamese caused President Johnson to "hint" about sending American combat units to Vietnam.[6] The first ground action as a result of the Tonkin Resolution was used in February 1965, when President Johnson authorized General William Westmoreland to use US forces against the Viet Cong in retaliation to the attack on a US Army base at Pleiku, South Vietnam, that killed eight Americans. By January 1965, the United States had 23,300 US military personnel in Vietnam.[7]

One day in early January 1965, I woke up with the realization that if I did not act to do something with my life, I would end up like my family predicted and expected: I would live a life that was worthless, pointless, and meaningless. With no job or college in my immediate future and living day to day on handouts from Mom and June, I had to decide to do something. I decided to give the US Army another try. If I was fortunate enough to get in, I would at least have a few years with a job making enough money to live on while I decided what direction I would take for the rest of my life.

Before I visited the US Army recruiter again to inquire if I could retake the entrance examination, I had found out that an individual could volunteer for the draft. I thought that this might be a better way of joining the US Army. Being drafted would only require me to spend two years in the military service instead of the normal three years for a person that enlisted. I still went to see the army recruiter again.

A different, more understanding and compassionate recruiter was at the station this time. I explained to him that less than a year earlier I had previously failed the entrance examination for the US Army. Our conversation touched on the topic of the voluntary draft. The standards were lower than enlistment standards, which would mean I had a better chance of getting into the army, he said. Without hesitation, he immediately confirmed that a lot of the young boys opted for the draft instead of enlistments, for a variety of reasons. Since I was only eighteen, I asked how long it would take to be drafted. If I waited for the normal process to take its course, it would take two to three years, because the government was drafting young boys in their early twenties, said the recruiter.

But, the recruiter informed me, if I volunteered for the draft, it might take only a month or less. The recruiter then told me that the draft board was located down the hall on the same floor as his office. I thought for a minute and then asked the recruiter to point the way.

Without further conversation, I left the recruiter's office and walked down the hall to the office of the Terre Haute draft board. I asked the man standing behind the counter what the procedures were to volunteer for the draft. He asked me if I was aware there was a war going on (meaning Vietnam) and if I was sure I wanted to be drafted. I replied, "Yes." He wrote down my address and said, "It's done. A notice from the draft board will be sent to you within a month." I was content when I signed up for the draft.

I went home that afternoon and told Mom, who gave her approval. If Mom had any idea about what the extent of the United States' involvement in Vietnam would become, she would have been against me going into the US Army.

I called Judy and gave her the news. Judy seemed to be okay with it but did not react with much emotion.

On February 10, 1965, I received my draft notice in the mail, directing me to report to the Armed Forces Examining and Entrance Station (AFEES) (as it was called in 1965) in Indianapolis, Indiana, on March 10, 1965. This process was easier and quicker than expected. I said, "I'm in the US Army now," or so I thought!

The author and his big sist-
ger, June- circa 1949

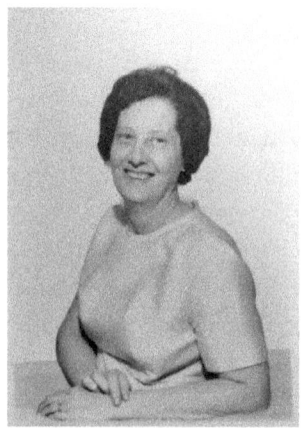

Mom, a great person and
staple of our family, circa
1967.

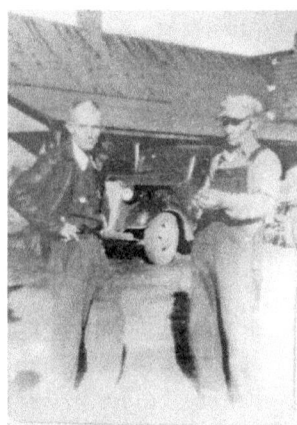

Dad is on the left. talking
with his brother Uncle Ted,
circa 1940s.

Grandma Anna Knight, circa
1930s.

Uncle Guy Knight, circa
1930s.

Uncle Bob Knight, circa
1930s.

My beauiful sister
June, 1961.

Author with his best
buddy Bruce, growing
up in Bicknell, Indi-
ana, circa 1950s.

Uncle Ted and Aunt
Louise, circa 1930s.

Dad with his sisters,
Bessie on right, Lottie
in rear, Gertrude to
his right, and Ida, at a
family reunion in the
early 1960s.

Hubert McAtee, recognized by his family on his ninetieth birthday—2011—a real American hero.

McAtee family, Nora and Hubert McAtee, and kids, Merilee, Marsha, Wes, and John, and their kids, circa 1980s.

Miller family, Evelyn, Marge, Midge, Phyllis, and boys, Roy and Tom, circa early 1990s. *

## 2

# The Awakening Years

Shaping My Persona

Fort Knox

Training Period in the US Army

*The US Army taught me to think, make decisions,*
*to learn, and to set goals in life*

On a chilly morning at 6:00 on March 10, 1965, I left the house and walked the two or so miles to the Terre Haute bus station. Once there, I found and boarded a chartered Greyhound bound for Indianapolis. There were about forty or so other noticeably excited but very nervous souls on the bus. As the bus started to move, a grinding noise could be heard each time the driver shifted gears. The bus driver headed east on Wabash Avenue, and soon we were out of Terre Haute. The seventy-five-mile trip to Indianapolis would take a little over an hour.

As we passed the city limit sign, I felt the emotion swelling up inside me, knowing it would be weeks before I would see Terre Haute and home again. My thoughts were filled with anticipation and anxiety of what was to come.

We arrived at our destination around 8:00 and immediately were ushered from the bus into a huge, cold, dimly lit room that was set up with a lectern in the front of several rows of neatly arranged folding metal chairs. A young soldier appearing to be in his early twenties instructed us to drop our suitcases and personal items that we were carrying next to a wall. Another somewhat older man in an army uniform barked out our names in alphabetical order and directed us to take the next available chair in the row until the last seat was filled, continuing to the other rows of chairs until the last person was called. Once we were all seated, it became eerily quiet. I thought the army guys were efficient in getting a large group of people that did not know each other, had never been together, and were from all walks of life to quickly and orderly move from the bus to the folding chairs in a matter of only a couple of minutes without any trouble.

Suddenly, I was startled out of my wits when I heard someone shout into a microphone, "*Welcome to the US Army!*" The statement came from a third soldier, who was standing in the front of the room near the lectern. The man behind the lectern was a sergeant, who began to tell his audience what to expect the rest of the day. He told me and the others that we were going to receive a complete physical examination and be given a battery of aptitude, skill, English, math, and mechanical tests that would determine our qualifications for our military occupation specialty (MOS).

Once he finished, the sergeant and other soldiers broke us up into groups of ten. The group of ten that I was in was escorted into another smaller room and given physical examinations that took the rest of the morning. We then ate lunch. After lunch, our group received a series of shots. For the rest of the afternoon, we were given written tests. At the end of the day, I was called into the office of the sergeant who had given us the orientation that morning. He told me that I had passed the physical examination but had not done well on the written tests. He further commented that I would have to submit to some additional testing the next morning. I was absolutely devastated with the news.

The army gave me an evening and morning meal ticket for a nearby restaurant and a voucher for a one-night stay at the YMCA down the street from the AFEES. I was then told to report back to them at 8:00 the next morning.

I checked in at the YMCA and headed to the restaurant to eat. I was worried, depressed, and troubled about the events of the day. I hardly ate my meal at the restaurant and spent the rest of the evening walking the city streets of downtown Indianapolis and pondering the possibility that I was not going into the army after all. If I couldn't get into the army, what was I going to do? I had spent the last month anticipating a two-year hitch in the army. For those two years, I would not have to worry about employment. It also gave me time to think and prepare for the future. I had told all my relatives and friends that I was going into the army. Now, based on what the army told me, it was a distinct possibility I would be humiliated to have to face my relatives and friends with the news that I did not qualify for the army. I went back to the YMCA and went to bed, but sleep did not come.

The next morning came quickly. I hurriedly showered and dressed, did not eat breakfast, and reported to the AFEES at precisely 8:00 a.m. I was directed to the same sergeant that had broken the bad news to me the previous day. He escorted me to a private first class (PFC) who administered me another series of tests, which I completed in about two hours. The PFC took my test papers, looked at them and then back at me with a cold stare, and told me to wait until he returned. I sat in this room, isolated from everyone, for about half an hour. Then the PFC came into the room with a grim look on his face. He approached me and said in a low, almost inaudible voice, "Do you really want to go into the army?"

I replied, "Yes!"

He said, "Okay. We'll complete processing your paperwork, and you will be headed for Fort Knox to attend basic training this afternoon."

He sent me to a room that had a lot of reading material and told me to wait until they called me. I was ecstatic! I had no idea what the results of the test were, but from the look on his face, I can imagine the scores could not have been that great. I no longer had to worry about what my friends and relatives would think. My emotions were now running in high gear. I was filled with a great deal of anticipation about what was going to happen next, mixed with a certain degree of apprehension concerning what to expect in basic training.

I waited for about two hours, and then another PFC I had not seen before escorted me to a group of about fifteen people. We were told to raise our right hands, and a military officer standing in front of the group told us to repeat after him, and I stated:

> I, Dietzel Morris Miller, do solemnly swear that I will support and defend the Constitution of the United States against all enemies, foreign and domestic; that I will bear true faith and allegiance to the same; and that I will obey the orders of the president of the United States and the orders of the officers appointed over me, according to regulations and the Uniform Code of Military Justice. So, help me God.

Shortly thereafter, our group was herded to a bus parked, with the engine running, just outside the door to the side of the building. We all boarded the bus to begin the approximate four-hour ride to Fort Knox, Kentucky, to begin army basic training. We arrived at the Fort Knox Reception Station at 11:00 on the evening of March 11, 1965. My life in the US Army had started.

The army did not waste any time to start training its new recruits as they ushered us off the bus, organized us into two columns, and then immediately marched us to a movie theater about a block from where we disembarked. We received another briefing on what to expect in the next few days. After the briefing, we were marched to a nearby barracks and assigned bunks. After settling in, it took about an hour or so to get some much-needed sleep. My first day in the US Army began about 4:30 in the morning on March 12, 1965, when a drill instructor entered our barracks and woke us up by pounding on an empty trash can and yelling for us to get out of bed. That morning would be the last day, for a long time, that I had breakfast in civilian clothes.

After "chow," as they call eating in the US Army, we began our transition into the army by marching in formation to a warehouse-type building a short distance from our barracks, where we received our military-issue clothing. Once we had stored our military clothing in our wall lockers and footlockers, we began in earnest to make the transition from civilian to military life. I realized that the transition became noticeable at the barbershop, where each of us lost all our hair.

Training to be a solider involved a combination of physical, mental, and cultural change. The army wants individual soldiers to think, act, and react as a team. The army requires steadfast loyalty and absolute commitment to the goals of the unit's mission. Commitment and loyalty were instilled in us early on and repeatedly reinforced during basic training. It was the first time that I understood what responsibility was and how it played a role in our lives. Not only did I learn about responsibility, I was taught to be responsible.

I was assigned to Company C, Tenth Battalion, Third Training Regiment (C-10-3) in the older section of Fort Knox. The barracks, which served as my home for the next eight weeks, were two-story wooden buildings built during World War II. Basic training was not easy, especially in the mornings after being awoken from a sound sleep in a warm bed and rushed to get ready for the daily run of several miles in all kinds of weather while most humans were still snuggled in their warm beds and content to sleep for a few more hours.

The army taught people how to lead, respect, trust, and evaluate others and to work as a team. For the first time, I felt like I had a real purpose and was developing a sense of importance in life. The training I received not only made me think about what I was doing but caused me to understand the consequences of my decisions, whether right or wrong. The long hours of mental challenges and physical conditioning brought a new, positive meaning to my life. The army's primary goal is to teach recruits how to become the best soldiers they can be and to work as a team. The secondary effect of the army's teachings allowed individuals to apply the acquired skills in leadership, trust, and responsibility to everyday life.

The eight weeks of basic training proved to be a key time in my life. I was now more positive than negative, looked for solutions instead of complaining, and became more self-confident around people. Not everyone thought the same way as I did. Some trainees felt they did not have to comply with the army's way of doing things. Other complainers cried to either get their way or because they did not see a reason for doing with they were told. To this day, I can recall a few of the members of my basic training unit complaining about the early mornings, lack of sleep, long hours, the harassment by drill sergeants, being homesick, and in general wondering why they had to go through the agony. The complaint group usually consisted of the draftees. A bunch of the folks were army reservists and National Guardsman, who joined their reserve and guard units in hopes of avoiding service in Vietnam. The real army enlistees generally did not complain much. I could understand the draftees complaining, but the others were volunteers with little or no reason to. Yet those that did not follow guidance or continued to think as individuals and not as a team were singled out by the drill instructors for extra training and in the correct ways of being a soldier.

One incident involved a draftee who had trouble or simply refused to properly make up his bunk in the mornings. He did not listen to fellow recruits who tried to help him. He was always being criticized during morning inspections for his lack of compliance. He continually kept up this practice each morning until he was singled out by our platoon drill instructor for enhanced retraining on how to make up his bunk. He was ordered to carry his bunk to the courtyard just outside the front door of the barracks, where every unit member could watch him. Once there, the recruit was ordered to properly make up his bunk twenty times. If he failed to make his bunk up to military standards, he had to tear the bed linens off and start over. Each improper attempt did not count as part of his twenty. Once this exercise was complete, the recruit never again had a problem making up his bunk.

A second incident occurred before basic training started. One of the recruits from Cleveland, Ohio, missed formation on the first morning at the reception station and attempted to go absent without leave (AWOL). He was located and returned to our group at the reception station. Since the individual happened to be my lower bunkmate, I was assigned to monitor him (my first official duty). I could keep him occupied by going to the movies in our free time and talking to him while we were in the barracks for about four days, but when we arrived at our basic training company, he was assigned to a different barracks. Somehow the platoon sergeant found out about this recruit missing formation at the reception station and that I was assigned to watch him. So, the platoon sergeant told me to continue watching him. I was never told how long this assignment was going to last.

To add to my frustration for having to watch this recruit, our company commander, Second Lieutenant (2LT) David L. Bowman, reported in his orientation speech to the new recruits that no one from his unit had gone AWOL since he'd become company commander. He never told us how long he had been company commander. He also had put out the word that he would not tolerate anyone going AWOL and that all recruits were responsible for reporting anyone who threatened to go AWOL and to do their best to try to prevent recruits from going AWOL. As fate, would have it, the very next morning, we were told by our platoon sergeant that a recruit (my ward) had taken off to parts unknown. The AWOL recruit was never seen again. Although circumstances prevented me from watching him that first night, mainly because we were in different barracks, I was the only one singled out as having failed my assignment to ensure that he did not take off. Subsequently, I had to do extra work around the barracks for the first week to make amends for my shortcomings. Therein lies another valuable rule. Rule Three: *You must find ways to accomplish even the most challenging tasks.*

Judy wrote infrequently, but reading her letters and getting caught up on what was happening in Terre Haute, Indiana, appeared to make time go faster. I called Mom each Sunday, and it felt good to hear her voice and talk to her a little, which ensured me that she was okay. During one of our telephone conversations, Mom told me that a nice fellow named Roscoe had stopped by her apartment and had given her a ten-dollar bill, telling her that it was the last payment owed to me for a loan I had provided him to help make a down payment on car. So, Roscoe was a little late with his last payment, but he still came through with what he promised. Mom's actions were a testament to her sincerity in trusting and treating people impartially and with respect. I thanked her and told her to keep the money.

As time passed, the training became more intense and focused on the mechanics of learning to be a soldier. We marched everywhere—to rifle ranges, to bivouac sites, and to isolated areas where we had to make our own way back to certain points by using our land compasses and maps to navigate to predesignated locations. There were times when I forgot what it was like to sleep in a bed under a roof. We experienced better weather in the latter part of our training due to it being the start of spring. Toward the end of training, the drill instructors started emphasizing that we had to pass a physical fitness test and soldier skills test to graduate from basic training. The drill instructors kept referring to area C41, which was the name of the soldier skills test site.

Every time a trainee failed to properly execute or follow through on a drill sergeant's orders or training instructions, he was reminded that if he made the same mistake at area C41, he would be recycled. Being recycled meant one of two things: you either flunked the training, or an injury prevented you from participating in the training. Either way, you had to repeat that training session again before graduating.

About six weeks into our training, the true meaning of what we were there for became more apparent and relevant than at any other time, when our commander, 2LT Bowman, announced to the company that he had just received orders for Vietnam. He advised us to put any doubts about why we were training recruits to fight in combat out of our minds. He said that our training was real and each one of us faced the possibility of going to war. Other cadres had talked about the possibility of war, but it was not until this point that we had a direct association or connection with Vietnam. We now knew an individual and could put a face to someone going to Vietnam.

The training wound down, and almost everyone passed the final tests held at area C41. There were a few fellows who were injured and could not complete the training, and two guys outright failed the soldiering skills tests. They were recycled and not seen again.

Within days of graduation, most of us received word of our assignments to advanced individual training (AIT). I was assigned to a supply military occupational specialty (MOS) at Fort Leonard Wood, Missouri, with a reporting date of June 15, 1965. Since I had volunteered for the US Army as a draftee, my choice to become a military policeman was thrown out the window, and I had to accept any job they decided to give me. The army gave me a two-week leave before reporting.

I spent the two weeks with Judy and Mom. Judy and I got to know each other a little better, but I did not detect any real sense of worry from her that I was going to be away for a while and might be sent to Vietnam. I also spent time at Mom's small apartment. Conversations Mom and I had over the two weeks I was at home, she voiced her worry about me going to Vietnam. I told Mom that I was going to receive training in the supply field and I might not even go to Vietnam, but if I did, I would not be on the front lines. This did not seem to appease her much. (Unbeknownst to me, I later learned that it was hard to distinguish where the front lines would be.) The time went extremely fast, and before I knew it, the time to report to Fort Leonard Wood arrived. I said my good-byes and boarded a bus for Fort Lost in the Woods, Missouri. No one was at the bus station to see me off.

On June 15, 1965, I reported to the reception station at Fort Leonard Wood, Missouri. The post is located near the Ozarks, just off Highway 66 (Interstate 44, which passes directly by one of the main gates of Fort Leonard Wood, had not been completed in 1965) near the small communities of Saint Roberts and Waynesville, in Pulaski County, Missouri. The post was named after Major General Leonard Wood, a physician who'd served as army chief of staff, the military governor of Cuba, and governor general of the Philippines.[8] It took about a day for processing at the reception station, and I was than assigned to my AIT company the next morning.

In 1965, the post still had an abundance of World War II–era buildings that were being used for office space, sleeping quarters, and storage facilities. When I reported to the AIT company, the drill sergeants were friendly, cordial, and not as forceful as those I had encountered in basic training. The basic training drill sergeants could be your best friend or worst enemy, depending on the situation; in comparison, our AIT drill sergeants appeared to be more human, caring, and patient. Since the training focused on supply, we were taught the basic process of equipment maintenance, first-echelon repair, and serviceability of army equipment. As the supply school proceeded into the latter weeks, we were taught the basics of acquisition and accountability. The supply course, which lasted six weeks, was primarily geared toward company-level supply. One sergeant first class (SFC) advised our class that to be picked for training in the supply MOS, you had to either score very high or very low on the general technical skills tests taken at the reception station.

About two weeks before completing the supply training, I found time on one weekend to visit Terre Haute. The bus ride ate up about eight hours of time due to the route requiring us to drop off and pick up passengers in various cities and towns along the way, causing me not to arrive in Terre Haute until after midnight on a Friday. On the trip to Terre Haute, while passing through Saint Louis, I saw the Saint Louis Arch while it was being built. The two sides independently reached into the sky, forming an incomplete arch had not yet been joined at the top. It was an awesome sight to see it in its uncompleted stage of construction. For almost fifty years since being completed, the Saint Louis Arch has been identified as the Gateway to the West and a must-see site for vacationers—one of the most viewed sites in our country.

I did not visit with Judy on that weekend, but I went to see Mom, who had moved into a room in a house on Chestnut Street in Terre Haute. I found Mom doing well, in good spirits, and healthy. I ate well that weekend and was sorry to have to say good-bye to her, whose company I thoroughly enjoyed. On my return trip, I flew in my first airplane from Terre Haute to Saint Louis, Missouri, and caught a bus from Saint Louis to Waynesville, Missouri.

Upon graduation from the supply school, about half of our class, totaling about twenty soldiers, received orders for Vietnam. Others were sent to installations throughout the States. I was one of only five who did not receive orders after graduating from the supply school. The five of us had no idea where we were going to be sent!

A few days after graduation, the first sergeant called me and one of the other guys into his office and asked if we would be interested in doing administrative work in the orderly room until our orders came in. Since I was bored doing almost nothing, I quickly agreed; the other person followed suit and accepted the assignment. Although I would never have imaged it, the decision to accept part-time employment as a company clerk had a very distinct and everlasting positive impact on how my early army career would take shape. I relished this assignment because it was the first job I'd ever had where I could use my own initiative, be creative, and be resourceful in handling situations and solving problems. Immediately, I began to tackle the administrative duties with an earnest, extremely enthusiastic excitement.

I graduated from supply school in late June 1965 and continued to be assigned to my AIT unit until the middle of September 1965 without orders for any permanent duty assignment. In July 1965, I was promoted to private second class (PV2). My work as a company clerk was praised by the primary assigned company clerk and the first sergeant. There was some talk about trying to get permanent orders assigning me to the company, but nothing ever came of it.

In the meantime, the Vietnam War was heating up. In May 1965, the first combat troops assigned to the 173rd Airborne Brigade arrived in Vietnam. At the end of July 1965, the 101st Airborne Division joined them in Vietnam, followed in September 1965 by the First Cavalry Division (Airmobile), and the buildup of combat troops continued.[9]

I was getting remarkably comfortable in my job when the inevitable finally happened. I received orders not to Vietnam but to Fort Bragg, North Carolina. I was scheduled to report to the Ninety-Second Chemical Company, Fort Bragg, North Carolina, on September 23, 1965. I had only a few days to clear up any personal matters and process out of Fort Leonard Wood. It took me another two days by train on the army's dime to reach Fort Bragg. The army saw fit to give me a sleeping berth, so the trip was smooth and relevantly relaxing.

Fort Bragg, named after Confederate general Braxton Bragg, was established in 1918[10] It is one of the largest army installations in American and home to the Eighty-Second Airborne Division, XVIII Airborne Corps, and the Special Operations Forces. I arrived at the Fort Bragg reception station on the morning of September 23, 1965. Personnel wasted no time in shipping me to the old division part of the post, where the unit was nestled in a small village of old World War II–type buildings. The battalion headquarters of the Ninety-Second Chemical Company was separated from the platoon, supply, dayroom, and orderly room buildings by a parade field. After processing through personnel, finance, and supply, I was assigned as a supply clerk in the chemical mask platoon. My principle duties involved preparing documents that established a paper trail that documented the intake, maintenance, and return to unit of repaired gas masks. Our platoon was responsible for ensuring that all members of units at Fort Bragg had a functional gas mask.

When I arrived at the unit, part of the platoon I was assigned to was temporarily assigned (TDY) to the Dominican Republic, providing direct combat support to the Eighty-Second Airborne Division in Operation Power Pack. On May 1, 1965, most of the Eighty-Second Airborne Division and its parent, the XVIII Airborne Corps, joined the United States Marine Corps, who had arrived in the Dominican Republic a few days before. For several years, the government of the Dominican Republic, politically and economically unstable, was experiencing internal strife from armed rebels over leadership, and the United States feared the Communist influence might lead to another Cuba. Based on this situation, President Lyndon B. Johnson ordered US forces to restore order. Armed conflict lasted a few months until both sides called a truce in September 1965.

During the armed conflict, there were 44 American soldiers killed, (none from the Ninety-Second Chemical Company), 27 in action, and 172 wounded.[11]

My platoon sergeant had informed me when I first arrived that there was a good possibility that I may be sent TDY to the Dominican Republic. The unit first sergeant put a stop to the TDY possibility when he selected me to be his next company clerk. This would not be the last time that a company first sergeant picked me for his chief clerk, which precluded me from performing duties in my military occupational specialty. When I processed into the Ninety-Second, my records reflected that I had served as a company clerk in my former AIT unit. The first sergeant jumped at the chance to bring me into the orderly room to receive on-the-job training in preparation to replace the current company clerk, who was getting ready to leave the army.

The company clerk I was replacing, a draftee, had served his two years and was looking forward to returning to his home in Georgia and studying business at a local college. He was a good teacher who taught me the ropes of the job. He knew the ins and outs of the system and was detail oriented, and his knowledge and insights of the job were a great help to me even after he left. As I settled into my duties as the company clerk, I worked directly for First Sergeant (1SG) Walter Miltenburger (Top, as I called him, the preferred name of all 1SGs in the US Army), who was a World War II and Korean War veteran. He told me stories about his time in the army and that he had been a major in the artillery until after the wars, when the army converted him back to an enlisted soldier.

1SG Miltenburger, a huge man, well over six feet in height, was always upbeat and positive. He was articulate when he spoke. If something did not go his way, he had a habit of looking you directly in the eye and giving what I called "the silent Miltenburger Look." His stare could make most junior enlistees cringe in anticipation of what was coming next. Captain Phillip P. Craig, the company commander, was soft-spoken, quiet, and always focused on business matters. He never got close to anyone, not even to his lieutenants or 1SG Miltenburger. He was cordial and responsive to my comments and questions, but he never engaged in conversation beyond the topic at hand. As time went on, I gained the confidence of both 1SG Miltenburger and Captain Craig, and they eventually referred all administrative questions from unit members to me.

One of the hardest duties of my job as the company clerk was to prepare the morning report for the unit.[12] This report tracked the personnel status of each officer and enlisted person. The report could not contain any misspellings, but since typewriters had no real correctional capabilities in those days, a slash marked through the wrong letter could be used up to three times per report. Each entry was to be prepared exactly as the regulation required. Other duties were to track all impending personnel actions, prepare all commander and first sergeant correspondence, and liaise with the battalion personnel sergeant. The duties and responsibilities were extensive, but the work provided me with an opportunity to make my own decisions.

I had been in the army for over six months now and was getting used to the culture, work, and interactions with people. I became more self-confident in dealing with job-related issues and gained the trust of my superiors, work colleagues, and others. I knew I still had a lot to learn, but I had come a long way since my days in Bicknell. The trip down the road to maturity was still some distance away, but getting shorter. I no longer felt intimidated by people and felt comfortable in my professional and personal surroundings.

In the mid-1960s when I went into the army, our country was in the beginning stages of a cultural and racial transformation. There was also a different approach to our health care programs. President Johnson had recently signed historical civil rights legislation, allowing greater liberties for minorities, and bills that drastically altered the way our country medically treated the elderly, poor, and disadvantaged. At the same time, US involvement in the Vietnam War was politically polarizing people throughout the country.

Internally, the army was suffering from the same effects of polarization as the civilian communities. The army had been desegregated by President Truman when he signed Executive Order (EO) 9981 on July 26, 1948, which allowed black and white soldiers to serve together in the same unit and gave blacks equal rights as that of whites. Full desegregation of the army was not complete until 1954, when the last all-black army unit (Second Ranger Company)[13] was deactivated. Even after 1954, racism and prejudices continued in the army. One of the more openly racial practices that the army had until the mid-1960s was to put the soldier's race on all assignment orders. Thus, incoming units were always aware of the newly assigned soldier's race before he reported in. This practice was an unnecessary policy that severed no real purpose at the time it was being used.

An incident I recall that had overtones of racism occurred one day when I was sitting in my office working on the morning report. I had received a call from an army captain from Fort McClellan, Alabama. He identified himself as a commander of a unit who had received orders that one of the Ninety-Second Chemical Company noncommissioned officers (NCO) was to be assigned to his unit. The NCO he was talking about was still on leave had not yet reported into the unit at Fort McClellan. The army captain wanted to know about the NCOs character, reputation, and soldiering skills, and if he had ever been in any type of trouble while assigned to the Ninety-Second. Since I knew the NCO, who was black, and considered him one of the best in the Ninety-Second, I answered positively to the questions. I had not seen a great deal of racism or discrimination in my short life while growing up in Indiana, but I could detect the army captain's subtle attempts to follow up with certain questions that had a hidden agenda. I felt that the captain's real concern was because he knew the incoming NCO was black! I ended the phone conversation by providing laudatory comments about the NCO in question and told the army captain he was getting a top-notch soldier who was extremely professional and competent. I often wondered whatever happened to that NCO—if he went to Vietnam or made the army a career! The *race indicator* of individuals was eliminated from orders altogether sometime in 1965.

In November 1965, I was promoted to private first class (PFC). When I became eligible for the promotion, Top came to me and told me to cut my own orders. Back in the 1960s, the company-level units cut their own personnel orders for PFCs. Using the stencil-type machine, I typed my own orders and made enough copies for the proper distribution to the appropriate offices needing them, especially the finance section, so I could get the pay raise. This pay raise came to a whopping $117 per month. This included $40 per month that I was sending to Mom.

During the mid-1960s, protests of the Vietnam War had not reached main stream society yet. Nevertheless, the US government somehow saw into the near future and started training some army units on techniques to control or quell a large group of protestors. This situation became apparent when Top called me into his office one day and informed me that I had been selected to attend riot control training. I was surprised but did not question his judgment or rationale of my selection. The training was one week long and would be conducted at a company classroom with field exercises such as riot formations and controlling protestors on the battalion parade field. We trained with full riot gear, gas masks, batons, shields, and rifles. We learned the various formations to control protestors and practiced methods on how to disperse them and take them into custody if needed. I never did find out why the army felt a need to train federal troops instead of National Guardsman for riot control or what their rationale was to focus on members of the Ninety-Second Chemical Company for that training. If demonstrations were to turn into riots somewhere in the country, would the Ninety-Second Chemical Company be deployed to that location to intercede? Whether the Ninety-Second would ever be deployed or not became a moot point to me.

About a week or so after the riot control training, I was in my office doing paperwork when the battalion personnel sergeant called. He asked if the first sergeant was in, and I replied, "No." He then started reading off some names of unit members who were identified for overseas assignments. After the fourth name, the battalion personnel sergeant paused for a few seconds and then in a low voice said, "And yourself." I asked him to clarify, and the battalion personnel sergeant answered, "All you guys are receiving orders for Vietnam." I asked when the orders would be sent to the unit, and he estimated about a week.

A few moments later, 1SG Miltenburger returned to his office, and I informed him that five guys had just received orders for Vietnam and that I was one of them. He was noticeably stunned that I was on the list and said he would inform Captain Craig. The news around the company and battalion headquarters that I was going to Vietnam prompted numerous phone calls from the various people I worked with. The battalion morning report administrator called and asked if it was true. The battalion assistant personnel sergeant called and the Ninety-Second's company supply sergeant called to wish me good luck.

A few days later, I received orders showing my assignment to the 344th Transportation Company, 394th Transportation Battalion, which was currently in Qui Nhon, South Vietnam, with a reporting date of February 2, 1966. It took me about three days to clear Fort Bragg and to thank and give my appreciation to those in the Ninety-Second Chemical Company and battalion headquarters that helped and guided me through my first permanent duty assignment. Although the duty at Fort Bragg was short, I gained a lot of valuable insights on how the army worked, and the knowledge I gained motivated me in future assignments.

On the morning of December 15, 1965, I departed Fort Bragg by bus and arrived in Terre Haute on the evening of December 16. For some unknown reason, the army had graciously provided me with a forty-five-day leave at home before I had to report to Vietnam. I stayed at Mom's small apartment and used the time to visit with the Miller and McAtee families. I saw Judy about twice a week, and it appeared that a long-lasting relationship might be developing, and I genuinely felt there might even be a future with each other after Vietnam. Time would tell. I enjoyed spending time with the family, especially the meals they prepared for me. With all the good treatment I was receiving, I had a fleeting thought that in some way it may be a prelude to something bad. However, I shook the feeling off and just enjoyed the time at home.

When I departed Fort Bragg, I was told to call for a port of call (time to report for shipment to Vietnam). In late January, I called Travis Air Force Base, where I was to catch the plane for Vietnam. They informed me that I was to report on February 4, 1966, to Travis. I was told that my first stop in Vietnam would be the Ninetieth Replacement Depot, Tan Son Nhut Air Base just outside Saigon. Even with the extra few days of leave, the time I spent at home still seemed short and went very fast. On my last night at home, I said my good-byes to the family and took Judy out to a nice restaurant for a good dinner. Judy and I kept our conversation to general topics and did not discuss our future, but she was reasonably talkative and did mention she would write me while I was in Vietnam. After dinner, I went back to Mom's apartment and went directly to bed.

The next morning, I caught a train (this was before Amtrak) to California. This was my first trip across the United States, and the scenery was beautiful. I made stops in Saint Louis, Missouri; Kansas City, Kansas; and Denver, Colorado. I traveled through the Rocky Mountains into Nevada to California. The trip took two and a half days, but it was well worth the time spent. I made it to Travis Air Force Base in plenty of time to catch my flight to Vietnam.

# 3

# Year of Responsible Decision Making

## Gaining Maturity

## Vietnam

*Life can be easy or difficult, but never predicable.*

Our flight to Tan Son Nhut Air Base, Vietnam, with stops in Honolulu, Manila, and Guam, took eighteen hours. As we exited the door to our comfortable, cool, air-conditioned plane, the highly pungent humidity hit us like a blast of heat from a furnace. Our pressed and starched khaki uniforms became wet and clung to our bodies. Immediately upon disembarking from the plane, we heard trucks, jeeps, and other larger vehicles passing nearby. A US Army sergeant wearing jungle fatigues and a holstered .45-caliber pistol around his waist started shouting directions for the enlisted men to go to the right and the officers to the left as we reached the tarmac. We ended up inside an area surrounded by sandbags about eight feet high. There were two doors—the one we entered and another on the far wall.

Once inside the sandbag bunker, the constant noise and reverberation of the traffic around us went unabated. What got our attention was the sound of a sudden and deafening explosion nearby. Of course, everyone thought it might be a mortar attack and that we had been directed to the small sandbag fortress for our safety. Then suddenly, the sergeant who had directed us into the sandbagged area walked in with a big smile on his face. As he headed for the door at the far side of the enclosed sandbag area, he said, "Follow me, men."[14]

The gaggle of men started forming a line behind the sergeant. Once we walked through the door, we found ourselves inside an actual building that had a huge counter in the middle of the room. The group was told to gather around the counter. Once we were all settled, a US airman in the middle of the room welcomed us to Vietnam. He then immediately informed us that the commotion we had just heard was caused by army engineers, who were building a road and had used the explosives to clear an area around the side of a mountain. Looking around the room, you could see the troubled and worried looks melt from the faces of the people who had just gotten off the plane. The purpose of meeting in the large room was to turn over our records. Most of us carried them with us on the plane.

We were told that if we had a direct assignment to a unit, we would be transported either by truck or plane within a day to our units. When the US airman got to me, he reviewed my orders and told me I had direct orders requiring me to report to Qui Nhon, Vietnam, about 385 miles north of Saigon. After checking everyone in, the US airman then asked if anyone in the group knew how to fire an M60 machine gun. There were not many who raised their hands. They were looking for perimeter guards for Tan Son Nhut. Once enough soldiers were identified and no more "volunteers" were sought, the airman told us not to worry, because everyone would get their chance at guard duty; it was a shared duty with all newcomers. He alluded that if we stayed at Tan Son Nhut for any length of time, most of us would eventually have our turn at guard duty. We were then briefed on procedures to follow in case the base was attacked while we were there. The main thing I recalled about that briefing was that since we were not assigned a rifle or other weapon, if an attack was launched by the Viet Cong (VC), we were to make it to our assigned bunks, pull the bed mattresses over us, lie on the floor, and pray. Fortunately, my time at Tan Son Nhut was for only one night, and no attack took place.

The next morning, February 5, 1966, I boarded a C-130 Hercules transport and flew to Qui Nhon, Vietnam, about two hours away. We arrived at the Qui Nhon airport in midmorning and was escorted to a holding area so that personnel there could process us in and arrange for transportation to our unit. Qui Nhon is a coastal city on the South China Sea, located in Binh Dinh Providence about 640 kilometers (about 385 miles) from Saigon (now called Ho Chi Minh City).

After personnel reviewed my orders, I was escorted to a deuce-and-a-half-ton truck nearby and told to hop on for a short ride to the 394th Transportation Battalion located at Qui Nhon, South Vietnam. The actual city of Qui Nhon was about a half mile to the north. In all, there were seven or eight of us headed to the 394th. The trip to the 394th took us about three miles from the Qui Nhon airport to a road paralleling the beach. For as far as the eye could see, the US military presence was obvious. We zipped by US military facilities, personnel, and vast tent cities on one side of the road and the sandy beaches on the other side. There was a constant flow of military trucks, jeeps, and other vehicles whizzing by.

I wondered if all the vehicles had an actual destination or were they just traveling up and down the road in long convoys, trying to confuse our enemy. In the distance, I could see the pure beauty of magnificent and pristine mountains reaching the deep blue sky. The ride took us about fifteen minutes. I could not help but notice how beautiful the beach was and wondered if I was in a war zone or if the US Army had mistakenly sent me to a vacation resort instead. One thing that separated that feeling was the pungent odor in the air of dead fish and decaying vegetables combined with a slight salty seawater aroma.

When we arrived at headquarters, 394th, the driver pointed toward a large tent located on the beach side of the road and told us to pile out and report. The group of us walked the short distance to the tent as directed. A personnel specialist named Matthew McCabe took our orders and one by one processed us in. I was the only one headed for the 344th Transportation Company; the rest of the soldiers were headed to other units in the battalion. McCabe told me that although he was assigned to the 394th Transportation Battalion, he was quartered with the 344th. McCabe advised that after he processed me in, he would take me to the unit and introduce me to the first sergeant.

Our walk to the 344th orderly room was short. I was introduced to First Sergeant John Howard. Howard had his hair close cropped and was heavyset, grossly overweight, and obviously out of shape. He was a polite man who enthusiastically welcomed me to the unit. As I was talking to First Sergeant Howard, I just realized that I was unfamiliar with the type of unit and mission of the 344th and even became more confused when I saw a large, funny-looking boat on wheels whizzing by. I inquired with First Sergeant Howard as to what kind of vehicle I had just seen. He informed me that it was a LARC-V (Lighter, Amphibious, Resupply, Cargo) five-ton vessel. He added that it was the mission of the 344th to transport men and supplies from ship to shore. As I was looking more confused, Howard said, "Yes, son, the army has boats—plenty of them. As a matter of fact, they have more boats than the navy."

I informed Top that I had never seen a LARC, had no knowledge of what a LARC did, and was surprised that the army even had boats in their inventory. McCabe and Top started laughing, and I started getting a sick feeling in my stomach.

I reckoned I was not making any points with Top, but when he regained his composure, he did ask me about my experiences in the US Army. I informed him of my supply training and work as a company clerk in both my AIT unit at Fort Leonard Wood and with the Ninety-Second Chemical Company at Fort Bragg. I started to feel a little better when I saw Top's face soften somewhat and his eyes light up. He told me he needed a second company clerk and asked if I would like to give the job a try. I could not believe my good fortune. I was not interested in working supply, did not know anything about LARC-Vs, thoroughly enjoyed working as a company clerk, and could not imagine having a better job in a war zone. I had never received any formal training in the administrative field, but every assignment I'd had since basic training had been as the unit's company clerk.

Top introduced me to J. W. Spoonemore, the unit's current company clerk, and said, "You two will be working together." I chatted with Spoonemore for a while, but he did not waste any time acquainting me on the duties and responsibilities of working in the 344th orderly room. Spoonemore told me he was from Dallas, Texas, and had been assigned to the 344th right out of personnel school.

"I have been in the unit for two months," Spoonemore made a point of telling me and that he was glad he was finally getting some help and looked forward to working with me.

As we were talking, McCabe reentered the orderly room and informed me he would walk me to the supply room to get my bed linen and to the unit armorer so I could pick up my M14 rifle. The grunts were the only ones being issued the M16 rifle at the time. As we walked through the unit area, I saw that everyone lived in GP medium tents that housed about sixteen to twenty soldiers each. The company commander, 1LT Michael Redman, whom I had not yet met, lived in a room behind the orderly room office. After I picked up my linen and M14 rifle, I spent some time getting my equipment, bunk, and personal items organized. I spent the rest of the day back at the unit orderly room, getting more familiar with the job. As I lay in my bunk trying to fall asleep that night, I thought of the day's activities and how lucky I was to have wound up being assigned to the 344th and been given the job I had. This feeling was intensified due to me being in a war zone, where soldiers were dying daily.

I spent about two weeks working with Spoonemore before I felt comfortable in the job. Spoonemore and I established our duties as we went along from day to day. Between the two of us, we agreed that I would take over the administrative responsibilities for the 253rd Transportation Detachment, whose members were augmented to the 344th Transportation Company. The 253rd played a direct support (DS) role by performing second- and third-echelon maintenance on the 344th LARC-V vehicles. They had a CW3 in charge of the unit and a CW2 acting as a sort of executive officer. I took over the management of personnel actions of the 253rd. Another duty was to prepare the weekly tonnage reports for the total tons of supplies, materials, and other cargo hauled by the LARC-Vs and the troop numbers being transported to shore from newly arrived ships.

The work was hard, the hours long, and the heat often unbearable in the open-air tent that served as our orderly room. Initially, I thought that I would have more interaction with 1LT Redman, because our desks were right next to each other, but that was not the case. Other than being introduced to him by Top, he rarely engaged in conversations. I did prepare most of his correspondence, but he hardly ever spoke beyond giving me instructions with what he wanted me to do.

Most workdays lasted from twelve to fifteen hours. My duties also included driving Top and a young lieutenant platoon leader to areas around Qui Nhon where the 344th operations were being performed. The three of us also had to visit the beach daily, where the LARC-Vs came out of the water with their cargo. The lieutenant, named Reed, was there to check on the troops while, most of the time, Top just went along for the ride. Top also thought that his presence would be a morale booster for the troops, because it showed his support. Besides, driving them there allowed me to compile information for the daily tonnage reports. It was not uncommon to work until midnight or later each day. As I became more familiar with my duties and responsibilities, I settled into a routine.

Shortly after I arrived at Qui Nhon, I convinced some of the guys to teach me how to drive a LARC-V. The LARC-V was an incredibly unusual, multifaceted vehicle. The LARC-V was an aluminum amphibious boat requiring a two-man crew, capable of carrying five tons of cargo or up to forty soldiers at a time. The LARC-V could travel at speeds from eight to ten miles per hour in the water and twenty-eight miles per hour on land. Measuring twelve feet in length, with a weight of nineteen thousand pounds, the LARC-V had a draft (the depth the boat stood in the water) of only three and a half feet, enabling it to navigate in shallow water.[15] It was the smallest among the US Army's fleet of amphibious boats. With no prior training under my belt, the efforts by those dedicated to train me took a while longer, but I finally got the knack of it. After I learned how to drive the LARC-V, I would occasionally go out to the ships with other crew members on board to pick up men and cargo.

In 1966, the city of Qui Nhon was still a relatively safe place to be in Vietnam.[16] The Koreans protected the US Army and the surrounding beach areas. However, occasionally, the VC would get close enough to lob a few mortars into a unit compound. One night a few weeks after my arrival to the 344th Transportation Company, I was in our dayroom tent, writing letters to Mom and Judy, when the VC dropped three mortars into our unit area, catching us by surprise. We were ordered to grab our M14 rifles and fall out to our assigned positions along the perimeter of the unit. We lay there with our faces in the sand for a couple of hours, but when no attack followed and no one was hurt, we stood down. We increased the guards that night and for several nights afterward.

The Eighty-Fifth Medical Evacuation (Medevac) Field Hospital was where the combat wounded were treated. The Eighty-Fifth was within a fifteen-minute drive from our unit area. Although Qui Nhon was safe, the surrounding area in the central highlands was where some of the heaviest fighting was taking place. Throughout the day, you could hear the distant sound of explosions, small-arms fire and the *whop-whop-whop* sound of the medevac helicopter blades as they ferried the wounded and killed in action to the Eighty-Fifth.

About two weeks after I arrived at the 344th, I saw firsthand how stress can eat at the emotions of soldiers in Vietnam. A staff sergeant (SSG) and acting platoon sergeant who deployed from the United States with the unit received a

"Dear John" letter from his wife. Not being able to handle the anguish of losing his wife of several years, he decided to end his life by shooting himself in the face with his M14 rifle while sitting on his bunk. I overheard Top Howard telling lLT Redman that the SSG was a good NCO and he did not deserve to have his life snuffed out by suicide. At a small memorial, Top Howard praised the SSG's work and life accomplishments in front of the dead NCO's platoon members. He told them that regardless of how bad things got in their lives, the method chosen by the SSG to resolve them was not the way to settle them.[17]

In early March 1966, while I was working on some reports in the orderly room, Top caught me by surprise when he came to my desk and told me to procure a jeep so we could take a ride along the beach road. Since we had not scheduled any trips for the day, I had no idea where he wanted to go, but I got a jeep, gassed it up, and parked it just outside the orderly room tent. Top and Battalion Sergeant Major (SMG) Thomas Brown, whom I had not met, came outside carrying their M14 rifles with loaded clips and got into the jeep. "Before we get on the road, you need to get your weapon," Top said. He added, "You will also have to get a couple of men to help you."

I asked Top, "What for?"

He replied, "To get the beer from the supply tent."

Still somewhat confused, I grabbed my M14 rifle, secured the fully loaded (twenty-round) magazine clip into the weapon, and placed it inside the jeep where it could readily be accessible if needed. I then went to the supply tent a short distance from where the jeep was parked. The supply sergeant, Thomas (Tom) Foley, who eventually became a close friend during our tour in Vietnam, looked at me with a smile. Tom pointed to a corner in front of the supply tent and said, "Is that what you are here for?"

I glanced in the area where Tom had pointed and saw at least ten cases of various kinds of American beers. Tom helped me load the beer into the back of the jeep, making sure to leave enough room for SMG Brown to sit. Once we had all the beer in the jeep, with Top in the front passenger seat and SMG Brown in back, I took off down the beach road in the direction Top pointed. I asked Top, "Where are we going?"

He replied, "We're going to have dinner with a priest."

I drove a couple of miles, leaving the US Army tent city in the distance. The road left the beach area and started up the side of a mountain, winding its way high above the coast, affording us a great panoramic view of the tent city and the busy port peninsula of Qui Nhon.

As I drove around a curve at the top of the mountain road, we were startled out of our wits when a very young and nervous Korean soldier appeared out of nowhere and started yelling in Korean, all the while pointing his rifle at us. When someone in a foreign military uniform points a rifle at you in a war zone, you are inclined to pray and see your entire life run through your mind. I did both. Almost as soon as the young soldier appeared alongside the road with rifle in hand, a Korean officer walked out of the jungle next to the road and told the young solider to lower his weapon. The Korean officer then very calmly waved at us and, in perfect English, told us to continue our way. This incident lasted only a few seconds, but it seemed like an eternity. Top and SMG Brown started laughing as we continued our trip, but I could tell, like me, they were very relieved that the incident ended well. Apparently, the stretch of road we were on was well guarded by the Korean White Horse Division against possible infiltration by the VC.

When we started down the other side of the mountain, I saw a Vietnamese village at the bottom. As our jeep got closer, I couldn't help but notice how unusual the Vietnamese people, who were standing on either side of the road, looked. They had various disfigurations on their limbs and faces. I saw an upper arm bone protruding from an open ulcerous wound on one man, and another man had a cavity where his nose should have been. Many more had abscesses, boils, and lesions all over their bodies. I looked over at Top and asked if the Vietnamese had been wounded or injured because of attacks from the VC.

"No, they all have leprosy," Top said. "That's why we are here. We are going to visit the priest at the leper colony, and he likes beer," Top said.

At that time, I had no knowledge of leprosy or anything about the disease. Up until talking with Top, I had never heard of the disease. Leprosy is a disease that affects the nerves and skin of the person infected. It can result in blindness, disfiguration of the face, kidney failure, and muscle weakness. Contrary to popular belief, leprosy is not that contagious. To catch the disease, one must live with the affected person for a long time. Contact with nose and mouth droplets from someone with untreated leprosy over a period can lead to leprosy. It takes about three to five years for symptoms to appear after coming into contact the leprosy-causing bacteria. Some people do not develop symptoms until twenty years later.[18] Top assured me that the short duration of our visit at the leprosarium would not put us in any jeopardy.

As we pulled up to a rather nice-looking building, I saw a priest standing in front, apparently waiting for us. Before I could stop the jeep, Top jumped out and shook hands with the priest. Based on their friendly handshake, it was obvious to me that the two men were not meeting for the first time. Several young Vietnamese boys gathered around the jeep, and SMG Brown pointed his finger at the cases of beer, and they started taking the beer into the building. The priest turned toward SMG Brown, greeting us in English but with a foreign accent, and shook his hand and then mine. Later, I learned that his accent was German. Top and the priest then turned and went inside the building with SMG Brown and me following.

We all walked into a large room, which had huge paintings of religious figures and churches hanging on the wall. The priest invited us to sit in chairs. Almost immediately, several nuns dressed in white habits swarmed around us. A nun, speaking in fluent English, asked me what I would like to drink. Other nuns, speaking in equally fluent English, asked Top and SMG Brown what they wanted. I was overwhelmed by the attention we were getting. When the nuns went off to fetch our drinks, I saw another nun give the priest one of the beers we had brought.

By being with two of the highest-ranking sergeants in my unit and a priest, I felt somewhat overwhelmed. I was a lowly PFC and had no religious background and nothing in common with the three men I was with. SMG Brown, apparently sensing my quandary, attempted to make small talk with me while the other two focused only on their conversation. Neither made any attempts to bring me or SMG Brown into their conversation. The priest and Top were having an intense conversation about religion. While working around Top for the short time I had been in Vietnam and hearing him using profanity on a regular basis, I would have never figured him to be religiously inclined.

The four nuns, one for each of us, were hovering nearby in case we asked for something in the form of refreshments. After about thirty minutes, an older nun appeared and invited us into a dining room for lunch. Shadowed by the attentive nuns, we all went to the dining room. I was in awe when I saw the table setting for four. The spread on the table was more like Thanksgiving dinner than lunch. Food consisted of salad, roasted chicken, vegetables, glasses of water, and, I found out later, a scoop of vanilla ice cream. I did not realize that Vietnam had food like this. I thought I had died and gone to heaven.

The priest and Top sat on one side of the table with the wall behind them. SMG Brown and I sat on the other side, facing the wall. The nun who had waited on me in the living room asked if I would like some wine (not specifying a type) with my meal. I was surprised. I had never had wine before, and there was no better time than now to have a glass, so I replied, "Yes." She returned with a white wine that was somewhat warm. Although I was not sophisticated in drinking wine, somehow, I knew that white wine should be chilled, so, in a very unsophisticated manner, I asked for some ice to cool the wine. This was the first real meal I'd had in Vietnam. When we arrived in country, we were warned not to drink water outside our unit compound for fear it was not potable. We had no trouble that day drinking the water. We ate like kings, stuffing ourselves, drinking wine, and having a hearty, good old time.

This scene was surreal, like a vacation resort more than a war zone, and the vision of the setting and ambience has stuck with me my entire life. Later, these feelings turned to guilt that I could not shake.

Once we finished our excellent meal, we were served coffee by the nuns. As we were drinking our coffee, SGM Brown leaned over toward me and asked if I knew why the priest was so captivated with 1SG Howard and, I replied, "No." SGM Brown pointed to the wall behind the two men. The wall had a huge mural of one of the Catholic popes. The face on the painting was unerringly like that of 1SG Howard. You could not tell the two faces apart. This is the reason the priest and 1SG Howard had such a good rapport with each other. My nun, apparently overhearing SGM Brown telling me about the mural depicting a pope in the likeness of 1SG Howard, commented that they all looked forward to having 1SG Howard pay them a visit because it gave everyone at the leprosarium a mystical feeling. She added, "We are all in awe as to how similar the two look."

After lunch, the priest, 1SG Howard, SMG Brown, and I, followed by the four nuns, walked to the beach. One of the nuns made sure that the priest had a beer with him as he walked. The priest and 1SG Howard were continuously engaged in conversation with each other, and SGM Brown, the nuns, and I were merely present with them. The beach was called Queen Beach, named for the wife of Bao Dai, the last emperor of Vietnam. I took photographs from a camera I had brought from the United States that captured Top and the priest walking on the beautiful South China Sea beach. Once the priest and 1SG Howard finished their conversation and said their good-byes, 1SG Howard, SMG Brown, and I jumped into the jeep for the drive back to our base camp. As we started our drive up the side of the mountain, I stopped the jeep and snapped more photographs of people at the leprosarium and the scenery around the compound to capture the beauty of the area. As we continued up the mountain, we all waved to the priest, who, incidentally, was drinking another beer. We did not have any trouble with at the Korean security guard post as we returned to the 344th. What a day!

Over the years since that trip to the leprosarium at Quy Hoa, just outside Qui Nhon, I had done some research on the place and found that it was started by Paul Maheure, a French Catholic priest, in 1929, when he brought thirty leprosy patients to the area. Franciscan nuns joined the leprosarium over the years, and they all helped expand the facility into a neat, clean, fully functional hospital that treated leprosy and other skin diseases. The Japanese left it alone when they invaded the country in 1945. Between 1954 and 1959, the French ensured it was not attacked during the First Indochina War. During the Vietnam War (1959–1975), the United States unofficially supported the leprosarium. It appears that during the American presence in Vietnam, neither did the Viet Cong nor the

North Vietnamese Army do harm to the leprosarium. On August 26, 1999, the Quy Hoa leprosarium was renamed Quy Hoa National Leprosy Dermatology Hospital.[19]

Spoonemore and I continued to work twelve- to fifteen-hour days, getting only four or five hours of sleep each night. I took Sunday mornings off while Spoonemore rested on Sunday afternoons. I considered the work to be easier as time passed, but conditions continued to be hot and muggy. I slipped away for a couple of hours each day to the beach and helped drive LARC-Vs from ship to shore. The LARC-Vs were workhorses in moving supplies, materials, and, on occasion, men from the ships in Qui Nhon Harbor. The area around Qui Nhon was a beehive of activity.

In March 1966, I took a break and went over to the Eighty-Fifth's Evacuation Hospital, a short distance from the 344th base camp, to see a solider that went through supply training with me at Fort Leonard Wood, Missouri, and a fellow Hoosier. I had run into him on a previous trip to the Eighty-Fifth Evacuation Hospital post exchange (PX). We were not particularly close, but it felt good to know someone in Vietnam that I had known previously in the States.

In September 1965, the Eighty-Fifth Evacuation Hospital had set up operations in Qui Nhon. When I arrived in Qui Nhon, much of the hospital compound was made up of tents, but Quonset huts gradually replaced the tents.[20] The 344th arrived at Qui Nhon about two months before the 85th.

As the soldier and I stood talking just outside his tent, we heard the familiar *whop-whop-whop* sound of medevac helicopters (Hueys) as they appeared flying over the trees. They were whizzing toward the Eighty-Fifth Evacuation Hospital compound landing zone. As the first chopper touched down, medics from the Eighty-Fifth retrieved three wounded soldiers from the craft and swiftly transported them on litters to the emergency Quonset hut nearby. A moment later, a second chopper landed with a loud thump, and medical personnel rushed to remove several soldiers from that Huey and ran with them on litters into the emergency Quonset hut.

The medical personnel seemed to take longer in extracting the four soldiers from the third Huey. One soldier was screaming as he was carried off the Huey, yelling at the medics, "Take it easy! My stomach is all shot up!" Medics placed another wounded soldier lying on a litter on the ground near where I was standing. The soldier did not speak, but stared, stoical, directly at me. He had a gaping wound in his right upper arm, probably caused by a bullet fired from a VC AK-47. I felt like I should reach down to him and attempt in some way to comfort him, but I froze and just stared back at him. Seconds later, the medics grabbed his litter and rushed him away for treatment. As the soldier was being taken away, he moved his head in my direction. He kept looking directly at me without saying a word. Two other soldiers were pulled off the Huey in body bags and taken toward the mortuary tent. This scene destroyed all feelings of security and safety I had felt about Vietnam. I truly knew now that we were not in a vacation resort where everything was white sandy beaches and all was well. We were in a war!

Later that night as I lay comfortably on my bunk, inside my secured tent, I could not get the image of seeing those poor, unfortunate soldiers, wounded and killed, out of my mind. From that day forward, I felt a tremendous sense of remorse for not having to go through the hell that our infantry and other fighting soldiers had to endure and a feeling of relief for not having to. I thought, *Here I am, a nineteen-year-old kid from Terre Haute and Bicknell, Indiana, in a war, having no feelings of fear or worries about facing the enemy in battle, but having the constant emotion of despair for not doing so.*

About a week after experiencing the horror of seeing those poor ill-fated killed and wounded soldiers being off-loaded from the medevac choppers, Top came to me and said they needed an administrative presence at the detachment in Da Nang, where we had several LARC-Vs helping the US Navy. By the end of June 1965, the unit had received the task to send one of the LARC platoons up to Da Nang on a thirty-day temporary change of duty to help the navy deliver ammunition to the air force. Every thirty days, they received another thirty-day extension and had remained there ever since. As Top related the origins of the 344th being in Da Nang, I had just poured my first cup of coffee, and Top continued to tell me that 1LT Robert Baker, the detachment commander, needed help. He then told me he thought I was the right guy for the job in Da Nang.

He sugarcoated it by saying that I would technically be the acting 1SG of the detachment. Me, not being long in the US Army and hadn't recently fallen from a turnip truck, clearly understood that a PFC could not in reality be considered the top soldier. I may have all the responsibilities, but I would not have any authority for the job. My thoughts on the manner were never considered, however, because Top had already decided I was going to Da Nang. Top told me to pack my bags and catch a C-130 for Da Nang the next day. Top also informed me that rumor had it that the entire 344th Transportation Company was moving to Da Nang in a few weeks, and I had been chosen to be the advance man to get the headquarters prepared for that move.

Top told me that one of my main duties was to seek out a site for a new headquarters that could house him, Spoonemore, 1LT Redman, and me. I told Top I would try my best.

I updated Spoonemore on what I had been working on and fed him in on the information I had received from Top about the move to Da Nang. Spoonemore did not act very surprised to hear about the move. I then drew some necessary items, such as a poncho, canteen, and ammo for my M14 rifle, from supply.

I needed these things, because Top and others had informed me that conditions in Da Nang were far more primitive than in Qui Nhon. A driver took me to the Qui Nhon airport for the trip to Da Nang. As I waited to load my gear onto the C-130, I noticed that six captured VC were crouched down in a row on the tarmac about fifty feet from where I was standing. There were two US Army soldiers with M16 rifles standing guard over them. As I stood there staring at them, wondering where they were being taken, I heard a sergeant barking orders at them to get on the plane ASAP.

Da Nang was second only to Tan Son Nhut Air Base as the busiest military airport during the Vietnam War. Da Nang was in I Corps and home to the Third Marine Division since they'd landed in 1965. The Da Nang airport (originally named Tourane Airport by the French) had been built by the French colonial government in the 1930s as a civilian airport. The French used the airport during the First Indochina War (1946–1954). During the Vietnam War (1959–1975), the name changed to the Da Nang airport.[21]

After an hour-and-a-half flight of about 172 miles aboard a US Air Force C-130 Hercules, I arrived in Da Nang on April 5, 1966. I was picked up at the Da Nang airport by 1LT Baker, who smiled as he extended his right hand to welcome me to the 344th Transportation Company, First Platoon Detachment at Da Nang. I shook his hand and threw my duffel bag in the backseat, keeping my M14 rifle in hand. As he drove to our platoon area, located on the south edge of the airport, he did not brief me on what my duties and responsibilities were to be. Instead, he told me that on top of trying to conduct LARC-V operations from ship to shore and dealing with the VC, travel in and around Da Nang would be limited. Waving his right hand in the air to accentuate the meaning of his comment, he said that Da Nang was experiencing an ongoing Buddhist uprising with young university students supporting them. The apparent cause of the disturbances had its origin with the current Vietnamese government having a hard time assimilating certain elements (the Buddhists) into the mainstream of society and deciding on a date for free elections. I consider the matter of politics to be way beyond my element of concern, so I just listened to him.

"The marines keep the area secure from the Viet Cong, but sometimes that security interferes with routes the LARCs take to the beach and to avoid the protests," said 1LT Baker. As lLT Baker drove out of the protected area of the Da Nang airport, we passed a marine patrol walking on both sides of the road. They looked like a bunch of ragtag, tired, shattered, and unkempt marines. I wondered how long they had been on patrol and if they'd had any contact with the Viet Cong.

A short distance down the road, we arrived at a checkpoint manned by three marines. One was positioned in a bunker surrounded by sandbags, armed with a .50-caliber machine gun, and the other two standing next to the side of the road had M16 rifles. The checkpoint was located on a raised curve in the road with the Da Nang airport on one side and a jungle area on the other. The road was being cleared by a group of marine engineers using a bulldozer. After the jungle area was cleared, the marines would have a better strategic vantage point of the entire surrounding area. 1LT Baker stopped the jeep, and the marine standing closest to the road, who appeared younger than I, looked us up and down, and without saying a word, he motioned with his M16 rifle to proceed.

Another checkpoint about a half mile farther down the road was manned by the US Army. "The marines protect the outer limits of our area, and the US Army secures our base camp," said 1LT Baker.

Once through the US Army gate, we traveled another hundred yards or so and pulled up to a GP medium tent with a rudimentary sign in front identifying it as the orderly room of the 344th Transportation Headquarters. "You can store your personal belongings in the room directly behind the detachment headquarters tent," said lLT Baker.[22] "You can also bunk down in the rear room until other arrangements can be made," he said.

It took me about five minutes to get my things stored, and I joined lLT Baker in the front of the tent. There were two small offices, one for 1LT Baker and the other for use by a clerk. The work area contained only the essentials: a field table for a desk, an old, brown Royal typewriter, and a straight-backed metal chair. Baker's office contained a field table, a straight-backed metal chair, but no typewriter. A field telephone was positioned in the doorway between the two offices, suggesting its use was to be shared.

1LT Baker motioned with his hands for me to sit down. As I sat in the metal chair, Baker pulled the chair from his office, placed it next to mine, and started talking. "I requested a clerk be sent up from Qui Nhon to help with the damn paperwork," said 1LT Baker. "There will be other duties as assigned, of course, but your primary tasks at hand will be to do correspondence, prepare reports, and run messages from the detachment headquarters to the beach area where the LARC-Vs were operating," he said. "I want you to administratively organize the detachment," he said.

As I was listening to 1LT Baker tell me what he expected, I thought that I had landed another company clerk–type job, which was the only duty I had performed in the US Army. I continued to consider myself a very lucky young man to have this type of job, especially in a war zone.

I knew I would adapt quickly to the duties and responsibilities of the job. However, I still could not shake the feeling of knowing that there were young

American boys, most just like me, from cities, farms, and small towns that were being killed or seriously wounded in combat, while I was in the virtual comfort and safety of a garrison-type setting. I was truly blessed! I often stopped to consider how far I had gone from the days as a wayward, shy, and insecure kid with no focus to a young, maturing man in Vietnam. I had become less intimidated with people and more focused on the job, and I had developed new skills to communicate and gained greater confidence.

I took notice that 1LT Baker, unlike the other officers in the 344th Transportation Company that I had contact with, appeared to be in good physical shape. In my brief interaction with 1LT Baker, he came across as friendly, pleasant, respectful, and an earnest sort of guy, who seemed genuinely concerned about the men in his platoon. My impression was that he was going to be firm but fair to work for. I tried to sleep that night in my new surroundings, but the deafening, sharp, ear-piercing sound of jet engines on the runway a short distance from our base camp was boggling. The jets, fighters, bombers, and other types had a twenty-four-hour schedule of taking off and landing, and the sound became a constant source of irritation.

I immediately got to work contacting other unit clerks, both US Army and marines, to gather forms, office supplies, and other necessary items needed to complete the job I was assigned. Security was tight, and each time I ventured outside our compound to reach out to others, I had to go through several roadside security checkpoints. I was constantly on the field phone with Top and Spoonemore to brief them on what I had accomplished in setting up the headquarters. My search for a suitable office to accommodate Top, Spoonemore, 1LT Redman, and me ended with a decision to use the current tent we already had because it was the best location. Top concurred.

As the days went by, I continued to organize the orderly room and prepare for the company's arrival, a date that had not been announced. 1LT Baker was a hands-on leader who liked to be with his men. He was seldom in the orderly room, and two to three days would go by without seeing him. Early one morning, 1LT Baker did stop by the orderly room, and he asked if I wanted to go with him to the beach of operations. I did not hesitate. I grabbed my headgear and M-14 and followed him to the jeep. He insisted on driving, which was all right with me, since I did not know the area that well.

About ten minutes later, 1LT Baker pulled the jeep up to a small tent with three LARC-Vs parked nearby, located just outside the sandy beach area of Da Nang Bay. He was out of the jeep almost before it stopped. I followed him into the small tent, which served as the beach operations headquarters (BOH) of the unit. A sergeant immediately stood up and, without acknowledging me, greeted 1LT Baker. "Have you found the bombs yet?" asked 1LT Baker.

The sergeant replied, "No, but they are currently in the bay looking for them."

1LT Baker asked for a lift in one of the LARC-Vs to go see the searchers'. As we walked to one of the LARC-Vs near the tent, I overheard 1LT Baker and the sergeant accompanying us talking about two five-hundred-pound bombs falling off a LARC-V into the bay a few hours earlier.

We found a driver for the LARC-V and headed out into the bay to the area of the search. I had brought my camera and took plenty of photographs of the beautiful white sandy beaches and the mountains that seemed to touch the sky. Coupled with the beauty of the sandy beaches, distant mountains, and the sun shining in a cloudless sky, I thought the photographs would make some of the best majestic scenery. Acknowledging that he knew I was taking photographs of the area as we traveled to the search site, 1LT Baker turned to me and pointed in the direction of a mountain range in the distance. "That is Monkey Mountain to the southeast, and Marble Mountain to your south," 1LT Baker said. I learned much later in life that the caves at Marble Mountain are considered sacred; some of the largest were used as VC and North Vietnam military hospital sites during the Vietnam War.

It took us about ten minutes to arrive at the location, where three members of the 344th were in the water searching for the bombs. I also photographed the soldiers as they searched for the bombs. They were all in shallow water of no more than five feet or so, and one of them swam to the side of our LARC-V and told 1LT Baker that the search had not located the bombs. He told them to continue the search and report if they found them. The LARC-V brought us back to shore, and 1LT Baker and I went back to the orderly room, where he called lLT Redman with the news that the bombs had not been found.

I had been at the Da Nang detachment for about two weeks when I was ordered to go to the BOH to get some information to complete the tonnage report. I took the detachment jeep for the trip of about three miles. I obtained the information from the on-duty beach operations sergeant and just turned onto the main road from the beach headed back to base camp when I heard two ear-piercing explosions nearby going off simultaneously. Fearing the worst—that it might be the beginning of an attack on the beachfront—I stepped on the gas and drove as fast as possible to put distance between me and the explosions. I knew I was close to a marine checkpoint that I had gone through earlier to get to the BOH, and it took me a couple of minutes to get there. When I drove up to the checkpoint, two young marines advised me to take cover because they were expecting an immediate attack from an unknown size VC unit who had been spotted in the area. To play it safe, I was advised by one of the marines to stay with them until a patrol arrived to reinforce their position.

I pulled over and grabbed my M14 rifle, simultaneously glancing to check if my clip of twenty rounds of ammo was inserted as I jumped from the jeep. I slid down a shallow gulley alongside the road, next to a marine. Feeling a sharp pain in my left knee as I landed, I looked down and noticed my pants were ripped and my knee was bleeding. Ignoring the pain, I took up a prone position next to the young marine.

The marine nearest me immediately noticed that I had an M14 rifle instead of an M16 rifle. Acting extremely nervous, obviously due to the impending VC attack, he commented, "I thought the US Army was using M16 rifles like the marines."

I informed him that the US Army infantry had M16 rifles, but all support personnel were still using M14s.

The marines, still having the responsibility of manning the checkpoint, had placed themselves in a prone position near the barricade crossing the road. The marine nearest me advised me to scan the area to the right and said he would do the same to the left. All three of us were extremely anxious but stood fast at our locations. Then the inevitable occurred; small-arms fire was heard a short distance from our location. I thought, *this is it—my first firefight.* It was an odd feeling, but fear seemed to be replaced with a strong sense of fortitude to repel an up-until-now-unseen enemy.

Moments later, we were joined by a patrol of several marines, who took cover with me and the two marine guards. The marine sergeant leading the patrol advised the marine guards at the checkpoint that word had been received that another marine patrol was under attack near the jungles edging the beach just ahead. The sergeant of the second marine patrol told us they were ordered to reinforce the unit under attack. As we all cautiously gathered around the barricade, the sergeant leading the marine patrol received a radio call from his platoon leader, advising that there had been several marine causalities and to get their asses moving. Immediately after the radio call, a marine driving a jeep from an aide station approached the checkpoint.

One of the marine checkpoint guards lifted the barricade just in time to allow the jeep, bearing a Red Cross symbol, to speed through. The marine sergeant left two marines from his patrol at the checkpoint, one with a machine gun, and the rest of the men immediately got up and followed the jeep at a quick pace.

A short time later, the jeep with the Red Cross cover came racing back through the checkpoint carrying a seriously injured, unconscious, and bleeding young marine. One of the marines with the patrol returned in the jeep. The jeep stopping only long enough for the marine from the patrol to jump off as it sped toward the medical aid station. The marine that returned and told us that two mortars had landed near a squad of marines patrolling near the beach, killing three and wounding one. That wounded marine was being taken to the aide station for treatment. The marine that returned ordered the two marines left at the checkpoint to follow him back to the site of the attack, because they were in hot pursuit of Charlie. The three marines started running toward to catch up with their patrol. It appeared that the marine patrol that reinforced the first patrol had the VCs on the run in the opposite direction I was going. So much for the firefight; I was lucky that day. I felt a sense of pride that in a small way I had been prepared to take a stand against our enemy with a bunch of marines by my side.

I thanked the two marine guards, wished them luck, and got into my jeep and sped away. My injured knee hurt like the dickens, and when I arrived back as our base camp, the medics treated it and wrapped the wound with bandages. Later, the news came in that the VC had lobbed two mortars into a group of marines killing three and wounding one. Because of the attack, the US Army increased its guard presence around the beach, and the marines added more patrols in the area. As part of my duties to obtain information for the tonnage report, I continued to travel to the beach area, but I became more cautious and alert to anything unusual on my route.

Days at Da Nang were busy and full. Most of my work was conducted individually with no partner or assistant to help. I pretty much decided the priority on work projects and those that could be put on the back burner. I never allowed problems to fester or grow, and I tackled each situation with enthusiasm. Once I settled in on what 1LT Baker and Top wanted, they stayed out of my way and let me do the work virtually uninterrupted. I commandeered two new typewriters (don't ask where they came from) and two additional chairs from a unit that was deploying to another location and wanted to get rid of excess property. All this work seemed trivial when compared to what the American fighting men were doing in the war, but still a very essential requirement in the overall scheme of things.

One evening about 11:00, I had just left work for the day and was walking into my living quarters when I heard a loud burst of automatic-weapons fire nearby. It sounded like a burst from a .50-caliber machine gun. I ran down the PSP (pierced [or perforated] steel planking) walkway in between our personnel GP medium tents to see if others were concerned. A few fellow unit members came out of their tents, but none looked overly alarmed. One unit member said small-arms fire was often heard at night. He indicated that the fire could be coming from a marine patrol protecting the perimeter of the US Army compound. It was not the marines but who they were firing at that caused me concern, I thought. No other small-arms fire was heard during the night. I hugged my M14 rifle as I slept that night.

About two days before Easter (April 10) of 1966, I was excited when I received a letter from Judy. Knowing she would be there when I returned from Vietnam, I always got an emotional boost when reading her letters. I hurriedly opened it and read each word intently. She asked the normal questions of how I was doing and if things were going well. But about a third of the way through the letter (she never wrote long letters), she asked if it was all right for a guy she knew (she did not mention his name) to take her to an Easter party, adding that she knew I would understand. Understand? What on earth was she talking about? I did not understand and was hurt.

Judy and I had not made any significant plans for when I returned to the States; however, it was sort of understood (at least by me) that we were a couple and would continue to develop the relationship to see where it took us. I was obviously wrong, to say the least. Since I received the letter only two days before Easter, there was no way I could have responded to her, one way or another, whether it was okay or not, in time. Given that situation, I figured she would let the "boyfriend" take her to the Easter party, regardless of my feelings. I read the letter over and over, but the wording would not change; I was devastated. On Easter Sunday, even though I felt differently, I wrote Judy, telling her it was okay with me for her to go to the Easter function with the guy. I never heard from her again.

About a week into May 1966, I received a phone call from Top telling me that the 344th had received deployment orders and was scheduled to arrive at Da Nang in a couple of weeks. I informed him that everything was ready for their arrival. An LST (landing ship, tank) had been scheduled, but the planning and movement of the 344th's equipment, trucks, jeeps, LARC-Vs, materials, supplies, and personnel would be no easy task. I was glad that I was already in Da Nang, but as I found out, I would participate in a major unit move a couple of months later.

I spent the next two weeks keeping busy, ensuring that all the necessary equipment had been obtained and readied for the arrival of 1LT Redman, Top, and Spoonemore. Figuring that either Top or 1LT Redman would want to occupy my quarters in the rear room of the 344th orderly room tent, I made sure I had another place to bunk down at night in a GP medium tent next to the orderly room. I arranged a bunk for Spoonemore next to mine. 1LT Baker continued his activities and rarely stopped by the orderly room. On the occasions when our paths crossed, he would inquire as to any updates on the arrival of the main party of the 344th. I updated him when information became available. Shortly before personnel started arriving by airplane, a detail of men had been assigned by 1LT Baker to erect more tents, and others were given the task of coordinating for additional rations.

Top and the gang finally arrived in the middle of May 1966. It took about three days to get everyone settled into their sleeping quarters. The LST was off-loaded at the beach near the BOH, and a lot of personnel slept on their assigned LARC-Vs until space became available in the unit area. The unit was fully operational within the first week. With all the unit members now in Da Nang, things went back to normal. Spoonemore and I settled in a regular routine like what we'd had in Qui Nhon. One constant aggravation we had to live with was the ear-splitting noise of the F-105 Thunderchiefs, or Thuds, and McDonnell Douglas F-4 Phantoms taking off on their missions, especially at night, which prevented us from getting a good night's sleep. The Thuds were primarily bombers and the Phantoms dogfighters, but both were capable in either role.

Things ran smoothly for about a month, and then the wisdom of the US Army prevailed once again. In the middle of June 1966, the unit received orders for redeployment back to Qui Nhon. None of us were troubled by this decision, because we all felt that it was part of our tour in Vietnam. The constant changes are a part of the way of doing business in the US Army. Top held a meeting with Spoonemore and me about which one of us would repeat the undertakings that we had completed prior to the move to Da Nang. A decision was ultimately made by Top that Spoonemore would be the one to travel with the advance party that returned to Qui Nhon and I would stay in Da Nang. I took Spoonemore to the Da Nang airport a few days later. We bid our farewells and acknowledged we would see one another in a couple of weeks.

The unit spent the next two weeks preparing our equipment, materials, supplies, and vehicles to get ready for the move. It took two days to load the LST and another two days on the South China Sea to get back to Qui Nhon. The LST would go out into the South China Sea several miles to avoid coastal gunfire from the VC or the North Vietnamese Military (NVA).

Once we arrived at Qui Nhon, Spoonemore was one of the first people I saw when I got off the LST. He indicated the base camp was near where it had been before the unit vacated the space for the deployment to Da Nang. As he drove Top and me to the base camp, Spoonemore gave us the rundown on what to expect when we arrived. Once we arrived, I saw what Spoonemore was talking about. The base camp consisted of only a few GP medium tents, one that would serve as our orderly room. Several unit members from the advanced party were still working on erecting other GP medium tents. It took several days to off-load the LST and get everything relocated to the base camp from the beach. Spoonemore had everything positioned in the orderly room, which allowed us to set up operations almost immediately.

None of the local Vietnamese women who served as housemaids had been rehired yet. However, it did not take long before a group of local Vietnamese women showed up at the main gate to our base camp, inquiring as to when they could come back to work. I had volunteered for guard duty at the main gate for a couple of days and spent much of my time attempting to communicate with these Vietnamese women that it would still be a few days before they could come back.

It was about this time that I struck up a good friendship with Tom Foley, the supply sergeant. He informed me he was from Solon, Ohio, near Cleveland, and that he had been drafted into the US Army and served at Fort Ord, California, before being sent to Vietnam. We did not get much off time, but when we did, Tom and I spent it together. Since the supply tent was next to the orderly room, we also saw each other every day. Tom told me that while at Fort Ord, he had met a girl that he planned to marry when he got out of the US Army. He had no desire to make the US Army a career.

The 344th's stay in Qui Nhon was short-lived. About a month after we arrived back at Qui Nhon, battalion headquarters[23] informed 1LT Redman that the 344th had been tapped to deploy to Cam Ranh Bay. Cam Ranh Bay is a deep-water bay in Vietnam in the province of Khánh Hòa. It is located at an inlet off the South China Sea situated on the southeastern coast of Vietnam, between Phan Rang and Nha Trang, approximately 290 kilometers' northeast of Saigon (Ho Chi Minh City).

In 1966, Cam Ranh Bay was relatively safe from attack by the enemy. The base was the largest American presence in any one location in Vietnam and accommodated tens of thousands of soldiers, airmen, sailors, and civilian contractors. Cam Ranh Bay ended up being the main personnel processing center (Twenty-Second Replacement Detachment) for the Vietnam War. Cam Ranh Bay was designated by higher-ups to be well suited for the use of our LARC-Vs until the US Army finished constructing deep-water piers that would not be completed until late 1966. The LARC-Vs were needed to haul materials, supplies, munitions, and personnel from ship to shore until the piers were completed. The 344th had plenty of experience getting ready to deploy to another location within country, so it did not take as long to prepare everything to relocate to Cam Ranh Bay. The US Navy was getting used to us by this time, and the two branches worked well with each other to make this move the smoothest one yet.

The 344th arrived in Cam Ranh Bay during the month of July 1966, and the unit established a base camp on a couple of acres of sandy land on South Beach. We were administratively organized and ready to work within two days and operationally ready within one day of our arrival. Tom and I arranged to bunk in the same tent. It was during the assignment to Cam Ranh Bay that our friendship took root. The slack time was short, but we became very close, both professionally and personally. Tom was a good supply sergeant who worked hard and ensured that all equipment was serviceable and, if it was in short supply, he always found ways to get more of what was needed. He made sure replacement supplies were obtained as quickly as possible. He was equally liked by other 344th members and could work well with them and the senior NCOs and officers. Tom was very fortunate in that his duties did not include handling the LARC-Vs.

Shortly after the 344th arrived at Cam Ranh Bay, a few of their LARC-Vs were tasked to perform port security. This task required daytime and nighttime patrols not only in Cam Ranh Bay but up the many waterways leading inland around the area. The 344th's added responsibilities were stopping and searching sampans (small Vietnamese boats) for VC infiltrators, weapons, ammunition, and supplies that were being smuggled into the area. The added duties of port security were taking away from our primary ship-to-shore mission.[24] When the 344th started operations in Cam Ranh Bay, there was only one deep-water pier[25] (DeLong pier). This meant that LARC-Vs were in great demand to augment the mission of getting supplies, munitions, weapons, men, and other much-needed provisions from cargo ships to shore. By late 1966, Cam Ranh Bay had three DeLong piers and was the major logistical beach for II Corps.

Regardless of this added mission, the 344th settled down, and the US Army did not move any of our company assets or troops for several months. From mid-July to November 1966, the unit was fully operational on the south beach at Cam Ranh Bay. The sheer volume of duties and responsibilities continued to be tremendous and sometimes overwhelming for Spoonemore and me. The days were long, hot, hectic, and frustrating. Our worst enemy was the brutal weather that hampered our work productivity. Working conditions were horrific with the sweltering heat and high winds that blew sand all over the place. Sand blew into our orderly room on a regular basis. It collected in the drawers of desks and on the floor. The sand got on our papers, making it hard to work with the documents. It was impractical to attempt to clean the desks or sweep the floor, because as soon as you swept up a pile of sand, the wind blew in another pile.

One day, a multilevel bookshelf that stood directly behind me and was used to separate my desk from the commanders, holding heavy binders full of US Army regulations, guidance pamphlets, reports, other official papers, and materials, was propelled by a strong gust of wind onto my back. Spoonemore and 1LT Redman had to pull me out from under the rubble. I ended up with a three-inch laceration to the back of my head and some bruises, bumps, and welts to my back and arms, but I otherwise made it through the ordeal. I was treated by a medic and immediately sent back to work. These frustrations, inconveniences, and injuries were nothing compared to what the foot soldiers fighting in the jungles of Vietnam had to endure. However, the 344th's mission was just as important to the war effort.

It had been a year (the length of time for a tour in Vietnam) since the original members of the 344th had arrived with the unit in June 1965. Thus, they began rotating back to the United States to other assignments, and many new faces started to appear. One of the old-timers to leave the 344th was Top Howard. He went back to Fort Story, and his replacement, 1SG John Wimmer, came on board in mid-July. Wimmer was an older soldier, having served as far back as World War II and the Korean Conflict. He had retired from the US Army in the early 1960s but volunteered to come back on active duty to serve in Vietnam. Wimmer was also a candidate for warrant officer and was awaiting the US Army's decision on his selection. Wimmer was slender, had an affable personality, got along with 1LT Redman, and worked well with Spoonemore and me. As time passed, however, he rarely got involved in making any real decisions or running the company in a manner commensurate with expectations of a first sergeant's duties. Spoonemore and I took over as shadow first sergeants. On occasion, Wimmer would lie down on a cot and take extended naps during normal duty hours. I attributed his behavior and performance as short-lived until his warrant officer selection came through.

July 1966 was a busy month for the 344th. In late July 1966, 1LT Redman was promoted to captain, and I received a promotion to specialist four (E4). I enjoyed the raise to $175 a month, and it added to the amount I sent home to Mom for her and some extra to put in my bank savings. The unit continued with both ship-to-shore and port security operations with no causalities. The weather improved, and work conditions became somewhat more bearable.

In early August 1966, I received a care package from my sister June. June always had a humorous side to her, and the contents of the package reflected this trait. She had sent newspapers from Terre Haute, some peanut-butter fudge that I liked, and some girlie magazines, which were a favorite of Tom's. But the most unusual thing she included in the box was a red shirt with yellow polka dots. If I ever decided to wear the shirt (which I didn't), it would have made the VCs' job a lot easier for them to put me in their crosshairs. Also, included in the care package was a letter from June. She informed me that she had moved from Terre Haute to Raleigh, North Carolina, where she'd found a job working as a secretary for a land developer. She invited me to Raleigh for a visit when I returned from Vietnam.

One evening, I was at the BOH, finishing up the daily tonnage report, when one of the LARC-V drivers asked me if I would accompany him to the other side of the bay. He informed me he had to take several Vietnamese people back to their village. I readily agreed, and off we went. Darkness came quickly, and we found ourselves just out of radio range of the harbormaster. The jaunt was supposed to be a simple, short trip to drop off the group of Vietnamese and immediately return to the south beach. However, as we went farther out into the bay, the driver got lost, and he received no help from the Vietnamese, because they did not speak English. The LARC-V driver headed for the nearest visual lights in the distance but was surprised to learn they were farther than he realized. We continued for what seemed like an hour or so, but it was probably only fifteen to twenty minutes, and it became obvious that the group of Vietnamese people were getting more apprehensive about where we were headed. For what seemed like an eternity, we traveled toward the lights on the shore. At night when traveling in a large body of water with a small boat, one's perception of distance is often distorted.

With no warning, the LARC-V's huge tires hit some rocks, which threw the boat into a spin, causing the Vietnamese to get even more fearful than before. Several of them lost their balance, and it was a miracle that no one fell overboard. The driver eventually regained control of the LARC-V. The roar of the engine and the screaming, anxious Vietnamese trying to hang on to whatever they could get their hands on prevented the driver from hearing me when I yelled at him to slow down. We were entirely in darkness with the headlights of the LARC-V giving off very little light in front of us. I finally pushed my way through the group of Vietnamese that was standing between me and the driver at the front of the LARC-V. I tapped him on the shoulder, and he finally turned his face so we had eye contact. I asked him if he had any idea where we were going.

"I made the trip once before in the daylight, but at night, it's a different situation," the driver said. He admitted that he was unsure as to where he was going, but he indicated he had probably gone too far. He believed that by heading for the shore lights in the distance, he had passed the entrance to a small cove to get to the water's edge of the village. I suggested that we turn around and follow the shoreline for a while in hopes of seeing additional shore lights. He agreed.

We traveled in the opposite direction for another twenty minutes, and to our delight, we both saw lights on the shore to our left. We both agreed to turn in the direction of the lights. About ten minutes later, we came upon a small cove just as the driver had indicated. Once through the cove, we could make out a small gathering of Vietnamese villagers standing on the shore, waving at us. As we approached the shore, an older Vietnamese gentleman tugged my shirt sleeve and gave me a thumbs-up to indicate it was his village. After the driver pulled the LARC-V onto shore and let the group of Vietnamese people get off the LARC-V, the driver and I were extremely relieved that we had gotten them home. Now, we had to get back to the other side of the bay. We had been gone about an hour and a half and had no radio contact with the BOH. We had seen only a couple of small sampans on the water as we were making our way across the bay.

The driver carefully maneuvered the LARC-V from the shore back out into the bay. He was cautious to avoid any large rocks that might be in our path. Once we went back through the cove, he opened it up, and we headed for the other side of the bay. With good luck, the trip should take about an hour. "We have plenty of gas," said the driver.

I thought, *Thank God.*

We had an uneventful return trip back to the other side of the bay, and once we were a short distance from shore, our radio communication was restored. A voice from the BOH blared over the radio, "Where have you been? We almost shot you out of the water!"

The LARC-V driver related what had happened, and he was ordered to report immediately to the BOH once he came ashore. About ten minutes later, both of us were in the BOH.

The sergeant on duty at the BOH advised the LARC-V driver that a Coast Guard gunboat was tracking us on their radar. Since the LARC-V was in a restricted area, they were prepared to shoot and ask questions later. Fortunately, no action, other than monitoring the LARC-V, was taken by the Coast Guard. You never know how precarious certain situations become until they are over. Rule Four: *When venturing into the unknown, ensure everyone required is briefed.*

After the "lost in the bay" episode, things were relatively quiet for a while. Spoonemore and I routinely went about our daily work tasks and pretty much ran the full gamut of administrative duties for the 344th. Captain Redman was busy ensuring that the unit mission of hauling materials, supplies, personnel, and other provisions from ship to shore got done and that a small contingent of LARC-Vs were patrolling the port and waterways, making it safe for others to do their job. This mission continued uninterrupted for a couple of months.

Tom kept busy ensuring adequate supplies were brought into the unit on a regular basis. His days were as hectic as mine. It seemed that each day took three to complete one. For the short time in the evenings before we crashed into much-needed sleep, we relentlessly talked about home, family, and what we were going to do when we returned home after our tour in Vietnam. The time was passing fast, and I would be satisfied to just continue working at the pace we were until I left Vietnam. I received an occasional letter from Mom, who always was upbeat and positive. She spoke of family and health, without talking specifics about anyone. One thing she was consistent about in all her letters was that she could not wait until I got home. For every one letter from Mom, I wrote two or three to her. Just after arriving in Vietnam, I wrote a few letters to June and Nora, but that stopped after a month or so.

At the end of October 1966, I requested and received permission for a trip to Hawaii under the US Army Rest and Recuperation (R&R) Program. The

R&R Program allows up to a week for service members in a combat zone to take leave (vacation) to any location on an approved list of cities, which included Honolulu, Sydney (Australia), Hong Kong, Bangkok, and more; I chose Honolulu as my preferred destination. I was excited about taking the trip and relished in the thought of spending some time away from Vietnam in an American city and to eat a big, fat, juicy hamburger. As the old saying goes, *if it looks too good to be true, it probably isn't.* On the day that I was to depart, I had to take a flight on a C-130 from Cam Ranh Bay to Saigon, where I would catch a commercial flight to Honolulu. Tom dropped me off at the Cam Ranh Bay airport, we said our good-byes, and I told him I would see him in about a week.

As luck, would have it, the C-130 I was scheduled to take from Cam Ranh Bay to Saigon had been damaged when it received small-arms fire as it was landing at the airport, and the flight to Saigon was canceled. As the sun went down and the evening fell upon Vietnam, I still had not been able to get a second flight to Saigon, so I decided to head back to the 344th. I hitched a ride back to the 344th base camp and found everyone else already sacked out in their bunks sound asleep. I immediately crashed in my bunk and had no trouble finding sleep that night.

The next thing I remember was Tom waking me up at about 5:30 a.m. the following morning. "What the hell happened?" Tom asked.

I told him and a few of the fellows standing nearby that the plane to Saigon had been fired on as it was landing at the Cam Ranh Bay Airport and no other flights were available to get me to Saigon. When Tom left, I assumed he went to the chow tent for breakfast, but a few moments later, he came running back into our tent, short of breath, and said Captain Redman wanted to see me ASAP.

Not knowing what was up, I reported to Captain Redman, who was at his desk. Without hesitation and barely moving in his chair, he pointed to his driver, who was waiting next to his jeep, and yelled, "Get in! Johnson [his driver] will take you part of the way to Nha Trang about thirty-five miles down the road. There you can hitch a ride to the Ninetieth Replacement Center, where an R&R center is located. They can get you to Hawaii. Good luck!"

I tried to thank him, but he kept yelling, "Go, go, go!"

I ran to my tent, grabbed by personal bag, and hopped in the jeep. Johnson took me to a guard post on Route 1 a few miles from Nha Trang. I had to make the additional ten or so miles to Nha Trang, which was about fifteen miles north of Cam Ranh Bay.

As I jumped from the jeep, I thanked Johnson for his efforts and approached an American soldier waiting on the side of the road near a gate barricade. The soldier told me that he too was hitching a ride into Nha Trang, so we waited together. Shortly afterward, a deuce-and-a-half showed up, and the driver let both of us get in the back. Coincidently, the route the driver took directly passed the Ninetieth Replacement Center, where I was going. After driving several miles through heavy traffic consisting of military jeeps, trucks, and civilian vehicles, the driver let me off near the main entrance to the Ninetieth Replacement Center. Boy, what luck was that?

I found the R&R center to be in a huge garrison-type building in an area inside a compound surrounded by wire and a wooden wall. There were several wooden buildings on the compound, recently built to support the US military presence in Nha Trang, Vietnam.

I reported to a US Navy petty officer standing behind a counter and told him that I was there to catch a plane to Hawaii for an R&R trip. With a scowl on his face, he looked up and asked me why I hadn't gone through the proper channels to get the flight. I gave him a copy of my orders and explained my story. The petty officer empathically told me that there were no commercial flights headed for Hawaii for a couple of days.

I figured, *Well, that's it*, and I started thinking about how I was going to get back to the 344th that night. However, before I could ponder my situation any longer, he immediately asked if I was interested in going anywhere else. I told him I had not thought of it, but if it was possible, I might consider a different location. I asked him how much trouble it would be to get orders for another location. He told me, "Wait a minute. I'll be right back."

I saw him go to an inner office behind the counter and speak to a US Army captain. They spoke for a couple of minutes, and the petty officer returned and asked if I would like to go to Penang, Malaysia. I had never heard of the city or country, but my curiosity got the best of me, so I told the petty officer that it sounded like fun. The petty officer told me that I was extremely lucky—he was getting ready to board a flight for Penang himself.

"How does this make me lucky?" I asked.

"Your orders have been changed, and you are now authorized to board the same flight as I am," the petty officer said.

I was dumbfounded to say the least. I saw him write on the orders I had given him when I walked in, and he handed them back to me. All he did to change my R&R orders was to mark through the words *Honolulu, Hawaii*, and to write in ink *Penang, Malaysia*, and he told me to follow him. I could not believe what was happening. The petty officer who worked at the R&R center was scheduled to go on R&R to Penang. When I walked into the R&R center, he was just getting some last-minute tasks completed before jumping on the plane. If I had been five minutes later, what had just happened would not have taken place.

Penang, a state in Malaysia is located on the northwest coast of Peninsular Malaysia by the Strait of Malacca. It is bordered by Kedah in the north and east, and Perak in the south. Penang is the second smallest Malaysian state in area after Perlis and the eighth most populous. It is composed of two parts—Penang Island, the government seat and Seberang Perai on the Malay Peninsula.[26]

The airplane was literally just outside the R&R center building, about twenty feet from the rear door. We boarded a small two-engine prop run by the Vietnamese airline and took two seats over the wing, the petty officer on one side and me on the other; the flight took about three hours to get to Malaysia. We landed on the mainland and were met by R&R representatives at the airport. We boarded a bus that took us to a ferryboat, where we were given a short briefing about the island of Penang as we made the fifty-minute trip across the Strait of Malacca from the mainland to city of George Town on the island of Penang. Since I had been added to the group at the last minute, I was unable to reserve a hotel room at a more affordable rate and had to pay a premium price for a five-night stay at the Ambassador Hotel. Still, with the exchange rate being 2.96 Malaysian dollars to each US dollar, this was a great bargain.

On the plane, the petty officer had introduced himself as Marvin Wilson[27] from Milwaukee, Wisconsin. Wilson told me he had been in the US Navy about six years and was seven months into his tour in Vietnam. By coincidence, Wilson also was staying at the Ambassador Hotel, not because he liked paying more money but because he got a cut rate on a room by being associated with the travel market by benefit of his job with the R&R center. Although we got to know each other while flying to Malaysia and were staying at the same hotel, we made no plans to tour the city of George Town or the island together. We did end up eating dinner together a couple of nights at the hotel restaurant.

I spent the next five days traveling around the island of Penang and the city of George Town, sightseeing, eating and sleeping. The scenery was stunning, and Penang Island had gorgeous high ranges, multicolored plants, flowers, deep-blue streams, and rivers, and the city of George Town was clean and modern looking. The weather was sunny, cool, and somewhat breezy to the point I felt guilty about not having to work in the hot, sweltering heat of Vietnam. I could not believe my good fortune of being so young and experiencing such wonders in a far-off land. I took numerous photographs of the places, sights, and people I saw. The memories alone would be enough to sustain a person for a lifetime. One memory I will always remember is that I spent October 25, 1966—my twentieth birthday—in Penang, Malaysia.

A fact of life that always follows delightful happenings, like the one I experienced in Penang, is that they end. The morning of our departure, I said my good-byes to hotel staff, the taxi driver I had hired to drive me around the island to the many sites and locations I saw, and others who had helped me on the trip. I did not feel like a young kid from Bicknell or Terre Haute; I felt like a world traveler. In the hotel lobby, I hooked up with Wilson, who, like me, looked refreshed and rejuvenated. We sat next to each other on the flight back to Nha Trang and exchanged stories of the things and places we'd experienced and the people we'd seen.

It was around 10:00 p.m. when I made it back to base camp after most people had finished working for the day. However, when the jeep driver I had hitched a ride with let me out, I walked past the orderly room tent and saw Spoonemore still working. I went in to let him know how good of a time I had in Penang, but he was so focused on working that he, almost as an afterthought, looked at me and said, "Hi."

I dropped my bag, sat down at my desk, and asked what I could do to help. Spoonemore appeared tired, worn down, and on the verge of exhaustion. Suddenly, I lost my yearning to talk about my trip and started pulling documents from my in-box to determine what I could get started on first. I worked until five that morning and then went to my tent, changed into my fatigues, grabbed some chow, and returned to the orderly room. When I returned to the orderly room, Spoonemore, who had left just before I did, was already at his desk hard at work.

It took me about three fifteen-hour workdays to catch up. No one had completed the tonnage reports since I had departed on R&R, and I had to get creative in getting them caught up and submitted to battalion headquarters. The morning reports for the 253rd had also not been completed, but fortunately, not many personnel changes had occurred since I'd left, making it easy to catch up.

Spoonemore updated me on what had occurred in my absence. One thing that caught my attention more than anything else was a new rumor going around that the 344th was going to send more men to Vung Ro Bay.[28] Vung Ro Bay was about eighty-five miles north on Route 1, situated on the coast of the South China Sea, north of Cam Ranh Bay. Vung Ro Bay was about eighteen miles south of Tuy Hoa Air Base and the home of the 4th Infantry Division.[29] The 344th had deployed a platoon-size detachment to Vung Ro Bay a few months prior. The first thought on my mind was that I would be picked to deploy there. I kept my fingers crossed that that wouldn't happen. I had just three months left in country and wanted to spend the rest of my time at Cam Ranh Bay.

Well into November 1966, two weeks after hearing the news about Vung Ro Bay from Spoonemore, I felt I had dodged deployment there, because it was getting too close to my departure from Vietnam. However, Top Wimmer, his face drawn and ashen looking, came to me early one day in mid-November and gave me the unwanted news that my excellent reputation for being the advance man on previous deployments had placed me at the top of the list. He told me that I had been handpicked to go to Vung Ro Bay to take over the administrative duties there. Top Wimmer knew I did not want to deploy to Vung Ro Bay, but he had no choice in the matter; the decision had already been made by Captain Redman. I had the rest of the day to prepare my personal things and to collect needed supplies, materials, and other necessities. I was told there would be no assigned tent or any designated location where I could utilize space at Vung Ro Bay and I would be on my own. I felt proud that Captain Redman, Top, and other senior NCOs considered me as the best man for the job and knew I could handle the myriad of duties required, but I was not anxious to relocate to another base camp this late in my Vietnam tour.

At 6:00 a.m. on November 17, 1966, I gathered my personal belongings, supplies, and other things and threw them in Captain Redman's jeep, and his driver took me to the airport. I got everything on the waiting C-130, and we immediately took off for Tuy Hoa Air Base. The flight from Cam Ranh Bay to Tuy Hoa, including taxiing time, was about an hour and a half—approximately eighty-five miles. There was no one there to meet me upon arrival. I off-loaded my gear and asked an airman if I could store my belongings in a corner within his sight until I found transportation to the 344th detachment area. There was too much gear for me to hand carry, and I had absolutely no idea where to start looking for a ride. I began by asking the airman that agreed to watch my gear if he knew how far Vung Ro Bay was and if any ground transportation was available. The airman, without telling me how far Vung Ro Bay was and devoid of any sort of emotion about my quandary, muttered that I should check outside the terminal, where drivers usually congregated while waiting for new arrivals to take to their respective units.

The first several drivers I approached said they were not going to Vung Ro Bay. I kept going down the line and finally found a US Army PFC from the 119th Transportation Company who said he was going to Vung Ro Bay, but probably had a full load. He told me he was expecting eight soldiers with full gear to come at 10:00 from Tan Son Nhut. However, if I could squeeze on, he would gladly take me along; waiting until 10:00 meant another hour. I told him I would check back in about an hour to see if he had room. I checked with five more drivers, but none were headed toward Vung Ro Bay.

I found the PFC from the 119th, who was sitting in his truck smoking a cigarette, and said I would take him up on his offer for a ride. I dreaded him seeing me carrying my gear to the truck for fear he would think it was too much, but he did not say anything and even helped me put it on the truck. I pushed the gear all the way to the back of the truck. Luck stayed with me when the new troops arrived: there were only six men. Two of them had apparently been reassigned to other units and were not coming to Tuy Hoa. They all had duffel bags, and only a couple of them had additional bags of personal belongings. We had no trouble fitting everyone inside the deuce-and-a-half truck comfortably.

Vung Ro Bay, located in south Phu Yen Province, was about eighteen miles east on Highway A1 from Tuy Hoa. The short distance still took us about an hour, because the road was narrow with no shoulder and had potholes every few feet, making the driving conditions perilous. We went through two small rural Vietnamese villages along the route, consisting of straw-roofed huts and numerous street vendors selling everything from cigarettes to raw, uncleaned vegetables and unwholesome-looking, nasty, noxious-smelling fish. The street vendors, positioned close to the road, were eager to seize the opportunity to do business with any of the many US Army trucks and other vehicles passing by. The Vietnamese boys were shirtless, and the girls wore traditional ao ba ba silk pants and long-sleeved, button-down shirts. The girls' long shirts were split at the sides at the waist, forming two flaps, with two pockets in the front. The attire was simple yet versatile. In my travels throughout Vietnam, I noticed the general population wore the same style of clothing while laboring or lounging. The kids, selling nothing, were waving and stretching their arms out to see if they could catch any handouts as we drove by. I would become very familiar with one of these villages because of many trips up and down Highway A1 between Vung Ro Bay and Tuy Hoa Air Base.

We arrived at Vung Ro Bay about 3:00 in the afternoon. The imposing landscapes of the Truong Son Mountains from the crest of Deo Ca Pass on Highway 1A were breathtaking. The driver turned down a narrow, dusty road that wound its way down to Vung Ro Bay. The driver stopped on Alpha Beach, where trucks, jeeps, and other vehicles were parked. The driver informed his passengers that Bravo and Charlie Beaches could only be accessed by boat or helicopter. I found out that the 344th was located on Charlie Beach, in a small cove a short distance around a mountain from Alpha. Immediately after I got my gear off-loaded from the deuce-and-a-half, I noticed a couple of LARC-Vs parked on the beach. I got permission to secure my gear inside a tent that was used by the harbormaster. I was informed that the LARC-Vs belonged to the 344th and that the unit would be off-loading supplies from docked ships until about 6:00 that evening.

I asked one of the soldiers in the tent to radio a LARC to inquire if any were going to Charlie Beach before that time. The soldier pressed the radio mic and asked for anyone from the 344th to come back. A voice could be heard over the loud squelch of the radio that one of the LARCs already parked on the beach was getting ready to make a run to Charlie in thirty minutes or so. I was directed to one of the LARCs, where its driver was working on the engine. As we shook hands, I introduced myself as Dick Miller, and he replied, "Larry Bailey."

I did not know him, but he knew me from Qui Nhon and Cam Ranh. "I have been in country since March and was in the first group to be sent here in June," Bailey said.

I advised him that Captain Redman sent me to Vung Ro Bay to set up an administrative support section for the detachment.

"We need someone to take care of our personnel and personal matters," said Bailey.

I felt better after hearing Bailey's comment, because it validated my presence at Vung Ro Bay. Bailey mentioned that he would run me to Charlie Beach as soon as a couple of other soldiers from the 344th who were working nearby showed up. It took two trips to get all my gear to the LARC. I had it all loaded on the LARC before the others arrived.

We started for Charlie Beach about fifteen minutes later. Once we were well out into the bay, I could not help but notice how serene and tranquil the water looked. It made me feel like I was in a different part of the world. I felt like I was in an area where everyone came to relax and enjoy themselves and there was no war, death, or destruction, and then I was brought back to reality when I remembered the wounded and dead soldiers being hauled off the helicopters at the Eighty-Fifth.

I fired questions at the two soldiers riding with us about the area. Was it safe? Was the food good? How were the living conditions?

They both responded with essentially the same answers: it was relatively safe, the chow was decent, and apart from the living conditions being somewhat primitive, they felt comfortable. I asked them to clarify "relatively safe," and they indicated Charlie had snipers that occasionally took potshots at trucks traveling on Highway A1 from Vung Ro Bay to Tuy Hoa.

Things went quiet for a few moments, and then I felt a jolt as the LARC-V's engine growled and roared when it left the water and climbed onto the sandy beach. Bailey sped along the beach for a short distance and came to an abrupt, almost hurried stop in front of a sign indicating we were at the 344th Transportation Company. At the water's edge sat the compound of the 344th Transportation Company.

"Here we are, gentleman," Bailey barked.

"Where do I report?" I inquired with Bailey.

He gave me a funny, sort of amused look and told me he was not sure. Puzzled, I asked him who was in charge, and he said he reported to Sergeant Allen of the First Platoon. I then asked him who the ranking person was and where I could find him. "Staff Sergeant [SSG] Michaels," Bailey replied. "He usually is one of the last people to leave Alpha in the evening."

I went into a holding pattern until around 6:30 when Michaels showed up. While waiting on Michaels, I walked around the base camp area and saw three GP medium tents, a mess tent, and a couple of unmanned bunkers surrounded by sandbags. Since I found no tent or area used for supplies, I assumed that they were kept on Alpha Beach. Earlier, I had been informed by one of the soldiers that when not operational, four of the five LARC-Vs at Vung Ro were parked on Alpha and one, which shuttled men to work, was kept on Charlie. When Michaels showed up, we introduced ourselves. Looking somewhat indifferent, Michaels immediately explained, "I may be the ranking person at the 344th Detachment, but the unit leadership did not tell me I was the guy in charge, and no one told me you were coming. Since no one told me you were coming, I have no idea where you are going to stay."

I thought, *someone dropped the ball about me coming to Vung Ro.*

After I got some chow at the dining tent, I visited each tent to inquire if they had any space for another bunk. The last tent I checked had one bunk at the rear of the tent. I checked with the men around the bunk, who voiced no objection about me claiming ownership. I moved my gear into the back of the tent. The tent had no sides, but a wooden floor was a plus. From my bunk, I could clearly see the jungle reaching up the mountain directly behind the tent. Vung Ro was the most primitive base camp the 344th had in Vietnam, and I suspected my job here would bring some unusual challenges.

I introduced myself to Johnson, Fisher, and Collins,[30] the men nearest my bunk, and they all welcomed me to the detachment. Each person I introduced myself to in the tent said he was assigned to the First Platoon and reported to Sergeant Allen, but like Bailey and Michaels, none of them knew who oversaw the 344th Detachment at Vung Ro Base Camp. I decided I would try to get some sleep and worry about this predicament in the morning. I was exhausted from the activities I'd endured on the trip to Vung Ro, but before I crashed for the night, I had one more obstacle to overcome: I had to find blankets. No one knew where any were located. That first night at Vung Ro, I slept in my fatigues to keep warm and used my helmet as a pillow.

I awoke at 5:00 the next morning at the same time others were getting ready for their duty day. I went with Johnson, Fisher, and Collins to the dining tent. As we walked into the tent, I saw SSG Michaels at a table, already eating his breakfast. I got my food and joined him. "Good morning," I said.

"Good morning," he mumbled.

After a few minutes of silence, I readdressed the issue of who oversaw the 344th at Vung Ro Bay. SSG Michaels suggested I call headquarters at Cam Ranh to see if the commander or Top would know. Under normal circumstances, Michaels's recommendation would have seemed like a dumb idea, but since the chain of command at Vung Ro was so muddled, Michaels's suggestion seemed the most sensible way to resolve the situation of who was the boss.

After chow, I found a field phone and spent most of the morning trying unsuccessfully to reach Top at Cam Ranh. Finally, that afternoon, I got through to Top, who told me that I was to oversee the administrative, supply, and personnel duties at Vung Ro. "SSG Michaels, although the senior NCO at Vung Ro and technically the man in charge of the LARC-Vs and the men that operated them, is not your boss. You report to me," Top simply explained.

I told Top that he should let Michaels know he was the person in charge, because he sure didn't know it. I also informed Top that I had searched for a good location to work, but there wasn't any. I informed him that I was setting up operations in my tent and that I would get word to everyone who needed assistance with any personnel matters to reach out to me. Top thought that was a good start and that I should not be afraid to take the initiative to get the job done. Throughout the entire phone call, Top and I had a hard time hearing each other due to the bad connection. Rule Five: *If you are in a new job where your duties and responsibilities are not clearly defined, you should expeditiously concentrate on identifying the goals, objectives, and needs of your personnel; then set forth procedures to organize steps to achieve those goals and objectives and help your personnel.*

In future incidents, I would find myself in the same predicament like the one at Vung Ro of not having clear and concise guidance from leadership to get the job done, which had to be corrected by my initiatives. The US Army needs good leaders to function, and even a lowly specialist fourth class like me knew the Vung Ro detachment of the 344th had serious leadership problems. If we ever got attacked by the VC, there would be no one to organize a defense of our base camp; it would be every man for himself. What a way to fight a war.

I spent the next several days arranging a corner of the GP medium tent into a makeshift orderly room and supply area. I borrowed (and I am sticking to my story) a field table for my typewriter, which I'd brought with me. I begged, borrowed, and procured enough wood from the other units along the beach to build a rudimentary bookshelf on which to pile forms, documents, and a couple of binders containing reference regulations. I was now able to work on the tonnage reports that became one of my major duties, just as I had done at Qui Nhon, Da Nang, and Cam Ranh. SSG Michaels was glad that he was no longer responsible for the tonnage reports.

I prepared a notice to all members of the detachment that anyone having need of administrative, supply, or personnel matters could come to me. I coordinated with SSG Michaels and Sergeant Allen to ask their men what their needs and concerns were and requested information on morale and activities of the men when they were not working. I also advised the two that I had set up a makeshift orderly and supply area in the corner of my tent and was prepared to provide them with assistance. I suspected it would take a couple of days or more to get answers to my questions.

To my surprise, SSG Michaels and Sergeant Allen came back that evening with information they had received from their men. One of the main problems for the men was getting time off to find a place to purchase money orders to send to family members. Another issue with the men was not having a steady flow of beer to relax with in the evenings after a long day doing ship-to-shore trips with the LARCs.

"We have no ground transportation to go to Tuy Hoa to obtain supplies from the supply depot and PX," Allen said.

I asked Michaels and Allen, "How did you accomplish these tasks prior to my arrival?"

They told me that they would designate an individual, usually a person taken from duty during the day, to hitch a ride on another unit's deuce-and-a-half that was going to Tuy Hoa. This system did not always work, because they rarely knew the schedule when a driver from another unit was going to make the trip. The other units also had barely enough time to get their own supplies, let alone help the 344th with theirs.

"I will work on getting readily available ground transportation for a weekly run to Tuy Hoa," I informed Allen and Michaels.

I figured that once the ground transportation was procured, I could establish a time and place and method to collect monies from unit members and personally take it to the Tuy Hoa post office and purchase the money orders for them. Getting a vehicle would also help us with getting supplies, including beer for the troops. I began almost immediately to search for a vehicle for the detachment. I started by contacting Top in Cam Ranh to inquire if they could send us a deuce-and-a-half or a jeep. This effort failed, because the 344th had no vehicles to send, and even if they'd had one available (driving it up Highway A1 was out due to VC activity), it would take weeks to ship it to Tuy Hoa via US Navy LST transport. I am not sure Top Wimmer was putting forth the required effort to work through this problem and get us a vehicle. This was the last time I ever talked to Top Wimmer, because by the time I left Vung Ro for Cam Ranh just prior to going home, he had been accepted for warrant rank and had been reassigned from the unit. I did not pursue this angle any further and went to plan B.

I approached the NCO in charge of an engineer company and requested the use of a deuce-and-a-half one day a week for a supply and morale run for the 344th. He said he would ponder the request and let me know. I went to two other companies on Alpha Beach and was flatly turned down without even getting an offer to catch a ride with them whenever they would do supply runs into Tuy Hoa. I checked the motor pool on Alpha to see what other units I could approach to procure a vehicle. I thought that my request for the use of a vehicle was falling on deaf ears because of my position and rank. It could also be that most of the senior NCOs running their detachments had no vehicles to spare or those I talked to could not figure why the 344th did not have ready access to a vehicle.

From dodging combat to having the most coveted type of job, I always considered myself lucky in Vietnam. Well, my luck continued to be good in that when I returned to the engineer company a couple of days later to check on the NCO in charge's decision to use a deuce-and-a-half, I was informed that one could be made available to the 344th each Tuesday. I agreed to the terms of use and was anxious to get started on planning and formalizing the 344th weekly supply and morale trips. I advised Michaels and Allen that I had procured ground transportation for Tuesday of each week.

"I need a driver for a deuce-and-a-half," I advised Michaels.

He looked at Allen, and they both agreed that Bailey should be that person. They were elated of the news and immediately told their men that they could meet with me to coordinate money order runs. It took two days to meet with all the men who needed to send money home. Michaels, Allen, and I also collected small amounts of money from each man in the detachment so we could purchase beer at the Tuy Hoa post exchange.

On Tuesday, Bailey and I picked up the deuce-and-a-half from the engineers and started up the mountain toward Highway A1 and then onto Tuy Hoa. As we stopped just before turning onto Highway A1, a US Army lieutenant colonel (LTC) had his driver abruptly stop his jeep in front of our deuce-and-a-half, causing Baily to slam on the brakes. The US Army LTC then jumped out, ran back to our vehicle, heaved himself upon the floorboard, and stuck his head inside and, without explaining himself, shouted at Bailey and me, "I know what is going on at Charlie Beach, and you fellows had better watch it, because I am keeping an eye on you guys!" Then just as quickly, the LTC jumped off the floorboard, hopped back in his jeep, and drove off.

I looked at Bailey with a puzzled expression and asked, "What in the hell was that all about?"

Bailey returned my stare with an equally perplexed look. "I do not have any f....'ing idea what he was talking about," Bailey responded.

Neither Bailey nor I ever saw the LTC again. In retrospect, the LTC was probably the officer in charge of the Vung Ro Bay operations and had a skewed assessment of the activities at Charlie Beach because he did not live there or had never visited.

On the trip to Tuy Hoa Air Base that day, Bailey and I stopped at a Vietnamese eatery in a small village. We would travel through this village many times on the trip from Vung Ro to the airport during my tenure at Vung Ro Bay. Bailey parked the deuce-and-a-half on a side road so it would not impede traffic on the narrow thoroughfare. The building that housed the eatery was a small dirt hut with a tin roof. The inside dining area was dirty, upswept, and dark. There was barely enough room for five or six tables. We were lucky: no one was there, so we had no trouble finding a table.

I ordered some fried chopped fish (*banh mi cha ca*), and Bailey got some type of noodle soup (*mi quang ga*). The place was not an eatery where you would want to see the health inspection report, but the food tasted good. As we sat eating our food, a small Vietnamese girl about eleven years old came limping up to our table to ask for a handout. I noticed that her left foot was covered in a dirty dressing. She spoke little English, but I knew she was asking for food. I ordered her some pork and rice, and when it was brought to the table, she grabbed the bowl and started to walk off. I motioned for her to sit down with us so she could eat the food, to which she complied.

The girl was unkempt and wearing a raggedy, stained, dirty dress with no shoes. She was cute, nicely mannered, and obviously very hungry. She appeared very grateful that I had gotten her some food, which she immediately and enthusiastically dived into with gusto. The girl had beautiful blonde hair and was Eurasian in appearance. Although I was unaware at the time of the French's involvement in the Indochina war prior to the US conflict, in memory, I have long since concluded that she was the offspring of a French father and Vietnamese mother. Bailey and I continued to eat our food while watching the young girl devour hers. I motioned for our Vietnamese waitress to come to our table. I had previously determined she spoke at least limited English when we ordered our food. I asked the waitress if she knew the young girl, and she told me that she was an orphan who lived on the streets, and without asking, the waitress told us the girl had hurt her foot one night during a VC attack near the village. The waitress further explained that during the daytime, the girl hung around the restaurant begging customers for food. I asked the waitress what happened to her parents. With a look of anguish, the Vietnamese waitress softly responded, "Her mother was killed by the VC a few months ago, and no one knows if her father is alive or dead." Thinking how difficult the little girl's life had been, one could not help but to ruminate about her future.

After we finished our meal, I decided to take the little girl a short distance down the road to a medical clinic to see if they could at least check her foot. I told Bailey to wait for me in the truck, and off we went. The girl walked with a visible limp favoring her left foot. It took us only a few minutes to get to the clinic. We walked in and immediately ran into a Vietnamese doctor leaning against a wall, smoking a cigarette. Before I could ask him to check the girl's foot, the doctor sharply blurted out that they had repeatedly changed the dressing, but she refused to stay off her foot. The doctor explained that the girl was well known to his medical staff and they helped her as much as they could, but she would not listen to any advice they gave her.

*If the girl has no place to live and sleeps on the street, then how can she stay off the foot for any length of time?* I thought.

After the doctor got through talking, I asked him if there was anything else they could do for the girl.

He shrugged as if to say, "Nothing."

I thanked the doctor and asked him to tell the little girl that she needed to stay off her foot as much as possible. He uttered a few Vietnamese words to the girl and turned around and walked away. When I left that little girl that day, I wondered, with the war going on and her living on the streets, just how long could she survive. On future supply runs to Tuy Hoa, I stopped at the same restaurant to eat, but I never saw the little girl again. In the almost fifty years since I left Vietnam, I often think about that little girl and whether she made it through the war or had any type of productive life. I did not know it at the time, but the Mang Lang Orphanage was located near Tuy Hoa. I hope that someone thought of that orphanage and by some miracle sent the little girl there, but I will never know.

Bailey and I made it to the Tuy Hoa post office, purchased the men's money orders, and then drove to the Air Force post exchange (AAFES) on the air base. We obtained various comfort supplies for the troops like candy, cigarettes, and other commodities the men wanted. After loading the truck with our purchases, we were allowed inside a fenced-in compound where the beer was secured. We backed up the deuce-and-a-half next to the beer, where Bailey and I loaded the truck. We had enough money to purchase twenty cases of beer. I had no accurate account of just how many cases of beer got onto the bed of the truck that day, but I know it was more than twenty. We got back to the 344th and off-loaded the beer and got the money orders to the men before dark. The men of the 344th had a good time that evening celebrating the spoils of war.

Eventually, I settled into a daily work routine at Vung Ro of managing supplies, completing the tonnage reports, and seeing to the needs of the men of the 344th. The weekly trips to Tuy Hoa continued without any real glitches. The trips were uneventful (no snipers or other enemy interference). The scenery along Highway A1 from Vung Ro to Tuy Hoa was purely gorgeous; the backdrop of the beautiful mountains and pure, dark green, watery rice paddies with an occasional roaming water buffalo was a sight to behold. I took many photographs of the scenes that capture memories that I would treasure for the rest of my days.

Although things at Vung Ro were good with the daily ship-to-shore mission running smoothly and having few disruptions, the morale of the men was high, but that was soon to change because more and more troops were pouring in. The increase in personnel caused a strain on the comforts of home. The base camp had a shortage of space to put up more tents and to build more latrines and shower facilities, which altered nightly routines. I did not see this as a 344th problem to fix because the 344th manpower pretty much stayed the same. However, the 344th had to share the latrine and shower facilities with other units on Charlie. The 344th's mission was requiring our men to work fifteen-hour days, which prevented them from taking off to commit to constructing more latrine and shower facilities. I was holding my breath, hoping that the in-charge guys at Vung Ro would not direct our troops to work in the evenings. I skirted the issue of no available showers by taking a dip in a small freshwater stream located about a quarter of a mile from the main beach area on Charlie Beach adjacent to the jungle. When others found out what I was doing this, they joined me. The isolated clearwater stream was the home of many snakes and other odd-looking creatures, but they seemed to stay away from us when we used their facility.

In late November, it started raining at Vung Ro and did not stop for several days. Some say it was the monsoon season. Monsoon season is roughly May through October, but you can count on one thing in Vietnam: it can rain at any time of the year. For two or three days, it rained so hard that water started rushing down the side of the mountain into our base camp, channeling its way around both sides of our GP medium tent, creating small ruts where sand was being washed away by the water. No one had any thoughts of what was about to happen next. During the hard, pouring rain one night, we were awakened about 4:30 to find our GP medium tent floating on water. We hastily got dressed and ran outside, bringing with us as many of our belongings as we could. We lost most of our personal belongings, as well as the 344th supplies, forms, and my field table. I had grabbed the typewriter as I left the tent, but all else was lost. We used LARC-Vs to get the gear that did not sink into the bay. It took two days for a small detail of engineers to fortify the base of the mountain with sandbags to stop the flow of water and set up a new GP medium tent to replace the one we'd lost. In the meantime, we slept on the beach, protected only by ponchos.

It was now December 1966, and my tour in Vietnam was approaching its end. The 344th's mission became more complicated when word came down from headquarters that one of our LARC-Vs was targeted for port security. Michaels identified two drivers who would go out on patrol with two military policemen into the bay and its waterways. We were now down to four LARC-Vs for ship-to-shore operations, but we were still able to sustain the mission. The men of the 344th worked hard and were dedicated soldiers committed to getting the job done. The system I had implemented worked well, and nearly all my time now was spent managing the administrative and supply functions of the 344th at Vung Ro. The 344th was fortunate in that no men were lost due to injuries the entire time I was assigned to Vung Ro. (This was not the case during the VC / North Vietnamese Tet Offensive of January 1968.)

On January 27, 1967, the same day a fire swept the Apollo 1 main capsule on the launching pad, causing the deaths of Virgil "Gus" Grissom, Ed White, and Roger Chaffee, I left Vung Ro aboard a C-130 out of Tuy Hoa, bound for Cam Ranh. I was carrying bulky gear and my M14 rifle. After landing, I looked around for my ride to the unit. As usual, no one was waiting for me to take me to the 344th when I got off the plane. This angered me somewhat in that I had informed the new company clerk by field telephone that I was returning from Vung Ro. Since the planes were pretty much on time, a ride would not be that difficult to arrange. I had no other choice but to try to hitch a ride to the unit.

Once outside the terminal, I could not find any suitable ground transportation, so, not knowing which way to go, I started walking toward the gate of the airport. Just outside, I stood on the side of the road, hoping someone would come along so I could hitch a ride to the 344th. I looked around, and to my amazement, I was standing next to a pole that had a bus schedule. It indicated that buses came by every forty-five minutes. Not knowing how long it had been since the last bus went by, I sat down for the wait, using my gear as a seat. About twenty minutes later, a bus with a US Army driver stopped, and as I started to board, the driver yelled, "Do not get on this bus with that rifle!"

With a look of astonishment, I looked up at him and said, "What?"

He said, "No rifles."

I angrily informed him, "We are in a war here."

Without answering me, he started shutting the door of the bus, forcing me to jump off the steps, causing me to trip and fall to the ground. While reclaiming my composure and dignity, I steadily got to my feet and calmly gave the bus driver the finger as he drove off.

While I was sitting down near the bus stop, contemplating what I was going to do next—either hitch a ride or walk to the unit (although that idea would be crazy since I did not know where the 344th was located)—I looked across the street, and to my astonishment, I saw an airman that I knew. It was not just a person I had met in the US Army—it was Dave Dombrosky from Bicknell, Indiana. When our eyes connected, he immediately recognized me as well. I rushed across the street, and we shook hands and kind of hugged one another. Although we did not run in the same circles back home, we were both elated to see each other. After seconds of howdy-dos and wows, he told me there was another person in his unit from Bicknell, Steve Faith. I told Dave that I also knew him. Dave took me to his unit, a short distance from where we stood, and located Steve. We greeted each other and said our hellos.

The three of us attended Bicknell High, but Dave was two years older, and Steve was one year younger. Nonetheless, we all thought it was extraordinary that three guys from the same small town in south-central Indiana would run into each other in a war on the other side of the world. The unexpected but delightful meeting ended abruptly when another guy I had known from Fort Leonard Wood saw me talking to the two outside their tent. The guy, named Miles, was driving a jeep down the road next to where we were standing and stopped to say hi. After a couple of minutes of conversation, I asked Miles if he would give me a lift to my unit. As I piled my gear in the back and jumped in, I bid farewell to the Bicknell boys, knowing I probably would never see them again. I told Miles I needed to go to the 344th Transportation Company but was unsure where they were located, since they had moved while I was at Vung Ro. Miles advised me that he would find the unit, and he sped off.

As we whizzed down the paved road, I was shocked at how the entire area had been colossally developed since I'd left for Vung Ro. Old, sandy roads were now all paved, and more barracks had been built to house the vast amounts of troops that poured into Cam Ranh. It took Miles about fifteen minutes to locate the 344th. As we pulled up in front of the 344th orderly room, I thanked Miles for the ride; we wished each other good luck and said our good-byes, never to see each other again. When I approached, I noticed several men milling around on the steps outside the door to the 344th orderly room. I knew one or two of them and said hi, but many of them were new. One of the soldiers I knew told me he thought I had already left Vietnam. "I've been deployed to Vung Ro for the last three months," I said. He also told me he was "short," meaning he was almost ready to leave Vietnam.

Inside the orderly room, I was shocked to find that Captain Redman, Top Wimmer, and Spoonemore were all gone. I reported to a new acting 1SG, a sergeant first class (SFC) who did not know me. The 344th had detachments at Da Nang and Vung Ro, and they functioned as separate units. I had to explain to Top that I had been one of two primary company clerks at the 344th prior to being deployed to Vung Ro for the last three months. I never did talk to the new commander, who was a 1LT and apparently had just arrived in country. I told the new acting 1SG that I had only six days left in country before my DEROS (date expected to return from overseas). The acting 1SG never was clear on what my duties would be for the remaining six days, so I just rolled up my sleeves and pitched in wherever I was needed. For the next six days, I routinely reported to the orderly room and did odd jobs for the new 344th clerks, both having been in the unit for only a few weeks; I spent a lot of time helping them with their duties. Tom and I spent a lot of time catching up on what had changed in the unit since I'd left.

To say I had good fortune in Vietnam is an understatement. Several factors in 1966 caused so many others to suffer, be killed, or become disabled. In 1966, the Vietnam War grew in scope, but Americans back home had not yet become preoccupied by it. By the end of 1966, US military strength increased to almost four hundred thousand,[31] and combat deaths totaled just over five thousand,[32] with another one thousand killed in non-combat-related incidents.

In 1966, Agent Orange was the most widely used herbicide in Vietnam. The dangers of Agent Orange, which was used to clear away the undergrowth alongside roads and around base camps and to eliminate cover so the enemy would not be able to get in close for attacks or ambushes, was not yet known. The use of herbicides in Vietnam undoubtedly saved American lives, but of course, the long-term effects it had on those individuals exposed to it would not be understood for many years. After the war, these consequences became more apparent.[33] Time will tell whether I may have been affected by Agent Orange, because the 344th had handled the chemical since their mission started in 1965, and I, just like most of the unit members, had undoubtedly been exposed to the deadly toxin.

I had come a long way since entering the US Army almost two years earlier. I'd matured in Vietnam far more than I realized at the time. I noticed subtle changes in the way I saw and reacted to my surroundings, but I did not recognize how significant my experiences had been on me since leaving home and serving in the US Army until later. I became more focused on the future and better understood suitable approaches to the way I handled situations, which paid big dividends in the way I was perceived by others.

I learned to be more assertive, responsive, and sensitive toward those I interacted with. I had been in Vietnam making and acting on my own decisions without direct supervision. Looking back on my time in Vietnam, I am amazed at my accomplishments in the US Army and how it helped my emotional strength and persona. It seemed so much more important and significant when you consider my early upbringing. My life expectations changed because of my Vietnam service. Once I left Vietnam, my goal was to succeed in life by getting an education and pursuing a lifelong career.

344th Transportation Detachment at Vung Ro Bay, South Vietnam, circa 1966. Photograph courtesy of the US Army Transportation Museum, Fort Eustis, Virginia.

LARC-V used by 344th Transportation Company for transporting supplies and men from ship to shore and later patroling the ports, circa 1966. Photograph courtesy of the US Army Transportation Museum, Fort Eustis, Virginia.

344th Transportation Detachment unit sign on Charlie Beach, Vung Ro Bay, South Vietnam, circa 1966. Photograph courtesy of the US Army Transportation Museum, Fort Eustis, Virginia.

344th Transportation Company Base Camp at Charlie Beach, Vung Ro Bay, South Vietnam, circa 1966. Photograph courtesy of the US Army Transportation Museum, Fort Eustis, Virginia.

View of 344th Transportation Company base camp at Vung Ro Bay from the South China Sea, circa 1966. Photograph courtesy of the US Army Transportation Museum, Fort Eustis, Virginia.

# 4

# The Learning Years

You Do Not Have to Be Smart to Graduate from College, Just Dedicated

Back in Indiana

*You must start early in life to determine what the value and worth your life will be*

On February 2, 1967, I left Vietnam and flew aboard a chartered commercial jet on a thirteen-hour flight via Tokyo to Seattle. I was then transferred by shuttle to Fort Lewis, Washington, where I was discharged from the US Army. I had no detailed plans when I got out of the service in 1967, but I knew I wanted to go to college and pursue a career. At that time, I had no thoughts of reentering the US Army for any reason. Times and situations always change in the future. Immediately after being released from active duty, I found a phone and called June in North Carolina and told her I had plenty of time on my hands and wanted to come see her.

"I'll make the arrangements," she said.

I grabbed a shuttle to the Seattle airport and caught a flight to Raleigh.

About six hours later, June picked me up at the Raleigh-Durham airport. She had arranged a room for me at a house next door to where she rented. When we arrived at her place, she introduced me to her roommate, Mary. We exchanged pleasantries, and moments later, June introduced me to my new temporary landlords.

While I was in Raleigh, Mary gave me a tour of the city, and June and I caught up on what was happening in our lives. June thought it was great that college was in my future, and she wished me good luck. I am not sure how serious June took me when I told her about plans for college.

I spent three weeks in Raleigh and then headed, by bus, for Terre Haute to see Mom. Mom was excited to see me back home. Mom arranged with her landlord to get me a room above her apartment, which she rented on Chestnut Street. About two months later, Mom and I moved to a larger apartment owned by the same landlord, across the street. It was not much, but it was comfortable and accommodated both of us. Mom and I spent time catching up on things, and I was glad to find her in good spirits.

Shortly after my return to Terre Haute, Nora and Hubert stopped by to see me. They were happy I had made it home in one piece, thinking the worst about Vietnam, I suppose. I told them I fared well in Vietnam and was lucky to not have seen any real combat. My family is not very inquisitive when it comes to asking about what is going on in your life or what the future holds for you. Our conversations were very narrow in scope and usually involved topics such as our health, what the weather was going to be tomorrow, or how this family member or that one was doing. In fact, in the hour or so that Nora and Hubert visited that day, they did not inquire about anything I had done in the last year, but I was still very pleased to be home.

I knew that to see other family members, I needed to get a car. I purchased a 1962 Chevrolet Impala convertible from a used car dealer at Thirteenth and Chestnut Streets, located about a half block from our apartment. Before I drove the car off the lot, I bought insurance from an agent whose office was in the same building. After paying cash for the car and spending money on insurance, I was almost busted. With two major priorities of finding a place to live and owning a car out of the way, my next step was to find a job.

I started my job search by visiting the Terre Haute employment agency on Ohio Street. They had me fill out an application asking for my employment history. This wasn't too difficult, since I only had dish-washing jobs at local restaurants and two years in the US Army. I turned in the application document and was told to take a seat and that someone would be with me shortly.

About one hour later, a man introduced himself to me as one of the employee counselors. He sat behind his desk and motioned for me to take the chair facing him. He browsed my application, looked me in the eye, and started to make small talk, most probably to establish rapport. He asked about army life and about my tour in Vietnam. Then he disclosed that he, too, was an army veteran and had served in the Korean War. He also told me that he was a member of the Veterans of Foreign Wars (VFW) on Thirteenth Street and asked if I would be interested in joining. I told him I was not even twenty-one yet and could not drink, even though I had been known to consume a few beers in the US Army. Since I was already aware that my brother, John, was the post commander at the VFW, I informed the gentleman of that. He then told me that John worked to get veterans jobs and that he would talk to him about me; John never did call me. The next time I saw John was in 1982, when he attended a party at June's house to welcome Elda, my second wife, to the family.

Like a lot of returning Vietnam veterans, I experienced the cold-shoulder treatment when applying for a job. On one referral, I went to the Weston Paper Mill on Nineteenth Street, went through the process of completing their application, and was interviewed by a member of the personnel staff. I was politely told that I qualified for employment with them, but they would not hire me because they were concerned that the time I'd spent with my reserve unit—especially "summer camp," as they called it—would interfere with my job schedule with them.

I called Chuck, my friend from high school, and we caught up on our lives. He was working at a local IGA grocery store making a dollar an hour. Since he worked from 11:00 a.m. until 8:00 p.m., he had plenty of personal time in the mornings, which he spent with me. Since Chuck was not making much money in his current job, he decided that he would join me in looking for work.

On March 3, 1967, Chuck and I both started working at Columbian Enamel, a local factory that manufactured roaster bases for cooking. To prevent friction burns, soap and other liquid chemicals were sprayed onto sheets of metal before being pressed (molded) into roaster bases and lids. Our job involved putting the recently molded roaster bases and lids into a furnace to burn the soap and liquid off before they were painted. Our section was called the "blitz." We were each given thick gloves to remove the roaster bases and lids from an incoming conveyor belt and place them onto another moving conveyor belt that pulled the framed metal through the furnace. We worked five days a week and received the weekends off. We were allowed one fifteen-minute break every two hours. The pay was modest, but decent for the times. Having this job made me want an education that much more.

In early March, I had applied for entrance to Indiana State University (ISU) shortly after I returned to Terre Haute. Besides being hired by Columbian Enamel and applying to ISU, I had joined the 604th Military Police (MP) Battalion, a reserve unit in Terre Haute. In 1967, draftees were required by the law to spend two years in the active reserves in addition to two years of active duty. Being assigned to the ready reserves (subject to recall) for two years covered the rest of the requirement of six years of service before being really discharged.

The 604th MP Battalion's mission was corrections. Instead of the transitional onetime monthly weekend drills on Saturday and Sunday usually conducted by all reserve units, the 604th conducted their drills one Sunday a month and every other Wednesday from 6:00 to 10:00 in the evening. This allowed its members to have every Saturday in the month off. Most unit members had no issues with the schedule and accepted it fully. Since the primary mission of the 604th was providing guard duties at US Army correctional facilities, training was the chief focus of the drills at the reserve center. The drills usually involved classroom lectures and time spent on ensuring equipment was cleaned and ready for deployment. Many unit members were civilian professionals in law enforcement from city, county, and state departments or correctional personnel from the local lockups and the Terre Haute federal penitentiary. The 604th routinely conducted their two-week annual summer deployment at the US Disciplinary Barracks (USDB)—or as some call it, the "Castle" at Fort Leavenworth, Kansas—where they supplemented the active duty MPs.

In mid-April, I received a letter from ISU informing me that I had conditionally been accepted into their Freshmen Opportunity Program (FOP). The proviso of ISU's FOP was that I had to maintain a C average to avoid academic probation. Academic probation meant that you had one semester to improve your grades before being dismissed from ISU and prohibited from reapplying for one year. Since my grades in high school were not considered high enough for ISU standards, the FOP was the only way to be admitted. I accepted this requirement with no reservations.

I scheduled my first classes for the summer semester of June/July 1967. Work, attending reserve meetings, hanging with Chuck, and visiting friends and relatives I had not seen in over a year occupied my time before starting classes.

I took my first trip to Bicknell shortly after I started working for Columbian Enamel to see Norman; however, I found that he had been in the US Army for about a year and a half and had been assigned to Korea for the past six months. I was excited about this development, thinking how surprised I was that he'd entered the US Army. I updated his mother, sister, and brother on my US Army tour and promised to visit soon. I learned from his mother that Norman would be returning to the States in about six months. I reckoned I would see him then.

The 604th was scheduled for its annual two-week training deployment. When time came for deployment, the unit was bused to Fort Leavenworth, Kansas, from Terre Haute. The bus trip to Kansas reminded me of my dad's trip from Kansas to Indiana back in the late 1890s. I bet it took him a lot longer than nine hours to make the trip by horse-drawn wagon. We arrived at Fort Leavenworth on a Sunday evening in mid-May 1967. We settled into our quarters and were given last-minute instructions on where to report the following morning.

I was assigned to Wing 3M, known as the Administrative Segregation Unit (ASU). 3M was where prisoners were held, pending a hearing on incidents they were involved in or for suspected infractions of Fort Leavenworth's rules or regulations. My first day of duty involved waking the prisoners for morning chow. To say the least, the prisoners that were slow in getting out of their bunks were somewhat argumentative when told to get moving. On one occasion, two MPs had to enter an inmate's cell and physically pull him out of his bunk. Later that day, I found myself the only person in the Operational Control Rotunda (OCR). The MP guards and officer in charge (OIC) of the wing were conducting their rounds, and the lunch meal was being served. The OCR had telephones for communication to other locations in the DB and limited records of the inmates that were temporarily housed on wing 3M.

While waiting for any incoming calls, I suddenly heard a loud scream and people yelling. My view of the disturbance was obstructed by a wall. To see what was happening, I walked outside the OCR and discovered that two MPs were attempting to restrain one of the inmates. The OIC was standing off to one side with his back to me. As the scuffle ensued, the OIC turned in my direction. "Get down here ASAP and give us a hand!" he yelled.

I rushed to the commotion and observed the OIC had blood running from his nose. I overheard the OIC say to the prisoner on the floor, "You have just earned another six months' confinement for hitting an officer."

Gasping for air, the inmate, a huge burly-looking man, obviously exhausted from the struggle, blurted out, "I got fourteen years for killing a Vietnamese farmer. Another six months is nothing."

I saw that the two MPs each held an arm and were trying to force the prisoner down on his stomach, but the inmate was too strong for them. The inmate's wrestling abilities, strength, and survival instincts were propelling the momentum of the fracas in his favor. The inmate was using his unrestrained legs as weapons and hurled a rock-solid kick to the groin of one his antagonists, causing the MP to cry out in pain. I stooped down and grabbed the inmate's left ankle with both hands, swung the limb over the top of his right ankle, and pressed down, hard. The inmate screamed in agony. "You got me! I give up!" he howled. The inmate, now calm, was handcuffed from behind and pulled to his feet. The MPs then escorted him to solitary confinement.

I found out later that the inmate received a fourteen-year sentence for shooting and killing a Vietnamese with his M16 rifle. The inmate had been placed in the ASU, pending a hearing to determine his culpability in an assault on another inmate. The disturbance that caused him to be pulled from his cell originated when he tore the sink from the wall and set fire to his mattress and bed linens to protest bad-tasting food. He was obviously a very disturbed individual who suffered from antisocial predilections.

Another incident while I was at the USDB involved an inmate, a former SSG, who had killed a fellow soldier in a bar fight in Korea. The SSG struck his opponent with his fist, knocking him to the floor, causing the soldier's head to strike a protruding pipe of a heater, resulting in his death. The inmate had served about two years of a nine-year sentence for involuntary manslaughter. The inmate had been a model prisoner during his time at the USDB and was even awarded trustee status and privileges to sleep in one of the better-kept buildings, away from the main prisoner population. His case was pending review by the court of military appeals. The inmate sat around for several months waiting to hear the results and hoped that the appeal would reduce his sentence or more; the decision could result in his release from the USDB. The eventual day came when he found out that the courts had upheld his original sentence and ruled that he must remain incarcerated for the duration of his sentence.

After being told of the court's ruling, the inmate calmly stood up and walked back to his living quarters and sat on his bunk. Witnesses say the inmate became almost catatonic as he looked straight into the distance with a strange stare. No one knew what was going on in his head or how he was digesting the information he had just heard. He was overwhelmed with raw emotion. Feelings of hopelessness and the rage boiled up inside him, causing him to go berserk.

Like a crazy man, he started grabbing at anything not secured and flinging it as far as he good. He tore his bunk apart and picked up an iron bedpost and started swinging it at those around him. He swung at things that were breakable, all the while yelling and screaming, "I did not deserve this! I did not deserve this!" Several MPs were finally able to forcibly remove the iron bedpost from his hands, physically restrain him, and effectively carry him from the building for medical evaluation and almost certain solitary confinement. I have thought about this individual many times over the years and wondered how he adapted when released from the USDB.

The rest of my two-week tour at the USDB was routine and uneventful. The experience opened my eyes to inmate life and how they survived while incarcerated. Although the two weeks spent at the USDB were short-lived, I cannot forget some of the prisoners I encountered there. There was a US Army captain who was serving sixty-five years for rape; purportedly there was a former MP who was serving a life sentence, pending transfer to a federal penitentiary to finish out his sentence, at the USDB for killing a fellow MP at Fort Gordon, Georgia. He then hacked up the MP's body, frying some of the parts and eating them.[34] There were other murderers, rapists, and even prisoners that probably did not belong at the USDB, such as those that had gone AWOL. However, since the Vietnam War was ongoing at the time, going AWOL was looked at in a different light than it is today. In the 1960s, the more serious charge of desertion was associated with some AWOL cases. The 604th MP Battalion's two-week tour at Fort Leavenworth came to an end, and we were all grateful to be homebound.

Back in Terre Haute, I was anxious to get started with classes at ISU. I had enrolled in two basic 101 courses—one English, the other sociology. The studies would take me through June and July 1967. Largely through a gift from Uncle Sam, in the form of the GI Bill, I would receive $250 per month if I attended college full-time. That sum made college affordable in the 1960s. I was somewhat concerned, however, that I may have a rough time adjusting to the rigors and stress of studying. Having the mere desire to succeed was there, but did I have the proper discipline to do well in the classes? I would soon to find out.

Timing of the classes was my first consideration because I was scheduled to take one class in the morning and the other in midafternoon Monday through Friday for an hour each day. I was currently working Monday through Friday during the day at Columbian Enamel. I also had to think about how to fit my reserve training each Wednesday evening into the schedule. I devised a plan to change my schedule at Columbian Enamel to the night shift, which had me working from 11:00 in the evening to 7:00 in the morning each weeknight. This way, I had the whole day for classes, and each Wednesday, I could make my reserve meeting before I had to be at work. The problem with this hectic schedule was that it did not leave me any significant time to study or sleep. I figured I was in for a bumpy ride, to say the least.

At the end of July that summer, I was one tired puppy, but I did pass both classes and kept perfect attendance at ISU, Columbian Enamel, and all my reserve meetings.

The Miller luck again took hold before I started the fall semester in 1967. Congress had ruled that draftees and two-year enlistees who spent two years on active duty no longer had to devote two additional years to a reserve unit, so I sought and received a discharge from the active reserves. I left the 604th under good circumstances with the leadership. This was a tremendous relief for me, because my schedule now allowed adequate time for study and sleep while going to classes. Before starting the fall semester 1967, I tentatively decided on a major in criminology and was leaning toward a career in corrections or law enforcement. This decision was partially based on my experience with the 604th MP Battalion.

I had been working nights at Columbian Enamel for about three months when a good-looking young girl from the press section caught my eye. Our eyes lingered toward each other, and over a few weeks, I built up the nerve to ask her name, and she replied, "Melitta Marie Collins, but I go by Sandy." Later, I found out that she went by the name of Sandy because her maiden name was Sandin. Throughout our time together, I called her Melitta. In her own way, she was attractive and seemed pleasant, but her overall demeanor was rather guarded. It took me another month before I had the nerve to ask her out on a date, which she warmly accepted.

Our first date was dinner at the upper-scale Nat King Cole restaurant in Indianapolis. Back in 1960s, you could buy a decent-size steak dinner for two for under fifteen dollars. I spared no cost in making our date a memorable one. During dinner, we talked about our lives. She informed me that she'd gone to Terre Haute to study physical education at ISU. She completed almost two years of studies, and during that time, she met Bill Collins, a fellow ISU student. They were married and had a son named Robert, who was about two years old. Melitta told me that her parents did not like Bill, because they felt he was not ambitious enough. She told me that they had gotten married without telling their parents. This did not do much for the bad feelings her parents had for Bill. Not wanting to upset her parents any further, she ended the marriage.

After that first dinner, we pretty much dated on a continuous basis. During that time, I must admit that we had some ups and downs in developing the relationship, but we generally could get along to where our affections for each other grew.

I recall the first time I met Melitta's parents, Bob and Mary Sandin, in September 1967, when they visited Melitta at her home in Terre Haute. They had driven down from Michigan City, Indiana, for the weekend. They both were in their forties, and from the start, both acted taut, curious, and withdrawn, but not ostentatious. I found out that Bob ran his own hardware store in Michigan City, and Mary was a housewife. Bob had made a fortune selling mobile homes earlier in his life. I was not sure what they thought of me on that night, but I purposely presented myself as I was and did not go out of my way to make a false impression of someone I was not. I was honest and straightforward with them. I introduced myself and told them I was from Terre Haute, had been in the US Army, and was currently going to college at ISU. The conversation with them was strained and somewhat contrived, but friendly. I noticed that Melitta did not contribute much to our discussion and throughout the night was extremely aloof.

When I left them that night, I felt like I might be out of their social league and probably left them with thoughts of, *I hope our daughter does not get involved with this guy; he is sort of a step down from us.* How accurate this assessment was, only time would tell? Since I was ready for a permanent relationship in my life, I could hardly wait until I saw Melitta at work so she could tell me what her parents thought about me.

When I saw her again, Melitta was limited about how her parents felt about me. Her reaction to my question almost went unanswered, not as if she did not want to tell me what they thought but more along the lines that she did not want to talk about it.

As I got to know Melitta better, I gradually discovered that her frame of mind was sort of atypical. She rarely, if ever, elaborated on things, and I started noticing little subtle restraints about openness. I also observed that Melitta had a habit of spontaneously going into tirades over things that to others were inconsequential. It was as if she was afraid to express herself or talk openly about things that affected her and kept them bottled up inside until it got too much for her, and then she exploded. Later in our relationship, this issue became a point of contention between us. Even though this controversy existed, at the time I felt it was not serious enough for us to break up.

Through the years, I pulled bits and pieces out of Melitta about her early childhood that made me realize she had a good reason to suffer from a form of anxiety that prevented her from showing affection to others. I found out that she was born in a German prison camp near Munich in 1943, where her mother, Mary, had been incarcerated while pregnant with Melitta. Since Mary was a German Catholic, apparently, this camp was a political prison for people that fell out of grace with the Third Reich and was not a concentration camp. I thought that as time went by, I would gain her trust to where she could find the confidence to freely express her own self. However, her silence only became worse in the future.

I overlooked my concern for Melitta's emotional health because I was blinded by my affection for her and wanted the relationship to grow. We continued to date and became closer as a couple. In the fall of 1968, Melitta accepted my proposal of marriage, and we agreed on a June 1969 wedding. Since she was Catholic and had previously been married in a civil ceremony, she had to have her first marriage annulled. She also had to attend marriage classes with a priest. Although I had sporadically attended a Nazarene church as a child, I had no real religious affiliation. Therefore, I also was required to take classes. We scheduled our wedding date for June 29, 1969, at Saint Patrick's Catholic Church at Fourteenth and Poplar Streets in Terre Haute. This was the same church where my sister June married her first husband, Chuck Hanley.

About the same time, my studies at ISU were getting more intense, so I decided I needed to change to a job that would provide me a more hassle-free way to make money and would allow more time to study. Melitta was unwavering in her feelings that I should not quit my job. I never found out the real reason why she was so dead set against me leaving the Columbian Enamel job. This was the first time she'd interfered with anything in my personal life. I explained to her that I was glad that she had some concerns but that the job was not a career position. Graduation from college took priority, and if a better situation helped, it was a good thing.

It appeared to me that she was more concerned as to how my decision would affect her than me. I was troubled by her feelings, but more importantly, I was having a hard time understanding just where she was coming from. I also had a hard time trying to make her understand that this decision made sense and could only be viewed as a normal bump in the road for any college student. I told her this did not mean I would not get another job before leaving Columbian Enamel. Over Melitta's objections, I sought employment elsewhere. Before leaving Columbian Enamel, I easily landed a job, the pay of which was comparable, as a surgical room orderly at Saint Anthony's Hospital in Terre Haute. The new job provided a better work schedule, the environment was cleaner, and it allowed me to leave work and go to class without taking a shower. The new job was more relaxed, and since the hospital was a training facility and because of the mere nature of my duties, I was allowed time to study while at work.

As I entered my junior year at ISU, I had committed myself to a degree in criminology. My overall grades were scarcely above average, but I maintained a 3.00 GPA in my major, so it looked like I was on the way to fulfilling the goal I'd set for myself after leaving the US Army of getting a college degree. Not bad for an almost high school dropout. I worked very hard to keep my grades up and often would pull all-nighters to get ready for tests. All-nighters infuriated Melitta, because she would often stop by my place early in the morning after she got off work to see me. She had a peculiar habit when she came to my apartment of routinely touching lightbulbs to see if they were hot. If they were hot, she knew I had been up all night.

All-nighters were not the only thing that upset Melitta. When scheduling my classes to start my junior year, I decided to take a course in constitutional law. Just to make her aware of what I was doing, I routinely discussed the scheduling of my classes with her. When I signed up to take a class in constitutional law, she went nuts! "You can't take that course. It is too hard, and you have to spend a lot of time studying, and you will flunk it," she blurted out. Her refusal to support me on this matter and my vigorous attempt to justify taking the course exploded into a heated argument, which almost resulted in me breaking it off with her. This was another incident where she, for no perceptible reason, became enraged to the point of being physical, and she started shoving me. It took me a few days to cool off before I saw her again. To appease her, I gave in and canceled the constitutional law course. My love-hate relationship with Melitta was routinely hampered by her aloofness and peculiar outbursts of erratic behavior, but my bond with Robert, her son, was strong. I often took him for rides around town, and we would stop for ice cream.

Throughout the rest of 1967 and 1968, we occasionally visited Bob and Mary on the weekends, and they would in turn drive to Terre Haute and spend weekends with us. When in Terre Haute, Bob usually took us out for dinner on Saturday nights. The Bierstube German restaurant in north Terre Haute was their favorite. On a few occasions when Melitta, Robert, and I would drive to Michigan City to visit the Sandins, they would take us to Saugatuck and Douglas, Michigan, where they had a summer home near Lake Michigan. These trips were very relaxing and enjoyable for the most part. Melitta and I would spend most of the day swimming in the lake nearby.

The visits were not all peaceful and without incidents involving Melitta's emotional weirdness. Melitta was a different person while visiting her parents' summer home. She would often become more distant and shut people out. She would act as if she were mad or perturbed about something. On one occasion, we were standing in front of the summer home at the lake's edge, and for no apparent reason whatsoever, she punched me, grabbed and held my arms, and then bit me hard on the chest. Since Bob and Mary were close by sitting in the sunroom watching us, I friskily and firmly shoved her away from me and pretended to playfully wrestle her to the ground. She never gave me a reason why she bit me, and when I tried to talk about it, she would shut me out and not say a word. I should have seen the writing on the wall and anticipated the obvious problems that I would have concerning her strange behavior, but I chose to ignore the situation, because I genuinely cared for her.

A few days after we got back from visiting Melitta's parents, things settled down between Melitta and me. In earnest, we started talking about the wedding and where we would live. I occupied only a room across the street from Mom, and Melitta rented a small US government–subsidized row house, neither of which was a fit for a married family. As fate, would have it, Melitta informed me that a coworker at Columbian Enamel who was moving to Texas with her family was interested in renting their home. A few days later, we inspected the property located on Thirty-Fifth Street in Terre Haute. We both immediately liked the place and found out we could afford the rent. The family agreed to rent the house to us, and within a week, we moved in.

I informed her that I was going to visit Tom Foley, my army buddy from Vietnam. She gave me a strange look of displeasure about my planned trip, but she did not voice an objection. Solon, Ohio, a short distance from Cleveland, was about 350 miles from Terre Haute. I made the trip in about seven hours.

I found Tom in good health. We talked some about our time in Vietnam and about what had occurred since leaving. After he returned, he'd gotten married to the girl he had met at Fort Ord. He had a nice home, had joined his father's ironworks company, and already had a child. Life was very good for him. I told him about college and my pending marriage to Melitta. I took the opportunity during the visit to ask Tom to be my best man at my wedding; he accepted. When I returned to Terre Haute, I felt good about the visit to see Tom, and I'd thoroughly enjoyed meeting his wife.

When I got back from the trip to see Tom, Melitta and I started putting the list of attendees together for our wedding. Melitta anticipated that her parents, aunt, and grandmother would be attending from Michigan City. I told her that my relatives from the Terre Haute area and Tom and his wife from Solon, Ohio, were coming. I began telling Melitta that Tom and his wife would need a place to stay, and before I could finish, she immediately stopped me in midsentence. Nervously shifting in her chair and with a frown on her face, Melitta instantly remarked, "Not our responsibility!"

I looked at her with disbelief and bewilderment that she would even think it was not our responsibility. "I invited Tom and feel it is our obligation to provide him and his wife with a place to stay while attending the wedding," I pointed out.

Melitta, her eyes wandering around the room, started shutting me out. I decided I would handle this issue on my own later. We had decided that her parents, aunt, and grandmother could stay with her at the house. Everyone else was local and would not need any overnight accommodations. Richard Meredith, a friend and fellow classmate from Gerstmeyer High School, and Larry Jerrell, a fellow classmate who had moved to Terre Haute from Bicknell way before I did, agreed to serve as ushers. The day before the wedding, Tom, his wife, and baby girl drove down from Solon, Ohio, and they settled into the Travelodge Motel. Melitta's parents and grandmother and Bob's sister Helen drove down from Michigan City.

The night before the wedding, Tom and Richard, thinking that I just could not get married without a bachelor party, took me out on the town and tried to get me drunk. It didn't work, because I was not in the mood, but the three of us had a lengthy talk about marriage, old times, and the future. Later that night, with Tom driving, we dropped Richard off at his house. On the way to my apartment, Tom and I talked about marriage and how well he liked it. I was quiet and let him do most of the talking, but I listened to what he was saying. He dropped me off, and I immediately changed into the suit I was going to wear to the wedding in a few hours. I laid down on the bed and tried to get some much-needed rest, but sleep never came.

The inevitable day came, and Melitta and I were married on June 28, 1969. The wedding reception was held at the Albert Pick Motel in Terre Haute. I drove Melitta to the reception in her old, red Corvair sedan. The guys—Tom, Richard, and Larry—had used soap to write *NEWLYWEDS* on the back window and tied tin cans to the back bumper. The dinner was hosted by Bob Sandin. Before the reception was over, Melitta, unannounced, took off to go clean up her car, probably because she was embarrassed to be seen in it. She never returned to our wedding reception, and I caught a ride with her dad to her house on Thirty-Fifth Street in Terre Haute.

While waiting for Melitta to return home, I suddenly realized that Tom and I had said our good-byes, and he'd left for Ohio without me paying for his motel room. This upset me, because it was my intent to pay for motel room while he stayed for the wedding. This was a problem I would have to handle later, because Melitta's family made it known they wanted to leave and did not wait for her to return. Finally, she made it to the house about fifteen minutes after her family left. We got involved in a heated argument over her disappearance, and she stormed out of the house and was gone for over an hour before returning without an apology. What a way to start a marriage. When I asked why she'd left the wedding reception, she said she had to clean her car before it got dark!

Now, I was officially a married man, and life as I knew it would never be the same. I slowly adapted to my new lifestyle as being a husband to Melitta and a father to Robert. I thoroughly enjoyed our first year together as a family. I became proficient at juggling a full-time job, taking fifteen hours of classes each semester, and working in the role as a husband and father. I endured Melitta's unusual idiosyncrasies as her normal way of interacting with people. In the back of my mind, I anticipated a very bumpy, roller-coaster ride into the future.

I had some of my best grades during the last semester of college. It was getting close to decision time about where I was going to seek employment. During the time at ISU, I had developed a camaraderie with a group of fellow criminology majors who had the same aspirations and goals as I, and we exchanged information on who was hiring and who was not. Some wanted to pursue corrections, and others wanted law enforcement as their chosen careers. I had changed over the years from possibly working in corrections to a career in law enforcement; that ultimately would lead to a position as a criminal investigator. I was scheduled to graduate in June 1972, but I thought that my search for employment should begin earlier. I started sending résumés to police departments throughout the country. Most of the departments contacted provided negative responses, citing residency and experience requirements. However, in December 1971, the Saint Louis Metropolitan Police Department reached out to me and invited me in for an initial assessment.

During this time, I was among a group of three from ISU that were the first criminology students to start and complete an internship program with the police department in Terre Haute, Indiana. The internship lasted six weeks and involved learning all aspects of the police officer's responsibilities to include patrol, interaction with citizens, responding to crime incidents, report writing, and other duties that spring up during a normal work shift. I was assigned to a two-man patrol car consisting of one senior Terre Haute Police Department (THPD) veteran and a young second-year newbie named Dan Rose from Ohio, who had moved to Terre Haute a few years earlier to study business at ISU. Both THPD officers were very informative and took their jobs as policer officers very seriously, and I learned a lot about police work from them both. The situations we responded to were as wide ranging as could be, from the very simple dispute between two neighbors over property lines to serious crimes involving burglary or assault. There were no set rules of the internship, but we had to sign a letter that we accepted liability for our actions while working on the internship in case we were hurt or injured in any way.

A typical eight-hour shift would be mostly routine, with one or two incidents of rapid, pulsating action packed with excitement, making the evening meaningful. I recalled one incident around 11:00 p.m., where the radio dispatcher radioed to our patrol car that a Laundromat alarm had gone off, indicating a possible break-in. This was my first experience with any type of criminal investigation, and I called it the Case of the Scared Burglar:

THE CASE OF THE SCARED BURGLAR
If you commit a crime, you can never hide from the police; they will always find you

We sped to the scene doing eighty to ninety miles per hour down Third Street. A short distance from the site, THPD Officer Rose turned off the police car's oscillating overhead flashing lights. As we entered the parking lot of the Laundromat, three people were milling around near the front door. Both THPD officers got out of the patrol car and, with their hands on their service revolvers, confronted the individuals. The three were identified as the owner of the Laundromat, his wife, and his son. The THPD officers found out that they lived in a house directly behind the Laundromat and heard the alarm when it went off. Apparently, when someone entered the Laundromat by force, the alarm was set to sound in their house. The THPD officers were told by the owner that he immediately raced to the front door of the Laundromat building and found it had been tampered with by someone who might still be inside.

While all this was going on, I remained sitting in the backseat of the THPD patrol car. When the owner saw me, thinking that I had been picked up by THPD officers in the area as they were responding to the scene, he attempted to open the door. Apparently thinking I was a suspect, the owner was going to dish out some old-fashioned justice, but Officer Rose grabbed the owner's arm before he could reach the door handle. Officer Rose politely told the owner that I was with them, and he backed off. After that situation was resolved, the other officer called for K-9 backup. When the K-9 unit arrived, the dog handler entered the Laundromat with the police dog in the lead, followed by both THPD officers. I followed them into the building. I probably should have stayed outside until the building was either cleared or they found the perpetrator (perp), but no one stopped me. I looked over my shoulder as I entered the Laundromat and saw that the owner, his wife, and his son were directly behind me.

The THPD officers and K-9 unit looked throughout the building and found nothing. Then the police dog alerted by barking and jumping up on his hind legs, touching his front paws to the door to one of the dryers. The THPD officers started opening each dryer door, but found no one. Then the senior

THPD officer looked up on the top of the dryers. There he was, a young, white, male perp, lying in a space about two feet between the top of the dryers and the ceiling.

"Get down from there right now," one of the THPD officers ordered.

"Okay, okay, but please call the dog off," the perp pleaded.

As the perp started climbing down off the dryer, the dog handler had to restrain the police dog, who was voraciously barking and lunging at the guy. The perp hesitated and again pleaded to have the police dog removed before he got down. The handler then took the police dog outside and placed him in the K-9 unit. The perp then climbed down from the top of the Laundromat dryers and was immediately placed in hand irons by Officer Rose and led to the patrol car. Once we were convinced there were no other perps involved with the break-in, the two THPD officers got the information they needed from the owner of the Laundromat and headed off to the Terre Haute police station to process the perp. THPD Officer Rose sat in the backseat with the perp while I rode in the front. I got a firsthand look at how police dogs were used during investigations. They are true assets to a police officer.

Another incident I observed as an intern with the Terre Haute Police Department involved a family dispute, where the wife stabbed her husband during an argument. I will always remember the Case of the Grandfather Who Drank Too Much:

THE CASE OF THE GRANDFATHER WHO DRANK TOO MUCH
Alcohol is never the answer to problems

Our patrol car was dispatched to a residence on the southeast side of Terre Haute. When we arrived, the two THPD officers were confronted by a hysterical woman, gasping for breath and saying, "He stabbed me! He stabbed me! He is in there! He is in there!"

The two THPD officers rushed into the house, with me in pursuit. Again, I probably should not have followed them into the house until the situation was defused, but the THPD officers seemed comfortable with me riding with them, and there was a sense of trust built up between the three of us. The THPD officers and I had many long and in-depth conversations about how police officers should react in stressful situations. After all, I had signed a note of legal responsibility for my own liability when starting the internship.

Once in the house, the senior THPD officer went right into the bedroom, and the other went into the living room and then the kitchen.

My attention was diverted to a young, boy about ten, sitting on the couch, crying. As I approached the youth, the senior THPD officer from the bedroom yelled, "I found him underneath the bed!"

THPD Officer Rose went from the kitchen and quickly joined his partner in the bedroom. As I comforted the youth on the couch, the woman, who had remained on the front porch, came into the living room. At the same time, the two THPD officers were coming from the bedroom with the man in hand irons. The man looked and smelled like he had been drinking alcohol. His eyes were bloodshot, and his speech slurred when he spoke. He was somewhat argumentative but seemed to follow the THPD officers' instructions when told to sit down in the chair alongside the couch, near where the boy was sitting. Directing his question to the woman, Officer Rose asked, "What is your relationship with the boy?"

"He is our grandchild," she proudly acknowledged.

With everyone in the living room, things appeared to be calming down somewhat, but it all started again when the wife accused the husband of stabbing her. Officer Rose asked her to show him where she was stabbed. The woman raised her right arm and pointed with the forefinger of her left hand and said, "Here."

We all looked at her arm and saw nothing to suggest she had been stabbed. Officer Rose asked the woman, "What did your husband use to stab you?"

"A pencil," she said.

The husband then started in on her by stating, "You are a crazy woman."

The THPD officers then separated the two, Officer Rose escorting the wife into the kitchen while the senior officer stayed in the living room to talk with the husband.

The senior THPD officer asked the husband, "Why did you stab your wife with the pencil?"

"I got mad at her because she is always on to me about everything I do," he replied.

"Where is, the pencil used to stab your wife?" asked the senior THPD officer.

"In the bedroom," the husband answered.

"Can you show me where it is?"

"Yes," the husband replied as they headed toward the bedroom.

They both returned moments later with the senior THPD officer carrying two pieces of a pencil. At the same time, Officer Rose returned to the living room with the wife in tow. Both followed instructions to sit down; the husband sat in the same chair alongside the couch, where the boy was still sitting, and the wife went to a second chair across the room. With things calming down between the two, but still potentially volatile, the THPD officers had to decide how to end the present situation to the benefit of all involved. The two THPD officers and I grouped near the front door, where I listened to them ponder whether to let the two cool off for the night or arrest the husband for assault. Since the husband did not use a knife but a pencil instead to stab his wife, the entire incident was deflated from a possible charge of attempted murder to an assault. Officer Rose offered up a situation where the incident could even be considered a domestic quarrel between the two. You must realize it was the 1970s, and things were perceived differently from the way they are under today's legal system rules. Today, without hesitation, the THPD officer would have no choice but to arrest the husband for domestic assault and possibly public intoxication, since part of the argument occurred in their front yard. In this case, however, the two THPD officers chose to consider the incident a domestic quarrel between the two with no injuries, thus quelling the matter by making no arrests. I often wonder what happened to that young boy sitting on the couch during the entire ordeal.

During the internship, I also observed how THPD officers handled intoxicated people. One evening when THPD Rose was absent, the senior THPD officer and I rode together. Except for a car accident and a call to settle a neighbor's dispute over property lines, things were quiet. Then, about 10:00 p.m., we were dispatched to the Wagon Wheel restaurant on South Third Street to check on a man who had fallen asleep at the food counter. When we arrived, the senior THPD officer and I walked into the restaurant and immediately saw a young, white male with his head lying down on the food counter, not moving and apparently asleep. The waitress behind the counter indicated he was the individual they'd called about and wanted him removed from the restaurant. This incident is embedded in my memory as the Case of the Passed-Out Drunk:

THE CASE OF THE PASSED-OUT DRUNK
When you drink alcohol, you should always be very selective where you choose to sleep

The senior THPD officer approached the unresponsive individual from behind, and in a seamless, smooth motion, as he'd obviously done many times before, he placed hand irons around the slumbering drunk's wrists and pulled him off the counter stool onto his feet before he knew what was happening. Once the person figured out he was being forcibly manipulated, he became combative and started attempting to get free from the officer's hold. He had no luck; the senior THPD officer was stronger, more alert, and very capable of handling the man. The senior THPD officer told me to get the back door of the police car open. So, as he was walking the man, who reeked with alcohol, out the door to the patrol car, I opened the driver-side door, reached into the back, and unlocked the door. The senior THPD officer was right there and immediately threw the man, ensuring he didn't hit his head as he placed him into the backseat. The whole affair took about two to three minutes. We escorted the man to the drunk tank at the Terre Haute police station. The affable senior THPD officer told me I could do the police report on the incident. Although not a sworn police officer, this was my first written police report. The written report must have been acceptable to the patrol supervisor that night, because I never heard anything from him or the senior THPD officer. As a matter of fact, the senior THPD officer praised my writing skills; of course, he signed it before giving it to the desk sergeant.

One of the most significant investigations I was associated with occurred prior to my internship with the Terre Haute Police Department. It involved the shooting of a young female by her husband. I called this the case of the abusive mother:

## THE CASE OF THE ABUSIVE MOTHER
Good or bad behavior is always scrutinized by someone

I was working for Saint Anthony's Hospital when an ambulance brought in the shooting victim, who was dead upon arrival. One of my jobs required me to transport dead bodies to the basement morgue, a job that I did not relish. For some reason, I had already taken the dead female to the morgue prior to a detective from the Terre Haute Police Department arriving at the hospital. The confusion was due to a couple of Terre Haute uniformed officers visiting the emergency room, taking notes, viewing the body, and leaving without informing any hospital staff that a follow-up visit by a detective was forthcoming. Sure enough, about ten minutes after removing the body to the morgue, a detective showed up requesting to view the body.

I escorted the detective to the morgue and positioned the body onto a slab so he could take photographs. The twenty-three-year-old woman was shot in the forehead by her husband during an argument about the wife's abusive treatment of their three-year-old son. The experience was the first time I had seen a dead body that was not in a funeral home.

I had an incredible and worthwhile experience during my internship with the THPD and benefited greatly from the program started and sponsored by ISU. I had many lengthy and pointed discussions about the philosophy of law enforcement with THPD officers. Most of the THPD officers were very amenable to my persistent prying and everlasting quest for answers to questions about the field of law enforcement. Times are different now; the mores of society and its culture have changed over the years. Back in the 1970s, there were few if any cameras at businesses, stores, ATMs, and other facilities that depicted real-time actions by people, especially those who committed crimes. One could argue that back in the 1970s and earlier, the police could work with impunity. Police officers must be on their toes and watch every step while they perform their duties. However, there was then—and there still is—a fundamental desire by the majority in law enforcement to do what is morally right.

I thought Melitta was supporting me on the decision to work in law enforcement. She never voiced any objections or concerns about my career until the Saint Louis interview. Suddenly, her defiant attitude against police work came to the surface. As I anxiously waited a call from Saint Louis for an initial interview date, she became more vocal in her opposition for me to pursue any type of career in law enforcement. Her objections and insolent behavior resulted in another quarrel between us. I tried to rationalize with her that the efforts I'd expended in working on my degree should not be in vain. When I tried to talk to her about her feelings, she again shut me out. I sought from her some form of understanding as to why she hadn't voiced her feelings before. Melitta had no empathy or concerns that I had just spent over four years on law enforcement studies at ISU. She was also nonresponsive to any discussions about the matter. It was at this juncture in our relationship that I seriously questioned the wisdom of us continuing the marriage. However, another factor not foreseen by me would soon change my view on our marriage.

I decided to pursue the interview with the Saint Louis Metropolitan Police Department. In early mid-December 1972, I traveled to Saint Louis and officially applied, passed their entrance examination, and cleared the psychological assessment phase of their hiring process. I passed the general physical but was told that my eyesight was not acceptable, and they declined to further process me for a police officer position. I was not satisfied with their decision concerning my eyesight, so I decided to get a second opinion. Back in Terre Haute, I saw an ophthalmologist, who examined my eyes and explained to me that I had twenty-twenty vision but that the two eyes functioned differently from those of most people. Unlike most people, who are born with what he called "normal vision" and see the same distance from both eyes at the same time, I had "monovision." People seek surgery where one eye is corrected for near and one eye is corrected for distance vision. However, the ophthalmologist told me I was born with natural monovision, and that was why my eyes saw differently. My left eye sees long distances, and the right eye is nearsighted. I took this report back to the Saint Louis Metropolitan Police Department's human relations office, and they said they would review the report and inform me of their decision by a letter detailing their decision.

In early January 1972, I received a letter from Saint Louis indicating they had reversed their decision and approved my hiring. I was placed on an eligibility list and informed that I would be called when I was chosen for their police academy. After I informed Melitta that I had made the hiring list for the Saint Louis Metropolitan Police Department, she was incensed. I recall that in the same conversation that I told her about Saint Louis, she perfunctorily told me that she was pregnant.

Unlike her, I was ecstatic when hearing the news. I thought that a child would bring us closer together, and I welcomed the news with a great deal of enthusiasm, anticipation, and pride. Melitta's pregnancy brought a whole new perspective to me, and I was prepared to do everything I possibly could do to make our marriage work.

If Melitta was excited, she did not show it in her emotions. Things were going as well as could be expected for us at this point, and I was hopeful that major changes for the better would occur in our relationship.

I went to the see William Nardini, chairman of the criminology department at ISU, and informed him that I had been placed on the hiring list for the Saint Louis Metropolitan Police Department but did not have a date of hire. "The reason I am seeing you is to get permission to take my end-of-class examinations early so I will be prepared to accept the Saint Louis position," I told him.

He was very responsive and advised that he would talk to all my college professors to see if they would allow me to take the end-of-course examinations early. I heard back from Nardini about two days later, and he informed me that all the professors were on board with early testing and that I could schedule the dates with them. This process took about two weeks, but it was successful. In late January 1972, I was officially a college graduate with a bachelor of science degree in criminology. If it wasn't for the GI Bill, I would have never graduated.

I continued to work at Saint Anthony's Hospital while waiting on word from Saint Louis. I also searched for other viable employment. I would find out soon that the wait for Saint Louis took on its own life. Melitta's obsession for an additional few cents on the dollar kept her on the night shift while I continued the evening shift at the hospital. I had not noticed any discernable change in Melitta's attitude about me going into law enforcement; however, I knew I must consider the possibility that in order the make the marriage work, I needed to consider a change in career directions. I knew my options were open, but I had spent the last few years studying law enforcement, and if I did not pursue a career in law enforcement, the last four to five years would have been wasted,

Melitta and I spent most weekends visiting our families in Terre Haute and on occasions went to Michigan City to see her family. Melitta had not brought up the topic of our future in some time. I informed her that regardless of my decision on a career, Robert and the new baby would take priority over any job or activity. I accepted that a major change was in store for me concerning a career path, but I just did not know how much that change would impact the family. I did emphasize to Melitta that to find suitable employment, we might have to move from Terre Haute, but she did not respond to my comment; in fact, her reaction was one of indifference.

It was April 1972, and I was getting anxious, because I still had not heard anything from the Saint Louis Metropolitan Police Department. I contacted their personnel office, and they replied that my selection was pending two factors: one, the date of the next class; and two, a determination of how many police cadets would attend. They clarified that each class usually took thirty candidates, and if money was available, there were usually two classes per year. If funding was not sufficient, only one class during the current year would be scheduled. They did reveal that I was one of sixty-five candidates pending selection. Armed with this information, I thought that if I wasn't selected for the first class, there was a good possibility I may not be hired until the following year or even later. On top of this possibility, there was no guarantee of when the next class was going to start. Based on the uncertainty concerning the class date and Melitta's wishes that I not pursue law enforcement, I felt it was in the best interest of my family that I seek employment in a different field, regardless of what Saint Louis's future decision on my selection would be.

In mid-April 1972, I centered my job search in Indianapolis, where there would be far more opportunities, and narrowed my employment hunt to the field of insurance adjusting. I chose insurance adjusting because the position requires extensive contact, investigating, and interviewing of people to determine facts of an incident and independent investigations to prove the circumstances of a case. Fundamental skills in dealing with people, interviewing, and investigations are the same talents required by criminal investigators. Also, hopefully, working as an adjuster could quell Melitta's anxieties about the type of work I chose. I thought this decision would be a win-win for my relationship with Melitta; boy, would I find out differently.

On April 25, 1972, I had an interview with Walter Wykes, vice president (VP) of personnel operations for American States Insurance Company in Indianapolis. Wykes, a six-foot-four-inch, slender, good-looking fellow with a gentle, soft-spoken voice and somewhat forced smile, had a very friendly and cordial demeanor. After a second interview a week later, I was hired as an adjuster. I was assigned to their corporate headquarters at Thirty-Fourth and Meridian Streets in Indianapolis for training. I left my job at Saint Anthony's Hospital and took my first post collegiate position, and the pay was the best I had ever received.

When I told Melitta about my new job, she reacted with skepticism. Looking somewhat bewildered, she snapped, "You wanted law enforcement. I don't think you will stay very long in insurance."

I was stunned when I heard her response. Throughout our marriage, Melitta always reacted opposite of what was expected. But her surprisingly apathetic response to the news about the insurance job, a decision I'd made for her, shook me a little more than usual.

If we were going to continue being together, I needed to put all the pieces to Melitta's puzzled personality together. Regardless of what I did—make major changes in my career path, tolerate her rude and disrespectful behavior, and ignore or disregard her uncaring attitude toward almost everybody and everything—it did not seem to be enough. For almost five years, I tried to analyze Melitta's emotional state of mind without success. Talking or dealing with her in any way was always like walking on eggs; you put pressure on them and they would break. I concluded that I was just too immature or too green to be able to handle her problems. I thought I had as many problems with her as there could be at this stage in our lives. I never thought those problems would begin to swell in the future. Even with the issues we had, I had to find normalcy in our lives.

I found some comfort in working as an insurance adjuster. American States agreed to hire me on condition that after successfully passing their training program, I would be willing to transfer to any location where they needed me. This obviously meant that I would have to relocate from the Indianapolis office to another city. Of course, I agreed to this stipulation, thinking just maybe a change of scenery would help Melitta and me. The training had no certain time frame, but generally new adjusters would have to work under a supervisor for different sections—auto, home, or business—until it was felt they had acquired enough working knowledge of the business to work independently in the field. They even allowed me enough time off to look for local housing for my family. Indianapolis was seventy-three miles from my home in Terre Haute. I had to leave for work about 6:00 each morning to make the seventy-three-mile trip in time to start work at 8:00. It would be nice that Melitta and the kids could move to Indianapolis to shorten that daily trip.

The first time I talked to Melitta about moving, she told me that we should wait until I found out where they were going to place me. I thought her comment made sense, so we agreed that she would remain living in Terre Haute, and I would continue driving to Indianapolis each day until I was reassigned.

Melitta's decision to stay in Terre Haute had further-reaching implications affecting my future career than I'd ever imagined. From late April through the end of June 1972, I worked at the corporate office under some extraordinarily good people who had been in the insurance business longer than my lifetime. I gained a lot of insights into the way claims worked and what insurance policies covered. Under their mentorship, I handled numerous routine auto accidents, storm-damaged homes and business, and fire loses.

One case involved a nightclub fire where the entire building and its contents were destroyed. The loss to the building was estimated to be more than $100,000, and the contents had a determined value of $75,000. Arson was suspected, so I hired an expert in the causes and origins of fires to inspect the burned building. He developed proof that gasoline was used as an accelerant in several locations in the nightclub area of the building. I investigated both the owner of the building and the nightclub owner, who leased space in the building. I determined the owner of the building had nothing suspicious in his background that could connect him to the fire. However, my investigation of the nightclub owner disclosed that he owed the Internal Revenue Service (IRS) back taxes and had good reason to need more money. I acted as the liaison between the fire marshal and Indianapolis Arson Investigators in laying out the case for prosecution.

The nightclub owner was jailed, and I denied his claim. During the investigation, I spent over $10,000 to prove arson and was concerned when I turned in my report that I would be chastised for spending too much money. However, instead of being reprimanded for spending that amount of money, I received accolades from corporate for saving money by denying the claim. I would find that the primary goal of the insurance industry is limiting losses in any way possible. By spending $10,000, I saved $165,000 in payouts if the claim had been approved. A lesson well learned. This case further stirred my ambition to pursue a career in investigations.

In June 1972, my supervisor, Bruce Torrance, a tall, slender gentleman, informed me that the company wanted to send me to Madison, Wisconsin. I was dreading this moment because of the anticipation of Melitta's reaction, but the move was inevitable. That evening when I got home, I did not hesitate to let Melitta know about my job transfer. What was foreseen as an intimate night of celebrating the news over wine and dinner turned out to be a routine night of discontent when Melitta told me that she was not going to move. She used the excuse that she did not know how long I would be in Madison. Of course, she did not have a clue as to how long I was going to be in Madison. I tried to explain to her that all transfers of this nature could have changing consequences on family life, but to advance one's career, it is an acceptable risk. I reminded her that I changed career directions because of her. Shrugging and waving her arms in the air to give emphasis to her frustration, she screamed, "Until you find a permanent job, I will not move anywhere with you!"

Melitta's strange, quirky, and often violent outbursts, in my opinion, were a reaction to what she saw as life-changing events and deep-seated feelings of insecurity. These feelings were veiled deep within her emotional and psychological framework. I don't think she was concerned about moving as much as how it would disrupt her perceived secure life. I started guessing that she had a strong fear of being left alone if she moved from her current comfortable surroundings to a new location. I thought that maybe she was afraid to get close to people, because if she did, they would surely leave her. It is ironic that her feelings of insecurities prevented her from getting close to people, because she was afraid of losing them in her life, which drove them away. She would rather stay alone in Terre Haute, where she felt secure, than move to a new area and, in her mind, face the possibility of being left there by herself.

So, it looked like I was going to make the trip to Madison by myself. I wondered how her emotions would play out in future job transfers. At this juncture in our lives, I was tempted to bring up the possibility of a trial separation with Melitta. The timing, however, was not right due to the impending birth of our baby. I let the matter die, but in the back of my mind, I knew it would resurface in the future. I would still attempt to bring her to Madison soon once I found a house for us. In late June 1972, I packed the car, gassed it up, and headed for Madison, Wisconsin.

Madison is the capital of Wisconsin, having been incorporated in 1848[35] It is in Dane County, in the south-central part of the state. Madison is located about 125 miles northwest of Chicago and had a population of approximately 172,000 people in 1970, two years before I first arrived there.[36] Madison is the home of the University of Wisconsin and is known as the City of Four Lakes: Mendota, Monona, Waubesa, and Kegonsa.

I found the American States Insurance office in a small business park near a Travelodge Motel. I figured I would stay at the nearby motel while looking for a permanent place to live, for which American States offered to pick up the tab. The American States Insurance office was in the lower level of a small two-story building. The work area consisted of a large room set up for the administrative manager, one adjuster (me), one secretary, and one salesman. The chief adjuster (my boss) had his own office, and a regional sales manager occupied the other single office across the hall. Although there were six people near one another, the space was reasonably adequate.

I greeted Frank Clapp, my new boss, whom I had previously met at the corporate office in Indianapolis. I was familiar with his recent selection to be the chief adjuster in Madison. Frank was thirty-six years old, had a full head of hair, was slender in build, and had a revolting, nasty habit of moving his false teeth around in his month with his tongue. Every time you would engage Frank in conversation, the noise he made with his false teeth was very repugnant and distracting. I am sure that Frank was not aware of his distasteful habit that totally annoyed people.

Ruth Berta, a young, good-looking, thirty-ish redhead was our secretary, and Donna Paterson, a middle-aged, stern-faced woman who wore her eyeglasses on her nose, ran the office. The salesman, Carl Matthews,[37] a longtime employee, was very pleasant and talkative. Paul Berta, the regional sales manager, was married to Ruth, the secretary. Paul was a nice-looking young man who had the look of confidence and was friendly, open, and well mannered. I later found out that Paul excelled in baseball and tennis while in college. Except for Frank's bad habit, I thought that the entire team was going to be good to work with.

Almost from day one, Frank assigned me the bulk of the claim cases to work. The claims ranged from minor fender benders and weather-damaged homes to store robberies, thefts, and frauds. Frank's lack of good managerial skills slowly became apparent. I saw his position as a working manager and not, as he thought, in the purest sense, strictly a supervisor. There was too much work in the office for just one man. The entire southern part of the state of Wisconsin and eastern part of Iowa comprised our area of operations. Once I started working claim investigations, I would have to drive from the city of Madison to La Crosse, Wisconsin, about 140 miles, or from Madison to Dubuque, approximately 93 miles, or to Milwaukee, roughly 80 miles, to investigate a claim in a day. This travel schedule got hectic at times, and I unofficially started to lobby for a second field adjuster, to no avail.

Initially, I spent a large portion of my travel time meeting our independent insurance agents selling our insurance. They were not used to an adjuster in the field, and they usually took care of small claims themselves. "It's not personal," I informed them. I was visiting them to get to know them and was still learning the job, I told them. I advised that in the future with more experience, I would not see a need to visit their areas as much.

It was well into July 1972 before I took my first trip to Terre Haute to visit Melitta and Robert. My planned trips to Terre Haute were usually every other week. I would usually schedule a series of claim investigations in Milwaukee on a Friday afternoon. Then, once finished for the day, I would drive south approximately 275 miles to Terre Haute, arriving about midnight on Friday, to spend time with Melitta and Robert. I usually stayed until Sunday morning and then headed back to Madison for the week. Most of the visits involved either lunch or dinner on Saturday, with the evening resting at home. Melitta was rarely forthcoming with any real conversation, but instead would be very curt and abrupt in responses to my attempts to engage her.

I recall on one Saturday evening we decided to stay in for dinner. After our meal, I sat down to read the *Terre Haute Tribune.* As I held the paper open to the page I was reading, I was caught by surprise when, for no apparent reason, Melitta grabbed the paper from my hands. Without saying a word, she violently wadded it up and threw it in the trash can. She then stomped off into the bedroom and slammed the door shut. I slept on the couch that night and left early that Sunday morning for Madison without resolving whatever was eating at her. On the drive to Madison, I speculated that Melitta, possibly angry over me reading the newspaper instead of me taking the time to talk, was unable to channel her repressed frustrations, so she exploded into an uncontrolled frenzy.

Back in Madison, I kept myself busy by working twelve-hour days. To educate myself, I read insurance industry news reports, analyzed insurance trends, and read virtually every reference book in the office's library. I had an occasional dinner at a restaurant with Frank and his wife and with Paul and Ruth at their home. Paul and I spent time together watching sports on TV, and he attempted to teach me how to play tennis, but I was a poor student, and he quickly gave up.

Time in Madison was going by very slowly, but Paul and Ruth made it tolerable. They also kept me from starving, because I was sending most of my paycheck to Melitta. I had little office interaction with Frank, because he seemed to always be away at meetings with claimants or doing company business.

On weekends when I did not visit Melitta and Robert, I looked at several apartments but found they were too expensive for my budget. Subsequently, I found a real estate agent and provided him with a budget to find a rental home in the Madison area. On a Saturday morning in late July 1972, I received a call from the real estate agent, who informed me he had found a house in my given price range that rented for a hundred dollars per month in Deerfield, about twenty miles outside the city. He picked me up at the Travelodge Motel, and we drove to Deerfield. The house—a two-story, single-family home with basement—was located on a tree-lined street in an established neighborhood of equally good homes. I liked it right away, but I worried about what Melitta might think, or even worse, if she would even come to Wisconsin for a visit to see it.

"Before I decide, my wife needs to look at the house," I informed the realtor.

He gave me the usual salesman's pitch that if I didn't act soon, it would be gone. This meant I needed Melitta in Wisconsin as soon as possible. I knew this was not going to be an easy task.

When I got back to the motel, I immediately called Melitta and began the efforts of enticing her to come to Wisconsin. Once I'd convinced her to visit Madison to view the house, then I had to work on persuading her to stay. Since American States had encouraged me to bring her to Wisconsin at their expense, I told her to fly and I would meet her at the airport. Melitta agreed to visit me in Madison, but she beat around the bush about whether she would entertain the thought of staying.

She called me at my office on Tuesday morning and told me she had decided that she would travel to Madison on Thursday. I was less than amused when she told me she was coming by bus. I was mainly concerned about the health of her and the baby. The long ride in the cramped space of a bus could not be good for a seven-and-a-half-month-pregnant woman. I thought this was ridiculous, since American States would fly her to Madison and reimburse us for a two-hour plane ride. But this was Melitta in her purest form, doing things that did not make sense to others. In this case, I assumed it was too inconvenient for her to have purchased a plane ticket, and she probably also was thinking of saving money. Whatever the reason for her decision to take a bus instead of a plane was her way of doing things that only suited her.

At 5:30 Thursday afternoon, I picked Melitta up at the Madison bus station. I had hoped she would agree to stay at least a week, but when I saw she had brought only one suitcase, I immediately thought that the length of her stay would be far shorter than anticipated. Melitta left Robert at our longtime babysitter Barbara's house in Terre Haute, so his care was squared away. Although I would have liked to have seen Robert, the decision for him to stay in Terre Haute was a good one. I wished for enough time to convince Melitta that a move to Madison was in the best interest of the family.

On the drive to the motel, Melitta did not say too much and looked worn out. I asked her how she felt and if there were any problems with the baby. She responded, "No," with no further discussion. I did not get a response from Melitta when I told her that I had arranged for us to see the house in Deerfield the next afternoon. I got a sinking feeling that she did not even want to be in Madison. The greeting I got from her lacked the emotion of a wife that had not seen her husband for a couple of weeks. I dropped off Melitta's suitcase at the motel, and we went to dinner and then turned in for the evening.

Friday morning finally came, and I was anxious to let Melitta see the house I had found, but first I had to get some work done at the office. I went in and made some phone calls and appointments for the beginning of next week. About noon, I informed Donna, the office manager, that I would be showing my wife around Madison and would return in a few hours. I met Melitta at the Travelodge and took her to lunch. I informed her that my employment in Madison was likely to last a long time and that I felt good about it. I assured her that a career in investigating claims was a respectable substitute for investigating crime. The focus of my conversation was to convince her that moving to Madison had its advantages. I laid out some positive aspects of being in Madison. The first one, and the most obvious, was that the family would be together. Second, the job opportunities for her were far greater than in Terre Haute. The third reason was my career development would be more defined here in Madison.

As if she had not paid any attention to what I'd just told her, Melitta's only comment was that she had a stable job in Terre Haute and was afraid that changing employment now would not be in her best interests. I got the impression that she was not in favor of ever moving from Terre Haute and, further, was not a bit concerned for what I did for a living. It seemed hopeless, my efforts collapsing. Regardless of what I said, it would never be enough to sway her decision, due to her feelings of what I felt were insecurities. I started to get the feeling that Melitta had no problem and would even welcome the situation that we reside separately if I provided money to support her, Robert, and our unborn baby.

In any event, I decided to continue as planned and went through with showing Melitta the house in Deerfield. As we walked outside from the restaurant to my car, a dark blue sky and sixty-degree temperature made it a perfect day for house hunting, or in this case, viewing. Our meeting was scheduled for 1:30 that afternoon. As I drove through the city of Madison, I pointed things of interest out to Melitta, but she seemed detached or preoccupied and not the least bit interested. When we arrived at exactly 1:30, the realtor was waiting for us in his car. I introduced him to Melitta, and we all walked into the house. As we toured the house, I kept watching for any positive hints of excitement or curiosity coming from Melitta's expressions, but I saw none. In the fifteen minutes to tour the entire house, Melitta had no pertinent questions about the house, schools in the area, the community, or anything else for the realtor.

"If I have any further questions, I'll get in touch with you," I told the realtor as we got into my car. We had driven about two or three miles before I asked Melitta what she thought about the area. Not knowing what to expect from her, but being optimistic, I hoped it was positive.

"I thought the house was nice," she said.

Not to make her angry, I thought better about bringing up the fact that she had asked no questions about the cost to heat the house, where the schools were located, or anything about the surrounding area. Of course, I had previously talked to the realtor about these things and had answers for Melitta, but I had no illusions that she would ever ask about such information.

About 2:30, I dropped Melitta off at the Travelodge to rest while I went back to the office for a couple of hours. It was hard for me to concentrate on work because I was thinking of Melitta's apathetic reactions to the house and moving to Madison. I decided that instead of confronting her with further discussions about the move, I would take her to a leisurely dinner and a movie after I left work. I would also spend the weekend showing her Madison. I would work on convincing her it was a good move before she left for Terre Haute.

This effort was for naught, because Melitta broke the news to me over dinner that she had seen enough of Madison and was ready to go home; her decision deflated my enthusiasm over the whole situation. I knew I was up against insurmountable odds in convincing her to stay for a few more days, let alone to permanently move to Madison, so at dinner that evening, I agreed to drive her home the following morning. At least it would allow me to see Robert over the weekend.

At 8:00 on Saturday morning, we began the six-hour drive to Terre Haute. We arrived in Terre Haute about 2:00 that afternoon and got settled in, and Melitta went to pick up Robert from Barbara's. We spent an uneventful Saturday evening at home but talked little about the move to Madison. I was not in the mood for a long stay in Terre Haute, so I decided to leave for Madison about 9:00 on Sunday morning. Before I departed, I tried to one more time to engage Melitta about the move to Madison, but I could not get a reasonable answer from her. The only thing she said to me right before I left for Madison was that she would think about it. I fired one final shot at her before leaving that the longer it took her to decide, the less chance we would have of getting the affordable house rental in Deerfield. She said good-bye as if we'd had never had the conversation in the first place. The drive back to Madison was a painful one.

In Madison, I threw myself into my work. I made it a practice to visit all agents at least once. When I was required to go to Dubuque, Iowa, I usually stayed overnight. I started getting a good reputation for closing claims quickly and that were cost effective to the company. The predominant claim investigations I worked were routine car accidents. I investigated a few bond forfeiture cases and conducted liaison with numerous police departments in Wisconsin when the company had insurance payouts due to loss from robberies, thefts, and non–auto accident bodily injury claims.

On days that I would see Frank, he always appeared busy in his office, and he rarely talked about details of what he was working on. I would catch him for lunch maybe one or two days every week or so. I took the opportunities during these lunches to update him on the status of Melitta's move to Madison. I purposely was straightforward with him about her reluctance to move to Madison, but I was unaware he was keeping the home office posted on this information. Later, a home office VP would confront me about my situation with Melitta.

I was pretty much on my own as far as the investigations were concerned. I rarely received any feedback or oversight on my investigations, and Frank never intervened in any of them. The only time that I did receive feedback, a VP review claims analyst from the home office reviewed one of my investigations on the damage to a van involved in a head-on collision with another vehicle. I totaled the 1972 Chevy van and paid the claimant $4,500 (my company spending limit without higher authorization was $5,000). The analyst fired back a review report on the claim and advised me that I could have saved more money if I had tried to repair the chassis. His opinion was based on the review of photographs submitted with my report. I was not sure how the review analyst came up with his decision, because the photographs did not show the chassis in any detail. Further, the analyst was not armed with the information obtained from the chassis tech that it was too problematic and the cost too high to repair the car frame, so he suggested scrapping the vehicle. The tech further advised that repairing versus scrapping the vehicle could have resulted in poor wheel alignment and structural damage. There was also extensive body damage to the van, and I continued to stand by my original decision to pay the claim. I heard nothing more from the home office on this claim and the review. Based on this case, I made a recommendation to the home office that all documents should be included with the adjuster's report so reviewers could have all the evidence to support findings in the field. Shortly thereafter, the home office made it a policy to include all documents and notes with the field adjuster's reports.

Time passed quickly. It was already mid-September. I continued to reside at the Travelodge, and Melitta had not given me a decision to move to Madison, so we lost the proposed rental property in Deerfield to another party. No one, including Frank or the home office, had approached me verbally, in writing, or by telephone about the time it was taking to find a permanent residence. When I was assigned to Madison, the home office never gave me a time frame for finding a house or apartment. I continued to search for a less expensive place for myself, where I could live without Melitta and Robert.

On September 28, 1972, a Thursday, Christopher Dietzel Miller was born at Union Hospital, Terre Haute, Indiana. He was a big baby, weighing 11.4 pounds at birth, and was in excellent health. June, my sister, had called me at my motel room with the exciting news about Chris's birth. I immediately called Frank at his home and told him the news. He gave me the rest of the week off so I could go to Terre Haute. After hanging up from speaking to Frank, I called Bob and Mary Sandin and told them the news of Chris's birth. I agreed to pick up Mary the next day in Michigan City on my way to Terre Haute.

At 6:00 Friday morning, I left Madison for the approximate two-and-a-half-hour drive to Michigan City. I picked up Mary at 8:45, and we headed for Terre Haute, arriving about 12:30 in the afternoon. We went straight to Union Hospital and saw Chris for the first time. He was an adorable little baby with very strong lungs. I was extremely proud of him, and I thought he was the cutest baby in the nursery. We then checked in on Melitta, who was in good spirits and resting well. We were informed that she and Chris had to stay in the hospital for one more night, and they could be taken home on Sunday. June was at the hospital when we arrived but could not stay long, because she had to go home to care for her baby, Charlie, who was born three weeks earlier. We stayed at the hospital about two hours, and then I dropped Mary off at our house and went to see June and her newborn baby, Charlie. Charlie was a cute baby and, like Chris, had strong lungs.

We brought Melitta and Chris home on Sunday morning, and before I left for Madison late that afternoon, we had a light dinner. I asked Melitta how long she planned to stay off work, and she told me about a week. I told her that was too short and she should consider at least two to three weeks, but it was to no avail; Melitta never listened to anyone. Mary decided to stay a week, helping Melitta care for Chris, and Bob would pick her up the following weekend. I told Mary that I would be home the following weekend.

I spent the next week in Madison getting as much work done as possible. Friday afternoon, I drove back to Terre Haute to spend the weekend. I got home about 7:00 that evening, and Bob drove down from Michigan City the next day. Melitta, her parents, Robert, Chris, and I had a good visit. Bob and Mary were still at the house when I left for Madison at 2:00 on Sunday afternoon.

Except for Chris being born, nothing much had changed. Melitta was still reluctant to move from Terre Haute, I had found no house or apartment, and I continued to work approximately twelve-hour days to stay busy. The insurance business was getting hectic, to say the least. The workload was tremendous, and it did not look like American States was going to hire any additional adjusters for the Madison office. There were rumors flying around the office that Frank was falling out of favor with the home office and that his dismissal was looming. For all practical purposes, I was the only person handling claims in Madison. Frank, as usual, spent most of his time away from the office and would not call in, so no one knew where he was.

It was mid-October 1972, on a Friday. The weather was windy and chilly, and leaves were falling from the trees. It had been two weeks since I'd last seen Melitta and the kids. Instead of leaving for Terre Haute that evening after work, I decided to wait until early Saturday morning. About 7:00 the next morning, I drove to Terre Haute for a shortened weekend to see Melitta and the kids. I arrived at our house at approximately 1:00 that afternoon. Not thinking anything of it when I found no one there, I unpacked and settled in to rest until they got back. When I woke from a short nap, I saw that it was almost 3:00, and there was still no one at home. I decided to go visit Mom and found her well and in good health. Mom did not know where Melitta or the kids were. We talked for about an hour, and everything was okay with her. I went back to our house, but still no Melitta or kids. I killed more time watching TV until about 7:00, with no word from Melitta. I thought that just maybe she'd taken the kids to see her parents.

I put in a call to Michigan City, and Bob answered the phone. Bob said that Melitta had arrived at his house about three hours earlier. He then yelled for Melitta to come to the phone.

In the few seconds that I waited for her to come to the phone, I thought, *I don't want to make a scene while she is with her parents. I will just talk with her and politely hang up.*

Melitta got on the phone and, in her usual unsympathetic tone, said, "What do you want?"

Without telling her where I was, I said to her, "I just wanted to check on you and the kids to see how everyone is getting along."

Melitta, bypassing any information about Chris, perfunctorily passed on Robert's greetings, without being apologetic or the least bit remorseful about not letting me know she was going to her parents. If I had known she was going to be in Michigan City, I could have driven down from Madison to see her and the kids at her parents' house. She did not even ask me how I was getting along, but instead abruptly ended the phone conversation by telling me they were getting ready for dinner.

"I'll talk to you later in the week. Good-bye."

I became extremely hurt and angry at Melitta for being so thoughtless. Since it was late, I decided to stay at the house for the evening and head back to Madison early the next morning. To this day, I've never told Melitta that I was in Terre Haute that weekend to see her and the kids, and I have not heard her mention anything about it. I left for Madison at 6:00 the next morning.

The claim investigations continued to come in, and my best efforts to close cases to keep pace with the newly opened ones fell short. Rumors about Frank's impending demise with American States continued to circulate around the office and even spread to the field agents. I would often get phone calls from independent insurance agents asking if I knew when Frank's last working day would be. It was hard to believe that Donna, the usual chief office gossip coordinator, was mum. Then one day in mid-November 1972, Walter Wykes from the home office called, and I answered the phone. He extended pleasantries to me and then asked for Frank, who, by coincidence, was in. Since my cube was positioned directly outside Frank's office door, I could hear Frank talk, but I could not determine what Wykes was saying. I did find out that Wykes was coming to Madison on Monday, November 20, three days before Thanksgiving. Boy, if Frank was going to be canned, I personally thought the timing just before Thanksgiving was rotten on American States' part.

Neither Frank nor anyone else in the office mentioned the Wykes visit until the day before his scheduled arrival. Donna informed me that Wykes was due to arrive at about 4:00 on the afternoon of the twentieth and that he was staying at the Holiday Inn. I wanted to talk to Wykes and repeatedly attempted to reach him at his hotel after 4:00 and throughout the evening, without success. I was unaware that he had already decided to meet with Frank to presumably to talk about Frank's future with American States. I wanted to talk with Wykes about my future with American States. My talk with him would have to wait until the following day when he came to our office.

Sure enough, about 8:00 the following morning, Wykes was in Frank's office with the door shut. Everyone—Paul, Donna, Ruth, and Carl—was already in the office when I arrived. When I walked in, you could hear a pin drop. No one was talking or making any sound whatsoever. Shortly after I grabbed my first cup of coffee, Frank opened the door to his office and motioned for me to step inside. Up until this moment, I never considered the possibility that my head might be on the chopping block, as well as Frank's. I took my coffee with me and stepped inside and was offered a chair in front of Frank's desk. I had sat there a few times when I'd gone into Frank's office to brief him on claim investigations—that is, when he was in the office. Wykes was sitting on the side of Frank's desk. I sat down, and Wykes leaned over and shut the office door. I could just imagine what the others outside were thinking. Wykes, with that forced smile on his face, immediately began the meeting by telling me that American States and Frank were "going their separate ways."

Had I heard his comment, right? At that moment, I realized that Frank just got fired. Wykes then changed topics without missing a step. "Frank tells me that your wife doesn't like Madison and is refusing to move from Terre Haute," Wykes started.

Once I heard Wykes relate what he knew about Melitta, I immediately knew that Frank had spun the information I had given him about Melitta's lack of decision into a no about the move to Madison. This hit me by surprise! Frank's job required him to tell Wykes that one of his employees was having trouble with his wife wanting to move to the area, but he should have related the information accurately. Thinking back on this meeting, Wykes was right in his assessment, although Melitta had not specifically said no at the time of the meeting. Wykes was under the correct assumption that Melitta did not want to move to Madison.

Moving from Melitta to my performance, Wykes, without his traditional forced smile and looking more natural than usual, volunteered, "We like your work and want you to stay." He then brought Melitta back to the equation. "If you can work it out with your wife about the move to Madison, we would welcome you to stay. In fact," he reiterated, "we want you to stay."

I knew my answer to Wykes would be conditional at best, because I had no confidence about swaying Melitta's feelings about the move to Madison. I asked him to give me until the middle of December, and then I could provide him with a final decision about staying in Madison. He agreed. It looked like I still had a job until at least the middle of December. I walked out of that meeting feeling relatively good, but I knew the outcome would depend on Melitta's decision.

I went to Terre Haute that Wednesday afternoon to spend the Thanksgiving holidays with Melitta and the kids. Of course, when I got home that evening, I found no one at home, because Melitta had dropped the kids off at Barbara's house for the night while she went to work until 7:00 on Thursday morning. So, as usual, I spent the evening alone, uncertain what my future was going to look like. I would have to give Melitta an ultimatum, a chance for me to have a career or to stay in Terre Haute and face uncertainty about the future. Knowing almost certainly what her answer was going to be, I had to decide what direction I was headed.

The morning went to hell in a handbasket after everyone got home. We acknowledged each other and engaged in small talk. I held Chris for a while and placed him in his crib. Robert was still sleepy, so I tucked him into his bed, and Melitta and I exchanged small talk. Then she dropped a bombshell on me. She knew I liked to spend Thanksgiving at home, and we had done so in the past. However, she told me she'd accepted an invitation from one of her coworkers to come to her family's home for Thanksgiving dinner. I reminded her that we had earlier in our marriage decided that Thanksgiving was the only yearly holiday that we agreed to celebrate at home. Melitta fired back that she did not know if I was coming home or staying in Madison. I felt my blood pressure boiling up inside. I told her that we had discussed the Thanksgiving holiday two weeks earlier, and I had even asked her to invite her parents down from Michigan City.

She did not respond to my comments, nor did she try to defend herself. Further, our quarrel left in dispute how we were going to spend Thanksgiving. With nothing in the refrigerator, it looked like we were going to her coworker's home for Thanksgiving.

Later that day, we had Thanksgiving dinner at the coworker's home and stayed until 7:00 that evening. Once we got home, there was no mention by Melitta of the day's events, no apologies, no saying, "I am sorry; I screwed up," nothing. I thought my expectations of Melitta might be way too high. I had to make a big decision before going back to Madison. Should I confront her one more time about moving to Madison with the reinforcement to support the move by telling her about my meeting with Wykes? Should I forget about even bringing up the topic and just go back to Madison to give American States my resignation? If I did the latter, I would have to come up with an alternate career path that would either keep me in Terre Haute or one in which I would leave Terre Haute. Regardless of what my decision would be, I had to bring Melitta on board; if not, I anticipated a divorce was certain. I decided to give it one more chance at convincing Melitta that a move to Madison was in our family's best interest.

On the Friday after Thanksgiving, I brought the Madison move up to Melitta one final time. I gave her all the pros and cons about the move, without her showing any reaction. I then asked her, "Are you going to move to Madison for the sake of the family?"

She responded, "No."

That was it! She finally gave me an answer. The one I had been expecting all along. I thought, *we would not be in this position if she had told me her answer before I moved to Madison.* I asked Melitta, "What do you expect me to do?" She did not utter a response.

For the rest of the day, we—no, *I*—discussed what direction our future was headed. Melitta just sat in a chair next to me and stared into the distance without saying a word. I was not getting through to her; she was totally unresponsive. Finally, I told her that I was going to have to leave American States, and suddenly, she asked me, "What are you going to do?"

I could not believe what I heard. I had been delicately having a one-sided discussion with her about my career and our future together for months now without any input from her. Now that I told her I had to leave my current job because she refused to move with me, she asked, "What are you going to do?" Melitta had never provided me with any idea of what she wanted me to do. I thought, *she does not care what I do if I continue to provide money to her each month!* I was certain she did not even care if I lived with her and the kids or away from them, so long as I provided her with money each month!

If I was going to stay married to Melitta, I had to face the likelihood that we would live separately. This I did not want but, for the sake of the kids, would consider. I had to come up with the ideal job that would be equally satisfying to both me and Melitta. I considered several options, to include reentering the US Army and hopefully becoming a criminal investigator with the United States Army Criminal Investigation Command (USACIDC), routinely called CID. CID investigators had the title of special agent, like other federal law enforcement agencies. The advantages of entering the US Army would provide me with stability, and salaries in the military were on the rise.

The US Army would be less strain on the financial side of the house, because more than likely, I would be provided with less-expensive living accommodations. This decision also might be better suited to appease Melitta. The disadvantages of reentering the US Army would be that there was no guarantee I would be accepted into the USACIDC, although I could not think of any reason; I had the education and an investigative background with the insurance industry as pluses. The advantages of staying with American States was that I already had a job and I could continue seeing the kids. The major disadvantage of staying with American States was financial. I would have to fork over money for a place to live and still send money to Melitta and the kids, which I could not afford. I had for all practical purposes forgotten about the pending decision by the Saint Louis Metropolitan Police Department.

I discussed with Melitta the possibility of returning to the US Army as a criminal investigator, and she, as usual, was ambiguous in her response and feelings about my idea. I went over the advantages of such a decision with her and took the opportunity to suggest that the social environment in the military may be more to her liking and it would be easier for her to make friends and provide better security and stability for her and the kids. For the first time in many months, I thought I saw a twinkle in her eyes and felt like I'd touched an emotional nerve. She responded with a positive comment that she thought that was interesting. We spent the rest of the weekend talking about the possibility of the US Army as a career, but mainly it was a one-sided discussion. I did obtain her permission to follow through with my idea.

On Monday morning, the office was eerily quiet without Frank, but I settled in comfortably for a long day of tedious work. There was not much intraoffice chatter, so I could get a lot of work done. Alone at dinner that evening at the Kountry [sic] Kitchen, my favorite restaurant because it was close to the Travelodge, I devised a time schedule for letting American States know that I had made up my mind to leave the company on December 15, 1972.

That following Friday, Donna received word from the home office that David Crawford[38] from one of American States' larger offices in Fort Wayne, Indiana, had been chosen to replace Frank. Since no one in the office knew Crawford, everyone speculated on what type of person he might be. Comments from people in the office ranged from Crawford being a nice young man on the move up to another Frank. Paul and I refrained from making any sort of prejudgment on him until we met him.

That night, Paul and I met for a beer, and I told him that I was resigning effective December 15. He seemed to understand the reason for my decision and wished me well in the future.

"I will be providing Wykes my letter of resignation on or about the first of December, requesting a termination date effective the fifteenth," I told him. I figured he would tell Ruth, his wife, but I asked him to hold off on telling the others in the office until I could spring it on the new boss, Crawford; Paul agreed. Wykes received and acknowledged my letter of resignation.

Crawford arrived on December 7, 1972. He was a youthful-looking, slender-framed lad of about thirty, neatly dressed in a blue suit and light red tie. He told me he was married with two small kids. As expected, I was selected to be the one to show him around. This was good, because it allowed me plenty of time to break the news to him that I was resigning effective December 15, 1972. However, telling Crawford I was resigning was a moot point because he told me that Wykes had already relayed the news to him.

I was not surprised about Wykes's disclosure; it was the corporate way of doing business. I quickly formulated a somewhat-less-than-spectacular opinion of Crawford that evening. For starters, over dinner, he ridiculed my decision to join the US Army. He came just short of saying the army was for losers by implying people who joined the army were not motivated. And, as if I were not even present and he was talking to a third party, he said, "I cannot understand why someone in his right mind would want to join the army." He snorted. In my resignation letter to Wykes, I had mentioned I was considering joining the US Army.

I spent the last week and a half ensuring my investigative files were in order and all claimants and insureds were updated on their cases. I closed out the cases, and I handed Donna the open ones. On the morning of December 15, 1972, I bid my farewells to Donna, Ruth, Paul, Carl, and of course David. I felt good about leaving American States, mainly because I do not think I could have effectively worked well with David.

My unemployment was short-lived, because I saw the US Army recruiter the following Monday after I returned to Terre Haute. This time around, it was much different from the first time. I had education, experience, and a drive that was noticed by the recruiter. He was a young SSG, slender and in good shape, and he looked sharp in his uniform. He told me he had been in the US Army for eight years. We were on the same level when we talked. I explained in detail what I wanted to accomplish in a US Army career. I told him I was aware that I could not get a direct assignment as a CID special agent, but that was my primary goal. He worked over the next few days to get me processed into the US Army as a military policeman (MP). When he notified me that I qualified for military occupational specialty (MOS) 95B, MP, I was ecstatic. He asked me if I would still be interested in joining the US Army if I had to take basic training a second time. I did not hesitate to say yes.

The recruiter also could guarantee my request for an assignment to Fort Knox, Kentucky, for at least two years. The assignment to Fort Knox was welcome news, because the US Army's decision placed me only three hours from home. Of course, if I could get Melitta to change her mind about moving, the location of assignments in the future would become irrelevant.

For reasons, unknown to me, the young recruiter invited me and Melitta to his house for dinner with his wife, so on the evening of December 20, 1972, we spent the evening enjoying each other's company and swapping war stories about our US Army assignments.

On the evening of December 21, 1972, the night before I was to report to Fort Knox, Melitta, in her usual self-centered way, decided she did not need to stay home on my last night before entering the US Army, so leaving me alone, she kept her schedule, took the kids to Barbara's house for the night, and went to work. At 6:00 the morning of December 22, 1972, a rather windy, cold morning with the temperature just above freezing, I walked to the Terre Haute bus station.

I thought, *I have done this before.* I joined others for the bus ride to Fort Knox to hopefully begin my career in the US Army. We arrived at Fort Knox later that day and were processed into the US Army, and I was administered the oath of enlistment for the second time. A stroke of good luck occurred that day when the US Army granted me and all the fellow enlistees who took the oath with me a two-week leave during the Christmas holidays.

I used the time to spend with Melitta and the kids. Chris was now three months old and Robert almost eight years. We spent Christmas at home but took a few days to visit Melitta's parents in Michigan City and visited Robert and Ellen Lane, her uncle and aunt, and their kids, Jimmy, Lisa, and little Robert, in Northbrook, Illinois. It seemed that the major topic of discussion over dinner at the Lanes' home was my joining the US Army. Melitta's parents and the Lanes were not in favor of me going back into the US Army but were silent on the matter. You could feel the tension in the air.

Lisa had a rude and inconsiderate boyfriend over for dinner that day as well. Her boyfriend, who later became her husband, apparently aspired to be a movie director. With everyone sitting around listening, Lisa's boyfriend started a half-hearted conversation about my poor decision to join the US Army.

Lisa's boyfriend came up with an analogy to prove his point by telling me the services had more general officers today than they had during World War II. At the time, I was not sure his facts were correct, but the analogy was a bad one to use as an example of why I should not join the US Army. In my defense, I attempted to explain to Lisa's boyfriend and the others sitting around the room that my decision was based on several factors, and, of course, I could not openly tell Melitta's family that it was her feelings of insecurities that led me to the decision to return to the US Army in the first place. I became incensed over their conclusions about my decision. In fact, I thought it was none of their business. That trip was the last time I ever saw the Lanes.

After returning home from Melitta's parents' home that holiday weekend, I spent the last few days as a civilian with Mom, June, her son, Charlie, Melitta, Chris and Robert in Terre Haute.

# 5

# Focusing on a Career

Patience Is a Virtue

Fort Knox

*Be unwavering, persistent, and unyielding with aspirations and goals in life*

Two weeks' leave granted by the US Army went by extremely fast, and on January 15, 1973, after a week at the reception station, I found myself in basic training at Fort Knox, Kentucky, for the second time in seven years. At twenty-six years of age, I knew I had the mental and physical toughness needed to handle the many challenges of US Army training. Technically, the Vietnam War was still officially ongoing, but that was soon to change on January 27, 1973, when all warring parties ceased hostilities. Within six months, the draft would end, and only volunteers would fill the ranks of the US Army.

I was assigned to Company C, Fifteenth Training Battalion, Fourth Training Brigade (C-15-4). Our barracks were comprised of the new concrete buildings with individual cadre rooms and open bays for line soldiers. This was an upgrade from the old WWII-era wooden-framed barracks I'd lived in during my first basic training period back in 1965. The training had changed in the seven years since I'd first entered the US Army, but the basic premise was still to prepare men and women to be soldiers. New ideas, concepts, and principles were used by the US Army in its methods, equipment, and style of training. A major change was the use of the M16 versus the M14 rifle, physical training events, and more women being allowed into MOSs previously dominated by men. Now, trainees were required to do push-ups, do sit-ups, and run two miles for their physical fitness test. The first few days of training were used to select leaders within the unit. I was selected as the Third Platoon guide because of my prior service, and I ended up bunking in one of the cadre rooms with my first squad leader, a twenty-year-old from Chicago, Illinois. Platoon guides served as acting sergeants and the chief liaison to the cadre. I also had to make sure the members of my platoon completed all assigned details within the barracks and elsewhere.

Training this time around emphasized physical strength more than before. Mentorship was encouraged as well as leadership and organizational management. The basics of map reading, land navigational skills, small-arms battle tactics, and group team development were focal points of training. Instead of serving predominantly as instructors as they did in the 1960s, drill instructors now functioned more like mentors and counselors to the recruits. This new style of training improved morale, reduced AWOL, and created a better initial impression recruits had of the US Army. Although I do not recall ever seeing any statistics on why more recruits were staying in, I suspect that the new approach and training style used had created a more congenial environment for soldiers than in the past and has undoubtedly made a positive impact on the number of soldiers choosing careers in the US Army.

Although there were a few incidents involving some of the trainees getting stressed out because of the intense training or that they were away from home for the first time, overwhelmingly, the morale was very high. One morning as our platoon was getting ready to march to the rifle range, I took roll call in front of the barracks. One young trainee named Otis Johnson,[39] a nineteen-year-old from Mississippi, was missing. I delegated the first squad leader to take the formation on the road march to the range while I went to look for Johnson. I found him sitting next to a wall in the open bay area, fully dressed and ready for the march, with his M16 rifle in his lap. I carefully approached him and saw that his weapon was not loaded. I sat down next to him and asked him what the problem was.

Crying, he mumbled, "I can't take it anymore."

Speaking softly, I expounded on the fact that we had gone a long way and were almost finished with basic.

He told me he missed his family, especially his mother, and he wanted to go home. I spent the better part of an hour sitting with him, just talking about anything I thought would boost his spirits. Eventually, he stopped crying and told me he was sorry for acting the way he did. I said, "Anyone in the highly stressful training environment we are in can be pushed to the breaking point." I assured Johnson that he had done nothing wrong and that no one was upset with him for his actions. I took the unprecedented step of telling him to take the morning off and I would talk to him that afternoon when we got back from the range.

I hoped that he would take the day to reflect and be in a better frame of mind later in the day. It was a risk, because he could go AWOL, but I took it upon myself to make the decision to let him off to contemplate his actions. It was fortunate that we were not qualifying with the rifle that day, so I told him I would clear it with the sergeant. To remove one more obstacle to defuse any other means Johnson might have of dealing with his stress, I had him relinquish his M16 rifle to me. I told him to utilize the day to rest, reflect, and possibly seek out a chaplain's counsel to further discuss his feelings. I left him in the barracks and went to our unit supply room to turn in his M16 rifle.

As I was running down the street near the barracks on my way to catch up with the rest of the platoon at the rifle range, an NCO stopped me and asked where I was going with an M16. Although I know now, I didn't think at the time how unusual, suspicious, or uncommon it was to see a lone soldier running down the street with an M16 in his possession. Soldiers carrying M16 rifles are almost always marching in unit formations or being supervised by cadre as they are being used or cleaned by trainees. I provided the NCO, who was not from C-15-4, my story, which he was okay with and told me to be careful and go straight to the range. Once at the range, I told our platoon sergeant about my encounter with Johnson, and he told me I'd done the right thing. We never had any further problems with Johnson, and he graduated from basic with the rest of us.

Apart from Kentucky's cold winter weather, the eight weeks of basic training went by smoothly. On Saturday, February 17, 1973, toward the middle of the training cycle, we were given an afternoon off. Since Sundays were mostly down days anyway, this meant that the men could bring their spouses or parents down for an overnight visit. Since I had not seen the kids in several weeks, I decided to take advantage of this time off by inviting Melitta and the kids down for the weekend. I was surprised when Melitta accepted my invitation. I thought she might not want to come because of the 175-mile trip. Since I was committed to work that Saturday until noon, I suggested she schedule her trip to arrive at Fort Knox around 1:00. As I waited anxiously for her and the kids' arrival, 1:00 p.m. came and went. I waited another five hours and made two phone calls to our house before she showed up at 6:00 that evening. Although I was annoyed over her inconsiderate behavior, I took a deep breath and counted to ten when I saw Robert get out of the car. He came running up to me and gave me a big hug. Melitta then got out of the car and, with not even so much as a hug or kiss, perfunctorily greeted me by saying, "Hi."

"Where is Chris?" I asked.

Giving me no explanation as to why, she said, "I left him at Barbara's house."

I became furious with her. I told her that I thought she knew that I wanted to see both kids.

To add to my despair, Melitta brought with her mail I had received since arriving at Fort Knox. I thumbed through the envelopes and didn't see much of anything important, except one letter from the Saint Louis Metropolitan Police Department. Knowing what it was, I hurriedly opened the envelope and read the contents: "Welcome to the St. Louis Metropolitan Police Department. Your Training Academy Start Date Has Been Scheduled for February 5, 1973." The letter was postmarked January 8, 1973, the day I reported to Fort Knox. Saint Louis allowed almost a month to prepare for the academy. The irony of my acceptance to the Saint Louis Metropolitan Police Department was obvious: one, I was now in the US Army and could not accept the Saint Louis offer; and two, the letter of notification was received the week of January 8, 1973, but I did not receive it from Melitta until February 17, 1973, almost two weeks after I was scheduled to start training. Although it would not have mattered, in my several phone calls in January and February to Melitta since being at Fort Knox, she never once mentioned receiving the letter. At least I will have the memory of knowing I was accepted to the Saint Louis Metropolitan Police Department. However, looking back on Saint Louis's offer and my inability to take the job, I realize that all things that happen to you in life are for a reason.

Melitta and Robert did spend the night, but the visit still fell short of expectations. Instead of staying for most of Sunday, she told me she had to get back to Terre Haute, and about 9:00 that morning, she dropped me off at my barracks and left for home. That visit was the first time I had seen the family since I'd joined the US Army over eight weeks previously. Although the visit was short, I at least got to see them for a few hours.

Basic training ended the third week of March 1973, and the US Army kindly gave me another two-week leave before I had to report to Fort Gordon for MP school, which I spent with Melitta and the kids in Terre Haute.

In March 1973, I reported to Fort Gordon, Georgia, for MP school. Fort Gordon is located near Augusta, Georgia. It was established as an official US Army base in 1917 as Camp Gordon.[40] In 1973, the installation was home to both the US Army Signal Corps training center and the United States Army Military Police School (USAMPS). We were lodged in Brems Barracks, named after PFC Patrick J. Brems, an MP who was killed on April 1, 1966, in a terrorist explosion in front of the Victoria Hotel in Saigon.[41] MP training was to last a little over seven weeks.

MP school was a well-organized training experience. We received instructions in military police operations, road patrols, traffic stops, how to restrain people and the use of force, how to apprehend people, legal rights warnings, searches and seizures, completing MP police reports, interviewing techniques, duties and responsibilities at crime scenes, field tactical procedures, use of radios, court testimony skills, operating an M151 jeep, manning a traffic control point (TCP), convoy escorts, and learning the proper procedures for handling, firing, qualifying, and cleaning the .45-caliber pistol, and a brief overview of the Uniform Code of Military Justice (UCMJ). The training was wide ranging and was accomplished through a mixture of classroom and practical exercises. The training at the MP school was rewarding, and the instructors were knowledgeable, professional, and accommodating. I left Fort Gordon content that I had probably received the same level of training as I would have in any civilian police academy.

After graduating from MP school in mid-May 1973, I drove directly to Fort Knox, Kentucky, the home of the gold vault. In 1973, Fort Knox was also the home of the Armor Center and the 543rd Military Police Company. I was initially on orders for Headquarters and Headquarters Detachment (HHD) 194th Armor Brigade. HHD 194th had an MP detachment that primarily performed TCP duties when the tank units went to the field. However, another stroke of Millers' luck fell upon me. When I reported in to HHD 194th, I was informed that the MP detachment had stood down and all MPs were reassigned to the 543rd.

The 543rd MP Company was a unique unit in that it was a battalion-size company that policed all elements at Fort Knox. The unit was redesignated the 543rd MP Company on September 23, 1964, at Fort Knox, Kentucky. Typically, different MP companies made up a battalion-size unit. Different companies were assigned responsibilities for entities such as garrison patrol, running a post stockade, investigations, AWOL apprehension, physical security, and staffing the local provost marshal section. The 543rd had it all, to include one company commander, a 1SG, and the Fort Knox provost marshal; a colonel was even assigned to the unit.

I found the 543rd orderly room about three blocks from HHD 194th. My arrival was rather late in the day on a Friday, so the unit was in shutdown mode when I reported in. While a personnel sergeant was taking my orders and initiating documents to process me into the unit, I overheard two MPs that were in the room, talking about an incident that occurred only a few days before my arrival. They were talking about a young SP4 who had been stopped by an MP for suspicion of drunk driving (DUI). The SP4, a student at the US Army Armor School, was learning how to drive a tank. After the SP4 was cited for suspected DUI, he was released to his training unit, where the commander placed him on restriction for the rest of the weekend. However, still apparently intoxicated, he left his barracks without authorization and, set on retaliation for being stopped earlier that night, misappropriated an M60 tank from the motor pool. His ultimate target with the tank was to do some serious damage to the MP station.

The damage he caused was extensive. He initially missed his target and mistakenly smashed into a branch PX snack bar located in a small building next to the MP station. Realizing that the building he had just driven the tank into was not the MP station, he backed up and headed for the MP station. When he arrived at the MP station parking lot, he steered the tank toward several parked MP cars, rolling over them before crashing into the MP station as young MPs were escaping. After causing severe damage to the building, he backed the tank up and steered it toward the main road. By this time, MPs started following him in police cars but could not stop him. As the SP4 drove the tank around a traffic circle, he ran out of gas. Once the tank stopped, Jeffrey Peck, an MP who later became a CID special agent, climbed onto the turret and convinced the frustrated SP4 to exit the tank. Fortunately; there was no one hurt. After hearing this story, I thought that my assignment as an MP at Fort Knox was not going to be boring. The soldier was court marshalled and received eight years at hard labor and reduction of all pay and benefits. He was lucky, based on his actions he could have been tried for attempted murder.

The personnel sergeant completed processing me into the unit and advised me that it was too late in the day to get anything else done, so he told me to report to the orderly room at 8:00 sharp Monday morning for further instructions as to which platoon I would be assigned.

Since I was only four hours from Terre Haute, I decided to go home for the weekend. I arrived in Terre Haute about 7:00 that evening. I was home only a matter of minutes and saw that nothing had changed in the ten or so weeks since I'd seen Melitta and the kids. When I walked through the door, with a look of surprise, Melitta, with her usual lack of emotion, greeted me as I hugged the kids. I told her I was home for only the weekend and had to report to my unit Monday morning. One of the first things from her mouth was, "Since you are home, I don't need to take the kids to Barbara's tonight." I was right in thinking she was going to work that evening. We spent about an hour talking before she left for work. The weekend was typical in that Melitta went about her everyday routine as if I had not been there.

At 8:00 Monday morning, I reported to SSG George Hayes, the 543rd company clerk. He was a nice gentleman, about five foot nine and slender, had his hair cut in the flattop style, and wore eyeglasses. He completed what little paperwork on me was needed and then wanted to know about my background. I advised him that I had just recently reenlisted and had been in the US Army for only about four months, but I added I had been in for two years, including my year in Vietnam, in the mid-1960s.

"What was your job in the army?" he inquired.

I told him most of my experience was as a company clerk with the units to which I'd been assigned. He immediately asked me if I would be interested in working temporarily as his assistant company clerk. I thought, *here we go again.* This time, I hesitated and told him my goal was to work as an MP for however long it took to get experience to qualify for the CID. If I made it into CID, I informed him that I had plans on making the US Army my career. I told him I was afraid that if I worked as a company clerk, it might not give me the needed experience required.

Hayes started to negotiate with me. "This unit is as big as a battalion, and the work for one man is overwhelming. I need a good man to help me with that work. If Top approves you coming on board as a company clerk, I will let him know that it will be for only a short time," Hayes said.

"How short?" I asked.

Hayes said, "Let's say six months—that is, if you work out."

I paused for a second, thinking to myself, *Will I ever leave the army clerk business?* I asked Hayes if I could think on the matter for a couple of days while I was getting settled into the unit.

Hayes's response was perfunctory. "I don't see why not."

I indicated I would let him know my decision by Wednesday morning; he agreed. I requested the additional time because I wanted to verify what the CID and US Army regulations were before accepting the company clerk job.

I spent the next few hours researching CID and US Army regulations and found that I had the prerequisites needed to apply for CID. I got situated into a room in the barracks and informed Hayes that I would take the company clerk position for six months.

He obtained the 1SG's approval, and I began in earnest on Thursday morning to help Hayes in the orderly room. Introductions to the 1SG and commander were the first items of business. Hayes introduced me to 1SG Edgar Toler. Toler was a tall, slender man with gray hair styled into a flattop. Toler had a twin brother who was also a 1SG in the US Army. He spoke with a midwestern accent and came across as a stern, no-nonsense guy. But underneath his tough persona, there was a subtle affable way about him that made me think of him as a good man. The commander, Captain Michael Sudnik, an MP officer, came across as being pleasant, friendly, and approachable. I liked them both and looked forward to working for them.

Hayes was getting ready for an assignment to Germany in the next few months, so much of the work was systematically being transferred to me. Within a few weeks, I had taken over most of the duties and responsibilities previously held by Hayes. The transition of work went smoothly, and before Hayes's departure in early July 1973, I had everything within my control. Hayes and I became friends, and he occasionally had me over to his house for a home-cooked meal prepared by his lovely wife.

1SG Toler and I had an excellent working relationship, which made the job stress-free. He allowed me to function with minimum supervision. One day, I went to him and told him I needed help in the orderly room.

"Identify someone in the company that can help you, and I will have him reassigned to you," 1SG Toler said.

We brought in not only one new clerk but two. I liked the job as company clerk but dreamed of the day when I could work as an investigator, which I hoped would come soon. As I settled into the job, I got to know a lot of the MPs assigned to the unit. I also established a good working relationship with the PMO fellows. 1SG Toler gave me free rein to coordinate operational activities without going through him, which often sped up the process and allowed things to get done much faster. In retrospect, I became a surrogate 1SG.

I not only completed all the 543rd reports, including the old traditional morning report, but I became involved with personnel matters as well. A young, unhappy MP SP4 came to me one day and submitted a leave request that had been approved by his platoon sergeant. I reviewed his record and discovered that he had taken a considerable amount of leave in a short time, so I asked him why he was always going on leave. The SP4 told me that his father was ill and he was the only son of the family and had to return home to Illinois as often as he could to help on the family's farm. The SP4 was one of a handful of draftees left in the US Army, but he still had almost a year left on active duty. To compound the SP4's situation, his father's illness was serious, and he was not expected to live much longer.

I asked the SP4 if he had ever tried to obtain a compassionate discharge due to being the only surviving son. The SP4 said he had not tried to get out of the US Army because no one had ever told him he could. I told him to get letters from his minister, the doctors treating his father, and anyone else he could find that would support an application for a compassionate discharge. It took two weeks before he came back with all the letters of verification that what he was telling me was true. I prepared his application for discharge and submitted it to higher headquarters. About thirty days later, the application came back approved, and he was out of the US Army a week later. I was elated that I'd accomplished something that no other person in the SP4's chain of command had ever attempted.

During the summer of 1973, the US Army was transitioning from the old personnel accounting system for the status and actions of personnel (usually typing reports, including the morning reports), which took time to complete, to a more efficient way of doing things. I recall spending a week preparing mark-sense forms for each person assigned to the 543rd. Once each person's status had been identified on the mark-sense forms, any changes, such as TDY, AWOL, leave, hospital, reassignment, discharge, and so on, had to be recorded on the forms. The old traditional morning report had to concurrently be completed. This transitioning period took a year to complete. This new system was the forerunner to automation of the personnel manning system that revolutionized the way the US Army accounted for its people.

The year 1973 saw the end of hostilities in Vietnam but not a cessation of all the problems experienced by soldiers coming home from that conflict. One of the biggest for some soldiers involved the use of heroin. I had one MP confide in me that he had taken "skag" heroin throughout his tour in Vietnam. He told me it was as common among the people he ran with over there as it was to get up in the morning. I am not sure why he came to me to tell his story, but it made me think, *here is an MP, a person sworn to up hold the laws, and yet he is breaking them.* I was disappointed in the young MP, and although I did not interrogate him any further, I wondered if he was still using illegal drugs. I wondered just how many MPs had experienced illegal drug use and were still performing law enforcement duties. The information from the MP was unverified, but probably true. Based on his admissions, but without solid corroborating testimony or physical evidence and the elapsed time since his use, any case against him would be hard to prove.

I worked throughout the summer of 1973 making improvements in the administrative operations of the 543rd. One of our major projects was to make a temporary move from one building to another due to engineers making renovations and putting in new air-conditioning systems in the main MP barracks. The 543rd moved from their primary barracks to the Disney Barracks area of Fort Knox. The unit stayed in their temporary home until way after I left my job as the unit's company clerk. I stayed on as the 543rd company clerk from May 1973 to December 1973, just over the agreed time of six months. Within this time, I had submitted my CID application, and it was being processed. After the decision was made that I could leave the clerk's job and 1SG Toler knowing I wanted to begin my career as an investigator, he and Captain Ricky V. Wykoop, the new company commander, recommended me for an assignment directly to the Military Police Investigation (MPI) section.

On December 17, 1973, I went to a white, wooden, WWII-era, two-story building near Brave Rifles Road, Fort Knox. The first floor of the building housed the Fort Knox CID offices, and the second floor was occupied by MPI and, at one end, the CID evidence room. I parked my car in a space near the building and reported to SFC John Foster, a Vietnam veteran and NCOIC of MPI at Fort Knox. The MPI OIC was Captain Kenneth Woods, who also saw action as an MP in Vietnam. Foster was from Indiana, so we had something in common. They were good leaders to work for, and we had a good relationship. MP investigators assigned to the section at the time I arrived were SP4 Ronald Hostettler, a fellow Hoosier (from Indiana and who would become a close friend), Sergeant Wayne Hymes, Sergeant Alan Allen (yes, he had the same first and last names, but spelled differently), SSG Gresham (I can't recall his first name), Sergeant Casmire Blecka, SP4 Michael Otte, SP4 Charles M. Innes, and SP4 Chuck Hart. There were two or three other investigators in the office at the time, but they departed shortly after my arrival.

SFC Foster arranged for me to be issued MPI credentials (creds), and I was issued a Smith & Wesson .38-caliber revolver. Foster also provided me with a copy of Army Regulation (AR) 190-30 that covered the MPI program. The AR disclosed that MPIs usually investigated offenses that called for less than one year of confinement, like larcenies of $250 or less, simple assaults, and simple possession of small amounts of marijuana[42] and non-narcotic controlled substances. I found that CID had to be notified by MPI if they had a simple possession of a small amount of marijuana or another non-narcotic. CID was responsible for investigating the serious felony cases, such as murder, rape, aggravated assaults, and others. I studied the differences between the MPI and CID jurisdictions and responsibilities. I learned many important steps on how to investigate misdemeanor crimes in the US Army.

During our first meeting, Foster advised me that if I remained in the section long enough, I would be sent to MPI school at Fort Gordon. In Foster's briefing, he advised that the normal duty day for an MPI was twenty-four hours. SFC Foster also informed me that if the MPI did not pick up a lot of cases on his duty day, he or she could take a portion of the next day off. As I gained knowledge and experience and became more familiar with military investigations, I learned that the dedicated MPIs usually worked a full day after performing a twenty-four-hour shift.

I observed the actions of more experienced MPIs during actual interviews and interrogations of victims, suspects, and subjects. I educated myself on the proper report-writing formats of DA form 3975 (MP report). For about two weeks, I tagged along with the MPI duty investigator to gain knowledge and experience in processing crime scenes, interviewing witnesses, and in collecting, documenting, and proper handling of evidence. The first batch of cases I was assigned consisted of ten unsolved investigations that had been opened for several weeks. The leads in these cases had already been exhausted. It was my job to review them and, if no other possible leads appeared likely, to write the investigative reports as being unsolved. I was responsible for following up on any leads. When my first duty day arrived, I felt that I had only touched the surface of criminal investigations, but I was eagerly awaiting the start of a very interesting career.

On my first day of duty as an MPI, I recalled picking up at least six to eight cases. I picked up three barracks larcenies, one shoplifting, one minor simple assault, and one unfounded complaint. However, the case that sticks out the most was my very first complaint. I was driving one of MPI's finest inventory cars, a 1972 four-door plymouth sedan without any police or Kojak lights, back to the MPI office from the MP station. The MP desk reported that a suspected prostitute was loitering around inside a bowling alley. As I was responding to the scene, I ran upon a small traffic jam of three or four cars stopped at an intersection about a block from the bowling alley. I thought, *I will never make it in time before she leaves.* I was determined to personally handle my first-ever call to investigate a potential illegal action on the part of this prostitute in the Case of the Young Loitering "Prostitute":

## THE CASE OF THE YOUNG LOITERING "PROSTITUTE"
Things aren't always what they seem.
—Phaedrus, Roman poet

Without hesitation, I squeezed my car between the curb to my right and cars stopped at the red light on my left and proceeded through the intersection to my designation. I walked into the bowling alley to the sounds of people chattering and bowling balls rolling down the lanes, striking the pins. I approached a man behind the counter where they issued bowling shoes and bowling balls and asked to see the manager.

"I am the manager," he said.

"I have a report of a possible prostitute in the bowling alley," I told him.

"Yes," the manager said. "I called it into the MPs." He then pointed to a girl sitting at a table by herself. I went over to talk to her, and I noticed she had on a pair of mid-calf-length black boots, a very short blue skirt riding halfway up her thigh, and a sleeveless white blouse. Her hair was short but neatly combed, and she stuttered when she talked. She was dressed provocatively like a hooker, but then every girl had the right to look any way she wanted if it was not illegally indecent.

"What is your name?" I inquired.

"Jane," she responded.

"What are you doing at the bowling alley?" I asked.

She told me, "Waiting on my mother."

I looked at my wristwatch, and the time was 2:30 in the afternoon, so I asked her, "What time is your mother supposed to show up?"

"Two forty-five," she replied.

I went back to the manager and asked him, "How long has the girl been here?"

The manager looked at his wristwatch and then at me and said, "About an hour."

"Has she caused any trouble?" I asked.

The manager said, "Not that I know of."

"What made you think she is a prostitute?" I asked.

"Just look at the way she is dressed," said the manager.

I was not ready to kick her out just yet. I had no reason to detain or apprehend her. All she had done was to draw attention to herself because of the way she was dressed. I wanted to wait until 2:45 to see if her mother would show. About five minutes before her mother was allegedly scheduled to show up, the girl confronted a young boy about sixteen or seventeen years old who was bowling with a friend. I immediately approached the two and told the girl I wanted to talk to her. The young boy started to accompany her, so I motioned for him to stay put.

"I want to know what you want with my sister," the young boy said.

I stopped in my tracks and asked, "What did you say?"

"What do you want with my sister?" he said incredulously.

I felt an emotional churning sensation welling up inside my chest called embarrassment. My eyes focused on the girl with a look of surprise. "Why didn't you tell me this young man was your brother?" I asked.

"I am not here to meet him. I am here to me my mother," she said. Then the girl's eyes diverted from mine to the doorway of the bowling alley. "My mother just walked in," she said.

I turned and saw a middle-aged woman walking toward us. The mother, looking puzzled, asked, "What is going on?"

I introduced myself and showed her my MPI credentials. Ignoring her question, I told her there has been a misunderstanding and that nothing was wrong.

Before the mother had time to pry further, I tactfully separated myself from the three and walked over to the manager. I told him the young girl was not a prostitute. She was there to bowl a few games with her mother; I then walked out.

As I left the bowling alley, I was comfortable in feeling that the young girl, her brother, or her mother knew the real reason why I was there, and for that matter, they did not need to know.

When I returned to the MPI office, SFC Foster caught me as I walked past his office and said, "Get in here." Looking somewhat baffled, he informed me that the car I'd signed out earlier in the day had been identified by a concerned citizen as running a red light.

"Yep, that was me," I admitted. In my defense, I explained to Foster what had happened, and he told me not to worry that he would take care of any questions the MPs might have on the incident. As I left his office, I heard him say, "Good work, Miller."

Rule Six: *Do not rush into investigations with a mind-set that what was reported is always factual.*

As I became more comfortable with the investigative process, my confidence grew. SFC Foster started assigning me the older cases that still had viable leads. Including these older cases and counting the new ones I picked up during on-duty days, my caseload started growing substantially. I became the investigator of choice for walk-in complaints.

One young soldier, a PV2, was referred to MPI by his 1SG who was personal friends with SFC Foster. Foster called me into his office and asked if I could take on another case, and I agreed. Foster told me he was doing his friend a favor by taking on the case directly without any MP involvement. "You must report the incident to the MPs after you interview the victim," Foster said.

"I'll do it this afternoon," I told Foster.

This investigation was known as the Case of the Stolen Car Battery:

## THE CASE OF THE STOLEN CAR BATTERY
First Confession: The most insignificant case can be your most memorable

I called for the PV2 to come into my office. I completed a workup sheet on him and found he was from one of the maintenance units on post. Thinking this case was going to be a big one, I felt anxious with anticipation. My ego deflated fast when the PV2 (victim) told me at the beginning of the interview that his car battery had been stolen, so it was not going to be the big break in the case after all. Nevertheless, I obtained all the information that I could think of and told him I would keep in touch with him on the progress. In the meantime, I started the case by telling the victim to meet me in the parking lot where his car was parked. So, began my investigation of the stolen car battery. The PV2's 1965 two-door Chevy Impala was in a big parking lot used by members of his unit. The car was in the front row near the sidewalk where anyone walking by could reach out and touch it.

"When was the last time you parked your car, and shut off the engine?" I inquired.

"About 8:00 last evening," he said.

"Has anybody had anything stolen from their cars in this parking lot before?" I asked.

"Not that I know of," he said.

"What time did you discover your car battery missing?" I asked.

"When I was going to work, about 7:00 this morning," he said.

I had established the time frame of the larceny to be between 8:00 in the evening and 7:00 the next morning. I thought that since it was December, most of that time was covered in darkness. I also noticed there was a bright streetlamp located near the victim's car. I thought this would make it much harder to raise the hood and steal the battery without being detected by someone. Before I released the victim, I reiterated what I had told him before, that I would contact him if I found out anything.

Armed with the information I found at the crime scene, I located the unit 1SG, who incidentally brought the victim to the MPI office to report the crime.

I asked the 1SG if he would get with his platoon sergeants and put out the word to locate anyone who might have heard someone say anything about seeing people milling around the parking lot the previous evening. I gave the 1SG my MPI phone number and left for the office. I knew I did not have any real leads on this case, but I hoped that someone would come forth with information that might help.

It took two days, but I did receive a call from the victim's 1SG, who told me one of his platoon sergeants reported that he had found a young soldier who knew of another soldier that had trouble starting his car a few days earlier. The 1SG provided me with the person's name, and I asked him to send that person to my office at 8:00 the next morning.

The suspect showed up at his appointed time, and I asked him to sit down in the chair in front of my desk. The suspect, clutching his hat in his hand and acting very nervous, complied. I informed him of why he was called into the office and requested he be up front with me when answering my questions. He waived his rights and agreed to talk to me. I asked him a series of questions about his car.

"I understand that you had trouble with your car a few days ago, can you tell me what that trouble was?" I asked. I could barely hear him. I told him to please speak up.

"My car wouldn't start," he replied.

"Yes, I understand that would be a problem, but can you tell me if you isolated the problem as to why it would not start?" I asked.

Noticeably shifting in his seat, in a soft voice, he replied, "The battery was dead."

"Have you replaced the battery?" I asked.

"Yes," he replied.

"Where did you get the battery?" I asked.

"At a store in Radcliff," he said.

"What store was it?" I asked.

"I don't remember the name," he said.

"Was the battery new when you bought it?" I asked.

"No, it was a used one," he said.

I questioned him for another thirty minutes, and his answers continued to be vague. Finally, I came right out and confronted him with a direct question: "Did you steal the battery that you put in your car to replace the one that was dead?"

He denied the allegations. I informed him that I was going to get a search warrant to inspect the battery in his car and I would find out where it came from eventually.

He folded his arms across his chest and said, "Go ahead."

I interpreted his comment as permission to search under the hood of his car.

I could get the victim to look at the battery the suspect put in his car to see if he could identify it as his. I also could fingerprint the battery and send the prints to the lab. Maybe I could find some information on the battery that could identify where it had come from. These were all viable leads that could help us find the origin of the battery. I kept the suspect under wraps at the MPI office while MPI Ronald Hostettler and I went to check his car. We confiscated the battery as evidence and had the victim look at it without allowing him to touch it. The victim said the battery was his, but he could not provide any details to prove it was his.

I checked the battery for latent fingerprints but found none. I then thought of another lead I could try. I approached the suspect and asked him to take me to the store where he'd purchased the battery.

"I can't," the suspect said.

"Why not?" I asked.

"Because I didn't buy it. I stole it from someone's car," he said.

I obtained a written statement from the suspect, confessing to stealing the car battery. I then released him to a unit representative, wrote up my report, and reported it to the MP desk sergeant. It was unfortunate that it took several weeks before I could release the battery from evidence back to the victim, because the suspect was pending action under Article 15. The suspect eventually was administered an Article 15 under the Uniform Code of Military Justice (UCMJ) and received a hundred-dollar fine and fourteen days of extra duty and restriction.

Some investigations are extremely frustrating to the investigator, especially if you know you have the perp but there is not enough evidence to prove it. This was the situation in the Case of the Reluctant Sexual Deviant That Got Away:

## THE CASE OF THE RELUCTANT SEXUAL DEVIANT THAT GOT AWAY
The depraved will always be warped

Early one afternoon in late December 1973, during a scheduled duty day, I received a call from the MP desk sergeant who reported to me that two young girls, ages eleven and twelve years, reported they'd observed a white, male soldier masturbating in his car. They went home and informed their parents as to what happened, and their parents brought them to the MP station to officially report the incident. I briefly talked on the phone to each father and requested they escort their daughters to the MPI office. About thirty minutes later, the girls arrived with their parents. I advised the fathers that I would like to talk to their daughters separately, and they agreed. I had prearranged for a female investigator to sit in with me on the interviews.

I chose to interview the eleven-year-old first. She was a fifth grader at a nearby elementary school. For her age, she was very bright and articulate in telling her story. She claimed a white soldier pulled his car alongside her and her friend as they were walking home from school. The girl said that she and her friend walked over to the car after the man inside called them over. The car door window was rolled down, and she could easily see inside. She told me and the female investigator that the man was moving his hand up and down on his "thing," as she called it. The MPI office did not have any anatomically correct dolls at that time, so the female investigator pointed to the area of her body, and the girl said, "Yes. Down there."

I asked the girl if she could describe the man, and the only thing she could give us was that he was a white male, wearing a US Army uniform. She told us that she could not recognize him because she did not see his face. I then asked her if she could describe the car he was in. She told me the car was a two-door dark green older car. The young girl did not know the different models or years of vehicles.

I was satisfied that we'd obtained as much information from the eleven-year-old as we could, so we stopped and asked for the twelve-year-old to come into the interview room. We went through the same questions as we had with the first girl. The one thing the twelve-year-old was certain of was that she could not recognize the soldier because she did not see his face, but she said he had on SSG stripes. She said the car was a dark green, two-door model with a Virginia license plate, but she did not know the numbers. We finished with the girls and released them to their parents, and they left.

This case was going to be very difficult to crack.

After completing the report of the incident, in my mind, I came up with a few leads that might help. One, the girls were walking on the street near their neighborhood. It was logical to believe that the suspect might have been heading home at the time and day of the incident. Two, I could inquire with unit 1SGs in the area to determine if any of their soldiers had a dark green, older-model car. Third, I could conduct surveillance of the street during the time of the incident. Fourth, I could review MP, MPI, and CID records to determine if they had any suspects or subjects fitting the modus operandi. With the time, I was spending on my current caseload, it would be hard fitting into my daily schedule the surveillance, but I thought it could be possible to pull it off even on my duty days, because I was generally not working on current cases but out of the office anyway.

I started my investigation by reviewing MP, MPI, and CID records, to include field interview cards (FIC) MPs filled out on their patrols. MPI records were negative, and most of the subjects in the CID files had either been discharged or sent to Fort Leavenworth. The MP records did reveal the identities of a couple of people that warranted follow-up, so I jotted down the information in my notebook on the two individuals and placed it in the field folder that I carried around with me.

The next step was to produce a concise story contained on one sheet of paper describing the crime, and as time allowed, I passed them out to 1SGs of the unit where it was most logical that the perpetrator might be assigned. I started leaving the office about 3:00 in the afternoons and conducted drive-by surveillance in and around the area where the girls said the incident occurred. I expanded my search into the neighborhood where the girls were headed. None of this activity disclosed any new information on the case.

I called the units of the two individuals identified on the MP FICs and found that one had been honorably discharged from the US Army, but the other one was available for interview. I arranged with his 1SG to have him report to the MPI office. The individual showed up, and I observed he was a twenty-five-year-old white male. My investigation disclosed he had been assigned to Fort Knox for the past two years. FIC information reported that the individual was stopped by the MPs about three blocks from where the incident I was investigating occurred. I asked him why he had been in the neighborhood to start with. I already knew what he'd told the MPs that day—that he was looking for someone in the neighborhood. The MPs had failed to ask the name of the individual he was looking for. The individual related to me that he was looking for a fellow unit member who had a lawn mower for sale, and he was interested in buying it.

I asked him if he'd ever found the guy that had the lawn mower for sale, and he said, "Yes, and I bought it from him for fifteen bucks."

I followed up with the information he had provided, and I verified his story as being true. I fingerprinted him and took his photograph and then released him. I looked out my office window and observed him drive away in a small, light green, old Plymouth sedan.

Two weeks passed, and all I could get accomplished on this case were a couple of sporadic roving surveillances around the area of the incident.

One morning, about mid-January 1974, I had just arrived at the MPI office and already had a phone message waiting for me from a unit 1SG. I called the 1SG, who was from a support unit on post. He asked me if I was still looking for someone who drove a dark green, older-model car. With butterflies churning in my stomach, I immediately said yes. The 1SG said he had a SSG who had been in his unit for about six months and drove a dark green Oldsmobile Dynamic Holiday coupe. I ascertained the SSG's name and asked where the car was parked.

The 1SG gave me the location where the SSG's car was currently parked and told me he had not been informed that CID wanted to talk to him yet.

"That's good," I said. I informed the 1SG that I needed a little time before I brought him in for an interview, and the 1SG told me to give him a call when I was ready.

I immediately conducted a name check on the SSG and found something very interesting. The man with the green car had a record while assigned to Japan (Okinawa) of indecent exposure for masturbating in front of young girls about six years earlier. I thought, *this has got to be our guy.*

I then rushed to where the 1SG told me the SSG's car was parked, and I took several photographs of the vehicle. I noticed that the vehicle was a dark green, two-door coupe with Virginia license plates. I then drove around to various parking lots in the area and took random photographs of five more dark green cars. After I got the photographs developed, I then got in touch with the fathers of both girls and told them I had identified a suspect and asked if they could bring their girls by for a photographic lineup. They both agreed and scheduled them for the following day after school.

I anxiously waited for the SSG to arrive at the MPI office. Shortly after talking to the 1SG, the SSG arrived at the MPI office and asked for me. I warmly greeted him, shook his hand, and invited him into my office. I first asked him if he had driven his car to the interview, and he indicated he had.

"Good," I said. I started by being straightforward with the SSG and told him why he was being interviewed. He did not act nervous or apprehensive in any way, waived his rights, and consented to talk with me about the offense of indecent exposure. I then provided him with details of the case at hand, and he immediately denied any involvement. I then brought up the fact that he had been identified as being the subject of a similar incident in Japan involving young girls. The SSG had a real comeback for an answer to this question; he said that he was the victim of mistaken identity in the Japanese case.

I asked him, "If you are innocent, why were you given an Article 15 and fined for the incident?"

He alluded to me that he could not prove to the authorities in Japan that it was not him.

I interviewed him for over an hour, and he did not admit to any wrongdoing. He subsequently declined to submit to a polygraph examination. Knowing he was not going to crack on this one, I knew I had to gather strong evidence to make a case against him. I stopped the interview and fingerprinted, photographed, and dismissed him. When he left, I knew we had our man, but it was going to be tough proving it.

The following afternoon, the two girls came to the MPI office, and I showed them a photographic lineup containing our deviant suspect from Japan, the other person who had been stopped by the MPs, and four other individuals from our mug book files. The gas ran out of the case when neither girl could positively identify any of the photographs as the man they'd seen exposing himself. I further showed the girls a photographic lineup six dark green cars, including the suspect's that I had taken a couple of days prior. The eleven-year-old said she thought the suspect's car was the one she saw the man in, but she was not sure. The twelve-year-old could not select any of the cars in the photographic lineup. I had to go to Staff Judge Advocate (SJA) with the evidence I had. My meeting with them was poignant in that they said there was not enough evidence to bring charges against the suspect. Since there were no further leads on the case, I had no alternative but to shut it down and close the investigation as unsolved.

Within a month after being assigned to the MPI section, I had been promoted to sergeant. The promotion gave me a psychological boost of confidence, and the emotional high I was feeling seemed to give me a blast of energy. The entire MPI section at Fort Knox was extremely busy. I was learning as well as performing investigative duties. I dug in to my work with a zest of motivation I had not experienced. I volunteered for extra duty, and Foster assigned me cases that would normally go to the MPI that initiated them.

My busy schedule left me with little time to travel back to Terre Haute to see Melitta and the kids. I did fit in one visit during Christmas Eve and Christmas. Melitta and I never wrote letters to each other; thus, the only planning I could accomplish was by telephone and hoped she would stay on the same sheet of music when we agreed on something, especially a future planned visit. Unfortunately, those plans often got sidetracked, because Melitta would forget, was indifferent, or changed the plans without consulting me.

This was the case in late January 1974. My schedule allowed me to take time off for a weekend visit with Melitta and the kids. I had called her about a week earlier and told her I would be able to visit her and the kids the following weekend, and to my surprise, she voiced her agreement. I got home that Friday evening about 7:00. I had scheduled my arrival to permit time to be home before Melitta had to go to work, allowing me to be with the kids that night. However, a note was left on the kitchen table that read, "Had to go into work early. See you tomorrow." She did not even mention the kids, who had presumably been left at Barbara's for the night. Melitta arrived home with the kids about 9:00 that Saturday morning. Since she had worked the night before, I took care of the kids while she slept a good portion of the day. Melitta started stirring about 3:00 in the afternoon. When she got up, we set at the kitchen table and had a general conversation about the kids for a few minutes. I then turned the conversation to moving to Kentucky, but she had that distant gaze on her face and was not open to my suggestions. I saw that I was not getting anywhere and at that moment concluded that I would never convince Melitta to move anyplace other than Terre Haute.

As I drove back to Fort Knox that Sunday, I was unsure I could keep up the charade of being a married man much longer. Earlier on, I thought that I may be able to handle living separately, but my patience was running thin, to say the least.

After that weekend trip to Terre Haute, I buckled down and got some serious casework done. Case closures were on the rise, but the reduction of cases was short-lived. In February 1974, the MPIs, including myself, started picking up several cases each time we pulled duty. Just when I felt I was making a dent in my caseload, duty investigator day would come along and I would pick up more than I had closed in the previous few days. Each MPI in the office was seeing a significant increase in theft cases. There had been an increase in stolen property cases— or at least of reported thefts—from parked vehicles in unit parking lots and of personal items from individual wall lockers, so when a young chaplain's assistant reported that his wall locker had been broken into, no one initially disputed it. MPI put forth all investigative efforts to successfully resolve any crime that was reported to them. Investigators didn't judge the merits of any case on the surface. Instead, a full and complete investigation was conducted on each complaint. If there were any concerns about the legitimacy of the case, it would almost always be resolved through a thorough investigation. One case stood out from others in that it involved a person whose character and integrity was believed to be above reproach, as noted in the Case of the Worried Chaplain's Assistant:

## THE CASE OF THE WORRIED CHAPLAIN'S ASSISTANT
Short as life is, we make it still shorter by the careless waste of time.
—Victor Hugo

On a bright, cloudless, cold day in February 1974, I received a call from the Fort Knox MP desk sergeant, who reported that a PFC had complained that someone had stolen twenty dollars from his barracks wall locker. I requested the MPs transport the young PFC to the MPI office. Since I had a window view of the street running in front of the MPI/CID offices, I saw everyone entering and leaving the building. Watching victims, suspects, and even subjects walk into the building did not provide me with much knowledge about their character and demeanor, but it always allowed me to say that it was good to see them again when greeting them. This usually caught them off guard, which gave me an advantage at the start of an interview. The MP patrol dropped the PFC victim off, and I watched him from my upstairs window walking into the building.

As usual when I went to get the victim in the waiting room, I shook his hand to welcome him to the MPI office. I told him it was good to see him again. Looking perplexed and anxious, he said, "Hi."

The victim began his story that he had placed a twenty-dollar bill inside a small cardboard box on a top shelf of his wall locker earlier in the morning at about 6:30 and left for a nearby dining hall to eat breakfast. The victim said when he returned to his room from breakfast at about 7:45, he discovered his wall locker had been rummaged through and the twenty-dollar bill was missing.

"Did you lock your wall locker and the door to your room when you left?" I asked.

"No!" he said.

"Why?" I asked.

The victim related, "I locked my wall locker, but did not lock the door to my room."

"Was the padlock that had secured your wall locker found in your room?" I asked.

He stopped for a moment before answering, apparently lost for words or trying to come up with the best-case scenario. He said he did not remember if the padlock was in the room or not when he returned.

"Was the small cardboard box that contained the twenty-dollar bill still there?" I asked.

"Yes," he indicated.

"Do you have any roommates?" I asked.

"Yes, but he is on a two-week leave," the victim said.

It was at this point in my interview with him that I knew I should have gone to the scene before talking to him. I did not go to his room, because the beginning of the investigation started when the victim reported the crime at the MP station instead of the normal procedure where MPs go to the scene. The MPs or I should have gone to the scene before his interview, but that step was missed.

In any event, the way the victim answered the question about whether the padlock had been found after the break-in sparked my curiosity. I could understand if the victim had not thought about the missing padlock, but to come up with the answer that he could not remember seeing it just did not appear consistent with his other answers. I had a gut feeling about this case from that moment forward. His comment caused me to change directions from an interview to gather information to an interrogation. I started suspecting that the victim was being deceptive or not being forthright. The victim started hesitating more between answers. I turned up the pressure for him to answer the questions more directly. The victim started getting fidgety and looked uncomfortable sitting in his chair.

"What is the unit's policy on room and wall locker inspections?" I asked.

"What do you mean?" he responded.

"Do they have a set time in the morning for the inspections?" I said.

"Yes. It is 9:00 a.m.," he said.

Now, I made the decision to interrupt the interview and go visit his room. I inquired with the victim if his room and wall locker were locked. He responded that he locked both his wall locker and room door before he went to the MPs to report the larceny of the twenty-dollar bill. I then decided to take him with me back to his barracks to inspect the crime scene. As we rode in the car to his unit, the victim's face looked ashen, and he was silent most of the trip. Once we got to his barracks, I advised a clerk at the unit orderly room what we were about to do. When we arrived at his room, the victim took a set of keys from his front pants pocket, selected one of the keys, and unlocked his room. As I entered his room, I immediately noticed that his wall locker was also locked. I inspected the brass padlock that secured his wall locker and asked him to unlock the wall locker. Again, reaching into his pocket, he pulled out a set of keys and selected one from the ring and unlocked his wall locker. I noticed that he had several keys on the ring he carried in his pocket. I asked to inspect the keys on the ring, and he gave them to me. I asked him which key was for the padlock that had secured his wall locker before the break-in. I told him he should still have that key. He first looked at the keys on the ring but quickly told me that he had thrown it away.

"Did you understand that that key might be evidence if we ever found the padlock?" I commented.

He shrugged and commented, "I did not think of the key as evidence."

I handed the keys back to him and continued to inspect the wall locker. I found no evidence, such as scratches on the key hook on the wall locker or metal particles on the floor, to indicate anyone had tried to force open the doors.

I then painstakingly went to the victim's wall locker, and it was a mess. The top shelf had personal stuff, such as aftershave lotion and lather, mouthwash, razor, bottles that were open, and lids lying around inside the shelves. I had the victim point to where the small cardboard box was located that had the twenty-dollar bill. He pointed to a corner behind the personal items. No small cardboard box was found. Dirty towels were hanging inside the wall locker, and he had unkempt uniforms clumped up in the bottom portion of the wall locker. The wad of military uniforms and civilian clothes looked like they were ready for the laundry. My examination of his wall locker told me that the victim had not prepared for the 9:00 inspection.

"When and where did you purchase the padlock you currently have?" I asked. When he told me the PX but did not volunteer when, I asked him again, "When did you purchase the padlock?"

He again hesitated and was slow coming up with an answer. He eventually told me that he had purchased the padlock a while ago and kept it as a backup to the one that had been on his wall locker when it was broken into. I looked around on the floor, underneath his bunk, and found no padlock. "Where did you keep the padlock that you have now?" I inquired. He pointed to a desk in the corner of his side of the room. (The victim lived in a two-man room, and the individual living space was divided by wall lockers.)

"Over there in the drawer," he said.

I went over and looked inside the drawer and found an assortment of writing pads, pencils, pens, and other things that would normally be in a desk drawer, but I did not find what I was hoping for. I then scanned the room and found a trash can. I walk over and inspected its contents, but still did not find what I was looking for. My investigation of his room told me what I needed to know and convinced me the victim was lying. I told him to secure everything and requested he accompany me back to the MPI office to sum up the interview. He complied.

I brought the victim into my office and surprised him when I read him his rights for filing a false police report; he was stunned. I laid out the circumstances and explained to him the facts leading to the conclusion that I believed he had lied during his interview. One, his story about the second padlock was too convenient and appeared contrived. Second, his wall locker showed no signs of being tampered with. Third, his wall locker was a mess and was not ready for inspections. Fourth, he inexplicably threw away the key to the missing padlock before reporting the incident. When I asked him if he wanted me to continue, he lowered his head and said, "There is no need. You got me."

I asked him why he'd falsely reported the crime. He admitted that he had made up the incident, thinking it would prevent him from getting into trouble for not getting his wall locker ready for inspection. I told him it was going to cost him more than twenty dollars to recover from his foolishness. Later, I found out I was wrong about his punishment. His commander only gave him a letter of admonishment with no Article 15. The punishment would tarnish his reputation for a while, but hopefully he had learned a lesson. This case illustrates that people do not have to get involved in situations if they just follow rules and use common sense in everyday life.

In late March 1974, a new OIC was assigned to the MPI Section. His name: Major Augustine Vendetti, a Vietnam War hero who was a helicopter pilot that reportedly had been shot down a couple of times. Within a few weeks of taking over the OIC position at MPI, he became very popular with the MPIs. He was a leader by example, and although he was personable, he would not hesitate to resolve any issues with positive and stern action. Meetings with leaders are usually very intense or too businesslike, and at the end, you leave feeling like nothing was accomplished. Not the case with my first sit-down with Major Vendetti. He was a pleasant, straightforward, and extremely personable man who made you feel very comfortable and relaxed talking to him. He would get involved with cases only when needed, usually to intervene or be a buffer between browbeating senior NCOs or commanders of suspects or subjects being investigated. Major Vendetti vastly improved working relationships between MPI and CID. He outranked the 543rd MP company commander, but this situation never caused any concerns or issues with MPI assignments. He also was on equal footing with the CID commander, who was also a major. Their excellent working relationship influenced good camaraderie between the MPIs and CID special agents. An example of working closely together reminds me of two cases in which I personally assisted CID with the investigations. One was the Case of the Thief Who Wanted to Get Rich:

## THE CASE OF THE THIEF WHO WANTED TO GET RICH
If you are caught, stay caught

On a hot summer night in June 1974, I was the MPI duty investigator and working in my office catching up on paperwork from the day's cases. Around 10:45 p.m., I received a call from the MP desk sergeant to report that three civilians were caught stealing aluminum magnesium shell casings from a tank range located in a rural part of Fort Knox by two MP game wardens. (Aluminum magnesium shell casings are valuable, because the metal can be sold as scrap.) The MP desk sergeant also reported that as the MPs were transporting the three to the MP station, one of the suspects was shot in an attempted escape. I knew that the case was CID's from the start and that the MP desk sergeant only called me for notification purposes. I rushed downstairs and found CID duty special agent (SA) Robert Beightol in his office.

"I was just notified by the MPs about the shooting incident at the tank range," Beightol advised. I noticed he was in the process of putting together his crime scene gear. Beightol asked if I could assist him, and I said yes. Beightol decided to drive his assigned CID sedan to the scene, and I drove the MPI car. The decision to drive two cars was made due to the probability that one or both of us would receive other duty calls and would need our own transportation.

Once we arrived at the tank range, about five to seven miles away, we started looking for the MP game wardens. The night was dark, and visibility was limited. I was in the lead car, while Beightol followed closely in the CID sedan. Even with the bright lights on, I did not have adequate visibility. We turned off the main road onto a very narrow range access dirt road that was just wide enough for one car. After traveling about a half mile, I noticed in front of me the narrow width of the road over a deep ditch. As I traveled over the ditch, the weight of my car shook loose some dirt, causing the left side of the road to cave in. My car made it across this narrow stretch of road, but before I could alert Beightol by radio, his car rolled over the same stretch of road.

From my rearview mirror, I saw Beightol's car lights virtually shoot vertical into the air as the left side of his vehicle went off the edge of the road and landed partially in the ditch. I immediately stopped my car and ran back to assist Beightol out of his car. I was relieved to see he had not been hurt. With minimal help, he pulled himself out of the car. Because of its precarious position, his car had to be left for a tow truck. He hopped into my vehicle, and we continued to search for the MPs who had apprehended the civilians. When we found them, the game warden's jeep was parked in a drainage ditch alongside Heartbreak Ridge Road. As we drove upon the scene, we observed two MPs standing outside with two suspects in hand irons.

MP SSG Henry advised that he and the other MP had caught the three-putting aluminum magnesium shell casings into the back of their pickup truck. The three suspects were apprehended and placed into the back of the MPs' jeep. Two were handcuffed to each other, and the third was secured with his arms behind his back in hand irons. MP SSG Henry advised Beightol that as he and his partner were transporting the three to the MP station, one of the individuals in the back grabbed the gun of Henry's partner riding in the front. SSG Henry immediately pulled the jeep into a ditch alongside the road and jumped out, pulled his .45-caliber pistol, and emptied the clip into the radiator. He did this to prevent the suspects from using the jeep for their escape. The individual who grabbed the MP's gun was inadvertently hit in the head by one of SSG Henry's bullets. With the engine still running, the wounded man was thrown backward from the jeep into the ditch. Because of the motion caused by all who had exited the vehicle, the jeep jolted backward and rolled over the wounded individual.

Later, it was discovered during an autopsy that the man had serious injuries because of the jeep rolling over him, but his death was caused by a gunshot wound to the head. The subsequent investigation by CID disclosed that the suspect who'd jumped from the jeep and escaped up a hill was the brother to the individual who was killed. The next day, the individual that escaped turned himself into the MP station and, like the suspect who'd stayed in the jeep during the ordeal, was charged with theft of US government property. The suspects were turned over to the civilian authorities for processing and legal proceedings. An inquiry was held in the shooting death of the civilian. SSG Henry was later cleared from any wrongdoing in the shooting death of the civilian and allowed to return to duty as an MP.

The above case was the first investigation in which I had rendered assistance to CID, and it gave me some good insights on how the special agents worked. There were many other cases, but this one continues to stand out over others and is narrated as the Case of the Unknown Music Lover:

## THE CASE OF THE UNKNOWN MUSIC LOVER
My first CID case

Initiative consists of doing the right thing without being told.
—Irving Mack

It was another duty investigator night in early July 1974 when Special Agent Dennis Walker from downstairs came into my office and asked for assistance. He said he had just received a call from the MP desk sergeant about a housebreaking and larceny of a stereo unit from a soldier's room at one of the units on Fort Knox. Special Agent Walker indicated that he was backed up with two additional cases, and requested I go to the scene and get details on what happened. Since I had no pending duty calls, I agreed. He gave me the unit and soldier's name.

I arrived at the unit and met with the victim, a SP4, who told the following story. He had left his room about 6:00 to go play baseball at a nearby ballpark. He returned to his room about 8:30 and discovered that his stereo system had been stolen from his room. He said he purchased the electronics system about two months earlier at the Fort Knox post exchange for about $900.

"Where was your roommate when you went to play baseball?" I asked.

"He was with me. We play on the same team," he said.

"Was your room door locked when you left to play ball?" I asked.

"Yes!" he exclaimed. His roommate, who was standing nearby, verified that they had locked the room when they left.

"How many people have shown an interest in the stereo package?" I inquired.

The victim could not come up with a number, but he did indicate most of the men in his platoon knew he had the stereo equipment. I asked him to provide me with a list of names and bring it to my office the next day. He agreed.

My examination of the crime scene disclosed it was a typical two-man room with one door and a window. I examined the door and found no signs of tampering, so I focused on the most likely point of entry to the room: the window. I discovered the window was fully functional and that it could be raised from the inside or outside. Upon closer examination, I found no trace evidence on the windowsill. My outside inspection of the window revealed it was only a few feet from a public sidewall, and anyone walking by could look inside the room without creating undue attention. With no physical evidence found at the scene, I would have to rely on interviews.

I returned to the MPI office with the victim and took a written statement from him on the details of the crime. I then completed the preliminary report and gave it to Special Agent Dennis Walker with a briefing that the victim would drop off a list of people who knew he'd had the stereo system in his room. Special Agent Walker thanked me for my assistance.

About two days later, I was called into Major Vendetti's office and found Special Agent Pete Dedijer from the Fort Knox CID office sitting on the couch next to Vendetti's desk. Pete had the housebreaking and larceny case I had worked on for Special Agent Walker in his hands. Pete indicated that since the preliminary work on the case was thorough, for continuity purposes, he requested that MPI take over the case for completion.

Major Vendetti looked at me, and I nodded approval to the major and then back to Dedijer, and I said, "Okay, we'll take it."

This is how I ended up with my first CID case as an MPI. I conducted many follow-up interviews on the case but developed no more evidence or leads to identify who may have entered the room and stolen the $900 stereo system. It was closed out as unsolved.

Working with the Fort Knox CID was a good experience, and all the special agents were friendly, knowledgeable, and personal. Of the lot, Special Agents Beightol, James Mayo, Skip Core, Pete Dedijer, Frank Woods, Roy Williams, and their executive officer, 1LT Henry S. Matlosz, were the ones I worked with the most. Fort Knox CID was considered a large office at the time I was an MPI. I cannot recall one incident where I approached the CID special agents to ask for their insights into some investigative matter when they didn't stop what they were doing and take the time to explain in detail the reasons for the investigative steps. They were also friendly, personable, and eager to help. Other investigations that I conducted as an MPI probably fell within the purview of the CID but were never turned over to them for work. One investigation that fit this scenario was the Case of the Elusive Corvette and Missing Revolver:

THE CASE OF THE ELUSIVE CORVETTE AND MISSING REVOLVER
The cruelest lies are often told in silence.
—Robert Louis Stevenson

I was assigned one case that probably should have been investigated by the CID, but no one ever questioned the jurisdiction. It was reported by a young SP4 from an armor unit that one night when he was driving down Brave Rifles Road, he got into the right turn lane in preparation to turn right. As he proceeded into the lane, he came up alongside a silver Corvette driven by a man. As the victim approached on the right, the driver of the silver Corvette pointed a small-caliber revolver through the passenger-side window at the SP4. The SP4 immediately applied his brakes and turned right into a nearby parking lot and made a beeline in the opposite direction. The SP4 victim said the driver of the Corvette did not chase him. The victim reported the incident to the MP station, and I received a call from the MP desk sergeant about the complaint. I interviewed and obtained a written statement from the victim, who essentially reiterated the same information as he had to the MPs. The victim showed genuine concern about what had happened to him. He claimed not to have known the man in the silver Corvette and could not think of any reason why the man had pointed the gun at him. The victim thought the gun was possibly a .22- or .25-caliber Smith & Wesson revolver, but he was not sure. I made contact arrangements with the victim and advised him I would be following up on his compliant.

Moving in and around Fort Knox as an MPI provided an excellent opportunity to see many of soldiers driving the same cars daily; surely a new Corvette would not go unnoticed. I personally had seen a young soldier driving a silver Corvette on several occasions at various locations on the installation. I also recalled seeing a silver Corvette parked in the parking lot at the Fort Knox NCO club in the past.

In the 1970s, the enlisted and NCO clubs were still hot spots for entertainment, especially on Friday and Saturday nights. I decided that my next logical lead in this case was to conduct a drive-through of the parking lots at the clubs the following Friday and Saturday nights. I asked Ron Hostettler to accompany me on the drive-through.

The next Friday night about 9:00, Hostettler and I drove through the NCO and enlisted club parking lots, but failed to see the Corvette. We repeated this exercise on Saturday night and hit pay dirt; I observed a silver Corvette in the parking lot at the NCO club. I parked the car, and we went inside the NCO club and sat at the bar. I asked the bartender if he knew anyone who drove a silver Corvette. He told me that there was one regular customer who did. I had the bartender point the individual out to me. The man, who was dancing with a girl, appeared to be Puerto Rican.

"Do you know the man's name and unit of assignment?"

"No," he answered.

Because of the crowd, I did not want to make any move to take him into custody. I considered two alternatives: one, wait for him to leave and then follow him to see if he went to his unit; or two, apprehend him as he got near the silver Corvette. I did not like the first alternative, because the suspect might leave with someone and go to another club, maybe even off post, or if the person that left with him was a female, the suspect might go to her residence. I decided on the second option of taking him into custody for questioning when he left the NCO club, regardless if anyone walked out with him.

I told Hostettler that we might have a long wait, because the NCO club stayed open until 1:00 or 2:00 in the morning. Then we might have to wait longer, because our man inside might decide to talk with people at his table for a while longer. The manager of the club advised us that the music stopped at 1:00 a.m. and the customers could stay until 2:00 a.m. He started kicking them out at 2:15. We weren't certain that the suspect would stay until closing; we had to play it by ear. If we stayed at the bar, there might be a lot of situations that could occur that would blow our cover, not counting the fact of how suspicious we would look at the bar without drinking for several hours. So, instead of waiting at the bar, Hostettler and I decided to pull surveillance on the Corvette from our car in the parking lot. We relocated our MPI car to a more advantageous location to view the Corvette and settled in for a long wait. Someone was on our side, because we were rewarded with a gift of time.

About 11:30 p.m., the suspect exited the NCO club, and he was alone. We watched him slowly stroll toward the general area where the silver Corvette was parked. Hostettler and I waited with a great deal of nervous anticipation. The closer the suspect got to the Corvette, the slower he walked, and time seemed endless. Something started churning inside my stomach, and my binoculars were fogging up, making it harder to track the suspect. We weren't even 100 percent certain the suspect's car was the silver Corvette. I thought. What a letdown it would be if the person we were watching was not the owner of the Corvette. We only had the word of the club bartender that he drove a silver Corvette.

Suddenly, my heart skipped a beat, and I took a deep breath when the suspect came to a dead stop. He stood still for a few seconds and then lit a cigarette. He took several puffs off the cigarette and then continued to walk toward the Corvette. Finally, I felt an enormous euphoric sensation when the suspect pulled a set of keys from his pants pocket and started to unlock the driver-side door of the Corvette. Before the suspect could get the door open, Hostettler and I exited the MPI car and rushed over to where he was standing and identified ourselves as MPIs.

The suspect was stunned and blurted out, "What did I do?"

As I got to him, I told him he was being detained for questioning concerning an assault with a gun. I told him that a soldier had reported that someone driving a car matching his pointed a small-caliber pistol at him while they were driving on Brave Rifles Road.

The suspect immediately said, "It was not me!"

I thought, *the suspect didn't deny having a small-caliber pistol.* I informed him that I still wanted to question him about the case and asked permission to search his car. He agreed. Because of the nature of the crime being investigated and the probability that the suspect had consumed alcohol, I handcuffed his arms behind him and called the MP desk to have the suspect transported to the MPI office while I searched his car.

While waiting on the MPs, I ascertained the suspect's name and unit. Considering it was a Saturday, one of the busiest nights of activity for the MPs, they were quick to arrive at the NCO club parking lot. I requested Hostettler accompany the suspect to the MPI office while I continued the search of his vehicle. My search did not uncover any pistols or other contraband from the suspect's car.

Once back at the MPI building, Hostettler was waiting with the suspect in my office. I called Hostettler outside into the hallway to have a private conversation with him before talking to the suspect. As discussed at the NCO club parking lot, Hostettler attempted to conduct a telephonic name check from the US Army Criminal Records Center (CRC), using the duty agent from the CID downstairs, but he was unsuccessful. Hostettler ran the suspect's name through the MPs and found no record. Although it was approaching 1:00 in the morning, Hostettler agreed to stay with me during the interview of the suspect.

I advised the suspect of his rights, and he agreed to discuss the case with me. After obtaining his personal data and history, he remained calm, cool, and unemotional throughout the interview. The suspect told us that he was single and lived alone in an off-post apartment in Vine Grove, Kentucky, near Fort Knox. When asked where he'd gotten the money to afford a silver Corvette and the cost of an off-post apartment, he told us that he had recently reenlisted for six years and received a bonus of $12,000. That was later verified through the reenlistment NCO at his unit.

The suspect remained steadfast in denying that he had pointed a gun at the victim. The suspect denied owning any pistols or other guns of any sort. I asked him if we could search his off-post apartment, and he agreed. Hostettler and I spent an hour searching his Vine Grove apartment but came up empty-handed. I ended the interview by asking the suspect if he would be willing to submit to a polygraph examination to determine the veracity of his statement. He declined. Further investigations and background checks on the suspect failed to identify any information that associated him with a small-caliber pistol or linked him to any previous crimes; he was clean as a whistle.

Even though our investigation of the suspect did not uncover any derogatory information about him, the Fort Knox Staff Judge Advocate (SJA) went forth with an Article 32 (preliminary hearing).[43] The Article 32 was held, and the findings released about a week later determined there was not enough evidence to support proceeding to go to trial. All charges against the suspect were dropped. Sometimes you can put a lot of effort into an investigation and still come up short.

On June 10, 1974, a Monday morning, just after spending the weekend in Terre Haute with Melitta and the kids, I was called into Major Vendetti's office, and he advised me that they had a slot open for MPI school at Fort Gordon, Georgia, and he would like for me to attend. He advised me that the class was scheduled to start on July 8, 1974. I requested a day or two before I gave him my decision, because I wanted to check on the status of my CID appointment. He agreed.

But before I reached Ed Foster, the CID accreditation manager, I got word from personnel that I had received orders for the Thirteenth MP Company in Bangkok, Thailand, with a reporting date of August 15, 1974.

Wow, when it rains it pours!

Before that Monday morning, all I was thinking about was how to prioritize my investigations. Now, I was simultaneously facing two new assignment possibilities and one TDY period. Foster advised that my application to CID was still pending,[44] but that everything thus far had been favorable. I informed him that I had just been selected for MPI school and had received orders for the Thirteenth MP Company in Bangkok. Mr. Foster alluded that my acceptance was a foregone conclusion when he told me that all he could tell me was to sit tight and hold on. Mr. Foster's advice left me with little wiggle room. My predicament presented many problems. I could not make the decision to attend MPI school, because I was uncertain about the appointment to CID. Yet the time was short, because the MPI school was ready to start in a couple of weeks. I also was not sure if the US Army would allow me to ignore the assignment to Bangkok, pending CID's decision. Combined with this quandary, my ongoing difficulties with Melitta only added to my dilemma.

I sat down at my desk to ponder my situation. Attending MPI school at a future date would not be possible unless I could convince personnel to adjust the assignment date to allow enough time to complete the course. I considered the possibility that if personnel would adjust the date of assignment to the Thirteenth MP Company, a favorable decision by CID could be made before, thus taking precedence over Bangkok. In any event, I thought the decision to attend MPI school would alleviate my woes and best serve my goal—that is, if CID came through with a favorable selection. For some reason, if CID did not select me, then I would eventually find myself assigned to the Thirteenth MP Company as a school-trained MPI. Not a bad alternative.

On June 17, 1974, I informed Major Vendetti that I would accept the appointment to MPI school. The 543rd adjusted the reporting date to Bangkok to September 30, 1974, thus allowing me time to complete the MPI school with a few weeks to spare. Two days after I informed Major Vendetti that I would attend MPI school, I received TDY orders for Fort Gordon to report on Sunday, July 7, 1974. That weekend, I would take a trip to Terre Haute to let Melitta know about my TDY to Fort Gordon and eventual assignment to Bangkok. I had a feeling that it did not make much difference to Melitta where I was assigned if I continued to provide her with money.

On that Friday, June 14, 1974, my TDY status took a major detour. I received a call from Mr. Foster from accreditation, informing me that I had favorably been selected by CID as a special agent trainee. I was scheduled to attend the CID special agents course from September 4, 1974, through November 27, 1974, with a follow-along assignment to Fort Ord, California. Mr. Foster told me he would coordinate with the necessary people to rescind my orders to the Thirteenth MP Company and that I should coordinate with the 543rd MP Company to cancel the MPI TDY orders. I was elated to hear the news and was looking forward to attending the special agents course at Fort Gordon, Georgia. My selection for CID training was a major milestone in my life. I began to feel that I had finally accomplished a level of real success.

My only concern was Melitta, who would not budge one bit from her position that life was better in Terre Haute than any other place on earth. When the dust settled on my assignment predicament, I went back to work until shortly before I left for the CID special agents course. I continued to investigate a variety of cases that kept me very busy. It was okay to work alone, but on serious cases, you can usually find someone to assist.

One of my last MPI investigations gave me a little heartburn. It was my first significant drug possession investigation, involving five soldiers that were caught smoking marijuana just outside the back door to the Disney Barracks gym. This case also is on my list of most memorable investigations because it involved the apprehension of many soldiers at same time.

A call for backup is the most logical way of proceeding when the crooks outnumber the police. However, under the criminal investigative system the US Army had at the time—and more than likely still does—there was no investigator counterpart to call. At best, you could call an investigative colleague at his or her home, but back in the 1970s, there were no cell phones like there are today. The MPs were usually all on patrol, and if one unit did respond before an apprehension was made, the element of surprise was vastly reduced.

Another problem inherent with having MPs called as a backup unit was that it required the investigator to brief them after they arrived on scene. In this situation, an apprehension was mandatory because of the exigent circumstances. The narrative below details the Case of the Five Potheads from Fort Knox.:

## THE CASE OF THE FIVE POTHEADS FROM FORT KNOX
Taking no investigative action is the same as overlooking or allowing a crime to go unpunished

I was pulling duty, and the weather outside was beautiful—a cloudless, bright, sunny, and hot summer morning—so I decided to get out and enjoy the summer day. On my duty day, I usually drove around to some of the hot spots, like the enlisted and NCO clubs, the bowling alley, and the PX snack bars, where soldiers liked to drink and the potential for trouble was always present. However, since it was still early in the day, I decided to make liaison with some of the commanders and 1SGs in companies around Fort Knox. I completed these visits in about two hours, and the day was still early, so I checked in with the 543rd orderly room in Disney Barracks and talked to 1SG Toler and the others I had worked with for over eight months, finding them well. With the 543rd visit complete and still no duty calls for the day, I walked down to the Disney Barracks gym about a block away to check on one of the civilian workers who had previously passed on some information pertaining to the misconduct of a few soldiers.

I entered the gym through the front door and located the civilian worker. I spent about fifteen minutes or so with him, and he had no new news to report. I left the gym through the side door, which took me to within a few feet of a wooded area. The wooded area had been known to be a place where soldiers went to smoke pot. I caught a glimpse of a group of soldiers sitting down on the ground just inside the tree line and smelled that very familiar odor of burning hemp, so I went to check them out. As they saw me approaching, they all got up and started hastily walking away. Not putting too much thought into what I would do next or the consequences thereof, I found their actions and the emitting odor too suspicious to ignore, so I yelled, "Stop! Military police!"

Five of the soldiers stopped, but several others broke and ran through the woods. I did not pay attention to the soldiers that got away. I ordered the five soldiers that did stop to get out of the woods, and I told them to raise their hands and place them on the wall to the gym and not to move. Each complied.

Here I was holding five soldiers at bay with no immediate backup. Boy, what I was thinking? I had my handheld Motorola radio with me, so I called the MP desk for backup. The dispatcher indicated an MP patrol was on its way to my location. What appeared to be an eternity was only a few minutes, waiting for the

MPs to arrive. I did not take my eyes off the five suspects, but when the MPs placed them in handcuffs, an assortment of drug paraphernalia, such as pipes, aluminum wrappers, and bags of suspected marijuana, was found on the ground, apparently discarded by the five suspects. Ownership of the suspect marijuana and drug paraphernalia would be hard to establish without confessions from all five suspects.

It took me about thirty minutes to bag the items found on the ground. I was careful to place items in separate evidence bags to correspond to where each of the five were standing, in hopes that each man would confess to ownership of the stuff found. When I got to the MP station, the five had been placed in a holding cell, pending my arrival. With bags of evidence in hand, I called each one out individually for an interview.

Luck was not on my side that day, because only one of the soldiers admitted that they were all smoking marijuana in the woods, but he told me that he had not brought any to the scene himself. He was provided a joint by one of the others, whom he refused to identify. Prior to conducting the interviews, I searched each of the five and found minute amounts of suspected marijuana on two of the five.

When shown the bags of suspected marijuana and drug paraphernalia, none of the five admitted to ownership of any of the contents. I coordinated the case with the local SJA office, and they indicated they may be able to make a case, but it would be difficult. They would also try other forms of penalty, such as nonjudicial punishment. This case would not be adjudicated until after I left for the CID special agents course. The result was that all five received company grade Article 15s with fines and restrictions. There was not much that I could have changed in this investigation. In retrospect, once I had opened the door to the gym and saw the group sitting in the woods, it was obvious they knew who I was, because I was carrying a Motorola radio. If I took no action, the five that were caught would have also escaped punishment.

My last case as an MPI was significant not because of its command interest but because it hit you in the heart and was emotionally satisfying. The case involved the theft of a young girl's bicycle. MPI Innes and I received a call one evening from the MP desk, reporting that a young girl's bicycle had been stolen from Walker Junior High School in Fort Knox. We responded to the young girl's quarters and met with her father, Major Walter A. Gallup, from an armor unit, who related that their young daughter had come home a short time earlier from an event at her school, crying her eyes out, and told him and his wife that someone had stolen her recently purchased bike from the school grounds. Their daughter was devastated with the loss of her bicycle, which she had paid for with her own

money. Major Gallup requested we do all we could to try to find the bike.
With nothing else to go on, SP4 Innes and I left the Gallup's quarters with only
the description of the bike. We did not even have a clue as to which direction to
start. Thus, I present a narrative of my recollection of what occurred. I call the
investigation the Case of the Missing Girl's Bike:

## THE CASE OF THE MISSING GIRL'S BIKE

Mere thanks from a victim of a crime is a great feeling for an investigator

We left the quarters with the description of the bicycle we had received from
Major Gallup and began a search of the neighborhood. We drove up and down
the street where the girl lived with her parents, but we found nothing. We
expanded the search for two blocks in each direction, going slowly, looking in the
yards of homes as we passed.

After about twenty minutes or so, we were just about through and ready to
return to the MPI office when we noticed something lying on the ground. We
drove by a dead-end roadway that ended at the edge of a small wooded area about
twenty feet from the main street, and then we stopped, backed up, and turned onto
the dead-end road. There it was: a small girl's bicycle, which looked like the one the
Major Gallup had described. We put the bicycle in the trunk of our MPI car and
returned to the major's quarters. When we pulled up in front of the quarters, MPI
Innes and I got out of our car and unloaded the bike from the truck. Apparently,
Major Gallup saw us from inside his home, because as soon as we placed the bike
on the sidewalk, he came running outside followed by his very happy young daughter. You could not help but notice the glow of relief in the girl's eyes and her feelings of unadulterated joy. MPI Innes and I also became a little emotional when the
young girl said the simple phrase, "Thank you." I was overwhelmed with happiness
for her. We felt good going back to the MPI office that night.

There was no evidence anyone tried to steal the bike. Instead, it appeared to
be an incident, probably kids pulling a dirty trick by carelessly leaving it a short
distance from where they took it. The next day, I contacted SJA, and they concurred with the assessment. About a week after the bike was recovered and
returned, the other MPI and I received a letter of thanks from the girl's father,
which was sent through the Fort Knox PMO, Colonel Darrell D. Kasson, to the
OIC MPI, Major Vendetti. This was the first official recognition I received for an
investigation.

The rest of my time at Fort Knox was spent clearing my caseload. I considered the
experience I gained working MPI cases invaluable, and it better prepared me for

my career in CID. I knew now that I had found the career I was looking for. On August 23, 1974, I bid farewell to my colleagues at the MPI office and the 543rd MP company and departed Fort Knox for the last time.

I spent a week in Terre Haute with Melitta and the kids before heading for the CID special agents course at Fort Gordon, Georgia. I broke the news to her that when I was selected for the CID special agents course, my assignment changed from the Thirteenth MP Company in Thailand to Fort Ord, California. The new assignment, or its implications on us as a family, did not appear to have much impact on Melitta's feelings. At least the Fort Ord assignment would make it easier for Melitta and the kids to join me. I attempted to sway Melitta's mind that our separation would be much more difficult to tolerate with me being assigned to Fort Ord and her staying in Terre Haute. I explained to her that the distance between California and Indiana would make it virtually impossible for quick trips every week or so to visit her and the kids. She responded in her usual self-serving way that she had too much to lose by leaving her job. Her response was not surprising, but her excuses confirmed her lack of emotions for our marriage. My leaving the family in past occasions was not as difficult as it was going to be on this trip. There was a good possibility that I could be separated from the family for much longer, maybe up to a year before I saw them again.

I knew that divorce was on the table; however, the obstacles of the impending special agents course and reassignment to Fort Ord made it impossible to resolve at the juncture. Talking to Melitta for the past several days was like talking into the wind. My hearing difficulty (still experiencing numbness and a constant ringing in my left ear) did not make it any easier to talk with her. My state of mind concerning our marriage made it tough for me during the visit home. I had a hard time understanding Melitta's apathetic attitude toward our family's future and her indifference to improving her lot. Feelings of ambiguity over unsettled issues with Melitta created a somber mood during my trip to Fort Gordon.

# 6

# Career Path Interrupted

Learning Skills as an Investigator

Fort Sheridan

*Believing in oneself is a necessity to success and endurance as a professional*

On September 3, 1974, a Monday, I made it to Fort Gordon, got settled into quarters, found a restaurant in Augusta, and had dinner. After dinner, I took a drive around Fort Gordon and the surrounding area. I stopped and read a plaque near the post headquarters that contained a brief history of Fort Gordon. The installation has a colorful past dating back to 1917. It was named after John Brown Gordon, a Confederate general. The installation is a beautiful scenic military base occupying areas in the Columbia, Jefferson, McDuffie, and Richmond Counties in Georgia. With a full belly and after about two hours of driving around, I decided to call it a day. I went back to my quarters and, knowing I had a big day the next day, tried to get some sleep. I dozed, but sleep escaped me; I kept thinking about the future. I was about to launch a new and exciting career, but my marriage was in shambles and was probably not going to survive. After tossing and turning for several hours, I eventually fell into a deep slumber and woke up relatively refreshed and ready to start the CID special agents course.

In 1948, Fort Gordon became the training center for the military police and criminal investigations schools. In 1976, the training mission of these schools would eventually move to Fort McClellan, Alabama, where they remained until 1999, and in due course found a permanent home at Fort Leonard Wood, Missouri. In 1974, the CID school had recently enhanced their course curriculum requirements that changed the length of the training from eight weeks to twelve weeks. Two legendary CID agents, CW3 Raymond (Ray) Kangas[45] (known as "Dr. Death," due to his expertise in death investigations and training at the US Armed Forces Institute of Pathology [AFIP]) and CW4 James Squires (the course manager), were instructors when I attended the course. Ray and I would regularly come into contact in future assignments throughout our careers, and I attended his retirement celebration almost twenty-five years after graduation from CID basic.

On September 17, 1971, USACIDC, commonly known throughout the US Army just as CID, was established as a major command, vested with command and control of all CID activities and resources worldwide. CID is one of several in a group of military investigative agencies. Some of the other more notable agencies are the Naval Investigative Service (now known as the Naval Criminal Investigative Service, or NCIS) and the US Air Force Office of Special Investigation (AFOSI). The primary mission of the CID in the '70s was to investigate serious felony-level crime (murder and all unattended deaths, rapes, aggravated assaults, housebreaking larcenies, frauds, and any other felony crimes); collect, analyze, and disseminate criminal intelligence; conduct protective service operations; provide forensic laboratory support; and maintain US Army criminal records. The CID has a stellar reputation among other federal law enforcement agencies and is considered the FBI of the US Army.

The instructors, using their knowledge based on their own CID experience, taught the curriculum in a relevant, detailed, and meaningful way. They all contributed for a well-balanced and organized criminal investigations training program using classroom lectures, practical exercises, and individual participation. The instructors led us through a myriad of options on the proper steps of conducting criminal investigations. They covered subject matters such as actions performed at crime scenes, taking notes, photographs and making sketches, and how to link the perpetrators to the crime, like fingerprinting, casts, molds, and trace evidence that was both found and developed. We not only learned how to collect evidence but were taught the various ways of protecting and preserving it. Training also consisted of the types of surveillance, undercover work, interviews, interrogations, and report writing. We were taught aspects of the manual for courts-martial and the punitive articles covering crimes investigated by CID. To a limited degree, we received instructions on how to give testimony in court and were provided a cursory class, more along the lines of an introduction to protective services.

We spent a great deal of time on interviews and interrogations, which comprised a large portion of the criminal investigation process, in the era classes were conducted. The purpose of this training was to focus on obtaining details of the crime from the perspectives of the victim, witnesses, and hopefully suspects. We were taught that interrogation of any suspects was to determine if they'd committed the crime and what their intent was in doing so. Staged scenarios allowed us to practice interview techniques learned during training. Instructors did an excellent job teaching us how to identify and interpret body language, gestures, and facial expressions and to detect certain types of behavioral traits as indicators of truth or dishonesty from the person portraying our victims, witnesses, and suspects during mock interviews.

We trained and qualified with the .38-caliber revolver and familiarized ourselves with other weapons. One of those weapons was a Remington pump-action

Model 870 twelve-gauge shotgun. In those days, we did not have the sophisticated ear protection in use today. Instead, we used small, rubbery earplugs that you placed in your ear canal. I had the misfortunate on the range one evening when the kick from firing the M-870 shotgun jolted the rudimentary ear piece from my left ear. The earsplitting noise created by the blast caused numbness and internal hearing damage to my left ear. The doctors later diagnosed the hearing damage as an inner-ear injury or acoustic trauma. I did not know it at the time, but the injury to my left ear caused permanent partial hearing loss; I also developed tinnitus (ear ringing) in the left ear.

One of the student soldiers attending the CID special agents course with me was SP5 Guy Surian. Surian and I got to know each other through the course. When Guy was selected for the CID special agents course training, CID command chose to assign him to Fort Sheridan, Illinois, and they programmed me for Fort Ord, California, after graduation. About midway through the CID special agents course, the two of us got to talking one day about whether we might be able to switch assignments, since he was from San Francisco, California (near Fort Ord), and I was from Indiana (which is close to Fort Sheridan). We agreed to give it a shot and called CID accreditation to see if the transfer could be possible. Foster, to our surprise, was very amenable to the idea and told us he would work to make it happen. Foster requested we submit a request for the reassignments to make it official. Within a week or so, our transfers were approved; I was now headed to Fort Sheridan, Illinois, for my first CID assignment.

Guy and I never became close friends, but we would periodically run into each other on future assignments in CID. I saw no need to call Melitta to let her know about the assignment change from Fort Ord to Fort Sheridan now; it would not have mattered to her anyway. I just continued to do my best in the course by studying hard and trying to learn everything about the position as a US Army CID special agent as I could.

Our final exam was to process a death scene in a room, which took most of us an entire day to complete. We were required to evaluate the crime scene from the moment we entered until we finished our investigation. We were required to photograph the scene in detail and draw a rough sketch showing evidence measurements triangulated to focus on location of things. A detailed sketch had to depict where evidence was before being collected and bagged. Extensive notes were required on our observations, the weather conditions, and actions taken at the crime scene, which included enormous amounts of information. The training showed us how to organize and document each step during the process.

The CID special agents course was a very insightful, educational, and professionally rewarding learning experience. I was unaware of at the time but found out later through association and working relationships with other law enforcement colleagues that the CID special agents course stands at the top in the investigative profession.[46] The training I received at Fort Gordon armed me with valuable investigative techniques that stayed with me throughout my career.

On November 27, 1974, I graduated tenth out of thirty-three students at the CID special agents course and was sworn in as a probationary special agent.

I, Dietzel Morris Miller, do hereby swear that I shall support and uphold the Constitution and the laws of the United States; that I shall endeavor to discharge my responsibilities as a United States Army CID special agent in accordance therewith; that I shall at all times seek diligently to discover the truth, deterred neither by fear nor prejudice; and I shall strive to be worthy of the special trust reposed in me by my country, the United States Army, and the Criminal Investigation Command.

Since you must practically drive through Terre Haute to get to Fort Sheridan from Fort Gordon, I could spend the Thanksgiving holidays with Melitta and the kids before reporting in. I took this time to explain to Melitta that I'd switched assignments from Fort Ord to Fort Sheridan. I told her for at least two years, maybe a little longer, I could continue coming home every other weekend or so to visit with her and the kids. Melitta had no clue as to how close I'd come to spending lengthy periods of time away from her and the kids if I had not been able to switch my assignment. Then again, I am not sure it meant that much to her.

I spent a relatively ordinary couple of weeks at home, where I could see Mom and June for the first time in a spell, and I found them both in good health. I felt that the Fort Sheridan assignment, however long it lasted, and knowing it was for a fixed time, was a better deal than living in Madison, Wisconsin. It was closer to home and to Melitta's parents in Michigan City. I asked Melitta if we could possibly revisit the issue of her and the kids moving once we determined that CID was a worthwhile career. Her response lacked enthusiasm, but she did say yes. My spirits were not boosted much when I heard her perfunctory reply.

On December 9, 1974, I entered Fort Sheridan for the first time. The installation was surrounded on the south and west sides by the small town of Highwood and bordered on the east side by Lake Michigan. The city of Lake Forest was just to the north. I located the CID office near the south gate. Fort Sheridan had two gates, the south gate and the main gate on the west side of the installation. When I got out of my car, I viewed the outside of the CID building for the first time. The building was a two-story, wooden, WWII-type structure, and when I walked inside, I immediately observed that the first floor held the administrative staff, commander, and operations officer offices. I presumed the special agents' offices, polygraph, and evidence rooms were on the second floor.

I reported to the operations officer, CW3 Chief Milton G. (Gene) A. Wheaton, a slender, middle-aged man who was nearly bald and wore eyeglasses. My first impression of him was that he was a good, self-confident man who was friendly, cordial, and attentive. He did not hurry when he briefed me on the office and intently listened to me as I discussed my background and experiences. Based on my recent hearing damage, it was hard for me to decipher everything he was saying, but I thought the first meeting went well. Above all, he welcomed me to the office and took time to take me around and introduce me to the other special agents, commander, and staff. Mr. Wheaton told me he had assigned Gerald Siravo as my training agent.

The special agents in the office were Gerald (Jerry) Siravo, Ronald Gann, Art Koziera, Jim Kovac, Don Fisher, Stanley Stoner, and Dale Anderburg. SSG Ron Kornaick was the personnel sergeant, and SSG Nate (I can't recall his last name) was the unit's supply sergeant. The commander was Major Michael Muller. The office also had one military and one civilian secretary. All the folks appeared friendly and were open and welcoming; I instantly liked them all. The people were very helpful as I got settled into my work area, which I would share with Siravo. Since the position of special agent was considered a specialty in the US Army, all enlisted agents were specialists and not NCOs.

I arrived at Fort Sheridan with the rank of sergeant, but when I was selected for the CID program, my rank was changed to Specialist 5 (SP5). During my tenure at Fort Sheridan, Siravo and Anderburg would depart, and a new probationary agent named Gary Kral came over from the 204th MP Company, and a suspended probationary agent named Gerald Brennen came in from the Frankfurt, Germany, CID shortly before I departed Fort Sheridan. Another newcomer was Special Agent Ralph Blevins, who had just been accepted into the CID and had not yet gone to the CID special agents course. Special Agent Blevins and I would become close friends throughout our careers and into retirement. I continued to see him on occasions for CID dinners in the Washington, DC, area. Major Muller would eventually become the post PMO and be replaced by Captain Thomas McHugh, an extremely competent and dedicated MP officer who'd had a previous CID assignment in Japan. Captain McHugh would spend most of his military career in the CID, usually in command-type positions at field offices and districts. In the early 1990s, McHugh, then a colonel, retired from the US Army after serving in some capacity with the New Mexico National Guard. Chief Wheaton also retired, and CW3 Marshall Thomas replaced him.

I was issued my first .38-caliber snub-nosed Smith & Wesson revolver, handcuffs, twelve bullets, and a CID-issued holster by Special Agent Stoner. My first conversation with Siravo was about the situation with Melitta and that she might not be joining me anytime soon, or for that matter, maybe not at all. I informed him that due to my limited finances, I would like to find suitable quarters on Fort Sheridan to save money. Siravo indicated he would help me find a place to live. By 3:00 that afternoon, my first day as a CID probationary special agent, Siravo told me to take the rest of the day off to square away my personal matters. I left the CID office that day thinking, heck, they did not rush to dump a lot of cases on me, and I felt comfortable that I was in good hands with Siravo.

Fort Sheridan was a small installation north of Chicago. Fort McCoy, Wisconsin, about four hours to the north from Fort Sheridan, was open during the summer months (usually May through September) as a branch office. Special Agent Don Fisher was the agent that ran Fort McCoy when CID established its presence there during the summer months. However, there would be exceptions from time to time on who went up there to conduct investigations. The workload at Sheridan was light compared to the bigger installations, such as Forts Riley, Lewis, Bragg, Hood, Polk, or Carson. In retrospect, by being at Fort Ord, it would have more than likely given me greater potential to gain experience during my initial years as a probationary special agent. As it turned out, I did gain a good deal of experience in that I conducted a variety of criminal investigations while assigned at Fort Sheridan.

I located a Howard Johnson motel a few miles from Fort Sheridan and got some rest before finding a place to eat dinner. When I left the motel a couple of hours later, I decided to eat at a mom-and-pop-type restaurant directly across the street. I spent the rest of the evening relaxing and thinking about what was going to happen in the days ahead. That evening, I called Melitta moments before she left for work, so she did not give me a lot of time to talk. I had time to give her the Fort Sheridan CID office phone number and told her I would contact her when I found a place to live. She acted rushed and hung up before I could say good night to the kids. I settled in for a good night's rest and surprisingly slept very well.

The next day, I got to the CID office around 8:00 and was informed by Personnel Sergeant Ron Kornaick that I could bunk across the street in a CID-owned building until better arrangements could be made. My quarters were in a one-story, wooden, WWII-type building that had a huge front room as you entered the door, with a pool table in the middle that was apparently used by CID for a dayroom (recreational), and the rest of the rooms were set up as sleeping quarters. I am not sure if I ever told Special Agent Siravo or SSG Kornaick how grateful I was to them for arranging my living quarters.

I was the only geographical bachelor assigned to the office; the rest of the people were married. US Army regulations authorized military quarters for geographical bachelors (those that were married but serving in an area without their spouses). Moving to this building also greatly helped with my limited budget. I had only retained $50 every two weeks for myself and sent the bulk of my monthly salary (about $600) to Melitta and the kids.

I spent about two hours moving my personal things into a room in the building. I thought this also was not a bad place to live, because it was directly across the street from the CID office.

Later that morning, SA Siravo drove me around the installation and introduced me to the SJA lawyers, the post provost marshal, and the on-duty MP desk sergeant. I got the feeling that if Siravo had the time to take me on a personal tour of Fort Sheridan, he obviously did not have a high caseload.

On my second day at Fort Sheridan, Special Agent Siravo took me to lunch at a place called Stash's in Highland Park, a short distance from Fort Sheridan. Stash's had the best french fries and sub sandwiches I had ever eaten. The lunch that day started a weekly ritual of going to Stash's for lunch. Years later, while coming home from work one afternoon, I met a rider on a commuter bus from Washington, DC, to the park and ride in Prince William County, Virginia. The rider happened to be from Highland Park, Illinois. During our casual conversation on the bus that day, I told him about my weekly trips to Stash's. Excitedly, he said that when he was visiting home, he and his entire family still went there.

The first week at Fort Sheridan was all about getting settled in. Although I had yet to pull duty, I ended up with a few cases involving property thefts. I found all the investigative files handed to me to be well documented, with only one or two leads pending. I completed those leads and closed out the lot. Thus, my first group of CID investigations were done, finished, and so on; they were reviewed, and with only minor changes and suggestions by Special Agent Siravo, all passed scrutiny.

A good portion of the work at Fort Sheridan in the '70s involved leads from other CID elements around the world. Since a lot of the leads would take us to the inner-city slums and ghettos of Chicago, we attempted to always pair up with other agents in the office. It was common to leave the CID office in the early morning with a briefcase full of leads and not return until late in the evening, often after normal business hours.

Some downright comical incidents occurred on a few of those trips. One lead from another stateside CID office took us to the Cabrini-Green[47] housing project in the South Side of Chicago to interview a former soldier. Thus, began one of my first investigative ventures into the city of Chicago. Special Agent Koziera and I teamed up to make that trip. Special Agent Koziera was quiet, soft-spoken, an almost shy man who had a full head of blond hair, was muscular, appeared physically fit, and was always neatly dressed. He showed little or no emotion when confronted with pressure, but he was a good special agent, and I liked working with him. The first investigation we worked together required us to travel to the South Side of Chicago.

I fondly recall the humorous way we entered Cabrini-Green public housing project, one of the most notorious high-crime areas in the city of Chicago and probably the whole country. The case required us to locate and interview a tenant who was identified as a possible suspect in a case involving a housebreaking and larceny. I called the incident the Case of the Nervous Special Agent:

## THE CASE OF THE NERVOUS SPECIAL AGENT
The human brain can perceive or interpret sounds to fit the current situation a person is in

Cabrini-Green housing project was a well-known hotbed of crime and had a reputation for gang violence. Our assignment was to locate and interview a former soldier who supposedly had knowledge of a housebreaking and larceny being investigated by the requesting CID office. Special Agent Koziera and I drove to Cabrini-Green and found the best parking space possible. We started our long, uncomfortable journey toward the building where the guy was reportedly living. Just imagine the scene of Special Agent Koziera and me, both with worried looks on our faces and both anticipating the unexpected. We were the only two white people dressed in suits and ties in the middle of the courtyard of four buildings that made up the public housing complex. We could be directly and openly in the crosshairs of anyone who wanted to hurt us, and that activity was known to regularly occur in the project. Although we were CID special agents on official US Army investigative business, it would not require a great deal of imagination for anyone to think we were two of Chicago's finest coming to make an arrest.

Our edginess and apprehension during our hike from the car to the apartment intensified when we heard a loud noise that sounded like a gunshot. Within a nanosecond, Special Agent Koziera quickly stooped to the ground and placed his hand on his .38.

"What was that?" Koziera shrieked.

I turned and looked at Koziera without saying a word. Instead, I looked around to determine if I could locate the source of the noise. To my relief, I saw a group of construction workers near one of the buildings that surrounded the courtyard. Once my eyes were fixed on the construction site, another loud gunshot-like sound occurred. This time, I could figure out the source of the noise was two boards banging together as they were being removed from a truck and stacked in a pile by the construction workers.

Up to this point, the incident was humorous enough, but it got more hilarious immediately after we'd recovered from our reactions to the sound of the boards. A young man came strolling by, probably a tenant in the project, and said, "You guys are in the wrong neighborhood," as he walked past Special Agent Koziera and me. Hell, he did not have to tell us that, because we already knew it. We did not waste any time locating the person we'd gone there to interview, finding him, getting the information we came for, and hightailing it out of Cabrini-Green.

Special Agent Gary Kral grew up in Chicago and knew the city streets better than anyone. You felt comfortable with him as your partner. He related a story that when he was a kid in 1966, he rode his bicycle to the house where eight student nurses were killed by Richard Speck. The multiple murder case received worldwide media attention. The ten-year-old Kral was in the crowd that had formed outside the house where the murders had occurred as the police and medical people were removing the bodies. Special Agent Kral said that incident had a lifelong impact on him. The incident occurred a short distance from his home in Chicago. When I knew him, he was a very practically minded and educated special agent who used common sense and wanted to pursue a career in law enforcement. I enjoyed working with him and considered him a good friend. He would go out of his way to assist people if he thought they needed it. The incident we rolled on was another routine lead from a stateside CID office.

We were tasked to locate the father of a soldier who had confessed to a housebreaking and larceny of stereo equipment from a soldier's room on another US Army post. The perpetrator admitted to taking the stolen property home to Chicago and had told the requesting CID special agent that obtained his confession that the property could be recovered from his father. You never know what will happen when you start an interview. His father might be receptive or hostile, or he might find reason to hide the fact that he had the property, thinking he was protecting his son. What happened when we arrived at the perp's father's residence would, for a moment, make any investigator have second thoughts about his vocation. Hence, I present the Case of the Scatterbrained Special Agent:

THE CASE OF THE SCATTERBRAINED SPECIAL AGENT
Thinking before acting always assures the better outcome of your actions

It was a beautiful, sunny summer morning with blue skies when we began our trip to Chicago. Special Agent Kral and I had several leads to work on, which would take us to all parts of the city. Since one of the leads involved taking custody of stolen property that we did not want to cart around all day, we decided to do all the other leads first. Around 3:00 in the afternoon, we were finished with our leads except the one involving the stolen property. In the days of no GPS navigational devices, we had to depend on handheld maps. On this day, we had an advantage; Special Agent Kral knew how to get around in the city of Chicago, his boyhood home. We had no trouble finding the row house we were looking for. I parked the CID car in front of the residence, and Special Agent Kral and I proceeded to the second-floor apartment where the person we were looking for lived.

The occupant answered our knock, we introduced ourselves and showed him our CID credentials, and he invited us in to his apartment. We spent about thirty minutes talking to the elderly black gentleman and subsequently identifying and gathering the stolen stereo equipment that he had already placed in two boxes before we got there. Apparently, his son, the perp in the case from the other stateside installation, called and told him we were coming by and had explained the reason for our visit. With the evidence in hand, we thanked the man, expressed our appreciation for his cooperation, and left the apartment with each of us carrying a box containing the stereo equipment. As we approached the CID car, we noticed a group of men gathered around an abandoned car across the street. It looked like they were drinking liquor from a bottle wrapped in a brown paper sack. I thought, *this is nothing to worry about ... yet*. Still, not wanting to be in this situation, Special Agent Kral and I were anxious to get the boxes of stereo equipment in the car and drive out of the neighborhood as fast as possible.

When I reached into my pants pocket to get the keys to open the trunk of the CID car, I could not find them. I checked the other front pants pocket with the same results. Not quite to the freaking-out stage, I suggested to Special Agent Kral that he also check his pockets just in case I may have given the keys to him at some point. Special Agent Kral searched his pockets to no avail. Now it was starting to get to freaking-out time. Special Agent Kral, still carrying one of the boxes of stereo equipment, casually walked to the driver-side window and looked in. Calmly, he looked at me from across the roof of the CID car and said, "Dick, look inside!"

Not sure what he meant, I countered with, "What?"

He repeated himself, "Dick, look inside!"

I looked down into the passenger-side window. Suddenly, I couldn't swallow, and my breath swelled up inside my chest. Without looking up at Special Agent Kral, I said, "The keys!"

I heard him say, "No sh——!"

We then stared at each other for a good ten seconds without saying a word.

Speaking first, Special Agent Kral mumbled, "We have to get a clothes hanger somewhere." Undeniably, we were in a pickle.

Here we were in a neighborhood with unsecured stereo equipment in our hands and no means of unlocking our car. A group of potentially bad guys, all drinking liquor and possibly violent, loitered within twenty feet of us. We had an impossible task to act fast to find a means of unlocking our car without drawing undue attention to ourselves.

The group across the street probably heard every word we spoke and were watching our every step. Then, from out of nowhere, we heard a man's voice ask, "Do you boys need help?"

I thought, *Hell yes, we need help*, but without knowing where the help was coming from, I momentarily hesitated.

At the same time, Special Agent Kral and I looked upward and saw the same elderly gentleman we had just talked to leaning out his second-story window with a wire clothes hanger in his hands. Special Agent Kral acknowledged our need for the wire clothes hanger, and the elderly gentleman tossed it to the ground. I laid down the box of stereo equipment next to the car and went over and picked it up. It took me about ten seconds to straighten the clothes hanger wire and insert one end into the top of the driver-side window and to start working on lifting the lock. Knowing the cluster of men across the street was watching us, the hair on the back of my neck stood up as I worked. Fortunately, it only took me a couple of minutes (which seemed like an hour) before I could unlatch the lock and open the car door. It took Special Agent Kral and me less than a minute to load the boxes into the trunk and to skedaddle out of the neighborhood. The lead was successfully accomplished, but two young probationary agents were extremely embarrassed. Special Agent Kral and I had other experiences while at Fort Sheridan and those stories are worthy of telling later in this chapter.

Work at the Fort Sheridan CID office was not actually busy as much as it was steady. My first few duty days resulted in initiating investigations of perps that committed relatively minor crimes but were still in CID's purview, and they were easily resolved. As I progressed to the more serious, convoluted, and intricately involved investigations, I credited Special Agent Siravo for being a good trainer, mentor, and friend for taking the extra time to explain the complex process. Not only did he provide me with significant insight into the technical aspects of criminal investigations, he guided me into how to interpret legal issues and understand the people involved in the crime.

Special Agent Siravo reviewed the first case I wrote for CID. His review helped me hone my writing skills on how to properly title individuals and prepare narratives. I learned that the written CID report of investigation (ROI) is all about packaging. A well-written case that covers everything and is timely will face less scrutiny up the chain. A narrative of my first case will always stick in the back of my mind, because Special Agent Siravo taught me how to write the investigation on the facts instead of what was reported. I considered this the Case of the Spaced-Out Kitchen Cook:

## THE CASE OF THE SPACED-OUT KITCHEN COOK
Report what occurs, clarify what someone says

I was notified by the Fort Sheridan MP desk that two civilian kitchen employees had gotten into a scuffle at the post dining facility. The preliminary information indicated that a civilian cook, reportedly high on LSD, stabbed another civilian kitchen employee, and the victim had been transported to a local hospital. The suspect was combative when transported to the MP station. As I departed the office for the scene, one of our agents called the FBI because the suspect was civilian. Since all military installations are located on federal land, the FBI has primary jurisdiction and usually take the investigative lead.

I arrived at the dining facility and found two witnesses to the incident. One witness informed me that he saw two line cooks arguing with each other, but he did not know the reason for their spat. The witness told me that a kitchen supervisor told the two to lower their voices, but the two continued to quarrel. The witness said he left the area because he did not want to get involved in their dispute.

The other witness told me essentially the same information, but added that he saw one of the cooks take a knife from a nearby counter and slash the other guy on the arm. After the incident, the suspect laid down the knife on the counter and simply walked away. The suspect in the case had a reputation for using drugs and had confided with other employees that he often used LSD. When I examined the crime scene, I was surprised that there was no blood found on the floor or the counter where the knife had been placed. After processing the crime scene, I returned to the CID office to follow up with the FBI to see what they had ascertained from the victim.

Several hours had passed before I received a call from the FBI's Waukegan resident agency. I was informed that the victim had a superficial laceration to his left arm and was released from the hospital. The suspect had requested a lawyer. I was also informed that since the offense was not serious, the FBI would not be pursuing any prosecution of the suspect. This often occurs when the Assistant US Attorneys (AUSA) do not want to spend time on minor cases. Unfortunately, they make the determination on what is minor. This would not be the last time the AUSA would decline to prosecute perps on cases I'd investigated. The US Army can and did act on the civilian suspect by having him barred from Fort Sheridan; thus, he could not continue to work at the post dining facility.

When I wrote the case, I had titled the civilian cook for aggravated assault and possession and use of a controlled substance (LSD). I thought I had done a bang-up job until it was reviewed by Special Agent Siravo. He returned the report to me with a comment: "Where is the proof for possession and use of a controlled substance?"

After reading his comments and reviewing the statements obtained during my investigation, it was obvious that Special Agent Siravo's question had merit. I realized that my report did not identify any real evidence that the suspect had possessed and used LSD. I, like all others fresh out of CID basic, was young, untested, and had limited knowledge and skills; I had written the report without applying the necessary attention to detail that comes with time and experience. I rewrote the report to remove the offense of wrongful possession and use of a controlled substance and changed the narrative to indicate the suspect "was purportedly high on LSD when he slashed the victim's arm with a knife" to more accurately portray the facts disclosed. The write-up on this case introduced into my professional work philosophy a new rule. Rule Seven: *Report facts, not what someone reports as facts.*

Although Fort Sheridan was a small post, it still had all the amenities of a larger installation, such as commissary, post exchange (PX), bank, and other facilities and services. The assignment still brought many challenges to the job. The experience level moved slower than what occurred on larger installations, but there was still a sense of accomplishment when successfully completing each investigation. You learn from others and hope that their actions are in line with proper protocol or that they are going about the task as professionally as they should. Although not a crime, one incident at the commissary occurred that I had a role in which I called the case of the sick old sergeant:

## THE CASE OF THE SICK, OLD SERGEANT
Expect the unexpected more than the expected

I was returning to the CID office after conducting some interviews on cases when I overheard a radio call from the MP desk dispatching an MP patrol to the Fort Sheridan commissary to check on an unconscious man lying in the parking lot. Since I was coincidently driving by the commissary when the call was heard, I radioed that I was already at the scene and would check it out. Upon entering the commissary parking lot, I immediately saw a man lying near a car with the driver-side door open. I thought the man could be injured, possibly in a robbery gone bad; he could be passed out due to illness; or, even worse, he could be dead. I rushed to the prone man's location, abruptly stopped my car, got out, and knelt to check on his condition. The man, who looked to be in his sixties and grossly overweight, was lying on his back and unresponsive. I was ready to render CPR when suddenly I got a whiff of the most revolting and disgusting odor secreting from his mouth, followed by spewing liquids, gases, and undigested food as he began to regurgitate all over himself and on me as well. The problem: he was ridiculously drunk.

I turned him onto his stomach to prevent him from choking on his vomit. He opened his bloodshot eyes and attempted to speak. However, his speech was slurred and incoherent. I then checked his body for injuries he might have received during the fall to the ground, but I found none. An ambulance showed up, and before the medics loaded him into the back of the emergency vehicle, I retrieved his wallet from his back pocket and obtained his US Army identification card. It showed that he was a retired US Army SFC and had a local address. As the ambulance drove away, I checked the man's car and removed the keys from the ignition, secured the vehicle, and headed for the clinic to drop off his keys. This case was kept at the MPs' level to resolve.

Just like any other military installation, Fort Sheridan had a hodgepodge of crimes that CID investigated—crimes ran the gamut from the most violent and serious to the routine. But the goal was always the same: to put the perp away. I did get involved with significant, highly visible, and violent crimes involving aggravated assault with a weapon and robbery, bank robbery, and my first death investigation for the US Army. Some cases I investigated were more noteworthy than others, some were resolved quickly, and others took time. Cases that I worked with the FBI gave me a good understanding of how they handled cases and of their investigative techniques and processes. The FBI, although similar, handled somewhat different types of investigation than the CID.

The special agents of the FBI Waukegan resident agency were a great group of guys to work with. They were very cooperative, conciliatory with respect to investigative jurisdictional matters, and always ready to lend a hand when needed. One of their investigators, whose area of responsibility included Fort Sheridan, was FBI Special Agent Gary Harmmon. FBI Special Agent Harmmon was an excellent partner when it came to cases on which the FBI assumed primary investigative jurisdiction. He always made me feel like I was on his team and not just patronizing me because he thought he should. Harmmon was a former schoolteacher who had joined the FBI to satisfy a lifelong dream of working in law enforcement. Harmmon and I jointly worked several cases involving civilian perps. One of these cases was initiated by the FBI, who requested CID's investigative assistance. It involved an individual who repeatedly joined the US Army to collect money and then vanished, only to reenlist under an alias. The following narrative depicts the actions taken in the investigation I called the case of the soldier who could not make up his mind:

## THE SOLDIER WHO COULD NOT MAKE UP HIS MIND
Repeated enlistments in the US Army do not accelerate retirement

In early 1975, Special Agent Gary Harmmon reported to CID that the FBI was investigating an individual for fraud against the US government. The FBI's investigation had been initiated when the individual was arrested for an unrelated federal crime. The FBI investigation had also disclosed that the man was suspected of using various aliases to fraudulently enter the US Army. Special Agent Harmmon requested CID's assistance in establishing if any crimes were being investigated by the US Army with the names of the perp and any aliases he used. I found that three of the five names provided by Special Agent Harmmon had a history of offenses with the US Army, but the only crimes associated with the names were individuals considered either AWOL or in a deserter status (soldiers gone for more than thirty consecutive days).

Our joint investigation disclosed that the perp enlisted five times, stayed a few months, was paid during that time, and subsequently disappeared, only to repeat his actions under a new name a few months later. The evidence against the fraudulent enlistee was overwhelming, and the perp confessed to his wrongdoings and was given a home under federal government sponsorship for a couple of years. To alert all CID elements on this case, the methods used by the perp were reported to all CID elements through the means of a criminal information report (CIR), which documented the systematic fraudulent enlistments. CIRs were used to report criminal information evaluated as having investigative interest outside the operational activities of the initiating office.[48]

Working with the FBI would continue throughout my career with the CID; however, the Fort Sheridan experience with the agency was by far the best. The camaraderie made one feel good when working with special agents of other agencies. The cooperation with all federal law enforcement agencies is necessary for the successful completion of some investigations, but since the FBI has primary jurisdiction on all US military installations, CID works more with them than any other federal agency. Although I either assisted, jointly investigated, or in some form liaised with the FBI on several criminal matters during my tenure at Fort Sheridan, certain cases stand out more than others. The following investigations were certainly an example on how well the two agencies work together. Take, for instance, the Case of the Gun-Toting Former Soldier:

# THE CASE OF THE GUN-TOTING FORMER SOLDIER
Even in one's own home, no one is 100 percent safe

One evening around nine in mid-April 1975, when I was the special agent on duty, I received a call from the MP desk that an armed robbery had occurred in the Garrison Barracks. Fort Sheridan at the time had one four-story brick building that lodged the unmarried male and female soldiers. I responded to the scene and met with the responding MPs, who provided me with what they had ascertained so far. A perp, identified as an average-height white male brandishing a sawed-off shotgun, entered the building through a side door and robbed four soldiers (all males) of about $300. A witness saw the perp leave the building through a first-floor side door and run toward the main gate, which was about a quarter of a mile from the site of the crime. Since the crime occurred about ten minutes prior to the MPs' arrival and I had been on the scene for about five minutes, I directed them to call the main gate to see if the perp could be caught as he was attempting to leave the post. That request reached the MP at the main gate too late. The MP at the gate advised that someone fitting the description had walked through the gate only minutes before he was notified. If the MPs had made that call prior to my arrival, the perp might have been caught.

I obtained more information from the victims. The man appeared to know his way around the building. This indicated to me that he might have been a worker or maybe even a former soldier who'd lived in the building at one time. The perp accosted all four victims in the hallway of the third floor and demanded their money. In fear of being shot, each victim complied and handed over the money he had in his wallet. I planned for all four victims to report to the MP station for in-depth interviews within the hour. I chose the MP station over the CID office, because it was after nine in the evening and our office was closed.

In the meantime, while I was still at the barracks, I notified the police departments in both Highwood and Lake Forest, Illinois, by telephone and provided them with a description of the perp and requested they patrol the area where the perp was last seen by the MP in front of the Fort Sheridan main gate. As I was headed to the MP station, I received a radio call from the MP desk that Highwood police had pulled over a vehicle that had moments before been reported stolen, and they identified the man driving as fitting the description of our perp. Highwood also found a large amount of money on the individual and a sawed-off shotgun in the front seat.

*This must be our guy,* I thought.

I notified the desk to keep the four victims at the MP station until I arrived. I then informed the desk that first I needed to coordinate with the Highwood Police Department to gather more information about the man they'd caught driving the stolen car. Upon my arrival, I reported to the Highwood police desk sergeant, and he notified a detective that had the man in an interrogation room. I was escorted into a room adjacent to the interrogation room and observed, through a one-way mirror, the man being interviewed. The man confessed not only to stealing the car from a parking lot in Highwood but also to committing the robbery on Fort Sheridan moments before; the car was used as a getaway vehicle. I obtained the information on the perp, viewed the shotgun and money confiscated from him, and left for the MP station, knowing that we had our man.

I felt good when I informed the victims that we had caught the guy and recovered their money. The next morning, I notified the FBI, who assumed the investigation for prosecution. The man was charged with both a state and federal crime because he'd committed armed robbery on a federal installation and stolen a car in the city of Highwood. The perp was identified as a former soldier assigned to Fort Sheridan.

A second case involved a bank robbery at Fort Sheridan, which is narrated in the Case of the Crazy Bank Robber:

## THE CASE OF THE CRAZY BANK ROBBER
Not all law enforcement agencies receive the same type of training

One morning, all the Fort Sheridan special agents were gathered in a group on the second floor of the CID office engaged in a training class when the phone rang. Since I was the duty agent for the day, I answered.

"There has been a bank robbery at the Fort Sheridan bank," the voice on the other end breathlessly said. It was the MP desk sergeant reporting that a bank robbery had just occurred moments before.

I informed the MP that I would immediately head to the bank, and I hung up. I turned around and informed the group of special agents what I'd just learned. I gathered up the crime scene kit and rushed to the duty sedan in the CID parking lot with Special Agents Stoner and Kovac in tow.

The three of us arrived at the bank, and the employees were all gathered in a small cluster near the front door. The first thing that I did was separate them and advise them not to talk to the each other. I also informed them that the FBI would be assuming the case and that they would have to relate what occurred in detail to them.

Enroute to the bank, I had the MP desk call the FBI and inform them of the bank robbery. The responding MP patrol informed me that the perp had sped out the main gate, heading toward Highwood. Shots were fired as he departed the post. A second MP patrol initiated a chase of the perp's vehicle, and all local units (police departments in the area) were notified. About fifteen minutes after CID's arrival at the bank, the FBI special agents from the Waukegan resident agency showed up and were briefed on the information known to date.

A short time later, Harmmon, one of the FBI special agents to converge on the scene, received word from his office that the perp's car had spun out of control, leaving Interstate 94 near the Skokie turnoff. The Fort Sheridan MPs and the Illinois State Police were seconds behind him when his car left the road, and they apprehended him without incident. All the money, approximately $12,000, was found in the backseat of the perp's car. FBI Special Agent Harmmon, who had received the call when I was talking to him, said the perp was being transported to the Skokie police station. Harmmon briefed the other FBI special agents at the crime scene, and they decided to head for Skokie.

Before they left, Special Agent Harmmon asked me if I needed any help at the bank while they were in Skokie. I told him that keeping an FBI special agent on-site would be beneficial to shore up information and to gather any evidence that connected the perp to the scene. Special Agent Harmmon introduced me to a rookie FBI special agent who had been assigned to the Waukegan resident agency for only a week. Harmmon started to get into the FBI sedan to leave. He looked over at the rookie and directed him to assist me with processing the crime scene, and then he sped off for Skokie. CID Special Agents Stoner and Kovac were canvassing the nearby buildings to see if they could locate any more witnesses. I reached them via radio and told them that the perp had been caught and that additional canvassing would not be necessary.

The rookie FBI special agent started following me around like a baby chick. I had expected the FBI to have taken more control of the scene; however, since the perp had already been apprehended, I guess all they had to do was interview him and follow up with the interviews of the bank employees. CID had already conducted preliminary interviews with most of the bank employees. Because of our efforts, we discovered that the perp took custody of the money from the bank and ran out the front door and across the muddy grassy area in the front of the bank to a car parked on the street. I inspected the route he reportedly took and found several footprint impressions.

I had the equipment to take cast moldings suspected to be the perp's in the muddy, grassy area in front of the bank. I thought this would be a good job for the rookie, so I asked him, "Would you take cast impressions of the footprints suspected to be made by the perp?"

He locked his eye onto mine, and with a somewhat dumbfounded look on his face, he said, "They did not teach us how to make cast impression at the FBI Academy."

That surprised me to some degree, but I did not overtly react to his information. Until this moment, I had never considered how different the training was between the FBI and CID. At that time, CID investigated more of the traditional types of crimes one would see in a city or town police force, whereas the FBI handled mostly federal crimes, especially white-collar crimes. Just in case the FBI needed them as evidence, I ended up taking the cast impressions and released them to FBI that afternoon.

About two weeks later, FBI Special Agent Harmmon dropped by the CID office and advised us that the bank robber did not waive his rights and did not make any admissions. "I wish we could have taken him to trial," Harmmon commented. But based on the perp's unusual behavior during the interview, we brought in a psychiatrist to check his mental health. The psychiatrist determined that the perp was suffering from a form of schizophrenia. Special Agent Harmmon said they had enough evidence to take the man to trial, and they did present the case to the AUSA. However, after reviewing all the facts in the case and evaluating the condition of the perp, the AUSA decided not to prosecute in lieu of treatment. Harmmon added that the decision not to prosecute was further supported by the fact that no one was hurt in the robbery, and all the money had been recovered.

A third case in which the CID teamed up with the FBI was the theft of four new car tires from the auto body shop building at Fort Sheridan. The MPs had previously received reports from the manager of the Fort Sheridan auto body shop that tools and materials had been taken. Those incidents were all investigated by the military police investigations (MPI) section of the provost marshal's office. The MPI investigations did not result in any valuable leads on who was responsible for the missing property. However, the most recent case involved US Army property valued at several hundred dollars. As in the many MPI investigations I had conducted in the past, there was no signs of forcible entry into the building.

The lack of forcible entry into the building was indicative of an inside job. I knew then that my focus would be to check out every angle I could to determine if the break-in was linked to those working on the inside. When the obvious fits, work on it until there is no other path to pursue before going on to the next step. Cases that have the most leads should be reasonably pursued. If you come to a T intersection in a case, ensure that the right and left turns are both fully investigated before determining if they are the wrong paths. Then go to the next step. This investigation—another example of how well our two agencies got along—is depicted in the Case of the Spoiled Young Man:

## THE CASE OF THE SPOILED YOUNG MAN
Crimes can be solved by gut feelings

Late one morning in late March 1976, I received a duty call from the MPs that the Fort Sheridan auto body shop had been broken into the previous night, and four new car tires valued at $300 had been stolen. I responded to the scene and met with the auto body shop manager, who told me that he had locked the doors to the shop at 9:00 the previous night and opened the next morning for business at 8:00. When he left the building the previous night, he recalled seeing the tires on a display shelf shortly before locking the doors. He indicated he did not immediately discover the tires missing until after he had been open for about two hours. He provided a description of the tires, which were in the inventory for customers to purchase them. I asked him if any employees could have moved the tires to another location for any reason, and he said, "No. There is no one else working in the building."

My crime scene examination did not disclose any evidence of forced entry. There was no damage or wedge markings on the door, and none of the windows to the building showed any signs of being tampered with. When I examined the location where the tires had been, there were clear indications that something had been sitting on the shelf for a long period, because the shelf area was clear of dust. With no evidence of forced entry, I could not get it out of my mind that the theft might be an inside job. Yet I did not suspect the manager, because I felt he was being straight with me. I did not question the validity of his crime, but the perp had to have access to the building.

I obtained a list of more than thirty people who had worked on their autos in the past month from a sign-in ledger. I began my investigation by locating and interviewing each of the people on the list. I had interviewed several people, and they all appeared to be clean. Then I hit pay dirt; one individual I interviewed brought up the fact that the manager's son often came into the shop and worked on his car. I ascertained that the son had confided in two of the people I talked with that he needed some new tires for his car. The fact that he worked on his car in the shop at all opened the possibility of a separate potential crime because he was a civilian and not authorized. Another suspicious aspect of my findings was that the son had not registered his name anywhere in the ledger.

I continued to dig into the information I had ascertained and conducted a background check on the manager's son. The US Army Crime Records Center (CRC) had no record of him, but local police check in Highwood, Illinois, disclosed that he was twenty-two years old and had been arrested for a minor theft a few years earlier. The record showed he resided with his parents at an address in Highwood. Since it was still early afternoon when I found out this information,

I decided to take a trip to the address and have a look around to determine if anything stuck out from the norm.

As I drove by the house, I saw no cars in the driveway and none parked in front or near the house. I had a gut feeling that I should check behind the house. I thought that I might find a car parked in the backyard.

I was in luck. When I saw that an alley behind the house, I slowly drove by but did not see a car. What I did see caused my body to experience a sensation of exhilaration, however. The house had a detached garage, and the door faced the alleyway. I was also astonished to find that the garage door had windows that allowed someone to view inside without entering. I cautiously stopped my car and looked around before getting out. I slowly approached and looked through the garage door windows. What I saw next caught me by surprise; there they were, in their magnificent glory, leaning next to the wall inside the garage: the missing tires, no doubt about it. The day was still clear, and the brightness of the daylight emitting enough light to see inside the garage was so ever revealing. The tires were the ones stolen from the auto body shop at Fort Sheridan.

I hopped into my CID car and rushed back to the office to call Special Agent Harmmon at the Waukegan FBI resident agency. I figured that the sooner I contacted him and a decision was made on jurisdiction of the case, the less time it would give the suspect to dispose of the tires. I hoped that Special Agent Harmmon would assume the investigation because the suspect was civilian and the crime was committed on the Fort Sheridan installation. The value of the tires was not much, but the spirit of investigative camaraderie meant something to me; I prayed Special Agent Harmmon felt the same way.

After I briefed Harmmon on the details of the investigation, he did not hesitate to assume jurisdiction of the case. He did not shilly-shally around; he acted immediately. It was now almost 6:00 in the evening, but he wanted to act now. Within fifteen minutes, Special Agent Harmmon was sitting in my office at CID. We again went over details of the case, and he decided to go talk to the suspect at his home in Highwood.

Hoping that the suspect would give permission to search the garage, Harmmon confided with me that we might be on shaky ground if we had to use my observation through the garage window as the only reason for the search; I agreed with Harmmon. He further explained to me that he probably needed more information before trying to obtain a probable cause search warrant from the federal magistrate. Three other CID special agents were recruited from our office to accompany Special Agent Harmmon and me to the suspect's home in Highwood. We drove to the suspect's home in two cars; I went with FBI Special Agent Harmmon in the FBI vehicle, while CID Special Agents Fisher, Kovac, and Stoner went in the CID car.

Ten minutes later, we were all standing outside the suspect's front door as Special Agent Harmmon knocked. The suspect's dad, the manager of the auto body shop, answered and instantly recognized me; he invited us into his home. After Special Agent Harmmon informed him of the purpose of our visit, the gentleman's face turned red, and he bowed his head.

"I have been waiting for you guys to come by," he said in a chagrining manner. "I have allowed my son too many chances in life. I am afraid that I have spoiled him," he added.

We found out that his son was not at home, but the suspect's father gave us permission to search his garage. The search took only a minute before we found the stolen tires; now, our suspect was our perp. The perp's father denied knowing that his son took the tires, but he made an admission that he suspected he had but was praying that he had not. I thought that since the garage was used daily to park cars, how was it possible the suspect's father did not know the tires were there? One thing that might explain this was because the tires were stored on the left side of the garage, nearest his son's car; the father might not have noticed them. Or was it that he just did not want to know? Out of sight, out of mind.

As we were placing the tires, now considered evidence, in the trunk of the FBI vehicle, the perp returned home and, with a look of bewilderment, asked us, "What's going on?"

FBI Special Agent Harmmon arrested him on the spot, and we took a detour via the Highwood police station before returning to the CID office. The next day, the perp had his first court appearance and was read the charges of theft of US government property. At Special Agent Harmmon's urging, I attended the court appearance, and the perp was released on bail, pending his trial date.

This case was another example of the great working cooperation the CID had with the FBI in the '70s. To a lesser degree for me, it was the same way with the Fort Knox CID and FBI relationships. I recall that the Louisville, Kentucky, FBI had a desk at the Fort Knox CID office, where one of their SAs would spend every Wednesday liaising and coordinating criminal investigations. I was fully aware that the FBI would not have investigated this type of crime if it had not occurred on a federal reservation.

I continuously stayed busy at Fort Sheridan, doing criminal cases and leads for other CID offices and enhancing my investigative techniques. I found time in the evenings to take some graduate courses in criminal justice. I attended the Webster University satellite campus at Fort Sheridan. Funding for the graduate courses came from the US Army tuition assistance program and a few months of educational benefits left from the GI Bill. I attended courses from January 1975 to January 1976, but I stopped three hours short of acquiring a master's degree in criminal justice. During that year, Special Agent Kral and I took most of the classes together, but unlike me, he graduated with a master's.

On top of working and attending graduate courses, I was also able to fit some time in to visit the family in Terre Haute every other weekend. I had a long time ago acquiesced to the situation that Melitta was not going to move, regardless of where I was stationed. Whatever the situation was with Melitta, I always enjoyed going home to see the boys and visit with Mom and, on rare occasions, with Nora and Hubert. On one of my trips to Terre Haute in January 1976, the seed of a divorce was planted, but in her normal emotionless state, Melitta said little. Chris, now four, was growing like a weed, and eleven-year-old Robert was almost as tall as his mother. Both boys were well behaved, and neither caused any trouble. Both were enjoyable to be around. I hated leaving them on Sunday afternoons when I had to return to Fort Sheridan.

I had no trouble keeping busy conducting investigations at Fort Sheridan. One case that had significance in my career sticks in my mind, involving my first death investigation as a CID special agent. I received a call of a body found in a room in one of the buildings on Fort Sheridan. When I arrived, two MPs were on the scene and informed me of what they had ascertained thus far. They found a white male lying on the floor of a room, fully dressed in his US Army uniform. They had identified him as SFC Ralph P. Swanson,[49] assigned to a medical detachment in downtown Chicago, who inspected agricultural products sold to the US Army. The MPs ascertained that he had been found by coworkers who went to pick him up for work. When they could not rouse him, they forcibly entered his room when he did not answer the door. I call this investigation the Case of the Soldier Who Did Not Make It to Work:

## THE CASE OF THE SOLIDER WHO DID NOT MAKE IT TO WORK
Living with no one makes one's life lonely

The body of thirty-nine-year-old SFC Ralph Swanson was found in his room, lying dead on the floor beside his bed. He was found by coworkers who were picking him up for work. Swanson was a medic who worked in downtown Chicago and was a part of a team of US medics that inspected meat for the army. The day before he died, Swanson spent time doing routine inspections at area meat plants, and his interactions with coworkers were considered normal and ordinary. He was a bachelor and considered a loner with no known problems.

When I arrived, I observed the man lying on his back on the floor next to his bed, fully dressed in his US Army uniform. My initial examination of the body did not reveal any signs of trauma. My initial view of SFC Swanson lying on the floor, obviously dead, was unnerving, to say the least. I felt a sickening feeling in my stomach, like the sensation I had experienced in Vietnam when I saw the medics carrying dead soldiers off the helicopter at the Eighty-Fifth Medevac Field Hospital.

Based on the body's lack of rigor mortis and the warm room temperature, it appeared he had been dead for only a few hours before he was found. He had probably just showered, shaved, and dressed for work when he suddenly—and from all accounts, unexpectedly—died. My investigation disclosed from interviews that coworkers had found his room door locked, and they'd had to forcibly open the door by shoving it until the lock gave way. SFC Swanson's room was well kept, and nothing seemed to be out of the place. Other than the lock to the door being damaged by his coworkers, there were no signs of forced entry. It appeared that the man had died of natural causes, but an autopsy was needed to determine the cause of death.

It is strange how things work out. SFC Swanson most likely started his workday as usual by waking up at the sound of the clock alarm (on the bedside table), routinely taking his shower, shaving, and putting on his uniform, and he was waiting for his ride for work when he died, probably from a heart attack. Imagine, your day starts as usual, and within an hour after waking up, you die. Life is short, and most of us take it for granted. Our choices in life can determine how long we live. As we go about our daily activities, death is not on our radar screen, but one thing is for certain: eventually, death will catch us, often by surprise.

I called the Great Lakes medical facility and requested that an ambulance pick up the body. When they arrived, I released the body to them for transport to the morgue, pending an autopsy. After I finished examining the scene, I secured the room and returned to the CID office and prepared my preliminary report. I wrote that the body was found intact, fully dressed, emphasizing that there were no physical evidence of body trauma and that his death appeared to be from natural causes. I also put in my report that an autopsy was pending.

Early the next morning, I received a call from the pathologist, who said he had scheduled the autopsy for 10:00 that morning. I requested that Special Agent Kral accompany me to the autopsy, because, like me, he had never attended one.

On the day of the autopsy, Special Agent Kral and I arrived at the Great Lakes naval base hospital morgue about 9:00. Per my request, the pathologist waited until our arrival to start the postmortem. At precisely 10:00, the pathologist started his examination of the body. I observed medical assistants removing SFC Swanson's clothing. Obviously, the medical assistants had done this before, because it appeared they knew what they were doing. Each piece of clothing was identified and marked, to include boots.

The pathologist allowed Special Agent Kral and me to examine the body after his clothes were removed. The anterior side of the body, including the face, torso, stomach, groin, and legs, showed no signs of trauma. When the body was turned over, the posterior side of the body showed lividity; a bluish-purple discoloration of the skin was observed. The lividity, or livor mortis, was consistent with the position of the body when I'd first observed it. The pre-autopsy examination revealed no evidence of how SFC Swanson died. The autopsy took approximately one and a half hours to complete and focused on the heart. The findings were not surprising; the man had atherosclerosis (hardening of arteries) and traces of alcohol in his system. The pathologist told us that there were indications the man had been a heavy drinker. It was the opinion of the pathologist that the manner of death was natural and caused by a heart attack. This confirmed my suspicions at the scene of his death.

Two interesting side issues occurred during the investigation of the death of SFC Swanson. First, I was contacted by the Lake County medical examiner's office and told that it was a requirement to have the person pronounced dead by a medical authority and to be granted permission from his office before moving the body from Fort Sheridan to the Great Lakes naval hospital. Second, I was notified by the casualty officer assigned that while he was processing the SFC's personal effects, he found $1,300 in cash stashed in a pocket of a coat hanging inside a closet of the SFC's room. You always learn from mistakes, so in future investigations, whether I was investigating or managing their progress, I went that extra mile to ensure that the scene was completely searched before leaving. Hence, this investigation created a new Rule Eight: *When doing something for the first time, ensure all steps are taken before executing action.*

Fort Sheridan was a unique post because of its proximity to Chicago and the seven-plus million people in the metropolitan area and an additional two million or more in the area encompassing the five counties in northern Indiana.[50] Correspondingly, a large population of soldiers from the area was stationed in Germany. Thus, CID had several cases involving contraband and small amounts of illegal drugs, such as hashish, smuggled into the area in envelopes and packages that were addressed to their many associates, friends, and relatives. The contraband and illegal drugs sent from European US Army post offices (APO) were seized by US Customs coming into New York. The return addresses were always either faked or totally absent from the envelopes or packages. Since the items smuggled originated from APOs, CID's involvement was to identify the senders. SA Kral and I usually teamed up to conduct the investigative leads. These leads were always a welcome change of pace in that they usually required travel into Wisconsin or Indiana or downstate in Illinois.

The local police were brought into the investigations for reporting purposes only. Since the envelope or package sent by the soldier was seized by US Customs, the recipients never actually took custody of the substance and were not charged with a crime. These cases were time consuming but worth the trouble in that they identified soldiers stationed in Germany that were involved in illegal drugs. I never thought that any of these soldiers were major international drug smugglers or big dealers, but they needed to be identified so that unit commanders knew who in his or her unit was involved with illegal drugs. A couple of those leads were noteworthy, and one is recounted in the Case of the Talkative Girlfriend:

## THE CASE OF THE TALKATIVE GIRLFRIEND
If you are going to commit a crime, don't trust anyone

I was assigned one of the routine US Customs seizure cases out of New York. SA Louis Patalano, from the Fort Hamilton resident agency, usually handled the liaising with US Customs. Once Hamilton received the information from the US Customs, Patalano would send a request for assistance (RFA) to the CID office that covered the area where the sender addressed the envelopes or packages that contained illegal drugs (primarily hashish). This case, the first in a series of leads, involved the smuggling of a small amount of hashish to a female residing in the city of Elkhart, Indiana.

Armed with information on what US Customs seized and the intended address, SA Kral, who teamed with me, and I headed for Elkhart, Indiana, about one and a half hours from Fort Sheridan, depending on traffic around Chicago. We found the address on a tree-lined street consisting of modest homes, some with one-car garages and others without, but all had off-street driveways. We pulled up in front of the targeted house and noticed no cars in the driveway. As SA Kral and I walked up the steps to the front porch, we both wondered whether anyone was home. We found out almost immediately when Special Agent Kral knocked on the door. A vibrant, extremely attractive girl around twenty years old opened the door and asked what we wanted.

After we introduced ourselves, Special Agent Kral was the first to speak. She looked shocked when she heard SA Kral refer to her by name. I then explained to her the purpose of our visit. She momentarily hesitated but reluctantly let us in. There was no politeness in her demeanor, and she did not invite us to sit down, so we stood. Our questioning focused on whether she routinely communicated with a boyfriend, any friends, or relatives in the US Army stationed in Germany. With a look of sheer panic, she nervously said no. Her answer appeared to be contrived.

Being more direct, I asked, "Have you ever received any letters from someone you know who is in Germany?"

She took a moment to answer. "Well, I do know someone in the army, but I haven't heard from him in a while."

Noting that she did not actually answer the question, unsympathetically, I repeated, "When was the last time you heard from him?"

Struggling for words, she claimed to not remember the last time they talked. It was clear she was not being straightforward with us. We asked a few more questions without getting any specific answers from her. We then hit her with the bombshell. I told her that US Customs had seized a letter addressed to her from a soldier in the US Army stationed in Germany and that the envelope contained a small amount of hashish. I implied that we knew the identity of the soldier who sent the letter to her, hoping that she would come clean. This question might have opened the door for her to say it was possible, thinking that would eliminate her as the person we wanted to talk to, but she denied that possibility. I changed the tone of the interview. We initially started the questioning that was more aligned with interview techniques. To gain an advantage and put more pressure on her, I considered using an interrogative approach and what-if questions. The tactic worked.

I informed her that smuggling was illegal and just having knowledge of the crime could get a person in trouble. I then told her that the military could not prosecute civilians, but if they were implicated in a crime the US Army was investigating, civilian police could be brought into the investigation. However, if that civilian knew something about a crime committed by a soldier and provided details to army investigators, leniency would be considered. If the civilian did not help, then the army would provide information on that person's involvement to the civilian police, and a parallel investigation would be initiated. We also could bring in the FBI on the case if warranted, I told her.

I summarized my questioning by saying that in this case, the US Army's main objective was to identify the soldier who'd smuggled hashish into the United States, which was a serious offense, and was not to be concerned about any civilian involvement. After a short time, we hit rock bottom on our interview strategy; our ammunition was quickly running out. If she did not provide the identity of the soldier soon, we were at tail's end. Special Agent Kral and I looked at each other, knowing we felt the same way. If I had not convinced her by now to tell us the identity of the soldier after what I had just gone through with her, then Special Agent Kral and I would have to pull something extra out of the box to get it done.

At this point, the girl continued to deny that she knew anyone who would want to send her any hashish and started insinuating that we leave. I instinctively thought of one last-ditch effort. I directed a specific comment to her: "If you do not tell us who you know in Germany, I will contact the Elkhart Police Department and tell them to initiate an investigation into your involvement with illegal drugs."

Creating a scenario to make her think she could possibly be investigated by the police, I picked up the wall phone located just inside the doorway to the kitchen that was visible from the living room and pretended to call the Elkhart Police Department. As I pretended to speak into the phone, like a Bob Feller fastball, she bolted toward me, hysterically screaming, "Hang up! I will tell you who he is, just don't call the police!"

Well, we spent another fifteen minutes talking to her about her former high school boyfriend, who had been in the US Army for two years. She gave us his unit address and provided some bonus information. She admitted to sporadically smoking pot at local parties and, on occasions before he left for Germany, with our soldier. To our disbelief, she also confided in us that since the soldier had been in Germany, he had repeatedly sent small amounts of hashish to her. Once she opened about our soldier, she told us his complete history of drug use. We exceed our expectations by obtaining additional information about the soldier's illegal drug usage that I suspect came in handy to the investigators in Germany.

As we left her house, she meekly asked that we not say anything to the Elkhart police.

As we drove away, Special Agent Kral and I looked at each other and grinned. If she'd only known, we were bluffing with the fake phone call to the Elkhart police! Thinking back to the interview with the girl, I have often wondered what would have happened if she had called our bluff.

Most of these types of cases ran the same. Special Agent Kral and I would use various methods to get the recipients to tell us who'd sent them the hashish. The problems we would run into were usually the same.

Another major problem with these cases involved encounters with angry family members, especially mothers, who felt strongly that CID or law enforcement in general should not be bothering their kids for such a minor, insignificant incident involving the personal use of drugs. Right or wrong, these soldiers were violating the law, and to allow them to continue sending hashish or any other illegal contraband to a girlfriend or buddy would be a violation of the law. No one should be eliminated from being investigated if he or she commits a crime, however small or insignificant it may be. Laws are created and enforced for a purpose of making society safe.

Another noteworthy investigation Kral and I worked is recalled in the Case of the Angry Mother:

## THE CASE OF THE ANGRY MOTHER
Justice does not always please the public

Special Agent Kral and I ran with another similar lead request from Fort Hamilton to locate a girl who was the intended recipient of an envelope containing hashish. This time, the address was in a suburban area in northern Illinois. This lead was almost identical, as were others we investigated, in circumstances as the first one we'd investigated. Similarly, the sender did not identify himself on the confiscated envelope, and all we had to go on was the recipient's address. We found the address located on a city street in the small town of Naperville, Illinois. The difference from other cases of this nature was the actions of the mother of the girl we went to interview. She was extremely hostile and kicked us out of her house.

When we first arrived at the house, we were met by a college-aged girl. We explained why we were there, and she invited us into her home. From the start, the girl indicated her willingness to be honest and up front with us. She immediately told us the identity of her friend stationed in Germany, but she denied ever receiving any contraband or illegal drugs of any kind from him. The entire interview took about fifteen minutes—a slam dunk, we thought.

We were just about ready to leave when the girl's mother returned from shopping. She walked into the living room carrying sacks of groceries. She walked past us into the kitchen, placed the sacks of groceries on the counter, and returned to the living room. She wanted to know why we were in her home. Before Special Agent Kral or I could tell her, the girl told her mother the purpose of our visit. Her mother did not immediately say anything. Without warning, she went into a tirade about why we were not out chasing the big drug dealers in the world. She continued by lecturing us on the evils of accosting young, innocent kids who did no wrong, and how dare we harass good citizens and so on. Her behavior became more and more irrational, and she started pacing back and forth between the front door and the kitchen, demanding an apology for our actions. Our attempts to justify the legitimacy to the woman fell on deaf ears.

We were looking for an opening to make our way out of the house, but the tempo of her pacing back and forth increased, and she stood directly in front of us, making our exit virtually impossible. Each time Special Agent Kral or I got close to the door, she stepped between it and us and continued her rant and raving criticism of our visit. Even her daughter tried to calm her down, but it appeared that she was so enraged that she did not notice. Finally, I told the woman that we were leaving and she could register her complaint with the Fort Sheridan CID office. It took us another couple of minutes of having to listen to her condemnation of our investigation before we positioned ourselves next to the door to enable our exit. This case was one of my most frustrating in that there was no rationalizing our mission with this woman.

I felt that Special Agent Kral and I had earned our money the day the angry mother verbally battered us. Thinking back, I realized that the angry mother did not, even one time, tell us to leave her house, and we never gave her the phone number to the Fort Sheridan CID office, nor did we hear from her again. In retrospect, I could understand why the angry mother felt the way she did. Her mind-set was totally different from ours; she did not consider it a major crime for youths to indulge in minor use of marijuana—or, in this case, hashish. On the other hand, our mission was to identify a soldier who'd possessed and probably used illegal drugs—someone that had an ultimate responsibility to be clearheaded and alert around his soldiers when they conducted training or, heaven prohibit, were in perilous situations.

In our tenure at Fort Sheridan CID, Special Agent Kral and I must have investigated at least ten or so of these types of leads, but the two mentioned above were the most unusual cases of them all.

If we had to travel far distances on leads, usually only one CID special agent would make the trip. There was one lead that was assigned to me that took me about 150 miles to a small town in central Illinois to locate and interview a suspect in a sexual molestation case that occurred in Germany. These types of leads were not usually ones that special agents sought, because the time involved in completing the trip and interviews were usually too short to qualify for TDY. The investigation was memorable in that it involved some very unusual sexual activities by our person of interest. He had already been discharged from the US Army under other-than-honorable conditions and returned to his hometown. I was going into the interview cold, because I had not talked to him over the phone. The lead from Germany did not identify a phone number. I had only an address in a rural area and hoped that the local sheriff's office could help me locate the individual with their resources. I had tried to contact the sheriff's office prior to my departure from Fort Sheridan, but the dispatcher said everyone was on calls, and she had no knowledge of the name I gave her. The dispatcher also informed me that the department's records clerk was on vacation, so my entire trip to his hometown might have been a waste of time if he had relocated. I call this lead the Case of the Young Pervert:

## THE CASE OF THE YOUNG PERVERT
You never know what an interview will reveal

I traveled to a small town in central Illinois and contacted the local sheriff's office to arrange a location for the interview of the suspect in a case investigated by a CID office in Germany. The sheriff offered a small interview room for my use. His department also allowed a deputy to accompany me to the suspect's home and assist me in escorting the suspect to the sheriff's office for the interview. This worked out well, because it added legitimacy to the interview in that I was a US Army CID special agent investigating in a civilian environment.

The suspect, a white male, had grown up on a farm just outside of the small Illinois community. The originating German CID office reported that he had spent only a couple of years in the US Army before receiving a general discharge for unsuitability. The deputy and I met with him at his parents' farm, and he agreed to go with us to the sheriff's office for the interview. The originating CID office had requested I locate and interview the individual as a person of interest in a sexual molestation case involving a fifteen-year-old German boy.

Apparently, the German boy hung around the unit's barracks and did odd jobs, like shining shoes and sweeping floors for the soldiers. The information we had to work with reported that person(s) unknown had attacked the boy in the barracks during the daytime when the soldiers were at work. The boy was a regular in the barracks, and his presence was nothing unusual. The boy was found lying on the floor in a utility room. The victim gave a verbal statement to the CID in Germany that he was approached from the rear and dragged into the utility room and sexually assaulted. The boy claimed that he did not see the attacker's face. Our suspect had been in the unit for a little over a year, so there were some elements of the boy's statement that were questionable, and there appeared to be more to the incident than what was reported. If our person of interest denied any involvement, I was to offer him a polygraph.

We arrived at the sheriff's office, and I made sure the man had a drink, and I allowed him to smoke. (In those days, people could smoke cigarettes inside most buildings.)

I started the interview by getting some pertinent information about his personal history and time spent in Germany and working on establishing rapport with him. I explained to him that he was no longer under military jurisdiction, so he did not have to talk to me, but he volunteered to answer questions. He admitted knowing the young German boy and that the boy had been assaulted before he left Germany, but he denied committing the crime. Our person of interest waffled on some answers to my questions were vague during the entire interview. It was difficult to get a read on the person who appeared nervous, edgy, and consistently shifting in his seat throughout the interview.

I spent about an hour or better on the interview and felt I was getting nowhere with him. I started pressuring him about his moral character and that there were standards for the way one conducted his life and the value of realizing right and wrong in our society. This line of questioning seemed to be getting to him, but he continued to deny any involvement or knowledge of the crime. I was down to my last bullet when I then shot a direct question at him: "Have you ever done anything in your life that you were personally ashamed of?" Expecting his answer was going to be no, I was shocked at his response.

In a matter-of-fact attitude, he voluntarily admitted that when he was thirteen years old, he had sex with a sheep. However, revolting and nauseating his story was, I did not want my repugnant feelings of revulsion and disgust show in my facial expressions. I immediately considered the secret, private matter he had just confided with me as an indication he was being straight up and honesty with me. Why would he admit to something so distasteful? What was his objective in doing so? Why would he be willing to admit to doing this repulsive thing and not talk about the incident in Germany? I pondered these questions. It could be that, like he'd said, he had nothing to do with the incident in Germany.

I spent another thirty minutes with him, and he provided no more pertinent information, and I considered the interview to be over. The last question I had for him before completing the interview was to ask him if he would submit to a polygraph; I was not surprised when he said no. If he would have confessed to the sexual molestation incident, there would have been a jurisdictional issue. Based on the extradition treaty with the United States and Germany, anyone committing an offense of sexual assault upon a child is subject to extradition. Since our person of interest was now a civilian, he could be subjected to German law because the victim was a German citizen. I suspected that our person of interest was unaware of this situation, and it was highly unlikely that he denied the crime for fear of being extradited to German. There will always be that hint of uncertainty that will remain with me on whether he committed the offense.

On October 10, 1975, an incident occurred that changed my point of view on whether I wanted to make CID my career. It all started one morning when Special Agent Kral and I bundled up some leads and headed for Chicago. One lead involved a scenario like others we had previously completed with no problems. It involved a RFA from another stateside CID office, where we had to find a relative residing in a residential neighborhood in South Chicago. Our mission was to locate and interview the relative, confiscate the stolen property given to him by the perp, and bring it back as evidence. The address for the relative was 302 South Yates Street, Chicago.[51]

Special Agent Kral and I found the 300 block of South Yates Street but could not make out any address numbers on the houses as we drove by, so we decided to go house to house until we found 302. We parked our car in front of where we suspected the house might be. This house was adjacent to a vacant field, where we suspected a house had previously stood before being demolished. We entered the front door and immediately saw the number 304 nailed to a wall on our right. Not discouraged, we walked up the stairs and knocked on a couple of doors, and the people that answered told us they did not know anyone by the relative's name. Inquiries with the people also did not disclose any information about the address 302, so we left the house and checked next door and found it to be address 306. We checked the house located on the other side of the vacant field and found its address to be 300. We'd made a critical error by assuming the address 302 probably belonged to the house that formerly occupied the vacant field. We left the neighbor without finding the relative or the address 302.

Since the case was assigned to Special Agent Kral, I told him it would be a good idea to call the USPS to determine if they could provide confirmation that 302 still existed. Special Agent Kral checked with the USPS, and they provided him no relevant information, so he submitted his report indicating the address could not be found.

About a week later, both of us were told to report to the operations officer at that time, CW3 Marshall Thomas. We were shocked when he advised us of our rights for falsifying official documents related to the report that Special Agent Kral had submitted. Apparently, the operations officer had received a call from the originating CID office indicating that the address was a legitimate one and the relative had been waiting on CID to come by his house to obtain custody of the stolen property. Once that information was known to the operations officer, he and Captain McHugh went to the address on South Yates and found it at the same location where SA Kral and I were. The address 302 was located on the left of the foyer that SA Kral and I had been in, but that the address was obscured from the front entry.

I was incensed at our predicament, because there was never any intent to falsify any official document. I will concede that we blundered in assuming several things. It had been reasonable to think that the vacant field used to be where 302 stood, and not one individual we interviewed acknowledged knowing either the person we were looking for or if the 302-address existed. Kral, an inexperienced probationary special agent, probably should have contacted the case agent at the other CID office to have him verify the address, which would warrant another trip to the Chicago neighborhood. Short of this, the error could have just as easily been rectified by the operations officer chewing our butts and being told to complete the RFA as requested.

I thought the decision to advise Special Agent Kral and I of our rights was somewhat extreme. The whole incident was cleared up, and no formal charges were ever brought against Special Agent Kral and me. However, to rub salt in the wound, so to speak, I was ordered to go to Chicago and complete the lead myself; considering the case did not even belong to me in the first place, it was somewhat over the top. This incident stuck with me for some time, and it was one of the reasons that caused me to consider leaving the US Army.

The operations officer came to me one day and told me that he was unaware that I was still a probationary special agent when the incident occurred. Although

I never spoke with Chief Thomas about it, I thought maybe, therefore, I was singled out to complete the lead by myself, with the thought that I was a fully accredited special agent and should have known better than to make a silly mistake. One month later, I successfully completed my probationary period and was accredited as a special agent.

In retrospect, I have often looked back on this incident and pondered all the circumstances. The thought of what had occurred made me realize over the years that an investigator must pay attention to detail, be persistent, and cover all bases in an investigation before ending it and never ever assume anything. In the aftermath of the incident, Special Agent Kral made the decision to leave the US Army when his tour of duty at Fort Sheridan was completed. I personally do not know if Special Agent Kral's decision to leave CID was made based entirely on this incident, but circumstances suggest it. The CID lost an excellent and very professional special agent when he left.

It is sort of ironic that I'd just recovered from an unofficial internal investigation concerning the lead in Chicago when I was assigned to investigate the larceny of a fellow CID probationary special agent's credentials, service revolver, and ammunition from his off-post quarters. The CID probationary special agent was assigned to our office a few months prior to the incident and had just been reinstated as a special agent after a two-year suspension for an internal inquiry in Germany. He spent those two years sitting in a CID office doing absolutely nothing but coordinating with his attorney. He was eventually cleared to go back to work and had been reissued his CID credentials and service revolver with ammunition about a week before the theft. He had pulled one duty night and had a small caseload when the incident occurred. The probationary special agent had lived with his girlfriend in an apartment in Wheaton, Illinois, just west of Chicago, for only a couple of months when the theft occurred. This was the first case I had to conduct involving another CID special agent, but it wouldn't be my last. I called this investigation the Case of the Nervous Drug Dealer:

## THE CASE OF THE NERVOUS DRUG USER
To get results, you need persistence

The case was initiated when Probationary Special Agent Steven Blackburn[52] called the Fort Sheridan CID office early on the morning of June 22, 1976, and reported that someone had broken into his ground-floor apartment and stolen a briefcase containing his CID credentials and his assigned service revolver. Chief Thomas (now promoted to CW4) directed Special Agent Kral and I to the scene of Special Agent Blackburn's apartment to get details of what had occurred.

Special Agent Blackburn was waiting for us when we arrived. He informed us that he and his girlfriend had gone to bed around 9:00, and when he got up around 6:00, he discovered the screen on the patio door had been cut and someone had entered the apartment. The briefcase containing his CID credentials, a loaded service revolver, and extra ammunition had been stolen, but nothing else was missing.

Our crime scene examination revealed that the screen to the patio door had indeed been cut from the outside. A glass door had been left unlocked and showed no signs of being tampered with. I asked Special Agent Blackburn if he'd reported the incident to the Wheaton police.

"No, I have not," he said.

"Was the service revolver loaded?" I asked.

"Yes, it was," he responded.

After a series of questions, I asked him if there had been any other break-ins reported in the apartment complex.

"None that I know of," he responded.

I followed up with questions about his associates and about everyone who had visited him.

"An eighteen-year-old kid who lives upstairs has visited on a few occasions," he said.

"You should leave and go to the CID office, because Chief Thomas wants to talk to you," I told him.

His girlfriend stayed behind, but out of the way of our investigation. We completed our crime scene examination, took photographs, and decided our next move would be to report the incident to the Wheaton police in person.

A short time later, we arrived at the Wheaton police station and asked to speak to a detective, who met us in the lobby of the station. Both Special Agent Kral and I showed our CID credentials and introduced ourselves to him. He invited us to his office, where we sat down and briefed him on the break-in. He made a few phone calls while we were seated in front of his desk, and after the last one, he told us that they would put a man on the case, but it would be a low priority due to their other commitments. The detective cleared it with his department chief that it was okay for Special Agent Kral and me to canvass the neighborhood of the apartment complex where Blackburn lived. We left the detective with the agreement that we would brief him on our findings. I was very disappointed with the detective's lacking sense of urgency about the crime. Here we had an unknown person in the custody of a federal agent's credentials and loaded service revolver, and the civilian detective did not seem to care. I acquiesced to the feeling that we were not going to get much help from the Wheaton police.

On the trip, back to the Special Agent Blackburn's apartment, I contemplated which direction to take on our investigation. The first thing was to interview the eighteen-year-old that had visited Special Agent Blackburn's apartment. We would then go where the information took us. I contacted Special Agent Blackburn's girlfriend, who told us where the eighteen-year-old lived. We knocked on the door to his apartment, and a young attractive girl opened the door and asked what we wanted. We requested to speak with the eighteen-year-old.

"Why do you want to talk to my brother?" she said. She added that he was not at home.

She had a worried look on her face, and I wanted to know why. I asked her where her brother was, and she told us, "He is running the streets."

"When will he return?" I asked.

"I don't know," said the girl.

"How does your brother spend his days?" I asked.

"He often goes to work out in the gym."

"Where is the gym?"

"It is in the basement of our building," she hesitatingly informed us.

We told the girl that we would be back later in the day to talk with him. She shut the door without saying anything.

Special Agent Kral and I found the gym and conducted a search of the area where the girl said her brother spent time. Special Agent Kral took the workout room while I looked in the sauna and shower areas. I did not find the kid's name of any of the gym lockers. I searched the swimming area, but nothing stood out. I searched inside a cabinet where towels were stored but found nothing. Afterward, Special Agent Kral and I contemplated where to go from there. We both concluded that locating and interviewing the eighteen-year-old was our only real lead. I contacted Chief Thomas at the office and updated him on the case. I thought, w*e have plenty of work to do in a very short time.*

We returned to Special Agent Blackburn's apartment and reinterviewed his girlfriend to see if we'd missed anything. She could not tell us any more than what we already knew, so we left her at the apartment and drove around the area for a short while, discussing what our next move was going to be. We decided to try the boy's apartment again to see if he had returned home. We didn't have enough on him to officially call him a suspect, but he was the nearest we had to one. We parked our car in a space provided for visitors and walked up the outside staircase to the second-floor apartment where the kid lived. Before we could knock, and without warning, the door flew open.

There, standing in the doorway, was a different girl in her mid- to late twenties that we had not seen on our earlier visit to the apartment. "Saw you parking your car and knew you were coming to our place. What do you want now?" she barked.

I spoke up first and told her we stopped by to see if the eighteen-year-old had returned home.

"My brother is not at home," she curtly informed us.

After her comment, I thought, *Hey, he had two sisters living in the apartment, and they both are acting very strange.* Both Special Agent Kral and I had a feeling there was something odd in the tone of her voice. We had a gut feeling that both girls were hiding something from us. The girl we had talked to on our earlier visit stepped into the conversation.

"It is imperative that we talk to him," I urged.

"He comes and goes on his own, and most of the time we don't know where he is," the older girl replied.

I strongly urged her to reach out to her brother and explain to him that we wanted to ask him some questions about where he was the previous night. Both girls suddenly changed attitudes.

The older girl's eyes got teary, her voice started to crack, and she covered her face with her hands. In a soft, almost inaudible voice, she said, "I don't want him to get into trouble."

I had a rushing sensation spill over my body; well, I did believe we were getting somewhere.

Suddenly, the younger sister joined in and said, "I guess you guys should come in."

Special Agent Kral and I followed the two girls into the apartment and were directed to the couch. When we both sat down, the older of the two told us that her brother had mentioned something to her and her sister last night that he had "fixed his problem."

"Can you please elaborate?" I urged.

With the younger sister quietly sitting in a chair near us, the older sister, who was still standing, admitted that their brother was involved in illegal drugs. Special Agent Kral and I were astonished to hear the story she began telling us.

She told us their brother was having trouble at home and was kicked out because he was using drugs. She and her two sisters let him move in with them until he could hopefully get his life back on the right track. I stopped her momentarily to clarify that there was a third sister living at the apartment with them, but who was currently at work. She continued that shortly after their brother moved in, he met Special Agent Blackburn and his girlfriend. He started spending time with them in the evenings at their apartment. He found out that our probationary special agent was an investigator, and the girl told us that their brother told them he thought that Special Agent Blackburn was gathering information on him about his illegal drug use. Then she brought down the hammer. She told us their brother had confessed to them that he had broken into Special Agent Blackburn's apartment and stolen a briefcase that their brother thought contained information about his illegal drug involvement. Special Agent Kral and I were stunned beyond belief.

The girl continued with her incredible story by indicating her brother saw us at Special Agent Blackburn's apartment earlier that day and knew we would eventually find out about him. Suspecting he would be arrested for breaking into the apartment and stealing the briefcase, he fled their apartment without telling them where he was going. I jumped in and asked the girl if there was a possibility she knew where her brother was hiding, and she said no.

"Do you know if he has the briefcase with him?" I asked.

She said, "I think he does, but I am not sure."

I then leveled with the two girls and told them the US Army's involvement was not about the break-in as much as our commitment to recover the contents of the briefcase. I told them that it contained the CID credentials and a loaded .38-caliber service revolver. They appeared genuinely surprised at this information, and both expressed concerned about their brother's safety. I also explained to them that if we obtained the briefcase and all its contents, we would not take their brother into custody. It was still a possibility that the Wheaton police might investigate the incident; however, they had expressed a lack of interest in the case. The girls seemed upbeat after I explained the US Army's position on the case, and they agreed to help us locate their brother and recover the briefcase and its contents. I told them that their brother did not have to meet with us if they coordinated the transfer of the briefcase and all its contents to us. I told them that the agreement was only good if all the stolen property was returned. If any part of the stolen items was not returned, we did not have to bring in the Wheaton police, but we would seek the assistance of the FBI. I explained to them that US Army materials and equipment were considered federal property and the feds could bring charges against their brother.

They immediately started making phone calls to locate their brother while we waited anxiously at the apartment. Leaving Special Agent Kral at the apartment, I went to Special Agent Blackburn's apartment to use his telephone to call Chief Thomas and update him on the case progress thus far. Chief Thomas was ecstatic when he heard the news and told me not to return to the office without the weapon and CID credentials; I promised I wouldn't. I then rejoined Special Agent Kral and the two girls at their apartment.

It was now 5:00 in the afternoon, and we still had not heard from the girl's brother. Special Agent Kral and I did not want to leave the apartment for fear of missing the brother's call or, even better, his return and the possibility of losing the girls' cooperation, so we volunteered to spring for a pizza for the girls' dinner. They were all for the idea and ordered one that was brought to the apartment. As everyone was eating a slice of pizza, the third sister, who apparently was older than the other two, returned home from work. She was pretty put out by us being in her apartment and wanted to know what was going on. When the two sisters told her the reason why we were there, she did not look happy but acquiesced to the situation.

About forty-five minutes later, the telephone rang. The older sister answered the phone, and she then went silent. We heard her say, "Yes, they are still here."

"Where do we meet you?" she asked. She then hung up the phone and turned to Special Agent Kral and me and informed us, "Our brother requests that one of us [meaning one of the sisters] meet him in the parking lot at 7:00 p.m. sharp."

We had about fifteen minutes to decide what action we should take. I immediately thought that Special Agent Kral and I both should rush to the parking lot before he got there and position ourselves where he could not see us and attempt to apprehend him at that point. However, this was a bad idea, because the sisters might see our actions as a threat to their brother and warn him before we could get to him. I also thought that if the brother showed up in a car, he had the advantage in any attempt to get away. I wanted to avoid a car chase, especially in a civilian area, so we decided to stick to the original agreement and let one of the sisters meet with the brother to retrieve the stolen property. The time came, and it was decided between the three sisters that the oldest would meet their brother in the parking lot. We didn't know if the brother had arranged any type of signal to indicate he was waiting for her or that she would be in the parking lot at the time he said he would be there. The oldest sister left the apartment and was gone for a few minutes, which seemed like a few hours. It seemed that I held my breath the entire time she was gone.

Finally, I forcibly exhaled a blast of air when I saw her walking through the door carrying the briefcase. Special Agent Kral immediately grabbed the briefcase from her hands, set it down on the kitchen table, and opened it. Our hearts beat fast, and there was tension in the air. Then Special Agent Kral pulled out the probationary special agent's CID-issued holster encasing a loaded .38-caliber service revolver. In his other hand, Special Agent Kral held a set of CID credentials, and I looked inside the briefcase and observed an extra cylinder of .38-caliber rounds; we'd gotten everything we'd come for. As a final question for the girls (since neither saw the briefcase earlier that morning), I asked them if their brother confided in them about where he had placed the briefcase while still at the apartment. The oldest girl, who had retrieved the items from her brother, told us that he had mentioned that he'd kept the briefcase underneath the cabinet sink where the towels were stored in the sauna room of the apartment complex gym.

When I heard this, my heart sank in my chest. I had looked inside the cabinet underneath the sink. I recalled seeing two doors on the cabinet, I had only opened the left side. Although the cabinet had two doors, the inside was open. I had glanced to the right, but saw nothing. We already knew that the brother had left the apartment shortly after we arrived. The brother must have removed the briefcase when Special Agent Kral and I were obtaining preliminary information from Special Agent Blackburn and his girlfriend. I did not conduct my search of the sauna room cabinet until after we'd returned from the Wheaton police station. I figured the time in between these two events—the brother removing the briefcase and the time I conducted the search where it had been stored—was about one hour. Sometimes luck is on your side, and sometimes it is not. We thanked the girls for their cooperation and left the apartment.

It was now past 7:30 p.m., and I figured the Special Agent Blackburn had returned from the CID office by now, so as a courtesy, Special Agent Kral and I decided to stop by and brief him on our investigation. Knowing that he was facing more scrutiny because of this incident, our visit was the least we could do. Special Agent Kral knocked on his door, and Blackburn's girlfriend answered. Special Agent Kral held up the briefcase, and she screamed, "It's over! It's over! Thanks, guys. We really appreciate it." Special Agent Blackburn then entered the room and saw we had the briefcase. He knew we could not give him anything inside the briefcase, including his weapon or CID credentials, because it was now evidence. He acknowledged our efforts and thanked us. I told him I would see him in the morning and left for the CID office.

On the way to the CID office, I called Chief Thomas, who was waiting at his desk. We informed him that we were coming home with the briefcase, weapon, and CID credentials. He said, "Good job. Come home and get some rest." What a day we'd had.

In the aftermath of this investigation, Special Agent Blackburn was relieved from CID duties and given the option to choose between court-martial or being administered an Article 15 under the provisions of the UCMJ. If he chose the Article 15 route, he would also be drummed out of the US Army, which was his decision. Special Agent Kral and I both received Army Commendation Medals for achievement because of our investigation of this incident.

After the Blackburn case, things at Fort Sheridan returned to normal, and I continued to work a full investigative agenda. It was rare that Fort Sheridan had housebreaking and larceny incidents, but one did occur in the spring of 1976. A young soldier broke into the base PX and stole some stereo equipment. It was officially my first such case. I had conducted numerous break-ins as an MPI and had completed one CID-level housebreaking and larceny case as an MPI while stationed at Fort Knox. But this crime was my first break-in as a CID agent.

It came with some twists and turns, and support from our local SJA office fell short. The perp in this investigation had some serious family issues when he left home to join the US Army. The perp was essentially a good kid who'd made some bad judgments in his life. He had a good record while servicing as a clerk in the US Army, and from all accounts, he was well liked by his commander and 1SG and from all accounts, he got along well with his classmates, schoolteachers, and friends. His problems surfaced again during the investigation of the theft of stereo equipment from the Fort Sheridan PX. My investigation developed the young soldier as a suspect in the PX break-in. When he was interviewed, it was revealed that he and his father did not get along well. I call this investigation the Case of the Scared Young Soldier:

## THE CASE OF THE SCARED YOUNG SOLDIER
There is nothing you can do to keep your man if not supported by the local SJA

I received the notification from the MP desk that a housebreaking and larceny had occurred at the Fort Sheridan PX. The PX was in one of the historic stone buildings on the main post. I packed up the crime scene kit and headed to the scene.

Upon arrival, an MP patrol briefed me on what they had ascertained from talking to the PX staff. Apparently, a first-floor display window had been broken, and one entire stereo unit, still in the box, had been taken. The value was more than $500.

I conducted a crime scene examination of the break-in, which revealed that the display window glass had been broken from the outside. I took fingerprint impressions and interviewed staff members. I questioned the store manager, who stated, "I locked up the store at 6:00 last evening and opened for business today at 9:00 a.m. sharp."

I left the crime scene at the PX with no real leads to follow, I would continue my investigation by completing the interviews with PX staff members and canvass any buildings that might have been opened late the previous night. It took me about a week to complete these leads, which failed to develop into any viable leads. The case was getting cold fast, and the doors were slamming shut at every turn. I conducted checks for any similar crimes committed and found that there was no record of the PX at Fort Sheridan ever being broken into. I checked with late-night MP patrols, and they had no record of field interview cards on any suspicious activity being filed on anyone.

I was at a dead end until the unexpected happened. I was sitting in my office, working on reports one late afternoon, when our secretary told me to pick up the phone. The party on the other end said, "I got some information about the PX break-in. Who can I talk to?" Since Fort Sheridan was a very small US Army installation, anything that happened on the post would get around to everyone within a short time.

"It is my case, and I am the guy you need to talk with," I informed him.

"I do not want to come to the CID office. Can I meet you somewhere?" he asked.

I suggested that we could meet at the restaurant in Highwood in fifteen minutes. He agreed.

About fifteen minutes later, I found myself sitting in a booth at the restaurant in downtown Highwood, Illinois. I asked to be seated in a location where I could watch the door. I had to wait only a short time, when a young, black man, looking much like a soldier but wearing civilian clothing, entered the restaurant. We immediately made eye contact, and he walked over and sat down in my booth, facing me.

"I know you are a CID agent, because I have seen you around the post," he said.

Trying to make a funny comeback and soften the atmosphere, I commented, "Well, I am not working undercover."

He chuckled and seemed to feel more at ease.

"What do you have for me?" I inquired.

"You need to check the trash bins in the alley behind the personnel barracks at Fort Sheridan. I think you will be surprised at what you find," he replied.

"Can you provide me with anything else?"

"Yeah. Check the guy in room 302. You'll see that he has a new stereo set."

Before I could ask him any further questions, he abruptly got up and walked out of the restaurant. I momentarily sat there and digested what the man had just told me and wondered what motive he had for telling me the information. If it all panned out, the man might have just solved our PX caper.

I immediately returned to the Fort Sheridan CID office and briefed Chief Thomas on what I had ascertained. He told me to follow up on the lead. I got Special Agents Kral and Kovac to accompany me in the CID vehicle to the alley behind the personnel barracks. About halfway through the alley, we drove up next to two large trash bins, got out of the car, and looked in. All three of us were pleasantly flabbergasted at what we saw. Inside both trash bins, there were pieces of discarded cardboard boxes with pictures of a stereo like the model that had been stolen from the PX. We confiscated all the pieces of the cardboard boxes and placed them inside the trunk of the CID vehicle. I felt that finding the cardboard boxes that were believed to have contained the stereo equipment stolen from the PX would give up enough probable cause to search room 302.

We left Special Agent Kovac at the scene to catch any possible activity that might come from room 302, while Special Agent Kral and I went to get a ruling on the possibility of a search warrant from SJA. We met with Captain Stephen Stainish at the SJA office and briefed him on what we had. He advised that he thought there was enough credible information that established probable cause that the young soldier was involved and a search would be legal.

We returned and married up with SA Kovac and, seconds later, found ourselves at the door to room 302 in the personnel barracks at Fort Sheridan. When we knocked, a young, white, male soldier opened the door and, looking somewhat puzzled, asked what we wanted. We showed our CID credentials, introduced ourselves, and informed the young soldier of the purpose of our visit. He let us in, and all three of us immediately saw a stereo set sitting next to the wall near his bunk. Making sure his rights were not violated, SA Kovac took custody of the young soldier, now considered a suspect, while SA Kral and I confiscated the components to the stereo unit. While SA Kovac brought the suspect to the CID office, SA Kral and I loaded the confiscated property into the CID car and headed for the office. Once at the CID office, we placed the suspect in the interview room while we released the stereo property to the evidence custodian.

I conducted the interrogation of the suspect, who up until this time was very cooperative. He waived his rights and consented to talk. He acknowledged that he knew the stereo equipment taken from his room had been stolen, but he denied he was the one responsible for breaking into the PX. I attempted to get him to understand that he was still in trouble and that it would only go in his favor if he revealed how he'd obtained the property. He refused. I told him we had enough to submit a report to SJA for the offense of possession of stolen property, but he continued to deny stealing the property. I assured him that if his fingerprints matched the prints found on the cardboard boxes and at the scene of the break-in, it would be hard for him to deny he was involved. I started to get a gut feeling that there was something he was not telling me, possibly the real reason for not admitting to the crime.

I continued with the interrogation well into the evening hours with not much progress. To gain more rapport with the suspect, I started pressing him for information about his abilities and goals in life, and I even touched on childhood relationships with family and friends. This line of questioning apparently struck a nerve with him, because he gradually opened the door and started talking about his strong-willed father. I turned the direction of my interrogation into questions about his relationship with his father and what his father would think about his predicament.

"He would beat my ass," he bemoaned.

"How is your relationship with your father now?" I asked.

"All I know is that I don't want to let him down," he indicated.

Many times, in the interview, I felt the suspect was getting ready to completely confess to his crime.

"I can't let my father know about this situation," he gave in.

I took his answers as an admission of guilt, but I felt it was short of a confession. I sprinkled salt on the wound when I told him that our evidence was enough to prosecute him. I also informed him that there was no credible information that would suggest that anyone joined him in committing the crime. He remained silent.

It was around 9:00 p.m. when I stopped the interrogation and released him to the MPs to have him returned to his unit. As I left the MP station that evening, I thought that he might be an AWOL risk. There wasn't much we could do at this hour, because SJA had closed shop. Any coordination with them would have to wait until the following morning.

I arrived for work at 7:00 a.m. sharp and called SJA but received no answer. When Chief Thomas came to work, I briefed him on the case to date. He agreed that we had enough to place the suspect in the title block of the CID ROI for housebreaking and larceny. I also advised the chief that I was worried that the perp was an AWOL risk. Chief Thomas concurred with me that I should coordinate with SJA about possible confinement, pending trail.

About 9:00, I found myself sitting in Captain Stainish's office discussing the merits of confinement for the perp. We went over the entire investigation to date, and I reiterated that it was a strong likelihood that the perp would go AWOL if allowed to remain free, pending an Article 32 (equivalent to a civilian grand jury indictment) hearing and subsequent court-martial. Captain Stainish pondered the situation and told me he would get in touch with me when a decision was made. In the end, SJA ruled that confinement for a nonviolent crime was inappropriate in this case and the perp should remain free. This decision would come back to bite us in the butt.

To shore up loose ends in the case, we identified two unit members that the perp confided in that he in fact did break into the PX and steal the stereo equipment that was found in his barracks room. These witnesses put a lid on our case, and I submitted a final report to SJA for their action.

About three weeks passed before an Article 32 hearing could be scheduled. About three days before the Article 32 proceedings, the perp had reportedly gone AWOL. Everything was put on hold, pending his return. Several months later, my assignment at Fort Sheridan was completed, and the perp in this case had still not been returned to active duty. It is common for perps to remain free, pending legal proceedings for nonviolent crimes. Perps that are awaiting legal proceedings have not been convicted of a crime yet, so their movements are virtually unrestricted. If a perp wants to run, there is not much in his way to stop him.

The last week in June 1976, anticipating my departure from the US Army in August, Captain McHugh and Chief Thomas selected me to be a support agent on a secretary of defense (SECDEF) security detail in Chicago. The SECDEF's trip was an in/out visit to see the editor of the *Chicago Tribune*. SECDEF Donald Rumsfeld had served in the House of Representatives in the 1960s, representing Illinois. This was my first security detail, but it would not be my last. I was assigned as an advance agent, one who checks security at locations prior to the principal's arrival. On this mission, I was to check the security of the Tribune Tower and the elevators used, as well as inspect the meeting room where the host was to receive the SECDEF during his visiting. Skip Web and another agent, two personal security unit (PSU) special agents from CIDHQ, as it was called back in the 1970s, supervised the detail.

Special Agent Web from PSU and Special Agent Stan Stoner from the Fort Sheridan CID office picked the SECDEF up at Midway airport and drove the SECDEF into downtown to Tribune Tower at 435 North Michigan Avenue. I had conducted my inspection of the inside of the building and the route selected, and I met with key people who were assisting the editor. I was reconfirming the route that SA Web had previously chosen. The SECDEF arrived on time, met with the editor of the *Tribune*, and departed. The entire mission's activities took about an hour and a half, and the SECDEF left without incident.

I was intrigued with the SECDEF security detail and thought that the job had merit. I was fascinated with the job, but I put it out of my mind that someday I might be assigned to the detail in Washington, DC. Since I was pending discharge in August 1976, but contemplating, at a risk, to reenter the US Army CID, the future was in doubt, and any decision about my career direction would be put on hold until I settled my personal affairs.

Although I had made up my mind to leave the US Army, SSG Kornaick approached me about my feelings of attending a two-week Drug Enforcement Administration (DEA) course in Pittsburgh, Pennsylvania, in early July 1976.

"What about my impending discharge?" I bemoaned to SSG Kornaick, because I wanted to go.

"I have checked with the other agents in the office, and most had already taken the course. I figured that since you have done a good job here, I thought you might want to add it to your résumé," SSG Kornaick said.

"I appreciate it, and if you can make it happen, then send me," I told him.

SSG Kornaick's unique negotiating abilities were successful, and I was scheduled for the course in Pittsburgh for two weeks. The course was excellent training not only for those who were assigned to drug investigations but for law enforcement officers in general. The training involved the identification of drugs, surveillance techniques, interviews, interrogations, court testimony, and other aspects of drug investigations. The training I received from the DEA at this course would benefit my career for many years.

After I returned from Pittsburgh, I resumed responsibilities for the investigations I had in the summer of 1976. The workload was light, which allowed more time for me to visit the kids in Terre Haute. On a visit to see her and the kids in late March 1976, I gave Melitta an ultimatum to either join me at Fort Sheridan or get a divorce. She chose divorce and filed later that month, so I returned to Fort Sheridan after that visit and awaited the divorce process.

In June 1976, I received a nasty call from her attorney, accusing me of missing a pre-divorce hearing at her office the day before. I politely told the attorney that if I would have known about the meeting, I would have done my best to be there. I told her that I was never informed about a scheduled meeting. I further pointed out that I should have received some formal notice from her office. The attorney decided not to answer my comment, said good-bye, and hung up. It was typical of Melitta to either forget or simply ignore things she should act upon, such as with the meeting with the attorney.

During the entire assignment at Fort Sheridan, I sent a $600 allotment each month to Melitta for her and the kids. Throughout that time, I lived on $52 every two weeks. One could only imagine what kind of lifestyle I was living. There was one occasion that I needed gas for my car and had no money. I put $10 on a MasterCard that Melitta and I jointly obtained a couple of years prior. Since the billing statement went to our house address in Terre Haute and not to my address at Fort Sheridan, I never saw it. Well, Melitta ignored the bill, and when I attempted to use the MasterCard again, the business proprietor confiscated the card at the request of the credit card company. This situation was extremely embarrassing and inconvenient, and it could have easily been avoided if only she would have sent me the bill; I would have paid it.

My time at Fort Sheridan was slipping by fast, and I found myself facing a major dilemma that was further complicated when I received orders for Baumholder, Germany. Now I was facing three distinct situations that created one gigantic quandary. One, my pending divorce; two, whether to accept the assignment to Baumholder; or three, leave the US Army. I did not want to be in Germany with ongoing divorce proceedings or leave the US Army and a prospering career with the CID. I was in a real pickle. Of course, by leaving the US Army, I would eliminate the problems.

Thinking about the long haul, I could leave the US Army, get the divorce, and then reenter the US Army. Was the risk worth the effort? If I got out, I would have to start developing a new career at the age of thirty. If I left the US Army, could I return to the CID? I had to base my decision on my most serious issue: obtaining the divorce from Melitta. If I kept things status quo, I would always be living apart from the family due to Melitta's refusal to move wherever I was assigned. Plus, if I remained married and kept the career I sincerely wanted, would my quality of life be any good? If I ended the marriage, I would finally be free to pursue a career I wanted and felt strongly that that decision would bring with it the quality of life I was looking for. I thought of one final advantage of divorce: it would allow me better quality time with the kids. I finally decided that the best way to handle my predicament was to leave the US Army, obtain the divorce from Melitta, and pursue all possible efforts to reenter the US Army to continue my career in CID. This decision was the only true one to choose.

On August 20, 1976, I received an honorable discharge from the US Army and returned to Terre Haute, Indiana, for what I hoped was a very short time. Mom arranged with her landlord to let me rent a room next to her for a month or at least until the divorce was final. A couple of days after I got settled into my new digs, I called Melitta and asked when I could drop by to pick up my personal items. Her answer gave me a shock, but then again, it was typical Melitta style. She told me she had given all my clothes to Goodwill, burned my photographs from Vietnam, and tossed out other personal items.

The divorce hearing was scheduled for 10:00 a.m. on September 12, 1976, at the courthouse in Terre Haute, Indiana. I had no money to retain an attorney, so I represented myself. Melitta, her attorney, the presiding judge, and I were the only ones in the courtroom. Melitta's attorney presented her case to the judge. When she mentioned the date of our marriage, I was set back somewhat. The date we got married and our son's birthdate were both wrong. I kept that information to myself, because I knew these inconsistences might cause a delay in the proceedings, pending amendments to the petition submitted by Melitta. I did not want this. The judge ruled in her favor and ordered me to pay child support. The proceedings took about fifteen minutes.

It took me almost two months before I found work as an adjuster with the Meridian Mutual Insurance Company in Peru, Indiana. The employment couldn't have come at a more opportune time, because my mustering-out money from the US Army had run out. On October 10, 1976, I made the move to Peru, found a small apartment, and started work. The work was mundane at best, but the employees were good people. Most had worked in the insurance business for some time and enjoyed what they did for a living. My immediate boss, Bruce Bonencamper, had an affable personality and was good to his employees. There were three adjusters assigned to the office: Dennis Cripe, Greg Huey, and me.

We all shared an office with two other employees, a regional insurance sales rep and the office secretary, Jane Henning.[53] The branch office was in Peru, Indiana, but I worked the entire Miami and Wabash Counties in Indiana. I investigated claims involving auto accidents, thefts, fires, home, and embezzlements. The caseload was incredibly staggering with way too many claims and too few adjusters, but the employment kept me occupied and paid the bills. Melitta had created some unexpected debt I was unaware of, so most of my salary went to these bills. I planned to work for Meridian Mutual until after the new year and then concentrate on returning to the US Army.

The distance from Peru to Terre Haute was about 150 miles. One of the perks of the job was having a company car to use for both personal and business travel. The only difference between using the car for business was that gas was paid for; while conducting private travel, the bill was on you. On most weekends, I had enough time to visit with Chris, Mom, and other relatives that I had not seen in a while. On one occasion, I could bring Chris back to Peru for a two-week visit. We got along great, but work took most of my time. Although I had arranged for Chris to stay with a babysitter during the day, I thoroughly enjoyed the evenings with him. It was a very hectic time, but I managed. After returning Chris to Terre Haute, I had to spend a week in Indianapolis for training. The training was very useful for my work, and I considered it worthwhile.

In March 1977, I felt it was time to start focusing on what I had to do to let the CID know I wanted to come back. It was easier than I'd thought, due to a lot of help from Chief Thomas. I called and ran the idea by him, and he told me he would check and get back with me. The very next day, he called and gave me step-by-step instructions on how to reapply for CID, procedures that were provided to him by CID command headquarters. I was required to seek the assistance of a local recruiter to gather qualifying information to be submitted to the command to evaluate my qualifications for a direct assignment to CID. This process bypassed the routine steps required by an enlistee entering the US Army. The information gathered had to be entered onto a lengthy questionnaire that the recruiter was to obtain from CID command. Once CID command evaluated the information, a decision by them would be made, with the recruiter being used as the conduit.

The day after Chief Thomas's phone call, I went to see the recruiter in Peru. I told him what I needed. Looking somewhat confused and hesitant, he reluctantly complied. It took him two days to coordinate the efforts and get the questionnaire telefaxed. He called me and told me to report to his office the next morning to start the process. I showed up as scheduled, and it took about two hours to complete the questionnaire. He said he would process it and contact me when he heard from CID command. The recruiter, a staff sergeant, looked at me and said, "You must know someone really high up, because I have never processed anyone with prior service like this before."

I assured him that I did know some swell guys in the US Army, but they were a long way from being higher-ups. I thanked him and told him I would anxiously wait for his call. I wanted to get the approval in hand before letting Meridian Mutual know that I was resigning.

It took five days, but when the recruiter called me with the good news that CID had approved my application to reenter the CID program as a special agent, I was ecstatic. As I was celebrating over the phone, my emotional outburst of cheerfulness was apparent to the recruiter. He then interrupted my excitement and said, "It comes with stipulations."

I stopped and asked, "What stipulations?"

"You have to drop down one rank to SP4 and volunteer for a one-year tour in Korea," the recruiter said.

I thought for a nanosecond. "Let's do it," I said.

That afternoon, I broke the news to Bruce, my boss at Meridian Mutual, that I would be leaving the company. Bruce said he understood my decision but was sorry to see me go. He told me that he had just put me in for a pay raise. Knowing that it would not happen, but making the offer anyway, I told him to split the raise between Dennis and Greg because they deserved it. He laughed and wished me good luck.

It took another week to get everything coordinated. I spent another two weeks completing the cases I could and assuring that all the information on the ones remaining open was well documented. The afternoon on my last day, I bid my farewells to everyone and, that evening, attended a small dinner party with Dennis and Greg at a local hangout. I thanked them for their assistance, friendship, and mentorship while at Meridian Mutual and departed Peru the next morning, March 11, 1977, to spend a few days with Mom, the kids, and relatives.

On March 18, 1977, I was required to process back into the US Army at the reception station in Fort Knox, Kentucky, before going to South Korea. On March 21, 1977, shortly after I arrived at Fort Knox, I was administered the oath of enlistment for the third time and was required to stay at the Fort Knox reception station for several days before the US Army decided to authorize leave, pending a port call date (date to arrive overseas). I spent the leave in Terre Haute with family. The time went by slowly, and I was beginning to wonder if the US Army had forgotten about me, so I called the point of contact at Fort Knox that was given to me when I was placed on leave and was told to be patient. On May 2,

1977, I received orders for South Korea with a scheduled port call date of May 9, 1977. The US Army mailed me a commercial plane ticket from Indianapolis to South Korea.

June drove me to the Indianapolis airport, where I caught a flight to Los Angeles. On the flight across the country, I had time to think about how lucky I was to again latch onto a career that I'd almost given up. Hopefully, this time, I would be consistent and make the right decisions and steer all aspects of my life, personal and professional, in the right direction.

**Graduation CID Basic November 1974. I am in the middle second row from top.**

# 7

# Career Back on Track

### Picking Up Where I Left Off

### Korea

*Do not give up on success*

On May 10, 1977, about 10:00 p.m., I arrived in South Korea aboard a commercial flight from Indianapolis via Los Angeles and Manila to Osan Air Base; time in the air was approximately eighteen hours.

On the bus ride into Seoul, I had a lot of time to think of where I stood in life and where I was going. It felt like light-years ago when I'd left Terre Haute, Indiana, to join the US Army in March 1965. Coming to Korea was the closest I had been to Vietnam since leaving that country ten years earlier. President Carter was talking about reducing troop strength in South Korea. If a reduction in troops did occur, I hoped I would first be able to complete a normal tour (a year).

As usual, when I arrived at Camp Corner, the personnel building for Yongsan, luck was not on my side; no one was there to meet me. I noticed an MP standing near a counter as I walked into the terminal. I thought that he might tell me how to contact the local CID office. He had the number on a list at the counter. I did not realize it at the time, but the Yongsan field office (as it was called back then) was only a block from the building where I was. Using the phone at the counter, I called the number the MP provided.

A sharp, distinct, and professional-sounding voice answered, "Special Agent Patrick. Can I help you?"

I informed him I was a new special agent just arriving from the States and wanted assistance in getting to my CID unit. He advised me he was the duty agent for the evening and that he had time to pick me up within five minutes. He instructed me to meet him outside in front of the building. As I hung up, I suspected that no one informed CID I was coming, so I probably would have to arrange for a hotel room for the night.

Special Agent Patrick was right: I had only time to grab my bags and walk to the front of the building, and within a minute or two, he pulled up in a white Chevy four-door sedan. Special Agent Patrick was stocky, had a thinning hairline, and was very talkative. We introduced ourselves, and he helped me place my bags in the backseat of the car. (That introduction was the beginning of a long friendship between the two of us that would last thirty-five years, until Dick's untimely death in March 2012.) He told me that he had not been notified I was due to report in.

"Usually, special agents have sponsors to pick them up," he commented.

I filled him in on my story and how I'd ended up in Korea. He said he now understood why no one was there to pick me up.

"I think there is a bed available at the monastery," he said.

I thought, *I am not a man of the cloth. What is he talking about?* "What is the monastery?" I asked.

"That is where all the geographical bachelors live on their tour in Korea."

Our car sped through the south gate of Yongsan and traveled across a major highway into a housing area. Moments later, Special Agent Patrick turned off the main road and drove around a public swimming pool and stopped in front of a grayish-colored house sitting on a small hill directly behind the pool. Special Agent Patrick helped me carry my bags inside.

Almost immediately after we entered the living room of the building, a drowsy-eyed man entered from one of the five bedrooms in the house. His stocky frame loomed over me as he reached out to shake my hand and introduced himself as Larry Swails.

"Who are you?" he asked.

"Dick Miller," I answered. I then reiterated my story to him. After I was through talking, he stared at me with a bewildered look on his face, creating an awkward few seconds of tension.

Then, pointing with his index finger, he said, "You can take that bedroom there."

The bedroom he pointed to was next to his. As I moved my bags to the bedroom, Special Agent Patrick left the house. SA Swails agreed to escort me to the CID office the next morning. Although I did not know it at the time, much later in our lives, I would consider Larry a good friend well beyond retirement.

The Yongsan field office was colocated with Seventh Region CID at Camp Corner, South Korea. Yongsan had a general meeting at 6:30 the next morning. While getting ready for work, I met the other three SAs residing in the house— Larry Melcher, Beatty Spurr, and Chuck West. They were all very friendly, and each welcomed me to Korea. The mode of travel to the CID office was walking; it took all of us about fifteen minutes.

Yongsan Garrison was crime, black market, fraud, and drug suppression teams. I was surprised to find so many SAs assigned to the office, but I was told on the way into the office that there was plenty of work to go around. I found out later that Special Agent Swails had sent a message to CID command to verify my identity and inquire if my assignment to the unit was legit. Originally created as an Imperial Japanese Army garrison in the early decades of the twentieth century, at the time, the Japanese garrison was on the outskirts of the city in mostly undeveloped land. Since then, the city of Seoul had enveloped the garrison. The United States took over the garrison after the Korea War, and in the 1970s, the installation served as the home of MILPERCEN and headquarters for the Eight United States Forces, Korea. The garrison consisted of two main parts, Main Post (North Post) and South Post, which were divided by a four-lane boulevard that linked two Seoul districts together. Most of the post housing was located on South Post.[54]

The first day, I met with the operations officer, CW4 Brian Smith—tall, medium built, with a full head of hair, and who wore eyeglasses. He was engaging, and from the way he talked about criminal investigations, I got a sense that he was knowledgeable in the field. He gave me his philosophy and how he expected things to go. He was surprised that I was coming directly into the CID from civilian life, and he told me, "Maybe you're not ready to make up your mind about a career."

I spent the next thirty minutes or so trying to convince him that I did want to make the CID my career and explained the history behind my decision to leave the US Army a few months prior. He seemed to accept my explanation and welcomed me to the unit. He indicated that I was going to eventually work for Special Agent Spurr, whom I had already met at the monastery earlier that morning, on the black-market team. Black market would be interesting, I thought. Chief Smith concluded our meeting by telling me he wanted me to help SA Baker in the evidence room, pending receipt of my CID credentials. I felt that the meeting went well and hoped, once I was reissued my CID credentials, I could live up to Chief Smith's expectations.

I was then escorted to the black-market team located in an outer building behind the main CID office and met with my new team chief, Special Agent Beatty Spurr. Spurr looked to be in his mid-thirties, was almost bald, and came off as a pleasant and friendly guy, though somewhat reserved. I filled him in on my story, and he gave me a team chief's expectation of how he wanted the investigations to be completed. He provided me with a brief orientation on how black market cases were worked. I told him that I could not start working until I'd received my credentials from CID command. I noticed when I walked into the black-market team's office that Special Agent Patrick was sitting at one of the desks, so I presumed he was a member of the team. When the meeting with Spurr was finished and as I was getting ready to leave, I looked over at Special Agent Patrick and thanked him for helping me the night before. Without saying anything, he nodded in acknowledgment of my appreciation.

I was then introduced to Special Agent Danny Baker, the unit evidence custodian. Chief Smith had apparently already informed Special Agent Baker that I
would be helping him until I received my CID credentials. Special Agent Baker
was happy that I was going to assist him. He laid out the rules of our working
together. Since a strict adherence to the chain of custody had to be maintained
and everything he had needed to go somewhere, he was required to lock the evidence room door. Therefore, since I was not even a CID-credentialed person yet,
I had to leave the evidence room and either find a place to sit or do something else
until he returned. As I later found out, the drill of Special Agent Baker leaving
and me having to find something else to do until he returned occurred over and
over during the day. I could have been doing something far more productive than
standing next to Special Agent Baker for an indefinite period. But this exercise fell
into the area of "do what needs to be done." It would take about two months
before I received my CID credentials and could work independently.

I learned after only a few days in Korea that I was not officially back in the
CID yet. CID command had to complete an update on my background before
reinstatement. I was called into the personnel department and required to complete more forms on my previous employment and to provide a list of references
and places where I had lived while on hiatus from the US Army. I was prepared
to hang in there, however long it took. In the meantime, I had received permission to become a full-time resident at the monastery. This allowed me to personally get myself settled, but I was more interested in getting to work.

I did not learn a lot, nor was I expecting to by being an assistant evidence
custodian, which was not an official job within CID. Most of my work with Special Agent Baker involved running errands and was mundane and nonproductive.
I guess it did keep me out of people's way until I was cleared to start working.
During our time, together, I got to like Special Agent Baker as a coworker, and
we got along well.

About two weeks after they sent my application to CID, I started checking
with personnel on the status every few days. Whatever. It killed some time.
Finally, in June 1977, I was officially reinstated as a CID SA and reissued my
CID credentials and another .38-caliber service revolver. I then joined the black-
market team as an investigator.

Conducting black-market investigations in Korea was unique and always
interesting. A black market or underground economy is a market in which goods
or services are traded illegally. The term *black-market* is used to identify goods
sold that circumvent the established customs tax laws, rules, and legal procedures
set up by a government. Things that are popular on the black-market include
alcohol, food, electronics, and even hair spray, shampoo, and other household
items. In the 1970s, there were procedures in place to limit the number of items

that soldiers could legally purchase. A ration card had to be used to purchase most of those items and all high-dollar-value merchandise, such as stereo equipment, and other things known to be popular with the locals. One of the most popular liquors that soldiers could make money on was bottles of Johnnie Walker Red and Black. They could purchase a bottle for under twenty dollars and sell it on the black market for up to a hundred dollars.

There were several ways one could sell items on the black-market in Korea. The most prevalent method involved soldiers using their own ration cards to buy items from the commissaries and PXs and then sell them to Koreans. A second method was using a fraudulent ration card manufactured by a small organized group of Koreans. The Koreans had the talent to develop US ration cards that, upon inspection, looked genuine. The third most popular and widespread way to obtain black-market items was smuggling the merchandise into Korea. Black-market cases were some of the most frustrating investigations conducted by CID. Most of the cases involved endless leads that often did not pan out.

I got my first batch of black-market cases in early July 1977. I would thoroughly review every case file to ensure I understood the parameters of each investigation. I kept close to Special Agents Patrick and Spurr and was not afraid to ask them questions before proceeding on my own. Their help kept me on track and saved me from wasting valuable investigative man-hours with unnecessary leads. I will forever be indebted to both for their assistance.

I worked assiduously on every investigation throughout the summer of 1977 and had a good degree of success. However, some of the investigations were too ingrained into the Korean culture to solve. There were way too many people involved in black-market rings, which made it virtually impossible to identity the main perps. Black-market cases were in a lot of ways more difficult to resolve than narcotics investigations. There were too many organized clusters of Koreans involved in these types of cases, and they were thoroughly embedded into the Korean criminal culture. Most of our success came in the form of identifying the lower-end perps: the soldiers.

In the fall of 1977, Special Agent Spurr, who would go on to become an accomplished computer expert and photo analyst for the CID crime lab, was reassigned to take over as the special agent in charge of one of the Second Division areas, and Special Agent James Busha took his place. We all missed Special Agent Spurr, but Special Agent Busha was also a good team chief and a good person to work for. He was professionally competent, had an even temperament, and was a mentor to the team. He was also well liked by everyone. He joined the team that included SA Patrick, SA Ed Rall, and Lonnie Sapp. The team acquired two new members in the summer of 1977: a new probationary agent named Chuck Clark and Special Agent Jeffrey Stevens from Fort Carson. Our two Korean national criminal investigators were a Mr. Han and the legendary Korean CID agent Sam Mo Chong. The Yongsan black-market team was a close-knit group of professional investigators who worked tirelessly to seek out and identify those involved in one of the oldest crimes known to man—crimes that involved fraud or outright larceny and theft of other people's property. The criminals never ceased in developing methods and ways of stealing from others.

Most black-market cases were similar in content and outcome; the same steps were used to investigate, and one investigation was not any more unique than the other. However, in October 1977, there was one joint American-Korean investigation where the entire Yongsan black-market team was used to assist the Seoul Customs House (equivalent to US Customs, now a part of the Department of Homeland Security). The case focused on the operations of a major smuggling ring involving Korean, Japanese, American, British, and Chinese nationals. The Yongsan black- market team spent considerable time assisting the Seoul Customs House on the case, in which they took the lead but allowed our team a lot of leeway to go our own direction in the investigation. The Koreans were very easy to work with and often took notice of CID's expertise in various investigations. They had no trouble sitting down with CID to talk about jurisdictional issues under the status of force agreements signed by them and the United States.

This case stood out because it was the first time the whole Yongsan black-market team was involved in a joint investigation with the Koreans. It was also an investigation that would bring laudatory comments from the Seoul Customs House. I called the investigation the Case of the International Smuggling Gang Inc., which the black-market team investigated as a unit:

## THE CASE OF THE INTERNATIONAL SMUGGLING GANG INC.
Anything sold illegally is always more valuable than legally sold goods

The Seoul Customs House came to the Yongsan CID black-market team and requested assistance with an ongoing investigation involving an international criminal enterprise that was responsible for smuggling Chinese-grown deer horns into the Republic of South Korea. The deer horns, once processed into a fine powder for consumption, have long been thought of as an aphrodisiac. Taking the deer horn powder is thought to boost testosterone levels, resulting in an increased in sex drive; however, some believe its popularity outranks its effectiveness. There is some credible information that the deer horn substance can be used as an anti-inflammatory drug to treat rheumatoid arthritis, osteoarthritis, and other health-related issues. Deer horn powder is extremely profitable, and criminals are willing to take the risk to sell it on the black-market.

The Koreans planned and the joint CID / Korean task force executed the operation. It took us about a week or so to set the operation into motion. Each member of the black-market team had a role; mine involved watching the criminals' activities from about thirty feet away, sitting on a park bench, posing as a tourist, with a female soldier from CID as my partner. Other SAs teamed up with Korean agents at other vantage points in operation. After several days of covert surveillance in downtown Seoul, we arrested Korean, Japanese, American, British, and Chinese nationals, all members of the gang, in the act of transferring about 150 kilograms of illegally smuggled Chinese-grown deer horns worth an estimated value of 150 million won (estimated $2.5 million USD in 1977) on the local commercial market.

Because of our successful investigation, the entire Yongsan black-market team was invited, by Ok Se Yong, director of the Seoul Customs House, to his office, where he presented us with letters of appreciation and a plaque commemorating the successful results of the investigation. He also officially and publicly thanked all of us for our performance during the joint investigation and for the successful arrest of the international group of smugglers. He concluded his remarks at the ceremony by telling those in attendance that the joint investigation was representative of the mutual friendship and cooperation between departments of the Republic of South Korea and the United States of America.

Although I was assigned to the black-market team, I was still required to pull duty about once every week and a half. Usually if I picked up any general crimes cases, I would only be required to conduct the preliminary. Any follow-up investigation required would be conducted by a member of the general crimes team. Some of those preliminary investigations were complex and intense, but I always had the right attitude of "do what needs to be done." Some you wanted to get rid of as soon as you arrived at the crime scene. Yet others you may not want to keep often required many hours of criminal investigations before they were even ready to be turned over to an investigator from the general crimes team. One such investigation that occurred early in my tour at Yongsan that I did not particularly want to keep involved a Korean pedestrian traffic fatality. My portion of the investigation required me to take photographs of the deceased Korean. I call this investigation the Case of the Man Who Did Not Know He Was Dead:

THE CASE OF THE MAN WHO DID NOT KNOW HE WAS DEAD
Death is certain and permanent, or is it?

It was a cloudy, overcast day in June 1977. I was catching up on some long-overdue reports and looking forward to going home. I was hoping for an equally easy, uneventful evening. However, agents never have control over what they wish for and what they get.

About 4:00 that afternoon, Chief Smith called me into his office to advise me a soldier driving a US Army deuce-and-a-half truck had struck and killed an elderly Korean gentleman as he rode his bicycle on a street north of Seoul. Chief Smith reported that when the elderly Korean was hit, his body was propelled more than fifty feet into the air before landing on the heavily trafficked roadway; he was pronounced dead at the scene. The solider driving the military vehicle was being interviewed by the CID duty agent, and the dead Korean was currently at a morgue in downtown Seoul. As part of the overall CID investigation, Chief Smith directed me to go to the morgue and take pictures of the deceased Korean.

I asked Special Agent Jerald Unruh (Jerry) if he would accompany me to the morgue to take photographs of the deceased man. He agreed. It took us about forty-five minutes to navigate the winding, narrow roads in Seoul before we arrived at the morgue. As I parked the CID car, I couldn't help thinking of how easy it would be for any driver to accidently hit a pedestrian or a person riding a bicycle on the side of the road due to the conditions and width of the streets. I wondered if the Koreans had any real safety standards that were enforced. I felt for the soldier who'd struck the Korean, and I am sure he had no intentions of any wrongdoing; unfortunately, he would probably have to face a trial to find out his fate. I could only imagine that the old man started his day like any other and rode his bicycle up and down the same street for years without any incidents, except for today. I gathered the case containing our new 35 mm Canon camera that had just been placed into service by CID. This camera was a welcome replacement for the huge box camera we'd used before.

As Unruh and I walked into the morgue, we were surprised to find quite a few family members already sitting on benches, mourning the loss of their loved one. The elderly man had been dead for only a little over two hours, and to have so many people now at the morgue was unexpected. Over to the side of the room, we found a Korean employee of the morgue who spoke good English. We told him why we were there. He acknowledged the purpose of our visit and directed us to where the body was lying—on a slab in an unrefrigerated room. The room had a large opening, which made it possible to view of the body from the adjoining room, where family members were sitting. As Unruh and I made our way through the throng of people and entered the room where the body was located, I noticed there were no windows or artificial lighting in the room; it was dark, and I could barely see the body on the slab. As I pulled the camera from the case, I could not help noticing that the people in the connecting room could see everything Unruh and I were doing and probably overheard every word we said as well.

The body was lying in a dark room with no refrigeration, a condition that certainly would affect a determination of the time of death; I had to resort to taking photographs with a flash and hoped that my f-stop settings were correct. As I exposed the photographs of the dead Korean in the dark, the flash gave the appearance one would see in a light show on a stage or in slow motion by using intermittent illumination. This effect presented an illusion that the body was moving, but of course, this was not possible because the man was deceased, and we all know dead people do not move, or do they? I momentarily stopped taking photographs to get a visual of the body, and I noticed the fingers on the dead man's right hand twitching ever so slightly, but they did move. I immediately thought that maybe my eyes were playing tricks on me or my eyes had not adjusted to the flashing light of the camera. The longer I looked at the body, however, I was positive it moved. Then the left leg moved. This startled me, and I yelped as I jumped back. I stood there for a few seconds and saw no further movement, but I continued to have visions of the dead man moving. I figured that I had taken enough photographs, and I practically ran from the room.

I hoped the man's family had not seen the dead man's movement. It would be hard to explain to his family that he was dead. You can just imagine what they would think. The proof of the pudding, so to speak, came when we had the film developed. Surprisingly, most of the photographs turned out well; some were a little grainy and blurry but usable.[55]

Since that date in the Seoul morgue, Jerry and I have become friends and have remained in contact throughout the years. Jerry and I kept contact though work-related matters later in our careers, and to this day, we continue to have dinners with fellow retired and active duty CID agents. Occasionally, we will talk about the incident that occurred a long time ago, of the dead Korean national in the morgue that did not know he was dead.

In the fall of 1977, I was promoted to SP5 by the commanding general of USACIDC, Brigadier General (BG) Paul Timmerburg and CID Command Sergeant Major (SMG) Edwin King. BG Timmerburg and SMG King were on a visit to Korea at the time. For the rest of 1977 and the spring of 1978, I stayed busy working black market cases. For the most part, the investigations were routine and time consuming. One case involved a man named John Swain, the true name of a Second Infantry soldier. However, I verified through my investigation that he had left Korea almost a year before I'd gotten into country, and the use of his ration card was as recent as two weeks prior to me opening the investigation. The ration card that had been manufactured by the Koreans was of such good quality when used that it could not be detected as being counterfeit. Several soldiers were involved with the use of Swain's card to purchase black-marketable items, and the amounts totaled into the thousands of dollars. Although many alerts had been put out to the commissaries and post exchanges throughout Korea, no viable leads were generated. The case was not closed when I was transferred from the black-market team in the spring of 1978. This type of case was a typical black-market case we investigated and conceivably could go on forever, usually without being solved.

Social life in Korea was active. Every Friday afternoon, we could take off early and play volleyball and have a cookout. Some agents played cards, other just watched, but everyone had something to do. There were plenty of good restaurants in and around Yongsan. If you wanted to go out on the town, the Itaewon district of Seoul was the closest to the Yongsan military base. Bars, nightclubs, good restaurants, and shopping were abundant. If you wanted a date for Friday or Saturday night, there were plenty of Department of Defense schoolteachers or Red Cross workers that would gladly accept your invitation for dinner at the Embassy Club on South Post. The Embassy Club was the best place to eat a tasteful, quality American meal, especially on a Friday or Saturday night. It was a sophisticated and elegant dining atmosphere.

Entertainment and fun were always our goals on the weekends. However, there was one evening, August 19, 1977, a Friday night, that was a rather somber, gloomy date night. On this evening, my date, a lady from the Red Cross, and I ate dinner in almost total silence because Elvis Presley had died three days' prior on August 16, 1977. The world of music would never be the same.

In the 1970s, Korea had a curfew from midnight to 4:00 a.m. However, some soldiers and, on occasion, CID agents would circumvent the curfew by spending the entire nightly curfew hours at bars that would remain open. One such bar in Itaewon was in the basement of the Hamilton Hotel. They catered to their guests, the locals, and soldiers every night. I never received any mail from home, but on occasions, I wrote Mom letters to let her know how I was doing, and I would call her about once every month or so to check on her. I also became good friends with my roommates, Theo Anderson, who became the Yongsan field office's chief of investigative support (CIS), and Jeffrey Stevens, a fellow member of the black-market team.

One day, I was in Captain Baker's office with operations officer CW4 Brian Smith, discussing the progress of a case I had been working on, when CW4 Smith brought up the subject of me applying for warrant officer.

"Have you put in your paperwork for your warrant?" CW4 Smith asked.

"No, I have not," I replied.

"Well, I think it is about time to get the application completed, and we'll endorse it up the chain," CW4 Smith added.

His comments made me feel good, sort of refreshed and enthusiastic about a career in CID. I informed the two that I would have the request completed and turned in within a week.

I became interested in working narcotics cases, so I applied to attend the DEA Training Academy in Washington, DC. In March 1978, the application was approved with a tentative date of attendance for June 1978. Acceptance at this school determined the direction my career would take for several years into the future. In fact, well before I left Korea, I was transferred from black-market to drug suppression. I accepted this new assignment with enthusiasm. I wanted to learn the ropes on how these types of investigation were conducted.

When I took the lead on the Yongsan Drug Suppression Team (DST),[56] it had not been very productive. The team had no ongoing cases at the time, and I was the only member of the team, having replaced my predecessor, who'd gotten fired and transferred back to the MPs. My analysis of the lack of production of drug cases was quick and to the point. We needed good confidential informants to help develop criminal intelligence on drugs in the Yongsan area. I spent the first two weeks reviewing older drug investigations and trying to get ahold of the current drug trends in the area. I checked with the MPI section of the 142nd MP Company to determine how their level-three drug operations were going and found they had many health-and-welfare seizures resulting in soldiers receiving Article 15s or, worse, being court-martialed and sent to jail. There did not appear to be much coordination between CID and MPI prior to my assuming duties as the Yongsan CID drug team chief.

I met on a regular basis with SP4 William Bryant, MPI, 142nd MP Company, for exchanging information about crime trends, health-and-welfare inspections by unit commanders, and what MPI sources were providing. MPI Bryant and I would also conduct surveillance in and around Itaewon in efforts to develop criminal information on possible drug dealers selling to soldiers in the area. I sought the assistance of unit commanders and 1SGs as well.

One of the first investigative actions I pursued after being assigned to the Yongsan DST was to interview a soldier from one of the maintenance units who had been caught with marijuana in a command-directed health-and-welfare inspection. This effort paid off, because it produced the first legitimate confidential source (CS) for drug information that Yongsan had had in quite a while. I informed the CS that I was only interested in his source of marijuana. I explained to the CS that in exchange for any legitimate information he provided me about his illegal drug connections, I would let SJA and his commander know he had cooperated and that things might go a little easier for him if he chose to cooperate. It did not take him long to consider his options. He agreed to cooperate and gave me details on where he'd purchased the marijuana found in his room during the health-and-welfare inspection.

The CS, who was elevated to a Confidential Informant (CI); a CI are those individuals that are documented informants and on occasions are paid money, admitted that he had bought the marijuana from a soldier at the Incheon Hotel in Itaewon. He informed me that on the night he'd purchased the marijuana, he had met the dealer in a bar in Itaewon. After a few beers, their conversation led to marijuana, and the source implied to the soldier that he had not had any good, strong marijuana since being in Korea. The source said the soldier told the source that he knew where he could get some good "stuff," as he called it. The soldier then told the source if he wanted some, he could get it for him. Instead of the soldier taking the money from the source, going to get the marijuana, and bringing it back, the soldier took the source to his room, located on the fourth floor of the hotel a few doors down from the bar.

The CI told me that when they got to the soldier's hotel room, he saw several small, white paper packets, which turned out to contain marijuana, lying on the bed. The soldier informed the CI that he wanted ten dollars a packet. The CI agreed, and he provided the soldier with twenty dollars for two packets. The CI told me that they then left the hotel room and returned to the bar. The CI said he had purchased the marijuana about a week earlier from the soldier at the hotel. The first thing I thought of was whether the soldier was still selling marijuana from the hotel room. I instructed the CI to do some checking to determine if the soldier was still operating from the hotel room.

The following day, I received a call from the source, who indicated he had run into the soldier the previous evening at the same bar where they met the night he purchased the marijuana. They had a beer together and then went their own way. The CI had also determined he was still in the hotel room, but he did not say how long he would be there. The fact that the soldier was still in the hotel room after more than a week should have triggered my mind into wondering why he was still there. Was he on leave? Was he AWOL? Was he in the US Army? However, I was too focused on catching the "soldier" in the act of selling marijuana to think of anything else.

The CI did not provide any new information about the drug-dealing soldier, but he indicated he was told that he could get marijuana anytime he wanted it. I had no reason to doubt the validly of the CI's information, but an investigator must take all accounts into consideration when dealing with people that have been on the other side of the law. I directed the CI to meet me at 9:30 a.m. sharp at a small café across the street from the Incheon Hotel. He told me he would be there. This case was my first drug investigation in Korea and is most noteworthy for the many twists and turns it took. I called the investigation the Case of the Drug-Dealing Judo Artist:

## THE CASE OF THE DRUG-DEALING JUDO ARTIST
Appearances are not always what they seem

Since the location of any potential controlled purchase of drugs or apprehension of a criminal would most likely be in Itaewon, I needed to get the Korean police involved. I stopped at MPI Bryant's office and told him that a CI had contacted me and reported a soldier was selling marijuana out of a hotel room in Itaewon. I informed Bryant that we also needed to get the Korean police involved because the operation most probably would go down outside the Yongsan military installation.

MPI Bryant coordinated with the 142nd MP Company's Korean national criminal investigator (KNCI), Mr. Kim. KNCI Kim's office was in the PMO building, down the hall from MPI Bryant's. After I finished briefing MPI Bryant, he called KNCI Kim, who joined us in Bryant's office. After Mr. Kim was briefed, he agreed to accompany us to meet with the source near the Incheon Hotel in Itaewon.

KNCI Kim, MPI Bryant, and I left the PMO in the CID car and drove the short distance to meet with the CI at a small Korean café just inside the Itaewon district of Seoul. The source was sitting at a table directly to the right as we entered the establishment. I'd chosen the café because it was directly across the small, narrow, alley-like street from the main entrance to the Incheon Hotel, and you could see anyone leaving or entering the place. Fortunately for us, it was only 10:00 a.m., and there were only two other patrons sitting at a table far enough away so they would not be able to hear our conversation. We all sat down with the CI, and I introduced KNCI Kim and MPI Bryant to him. As I began going over information with the CI, a young Korean waitress came to the table to take our order; we all asked for Cokes. As soon as we got back into our conversation, we had to stop talking momentarily when the waitress delivered our drinks. It is very common for Korean female waitresses to help soldiers with illegal activity, such as dealing drugs.

For the benefit of KNCI Kim and MPI Bryant, I asked the CI to go over the original information he had already provided to me. He reiterated his comments that a US Army soldier was selling marijuana out a room in the Incheon Hotel. Good luck was again on our side. The source told us that just prior to our arrival at the small café, he could see the soldier through the window next to the table where he was sitting. This was good news; he was more than likely in the room at that moment. But first, I wanted to do a quick check inside the hotel to determine if any escape routes could be used by the soldier. While KNCI Kim stayed with the source, MPI Bryant and I went into the hotel.

The hotel building was constructed of brick, probably built before the World War II, and on a scale from one to five, five being the best, the hotel would be given one star. The hotel was used mainly by soldiers staying overnight in Itaewon. Our inspection of the hotel revealed there were no elevators in the building, only stairs leading to the next floor. We walked up the first flight of stairs to the second floor and noticed there were rooms on both sides of the hallway. We walked the entire hallway to check on other exits. The hallways ran in a square from the stairs leading to the floors back to the same set of stairs. There were no doors that could be used for an escape. We inspected all six floors of the building and found the hallways were the same. On the sixth and last floor, we did find a small set of stairs leading to the roof of the building; when we checked it, the door at the top was locked from the inside. We were satisfied we had seen enough of the building to be prepared for any attempted escape by the soldier.

MPI Bryant and I rejoined the CI and KNCI Kim at the café. Luck was still with us, because KNCI Kim informed MPI Bryant and me that the soldier had not been seen leaving the hotel. I went over the final details of the operation. My plan was to take down the drug dealer and not conduct a controlled buy from him. I advised the source to stay put while MPI Bryant, Mr. Kim, and I went to the drug dealer's room. The three of us walked to the fourth floor of the Incheon Hotel and positioned ourselves at the front of the door to the dealer's room. I stood to left side of the door, MPI Bryant the other, while KNCI Kim placed himself behind MPI Bryant. I knocked on the door, and it opened almost immediately.

A bulky, well-built, black male, dressed in civilian clothing and who looked to be in his mid-twenties, appeared at the door, holding it open. "What do you guys want?" he asked.

"You," I responded as I pulled CID credentials from my jacket pocket with the badge showing.

Before I could identify myself by name and that I was with the CID, the man yelled, "Oh, sh———!" He released the door and instantaneously placed his hands on my chest and forcibly shoved me hard, propelling my body backward, knocking me to the floor. As I hit the floor, the uncontrolled perpetual movement of my body continued to hurl my head into the wall on the other side of the hallway with such force I saw stars. His actions were so quick that I did not have a chance to react to his assault. It took me a second or two to regain my senses. As I slowly pulled myself up from the floor, my vision was somewhat blurred, but I could still see the suspect using extraordinary strength to slam himself into MPI Bryant with such force that it knocked Bryant to the floor. With both MPI

Bryant and me out of commission for a second, KNCI Kim gave chase as the suspect attempted to run toward the stairs.

When I could stand on my own two feet, I reached down and helped MPI Bryant to his feet. We looked at each other, and I mumbled, "What the hell did we run into, a buzz saw?"

MPI Bryant just nodded, and we both knew what we had to do. I went left, and MPI Bryant turned right, in the same direction that KNCI Kim had run after the suspect. As we chased him in the hallway, both of us kept yelling, to no avail, for him to stop. The four of us ended up colliding into each other near the staircase. Using both arms, MPI Bryant grabbed the suspect's right arm, and I clutched onto his left while KNCI Kim backed off.

The real fight now began; the suspect continued to struggle as we tried to restrain him. We were both losing the battle. MPI Bryant, finding as much strength as he could, held on to the suspect's right arm, and using all the power my muscles could muster, I tried to pull his left arm behind him, without much success. Using all my strength, I relentlessly held on to his left arm. My efforts brought my body to the point of exhaustion. Momentarily relaxing my grip, to readjust my hold, I inadvertently enabled him to partially free his left arm from my grasp. He took advantage of his temporary mobility to turn his head at a right angle and sink his teeth into my right arm and took a mouthful of flesh, making it bleed. The subsequent pain to my arm caused me to reduce my grip even more. Instantaneously, the suspect had the staying power combined with enough strength left in him to remove an Afro pick from his hair, hold it in his hand, and, with one downward swipe, slash the side of MPI Bryant's left ear, causing a long laceration between his left ear and cheek. Bleeding profusely, MPI Bryant did not let up on his efforts to subdue this violent wild man.

While all this was going on, KNCI Kim removed the belt from his pants and started striking the combative man in his upper torso. I am not sure if KNCI Kim realized it, but each time he struck the suspect with his belt buckle, it struck either me or MPI Bryant, and we also felt pain. The tide suddenly turned in our favor when the suspect became winded and his strength started fading. It seemed much longer, but after about five minutes with him dragging us around the hallway like rag dolls, fatigue set in, and we finally subdued the man. He eventually gave up and allowed us to secure his arms behind his back with handcuffs.

We got him to his feet and walked him back to his room. Once inside the room, the suspect was placed in a chair, and KNCI Kim watched him while I attended to MPI Bryant's lacerated left ear. It appeared that he would require stitches to close the wound. Using my radio, which miraculously had not been jerked from my belt during our struggle, I called the MP desk and advised them of what happened and requested CID be notified.

I then turned my attention to the suspect. I pulled him up from his chair, and as I held him, I searched his pockets and found no identification.

"What is your name?" I firmly asked.

"My name is Daniel Apaqya,"[57] he responded.

"What unit are you assigned to?" I inquired.

"Ha, but I am not in the American military," he quickly commented with a discreet smile on his face.

"What do you mean you are not in the US Army?" I recoiled.

"That is correct, sir," he retorted.

"Well, where are you from?" I probed.

"I am from Ghana, West Africa," he said.

"Where is your identification?" I pushed.

"In the top drawer." He was gesturing with his head.

I went over and opened the drawer and found his Ghanaian passport with other visa-type documents that showed he'd legally entered Korea. A stamp showed that he had been in Korea for about two weeks. I wondered how he could establish an illegal drug connection so quickly. I also wanted to know why he'd come to Korea in the first place. However, I had more pressing issues at hand. I needed to get MPI Bryant to the 120th Evacuation (Evac) Hospital to have his wound treated; I was not so much worried about my injuries. I had to also deal with Apaqya. It took MPI Bryant and me about ten minutes to gather up the suspected marijuana from the suspect's bed and search the room for other contraband; we found none. We secured the dope in a bag for transportation to the CID office.

We escorted Apaqya to the CID car and placed him, still in handcuffs, in the backseat. MPI Bryant, holding on to the seized marijuana, got into the front passenger's side, and KNCI Kim got into the back with Apaqya. Once they were in the car, I went back to the café where we left the CI. There, I spent a moment to debrief him and told him to call me the next day. I then joined the others waiting for me in the CID car and drove to the MP station. I made sure that Apaqya was kept under watch by the MPs while I took MPI Bryant to the 120th Evac.

At the 120th Evac emergency room, both MPI Bryant and I were seen by medical personnel. As we were being treated, Special Agent Kerri Nelson arrived from the CID office and took pictures of our wounds. MPI Bryant's injuries were more serious than we'd thought. He required stitches to close the wound near his left ear. I had my wounds treated without requiring stitches. As we departed the 120th, MPI Bryant, with a big smile, jokingly stated, "I am never going to help you with a bust again."

I smiled and said, "Sure."

I dropped off MPI Bryant at the MP station and immediately went to KNCI Kim's office to thank him for his assistance, a gesture he appreciated. I then picked up Apaqya and escorted him to the CID office for further questioning. On the drive to the CID office, Apaqya was talkative, but I detected that he was being evasive about many things.

At the CID office, I turned the marijuana and Afro pick into Special Agent Danny Baker, the evidence custodian, and joined Apaqya in my office, where I had left him. I needed to know a few things and hoped Apaqya would provide the answers. To establish rapport with him, I removed the handcuffs and allowed him to relax a little and take a drink of the soda I had brought to him and then got down to business.

Before questioning him, I stared at him for a solid minute without saying a word. His reactions as I went through this exercise showed me he was nervous, probably thinking about what the US Army could to do to him. I am sure he was unaware of our jurisdiction over his case. KNCI Kim was coordinating with the Seoul police on what their role would be in his case. Apaqya was not only facing charges for possession and distribution of illegal drugs but also looking at assault, attempting to flee a police officer, and whatever else the Koreans could come up with. Hopefully, he would be cooperative.

"Why did you come to Korea?" I started.

"I came to Korea to learn tae-kwon-do. I have a black belt in another form of judo, and I wanted to learn from the best and to broaden my skills with the sport."

*Damn, no wonder Apaqya could drag MPI Bryant and me around the hallway of the Incheon Hotel with such ease.* Inquiring about his background, I asked him what he did in Ghana.

"I worked for my father, who owns a beer brewery," he said.

That seemed like a good job, I told him, and he nodded in agreement. "How long have you been in Korea?" I asked.

"I have permission to spend up to six months, if they let me," he responded.

"How old are you, Mr. Apaqya?"

"Twenty-four," he replied.

I spent about thirty minutes taking notes on his background and holding off any questions about his illegal drug connections until the right moment. I did this with the sole purpose of making him feel more at ease. If he was more comfortable, he would be more likely and willing to talk. When I saw an opening, I started slowly digging.

"Have you stayed at the Incheon Hotel the entire time you have been in Korea?" I asked.

"Yes."

"Where are your tae-kwon-do lessons?" I inquired.

"In Itaewon, near the Incheon Hotel," he readily provided.

"Is that why you decided to stay at the Incheon?" I asked.

"Yes."

"Have you made any friends since arriving in Korea?"

"Yes. I have been dating a girl from Itaewon," he indicated.

"How did you meet her?" I quizzed him.

"At the Hamilton Hotel."

"Where do you two go?"

"We mainly see each other at the bar downstairs in the Hamilton Hotel."

"How have you been making a living while in Korea?" I inquired.

"My father provided me with money to live on, and it was agreed that when I am short, I contact him and he sends me more money."

"How long were you intending to stay in Korea?" I asked.

"About two months," he responded.

Thinking I had enough background and established rapport to be more direct, I now focused on his drug connections. "Who did you obtain the marijuana from?" I asked.

Bowing his head and looking at his folded hands in his lap, he quietly responded, "A Korean at the Hamilton Hotel."

"Do you know what the Korean's name is?"

"No. I met him the second night I was in Korea. We had a few beers together at the bar. Once he found out I was not an American soldier, he asked me if I wanted some marijuana. He then told me that he had plenty of marijuana and would sell me some. Over the rest of the night, we talked, and at one point, he left the bar and returned about fifteen to twenty minutes later. At this point, he showed me several small, white packets of marijuana and told me I could even make a lot of money by selling it myself." Apaqya continued his story by telling me that if he had not been feeling the effects of the beer that night, he probably would have ended the conversation with the Korean right there. Instead, however, he ended up purchasing the marijuana from the man.

"How many American soldiers have you sold marijuana to?" I asked.

Holding up three fingers on his right hand, he said, "Three."

I figured he was being partially truthful in that he had bought the marijuana and sold some to soldiers. I was not so sure that he was telling me the whole story of his involvement. Had he come to Korea specifically to sell marijuana? Was he telling me the truth when he claimed to have made a chance encounter with a Korean drug dealer?

Who knew? But at that moment, the Korean police showed up and took custody of Apaqya and ushered him off to their station in Itaewon for further questioning. Prior to them leaving the CID office, I also released the marijuana we had seized from Apaqya at the Incheon Hotel to the Korea police to be used as evidence in the case again him.

After his arrest by the Korean police, I never heard any further information about his case. Shortly after he was released to the Koreans, I left country for my assignment to Fort Riley, Kansas, and was never contacted to appear in court or for any other information concerning the case. I guess the Koreans' case against him was tight because he had been caught with the marijuana in his possession.

When I took over the DST, I knew it was for only a few weeks, because I was scheduled to rotate to the States. About a week before I left, SA Michael H. Curlee was assigned to take my place. Mike had been in Korea for some time but had prior experience working undercover cases. Mike, who was over six feet and solidly built, was a person who could handle himself in any dangerous situation. He had a low-key personality and was never known to lose his composure. He was well liked by others, and I wish I'd had more of an opportunity to have worked with him, but the short time I had left in Korea prevented this from happening. Our paths never crossed again. I heard Mike had retired in the late 1980s from the CID at Fort Lee, Virginia, and became a private investigator. Unfortunately, Mike was taken from us way too early by cancer.

In the short time, in between me leaving the DST and my departure from Korea, I was utilized as a catch-all man. While in this temporary status, Seventh Region informed me that the DEA school that I had been scheduled to attend in June 1978 had been delayed until January 1979. I was given a choice of either extending my tour at Yongsan or departing Korea as scheduled for Fort Riley. If I chose to proceed with my assignment to Fort Riley, I would still be able to attend the DEA school in January 1979. I chose to leave Korea on time and wait for the DEA school while at Fort Riley. About two weeks before I was scheduled to depart Korea, I received notification from CID command that my application for warrant had been approved. My appointment date had been set for July 28, 1978.

In the meantime, during my time remaining in Korea, I was used to help other agents interview people on their cases. The cases I helped with were usually those on their way to being cold cases or those investigations that had command interest. Many of the interviews or investigative activity required were found when I was given the case files for review.

However, one case I became associated with was an ongoing death investigation of a young black soldier named James Andrews,[58] who was found dead in a wooded area, with his hands tied behind his back, hanging from a tree. The investigation focused on whether he'd committed suicide or was murdered. If he'd committed suicide, there was nothing at the scene that could have been used by the victim to stand on and then knock away as he hanged himself. Having his hands tied behind him with rope was also inconsistent with a person who'd hung himself in the act of suicide.

> In a suicidal hanging, there is a characteristic inverted V bruise on the neck, which corresponds to the rope pressure. With strangulation, such as in murder, this bruise appears in a straight-line fashion around the neck, which corresponds to the pressure causing asphyxia.[59]

If Andrews had choked, his neck would show straight-line bruising and internal damage instead of breaking his neck, indicative of hanging. Because of the recency of death, the interview I conducted on this case was without the benefit of an autopsy.

This case is on my list of most memorial investigations because of the unusual circumstances surrounding the death, and I had an unexpected run-in with Sergeant Samuel Jennings, the person I'd interviewed as a witness in a case at Fort Riley, Kansas, several months later during a drug investigation. Since the US Army has a somewhat closed society compared to the general population and the chance of an individual running into the same person in a follow-up assignment is not that unusual, I am sure this situation has occurred before, but not to me. I call this investigation the Case of the Man Who Committed Suicide, or Did He:

THE CASE OF THE MAN WHO COMMITTED SUICIDE, OR DID HE?
When working undercover, always anticipate the unexpected

In early May 1978, I was sitting in my office, daydreaming about my impending assignment to Fort Riley, Kansas, and that my tour in Korea was coming to an end, when SA Willie Daniels, the Yongsan field office general crimes team chief, came waltzing into my office. Willie, as he was called by the senior agents in the office, had a stellar reputation within CID. He was older, or at least he looked older than other senior agents. He always had the habit of chewing on a cigar, and although I am sure he had, I can never recall a time when I saw Willie light the cigar, only that he had one in his mouth. Since I was still a junior agent, out of respect, I always addressed him as Mr. Daniels.
Without elaborating, he blurted out in his usual gruff voice, "Miller, I want you to do an interview for us. We have several people in the waiting room, and the team needs help interviewing them."

I asked to be briefed on the case, and he sent in another agent from the general crimes team, who brought me up to date on what their investigation had developed so far. The agent told me the investigation had not identified any information to indicate the death was other than a suicide. The agent advised me that the bruising and markings on Andrews's neck were consistent with hanging.

I was assigned to interview a Sergeant Samuel Jennings[60] from the Second Infantry Division. Jennings was not a suspect but a person who was assigned to the same unit and knew the dead soldier. I was supposed to gather as much information about the dead soldier's personality, activities, and associates as I could.

I brought Sergeant Jennings into the office and sat him next to my desk. Sergeant Jennings was a young-looking man in his early twenties, appearing to be in good physical condition and confident in his demeanor. I started by letting him know the purpose of the interview was to gather background information about Andrews. At the time of the interview, I was unaware of the type of information filtering down to the unit about the manner of Andrews's death. I asked a series of questions about the dead soldier's attitude. Sergeant Jennings appeared to be cooperative and sincere when answering my questions. My questioning went something like this:

"How well did you know Andrews?"

"Not well. I only knew him from running into him at unit functions or in the mess hall."

"Did you ever have a conversation with him about how he felt or get a feel for his emotional state?" I asked.

"No. Like I told you, we were not very close," responded Jennings.

"Was Andrews having any financial- or martial-type problems?"

"I have no idea," Jennings replied.

"Did you know some of the people he ran around with?" I inquired.

"No. As I said before, I did not know him that well."

"Are people talking about his death in the unit?"

"Yes. Everyone is thinking he committed suicide," Jennings fired back.

"Have you heard of anything else concerning how he died?" I asked.

"No. As I said, everyone thinks Andrews committed suicide," Jennings reiterated.

I had spent about forty-five minutes talking to Jennings and felt he was being truthful about everything I asked him, and I did not think he had anything else to offer. I decided the interview covered everything needed and terminated it without any concerns, so I thought. I would not feel the full ramifications of this interview until a few months later at Fort Riley, Kansas. I left Korea a short time after this interview without knowing if the soldier hanging from the tree was murdered or did in fact committed suicide.

Another investigation I worked occurred only two days before I was to leave Korea. It involved a fatal traffic crash of a Second Infantry Division soldier from Camp Casey. It was May 5, 1978, a Friday afternoon. I was in my office finishing up agent's investigations reports (AIR) on a couple of cases I had when I received a call from the duty agent. He told me he was calling from a crime scene he was working on involving an aggravated assault. The duty agent asked if I could go to the 120th Evacuation Hospital and take photographs of a soldier who had been killed in a jeep accident on a narrow road north of Seoul the night before. The deceased soldier had been medevac'd from the scene of the accident to the 120th, where an autopsy could be performed. I was also requested to check with the pathologist to determine the time an autopsy would be performed.

I was assured that I would not have to attend the autopsy, because the Camp Casey CID had the case and would be sending an agent from their office. The duty agent further justified his plea for my help by letting me know he already had three investigations backed up and that he would be spending the rest of the day on them. I asked him if he had tried to get another agent in the office to help him.

"Yes, but it is Friday, and all of them have already departed for the weekend," he said, pleading his case to me.

I empathically agreed. This case was significant; it was the last investigation I was involved with during my tour in Korea. My involvement with the case occurred on a Friday afternoon, and I was due to leave Korea the following Monday. Most cases do not go as smoothly as you would like them to, and this one was no exception to the rule. I called the investigation the Case of the Soldier Who Went Home Before His DEROS:

## THE CASE OF THE SOLDIER WHO WENT HOME BEFORE HIS DEROS
Destiny rules everything in your life

I wrapped things up at the office and hopped in a CID car for the ten-minute drive to the 120th. I went directly to the morgue and found a hospital medic cleaning a slab, apparently getting ready for an autopsy. I asked to see the body they had brought in the night before. The medic motioned for me to follow him into the next room, where the body was lying in a refrigerated drawer.

When the morgue attendant pulled the body out for viewing, I noticed it had not been prepped for an autopsy yet. In fact, the deceased soldier's body was still fully dressed in his fatigue uniform. I examined the body from head to toe and found no visible injuries. I inquired if an autopsy was scheduled, and the attendant indicated he did not know. He provided me with the name of the pathologist who was most likely to perform the procedure. I exposed photographs of the deceased soldier while he was lying on the slab in the morgue. More photographs of any injuries would have to be taken during the autopsy.

After exposing photographs, I located the pathologist's office. He was not in but due to be back later in the afternoon. I returned to my office and telephoned Camp Casey CID and informed them that the autopsy had not yet been scheduled, but I should have that information by late afternoon.

Finally, at 4:00 p.m., I was notified that the autopsy was scheduled for 9:00 on Monday morning. I informed the Camp Casey agent, who would be attending the autopsy, the time and date and advised him that I had taken some photographs of the body. However, they did not depict anything of evidential value, and more photographs would have to be taken at the autopsy. This case involved another example of how a person's life is so fragile and can change in an instant. The poor, ill-fated soldier had no inkling when he'd hopped into his jeep the night of the accident that it would be his last, that in a few moments his life would disappear, especially quickly, cease to exist, come to an end, and he would meet his maker. I left Korea without knowing the exact cause of the soldier's death.

My Korean tour was a good experience that allowed me to nourish and hone my investigative skills. It also was the start of what I'd hoped to be a lasting career in criminal investigations. Korea involved a series of firsts for me. It was my first US Army assignment after my divorce, my first overseas CID assignment, and my first supervisory CID assignment on the DST. Fort Sheridan provided an increase in investigative knowledge; Korea offered an invaluable degree of investigative experience.

The most significant difference between Fort Sheridan and Korea was the caseload and variety of investigations. A large portion of investigations at Fort Sheridan involved leads mostly into Chicago, and many duty days were case-free. Korea provided an in-depth picture of what a CID special agent's job is all about, and agents virtually never slept on scheduled duty days. One thing consistently brothering me was my ever-deteriorating hearing. So far, I could deal with the problem without major consequences.

Some good events occurred while in Korea. Special Agents Kerri Nelson and Ed Rall and Special Agent Michael Curlee and Glenda, the Yongsan field office army clerk, were married. I had developed lifelong friends that I continue to have contact with today. I always wanted to work narcotics cases, and the assignment in Korea afforded me the opportunity to begin this phase of my career. I was approved for attendance at the DEA training session in Washington, DC, to begin in January 1979 and selected to be promoted to warrant officer one at the end of July 1978.

A few days prior to catching the state-bound bird across the Pacific Ocean, I was approached by my former team chief, who never supervised me, and advised that since I was not an officer, I would not be put in for any type of medal. However, the customary procedure, he said, was to give all enlisted people a certificate of achievement signed by the region commander. He asked me if I had any problem with this policy, and I informed him that I did not. In retrospect, this policy was flawed, because it meant that all enlisted men and women who deserved service and achievement medals would not receive them, but officers would benefit from this policy at the expense of the enlisted soldiers.

At the time, I departed Korea, my career stood solid and was running smoothly down the track. I now had two great CID assignments under my belt and was truly looking forward to continuing my good future in a gratifying career at Fort Riley, Kansas, but since I had been selected to attend the DEA national academy in January 1979, I was offered the opportunity to extend my Korean tour to coincide with the starting date of the course. I respectfully declined that opportunity and requested to leave on my original DEROS.

On May 9, 1978, I boarded a commercial flight at Osan Air Base and began the long journey to Indianapolis, Indiana, via stops in San Francisco and Minneapolis. I was finally leaving the Land of the Morning Calm. It had been a good assignment, and I had turned up the burner on my investigative career.

The Yongsan CID black market team being recognized by the Seoul Customs House for out-standing work on a case that netted the seizure of in excess of 150 million won (Korean money) in ground-up deer horns (an aphrodisiac), smuggled in to avoid Korean import taxes by an American, Chinese, British, and Japanese smuggling ring. The special agents of the team—first row from left to right: Team chief James Busha, Walter Edwards, Dick Patrick, Jeff Stevens, KNCI Han. Back row from left to right: Lonnie Sapp (face hidden), Dick Miller, Ed Rall, Glenda Curlee, and KNCI Sam Mo Chong. Edwards and Curlee were not members of the team but brought in specifically for the investigation.

The author obtaining a confession from a soldier in a black market case, Yongsan District, circa 1977. Notice Special Agent Jeff Stevens sitting in front of me, working diligently.

Author getting promoted to SP5 by BG Paul Timmerburg and CID SMG Edward King, summer 1977 at Yongsan District.

At Yongsan District, saying farewell to Special Agent Larry Melcher, who was headed back to the States. He is being presented a plaque by commander Captain Robert Baker with the author (left) and Special Agents Willie Daniels (sitting) and Chuck West looking on.

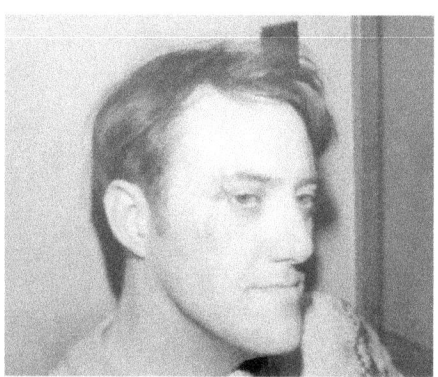

Author at 120th Evacuation Hospital in Seoul, getting treatment after arrest of West African drug dealer, circa 1977.

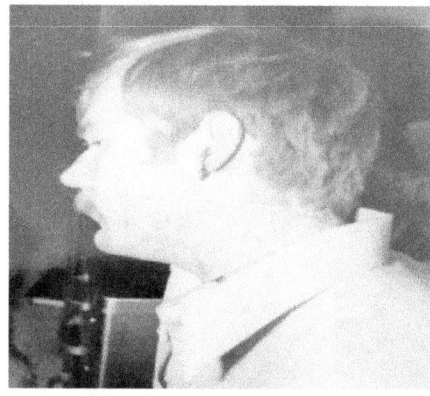

MPI Bryant at 120th Evacuation Hospital in Seoul, getting treatment on his ear after arrest of West African drug dealer, circa 1977.

# 8

# Career Going Forward

New Venture, New Friends, Enhancement of a Career

Fort Riley
*Never languish on your laurels, but build on them*

*A*fter an exhausting thirteen hours in the air and more than three hours of layovers, my flight arrived at the Indianapolis airport at precisely 12:45 p.m. on May 9, 1978, and June, her son, Charlie, and Chris were waiting for me. I was ecstatic to see them. I had previously arranged to pick up a new Chrysler at a local dealer not far from the airport. The car was ready for me when I got there. Chris and Charlie rode to Terre Haute with me, while June followed in her car. It was good to be home for a while. After spending a week and a half with Mom, Chris, Robert, and relatives, I headed by car to Fort Riley to begin another venture.

I took two days to make the five-hundred-plus-mile trip from Terre Haute to Fort Riley. My first sight of Fort Riley was when I crested a hill on I-70, about two miles from the main entrance. It was an awesome sight to behold. The view from I-70 of the sprawling plains was breathtaking; one can see for miles, yet Fort Riley was mostly concealed by trees and brush. The beauty of the area was like a painting. I turned onto the access road, crossing over the Kansas River into the Marshall Army Airfield area of Fort Riley. After I found out I was being assigned to Fort Riley, I researched the history of the installation and ascertained it was named after Major General (MG) Bennett C. Riley, whose career spanned from the War of 1812 to the Mexican-American War. MG Riley also served as the last territorial governor of California. He died in 1853 and is buried in Buffalo, New York.[61]

My initial information on the location of the Fort Riley CID office placed it in a building on Marshall Army Airfield, off the access road directly to the right. I drove around until I found a two-story, wooden, World War II–era building at the end of the airfield. I got out of my car, and as I approached the front door, I saw a sign that told the visitor the CID office had moved to another building in the headquarters section of the installation. I jotted down the new building number. About ten minutes later, I found the CID office that was now located in a two-story stone structure fitting the style of others like it in the area.

Because of the time and the probability that most of the agents and support personnel had gone home for the day, I debated whether I should check in immediately or wait until the next morning. I decided to at least check to see if the duty agent was in. I entered the unlocked building, which indicated to me that there were people inside. I immediately encountered a tall, slender man in his thirties, who came out of an office near the entrance and asked what I wanted. I introduced myself. In a friendly manner, he replied, "Hey. My name is Joe Hite. I am the duty agent. Welcome aboard. We heard you were due in soon."

Joe invited me into the office he had just came out of, which served as the duty agent's room. The moment I walked into the room, I saw a stack of about five or six case folders lying on the desk. This delighted me, because I liked to work.

"Have you had a busy duty day?" I inquired.

"Yes, it has been that kind of day," he responded.

Joe sat down in his chair, and I sat in the only other chair in the office. He gave me an overview of the office—who the agents were, operations, commander, and who was assigned as support staff. He informed me that he had been assigned to Fort Riley for almost a year. We continued with small talk, and I then told him I should get a place to stay for the night. To determine the time that I should report in the morning, I asked Joe if the office had the customary regularly scheduled morning meeting; he indicated it was at 8:00 a.m.

I asked for directions to a good motel, and he said, "I'll do better than that. I will show you where we usually put people when they visit." Without telling me the name of the motel, he commented, "It is a good place to stay and has an on-site restaurant."

I followed Joe in his car a short distance to the Hilton Inn just outside of Junction City, the town next to Fort Riley. I invited him to dinner, but he declined, indicating he wanted to get some work done before he got another duty call. I thanked him for his assistance, and he headed back to the CID office. I had no trouble getting a room and was also in luck; the restaurant was open until 10:00 p.m. I ate a good meal, and anticipating the next day being a busy day, I turned in early and slept like a baby.

The next morning, I arose at 6:00 sharp, put my best suit on, got ready for the day, ate a leisurely breakfast in the hotel restaurant, and headed out for my first day at the Fort Riley CID office.

It took me about fifteen minutes to drive to the CID office. I arrived at 7:45 a.m., and the first person I met when I walked through the door was SA Floyd Kelley, the chief of investigative support (CIS). CIS Kelley, a stern-faced individual dressed in conservative sports jacket and slacks, dispensed with small talk and told me he was headed for the morning meeting, which was held in the basement of the building. I followed him downstairs and saw the entire office of agents milling around, waiting for the meeting to start. I did not recognize anyone from previous assignments. The introductions would come later, because the meeting immediately started as I entered the room. The meeting was routine and involved the usual briefings of new information about office procedures and so on, as well as what cases were initiated the day before. It lasted about thirty minutes. This was a good sign that the meetings served their purpose. After the meeting broke up, everyone started heading to their offices for the day's work.

A couple of agents started walking toward me, but before they could introduce themselves, CIS Kelley immediately stepped in front of me and, with no exchange of pleasantries, told me, "Check with SSG Ed Devall, the supply sergeant, to see if your weapon has arrived."[62] He then introduced me to the operations officer, CW4 (SA) Jearl E. "Bucky" Ballow, who asked me to come to his office. Chief Ballow, a tall, stoutly built man who was in his retirement assignment, took about thirty minutes to give me his spin on the makeup of the office. He then introduced me to the commander, Lieutenant Commander (LTC) Donald Evans, who was already busy working the telephone but stopped long enough to shake hands and welcome me to the office. Chief Ballow advised me that he was assigning me to General Crimes Team (GCT) A and that my boss would be SA Ronald E. Corbett. Team Chief of GCT-B was SA Richard (Dick) Dawson.

Chief Ballow called SA Corbett to his office and introduced the two of us. SA Corbett then took me to meet the members of GCT-A. I was happy to learn that Joe was a member of the GCT-A and that my desk would be next to his. Joe and I would develop a good friendship that would extend beyond Fort Riley to Germany and into retirement. Others on the team were SA Jennet (JJ) Johnson and SA Ralph Wayne Staley. SA Raymond Lyons, fresh from the CID basic course, would join the team later, but he fell into some trouble and was released from CID. Finally, SA Donald Shanley and SA Timothy Graham joined the office after my arrival. Don served as the assistant operations officer. SA Corbett introduced me to Team Chief Dawson, SA Jose (Joe) Chavez, and SA David G. Ownby. The drug team was run by SA David Deitz. Others would come and go, but the agents mentioned are the ones I developed good working relationships with, and I would run into them periodically throughout the rest of my CID career.

Each GCT was divided into sections that were further separated into smaller areas that agents handled. SA Corbett chose to assign me to units that were clustered in or near the post headquarters. My area of investigative responsibility included incidents involving MPs, several tenant units, and Camp Funston, the location of the US Army Correctional Training Facility (CTF), commonly referred in the 1970s as the US Army Retraining Brigade (USARB).

USARB was a program designed for soldiers who had committed what was mainly considered purely military-type crimes, such as AWOL, poor performance, and other such infractions, some criminal in nature, where the offense gained the subjects fewer than two years, but primarily one year in confinement. The US Army opened the program in 1968 to rehabilitate and retrain soldiers who seemed worthy of a second chance. Once they successfully completed the course, they would be returned to duty.

USARB was broken down into units with designation of unit one, two, three, and so on. From what I recall of the organization, the training was designed to see how the soldier's performance was when he was placed under sustained physical and mental stress within a stringent military environment. The various elements of training included evaluation, counseling, basic educational skills, problem identification, motivational training, and adventure training. Ongoing postgraduate studies by USARB staff of the soldier's performance after his release from the program determined the success of the USARB's mission.

It took me about two days to get settled in and gradually start receiving cases. I pulled my first duty day about a week later. Other than initiating more cases per duty night, the work was the same as my other CID assignments. Within a month, I was receiving an average of five cases per day, with other agents picking up few to no cases. It appeared that each duty agent would pick up cases that fell into my area of responsibility. I felt uncomfortable bringing this issue up to Chief Ballow, but I did discuss the trend with Team Chief Corbett. He acknowledged that most cases appeared to occur in my area of responsibility.

There was another observation about the caseload as well. I was receiving an inordinate amount of small, insignificant housebreaking and larceny cases. As an example, one involved the theft of a jar of peanut butter and a loaf of bread from a dining facility at USARB in Camp Funston. Another investigation was initiated as a housebreaking and larceny of a barracks at Camp Funston. In this case, there was evidence that a break-in did occur. A screen had been cut, and trace evidence showed person(s) unknown did gain entry to the building, but there was nothing stolen.

I felt these types of minor crimes should best be handled by MPI and that CID should concentrate on the more serious crimes. To conduct a thorough investigation, I had to consider the possibility of interviewing hundreds of suspects. The crime involving the missing jar of peanut butter was probably committed by some poor young soldier who'd gotten hungry during the night of the incident and knew what he was looking for. Fort Riley CID did not have any formal memorandum of understanding (MOU) with the provost marshal. This would eventually change in the future. A large portion of my caseload in the post headquarters area would have been identified as being cases that fell into this category and it would be reasonable to delegate the investigation to

MPI. If a modified MOU, allowing housebreaking and larcenies of $250 or less, were in effect, the CID caseload would have been much better managed. (MOUs at the time involved thresholds of $500 and covered most thefts.)

In early August, Special Agent Donald Shanley reported to Fort Riley. Right away, I saw Don as a leader and mentor. He immediately connected with all the agents in the office. He was coming off a tour in Heilbronn, Germany, and did not waste any time pitching in to work.

In early fall 1978, Chief Ballow was selected to attend a service training school at Fort McClellan, and Don did a superb job as the temporary operations officer. About the same time, my caseload had ballooned upward to over forty cases at any given time, most involving minor thefts and having few leads. Under Don's skilled management techniques and direction, agents in the office worked together to successfully reduce the caseload. All agents in the office worked diligently to complete all the leads possible and close out the less significant cases that were taking up valuable time, which allowed all agents to dedicate themselves to the serious investigations.

In June 1978, I was assigned to conduct a crime prevention survey (CPS) of Camp Forsyth. Forsyth was one of four major locations on the Fort Riley post. The others were Custer Hill, where the First Infantry Division troops and family were housed; the main post, Camp Whiteside; and Camp Funston. Forsyth was more isolated and an out-of-the-way place for the Fort Riley headquarters staff to have a quiet beer (or two) before heading home for the evening. Well, it was my assigned duty to check the club out for any type of crime trends. My reputation at Fort Riley took a significant surge south in the conduct of what I called the Case of the Angry First Infantry Assistant Division Commander Who Couldn't Get Another Beer.

## THE CASE OF AN ANGRY ASSISTANT DIVISION COMMANDER WHO COULDN'T GET ANOTHER BEER

Special agents are better off knowing who is drinking at the officers' club before undertaking actions on the operation of the facility while conducting a crime prevention survey

Part of the assigned duties for a US Army CID special agent is to conduct CPSs to identify any potential crime trends, system flaws, and actual criminality and to generate assistance by indicating what type of corrective actions should be taken on vulnerabilities found. In June 1978, I had been assigned to conduct a CPS on the operations of the Camp Forsyth branch of the post officers' club system. This was my first CPS, and before I set out for my inspection of the club, I wanted to do enough research so I would not come across as a numskull, so I had done my homework on the club and read the manuals of club management.

Back in the late 1970s, the US Army club system was still a mecca for entertainment of the troops, and on certain nights, they would schedule happy hours for reduced drink prices, usually at half-price between 4:00 and 7:00. During the happy hour period, club personnel were required to use a separate cash drawer to account for the receipts of reduced-price drinks and another preset cash drawer for regular-priced drinks. My first step was to spend a couple of nights at the bar in a semi-covert status as a patron so I could observe the actions of the bartender and wait staff. My efforts revealed that they were not using a separate cash drawer for happy hours. The third night, I decided to do a quick accounting of the money in the happy hour cash drawer, but I did not imagine what would occur when I followed through on this task.

The third night landed on a Friday. I entered the club at about 4:00 p.m. and sat at the bar as usual. The same bartender who had been there the previous two nights greeted me. Obviously from me being at the bar the previous two nights, he recognized me.

"You want your usual?" he asked.

"Yes," I responded.

He gave me a draft beer, and I nursed it just like the previous two nights. I planned to observe him, the wait staff, and the patrons of the club until about 7:15 p.m. The time was significant because it allowed enough time after happy hour to end to see if the bartender would insert a new cash drawer for use for receipts of the normal-priced drinks. If not, I would shut him down, pending this action.

At precisely 7:15 p.m., the bartender had not changed the cash drawer, so I confronted him, explained what was taking place, and advised him to change the cash drawers.

"I can't," he said.

I asked, "Why?"

"I do not have a second cash drawer prepared," he responded.

"You do know the club management rules and regulations require a second cash drawer to be ready after happy hour ends," I explained.

"Yes, but it has always been the club's habit to use one cash drawer," he said.

In the meantime, drink requests kept coming in, especially from a table with about ten junior and midlevel officers in uniform and one colonel. Unfortunately for me, the colonel was none other than Colonel (P) John (Jack) T. Quinn, assistant division commander of the First Infantry Division. The (P) is his rank meant he was being promoted to Brigadier General.

Apparently, Colonel Quinn had brought his staff to the club for drinks, and he was not very happy that I'd stopped the flow of beer to their table. Although I was conducting my CPS investigation of the club correctly, it did not matter to Colonel Quinn, who, without speaking to me directly, decided to call LTC Evans, my commander, and inquire as to what the hell I was doing. Fortunately for me, LTC Evans stood his ground and advised Colonel Quinn that his agent was conducting a CPS within the required US Army rules and regulations. When Colonel Quinn ended his conversation with LTC Evans, he then gave the phone to the bartender. Politely, the bartender was considerate enough to speak to LTC Evans before hanging up. LTC Evans asked to speak to me. I took the phone from the bartender's hands and addressed LTC Evans.

"You are not going to the NCO club, are you?" LTC Evans asked.

Hoping that he was joking, I said, "No."

"Good. I briefed Colonel Quinn, and not only is he extremely angry, he is put out by CID's activities and said he would take the issue up with MG Kaplan, the division commander, Monday morning," LTC Evans said.

*I can hardly wait to see how this turns out,* I thought.

Strange things happen in the US Army, but my good fortune prevailed in a lot of ways. LTC Evans, who routinely attended First Infantry Division weekly staff meetings, commented to me later that Colonel Quinn never brought up the subject again. More than a year later, in August 1979, I personally briefed MG Kaplan on the Fort Riley drug suppression operations, and guess who was in attendance? Colonel Quinn. But the matter of the actions I took while conducting the CPS at the Forsyth officers' club never surfaced. After a long and industrious career, John T. (Jack) Quinn retired as a brigadier general in June 1986 and died of natural causes on December 24, 2006.

During the summer months, the US Army conducts six-week summer training camps for Reserve Officer Training Corps (ROTC). Army ROTC is one of the most demanding and successful leadership programs in the country. The training a student receives in army ROTC teaches leadership development, military skills, and career training. Courses take place both in the classroom and in the field and are mixed with normal academic studies. Additional summer programs, such as jump school, may also be attended. Upon completion, an army ROTC graduate is given a commission as a second lieutenant (2LT).[63] During the summer of 1978, I investigated the theft of an M16 rifle from an ROTC unit during one of their bivouacs. I call this investigation the Case of the Wannabe Commissioned Officer Who Had His M16 Stolen:

## THE CASE OF THE WANNABE COMMISSIONED OFFICER WHO HAD HIS M16 STOLEN
Some cases are just not solved

It was a hot day in mid-June in 1978, when one group of university ROTC students was deployed to Fort Riley on its annual six-week summer camp. Their training was routine but stressful and involved the usual topics of leadership, military tactics, battlefield strategies, and military careers. Part of this training involved bivouacking for a few days. The ROTC students were dressed in full battlefield fatigues, backpacks, canteens, and assigned M16 rifles. On their first night in the field, the group set up a base camp in a remote training site on the northern part of Fort Riley. Everyone was scurrying around getting last-minute chores completed before turning in for the night. Guards were scheduled to provide roving patrols in the area, where the men positioned their two-man pup tents. Instructions were given to the men to keep their M16 rifles and other equipment inside their tents as best they could when they were sleeping. About 11:00 p.m., the bulk of ROTC students had crawled into their tents, and the only movement was the guards walking up and down the rows of tents.

At 5:00 the next morning, the men started slowly climbing out of their tents and performing the tasks to get themselves ready for the new day of training. Shortly after one of the ROTC students woke and was exiting his tent, he noticed that his assigned M16 rifle was not where he'd laid it the night before. He thought the M16 had slid underneath his air mattress, but when he checked, he did not find it. He scrambled in and around his tent in a desperate attempt to locate the M16, without success. His tent partner's M16 rifle was not missing. The panic-stricken ROTC student checked with several of his colleagues that had their tents close by, but they all had their M16s. After about thirty minutes of searching, he gave up searching and reported his M16 had been stolen. The theft of the US Army's primary infantry weapon could not be treated lightly.

The investigation took several weeks, and no suspects were identified. We eliminated the ROTC student as a suspect; the victim's tent partner and others that were settled in close to the victim were also discarded as suspects. Our investigation did not disclose any leads at all. We checked with support units who assisted the ROTC group to set up their camp and did an intensive canvass of the area, including ranges and range personnel. Local pawnshops, known military equipment stores, gun dealers, and hunting clubs were all checked, with no leads developed. The CID ran several polygraph examinations, with no indication that the people interviewed were not telling the truth. The case was one of the most frustrating investigations of my career. Even after the case was closed, each time I came across the slightest bit of information that might lead to anyone, however remote, I followed up on it. It is frightening to know that there is someone out there who has possession of a US Army M16 rifle. It is also scary that the motives of the person or persons responsible for the theft of the M16 rifle are unknown.

On July 28, 1978, I pinned on my warrant one bars, and Special Agent Hite was promoted to SFC in back-to-back ceremonies at the Fort Riley CID office. The two of us held a party that was attended by most people at the office. I felt good about obtaining warrant and was satisfied that the promotion fit right into the steady upward swing of my career. I continued to be assigned multiple cases almost daily. I rolled up my sleeves and charged ahead, resolving them as swiftly as I could. The summer of 1978 was fast paced, the weeks and months running into each other at a speed I had not felt before.

In early September 1978, CID command sent word that the DEA course I had been approved for in Korea, but that had been delayed, was scheduled from January 3, 1979, through March 16, 1979. With the DEA training date now set, Chief Ballow decided to reassign me from GCT-A to be the team chief of DST. I could pick one other agent for the team, so I chose Joe, who had expressed an interest in narcotics investigations. We both started our new duties immediately.

Unlike the temporary assignment as the Yongsan District TC DST, the Fort Riley TC DST was permanent. This new assignment offered me a chance to apply my personal managerial talents to the team's activities. One of my first initiatives was to review the DST's overall operation for the past year. The review disclosed that the DST had made enough cases, but an in-depth analysis revealed that the investigations were based on opportunity and not planning. There was no information being gathered to identify what illegal drugs were being used and sold by soldiers. There was no big picture showing the extent or impact illegal drugs had on the troops at Fort Riley. There was no organizational structure to identify establishments where drugs were used or sold, no confidential sources or informants, and there were no specific targeting techniques used for identifying drug dealers. After about a week, I made it the DST's main objective to increase sources and improve drug intelligence procedures. Information developed indicated that the obvious drug of choice was marijuana, but other drugs were available to soldiers on a smaller scale.

Enhancement of the source and criminal drug intelligence programs was only a start. We had to design a program that would let us utilize those sources and intelligence-gathering information to initiate drug investigations. Thus, enabling the DST to produce the whole picture as to the extent illegal drugs impacted Fort Riley's mission effectiveness. SA Hite and I started by soliciting other agents for information on victims, suspects, and subjects of their investigations, to turn them into viable confidential sources. The initial phase to develop the drug suppression program at Fort Riley involved the formulation of a reliable foundation of information that identified units, nightclubs, or bars in the surrounding cities of Junction City and Manhattan, Kansas, and other areas that are associated with illegal drugs. As part of our program, coordination with the civilian police departments in the area and the Kansas Bureau of Investigations (KBI) was conducted.

I concentrated on the units at Fort Riley while Special Agent Hite worked the civilian communities. Special Agent Hite was primarily successful in developing information on illegal drug activities in the Manhattan, Kansas, area. Manhattan was the location of Kansas State University, but due to the age of the students, it was very hard to infiltrate any groups to gather criminal intelligence information concerning illegal drug usage; there was also the legal aspect of our job to consider.

Our initiatives started to pay off when, in late September 1978, the MPI section at Fort Riley provided me with information that a young First Infantry Division soldier admitted to an MP investigator that illegal drug activity was widespread in his unit. I scheduled the young soldier for an interview, which was made possible by the newly implemented intelligence-gathering strategy of cooperation between MP and CID. The soldier came to the attention of MPs after he was found in possession of a small amount of marijuana during a command health-and-welfare inspections of his barracks. The soldier reportedly knew about illegal drug activity in his unit and was willing to provide information on others involved in exchange for leniency in his case.

I brought the young soldier to the CID office for an interview. Surprisingly, he was extremely cooperative and provided the following information about two of his unit members that were using and involved in the sale and distribution of heroin, cocaine, and marijuana. The soldier identified the two: a black male named Samuel Jennings and a white male named Ronald Murphy.[64] The soldier said that Jennings had told him that he had a source for heroin and cocaine while Murphy only dealt with marijuana. The investigation that was initiated based on information and assistance provided by the soldier was probably one of the most bizarre and unusual cases that I have ever been associated with. I call this investigation the Case of the Suspected Drug Dealer Who Knew Too Much:

## THE CASE OF THE SUSPECTED DRUG DEALER WHO KNEW TOO MUCH
Criminal investigations are jam-packed with surprises and frustrations

The interview of the soldier, who was eventually classified as a CI, took place on a bright, sunny Monday morning in late September 1978. The CI, a known user of marijuana, provided information on Jennings and Murphy from his unit, who were involved with the sale and distribution of illegal drugs. After a thirty-minute interview, the CI agreed to fully cooperate with the DST and to introduce me to the two drug dealers. I took a sworn statement from the CI detailing our meeting, his knowledge of the drug dealers, what he knew of their activities, and his voluntariness to cooperate with the investigation. After I finished the statement and had him sign it.

I instructed the CI to contact both Jennings and Murphy and tell them that he had a friend who wanted to buy some drugs for him and his girlfriend. I advised the CI that initial introductions did not necessarily need to involve any controlled purchase. This would allow me to at least have facial recognition of the two dealers and to gain their confidence and establish rapport for future meetings. Also, I advised the CI that I wanted him to influence the location and time the introductions would take place. I realized that this situation would more than likely occur only in a perfect scenario, but with the maximum effort put forth to focus on keeping control of the situation, it could happen.

My plan of action was to develop as much information on Jennings's and Murphy's backgrounds as possible and then make one purchase of illegal drugs without apprehending them. A second controlled purchase would only be considered as the investigation dictated. This method of operation allowed me to eliminate the source from any future association with me and to gather evidence of trafficking by the dealers. The goal was to identify the dealers' source of drugs. CID's policy usually allows a second controlled purchase of illegal drugs as necessary to establish a pattern for distribution. I advised the CI to attempt to arrange the meeting in daylight hours for better control. Finally, I told the CI not to make the introductions close together; we needed time to evaluate and act separately. I gave the CI until the end of the day to contact me to let me know how his efforts to arrange the introductions with the dealers went. In the meantime, I wanted to focus on gathering as much information as I could on Jennings and Murphy, to include reviewing their personnel files. In the back of my mind, I kept thinking that I had heard Jennings's name before but just could not recall where.

The best-laid-out plans are often disrupted. Later in the afternoon on that Monday the interview of the source took place, my investigative plan hit a snag. Chief Ballow called me into his office and informed me I had been selected to conduct an internal inquiry on another agent at Fort Leavenworth that had his CID badge and credentials stolen at his off-duty job at a local hospital. This inquiry took me three days and sidetracked my drug operation of Jennings and Murphy. After I completed my investigation of the stolen badge and credentials, I returned to my office on Wednesday about 4:00 p.m. and found multiple phone messages from the CI; presumingly about Jennings and Murphy.

I spent the next two hours attempting to reach the CI by phone without success. I used the intervening time to work on the report pertaining to the stolen badge and credentials investigation. About 6:00 p.m. as I was making headway with the report, the phone rang. I answered.

"Where the hell have you been?" blurted the source.

"I got called to Fort Leavenworth on an investigation," I informed him.

"I'll bet," he said incredulously.

"Have you been able to arrange the introductions of our two dealers?" I asked.

"Yeah," said the CI. "I did."

I inquired about the details, and the CI said, "I had it all taken care of, but when I couldn't get ahold of you, I had to cancel the meetings."

Thinking that without the introductions of the two suspected drug dealers, no case could be made on their activities, I asked the CI, "Can we reschedule?"

"I thought you would never ask," the CI responded. "How long are you going to be in your office?"

"I have a lot of work, so it will be a while," I told him.

Before I got another word in, he hung up. *Damn*, I thought, *I do not do well with the unknown.* I wanted to remind the source not to pressure the two because they might get suspicious as to why he was after them for the meetings. I wanted the CI to keep it simple. Since the CI had no private telephone, he usually called me from a telephone booth near his barracks; even though I had the number, I could not risk calling him back, for fear of someone else answering.

Luck was not on my side. It had been about an hour since the CI and I had talked on the phone when he called again.

"I have the meetings set up!" the CI excitedly shouted into the phone.

"What?" I asked.

There was a short pause, and then I heard the source said, "I had to set the meetings up tonight, because our unit it going to the field in the next few days."

"When are the meetings?"

"I called Murphy, and he said he would meet you at 8:00 near the Camp Funston MP station parking lot this evening, while Jennings said he would meet us at a bar on Sixth and North Jackson in Junction City about 9:00."

*Hell, this is great*, I thought. No time to put a surveillance team into operation. Possibly the meetings would simply be introductions. I still wanted to complete my background checks on both Jennings and Murphy to find out as much as possible about them.

Fifteen minutes later, I picked up the CI at the agreed predesignated location and drove to a sheltered spot in a parking lot behind a building on post headquarters. Once we settled in at the out-of-the-way location, I turned to the CI, who was looking smug and beaming with confidence.

He said, "I talked to both Jennings and Murphy not more than a half hour ago, and they both agreed to meet with me and you tonight. I am not sure if Jennings has any cocaine or heroin on him, but I saw Murphy with a bunch of marijuana wrapped in baggies, and I think he wants to deal tonight; Jennings is more cautious than Murphy."

I looked at the CI and then at my watch, which indicated it was 7:25 p.m. We were about twenty minutes away from the location where we were scheduled to meet Murphy.

"I want to reach the parking lot of the Camp Funston MP station before Murphy," I told the CI.

There was an advantage to arriving before Murphy: a quick check if any counter surveillance measures had been set up. Arriving before any controlled buy went down could also result in determining if any obstacles that might interfere with the operation were present.

On our trip to meet Murphy, I advised the CI to introduce me as Frank Anderson. I had a fake ID card identifying me by that name. Traffic was light, and we made the trip in fifteen minutes. As I pulled into the parking area of the MP station, I thought Murphy was brazen if he wanted to sell drugs within eyeshot of the MPs. I wondered what Murphy's reasoning was for meeting here; maybe an MP was his CI for the marijuana? I passed several parked cars and asked the source if he saw Murphy.

"He is not here yet," the CI replied.

*This is the reason that you must always control the location of any controlled buy of drugs*, I thought. I then pulled into a parking space, allowing enough room for another car to pull alongside. "Since he does not know what car we have, I suggest we get out and act like we are having a conversation near the car so he can see you," I told the CI.

"Okay," the CI said as he got out of the CID undercover car, a black-over-red 1972 Mustang.

About five minutes later, a white male, appearing to be in his mid- to upper twenties with a soldier's haircut, driving a dark blue older Dodge sedan, pulled up next to where the CI and I were talking. A white male passenger who looked like a soldier was with him. They were both in civilian clothes.

In an almost inaudible voice, the CI said, "It's Murphy."

The man identified to me as Murphy lowered the driver-side window and acknowledged the source by saying hello. The CI returned the greeting without any fanfare and somewhat robotically introduced me as Frank. I took a deep breath, hoping that the source's quick introduction did not raise any concerns with Murphy, and asked, "How are you guys doing?" making sure Murphy's passenger was brought into the loop. To add credibility to his intentions and to avoid any future concerns a defense lawyer might have about entrapment, I wanted Murphy to start the conversation about his ability to sell me marijuana.

Murphy directed the conversation to marijuana and, in a straightforward manner, indicated to me that he could sell me some.

"How much are you asking?" I inquired.

"A hundred dollars a bag," he replied.

"Too much," I told him.

Murphy quickly added, "But I have five smaller bags inside the bag. I can sell you a smaller bag for twenty."

Thinking that his offer for the hundred-dollar bag would be more of an indication that he was dealing, instead of helping a friend, so I decided to go for it.

While our negotiations were going on, I told Murphy that I did not like the idea of making the deal in the MP's front yard.

"I chose this place because I do not live far from here, and I have sold marijuana to others in the parking lot," Murphy explained.

To distract any suspicions on Murphy's part and to enhance rapport with him, I told him I wanted to deal at another place. My real reason for suggesting another location for the deal was to reduce the chances of MP interference. He agreed to follow me in my car.

With the CI in the passenger seat of my car, I got into the Mustang and drove to an out-of-the-way section of a parking lot about two blocks from the MP station at Fort Funston Murphy pulled his car alongside mine so that his driver's window was next to mine. As he rolled his window down, he motioned for me to do the same; we were within reach of each other.

Without any overture of conversation or hesitation, Murphy asked, "How much do you want?"

I was ready to engage him conversation before bringing up the deal, but his quick, to-the-point offer made that unnecessary.

"Can I have a hundred-dollar bag?" I replied.

Murphy reached out from his car window with a bag, containing what he purported to be marijuana, in his hand. I took the bag from him and inspected the bag before giving him any money. My inspection of the substance disclosed it looked and smelled like marijuana, so I gave him five twenty-dollar bills in contingency funds (.0015 funds).[65]

Murphy took the money and said, "Thanks."

"If I like this stuff, can I get some more?" I asked.

"Sure. Just let me know," he said.

We then departed the area driving in separate directions.

I secured the bag of purported marijuana underneath my seat and turned to the source and asked, "What time are we supposed to meet with your other guy?"

"At 9:00," the source said.

I looked at my watch, which indicate it was 8:45. Feeling somewhat concerned on how the time was affecting our meeting, I said, "We have fifteen minutes. Is there any way you can get ahold of this guy to let him know we are running late or possibly change the meeting time until tomorrow?" I was implying to the CI that I did not want to meet with the other guy tonight.

"No!" the CI said.

I had an odd feeling about this meeting, because the name *Jennings* had a familiar ring to it. However, I could not recall specifically where I had heard it. There were a lot of people in the world that have Jennings as their family name, and after all, the name is not that uncommon. I decided to brush off the meeting with Jennings and told the source to arrange another meeting with him the following day. I dropped the CI off at a predesignated location and told him to call me with any information on a new time and date we could meet with Jennings. I then returned to the CID office, secured the marijuana in the temporary evidence locker, and called it a night.

About 10:00 the next morning, I received a call from the CI, who indicated that he had no problem arranging a new meeting at the same location with Jennings. The CI had arranged the meeting for 8:00 that evening. The CI agreed to meet me at our predesignated location about 7:00 p.m. to go over any last-minute details before we went to see Jennings. I got tied up for the rest of the day with SJA on other cases and with scheduled interviews. Joe was on a two-day leave and not available to assist me on the investigation. These circumstances and activities prevented me from going to personnel to review Jennings's record, which later proved to be a big mistake. CID special agents are assigned to locations around the world.

It is not uncommon to run into a fellow agent at another assignment but rare to meet people you have already interviewed on previous investigations you have worked on. But I could not shake the feeling that Jennings was a person that I had run into before. The following short narrative is a reflected summary of what took place when the source and I met Jennings that night. I call our encounter the Case of the Man in the White Suit and Pink Tie:

THE CASE OF THE MAN IN THE WHITE SUIT AND PINK TIE
You never know for certain, regardless of planning, what to expect

The CI and I met on schedule and shored up any uncertainties about what actions to take with Jennings.

"Do you think Jennings is suspicious about why we did not meet him last night?" I inquired with the CI.

"No. I told him you were called in to work and could not make it," he related.

During our drive, we discussed the meeting with Jennings and the events of the previous night with Murphy. The CI did not appear to be concerned about the meeting with Jennings and said there were no repercussions from the previous night. *It looks like things are going our way*, I thought. What I suddenly saw next, as we approached the location where Jennings said he would meet us, caused me not to feel that way anymore.

The source, pointing his forefinger, said, "There he is." Before the source even said anything, I had already seen the man whom I presumed was Jennings.

The image I saw fit New York City, not Junction City, Kansas. There, standing in front of a club frequented by Fort Riley soldiers, stood a black male, dressed in an ostentatious white suit with a white hat, pink tie, and flashy black shoes, holding a walking stick. I was shocked at the way this guy was dressed. If this person wasn't a drug dealer, his appearance sure stood out and made you think. Can you imagine? There we were in the heartland of the Midwest, and the man sure as hell looked the part. I had a nervous, churning sensation in my stomach that I had never felt before. As I stopped the Mustang at the curb directly in front of Jennings, I looked at the guy as he acknowledged us. This meeting was going to be very interesting, to say the least—I just did not know how interesting.

Jennings swaggered over to the Mustang, and before I could say anything to the source, he jumped out and held up the seat so he could get into the back. Immediately, I thought, *Wow, this is a big mistake.* I should have told the CI to get in the back and let Jennings in the front passenger seat so I could have better control of the situation.

With Jennings in the back and the CI in the front, I took off in the Mustang. As I had planned, after the source introduced us, I would take over any conversation that ensued and enter any negotiations for a drug deal (in this case, Jennings reportedly dealt with cocaine and heroin), leaving the CI out of the picture. Prior to meeting with Jennings, I had decided to push the CI for setting up a heroin buy.

However, the CI did not even get through his introduction when I felt something hitting me on my right shoulder, causing a sharp pain. After a nanosecond, I realized that Jennings had struck me with his cane.

"What the hell did you do that for?" I shouted.

"You don't remember me, do you, Miller?"

I turned around to look at his face. *I'll be damned*, I thought. The moment I saw his face, it was like a lightning bolt striking me. Samuel Jennings was the man I had interviewed about a death investigation involving a man hanging with his hands tied behind his back from a tree shortly before I left Korea. To hold on to any hope that my cover could somehow be protected, I still answered, "No, I don't." It had to be the ridiculous suit he had on that caused me not to recognize him.

"You interviewed me in Korea about a dead man from my unit," Jennings threw at me with a faint wildness to his voice. Ever since I'd heard the name Samuel Jennings, I'd had an inkling I had run into him somewhere in my past. When I saw his face up close, the memory of the interview flashed before me. The interview of Jennings about the questionable suicide was now as clear as a star shining on a brisk, cloudless night. *Now that Jennings knows the source is working with me*, I thought, *where can I take this from here?* My cover was blown. The CI was now forever associated with the CID, and his tenure in his unit would soon become precarious at best.

Jennings forced a quick decision when he repeatedly started banging his cane on the seat next to him and yelling for me to stop the car and let him out. I instantly had two things to think about. One, whether I should do something about Jennings striking me with his cane, which technically was an assault. And two, how to handle the situation with the CI. I was mainly concerned about the CI's safety. It was obvious that the source would be branded a snitch, and his life would be in danger once the news got around about him helping the CID.

So, I made the decision, right or wrong, to let Jennings out of the car and spend my time assessing the damage to our operation and what actions I would take to protect the CI from harm. After we let Jennings out of the car, I drove directly to the Fort Riley CID office, where I debriefed the CI. He informed me that neither Murphy nor Jennings lived in his barracks.

The CI said, "Murphy resides off post with his wife, and Jennings, who apparently has a girlfriend, usually stays at her apartment."

"This is good," I told the source.

Because of the late hour, I decided to allow the CI to return to his unit for the evening and assess the situation the next day. I drove him to his unit and instructed him to get in touch with me at 8:00 a.m.

About 7:30 a.m. the next day, I called the CI's unit commander, but he was not available, so I talked to the unit 1SG. I fully briefed him on the circumstances surrounding the CI's involvement and cooperation with the case against Murphy of his unit, and I also explained the situation with Jennings. The 1SG said he would fully cooperate with the Murphy and Jennings investigation. I advised him that we needed to bring the unit commander into the loop and that he should anticipate the possibility that the CI might be transferred to another installation for his own protection. I ended my conversation with the 1SG by requesting he keep the case against Murphy under wraps, pending CID's action and to allow the CI the freedom to work with CI. The 1SG agreed.

Meanwhile back at the CID office, I briefed Chief Ballow and LTC Evans, who both came on board that a transfer, if needed, would be the appropriate action.

About 8:15 a.m. after I had just returned to my office from briefing Chief Ballow and LTC Evans, the phone rang. It was the CI.

He whispered, "Jennings told Murphy, and they both have already confronted me about what happened."

"Did they threaten you in any way?" I asked.

"Yes, they did," answered the CI.

"How did they threaten you?" I quizzed.

"Jennings did not say much but agreed with Murphy when he told me that he was going to beat the sh—— out of me. Murphy then told me that he was going to tell everyone in the unit that I am a snitch. What should I do?"

I told him to hold tight and I would get back with him as soon as I could.

I updated Chief Ballow and LTC Evans on what the CI had told me, and they directed me to start the process under the Informant Threat Transfer Program to facilitate the CI's reassignment. I contacted CID headquarters to request the CI be placed in the threat transfer program. I made all the appropriate coordination with CID headquarters, the staff judge advocate (SJA), and the US Army Military Personnel Center (MILPERCEN). The SJA had no issue of reassigning the CI, because I had made the purchase of marijuana from Murphy, and the CI probably will not have to testify in any future court-martial. The process for the source's transfer was put into motion. Later in the day, I packaged the marijuana and had it shipped to the crime lab at Fort Gillem, Georgia, for analysis.

The process of arranging the reassignment of the source took about two days. In the interim, due to the imminent threat and continued harassment of the CI by Murphy, Jennings, and others in his unit, I contacted the CI and informed him that I would be placing him in a local hotel, pending his reassignment orders. I instructed him to get his personal affairs in order. We eventually got the CI away from Fort Riley. He ended up being reassigned to an installation on the eastern seaboard, and with everyone doing their part, the transfer went smoothly.

About thirty days later, I received the crime lab report indicating that the substance I'd purchased from Murphy was in fact marijuana with a concentrated THC content of about 8 percent. Armed with the crime lab's findings, I brought Murphy into the Fort Riley CID office for interrogation. Murphy did not waive his rights and requested a lawyer; he was released to his unit commander. Unfortunately, the unit commander decided to take the low road on punishment and opted for an Article 15 under the Uniform Code of Military Justice instead of court-martial. If Murphy opted for a court-martial or his commander would have recommended one, he faced substantial fines and a bad conduct discharge. He got off with a slap on the wrist. No prosecution, but under the UCMJ he was fined and restricted to his unit for 30 days under the proceedings of Article 15.

In late summer 1978, I brought Chris out to Fort Riley for a visit. He was now six and growing fast, and we enjoyed a satisfying two weeks with each other before he started school in Terre Haute. He was developing into a bright young boy who was amenable to any activity I suggested. We took a trip to old Dodge City, Kansas, and toured the surrounding prairies in the state. I felt like one of the characters in James Fenimore Cooper's historical novel *The Prairie*. When I took him back to Terre Haute, I was confident that he'd had a good time. I enjoyed our time together, and it was a sad day when I had to go back to work.

After Chris left, I devoted my entire time to work. Special Agent Hite and I continued developing confidential sources and informants in and around the Fort Riley area. This effort produced various bits and pieces of information on how the illegal drug trade worked. We were now able to start targeting specific people that we suspected were involved with illegal drugs. The nucleus of our efforts came from developed sources, unit cadre personnel, and intensive intelligence gathering. However, sometimes it does not matter how hardworking or innovative an investigator is in developing information; there is always that one opportunity that comes the investigator's way without any effort on his or her part whatsoever.

I had interviewed a walk-in SSG soldier from the First Infantry Division on Custer Hill who said he wanted to help us fight drugs. The SSG told me that he was at a bar on Washington Street in downtown Junction City a few nights earlier and had a conversation with a white male who claimed to be able to sell him heroin. The SSG told me that he declined the man's offer, using the excuse he had no money on him at the time.

"What is your motive in wanting to help the CID?" I inquired.

"I am tired of seeing many of the young soldiers in my unit coming to work or getting booted from the US Army for using illegal drugs," he said.

"How bad is illegal drug use in your unit?" I asked him.

"It is pretty bad, and I am afraid that the soldiers who come to work that are high on drugs pose a real safety problem in the unit," he ardently stated.

"Is the man you met in the bar the other night in any way connected to your unit drug problem?" I asked.

"I really don't know, but if we could get this guy I met, then that is one less dealer we have to worry about," he said.

I got the impression that the SSG thought he was already on the DST.

Based on what he had told me, I initiated a CID inquiry into the SSG's information. The following narrative reflects what occurred during the investigation. I call the inquiry the Case of the Civilian That Got Away with It:

# THE CASE OF THE CIVILIAN THAT GOT AWAY WITH IT
Thoroughness is the key to a successful investigation

I registered the SSG as a CI and then asked him, "Do you think it is possible to meet with this guy again?"

"Yes. I have seen him in the bar before," the source responded.

"Did he appear to be civilian or a soldier?" I anxiously asked the CI.

"He came across to me as a civilian," the CI replied.

"Can you describe the man?"

"He is about five foot nine inches, weighs maybe 215."

Weighing 215 pounds was a good indication that he was not a soldier. *Way too much weight*, I thought.

"Do you know what the man's name is?" I asked.

"No," said the CI.

"Attempt to get his name," I told him. Without letting the CI respond, I rapidly fired other questions at him. "Approximately how old do you think the man is? How often do you see the guy in the bar?" I asked.

Answering my last question first, the CI said, "I usually see him each time I go to the bar, which is about twice a week. I guess the man may possibly be in his mid- to late thirties."

"Does the man drink alone, or is he engaged with others?" I asked.

Talking to many bar patrons would be a strong indication that he was dealing, but if he sat alone, there would be a good chance the man was blowing smoke about his ability to get heroin.

"I have seen him talking to others in the bar," the CI said.

"See if you can get information about where the guy works," I added. The CI seemed somewhat overwhelmed and had a look of awe that I'd brought up so many questions.

"Boy, there is a lot of stuff you have to know in your job," the CI remarked.

"Yes, there is," I briskly responded.

I worried that I may have overloaded the CI with the amount of information I wanted him to obtain from the man at the bar. Therefore, I reemphasized that his approach for gathering the information should be slow and not rushed. If additional information was needed, other meetings could be arranged. I advised the CI not to go into the bar and immediately start quizzing the man to get the required information but to methodically seek answers. A painstaking, especially slow and careful approach was the best way to reduce the chances of a suspect getting suspicious.

I thought the case had potential, so I arranged for the CI to go to the bar that evening. I told the CI I wanted him to meet with me at the CID office at

6:00 p.m. so we could go over any last-minute details of what he should say. I thought that since the guy he was meeting was more likely a civilian, I wanted the CI to entice the man to come onto Fort Riley for any controlled buy setup. We had about three hours before the CI was to go to the bar, so before I let him go, I set the time at 7:00 p.m. for him to meet the man at the bar; that gave us an hour to shore up any details. I stressed to the CI that I did not want him to make any deals inside the bar—or, for that matter, within the jurisdiction of Junction City. It was illegal to generate drug cases on civilians in the United States off the military reservations.

At most, information that is developed on civilians must be provided to the civilian law enforcement department having jurisdiction over the area where the information pertained. The law that governs these situations where the US Army cannot enforce civilian law dates to the 1870s, during the reconstruction period after the Civil War. The law was enacted after issues with martial law was declared in the South after the Civil War. The legislation that prohibits the US Army from enforcing civilian laws or even investigating civilians is called the Posse Comitatus Act.

> The Posse Comitatus Act outlaws the willful use of any part of the Army or Air Force to execute the law unless expressly authorized by the Constitution or an act of Congress. The Posse Comitatus Act mentions only the U.S. Army and U.S. Air Force, but it is applicable to the U.S. Navy and U.S. Marines by administrative action and commands of other laws. The law enforcement functions of the Coast Guard have been expressly authorized by an act of congress and consequently cannot be said to be contrary to the act.[66]

The CI showed up at precisely 6:00 p.m. at the CID office as directed. Since our initial meeting hours before, in my mind, I had formulated a tentative plan on the time, location, and area, but not the date. I left that decision up to the CI and the target when to attempt to meet on Fort Riley. I reiterated my concerns to the CI about being too aggressive in his attempts to obtain the information from the alleged heroin dealer. The investigative plan focused on determining if the man in the bar could deliver the heroin as promised, to accumulate enough evidence to verify if he was a major dealer to soldiers at Fort Riley, and third, to bring the Junction City Police Department into the picture with a focus to conduct a joint investigation. To accomplish these objectives, I first had to establish a military connection; this step would be satisfied if he delivered the heroin in a controlled buy.

It was now 6:30 p.m., time for us to get to the bar. I instructed the CI to follow me in his car. The drive to Washington Street in downtown Junction City from the Fort Riley CID office takes about ten to fifteen minutes, which would place us at the bar at about the time I had suggested to the CI that he meet the suspect. I was right on the money; when I found a parking spot on Eighth Street near the intersection of Washington, it was 6:45 p.m.

I parked my car where I could view the doorway to the bar; the CI pulled in behind me. He joined me in my car, and we had a few minutes to discuss any last-minute details before the meeting. Except for a few cars traveling on Washington, there was virtually no activity around us. Since I was well known by numerous people at Fort Riley, I did not want to risk going into the bar for surveilling the CI when he met with our target, out of fear someone might recognize me.

The plan I had devised involved a controlled buy of heroin without an apprehension. I briefed the CI on details of the planned operation. I explained to the CI that on the day of the deal, your job brought you to the area around building 647 at Camp Forsyth.[67] I chose Camp Forsyth because most of the buildings were abandoned and there would be fewer people in the area. I had previously inspected building 647 for a possible location for the Fort Riley DST team office and knew it was vacant. This location, I thought, would make an excellent site for a controlled buy.

Before he left, I again voiced my anxieties and stressed to him to be careful with his approach of the target. I told him to wait for the target to offer to sell him the heroin. Even the most casual dealer would get suspicious if someone he did not know well asked him for a large or significant amount of the drug the first time.

The moment had arrived for the source to go inside the bar. The source did not act nervous or anxious, but exhibited a sense of confidence. I got the impression that he seemed to genuinely want to help, instead of just wanting to play cop. As he opened the door, the CI gave a thumb-up. I broke his momentum from exiting the car by grabbing his shoulder. With a concerned expression, I looked directly into his eyes.

"One other thing. Make your conversation flow naturally; don't rush," I implored. "Seize the moment. When you find an opening to ask a question, take it."

"Gotcha," he said as he slid from the seat of the car.

I watched the CI make his way across Washington Street and up the steps and into the bar. I hoped our target was inside waiting on him and that he was gullible enough to fall for our ruse. I watched the bar entrance continuously, while at the same time being alert for any suspicious activity around me. About forty-five minutes later, I was relieved when I saw the CI leaving the bar. As the CI got into the car, he blurted out, "The guy was there, and we had a nice long talk."

I could tell the CI was excited, so I did not interrupt him when he spoke.

"His name is David Henderson,[68] and he lives in Grandview Plaza. He is a local boy. Went to Junction City High School. I didn't get his age, but he said he graduated in 1970," the CI eagerly reported. "He told me that he works on Fort Riley, so it was easy to convince him to meet me on the base somewhere," the CI enthusiastically stated.

"Was a deal set?" I asked incredulously.

"He told me he had a fresh shipment of 'H' in and could get me a packet by Wednesday and meet me next to building 647 at Camp Forsyth around noon."

Since it was Monday, that gave us two days to get ready. I was skeptical about the alleged fresh shipment of heroin. If Henderson had the stuff, I didn't believe it would take him that long to sell a single packet of heroin. Of course, he might have something to do, but I doubted it. It sounded more like he had to get in touch with his source to get the stuff before he made a deal with my CI.

My next move on this case took me to the Civilian Personnel Office (CPO). I did not want the same thing to happen as the Jennings case. If I knew this guy, or if he had previously dealt in any way with the CID, I wanted to know about it. I found out through a review of Henderson's personnel record that he was a US Army civilian employee (DAC) who worked for the post engineers doing odd maintenance and labor-type jobs around Fort Riley. I then checked with the MPs, who had no record. I took a trip to Junction City Police Department and talked to their detectives, who knew Henderson's name. A research of their records and found that Henderson had a record for minor possession of marijuana and a couple of nonmoving traffic violations. Henderson's record fit his profile as a small-time nuisance to the area. The basis for the US Army connection to his case was tied to his selling of illegal drugs to soldiers and not that of a big-time drug dealer. A deal that took place on Fort Riley would establish that connection.

On the day before the controlled purchase of heroin was to take place, I obtained the keys to building 647 at Camp Forsyth from the Fort Riley property management office; they remembered me from my previous visit to their office. I was not concerned about what the people at the property office thought about my inspection of building 647. I figured they believed I was giving the building another once-over to see if it fit CID requirements for occupancy.

Once I had the keys, I took a trip to building 647 and inspected the inside and immediate area outside of the building. I made the determination that the best way to observe the controlled buy from Henderson was to view it from inside building 647.

I would have the CI park his car with the rear end facing toward building 647, and then I would have the CI raise the trunk lid of his car. To any unexpected witnesses, this would give the illusion that the CI and Henderson were talking about something inside the trunk as the heroin and money were transferred. I would observe the transaction from a cadre window.

My concealment was enhanced because the cadre room window had been painted over. Once I had chosen the cadre room for my surveillance point, I used a key to scrape away a small amount of paint, clearing the way for me to view the source when he met with Henderson through the glass. I not only wanted to witness the transaction but to photograph it as well, so I brought the CID Canon 35 mm camera with me.

At 10:00 a.m. on Wednesday, the CI arrived at the CID office as directed. Prior to leaving for building 647, I briefed the CI on how the deal was to go down.

"Once you see Henderson approaching, ensuring that he sees you, I want you to get out of your car and raise the trunk lid," I instructed.

"I understand," the CI said.

"Let's get going."

It took us about fifteen minutes to get to the parking lot of building 647. The CI parked his car with the rear end facing the building, as I had instructed. To get my car out of sight, I parked on the other side of the building. I advised the CI that while the buy was taking place, I would be observing from inside the building.

"If anything goes haywire, I'll be on Henderson so quick he won't know what's happening," I assured the CI. I asked the CI to come with me to the cadre room, where I would be conducting surveillance on his and Henderson's meeting. I informed the CI that I had to thoroughly search him and his car before he met with Henderson. Once this was done, I gave the CI a twenty in .0015 contingency funds for paying Henderson for the drugs.

It was now 11:15 a.m.—time to get in position and wait for Henderson's arrival. The CI got into his car, and I positioned myself inside the cadre room on the north side of building 647.

At 11:55 a.m., I spotted a white male driving an older white Ford pickup truck into the parking lot, getting out of his vehicle, and start walking toward the CID vehicle.

*This has got to be Henderson*, I thought.

I wanted to take a photograph of the truck's license plate, but it was not visible from my position. I then observed the CI get out of his car, walk behind it, and open the trunk, exactly as I had instructed him to do. As the trunk lid flew open, Henderson joined the CI behind the car. I immediately began taking photographs with the camera of their meeting, hoping that the man would not hear the noise of the shutter each time I took a photograph.

About a minute into their conversation, which I could not hear, they both turned their backs to me and appeared to be reaching into the trunk of the car. Then, almost immediately afterward, they both stood up and talked for a few more minutes, and then Henderson left. Damn. I hadn't seen the actual transfer go down. I took photographs, but it only showed the two meeting, I did not catch the transaction. I waited a couple of minutes until Henderson drove away in his truck, and then I left building 647, securing it with the keys I had obtained, and headed to the CID Mustang, all the while keeping alert for any signs of Henderson returning to the area.

I met up with the CI at a predesignated place a short distance from building 647. We both got out of our cars, and the CI immediately gave me a small white packet of white powdery substance. I harshly criticized the CI's actions for making the exchange without me seeing it, sharply scolding him, "You were supposed to arrange the transfer so I could see the exchange!" I found nothing that would compromise the investigation when I searched the CI and then debriefed him and sent him on his way.

I returned to the CID office and packaged up the suspected heroin and shipped it to the US Army crime lab at Fort Gillem. Three weeks later, the results were received, indicating that the substance in the white packet was in fact heroin, but it contained only 1 percent pure heroin. This was an indication that the substance purchased from Henderson was cut so many times that it was suspected he was not a major drug dealer but instead probably a user himself. The case was brought to the attention of the DEA, but the agency declined to pursue the matter. The US Attorney showed no interest in the case as well. The Junction City Police Department indicated they would pursue an investigation of Henderson, but CID never heard any more information about their efforts. Henderson was a person who got away with selling heroin and was never prosecuted.

In October 1978, I received my first evaluation as a new warrant officer one (WO1). The evaluation was outstanding, so I guess they thought I was doing a good job.

The DST kept up the momentum in our efforts to suppress the flow of illegal drugs into Fort Riley. Special Agent Hite and I were still the only working agents on the team, and it would be a while before we could recruit any MPs to assist in our efforts. The Fort Riley DST continued to routinely initiate level-two drug investigations throughout the rest of 1978. Elements of CID reserve units from Kansas, Missouri, and a few individual mobilized augmentee reservists (IMAs) worked with the Fort Riley CID office during 1978, and I acquired one for the DST. He was a Kansas City, Kansas, police patrolman who was a reserve warrant officer two that spent two weeks with the team, and his help was invaluable in our drug suppression efforts.

On January 3, 1979, I started training at the Department of Justice national DEA academy at Fourteenth and I Streets in Washington, DC. The school was designed for intensified training in law, targeting suspects, surveillance techniques, probable cause searches, seizure, and handling of evidence, identification of the various illicit drug use and prescription drug abuse, undercover operations, firearms training, liaison between law enforcement departments and agencies, various other law enforcement activities, and public speaking.

I thought the training was on the mark and very relevant to our drug investigative efforts in CID. I wrote an after-action report to the policy, plans, and training doctrine at CID headquarters that provided laudatory comments for the course and supported efforts to continue to send our CID special agents to the training. Since part of the requirements of the course was to train and qualify with service weapons, I made a recommendation to allow CID special agents to use their own .38-caliber revolvers when attending the course. (The .38-caliber snubnosed Smith & Wesson revolver was the main CID-issued weapon at the time.) CID special agents were one of a few departments where their personnel did not bring their service weapons to the course. I never heard from the policy, plans, and training doctrine at CID headquarters about my recommendations.

On March 19, 1979, I resumed my duties and responsibilities at Fort Riley. The day I returned, I met Lieutenant Commander (promotable) John T. Thompson Jr., the new commander who replaced LTC Evans after he retired. LTC (P) Thompson was a tall, slender, personable man who made a good first impression on me. He invited me into his office, where we talked for about forty-five minutes or so about my career, my future in the US Army, and the current condition. He assured me that I would continue as the team chief of the Fort Riley DST for the next few months. Throughout our association together at Fort Riley, LTC (P) Thompson would be a staunch supporter of the DST efforts.

"Can I do anything for you?" Thompson asked.

"Yes. The DST is very active, but there is only me and SA Hite to do the job," I told him.

I did not expect his answer when he said, "I'll see what I can do for you."

He concluded our meeting by touching on the Drug Suppression Survey Program (DSSP) assessment report done annually by each CID office. The report was intended to show the Fort Riley commander an accurate assessment of the availability of illicit drugs and narcotics available to his troops. "I want you to conduct the exit briefing to MG Kaplan, commander of the First Infantry Division, on August 10, 1979," he said.

"Yes, sir. I can handle that," I proudly replied.

Throughout spring and into the summer of 1979, Fort Riley DST efforts continued to focus on the identification of level-two drug traffickers. The development of sources was enhanced, which became the cornerstone of the DST program. During this period, SA Hite started making inroads into the illegal drug trafficking by US soldiers in Manhattan, Kansas. I was taking innovative approaches of gathering intelligence on the drug-trafficking patterns in and around Fort Riley. I increased the number of soldiers being interviewed, which produced a tremendous quantity of valuable information about illegal drug activities.

Other steps in gathering information were through surveillance of bars in Junction City that were known to be the locations where patrons could hook up with dealers, and from spot-checking residences of soldiers, we had previously developed information on their suspected illegal drug involvement. By checking license plate numbers of visiting cars parked at these residences, we confirmed the association of other known suspects involved with illegal drugs. Starting with a bare nucleus, Special Agent Hite and I formed the DST into a viable, practical, working drug suppression program. We produced outstanding results in the drug intelligence-gathering process and developed information within the adjoining civilian communities that supported our interdiction efforts. The number of law violators apprehended and illicit drugs seized increased far beyond the combined total of the two previous years.

Shortly after I took over as head of the DST, I had heard rumors that there were large fields of wild marijuana growing in isolated areas on the Fort Riley installation, so on a very hot day in late June 1979, I finally took some time to see for myself. Each time I had an hour or two to spare from my busy daily investigative activities, I would drive around the post looking in remote areas for the purported marijuana fields. A couple of days into my search, I hit pay dirt when I followed a narrow dirt road just off Henry Drive, adjacent to the Kansas River, near the entrance to Fort Riley from I-70. There, I discovered a large multiacre field of tall, wild-growing marijuana plants.

I spent about an hour walking the field, and there did not appear to be any evidence that anyone was working the field; the plants were wild and untended. Driving back to my office that day, I thought of an idea that would put the DST on the map, so to speak. I would recommend to the chief and commander that with the right kind of help, we could initiate a plan to eradicate or destroy the plants by pulling them up by the roots and burning them. If anything, our operation would have a positive impact on CID's drug suppression efforts. It would take a large-scale operation, probably involving not only the entire Fort Riley CID office but the support of the military police as well. I would have to devise an operations plan that would be reasonable and workable. It would require many working man-hours in setting up the eradication of marijuana operation.

A narrative below represents information of my recollection of CID's efforts in eradicating wild-growing marijuana on the Fort Riley installation in an investigation I named the Case of the Burned Evidence:

## THE CASE OF THE BURNED EVIDENCE
Regardless if it is wild ditch weed or marijuana, you sell it, you commit a crime

A major milestone in our drug suppression efforts at Fort Riley came in late June 1979 when I discovered approximately forty acres or more of untended large domestic plants of marijuana growing wild along the Kansas River just inside the Fort Riley installation, near the main entrance from I-70. Tetrahydrocannabinol (THC) is the active ingredient that produces a relaxed state and may heighten the senses when consumed. The domestic plants contain no more than 3–4 percent. The THC percentage, for example, in marijuana from Mexico, the main source for the United States, can be as high as 8–12 percent.

I came up with a plan to eradicate the marijuana plants that I found near the Kansas River. The plan had its risks. The greatest risk was information getting out to the public (general military communities) that could bring many soldiers and civilians to the area to pick the marijuana plants to use or, even worse, sell to others. The domestic plants, commonly referred to as ditch weed, were more closely tied to hemp instead of marijuana; they are two related plants that look alike, but were not the same. It is popularly remarked that you could smoke a joint made from domestic plants the size of a telephone pole, and all you would get is a headache and a sore throat. In any event, selling the domestic plants would still be considered a crime, because possession of the domestic plants is illegal, the same as the Mexican variety.

I briefed the chief and the commander, LTC (P) Thompson, on the plan, and they both were on board with it. It took about a week to plan, coordinate, and execute the operation, but the time was well worth it.

The DEA's Domestic Cannabis Eradication/Suppression Program (CESP) identified there were several categories of marijuana:

- *Cultivated*—Marijuana that is deliberately planted, grown, tended
- *Sinsemilla*—Seedless female plants found in plots where male plants have been removed

- *Tended Wild / Ditch Weed*—Wild marijuana that shows some human attention, such as mulching, feeding, watering, clipping, or harvesting
- *Untended Wild / Ditch Weed*—Wild marijuana that shows no signs of mulching, feeding, watering, clipping, harvesting
- *Processed Marijuana*—Smokable marijuana in the drying process, lose or packaged

CESP figures report that the DEA had seized or destroyed 4.7 billion feral hemp plants since 1984. That's in contrast to the 4.2 million marijuana plants it seized or destroyed during the same period. In other words, 98.1 percent of all plants eradicated under the CESP program were ditch weed. The DST plan was to utilize members of the First MP Company to assist agents from the CID in pulling the plants out of the ground and transporting them to a burn barrel a short distance away.

We planned to kick off Operation Burned Evidence for late June 1979 to allow enough time for pulling everything together, coordinating with the provost marshal to get sufficient men, equipment, and logistics to be put into place. CID obtained an M416 quarter-ton jeep trailer to haul the uprooted plants to the burn barrels. Throughout the day during Operation Burned Evidence, we pulled an estimated four thousand plants weighing several hundred pounds, all of which were destroyed by burning. The value of the plants, if they were pulled, dried, and sold loose or in packages on the illegal drug market, was estimated to be more than $1 million. Some involved with the operation felt the estimated value should be higher, but I reminded them that the plants were not cultivated and did not have the THC content needed for the high desired when smoking the weed. For at least six months after the operation, I sporadically checked the field and found no evidence that anyone had tampered with the area.

During my inspection of the marijuana field, I observed a small brown-and-white, spotted, long-haired dog with big brown eyes wandering in the area. When I saw him, I got out of my car and motioned for him, and the little guy started wiggling his tail and immediately came to me. He had burrs all over his body and was covered with fleas. He looked like he had not eaten anything for a while. I just couldn't leave him there, so I picked him up and took him back to the CID office. The next day, I had him deburred, sprayed for fleas, and washed; he looked like a different dog. *I can't keep the little guy*, I thought. For the time being, I decided to keep him secured at the DST building. I ended up naming the dog Narc.

At precisely 1:00 p.m. sharp on Friday, August 10, 1979, MG Phillip Kaplan's briefing of the Fort Riley DSSP was well received. He was responsive to what I had told him about the overall illegal drug picture affecting the troops at Fort Riley. He offered his support, and over a period of the next two weeks, through a series of inspired, spirited phone calls, based on MG Kaplan's interest in our efforts, the First MP Company provided the Fort Riley DST with two MPs. Since the division commander's briefing had gone well that afternoon, LTC (P) Thompson gave us the rest of the day off; we did not hesitate in taking him up on his offer.

That evening, a bunch of the guys at the office decided to go out for the three Ds: dinner, drinking, and dancing. Several of the agents took their wives, but I had no date. We had a favorite nightspot named Kennedy's Claim in Manhattan, Kansas, that we went to. It was a good place to have a good meal and a few drinks, listen to a live band, and dance. It was also a good location where single guys could hook up with single women. I had been fortunate a few times to date a few nice ladies I had met at the establishment.

The meal was excellent and the music was loud, and the guys were having a good time dancing with their wives. I found myself sitting alone at our table, while the others were dancing and having a good old time. I looked around but did not see any girls interesting enough to dance with, so I acquiesced just to sit and enjoy my drink.

Suddenly, I heard this voice. "Would you like to dance?"

I looked up and saw a very nice, attractive lady, possibly in her late twenties, smiling. She repeated herself. "Would you like to dance?"

"Sure," I said, almost tripping on the chair as I got up to escort her to the dance floor. It was good that she knew how to dance, because I am lousy on the floor. We stayed on the floor for a second dance, and when it was over, we started walking to her table. I then realized that I didn't know where her table was, so I asked her to join us. She consented but told me she first needed to tell her girlfriend what she was doing. We talked the rest of the evening, and I found out her name was Olga Vera, and she lived in Wamego, Kansas, about fifteen miles east of Manhattan. Before we departed that night, I asked her for a date the following Friday, to which she agreed. This chance meeting sparked a relationship that lasted for almost a year.

In late August 1979, Special Agent Hite and I welcomed SP4s John Stewart and Billy Brazell to the team. They both immediately had a positive impact on the number of cases initiated and enhanced our intelligence gathering. John had been in the US Army for only three years and Billy about two years. Their backgrounds varied. John had come right out of high school, while Billy was older and had even worked as a source for the Texas Public Safety Department (TPSD) in his home state. In his initial screening interview for the DST, I asked him how deeply involved he was with the illegal drug culture in Texas. He admitted that he had joined the US Army to get away from the crowd he was associated with in Texas, because he had testified against some of them. Both he and John were a welcome addition to the team.

Around the time that our team received the new people, SA Hite had shored up last-minute details of the drug operation he was working on with the investigators from the Riley County Sheriff's Department (RCSD). Through his personal efforts and the use of sources, he had identified several civilians and soldiers that were involved with the sale and distribution of marijuana and other illicit drugs in Manhattan and on Fort Riley. He had coordinated his efforts with the RCSD, who were working closely with him to culminate the perps' apprehension and arrests. The operation ran from the spring through the summer of 1979, and his efforts resulted in the apprehension of four soldiers from Fort Riley and twelve civilians from Manhattan. The drug operation removed a large amount of marijuana and heroin from the streets, and the local newspapers and television station picked up the stories, emphasizing the success and impact the operation had on the community.

The operation was bittersweet for me as the team chief of the Fort Riley DST. Shortly before the Manhattan drug operation, SA Hite came down on orders for Mainz, Germany. After Special Agent Hite's departure for Mainz, Chief Ballow replaced Hite with Special Agent Michael Burns. Burns brought with him a good deal of investigative experience to the team.

Olga and I were dating steadily now, and within a month, she had introduced me to her family. I thought the relationship was going in the right direction, and I thought she agreed with that assumption. She lived in a small house next to her parents in the rural area just outside of Wamego. Her father had a horse and a few other animals, including a dog on his property, which could be classified as a ranch. I got permission to bring Narc to the ranch. It would do the dog good, and the open area would enable him to roam the countryside. It was a good home for him, I thought, and I saw him every time I visited Olga.

Our investigative efforts into the illegal drug trade in and around Fort Riley were successful. We had the attention of the commanders, provost marshal, MG Kaplan, and the CID higher-ups. One could not ask for a better reputation. But there is no operation within the US Army that would be considered perfect. Just like all good things, they have hiccups and bumps. I would later experience the headaches of running a drug suppression operation at the same time as encountering my first real personnel conduct calamity. But for the latter part of 1979 and early 1980, times were good for the Fort Riley DST.

In the spring of 1980, we added Special Agent Joseph Herndon to the DST. He brought a wealth of drug investigation experience to the team, having served on DSTs in previous assignments.

Internationally, news that an angry mob of young Islamic revolutionaries had overrun the US embassy in Tehran on November 4, 1979, taking more than sixty Americans hostages, had put a damper on things in America just prior to the beginning of the holiday season. The hostage situation in Iran put pressure on the United States military to conduct operations to free the hostages. Prior to Iran's actions, the United States had no organized units capable of effectively conducting such a rescue, but it attempted one just the same. The Pentagon hurriedly put together a group of US Army and air force personnel, which failed in the desert outside Tehran. Some of the hostages were released during the crisis, but most were held for 444 days before being released immediately after Ronald Reagan took the oath of office as president. The US military threat was heightened during the crisis but had little impact on the CID operations at Fort Riley, though it was in the backs of all our minds as we carried out our duties.

During the crisis, to celebrate the Christmas season, we had the usual home parties and went out to dinners as a group and were enjoying the spirit of holidays the best we could. One evening while out to dinner with several fellow agents and their wives, Special Agent Dennis Jones asked me to pull duty for him on Christmas Day. Since I was single and he was married with children, I did not hesitate to accommodate him. I readily agreed to pull duty for that day with no anticipation of him returning the favor at a time in the future.

Christmas Day was a pleasant, cool but not cold, overcast day with no inclement weather conditions. In 1979, Christmas Day fell on a Tuesday, and I reported to the CID office at 8:00 a.m. sharp to check out the duty agent equipment and coordinate with the Fort Riley MP desk sergeant.

"Nope. Nothing going on," the desk sergeant informed me.

I spent the entire day at the office catching up on paperwork and got through the whole day without receiving a duty call. I decided to find some place to eat, but I was in trouble. I wasn't paying attention to the time, and before I realized it, it was past 7:00 p.m., and all my established eating spots were closed for the holiday, so I had to resign myself to the fact that I was going to eat my Christmas dinner in my BOQ room. I provided the MP desk sergeant with my contact number to my quarters, and after wishing him a merry Christmas, I retreated to my residence.

After a festive Christmas meal of a bologna sandwich with cheese and a glass of water, I settled in for what I hoped to be a quiet and restful evening reading or watching TV. By 9:00 p.m., I still had not received a call from the MP desk sergeant. I thought of all the soldiers on Fort Riley who were staying out of trouble and enjoying their days off with family and friends. I realized that Christmas Day without a duty call was just an imaginary dream, because the entire day felt like the lull before the storm. I figured there was a certainty I would get called out to investigate a crime before the evening was over. But since that call had yet to come, I decided to get some sleep, so I lay down on my bed and dozed off into a restful sleep. Then the inevitable happened. I was startled out of a soothing slumber by the sound of a ringing telephone.

I opened my eyes, and as I reached for the phone beside my bed, I looked at the clock; it was 10:30 p.m. I picked up the phone, and without any introduction, the man on the other end said, "There has been a violation of Article 118."

I made the quick assumption that the caller was the evening shift MP desk sergeant. Yawning, I asked, "What did you say?"

"A murder. A man has been shot in the barracks on Custer Hill, and he is not expected to live. He is now being transported by ambulance to Irwin Army Community Hospital with a bullet in his head!" the desk sergeant excitedly shouted through the phone.

"If he is still alive, then it's not murder yet, is it?" I commented to the MP desk sergeant.

"Yes, but indications are the victim is not going to make it," he said.

I was fully awake now and started throwing questions at the MP desk sergeant. "Is there a unit at the scene? Do we have a suspect? Give me the building number where the shooting took place."

The MP desk sergeant covered all the answers with quick, abbreviated remarks, adding that he would keep the MP at the scene. The MP desk sergeant added that the suspect, SP4 Olsen, was being escorted to the MP station.

"Keep him there until I can get to him," I stressed to the MP desk sergeant. I told the MP desk sergeant to isolate SP4 Olsen in a room with a guard and not to allow anyone to talk to him. "Could you also make sure an MP unit goes to the hospital to determine the condition of the victim?" I thought, *Well, I should have realized that it would be too good to be true to have an event-free night away from the crime.*

Prior to leaving for the scene, I called Don Shanley and briefed him on the details I had. Don asked that I call him if I needed any assistance once I'd evaluated the scene.

Within minutes of being called, I had dressed, driven the short distance to the CID office, placed the duty agent equipment in the trunk of the duty car, and was on my way to the scene.

The trip up Custer Hill was quiet with virtually no traffic, due to the Christmas holiday. When I arrived at the barracks where the shooting had reportedly taken place, there was a crowd of soldiers gathered outside the main entrance to the building. As I walked past them into the barracks, I heard a few comments like, "Look. There is CID. We need to be careful while he is in the building." The following narrative depicts my recollection of actions taken on that Christmas night and my personal thoughts on how the crime evolved. I called this crime the Case of the Soldier Who Lost at Russian Roulette:

## THE CASE OF THE SOLDIER WHO LOST AT RUSSIAN ROULETTE
It doesn't matter how much of a lull a CID agent experiences on a duty day—the action always seems to find him

The facts of the crime differ from an investigator's perspective of how it occurred until fully investigated. My perceptions of how this crime played out, combined with known facts, created the following scenario of events pertaining to the shooting of SP4 Bo'nes. Tuesday, December 25, 1979, a Christmas evening, was a brisk, cool, cloudless night at Fort Riley, Kansas. During the festive day, soldiers were mostly off and enjoying hearty dinners with their families and friends, and those young, single troops of the First Infantry Division residing in the barracks had equally delicious home-cooked-style meals with all the trimmings at the many dining facilities on base. After their fine dinners, their stomachs full, they all went about doing other things they either had planned or decided to do to culminate a good holiday.

SP4 Randy E. Olsen and SP4 Daniel L. Bo'nes[69] (pronounced *Bones*) were two of the many soldiers who'd had a good Christmas Day at Fort Riley. The two friends were also roommates that had known each other about a year. Both young men wanted to make the US Army their careers and had an excellent reputation within the unit. They were in a festive mood when they returned to their barracks room on that Christmas evening. They were content and satisfied after eating a delicious meal at the consolidated brigade dining facility. They both decided to stay at Fort Riley instead of going home for Christmas so they could save money for summer trips to see family and friends then.

Once in their room on the second floor of the barracks, SP4 Olsen, a young, blond-haired kid of twenty-one from the Chicago area, pulled from his wall locker a bottle of Bacardi rum that he had purchased at the class-six store a few days prior to Christmas. SP4 Bo'nes, twenty-three, from Puerto Rico, was waiting in anticipation of his first drink. The two had waited a whole weekend before breaking the seal on the bottle of the coveted rum. Because of the holiday spirit, it did not take long before they started feeling the effects of the alcohol.

It was now about 10:00 p.m., on Christmas evening and the two boys were well on their way to a night that would affect both their lives. While their moods were still festive, SP4 Olsen took an unregistered .25-caliber snub-nosed Smith & Wesson revolver from his wall locker and showed it to SP4 Bo'nes. SP4 Olsen, obviously under the influence of alcohol and with an unsteady hand, put a couple of bullets into the cylinder. He then pointed the gun to his head and pulled the trigger. Bo'nes gasped in anticipation of the gun firing, and he expelled air from his lungs in a sigh of relief when all he heard was a click, because the cylinder was empty.

"Goddamn it, Olsen. Don't point the gun at your head like that. You could kill yourself," a concerned SP4 Bo'nes barked. An argument ensued between the two over SP4 Olsen's handling of the revolver. When SP4 Bo'nes attempted to pull the gun from SP4 Olsen's hand, a struggle ensued for control of the revolver. During the physical exchange, SP4 Olsen's hand that was holding on to the revolver turned in a way that caused the gun barrel to point at SP4 Bo'nes's facial area. Then in an instant—*bang!*—a hot cloud of gas from the explosion of gunpowder, followed by a flame propelled a bullet from the gun, struck SP4 Bo'nes in the forehead.

I arrived at the scene about thirty minutes after the shooting. I found the charge of quarters, a SP4, trying to handle a barrage of phone calls from the MP desk, his commander, the 1SG, and just about anyone wanting to know details about the shooting. In between phone calls, I introduced myself and asked him to direct me to where the shooting occurred.

"Take the stairs up to the second floor, and the room is the third door to your left," he nervously responded, pointing with his right forefinger, and then he immediately returned his attention to the phone calls.

As I entered the second floor from the stairwell, I saw two MPs in the hallway just outside the door to the room where the shooting had taken place. They were doing what they were trained to do: guard the crime scene until CID arrived. The MP closest to me as I approached the room told me they had taken the victim to the hospital, and the shooter was in custody at the MP station. The MP then opened the door.

I stopped, took out the camera from the duty agent kit I was carrying, and asked the MP to watch the case while I took photographs of the scene. Before walking into the room, I gave the scene a once-over from the doorway. As I entered the room, I immediately took photographs, showing a panoramic view of the room. I noticed two wall lockers that separated the sleeping areas of the two occupants. Upon closer inspection, I noted that the wall lockers had the names of SP4 Randy E. Olsen and Daniel L. Bo'nes. Both beds could be viewed from the doorway. There were two writing desks, with various books and the usual personal office-type stuff one would use on them. The room was unkempt and in need of a major cleaning. I thought that the messy room was typical of single soldiers and not unusual in that it was a holiday period.

As I worked my way into the room, I noticed that two desk chairs were in the middle of the room facing each other. This was apparently where the shooting had taken place, but I was not sure, since there was no blood found at the scene. I observed a snub-nosed .25-caliber revolver on the floor next to one of the chairs. It took me about four hours to take photographs, draw a rough sketch of the room, and identify and collect evidence, including the revolver from the floor. My night had not even begun yet.

I needed to get a key to secure the room where the shooting occurred, and I wanted to interview SP4 Olsen. I finished my crime scene and shut the door to the room, requesting that the MPs continue to guard the room until I could get a key for the door. Both MPs did not look too happy about being required to stay at the scene. I don't much blame them, because it was 4:00 a.m., the day after Christmas, and they wanted to be home in a nice, warm bed.

Just before I departed, I stopped by the CQ's desk to tell him we needed a key to the door so I could secure it in case I needed to follow up on any search. He indicated he would try but that a lot of soldiers on holiday leave and the supply sergeant might be one of them.

"Just find someone that knows where the key is so that we can have the MPs secure the room," I told him and left the building.

I went directly to the CID office, secured the evidence confiscated at the shooting crime scene, and called the MP desk sergeant to have a unit bring SP4 Olsen to my office for an interview. About fifteen minutes later, the MP unit arrived with SP4 Olsen. I had concerns about doing the interview at this hour, but in any event, I had prepared for it. I was obviously concerned about what SP4 Olsen's physical state was; he had been drinking most of the evening leading up to the shooting. To mitigate this situation, he had almost five hours to rest, and I had been advised by the MP desk sergeant that he was observed sleeping in the holding cell at the MP station. Another concern was the status of Bo'nes. Was he seriously injured or dead from the gunshot? If Bo'nes was seriously injured but still alive, the offense would be *attempted murder*; if he was dead, it would be *murder*.

I decided to go ahead with the interview. Before I started the interview of SP4 Olsen, I called Irwin Army Community Hospital and spoke to an emergency room nurse that I knew, and she confirmed that Bo'nes was dead on arrival. I had SP4 Olsen brought to my office by one of the MPs who'd transported him to the CID office. I sat him down in front of my desk, not beside it. I chose this setting because in front of the desk, suspects cannot see what you are writing, they become more anxious, are less likely to lie, and the interviewer appears to be in charge, be less friendly, and have authority and power. If they sit to the side of the desk, suspects become more comfortable and relaxed and can see the interviewer as less intimidating and friendlier, and they are more likely to lie. At least this was my experience in previous interviews.

I asked SP4 Olsen if he felt okay to go through the interview, and he replied, "Yes."

I read him his rights for homicide and having an unregistered, loaded gun in the barracks. He waived his rights to counsel and consented to be interviewed about the shooting. He admitted to me that he and Bo'nes had gone to the dining facility to eat a Christmas dinner and returned to the barracks about 5:00 p.m., where they'd started drinking Bacardi rum from about 6:30 p.m. to about 10:00 p.m. About 10:00 p.m., and while intoxicated, he removed his .25-caliber snub-nosed revolver from his wall locker and showed it to Bo'nes. SP4 Olsen admitted he was influenced by alcohol when he pulled the revolver from his wall locker. He also admitted to putting a couple of bullets in the cylinder and pointing the gun to his head. Bo'nes immediately attempted to grab the gun from SP4 Olsen just before he accidently pulled the trigger.

"Although I had drunk quite a bit of rum at that point, I was never in any real danger of shooting myself, because I was careful to ensure that there were no bullets in the chamber; I had only been fooling around and never intended to pull the trigger. It was a combination of alcohol and being angry at Bo'nes for trying to get the revolver from me that caused my finger to pull on the trigger," he said. "But I swear I didn't have any intention of shooting Bo'nes. He was my friend, and we did everything together," he continued, crying.

"Where did you get the gun?" I inquired.

"From a street thug in Chicago when I was home on leave early this year," he lamented.

During the interview, SP4 Olsen was crying and showed genuine remorse over the incident. Once I completed the interview, I felt that if the circumstances were as SP4 Olsen described them, he would more than likely be charged with negligent homicide for the unintentional shooting of his friend SP4 Bo'nes.

I saw SP4 Olsen and SP4 Bo'nes as true friends who had experienced the ultimate tragedy of death. SP4 Bo'nes died, and SP4 Olsen would be living the death over and over until he died. If the events leading up to Bo'nes's death could be altered only slightly, what if the two returned to their barracks room and, instead of drinking, watched TV, played cards, or went to a movie? Everything is simple when you think of it as an afterthought. The chain of events that set this tragedy in motion started when SP4 Olsen bought the snub-nosed revolver in Chicago and brought it to Fort Riley.

With SP4 Olsen's statement completed, I released him to the MP station for processing. It was now about 8:00 a.m. on December 26, 1979. I was relieved that I could catch SP4 Olsen's commander by phone at the early hour. I advised him on the details on the case with a tactful recommendation that SP4 Olsen be kept in the barracks instead of being placed in confinement. My work on this case was far from being over, but I had a gut feeling the shooting had gone down just as SP4 Olsen had described it.

I had to attend the autopsy and send evidence to the crime lab. Since it was the Christmas holiday season, several days went by before the autopsy was performed. Christmas fell on Tuesday of that week back in 1979, and I recalled thinking that I would be lucky if I talked to SJA within the next couple of days. I was fortunate to find a trial counselor in his office later in the day and decided to see him in person. The meeting took place about noon, because the trial counselor was working only partial days. SJA ruled that CID should initially title SP4 Olsen with homicide and see where the investigation led us before a final decision would be made on the offense. Later that day, I was lucky to locate the pathologist at Irwin, who told me that he'd planned the autopsy of SP4 Bo'nes for December 28. Luck was on my side.

Friday, December 28, 1979, at 10:00 a.m. sharp, the autopsy of SP4 Bo'nes was conducted at the morgue at Irwin Army Community Hospital, Fort Riley. I inspected the remains of SP4 Bo'nes and took photographs of his body lying on the examination table, from head to toe. It was unnerving to see SP4 Bo'nes lying motionless on the table, eyes wide open, a look of shock frozen, probably instantly affixed, as the bullet entered his forehead just above his right eye, causing immediately death before his body collapsed to the floor. A narrow entrance wound with little blood spill could be seen on the right forehead area just above his right eye, consistent with an entrance wound from a small-caliber projectile. No exit wound could be found. There were no more markings on the body. His arms and legs were very flexible, indicating that he had been dead for at least thirty-six hours or better, which was consistent with the time frame the shooting occurred. Noticeable livor mortis, a purplish discoloration of the skin with intermediate white blotches, was seen on the posterior (back side) of the body, which was also consistent with the way it was found.

The pathologist took two hours to complete the autopsy, which resulted in finding the small projectile lodged in the frontal part of the brain, causing a significant amount of internal bleeding and damage. The pathologist said his report would reflect the cause of death to SP4 Bo'nes was blunt force trauma caused when the bullet pierced the skull and entered the brain tissue. The pathologist was briefed before the autopsy began on the circumstances of the case, and he left the manner of death to be determined by the CID, supported by their investigation.

The physical evidence supported what SP4 Olsen reported in his statement the night of the shooting. The crime lab found SP4 Bo'nes's fingerprints on the gun, which added creditability that he tried to get the gun from SP4 Olsen. The evidence combined with my testimony as to SP4 Olsen's actions and behavior showing genuine remorse over the incident during his interview influenced the jury in making their decision to convict SP4 Olsen of negligent homicide instead of involuntary manslaughter.

He was reduced to PV1, required to forfeit pay and allowances, and sentenced to one year of confinement. I feel the court got it right.

After pulling duty on Christmas night for SA Dennis Jones, I went back to managing the Fort Riley DST but was retained as the lead agent on the Bo'nes shooting investigation. I will never forget the sheer shock locked onto SP4 Bo'nes's face when I viewed his body at the Irwin Army Community Hospital that morning. Another young kid that would never have a full life. He would never get married, see or do things with his kids, never make decisions about family, money, or those actions that affect life, for he was dead.

During the spring of 1980, the Fort Riley DST continued to develop criminal intelligence about illegal drugs. Special Agent Burns and MPIs Brazell and Stewart and I worked well together, but good things do not last forever. One day in early March 1980, I was called into LTC (P) Thompson's office and informed that he wanted to get me more diversified experience.

*I am leaving the DST*, I thought, and I was right. LTC (P) Thompson, sitting behind his desk, looking very much the image of a commander, invited me to sit down on his office couch. That was something positive, I saw it in his face, because if I were in real trouble, I would be standing. When the commander calls you into his office and you do not know why, your mind always conjures up something negative.

"Dick, I want to run something by you," Thompson stated.

Well, he did not call me by my rank and last name, so I guessed he has something positive to tell me. I felt relieved.

"I like what you have accomplished on the DST," the commander started, breaking the silence.

*Very positive where is this going*, I mused.

"CW3 Dawson, TC of GCT-B, is being reassigned, and I want you to take his place."

The change in duty positions would mean that I would be leaving the Fort Riley DST. I thought that the move would only help my career; I would be a general crimes team chief, a position I saw as a step up the chain of command. But, hey, my mind started reeling with questions, like "Why me?" CW3 Dawson's team had a CW2 team member. Why not him? The move seemed to be a step in the right direction, so I told him I had no objections to the move.

"What about my replacement?" I asked.

With a slight hesitation, he replied, "Well, I haven't made a decision on that yet."

His hesitation led me to believe that he had either put some thought into who he wanted to take my place or that the decision had already been made and he was not ready to announce it yet.

Thompson gave me two weeks to make the transfer and to alert the members of the DST what was to transpire. He concluded our meeting by directing me to tell Special Agent Burns he was also leaving the team, effectively immediately; I thought this was rather a strange move, but I did not waste time pondering the reason for the change.

In early 1980, Chief Ballow retired, and CW4 Merlin Kuhlman replaced him as the Fort Riley operations officer. Changes in the office were gradual; the most significant change was set in motion prior to Chief Kuhlman's arrival. The major change involved the Fort Riley DST. After all the changes, I now know, but to this day, I do not understand why LTC (P) Thompson was not up front with me in his office the day he selected me to take over GCT-B. I found out that his decision after changing me to GCT-B was to select Don Shanley as the DST chief and send Special Agent Ownby and two other agents to the team as well. One way to look at the personnel change: it took four agents to replace me and Special Agent Burns.

Being away from the DST job allowed me more free time in the evening and to get to know Olga and her family a lot better. She had a seven-year-old daughter and five-year-old son. Her father ran and operated a Mexican restaurant in Manhattan. However, I was more into developing my career than having a permanent relationship. I was ready to let time set the progress of our relationship. She was sort of set in her ways and was not easily swayed by change. We spent our time dining out and socializing with mutual friends, but I sensed there were extreme differences in our personalities that I determined could make us incompatible for a long-term relationship.

While still technically serving as the TC of the Fort Riley DST, I started becoming more involved with the GCT-B. I started reviewing cases of members of the team and making decisions. CW3 Dawson had about one week left before he departed, which was the same time I had remaining on the DST. However, trouble does not wait for time. You can never plan your day without something coming along and changing it. One morning in early May 1980, as the office was gathering for the daily meeting, I received a call from the Fort Riley assistant provost marshal, Major William Smith.[70]

Without as much as a hello, he blurted, "This is Major Smith. Did you know one of your DST members was shot in a robbery attempt last night?"

"What did you say?" I responded.

"SP4 Brazell was shot in downtown Junction City last night by someone who tried to rob him," Smith said.

"Where is he now?" I inquired.

"He was shot in the left hand," Major Smith said.

"Where is Brazell now?" I asked again.

"He is being treated at Irwin."

As I disconnected from Major Smith, I immediately became suspicious as to the circumstances surrounding the incident. It just did not fit right that SP4 Brazell would even be in Junction City, let alone be the victim of a robbery.

Of course, I had to investigate the incident as if it had occurred as reported. It was my policy that if members of the DST ever needed help or assistance, to let me know; in this case, it didn't happen.

I let Chief Kuhlman know what had been reported and excused myself from the meeting. This was a very discouraging investigation for me, because I had grown to like SP4 Brazell. I was concerned about SP4 Brazell, whom I considered not only a DST member but a friend. I have recounted in the following narrative my recollection of what occurred in the Brazell shooting investigation, which I called the Case of the Careless and Unwise Military Police Investigator.

## THE CASE OF THE CARELESS AND UNWISE MILITARY INVESTIGA-TOR
Regardless of how good things are, there are always hiccups and bumps along the way

I headed for the DST office to pick up a camera so I could photograph Brazell's wounds and the area where the reported robbery had occurred. I parked in front of the DST office, and as I opened the door to my car, I immediately noticed what I believed to be blood droppings on the ground. I followed the trail, which led into the DST office and directly to SP4 Brazell's desk. Red droppings were also found on top of his desk. Based on the trail of suspected blood, it looked like the strange shooting of SP4 Billy Brazell had taken place inside the Fort Riley DST office and not while he was in downtown Junction City, Kansas, being robbed.

I immediately called Chief Kuhlman and informed him of my findings; he concurred with my conclusions that there was probably no robbery and the shooting was accidental. He told me to keep digging and put the pieces of the puzzle together.

The findings in this case were not surprising, to say the least, but were disappointing. SP4 Brazell came from Texas and, before entering the US Army, worked in some capacity, possibly as a drug informant, with local law enforcement agencies. I had put certain things together that SP4 Brazell told me over the few months he had worked for me that made me believe he may have gotten in too deep with a group of drug dealers in Texas and had to get out of the area for his own safety. The US Army was the best way he could accomplish this without a large expense on his part. Since working for me, he had been a little rough around the edges, but he generally was a good investigator.

Accidentally shooting himself showed a degree of carelessness, but trying to cover it up by fabricating that he had been shot in a robbery obviously aggravated the situation. Further, if my suspicions were correct and he had been intoxicated and accidentally shot himself in the DST office, it showed a gross lack of judgment. Did he use his military weapon, or was it a personal handgun? I had to piece all this together by sorting out facts from fiction.

I conducted a crime scene examination at the DST office. I took photographs of the suspected blood droppings, obtaining samples for lab analysis. After my crime scene examination was completed, my next step was to have SP4 Brazell interviewed.

SP4 Brazell was released later that morning from Irwin and returned to his MP unit. I arranged for another agent from the office to interview him. Besides me, Chief Kuhlman assigned three other agents to the case. One agent was to conduct an interview with SP4 Brazell, one agent concentrated on interviewing members of SP4 Brazell's MP unit, and another agent was directed to run down leads at local area gun stores to determine if he'd purchased a personal handgun. I would continue to collect evidence at the DST office and coordinate with the Junction City Police Department to get information on the reported robbery, if possible.

CID's investigation ascertained that there was no record found of him purchasing a personal handgun in the area. Investigation also disclosed that no robbery was reported to the Junction City Police Department on the night in question.

Several members of his MP unit knew him to have a personal small-caliber, possibly a .22 handgun. A couple of the MPs saw the gun and confirmed it to be a .22-caliber revolver. DST MP members were required to turn their service revolvers in to the arms room when not working. SP4 Brazell had followed policy and turned his service revolver in the previous evening when he'd gotten off work. An inspection of the arms room revealed the weapon was properly signed in, and an examination showed it had not been fired recently, and all SP4 Brazell's assigned ammo was accounted for. In addition to these findings, medical personnel at Irwin Army Community Hospital confirmed that SP4 Brazell had been drinking and appeared to be intoxicated when examined at the emergency room. Armed with this information, SP4 Brazell was interviewed, but when confronted with the overwhelming evidence that no robbery occurred, he did not waive his rights and requested a lawyer. The CID investigation concluded that SP4 Brazell probably, under the influence of alcohol, shot himself in the left hand accidently while at the DST office.

Although the CID case had substantial evidence that SP4 Brazell fabricated the robbery, apparently to cover up his mishandling of a personal weapon in the DST office, the Fort Riley SJA decided not to take the case to court-martial because, outside of his spontaneous admission that he had been robbed that night, we had no information from SP4 Brazell, the weapon used in the shooting was never found, and the practicality of prosecuting the case lacked merit. Instead, SP4 Brazell received a Chapter 10 general discharge in lieu of court-martial.

I as think back on SP4 Brazell's performance on the DST for the few months he worked for me, I realize he had the makings of a promising career with the MP corps. Another wasted opportunity gone.

After the SP4 Brazell case, things settled down for me. I had now transferred to the GCT-B and started getting involved with managing general crimes. It felt strange directing agents on how to conduct their investigations, and as a manager, it was a totally different world. I had yet to settle into any real style of leadership, and I still had a lack of confidence in my abilities to direct others, but time would be on my side.

The month of June 1980 was extremely hot at Fort Riley and a very busy one at that. In the middle of the month, I received orders for Heidelberg, Germany, with a reporting date of August 18, 1980. My tenure as TC of GCT-B would run about four months. I appreciated LTC (P) Thompson providing me the opportunity to work as a team chief until I departed Fort Riley.

June was also the month Thompson was promoted to colonel. He was promoted in a ceremony at post headquarters by MG Kaplan, the First Division commanding general. Several of us from the Fort Riley CID office were in attendance, as well as Colonel Thompson's family. Based on his promotion, Colonel Thompson received orders assigning him to be the commander of law enforcement command at Fort Carson, Colorado. He departed Fort Riley a few days after his promotion. I was receptive to his counsel and leadership, and I will always have fond memories of him.

My relationship with Olga was showing some major wear and tear. She started pressuring me to get married, and I was not certain that was the route I wanted to go with her. In early June 1980, to compound our already strained circumstances, Olga called me at my office one midafternoon, sounding hysterical.

"Slow down. What is the matter?" I said, trying to calm her down.

"My dad just shot Narc."

"What the hell for?" I asked.

"Dad saw him chewing the horse's bridle."[71]

"Damn!" I shouted. "Why didn't he just chase the darn dog away?" I stated. "Is he still alive?"

"Yes, after being shot, he ran underneath the house. I checked on him right before I called, and he is still there," she said.

I left the office early that day and drove the fifteen or twenty miles to Olga's in Wamego.

Once I got there, I quickly found Narc underneath the house. Poor Narc, shivering, scared, with a belly full of lead, barely able to hold up his head. What a way to end a pet's life. As I was recovering the dog from underneath the house, Olga came outside and watched. I picked up the little guy, and he did not look good. I carried him the short distance to my car and placed him in the backseat. Hardly acknowledging her presence, I got into the car and rushed him to the vet in Junction City.

After the examination, the vet said Narc's abdomen was severely damaged and he had a lot of internal bleeding; the prognosis was not good. "I could do exploratory surgery, but it would be costly, and there is no assurance I could save him. Or you could just put him down," the vet added.

I chose to put good old Narc down.

"That is what I would do," the vet said, acknowledging that I had made the right decision.

After the episode with Narc, I did not feel like going back to work and went home for the evening. I did not talk to Olga for a couple of days. She broke the ice and called me.

"Would you come over?" she asked hesitantly.

"I don't think it is a good idea. As a matter of fact, I suggest we not see each other for a while," I informed her with little emotion.

She said, "Okay," and without another word hung up.

I did not consider this a breakup exactly, but more like a "I want a rest from you for a while" type of situation. My lukewarm feelings for Olga transcended the shooting of Narc, although it may have been the catalyst that sparked my decision not to see her for a while and had more to do with her overall egocentric personality.

My time at Fort Riley was ending, and I was finishing up with my caseload, which I continued to carry even though I had performed duties as a TC for four months. I had sent a message to Second Region to alert them on my pending assignment. Officially, they already knew I was coming, but the purpose of my message was to determine if I had a sponsor. About a week after my inquiry, I received a message back from Second Region headquarters that SA Dale Anderburg had been selected as my sponsor and that he would be assisting me upon arrival in Germany. This was good news, because I had initially met Dale at Fort Sheridan.

Dale had been assigned to work economic crimes cases, technically stationed at Fort Sheridan but under the control of HQ CID command. At the time, I recall the people involved with this program were called Logcip agents. I seem to recall that Logcip stood for Logistics Criminal Investigative Program, but as time evolved, CID renamed the program economic crimes. I let Second Region know that I would advise them of my itinerary when I received my arrival information. *Hey*, I thought, *this is great*. It was the first assignment I had where I would have a sponsor and someone to greet me upon arrival at my new duty station. My orders assigned me directly to Second Region and not any sub office within Germany. I wondered what position I would fill at headquarters. Surely, I was not being considered for an assignment to level-one drug investigations; I thought this was improbable, because agents usually were not directly assigned to this unit. As I found out later, I was mistaken.

In my final months at Fort Riley, I also performed as duty agent every week or so and usually kept most of the cases I initiated. Chief Kuhlman directed that my last twenty-four-hour duty agent day would be on Saturday, June 21, 1980. Making June 21 my final twenty-four-hour duty day would allow me enough time to finish up my ongoing cases before I departed Fort Riley, which was now set for July 31, 1980.

As scheduled, on Saturday, June 21, 1980, I performed my last duty day at Fort Riley. It was a busy duty agent day. I investigated the usual housebreaking and larceny, an aggravated assault where one soldier struck another in a barracks fight, causing a rather serious laceration to his left cheek, and a reported rape of a female soldier. I had not identified anyone for the housebreaking and larceny, but the rape case was unfounded after I got the female soldier to admit she was angry at her boyfriend and tried to get back at him by accusing him of rape. Of course, a suspect in the aggravated assault had been identified when I got the call and had confessed to hitting the other soldier, causing his injuries. All in all, up to the time I finished processing the crimes, I considered my last duty day to be typical for a hot summer day. This would change later in the evening when my last typical duty agent day took a turn toward one of the most unusual duty days I had ever worked.

On the evening of June 21, 1980, I was in my office catching up on paperwork related to the cases I'd initiated during the day. About 9:00 p.m., MPI Duty Investigator Carol Henderson[72] dropped by to chat. MPI Henderson had a busy day as well and had just finished her preliminary reports on the investigations she was called out on during the day. Since I had also made good progress on completing my reports, I suggested to MPI Henderson that we take a drive around the post to check some of the hot spots where soldiers were known to get into trouble, like clubs, bowling alleys, and barracks parking lots. We had a routine on weekends, if time allowed, to also pick up soldiers, especially the ones suspected of being intoxicated, and drive them safely to their barracks.

After about an hour driving around the installation, we turned onto the road leading to Ogden. This access road took us by the Camp Funston area of Fort Riley. Along the way, we observed three soldiers walking on the side of the road, all apparently intoxicated, probably trying to make their way back to their barracks and an evening of partying. I slowed our vehicle and had MPI Henderson roll down the car window and ask them if they wanted a ride to their unit.

"Sure," one of the three responded.

I stopped the vehicle, and the three piled into the backseat.

"Where are you guys going?" I asked.

"Unit One at Camp Funston," responded one of them.

Unit One was not far from where we'd picked them up, and I started heading in that direction.

I had driven about an eighth of a mile when I observed another soldier, dressed in a bright red shirt and blue jeans, staggering alongside the road. I slowed down the vehicle and had MPI Henderson ask the young soldier if he needed a ride to his unit.

Slurring his words, he responded, "Yes. That would be okay."

Since we did not have enough room in the car, MPI Henderson told him we would be right back as soon as we dropped off these guys, pointing to the backseat. MPI Henderson told the lone soldier that it shouldn't be more than five minutes. He waved without verbally responding. It took about five minutes to get to Unit One at Camp Funston, where the three soldiers thanked us as they got out of the car. I immediately turned the car around and headed back to the area where we'd left the lone soldier in the bright red shirt.

When we got to the area, the soldier was nowhere to be found. Since the soldier was gone, we decided to call it a night and returned to the CID office. MPI Henderson left for the MP station, and I returned to my desk to continue working on other cases. I was hoping that the soldiers would be quiet tonight and would not commit any violent acts. I did have enough paperwork that could keep me up the whole night, but I was thinking about catching some shut-eye and lay down on the duty agent bed for a quick nap.

Around midnight, I was startled awake by the sound of the telephone ringing. It was the MP desk sergeant informing me that the railroad control center notified the MP desk that an engineer moving a train through Fort Riley, heading for Topeka, had reported seeing a man's head alongside the tracks near Camp Funston. There was no further information provided by the railroad engineer. I rushed to the MP station, verified the details, and discovered that the engineer controlling the train did not stop. I also ascertained that no MP patrol had been dispatched yet. I informed the MP desk sergeant that I was headed to the area to conduct a search. It was a warm night, and the area where the head was reported was not far from where MPI Henderson and I had last seen the soldier in the bright red shirt. I summarize in narrative format what investigative actions I took on that night what I call the Case of the Sleepy Soldier Who Lost His Life:

## THE CASE OF THE SLEEPY SOLDIER WHO LOST HIS LIFE
There is no way to stop what is inevitable

As I left the MP station and walked toward my car, MPI Henderson caught up with me and offered her assistance in the search.

"Come on. Let's go." I told her.

I drove a couple of miles down Huebner Road and turned on an access street to Camp Funston where I knew the railroad tracks crossed over. The location made me a little uneasy, because it was near the area where we had seen the soldier we'd promised to give a ride to his unit; however, he'd left that area before we'd returned. I parked the car, and MPI Henderson and I walked the short distance to the railroad tracks. I instructed MPI Henderson to take the left side of the tracks while I searched the right. Both in possession of long, black police flashlights to light up the area, we proceeded down the railroad tracks.

The two of us had walked about a quarter of a mile down the railroad tracks when I noticed in front of me what appeared to be a human body lying a few yards off to my left. As I approached, I froze when I saw that the torso was dressed in a bright red shirt. As I moved cautiously forward, I noticed the torso was missing a head.

"Hey, I found something!" I yelled at MPI Henderson.

She was a short distance behind and to the left of me. She joined me and immediately turned her head to one side. For a second, I thought MPI Henderson was going to lose it, but she hung in there and regained her composure. A closer examination disclosed the body had obviously received severe trauma and was grossly twisted and mangled. The right arm had been severed above the elbow, and most of his left hand was missing. I checked the pockets of the human remains and found his wallet. The wallet contained his US Army identification card that identified him as PV2 James Wilmore.[73] I placed his wallet and other personal effects into a plastic bag that I had obtained from a crime scene kit and continued walking a short distance when I saw the head by itself lying on the right side of the tracks. I radioed the MP desk and informed them of our findings. I requested an ambulance and an MP patrol to be dispatched to the scene. I further requested the MP desk to ascertain when the next scheduled train was due to pass through the area. In the meantime, I sent MPI Henderson back to the car to retrieve the crime scene kit. I continued to inspect the area where we'd found the body parts.

The MP patrol was the first to arrive at the scene, shortly followed by the ambulance from Irwin Army Community Hospital. I instructed the MPs to set up a perimeter from the intersection where the tracks crossed the small side road to a location I would determine once I inspected the entire area. I requested the MPs keep the ambulance team at bay, pending a determination on how broad the scene was going to be. I also requested for more MPs to help with securing the perimeter of the scene. After instructing them on what I needed, I requested MPI Henderson to accompany me down the tracks. We walked another twenty-five or so yards before we came upon a trestle.

The trestle, which had a wooden frame that crossed a small creek, was approximately fifty feet in length. About halfway across, I saw was appeared to be blood pooled in an area about four feet in diameter. To me this looked like the place where the train had struck Wilmore.

By this time, more MPs had arrived, and I assigned one of them to watch the bloodstained area. I also received a radio call from the MP desk sergeant, who related that the next train due to pass through the area was at 8:00 a.m. *Great*, I thought. *This gives us several hours of time without interruption to process the scene.*

With the origin of the scene believed to be on the trestle, this was where I started processing the scene. I took photographs using a 35-mm camera with a flash. However, I knew I would have to return in the daylight to get better shots showing a panorama view of the area. I observed what appeared to be scratch marks in the wood leading from the blood pool to the end of the trestle. These marks could have been caused by the victim's body being dragged across the trestle after he was struck by the train. It was hard to tell, because of the lack of light, but MPI Henderson was a tremendous help in holding the police flashlight while I inspected the area. I could get bits and pieces of torn tissue, bone fragments, and torn clothing off the trestle.

I radioed the on-site MP sergeant patrol supervisor and directed him to tell the ambulance team to bring a large body bag and gurney and join me on the trestle. The two medics took about ten minutes to reach my location with the gurney and body bag. I requested that since we had multiple body parts strewn over a rather large area that they maintain integrity of the torso and head while I secured the smaller pieces. As I worked my way to the victim's head, I photographed each piece of flesh, bone, and so on and supervised the medics as they placed assorted remains inside the body bags.

As we searched along the tracks, a portion of a left hand and the severed right arm were found. I photographed and allowed the medics to place the remains of the torso in the body bag. The terrain made it hard for the medics to move the gurney along the track, so they ended up carrying it with the assistance of two MPs. The collection of human remains went on for several hours. By the time, I was confident I had retrieved most of the human remains, it was 06:30 a.m. and daylight, so I retraced the scene from where the main body had been found to the train trestle for another closer look in the daylight. A few various remains were found that were placed in plastic bags. I subsequently released the MP patrols and followed the ambulance with the remains to Irwin Army Community Hospital.

Since it was a Sunday morning, I could not find a pathologist at the hospital, so any type of autopsy could not be scheduled until later in the week. I then left the hospital and dropped MPI Henderson off at the MP station, briefed the MP desk sergeant, and returned to the CID office and prepared the serious or sensitive investigation (SSI) report for distribution. What an unforgettable last duty agent day I had at Fort Riley.

I had seen dead bodies in previous death investigations and had attended autopsies where the remains had been cut open for examinations, but PV2 Wilmore's body was by far in the worst condition of any of them; he died a violent death. The horrific image of his remains will forever by embedded in my mind. I can also not help, but think that Wilmore's death could have been avoided if only he had waited for MPI Henderson and me that night. During the autopsy, his remains were so distorted that the investigation had to focus on toxicology results and what PV2 Wilmore's activities were before his death. I retained the PV2 Wilmore case for about a month before handing it over to another special agent for completion, due to the fact I was leaving Fort Riley for Germany.

On Monday morning, the autopsy was conducted on the remains of PV2 Wilmore that disclosed he had a high level of alcohol in his system at the time of death, rendering him legally intoxicated, which probably contributed to the circumstances that led to his death. There was nothing in my investigation that altered my belief that PV2 Wilmore lay down on the trestle, fell asleep, and was unable to react quickly enough to get out of the train's path when it moved along the tracks.

For some reason, I consented to take Olga to dinner and a movie in Junction City that Monday evening. I made the date to tell her it was all over with us; in retrospect, I now realize I picked the wrong venue for breaking the news to her, but my mind was made up. My plan to tell her our relationship was over changed when I walked up to the ticket booth to pay for the movie. As I was purchasing tickets to the movie, the attendant recognized me as the lead investigator at the train tracks the previous Saturday. He happened to be one of the medics that assisted me that evening. After a very praiseworthy commentary about my abilities and leadership at the scene, he let us see the movie without charge. This impressed

Olga, and for the rest of the evening, she would not stop talking about it. Until the man at the movie theater confronted me with his impressions of my actions the previous Saturday, I had not mentioned anything to Olga about my investigation of the man getting hit by the train. I let my decision to break up with her that evening slide. Olga tried her darnedest to rejuvenate our relationship, but a couple of weeks before I left Fort Riley, we met one final time, and I told her it was over.

It was now early July 1980, and I had my final duty agent day behind me and the date firmed up as to when I was leaving Fort Riley. The rest of my time would be utilized in finishing up cases I had been assigned. The new commander and Chief Kuhlman were very fair in allowing me enough time to get all the investigations done that I could. So, figuring there was enough time for personal endeavors as well, I brazenly went into Chief Kuhlman's office and asked for a three-day weekend. I informed him I would like to visit my son, whom I had not seen for quite some time; he consented. I used the time to drive to Indiana, where I convinced Melitta to allow me to have Chris for a few weeks. With Chris in tow, I drove back to Kansas, where he stayed with me for the rest of my time at Fort Riley. It was a good time for both of us, and he seemed to enjoy our time together.

After bringing Chris back to Fort Riley with me, I still had obligations to complete my cases, but we spent every evening together. My investigation into the victim hit by the train concluded that he was probably the same soldier that MPI Henderson and I saw alongside the road that night. We will never know for sure if it was him, because he was not recognizable due to the condition of his body after being hit by the train. A few of my cases had no leads, so I closed them as unsolved. There were also three or four that could not be closed, because leads were still pending. For the most part, I cleaned up the caseload without leaving any difficult investigations pending for other agents.

Finally, on July 28, 1980, the day before I departed Fort Riley, I was promoted to CW2 by the new Fort Riley commander. The last day at Fort Riley, the office had a farewell luncheon for me, and most of the people attended. A few got up and spoke about how they liked working with me and were looking forward to running into me in the future. They presented me with a plaque depicting my time and position at Fort Riley.

I will always have fond memories of my time at Fort Riley. I met and worked with a lot of very good agents, five of which earned their warrant bars in one big ceremony: Special Agents Mike Burns, David Ownby, Tim Graham, David Dietz, and Rick Deguise. I would run into each of them many times again before the end of my career, and Burns and Graham became life-long friends.

Fort Riley represented the third consecutive quality CID assignment. Before I departed Fort Riley, I got a message off to Heidelberg to let Second Region USACIDC know I would be arriving on August 18, 1980.

On August 1, 1980, with Chris in tow, I left Fort Riley, taking two days to drive to Terre Haute for a well-deserve break before heading off to Heidelberg, Germany. I spent a little over a week with Mom, June, and other family members, and best of all, I could be with Chris for the entire period of my leave. Chris, who within a little over a month would turn eight years old, was growing into a nice young boy with good manners and a disposition that makes a parent proud. Visiting with the family was good, but before I knew it, it was August 15. I made my way to Charleston AFB in two days and dropped off my car for shipment to Germany and then caught a chartered flight out of Charleston within two hours for Frankfurt, Germany, to begin a new phase in a very exciting and rewarding career in CID.

Destroying an estimated $1 million worth of wild marijuana at Fort Riley, orchastrated by DST, circa 1979.

MP from First MP Company, assisting CID DST with the eradication of marijuana field on Fort Riley, circa 1979.

Author getting promoted to CW2 at Fort Riley by the commander and secretary Tomie July 28, 1980.

# 9

# Pivotal Career Assignment

Greater Responsibilities, Improving Management, and Supervisory Skills

Schweinfurt, Germany

*Build on your accomplishments to make them better*

At about 10:45 a.m. on August 18, 1980, I arrived in Germany from Charleston, South Carolina, aboard a military-chartered jet after a seven-hour flight. Typical Millers' luck, no one from CID was at Frankfurt Airport to meet me when I arrived. I recall the day as being somewhat hot, with a mild breeze and blue skies. I waited at the airport terminal for some time in hopes someone from CID would show up, but they never came. I had to find alternate travel. I spotted a young SP4 soldier sitting in a deuce-and-a-half parked near the entrance. I approached him and asked, "Can I have a ride to Seckenheim Kaserne?"

"Sure. I am going right by there. Hop aboard," he replied.

I threw my duffel bag in the back and started to climb in.

"Hey, get up here in front with me," he directed.

He did not need to repeat himself. I got in, and we waited a few more minutes before his passenger, who was also in civilian clothes, walked out of the terminal and put his stuff in the back and got in beside me.

On the ride into Seckenheim Kaserne (post), which took about forty-five minutes, we talked about Germany, and they wanted to know why I was wearing a suit and tie. I told them I was a special agent with the CID, which sort of shut the lid on any more conversation.

I was dropped off in front of Second Region headquarters, got my duffel bag out of the back of the truck, and went inside.

The first person I meet was Sergeant Major (SGM) Curtis G. Ward. He was standing at the top of the steps when I entered the building.

"Where are you from?" he inquired.

"I just arrived from the States, and I am assigned to Second Region," I explained.

Looking puzzled, he inquired, "You mean you just got off the plane from the States?"

"Yes, that's right, and there was no one there to pick me up," I said, showing my frustration for having to find my way.

"Did we know you were coming?" he asked with a look of bewilderment.

Defending my position, I explained to SMG Ward, "Well, I thought I had it all taken care of. I sent messages to you guys but never received any reply."

"I need to check on this," he replied.

"Dale Anderburg was my sponsor, and we did communicate together, and I fired off a message right before I left Fort Riley, detailing my arrival date and time," I told him.

"Therein lies the problem. Dale is working in Israel. He has been there for over two weeks."

"Wouldn't someone else have gotten my message and acted on it?" I asked.

"I would think so," SMG Ward responded.

Discussing with anyone the reasons of why or why not someone was waiting for me were for naught, so I changed the conversation with SMG Ward to other things. He stopped me short and asked if I was hungry.

"Yes," I replied.

SMG Ward motioned in the direction of a staff sergeant who was sitting near where we were standing.

"Could you take this man to lunch?" he asked.

The SSG took me to a small German *Gasthaus*, and we ate a fine Deutschland meal of *jaeger schnitzel* and potatoes. When we returned to Seckenheim Kaserne, I met with the personnel sergeant, who verified my assignment directly to Second Region. I had no clue as to where I would be placed, but there was some inference that I was tentatively assigned to the level-one drug suppression team.

I had been a man without an assignment for about a week, doing absolutely nothing, when the Second Region operations officer, LTC Winston Campbell, called me into his office. Our conversation was straightforward and direct about my ultimate assignment.

"Are you interested in working level-one drugs?" he asked.

The question was not surprising and one I had been expecting since my arrival at Second Region. The question also confirmed what I had felt all along, that it was CID assignments officer CW4 Richard Greaves's intention of assigning me directly to level one. After all, my first two warrant officer evaluation reports contained laudatory narratives about my success and abilities to work narcotics investigations. With his question whirling around in my mind, I immediately tried to make sense of what I perceived to be the silent treatment I had experienced with certain agents. This perception caused me to have a great deal of uncertainty about the level-one assignment. Combined with having just gone through a week where no one from level one ever acknowledged, welcomed, or even introduced themselves to me created serious doubts in my mind concerning certain people's wishes not to have me on the level-one team.

I took the middle road and answered him the best way I could. "I don't want to spend the next ten years of my career working drugs," I informed him.

My answer was true, but in the back of my mind, I was thinking just the opposite. Looking somewhat surprised, he told me that Second Region could arrange for another assignment somewhere in Europe for me if I wanted it.

"Yes, I think that is best," I told him.

The entire conversation took about ten minutes. My actual thoughts and desires about working level-one drugs was somewhat ambiguous. I might have tried it if I'd felt the current establishment was more amenable to my coming on board. The decision I made that day changed my life for the best.

A short time later, LTC Campbell informed me that I had temporarily been assigned to the Schweinfurt resident agency. I immediately called Special Agent in Charge (SAC) John K. Boatwright and introduced myself to him. He was extremely polite in welcoming me to the office and very informative about what to expect. He indicated that when the orders were finalized, I should give him a call so he could arrange for one of the agents assigned to the office to pick me up at Second Region. I felt good about my conversation with SAC Boatwright and was looking forward to meeting him and the other agents in the office.

After arrangements for my temporary duty were taken care of, I put in a call to the Mainz resident agency and got ahold of Special Agent Larry Broadwell, an agent I had met in Korea. We talked for a while, and I asked about Special Agent Hite, who was supposed to also be at the office. He told me Joe was there waiting anxiously to speak with me.

Joe and I spoke for about fifteen minutes. It was decided that Larry would come to Second Region and give me a ride to Mainz for the weekend. It took Larry about an hour to drive the approximately fifty-five miles from Mainz. Larry and his wonderful wife invited me to spend the weekend with them. During the day, Joe and I used our time to catch up with our lives, and it was a good time for all. Sunday evening, Joe ran me back to Heidelberg.

On August 20, 1980, I called SAC Boatwright and told him I had received orders for a temporary assignment to Schweinfurt resident agency.

"I am sending Special Agent Lynn Muelhmeyer to pick you up. He should be there in about two hours," he said.

A couple of hours later, Special Agent Muelhmeyer picked me up at Second Region headquarters and drove approximately two hours to Schweinfurt, a city near the border of Czechoslovakia, about 135 or so miles from Heidelberg. The building that housed the Schweinfurt resident agency was in a small, three-story, multiple-family-style house in the little town of Niederwerrn, just outside of Schweinfurt. The CID office had found that the size and location of their building was considered inadequate, and about a week prior to my coming on board, they had moved to their current location from downtown Schweinfurt, Germany.

SAC Boatwright was sitting at his desk when Special Agent Muelhmeyer introduced us. He stood up and greeted me with a hearty handshake. He was a man about my height, in his mid-thirties, with a full head of curly brown hair. My first impression of him was that he was polite and friendly. I immediately liked him. SAC Boatwright took the time to thoroughly brief me on the operation of the office and took me around and introduced me to the other special agents—Ed Black, Larry Meyers, Bruce Maxium, and Roy Tuttle. The local national criminal investigator (LNCI) was Omar Luckhardt. Herr Luckhardt was a fifty-two-year-old German who had worked for the US Army since WWII.

After the introductions, SAC Boatwright placed me in the office directly next to his on the first floor of the building. He told me to take the rest of the day off to get settled in and report back to the office at 8:00 a.m. SA Muelhmeyer had arranged for me to stay where he was lodged at the Bier Hotel on the east side of Schweinfurt. I had a good meal with SA Muelhmeyer at the hotel restaurant and turned in early and had a restful night.

The city of Schweinfurt, Germany, has a unique and colorful history. The city was heavily bombed by the US Air Force during WWII, and a large portion of the city was destroyed. The Germans had established two military bases: one in the city of Schweinfurt they called Panzer Kaserne and the other just outside of Schweinfurt. The one outside Schweinfurt was a German airfield; both were originally built in the 1930s. The Schweinfurt resident agency supported these two major US Army installations in Schweinfurt and a third, Daley Barracks, in Bad Kissingen. The two installations in Schweinfurt: Panzer Kaserne, renamed Ledward; and Conn Barracks. Ledward was named in honor of LTC William J. Ledward, who was killed in action in Italy, June 1944. He was commanding officer of the Twenty-Seventh Armored Field Artillery Battalion. The US Army took control of Ledward Barracks in 1948. In 1947, the other installation in Schweinfurt was formerly a *flugplatz*, renamed Conn Barracks in honor of 2LT Orville B. Conn Jr. Lieutenant Conn was the first WWII casualty of the Sixth Cavalry Group, killed in action on August 10, 1944, at Normandy, France.[74] The Branch Office at Bad Kissingen, about 15 kilometers east of Schweinfurt was located on Daley Barracks. Originally named Manteuffel Kaserne after a German cavalry and political fame, Baron Freiherr von Manteuffel, was opened in the1930s. The US Army took over Daley Barracks in 1951. Daley Barracks was named after Technician Fifth Grade William T. Daley, who was posthumously awarded the Distinguished Service Cross for extraordinary heroism about military operations against the Germans. Daley Barracks used to be the home of the Fourteenth Military Police Criminal Investigation Detachment, which was deactivated in 1969.[75]

My first workday at the Schweinfurt resident agency was spent arranging my office and getting better acquainted with the other agents. I noticed the case board in SAC Boatwright's office showed that there were about fifteen cases per agent, and the ongoing investigations included deaths, serious assaults, larcenies, drugs—you name it, it was there. It looked like I was going to be very busy while assigned to the resident agency.

Our administrative clerk SP4 Kevin Merits's office looked like a disaster. There were case files all over the place, overflowing in his desk in-box, with stacks of case files on two different tables and several more stacks lying on top of his office filing cabinets. A closer look found a tall stack on the floor next to his desk. I thought, *Boy, I'll bet he is tired when he goes home in the evenings. He either lacks good organizational skills or he needs an assistant clerk to help him.*

I got settled in, and for the first two months, I was assigned to conduct general crime cases; and with the number of agents on board, twenty-four-hour duty agent days could be about once or twice a week. I found out just how busy the office could be. I initiated a variety of investigations, including a multitude of rape investigations, mostly reported on Saturday nights, and an unusually high amount of housebreaking and larceny incidents, aggravated assaults, and sexual assault cases. There were more rape investigations in Europe, than stateside. Inevitably, every Saturday night, our office was called to investigate a reported rape. About half of them were legitimate crimes; the other half were either unfounded or did not occur as reported, and most usually involved date-night situations.

The branch office at Bad Kissingen was just as busy for two agents as was the Schweinfurt office with six. On occasion, agents from Schweinfurt would have to travel the twenty kilometers or so to Bad Kissingen to assist with their investigations, because they were backed up. Two special agents assigned to the Bad Kissingen office were Ronald MacNelly and Erwin Forbes. Both were extremely talented and competent agents who worked hard to successfully resolve their investigations, but on occasions, they just needed Schweinfurt agents' help due to the sheer volume of cases that come into their office.

Deaths caused by driving while intoxicated (DWI) was another crime that was more prevalent in Europe compared to stateside. During my initial months at Schweinfurt, I investigated several DWI cases where personal injury, usually deaths, had occurred. The first DWI investigation I was called out on involved three young soldiers from the Third Battalion, Seventh ADA (Air Defense Artillery) at Conn Barracks. The case had personal ramifications for me well after the investigation was completed. The case is unique in that it was my first death investigation and I developed a connection with one of the young passengers, PFC Jonathan L. Trumwell[76] that survived. I call this investigation the Case of the Drunk but Remorseful Young Soldier:

## THE CASE OF THE DRUNK BUT REMORSEFUL YOUNG SOLDIER
It is stupid to drink and drive

It was a seasonally hot evening in mid-September 1980 when I got the call from the MP desk reporting a car crash had occurred near Conn Barracks. One of the soldiers was dead on arrival at the local Schweinfurt clinic. The driver and owner of the car was identified as PFC Stephen M. Williamson.[77] The initial report disclosed that PFC Williamson had attempted to take a corner on Niederwerrner Strasse too fast in his privately-owned vehicle (POV), causing him to lose control, propelling the car off the road into a tree. Fortunately for Williamson, he was not seriously injured, but tragically, his best friend and the front seat passenger in his car, PFC George L. McNeal,[78] was killed. To add to the gravity to Williamson's predicament, he was suspected to have been driving under the influence of alcohol. A third passenger, PFC Trumwell, was in the backseat of the car and received a hairline fracture to his right wrist.

Before interviewing the two survivors, I went to the scene of the car crash. When I arrived at the scene, an MP patrol was still there to protect the area until it was inspected. I pulled up and parked the CID sedan just off Niederwerrner Strasse just east of the main gate to Conn Barracks. I secured the 35-mm camera from the trunk of my car and approached the scene. The car, a blue older-model Ford, had crashed into a tree about fifteen feet from the road. It was obvious that the car was traveling at a high rate of speed when it struck the tree. The middle of the right side of the car was wrapped around the tree, with most of the damage being to the front passenger door.

After exposing photographs of the car, skid marks, and surrounding area, I went to the MP station to see if the other two occupants were well enough to be interviewed. The MP desk sergeant informed me that both individuals had already received medical treatment and were now at the MP station. PFC Williamson was in a holding cell, and PFC Trumwell was sitting on a bench in the hallway. I ascertained that all three soldiers apparently had been drinking. I requested the MP desk transport PFC Trumwell to the CID office so I could interview him. I requested the MP continue to hold PFC Williamson in the holding cell until I was ready for him. Under conditions when there is no death involved because of DWI, the driver would normally be interviewed by the MPs and then released to his unit, but since this case involved the death of PFC McNeal, the driver undoubtedly would be charged, depending on the evidence, with either involuntary manslaughter or negligent homicide.

An MP patrol brought PFC Trumwell to the CID office in Niederwerrn, where I interviewed him about the accident. His version had the three of them out drinking most of the evening at the Top Ten Club in downtown Schweinfurt. They all piled into Williamson's car for the ride back to their barracks.

"Once we were on the road, I fell asleep in the backseat of the car. I woke up when the car started to skid across the road," he said.

I asked him if Williamson had been driving the car, and he said, "Yes."

"You need to look at this incident as a lesson learned," I told him.

I could not believe his response when he said, "What do you mean by that?"

It was at this point I realized that he might not be aware that PFC McNeal had been killed.

"Are you aware that McNeal was killed in the crash?" I asked.

PFC Trumwell lowered his head, placed his hands over his face, and started to cry. Obviously emotionally distraught, because he had just been told he'd lost a good friend, he replied, "No, I didn't."

I summed up the interview and released PFC Trumwell to an MP patrol to be transported back to the MP station.

After I finished with PFC Trumwell, I had the MPs transport PFC Williamson to the CID office in Niederwerrn. It was 5:00 a.m., and it had been three hours since the accident occurred. I wanted Williamson to sober up before I interviewed him. I sat him down in my office for the interview at about 5:45 a.m. He looked okay, and to determine his condition, I engaged him in some small conversation unrelated to the car accident. Aside from being somewhat tired, as we all were, his voice was clear, and he seemed alert. I advised him of his rights for involuntary manslaughter, and he consented to talk about the car accident. Noticeably upset, he confessed to drinking and driving. He provided a written statement detailing the extent of his drinking that evening and the circumstances surrounding the car crash that killed his best friend, PFC McNeal.

The next morning, I attended the autopsy of twenty-two-year-old PFC McNeal. Upon my initial examination of PFC McNeal, I noticed a severe laceration to the right side of his head. His skull had been crushed, and there were several jagged lacerations to his forehead and right cheek. Glass fragments were imbedded into PFC McNeal's skin, cutting deep enough to have caused major internal damage. Once my examination of the body was complete, the pathologist took over.

The autopsy lasted about two hours, and the preliminary findings determined that PFC McNeal died from blunt force trauma to the brain, probably caused when his body was propelled forward with such force his head impacted with the window post dividing the front and back windows when the car struck the tree. Samples of PFC McNeal's blood were taken during the autopsy. About thirty days later, the toxicology report on PFC McNeal's confirmed that he had a blood alcohol level of .175, almost twice the legal limit to drive. The lab results of PFC Williamson's blood alcohol level were determined to be .210, more than twice the legal limit for driving.

A short time later, I ran into PFC Trumwell just outside the courtroom right before he was to testify in Williamson's trial. I noticed that there were no signs of the injury to his right wrist, but I suspected there might be some lingering psychological issues he was still dealing with because of PFC McNeal's death. I told him that he was a very lucky man to have survived the car crash with only a fractured wrist. I recalled what he told me in response: "Since the accident, I have spent a lot of time thinking about what happened and the choices we made that night. I have curbed my drinking and encourage others I am around to do the same. McNeal's death has caused me to change my drinking habits."

I thought for a moment about what PFC Trumwell said. "I hope you will use this incident as a positive step in reconsidering your actions when socializing in the future," I told him.

His final comment to me that day was, "You won't see me in a situation like this again."

As I walked away, I thought, *I hope not.* He seemed to be such a nice kid.

About forty-five days after the accident, PFC Williamson stood before a general court-martial and was found guilty of involuntary manslaughter instead of the lesser charge of negligent homicide. The factors that played a role in being found guilty of the more serious offense was due to his high blood to alcohol content exceeding .200, which increased his culpability and speed. He received a three-year sentence at the USADB, Fort Leavenworth, Kansas, was required to forfeit all pay and allowances, and received a dishonorable discharge from the US Army. Expensive price for a night out on the town.

Another investigation that I was involved with early in my assignment at Schweinfurt warrants attention because of the bizarre circumstances and total disregard the parents had for the health and well-being of their seven-month-old son. The incident was reported by the father, SP4 John Albert,[79] who called the MPs about 7:00 p.m. and said he found his seven-month-old son dead in his crib. Sudden infant death syndrome (SIDS) is usually what an investigator is thinking when he receives a call of this nature. CID's policy is to investigate all death cases until murder can be ruled out. SIDS, also known as cot death or crib death, is the sudden, unexplained death of a child usually less than one year of age. It requires that the death remains unexplained even after a thorough autopsy and detailed death scene investigation. This case was significant in that it was my first baby death, but it would not be the last. I called the investigation the Case of the Negligent Parents:

## THE CASE OF THE NEGLIGENT PARENTS
You must take responsibility to protect your kids

About 8:00 on a fall evening in 1980, I received a duty call from the MPs that a father had found his seven-month-old son dead in his crib. I gathered the duty agent kit and headed to the address given to me by the MPs in Askren Manor, a US military housing area, located in the city of Schweinfurt, Germany. I arrived about twenty minutes later and found an MP patrol and a medical ambulance at the scene. I asked the first MP, who was standing guard at the door to the house, "Where are the parents?"

"They are both sitting in the kitchen," he said.

"Where is the baby?" I asked.

"He is in the bedroom with the medics," the MP responded.

"What are the parents' names?" I asked.

One MP replied, "SP4 John Albert and Susan Albert."

As I walked toward the room where the baby was, I glanced through the doorway of the kitchen and saw the parents sitting at the table. Neither one of them was crying. Although many parents react differently to their child dying, the lack of emotion of these parents stuck with me. As I continued into the room, I assumed the baby was dead. I walked into what appeared to be a bedroom without an adult bed. The only furniture in the room was a small chest of drawers and a baby crib. Even with a lack of furniture, the room looked unkempt and did not appear to have been cleaned for a while.

My examination of the baby in the crib disclosed that the body was on its back, dressed in soiled diapers, lying on top of dirty linens that had not been washed for several days or longer and smelled to high heaven. The body appeared to be underweight, bloated, and swollen, which was indicative of malnutrition. There were no visible signs of body trauma, and the body had minimal stiffness. The facial and torso areas of the baby were purplish and cold to the touch, a condition indicative of onset of livor mortis. Livor mortis, or lividity (pooling of blood in the body), occurs from two to eight hours after death. Environmental conditions such as temperature can influence a ruling on the time of death. Heat would speed up the decomposition of the body, and the cold would slow it down, but it appeared that the baby had been lying on its stomach for some time after death for the lividity to form on the frontal part of the body. I applied pressure with my forefinger to the baby's stomach, and the purplish color momentarily disappeared. This situation also supported the assumption that the baby died less than three hours previously and had been moved since death.

Based on my examination of the infant's body, I suspected that the parents had seriously neglected the baby, but I knew further checks and a complete autopsy had to be performed before the exact cause of death could be determined. Lividity on the frontal part of body was one aspect that still bothered me. For lividity to appear on the anterior (front part) of the body, the baby had to be lying on its stomach for some time after death or at least placed on its stomach immediately following death.

Concerned, I asked the medics, "When you first came into the room, was the baby lying on his back or stomach?"

"On his back," one medic replied.

I then asked one of the MPs if they had moved the baby when they had arrived on the scene.

He responded, "Yes." He went on to explain his actions. "In the process of checking for signs of life, I repositioned the baby to where I could better perform CPR." With a perplexed look on his face, the MP commented, "I didn't do anything wrong, did I?"

"The welfare of the baby was the foremost concern upon your arrival, and any attempt to revive him was the right thing to do," I assured the MP.

This explained the lividity being on the anterior side of the body instead of the back side. The change in the baby's position from stomach to back occurred when the MPs were trying to revive him. Since there was no adult bed in the room where the baby slept, it appeared that the parents did not sleep in the same room as the infant. Combined with the baby's condition, the appearance of the house, and the probability the parents slept in another room all suggested neglect. Neglect might very well have had an influence on its death.

I walked back into the living room and stood for about a minute to take in a panoramic view of the entire area. There was a couch, TV sitting on the floor, and a small table with a telephone—nothing else. There was no carpet on the floor, no area rugs, or even photographs of family members or the baby displayed anywhere. The couch looked like it had been obtained by the parents on German Junk Day. Junk Day, which usually fell on a Monday of each week, was a program that allowed residences in Schweinfurt to put their unwanted furniture and other discarded property outside near the street. Anyone that came along could take the discarded items.

Now I know the reason why the parents were not sitting in the living room: they were probably more comfortable in the kitchen. I started getting the feeling that the parents had no money or managed what they had very poorly and did not take an interest in their home. I made my way into the kitchen, where the two parents were seated. I further became concerned and more suspicious of how the baby died when I saw the them drinking coffee as if nothing had happened. Neither of them was expressing any outward remorse, and they were not consoling each other. Both SP4 Albert, looking sloppy in his ill-fitted military uniform, and the mother, Susan Albert, hair uncombed, wearing an oversized sweater, an obvious attempt to hide her weight, and jeans with no shoes, were very quiet.

I introduced myself as Special Agent Miller and told them I was sorry for their loss. Barely audibly and without looking up, SP4 Albert said, "Thanks." Susan remained silent. I explained to them what was about to happen. I told them that CID was required to conduct a full investigation into the circumstances surrounding the death of their infant son. I told the SP4 Albert that as a part of the investigation, I would have to interview him in detail about his infant son's death, and because his wife, Susan, was a civilian, the German *polizei* would interview her. I did not indicate to the parents that I was skeptical as to just how their son died. I based my skepticism on the unkempt and unsanitary conditions of their home, their nonchalant attitudes, and the appearance of their baby being undernourished.

Before I left, I suggested that the medics contact their German medical counterparts and have them transport the body to the facility where an autopsy could be performed.

I brought the Alberts to the CID office in Niederwerrn and told them to have a seat in the waiting room until I called. I went to my office and called Chief Walter Beck of the German Kriminalpolizei (KRIPO) in Schweinfurt and briefed him on the baby's death. I told him I thought he might want to send one of his investigators to bring Susan Albert in for questioning about the circumstances surrounding the death of her son.

Just as I was preparing to interview SP4 Albert, I received a call from Chief Beck, who indicated two of his investigators were headed to the CID office to pick up Susan Albert for questioning. I told Chief Beck that she would be here. I delayed the start of SP4 Albert's interview until the KRIPO arrived. About a half hour later, Walter Schmidt and another fellow KRIPO investigator showed up and took custody of Susan Albert. The two KRIPO investigators transported her to the police station in downtown Schweinfurt for questioning.

After they left, I brought SP4 Albert into my office and spent about fifteen or twenty minutes reassuring him that his wife was in good hands and that the status of forces agreement (SOFA) between German and the United States required us to allow the Germans to interview all civilian family members that were associated with incidents investigated by CID. I then started on him by asking a few preliminary questions and completing an interview work sheet. I then told him what my investigation had revealed thus far. The examination of his infant son suggested that he may have been undernourished and that the exact cause of death would more than likely confirm that when an autopsy was performed by the Germans. His facial expressions changed. He lowered his head and looked downward.

I explained to him that regardless of what he told me in the interview, the evidence would speak for itself. I went through the various degrees of homicide but advised him that any charges would be determined after the investigation was completed and submitted to the SJA. I told him that he must first indicate he was willing to discuss his baby's death by waiving his rights to counsel, which required his signature on the rights waiver form. He consented and signed the form. I thought that I lost him when I observed him staring off into space. I told him that the truth was in his best interest.

"I guess you are right, Special Agent Miller. I am prepared to talk about John, my son," he said after raising his head and refocusing his attention to me.

This was the first time I had heard that his son was named John. "Okay, John, please tell me what happened to your son."

"Well, since John was born at the Würzburg US Army hospital, Sue, my wife, has had a hard time with him coming into our life. John was our first child, and Sue has never dealt with any baby before," he lamented. "I don't think either one of us was ready for a baby. Sue spent the entire day with John and cared for him at night, and I guess she got tired of him crying and being required to change his diapers," he said.

"Did Sue or you ever strike John or hit him when he cried?" I questioned.

"No, it wasn't like that; we never hit him or mistreated him in any way."

"What happened then?" I pushed him for a better answer.

"I guess you could say we neglected him. We did not feed him much, and when he cried, we did not pick him up and hold him or anything like that. Sue could not even get close to John because he smelled so bad."

"Did he smell bad because you or Sue did not change his diapers?"

"Yeah, that's the way it was; Sue just did not like to change John's diapers."

"Why didn't you change them?"

"I was working all the time, and when I came home at night, I needed to rest."

"Oh, was that the way it was?"

"Pretty much, I would say," he indicated with not much enthusiasm.

After I talked to SP4 Albert, I took his statement and released him to the MPs.

After SP4 Albert left, I sat in the chair at my desk for several minutes, staring at the wall. I couldn't get the image of what I'd seen out of my mind. That poor infant had no way to defend himself from the deplorable, filthy environment he was made to live in. The little guy was too young to even consider his miserable conditions, being totally reliant on his immature parents to care for him. He would never know what the world was like, would never go to school, have friends, or get married. Damn, if they did not want a child, why did they bring one into the world? The investigative profession brings the bad, ugly, and appalling aspects about human behavior to the forefront.

The next morning, I contacted Captain David Franks, Schweinfurt Trial Services, who advised me that depending on what the autopsy revealed, we had a case for at least negligent homicide and possibly even could get involuntary manslaughter. Three days later, Chief Beck came by my office and reported that the German autopsy showed that the infant was seriously malnourished and died from starvation. Chief Beck advised that Susan Albert confessed to neglecting her infant son and ignoring the basic steps of caring for her child. "The Germans are not going to prosecute Susan Albert for homicide," he said without elaboration.

After he left, I immediately briefed Captain Franks on their case against Susan Albert. Captain Franks indicated that his office was going to prosecute SP4 Albert for involuntary manslaughter. The process could take up to two months. The Germans deported Susan, and SP4 Albert received four years at Fort Leavenworth, a dishonorable discharge, and forfeiture of all pay and allowances. SP4 Albert and his wife, Susan, had the rest of their lives to think about what they had done to their infant baby, John. I hoped that if they remained married and had more children, they would grow up and would accept their responsibilities; I'll never know. Susan Albert was not prosecuted due to a jurisdictional gap in our laws that was not covered under the status of force agreement. The jurisdictional gap occurs when the host nation (in this case, Germany) fails to prosecute a noncitizen who committed a hideous crime of murder of another noncitizen. The United States will not seek prosecution due to the crime being committed outside its exterritorial jurisdiction. The fact that the crime took place on a US Army installation, land exclusively used by the US Army, does not qualify as US government exterritorial land.

About a month into my tenure at Schweinfurt, SAC Boatwright called me into his office and asked me to sit down. Although I had only known SAC Boatwright for about a month, I felt I could read him. When he called me into his office, I believed I had a good idea what he wanted. In the back of my mind, I knew SA Muelhmeyer was TDY to a service school, and I thought he wanted me to take over the DST while he was gone. On this day, I was partially correct when he spoke.

"I want you to take over the DST," he implored with a little sense of urgency in his voice.

I thought, *it will only be for a month. I can handle that.* "Sure, I'll run it until Special Agent Muelhmeyer returns from the States," I told him.

"No, I want you to take over the team permanently," he said.

"Oh," I said. "Have you brought SA Muelhmeyer in on your decision?" I answered back. Boy, what in the hell was I thinking? It was not my place to question SAC Boatwright about his decisions.

"No, but when he returns, I will bring him on board," Boatwright stressed.

*Well,* I thought, *here we go again.* I still enjoyed working drug investigations, but I wanted to see the light at the end of the tunnel, and of course, I would in the future. "Yes, of course I will take over the DST," I enthusiastically responded. I then asked SAC Boatwright what his main expectations were from the Schweinfurt DST.

"I want you to be proactive and make cases," he said.

"Okay, you got your man," I added. When I left SAC Boatwright's office, I thought, *I hope I can live up to expectations.*

The following morning, the first action I took on the Schweinfurt DST was to review the six open narcotics investigations. Two cases were initiated through health-and-welfare inspections; one was initiated based on a car stop where the driver was suspected of driving while intoxicated. A small amount of hashish was found when his car was searched. The other three cases, possession and distribution of hashish, were made through an informant buy. So, based on this review, 50 percent of the cases were initiated by using an informant. *Good,* I thought. *The informant looks productive and is currently active.*

One of my major goals while working drug investigations was to establish a viable network of informants. I met with the two assigned MPs, SP4 Eric Moore and SP4 Ray Punzalan, from the Third Platoon, 212th MP Company. They both had been on the team for almost a year and had a great deal of established knowledge of drug suppression in the area. In the meeting, I found that we had one female registered informant. All in all, my work was cut out for me. I decided it was best to keep both Moore and Punzalan to help make the transition from SA Muelhmeyer to me as smooth as possible. I could also use both SP4s Moore and Punzalan to help interrupt the information the DST already had on record.

On my first duty day as the DST TC, I called our only registered informant into the office to get to know her work habits and to assess her future with the team. I wanted introduce myself and to discuss her overall motivations as to why she wanted to be a criminal informant. Back in the 1980s and earlier, CID used a unique numbering system to identify their informants. The first four digits identified the office and the last three identified the informant used. It was always my main goal to protect our sources' identities. Most drug cases, however, require that sources testify in a court-martial, especially if they actively participated in the case. In most drug investigations, it is necessary to require our sources to testify. This means that the person whom the source orchestrated a drug investigation on would always know that the source assisted CID with the case.

Danger of drug dealer reprisals against sources is increased dramatically when they are in the same unit. However, contrary to what a lot of military soldiers think, CID does not have special agents working undercover in each unit on an installation. Working undercover narcotics investigations in the US Army is, in many ways, more difficult than similar cases performed by civilian police officers. It takes a tremendous amount of time setting up and coordinating a drug investigation. There are many factors that play a role in effectively creating a drug case on a soldier. I wanted to determine just how effective our registered female source could be in the future if we continued using her.

When I met the source, I ascertained that she was a local German girl named Petra Adler,[80] who had lived in Schweinfurt and the surrounding area most of her life. Her motivation for helping CID was primarily money. Although she was only in her mid-thirties, due to what I suspected was living a hard life on the street, she appeared much older. However, during my interview with her, she convinced me she had what it took to fit in with a much younger soldier population associated with illegal drug trafficking. She surprised me when she reached into her purse and pulled out a pipe and small piece of what she told me was hashish wrapped in aluminum foil.

"Where did you get this stuff?" I questioned.

"On the way to talk to you, I ran into this guy I know who is stationed at Conn Barracks, and he told me he had to get rid of it before he returned to his unit," she said matter-of-factly.

As I took custody of the suspected hashish, I pondered the future use of this source. On the very first day I met this girl and without speaking to her beforehand, she brought me some hashish. Now, my interview had to shift from interviewing her about her future as a source to interviewing her about the soldier who had given her the suspected hashish. I ascertained from this source the identity of the soldier she obtained the suspected hashish from and concluded our interview. His name was Johnny Parker,[81] and he was assigned to an air defense artillery (ADA) unit at Conn Barracks. I ran a local name check on him and had SP4 Moore review his personnel file to develop information we had on him.

The only reason Parker gave our source the small amount of hashish was to diminish the chances he would get caught with it in his possession—or he wanted something more from her than she was willing to provide him. I conducted a Becton-Dickinson field test on the substance and tested some residue contained in the pipe, which tested positive. The pipe and substance was then packaged and sent to our crime lab at Frankfurt. Their report, received about three weeks later, confirmed the presence of tetrahydrocannabinol.

When interviewed, Parker decided not to waive his rights and requested a lawyer. Requesting a lawyer did him a lot of good. He was given an Article 15 under the Uniform Code of Military Justice and required to forfeit pay and allowances for two months and was reduced in rank from SP4 to PFC. It is amazing how much one quick decision made by an individual can alter his or her career, life, or future.

My initial evaluation of this source was that she was being underused as a source. I changed that, and by the end of my tenure with the DST, this source had assisted the CID office in not only Schweinfurt; she had a good run in Würzburg, Kitzingen, Aschaffenburg, and Bad Kissingen as well.

I considered sources the cornerstone of any good drug suppression program. A DST must have sources that are streetwise, reliable, and basically honest; a lot of times, the latter is their shortcoming. An SA who runs a DST should always consider the fact that most drug sources have committed crimes involving illegal drugs themselves, for if they had not, they would not be able to infiltrate groups or gain the confidence of those who possess, use, and sell illegal drugs. Keeping in mind this information, DST members must be able to offset the sources' involvement with the drug elements when preparing for court proceedings.

To enhance our operation, blank dependent and active duty military ID cards were obtained from the Schweinfurt personnel center and used to give members of the DST fake names and identities. The list of blank ID cards was then logged into a ledger, and the issue and use of each ID card was strictly controlled by me. I established a policy that each of our DST members would assume an alternate persona cover story. Once they had decided what was best for them, being a civilian or military, I would prepare fake identities to fit each situation. When I took over the Schweinfurt DST, there were two MPIs assigned, and during my tenure, that number bloomed to as many as seven MPIs at various times, depending on actual need and commitments.

I obtained permission to alter my appearance, and I grew a beard to blend into the local German population so I could associate with those suspected illegal drug dealers who were selling to the American soldiers as well as to conceal my identity to those US personnel who were targeted for such activity. The cover story that I prominently used was that of a dependent husband in Germany with his wife, who worked for the US Army. Depending on the soldier's duty status, I would often change my backstory where my wife worked to diminish any likelihood that the suspects had knowledge of her work area and would do their own due diligence on me.

Even after taking over the DST, I was still required to pull duty agent at least one day a week and every other weekend. It was inevitable that on the weekend, usually Saturday night, I was called to investigate a reported rape of a German national female in one of the troop barracks. The scenarios were usually the same. Soldier meets German girl at a German bar or nightclub in downtown Schweinfurt that caters to the US military and takes her back to his barracks room with the hopes of having sex with her. When the German girl resists, the soldier is either too intoxicated to understand the implications of her refusal or does not consider her protest to be legitimate, and he goes ahead and has sex with her. After the act, she leaves the room and reports the incident to MPs or the German police. I investigated many of these types of rapes, and usually it was not a very good outcome for the soldier that wanted to have some fun. The soldiers often were court-martialed and received up to five years or more as guests of the US Military Disciplinary Barracks (USMDB) at Fort Leavenworth, Kansas. For a few moments of pleasure, a lot of soldiers changed or altered their future ways of life.

One night, Moore, Punzalan, and I were working a drug operation at Conn Barracks when I overheard a radio call from the MP desk to the CID duty agent that a soldier had killed another soldier in the barracks. Once I heard this over the radio, I called the CID office and received no response. Since our drug operations involved primarily surveillance and were not expected to materialize into anything else that evening, I made the decision to give my two subordinates a much-needed night off from work. I then headed to the MP station at Ledward Barracks. I ascertained that a sergeant from Company D, 703rd Maintenance Battalion, had killed a female soldier from his unit and was currently being interviewed by SAC Boatwright at the CID office.

The MP desk sergeant told me that the investigation was currently in the hands of CID but that MPs were still at the barracks protecting the scene until CID released them. The incident turned out to be a date gone wrong, and the maintenance sergeant ended up killing the female soldier he had been with at the Conn Barracks NCO club earlier in the evening. I thought this investigation warranted a detailed narrative because it was the first murder while I was assigned to Schweinfurt and the case had some legal twists and turns that played out in court and elsewhere. I called this investigation the Case of the Sergeant Who Wanted to Be a Mercenary:

## THE CASE OF THE SERGEANT WHO WANTED TO BE A MERCENARY
Life in prison does not necessarily mean life in prison

Susan E. Miller was born in 1947 and grew up in Portland, Oregon, in a middle-class northeast-side neighborhood, where she attended Sabin Elementary School and graduated from Grant High School in 1965. The actress Sally Struthers was one of her high school classmates. After high school, Susan worked at various jobs in Portland and was considered a typical girl who played softball and was well liked. Fed up with her life and probably seeing the possibility of no real future in Portland, she joined the US Army in 1974. After several years of hard work and dedication to duty and her country, she was promoted to the rank of sergeant E5. Her career finally brought her to Company D, 703rd Maintenance Battalion, in Schweinfurt, Germany.

Across the country at about the same time as Susan's birth, David N. Seeloff was born. He was raised in Lockport, New York, a small community near Niagara Falls. He, too, joined the US Army and was elevated to the rank of sergeant E5 and eventually assigned to the same unit as Susan. It was not only their mutual assignment to D Company, 703rd Maintenance Battalion, that aligned their fate but something far more sinister would intertwine these two young individuals forever.

It was an unseasonably warm evening on Monday, October 13, 1980, in Schweinfurt, Germany. Most members of the US Army had the day off and were celebrating Columbus Day at their homes, the downtown German *Gasthaus*, soldier hangouts, and at the various service clubs on Ledward and Conn Barracks. Those celebrating at the Conn Barracks NCO club also included Sergeants Susan Miller and David Seeloff. They both were drinking, dancing, and socializing with other unit members and, although not a steady couple, were seen snuggling and kissing each other. Miller and Seeloff were unaware of how their activities that evening would permanently alter their destinies.

Later, after the festivities wound down, the enamored pair went to Sergeant Seeloff's room on the first floor of Conn Barracks. After having consensual sex, Sergeant Miller complained about Sergeant Seeloff's lovemaking skills. Sergeant Seeloff, incensed by her comments, placed his hands around Sergeant Miller's neck and squeezed until she lost consciousness. Believing that he had killed her, he momentarily removed his hands from her neck. Suddenly, Sergeant Miller regain consciousness and started to move. Sergeant Seeloff again put his hands around her neck and pressed harder, making sure she was dead.

Sergeant Seeloff then crawled off the bed, looked at Sergeant Miller's body lying motionless, left the room, and, using the phone at the CQ (charge of quarters) desk, called a German taxicab. He hung up the phone and told the CQ, "Get ready. All hell is going to break loose in a half hour."

The taxi arrived, and Sergeant Seeloff instructed the driver to take him to the military police station on Ledward Barracks, some five miles away. At 10:25 p.m., Sergeant Seeloff walked into the military police station, located in the basement of the building next to the main gate, and approached the desk sergeant. The busy desk sergeant, working feverishly to finish the shift's blotter, did not want to be interrupted but perfunctorily listened when Sergeant Seeloff told him, "I need to talk to someone. I have a personal problem. I just murdered someone."

The desk sergeant, who hadn't had any calls of violence during the shift, told his MP clerk, "Take this man across the hall and see if you can render some assistance."

Across the hall in an interview room, Sergeant Seeloff began telling the MP clerk that he had killed a girl in his room on Conn Barracks. During his admission, the MP clerk started taking notes. A few minutes into his Sergeant Seeloff's admission, the MP clerk started believing his story, so he locked Sergeant Seeloff in the room and walked back to where the desk sergeant was. "I think this guy is serious," he excitedly reported.

At this point, the desk sergeant dispatched two MP patrols to Company D, 703rd Maintenance Battalion, on Conn Barracks to investigate.

Upon the arrival of the MPs, the CQ was not able to produce the right key to gain access to Sergeant Seeloff's room. The MPs then went outside to the window to the room, which happened to be cracked open, and tried to hoist the smallest of the MPs inside, but the window was too high. They went back inside and forcibly kept lunging against the door until it busted open. When the MPs turned on the light, they saw Sergeant Miller's lifeless body lying on the bed. An on-site MP notified the desk sergeant of what they had found, and he immediately ordered them to seal the crime scene and wait for further instructions and the arrival of CID. A short time later, more MPs arrived to assist with crowd control and securing the crime scene.

Later, members of the Schweinfurt CID office arrived and started processing the crime scene. While agents from the Schweinfurt resident agency were processing the crime scene, SAC Boatwright began the interview with Sergeant Seeloff. Sergeant Seeloff waived his rights and gave SAC Boatwright a complete confession of how he'd strangled Sergeant Miller in the barracks room after they'd had consensual sex. Sergeant Seeloff admitted that he became enraged because Sergeant Miller complained about his lack of lovemaking skills. He admitted placing his hands around her neck and choking her until she was unconscious. Sergeant Seeloff then told SAC Boatwright, "She started to move, so I pressed my hands tighter around her neck again until she stopped moving."

Sergeant Miller's body was transported to the Würzburg army hospital, where a couple of our CID agents from Schweinfurt attended the autopsy the next day. The autopsy confirmed the cause of death was strangulation and the manner of death was murder. Agents from the Schweinfurt CID office got to work doing interviews to establish information that would support the charge of murder.

The day after the murder, Susan's father, Alexander, was notified by a military officer and chaplain of his daughter's death overseas. He had just lost his wife (Susan's mother) a few months earlier.

Susan's body was sent back to the Fort Lewis, Washington, decedent affairs office and then on to Portland, Oregon, for funeral and interment, where many of Susan's high school friends were in attendance.

While the murder investigation was ongoing, Sergeant Seeloff was held in the detainment cell at the Schweinfurt military police station so he would be conveniently available to be transported back and forth to appointments with his psychologists.

At one point while meeting with them under MP guard, Seeloff went into a rage and broke the handcuffs placed on his wrist during an interview. After a few days, Sergeant Seeloff was sent to the correctional facility in Mannheim, Germany, where he was held while his US Army lawyers prepared his defense for court-martial. During his incarceration at the correctional facility in Mannheim, Sergeant Seeloff wrote one of his unit members to solicit his help to escape if the US Army decided to give him the death penalty.

The court-martial took place in March 1981, and even though he'd confessed, Sergeant Seeloff pleaded not guilty, but he was found guilty. He was sentenced to life in prison for the premeditated murder of Sergeant Miller plus reduction in rank to E1 and forfeiture of all pay and allowances and a dishonorable discharge. The reason he was found guilty of premeditated murder was because it became clear during the CID investigation and the trial that Sergeant Seeloff was fascinated with killing. He had told numerous people in his unit and the MPs, as well as during his confession, that he wanted to be a mercenary and that he wanted to see what killing someone was like. He also told the clerk and SAC Boatwright that it was fun killing Susan, and if he ever got out of prison, he wanted to be a mercenary. Several *Soldier of Fortune* magazines were also found in Seeloff's room.

Sergeant Seeloff was then transported to the Fort Leavenworth, Kansas, disciplinary barracks, where he immediately appealed his case into the federal court system, saying that the desk clerk did not read him his Miranda rights. His appeal was based on the statement made by the MP clerk that was introduced into evidence against him in the subsequent murder trial. On appeal, the court upheld the conviction, holding that the desk clerk had not interrogated the individual. Instead, there was an active volunteering, if not compulsion on the part of the individual, to tell what he had done. If anything, it was the individual who was questioning the desk clerk and trying to engage him in conversation. His statement was, therefore, admissible in evidence, and a sentence of confinement for life was upheld.

Seeloff lost the appeal and remained in Leavenworth for fourteen years and was released in 1994. When interviewed by a friend of Susan's after Seeloff's release, a former commander of Leavenworth said, "Life is really never life in the military." Mr. Seeloff then entered a "lifetime" parole until the year 2076 as a military parolee.

Mr. Seeloff returned to his mother's farm in upstate New York, where he seemed to live a quiet life until November 18, 2003. At some point prior to that date, someone tipped off Mr. Seeloff's federal parole officer that he had firearms on the farm. The US Parole Commission authorized a search of Seeloff's residence, vehicle, property, and person. On that date, members of the US Parole Office and the FBI raided the farm. They found numerous long guns, shotguns, and a Western Field M15D shotgun that had been illegally shortened. Seeloff went back to federal prison on a parole violation for four years. When he went back to prison, he again made a court appeal, saying that the search of his residence was illegal. The US district court in the western district of New York ruled against Mr. Seeloff. Mr. Seeloff was again released in 2008 after serving time for parole violation and is presumed to be still living in upstate New York.[82]

About once a week, I would take the evening off to have a nice dinner and socialize with friends and fellow coworkers with a few tasty German beers. My selected spot for this activity usually meant going to the Keller Bar, located in the basement of the Schweinfurt officers' club on Conn Barracks. One of the evenings I chose to take off was Saturday, October 25, 1980, my birthday. On this evening, there was a DJ spinning records. The enlisted, NCO, and officers' clubs were still popular nightspots that had plenty of nightly entertainment in the 1980s. The music was loud and beer flowing, it always meant fun for the mostly single helicopter pilots, a few maintenance warrant officers, a couple of CID warrants (Ed Black and me), and a few company commander captains. The fun factor consisted of the many single female Department of Defense (DOD) schoolteachers that always showed up at these events—and there were a lot of them in Schweinfurt.

That evening was a special night in that it was my birthday, but more importantly, the DST had initiated a couple of very challenging drug investigations just a couple of days before, and I had been working on them with little sleep ever since—and I needed a break. My intent for the evening was to eat a good dinner, have a beer or two, and go home to get some much-needed rest. My plan did not work out well. Just after eating, I moved to the bar to talk with fellow warrant officer CW2 Bob Mays, whom I had met shortly after arriving in Schweinfurt.

As Bob and I were talking, several DOD schoolteachers sashayed up to the bar as if they owned the place. The two of us tried to continue our conversation, but due to my bad hearing, the noise created by the group took care of my ability to listen to what the Bob was saying, so I just sat back and enjoyed my beer.

Within minutes after their arrival at the bar, armed with the drinks the bartender had just given them, most scooted away and went elsewhere. One smartly dressed, very attractive young girl in her late twenties or early thirties, with big, beautiful, marble-shaped brown eyes, smooth skin, and shoulder-length dark hair, was left sitting by herself about three seats from me. She did not appear to have been with the group of giggling girls that had just left. For the next several minutes, I periodically looked her way to see if anyone would join her, but she apparently was alone, sipping her mixed drink and minding her own business. Bob grabbed my attention and wanted to pick up where we'd left off in our conversation, just as if nothing had interrupted us.

I took my last drink and said good-bye to Bob, who had just ordered another beer. As I was walking out, a girl jumped in front of me and asked me to dance. *Why not?* I thought. When we finished, she acted like she wanted to continue dancing, but I wanted to get some sleep. But before I could think of an excuse not to, I saw the good-looking girl that had been at the bar earlier that evening. Immediately, I had my excuse.

"I would like to have another dance, but I promised the girl right over there," I said as I pointed to a table about five feet from us. The girl that had been at the bar was standing, talking to the people at the table. I thanked the girl I had just danced with and approached the other girl. "Would you like to dance?" I nervously asked.

"Okay," she said.

We danced a couple of tunes and found a table where we talked until the Keller Bar closed. I then walked her to her car, and we stood and talked for yet another two hours before we decided it was time to leave. During our conversation, she told me her name was Elda Guajardo and that she was from a town in South Texas called Freer, where she grew up in a family of four brothers and two sisters. She had gone to college at Texas A&I in Kingsville, Texas, and got her masters at Texas A&M– (formerly Corpus Christi University).

"I have always wanted to travel, so joining the DOD school system was the best way to do it," she informed me.

After that night, we started dating on a regular basis.

In February 1981, Elda and I decided to get married. We looked at engagement rings at the Schweinfurt PX, and Elda selected the one she liked most, but I did not buy it immediately. My strategy was to immediately return to the Schweinfurt PX without her and buy the ring, which I successfully did. When I gave her the ring, I wanted it to be a surprise. The situation arose when Elda wanted to take a bus trip to Paris, France. I hate bus rides, but my motive was clear; I had to sacrifice my comfort for my future, so I consented to this one trip.

So, in April 1981, we departed on that lengthy, thirteen-hour, backbreaking tour bus ride from Schweinfurt to Paris, and I carried the ring in my front pants pocket without her knowledge. Only the beautiful scenery of the German, Austrian, and French countryside and Elda's company made it bearable. Once in Paris, seeking the right moment overlooking the city of Paris skyline, I pulled out the ring from my pocket and had it in my hand when I proposed to her. With a surprised look on her face, she readily accepted.

We had a wonderful week touring the city and seeing all the historical sites and places, including the Eiffel Tower, the Louvre, and Versailles. The worst thing about the trip was the thirteen-hour bus ride back to Schweinfurt. When we got back from the Paris trip, I wrote Mom and told her about Elda and that I had asked for her hand in marriage.

After my involvement with the Sergeant Seeloff case, for which SAC Boatwright and other agents in the office deserve most of the credit for its resolution, I continued working level-two narcotics investigations. Our drug investigation caseload was increasing, and over a two-week period in October 1980, we increased our registered sources to four. For the next several weeks, our primarily investigative efforts were focused on specific targets, individuals who were suspected of possessing and distributing illegal drugs, mainly hashish, to US forces in our area of operation.

The DST was still lacking one major element of an effective operation: a good, solid targeting program, which was now my focus. I pulled in SP4s Moore and Punzalan, and we all started working on analyzing and correlating all the data from the previous year. Then we evaluated our sources' input to match with other criminal information we'd developed. Using this information, the DST could identify the local establishments in downtown Schweinfurt that most likely were places where soldiers could buy or hook up deals for illegal drugs. We documented the names of every soldier and civilian we talked to that we suspected to have an illegal drug connection and entered their names into the monthly raw data file. We then documented their names in an association chart with the establishment they most frequented.

The chart depicted not only their names and the places they mostly patronized but information ascertained from our discussions with them, and their names were crossed-referenced to the page number in the raw data file where the original information was initially reported by the DST member. An overall working identification chart was positioned on the wall in my DST office, entry of which was restricted to DST members only. (The DST office had two rooms—an outer one, used by the MP DST members, and an inner office, which served as my office.) A duplicate sheet identifying all the information collected on the individual's suspected illegal drug activities and connections was also placed into a binder; that was used to brief unit battalion commanders and sergeant majors and company commanders and their first sergeants. I had an informal policy that I would not brief anyone ranking lower.

This drug-targeting system started to pay off when we directed our sources' undercover activities specifically toward the individual soldiers that were previously identified. Our level-two drug investigations involving possession and distribution cases zoomed. The increase in drug investigations did not go unnoticed by the Würzburg district commander, LTC John D. Wilder, the operations officer, Matthew E. Moriarty, and the Schweinfurt community commander and assistant Third Infantry Division commander, BG Johnny J. Johnson.

Around this time, LTC Wilder was replaced by Major Markalee D. Brannen Jr. as the commander of the Würzburg District. I had originally run into Major Brannen at Second Region headquarters when I'd first gotten to Europe. We had a few small conversations during my short stay at Second Region, and I found Major Brannen to be an amiable and approachable commissioned officer, not knowing at the time that our assignments would bring us into contact on numerous occasions.

SAC Boatwright called me into his office one morning in early February 1981 and said, "BG Johnston wants to be briefed on the Schweinfurt's DST operations; more specifically, he would like to know the reason why cases are increasing in the community."

At the meeting with SAC Boatwright, I had brought a briefing book that I'd started a few weeks prior, which was constantly being updated with real-time information. "I am ready for any major command briefing at a moment's notice," I proudly proclaimed. "I am not only able to talk about the current cases, which units the perps were from, where they obtained their drugs, and the types of drugs used or sold but what the future investigative plans are for the DST," I enthusiastically advised SAC Boatwright.

"I will set up the meeting with BG Johnston as soon as I can," he told me.

One afternoon about a week after the meeting with SAC Boatwright, I got the word that the meeting with BG Johnston was scheduled for the following morning.

"I set up the briefing to take place right after my daily briefing with BG Johnston," SAC Boatwright told me.

I was given fifteen minutes with BG Johnston, but the briefing lasted over forty-five minutes. I explained to him that the reason he was seeing an increase in drug investigations in the Schweinfurt military community was that the DST had developed an excellent targeting system that identified the soldiers involved with illegal drugs before our investigation was initiated. I discussed with BG Johnston the DST's hard-earned efforts to develop criminal intelligence on our targets instead of just trolling for suspects. He seemed genuinely concerned about the extent of illegal drug use among the troops in the Schweinfurt military community. His response to my briefing made me feel it was well received.

The briefing gave BG Johnston some insights into how the illegal drugs affected the troops, not only professionally and performance-wise but financially as well. We left BG Johnston's office feeling we had truly gotten his attention about the drug situation in the Schweinfurt military community and that we had gained a friend.

About this time, USACIDC commander MG Paul Timmerburg made a visit to the Schweinfurt resident agency. The visit included a side trip to see BG Johnston. After that meeting, MG Timmerburg informed the Würzburg District commander, LTC Wilder, that BG Johnston requested to have CID conduct a special drug operation in the Schweinfurt AOR.

On March 2, 1981, a briefing was conducted on the tentative plan for a special drug operation for BG Johnston. BG Johnston obligated some Schweinfurt military community resources for the special drug operation. With the support of the USAREUR provost marshal, a special drug operation was warranted because the Schweinfurt military community was, at the time, USAREUR's number-one drug problem. I attributed this reputation to the hard work conducted by the Schweinfurt DST members and considered our efforts to be the main catalyst in getting the special drug operation started.

On March 3, 1981, the special drug operation, named Spring Cleaning, was submitted to the commander of the Second Region for approval. On March 25, 1981, Operation Spring Cleaning was approved up the chain by the provost marshal of HQ United States Army Europe (USAREUR), BG Leroy N. Suddath Jr.

An investigative planning phase was devised by a group consisting of the Würzburg District operations officer Moriarty, drug coordinator Wayne McNeely, the Schweinfurt resident agency, SAC Boatwright, and me. Brought on board were MPI resources from the Drug Suppression Operations Center (DSOC) in Mannheim, Germany, two CID special agents from outside the Schweinfurt area, and additional administrative help from the Schweinfurt military community. The primary thrust of this operation was to interdict illicit drugs intended for US forces personnel in the Schweinfurt military community area of responsibility and apprehending US Army personnel involved in this traffic. A secondary objective was to disrupt this flow by identifying and causing the apprehension of nonmilitary local and third-country nationals by the German Kriminalpolizei. The operation consisted of two three-man teams—one to target Ledward and Conn Barracks, and one team for the Schweinfurt downtown area. We had sources in place at all three locations.

On March 30, 1981, right in the middle of coordinating the first stage of Operation Spring Cleaning, our efforts took a backslide when a mentally ill twenty-five-year-old man named John Hinckley Jr. attempted to assassinate President Ronald Reagan in Washington, DC. Reagan's press secretary, Jim Brady, was shot and seriously wounded. Secret Service agent Timothy McCarthy and Washington, DC, police officer Thomas Delahanty were also shot in the incident, but all survived.[83] This senseless act created some tense days for the US military, but we all managed to get back on track.

I had already set in place targeting procedures prior to the implementation of the operation. I created name-card indexing of suspected traffickers and their associates by unit on an associates chart. This information was obtained through extensive undercover operations and research over a period from July 1980 to April 1981. About two weeks before the operation kicked off, I conducted a community-wide briefing with most of the assigned SMGs and 1SGs at the DST office. Although the SGMs and 1SGs were briefed on DST operations and requested to provide information to update current records on suspected traffickers, they were not informed that a special drug operation had been set in motion.

The names that the SGMs and 1SGs gave were incorporated into the existing index cards on file with the Schweinfurt DST, and names of personnel that had either been reassigned or had left the US Army were deleted. Criminal information reports (CIR) were prepared on those soldiers deleted due to reassignments and sent to the gaining installations. All existing target books and charts were updated and additional information added during the operation. The graphic charting of each targeted person and the relationships with each other on poster board by *Kaserne* / unit of residence was an ongoing process. This list also included the listings of German nationals and third-country nationals known or suspected as trafficking drugs in the area.

The commander of the Second Battalion, Thirtieth Infantry, LTC Barry McCaffrey, personally came to my office and sought an individual briefing on my drug operations within his unit. McCaffrey, who would later be one of the Desert Storm commanding generals and, after retirement from the US Army, become drug czar under Bill Clinton's administration, was provided with a detailed briefing on the criminal intelligence we had on the Second Battalion, Thirtieth Infantry. He was surprised at the depth of knowledge the Schweinfurt DST had on the extent of his unit's drug problem and offered his support for any operation we would direct clearing drug users and dealers from his unit.[84]

If it were not for the extensive prior investigative activity, where the identities of suspects, their associates, and locations of hangouts and units of assignment were discerned, Operation Spring Cleaning would not have been as successful as it was. But as the plan went into motion and the operation took hold, our expectations were exceeded. Over forty-eight people were apprehended for drug offenses, of which thirty-four were direct sellers of drugs. Out of the forty-eight identified, thirty-eight were military, nine were German nationals, and one was an American civilian. The balance consisted of conspirators or possessors.[85]

The German *polizei* were highly responsive to the joint actions during the Operation Spring Cleaning. There were several parallel investigations involving either American civilians or German nationals that were initiated during the operation, resulting in their arrest. Apart from one German national who had yet to be fully identified, all German arrests were made without complications.

One investigation led us to Frankfurt, Germany, where the German national was arrested while in possession of heroin. Our investigation revealed that the heroin was destined for the Schweinfurt military community. He received a jail sentence. Unfortunately, some of the German nationals in our operation were not prosecuted because of the small amounts of illegal drugs purchased or seized. Fortunately, of the nine who sold drugs to DST members working on Operation Spring Cleaning, three were on probation for previous offenses and were reincarcerated for the remainder of their original sentences. One German, who sold $6,000 worth of hashish, received a jail sentence.

US Army soldiers were the primary target for illegal drugs sold by German nationals identified in Operation Spring Cleaning. Of the thirty-eight soldiers who sold drugs during the operation, thirty-one were male, and one was female. All of them were either court-martialed or received nonjuridical punishment under Article 15 of the Uniformed Code of Military Justice (UCMJ). Of those court-martialed, all were required to forfeit pay, were reduced in rank, and received bad conduct discharges from the US Army.

After-action assessments of Operation Spring Cleaning showed it was a success. Because of the Schweinfurt DST, I recommended three individuals on the team for Army Achievement Medals and two for Army Commendation Medals. I was also awarded an Army Commendation Medal for Achievement for my overall supervisory role and actions during the operation. Because of the operation, we had one very happy Schweinfurt community commander.

One of the cases initiated during Operation Spring Cleaning merits a narrative of details for the unique circumstances of the investigation. I called this caper the Case of the Young Soldier from Two Countries:

## THE CASE OF THE YOUNG SOLDIER FROM TWO COUNTRIES
Positive identity does not always ensure you get your man

During Operation Spring Cleaning, one case stood out for its uniqueness. All criminal investigations involving possession, sale, and distribution of illegal drugs are similar in nature: the dealer has drugs, he sells drugs, he gets money. When apprehended, and interviewed, he both confesses to the crime and provides information about his source of the illegal drugs, or he remains silent and asked for a lawyer. One case involved CID Special Agent Reggie Smith, who came TDY from Mannheim to work on Operation Spring Cleaning. Reggie had a good deal of experience working undercover narcotics investigations and was a definite asset to the team during the operation. He was appointed as a leader of the team that worked undercover in downtown Schweinfurt.

One night, Reggie's team was working inside a bar in downtown Schweinfurt called the Top Ten Club, an establishment primarily catering to US soldiers. Criminal intelligence suggested that the Top Ten Club was a known hangout for those soldiers who wanted to score primarily hashish or heroin. The Top Ten Club was located on a city street in downtown Schweinfurt. The main entertainment area was in the basement of the building, where a small bar was directly to the left of the stairs. US soldiers and male and female German patrons, with beers in hand, would gather around an open dance floor that occupied most of the space. It was Reggie himself who struck up a conversation with a young man who appeared to be in his early twenties, was clean shaven, had short cropped hair, and had a German accent.

Reggie was not known by any of the German employees or patrons of the Top Ten Club because he was from Mannheim. His cover story was that of an American civilian working for the US Army and that he was new to the area. He was not known by the locals, and that was the primary reason Reggie was assigned to the downtown area team.

Reggie's actions and conversation probably trended as follows. Leaning again the bar sipping his beer, Reggie took a swig of beer and said, "You look German."

"*Ja*, I am," replied the German.

"Are you from Schweinfurt?" Reggie asked.

Without saying anything, the German national nodded.

"I am new in town. Where are the best places to go?" Reggie said as he tried to engage the German national.

"This is a good place," the German national replied without explanation.

Remaining silent, Reggie continued to sip his beer, making it last for appearances.

Then, without any prompting, the German national turned toward Reggie and introduced himself as Walter Kohler.[86]

Reggie, relieved that Kohler broke the ice, responded with his real name. "Hi. I am Reggie." Not wanting to waste time because Walter Kohler was not one of the names being targeted, Reggie wanted to direct the conversation toward illegal drugs, so without much preliminary dialogue, he moved precariously straight into a cat-and-mouse mode and cut to the chase. "Do you know where someone could get something other than a beer?" Reggie asked. Reggie thought that without further elucidation, Kohler would catch the implication of the question. But then again, if Kohler was not a dealer, he figured time was wasting.

Suddenly, Kohler answered, "*Ja.* I have some stuff, if you want it."

"What do you have?" Reggie asked.

"Hashish," Kohler responded as he reached into his pants pocket and pulled out a plastic bag containing several small wrapped squares purported to be hashish.

"How much?" Reggie inquired.

"Thirty dollars apiece," Kohler briskly stated.

Knowing that the price stated by Kohler was well within what street dealers were asking for hashish, Reggie responded, "Hey, I would like a couple of pieces of that."

"Follow me," Kohler voiced as he moved toward the stairs to go out.

Reggie consistently remained vigilant for anyone that might be tagging along behind them. Once outside, Reggie immediately felt a cool breeze of fresh air. Kohler motioned for Reggie to step into an alley near the building they had just come out of. Hesitantly, Reggie walked the short distance to the opening of the alley. Kohler, looking around for assurance no one was watching them, pulled the plastic bag containing the small aluminum-foil-wrapped squares from his pocket and held it in his hand.

Kohler then asked Reggie, "How much do you want?"

Reggie looked directly at the plastic bag in Kohler's hand, mentally estimating there must be about ten pieces of the stuff he claimed was hashish. Holding his forefinger and middle finger in the air Reggie said, "Two."

Kohler reached inside the plastic bag and grabbed two pieces of the stuff and gave them to Reggie. Reggie in turn gave Kohler three twenty-dollar bills. Reggie then thanked Kohler for the stuff and walked away. Over his shoulder, Reggie saw Kohler return to the bar.

Back at the CID office, Reggie examined the purported hashish. The pieces were a brownish, semisolid, paste-like substance that looked and smelled like hashish. Reggie then, using a Becton-Dickinson test kit, conducted a field test on the stuff he'd purchased from Kohler, which indicated positive for tetrahydro-cannabinol. He subsequently placed the substance in the temporary evidence locker. Later that evening, Reggie wrote his investigative report about the controlled purchase.

The next morning, Reggie and I went to the chief of narcotics investigation at the Kriminalpolizei, Herr Helmut Deutscher, and briefed him and his team on the investigation initiated on Kohler. Deutscher was an experienced undercover investigator, having worked his way up the chain of command to become the chief of the narcotics section, and he was an arch supporter of the Schweinfurt DST and had often expressed his fondness for the way the US Army CID worked drug investigations. Deutscher researched his records and found two minor offenses committed by a Walter Kohler—one for vandalism, and the other for simple assault.

I subsequently relinquished the two pieces of aluminum-foil-wrapped squares to Herr Deutscher. Deutscher produced the Kriminalpolizei's file on Kohler, which contained a mug shot. Reggie looked at the photograph and acknowledged it resembled the person who had sold the suspected hashish to him the night before. Herr Deutscher committed his staff to assist the Schweinfurt resident agency during Operation Spring Cleaning.

Three weeks later, after Reggie had left the team to return to Mannheim, Deutscher called my office and reported the German lab report came back indicting the substance sold to Reggie by Kohler confirmed it was hashish, the Schweinfurt Kriminalpolizei wanted to make an arrest. Deutscher and his team went to the address they had on record for Kohler and knocked on the door. A woman in her early fifties answered the door and identified herself as Anna Kohler, who verified that Walter Kohler was her son. But she added a strange twist to the investigation when she told Deutscher that her son was now in the American army, attending basic training at Fort Gordon, Georgia. Anna informed the German officers that she had once been married to an American soldier who used to be assigned to Schweinfurt, but they had divorced when Walter was a small child. Walter grew up in Schweinfurt but had visited the United States numerous times over the years and liked the country.

Walter being in the US Army was not the only wrinkle in this investigation. On the date the case was initiated against him (April 27, 1981), he was reportedly at Fort Gordon, attending basic combat training. A lead was sent to Fort Gordon to have Kohler located and interviewed. As anticipated, he denied being in Schweinfurt on the evening of April 27, 1981. The evidence we had that placed him in Schweinfurt on that night of was the testimony of Reggie. Any smart defense attorney could argue that the purchase of hashish on that evening was made in a dark area and the visibility was limited. His attorney would also contend that the person that sold Reggie the hashish could have provided him with a false name, possibly even knowing Kohler was in the US Army. How better to conceal his real name?

On our side, there was no documentation found at Kohler's basic training unit that showed he was at a specific site at Fort Gordon, but there was no evidence found that he was missing from his unit on that date, either. April 27,

1981, fell on a Monday, a regular workday for the US Army. This case baffled both the German police and the Schweinfurt DST and to this day has never been resolved. No action was ever taken on Kohler, for lack of evidence he sold hashish to Reggie, who was acting in an undercover capacity.

After Operation Spring Cleaning, the Schweinfurt resident agency DST continued to develop sources and sustained a steady flow of illegal drug cases throughout 1981 and well into 1982. The investigations involved offenders from various units in the Schweinfurt military community, and the military community leaders were very pleased with our drug suppression and interdiction efforts. Starting in the mid-1960s and running the early 1980s, illegal drug use by the American soldiers was at its zenith. The behavior of individual armed forces members mimicked that of the civilian population. This did not mean that every soldier in the US Army or other branches of the service were smoking dope, shooting heroin, taking narcotics, or consuming other mind-altering drugs.

In the Vietnam War, the US Army had the reputation of being dopers, heroin addicts, or junkies. The truth was that only a small percentage of US Army were users of marijuana and even fewer experimented with heroin. The illegal drug usage did increase in the 1970s and 1980s, topping out between 1980 and 1983. An early Gallup poll shows that during the '60s, only 4 percent said they had tried marijuana, but by 1985 (ten years after the Vietnam War ended), this figure had increased to 33 percent. In my twenty-three-year career in the US Army, twenty of those years with the US Army CID and six years working drug cases, the early 1980s were, in my opinion, by far the peak years of illegal drug usage by soldiers. Of course, it did not come to a complete stop after peaking in the early 1980s, but the US Army's tough stance on drug use and its urinalysis program drastically reduced the use of drugs by soldiers. The US Army urinalysis program set the foundation for fixing the drug problem in the US Army.

Criminal investigations are serious business, but there are times when you can't help but smile at what someone says, especially while that person has his or her best guard up during an interview. One of our drug investigations led the DST to SP4 Jason McGuire,[87] assigned to First Battalion, Thirtieth Infantry. McGuire was elusive, and regardless of what we tried, we could not develop enough evidence to initiate an investigation on him. McGuire came to our attention based on a source's information that he was involved with the distribution and sale of illegal drugs. As far as we knew from checking his background, he was a good soldier who did his job and was well liked by everyone, and the unit leaders had no idea he was involved with illegal drugs. Except for the source who steered us toward McGuire, efforts to develop information on him was limited. Working to gather enough information on this guy was tedious. Schweinfurt's

DST members working the streets, bars, and known hangouts for marijuana and hashish dealers and users did not identify McGuire, nor were the members of his unit known to be involved with illegal drugs. I called this investigation the Case of the Soldier Who Was Duped:

## THE CASE OF THE SOLDIER WHO WAS DUPED
Accidental admission is just as good as a confession

SP4 Jason McGuire was smart and effectively used his senses, and pulling the truth out of him would be all but impossible. McGuire was a good-looking kid, appeared sharp in his uniform, and was well liked by his commander and 1SG. Unfortunately, he liked to use and sell hashish. The Schweinfurt DST had developed information through a very reliable source that McGuire was one of the top sellers in his unit. The DST attempted, without success, to engage him in discussions about hashish at two different nightclubs in downtown Schweinfurt.

A review of his personnel file disclosed that he was scheduled for reassignment back to the States in two weeks, and time was running out for us to get anything on him. Considering it a very long shot, but not knowing where else to turn, I decided to bring him in for questioning. I would try not to revert to interrogation but to keep the meeting at the interview level. The interview was to focus on any information he would be willing to provide concerning sources for hashish in his unit. Thinking of how shrewd people thought this individual was, I figured he probably would not give me anything that would incriminate himself. I would conduct our interview like a conversation and would gradually slowly ease into the information we already had on him. I also planned to prepare a criminal information report and submit it to his gaining unit stateside.

About twenty minutes prior to the Specialist McGuire's arrival, knowing I would be busy the rest of the day and had little time for lunch, I grabbed a Kit Kat milk chocolate bar from my desk drawer. As I opened the wrapper, I took a bite from one of the bars, and I instantly got an idea. Back in those days, the Kit Kats had internal silver paper wrappings that look like the aluminum foil used by hashish dealers to wrap small squares of hashish, making it easier to price and sell. I thought that I might use the silver paper to wrap small squares of the milk chocolate bars to make them appear like small pieces of hashish. I broke up about ten pieces of the bars into small squares and wrapped them with the silver paper and placed them inside a clear plastic baggie. I then placed the clear plastic baggie in the main drawer of my desk.

Every good interview or interrogation requires an investigator understanding of how to read the person he or she is trying to get information from—how the person acts, his facial expressions in reaction to questions, what he does with his hands, arms, feet, and legs. To determine stress factors of the individual, I had to read signs of body movement. I would try to sum up SP4 McGuire before the interview started.

When I met him as he entered the CID office, it would give me the best opportunity to assess his reactions with less stress than he would have in a more formal meeting in my office.[88] I had to establish rapport with this guy before I started pushing him for more in-depth answers about topics that might incriminate him. I thought that if I did not gain an advantage during the interview, I would pull out the clear plastic bag of Kit Kats and throw it on my desk in front of the SP4 McGuire. I hoped that this ruse would entice him into making him think that we had something on him.

The ploy was risky and probably striking below the belt, but if SP4 McGuire saw something tangible in front of him, it might trigger some form of guilt response. I felt that I was going into the interview blind and had little hope that anything productive would come out of our discussion. The information about SP4 McGuire dealing hashish came from reliable sources, and I wanted to get the son of a gun. Experience had taught me that once the tone of a conversation turned toward being accusatory, it would be virtually impossible to stop and go back to interviewing the suspect. If this occurred, I would then expect to be forced to switch from a conversational or interview approach to an interrogation mode. If this happened, I would more than likely lose any advantage I had with SP4 McGuire. I was prepared to treat the suspect with an element of dignity and respect, which would go a long way toward him cooperating with me. I hoped I could catch him in a lie and, by using logic, would be able to get him to tell me the truth.

SP4 McGuire showed up at the CID office as scheduled. I happened to notice that he was well groomed, looked sharp in his uniform, and was very polite when responding to my greeting. We shook hands, and I invited him into my office and showed him where to sit. I had placed a straight-back chair directly in front of my desk for making the suspect feel more anxious or concerned during the meeting. As SP4 McGuire sat in the chair, he thanked me; I noticed he immediately shifted in his seat, becoming restless and unsettled.

Although I did not want to venture directly into an interrogation mode, I did not want to make him think he was coming in for an afternoon tea by sitting him in an easy chair where he could relax, either. If he was the top hashish dealer in his unit, as my source indicated, then he knew why he was being summoned by CID. I had to be prepared to advise him of his rights as our conversation progressed into his connection with illegal drugs.

Our interaction went something like this. Rapport was my foremost focus, so I started out asking if he wanted anything to drink. He declined. All CID interviews were required to be preceded by completing a CID Form 44 (interview work sheet). This form was designed to capture all personal data information, such as date and place of birth, unit of assignment, unusual physical characteristics, and any other information deemed necessary and relevant to the subject matter of the interview. I found out that SP4 McGuire was from central Illinois, where he'd attended schools and had several entry-level jobs before entering the US Army in 1975. He was a clerk in his company, and although he had reenlisted for a second term, he had not yet made up his mind whether to make the US Army a career. I was astonished that he provided information without asking why he was asked to come into the CID office. He was so responsive to my questions that I started getting the impression that SP4 McGuire was being a little patronizing with me during our talk.

I began by asking what he knew about illegal drugs in his unit. I purposely phrased my wording to not be accusatory, but along the line of whether he could help me.

"You know, there are a lot of illegal drugs being used by soldiers who are assigned to Ledward and Conn Barracks and the city of Schweinfurt. My investigation has revealed some of those illegal drugs are coming from the First Battalion, Thirtieth Infantry. I spoke with your 1SG and asked for names of the best troopers that he trusts. He provided me with your name as one of those individuals," I told SP4 McGuire. "I figured I should bring in those troopers and talk to them about what they have heard."

I discreetly observed his body movements as I informed him the reason he was brought into the CID office. I noticed that he looked worried, kept shifting in his seat with his arms folded across his chest. When I mentioned illegal drugs, I noticed that his eyebrows shot up, and he broke eye contact with me.

I changed directions of the interview and told him, "I called you in so that I can ask you a few questions about anything you might have heard or have been told about illegal drugs in your unit. Would you be willing to talk to me about what you know that goes on in your unit?" I continued to look for any reaction.

His arms did not move from his chest, nor did he reposition his feet in any way. He appeared to be masking his emotions the best he could.

"I don't know of any information concerning illegal drugs in the unit," SP4 McGuire said.

"Have you heard of any soldiers being involved with illegal drugs in downtown Schweinfurt?"

"Not really," he responded.

I continued this line of questioning for about thirty minutes without getting any significant information from SP4 McGuire. A few follow-up questions covered the area of whether SP4 McGuire knew of anyone who might have information on his illegal drug involvement in his unit. Questioning McGuire was very exhausting and was leading nowhere. We had the same information now as we'd had before we'd called him in for an interview—or *conversation*, as I preferred to call it. I had concluded that McGuire knew what I was trying to find out, but he coyly played with me, and he liked the game, so I had to try my ruse of the fake plastic baggie of hashish.

It was time that I changed the direction of my comments to him by focusing on his actual involvement with illegal drugs, specifically hashish, and telling him that we had information he was the primary source for the stuff in his unit.

"SP4 McGuire, I want to talk to you specifically about another area that I think we need to clear up," I told him.

When he heard this, he moved his legs from a wide stance, indicative of confidence, to more of a closed position with his feet under his chair, indicating he was uncomfortable. I saw his Adam's apple move as he swallowed, and his eyes avoided contact with mine.

"What do you want to ask me?"

Being straightforward, I asked, "Are you involved with illegal drugs in any way?"

Hesitating a second or two, he said, "Absolutely not."

"Are you sure? Because I have received information from a reliable source that you are involved with illegal drugs in your unit."

"I don't know who told you this, but I am not and never have been involved with illegal drugs."

It was time to play my hand. I knew that the quickest way to end any interview that has turned toward the interrogation mode unfavorably would be to use a poorly-thought-out bluff. But I considered using the prepared fake baggie of hashish to trigger some positive response from McGuire as a good bluff that might work. If it did not, I would be no further along than when he'd entered my office.

I then reached into the top drawer of my desk and pulled out the clear plastic baggie of silver-wrapped Kit Kat bars and threw it on my desk, where it landed directly in front of SP4 McGuire.

SP4 McGuire spontaneously blurted out, "If you think that hashish is mine, you're mistaken—I don't wrap mine that way." He immediately blushed and bowed his head. He instantly realized he had made a major blunder by indicating he was in fact involved the sale of hashish. I could not believe what I had just heard when he said, "All right, you got me, but it is going to be hard to prove anything."

The bluff worked as planned. Before I let him regain his composure, I charged headfirst into his unexpected statement. "If you don't wrap your hashish this way, then how do you wrap it?" I said as I stared into his eyes to pressure him to talk. I had now gained the advantage on him in our "conversation" about the hashish trafficking in his unit and wanted him to tell me more. He had lost the cocky attitude and confidence he had at the beginning of our meeting and now began defending himself with every word.

McGuire became silent for a few seconds and gave me the impression he was going to tell me more, but it would not come out. I had to be fast on my feet in my questioning and adapt to the different direction our conversation was going. In fact, we'd left the conversational part and entered the interrogation mode after the traumatic shift after his verbal blunder moments before. I pushed forward with several what-if questions about his use, distribution, and sale of hashish, even at one point telling him I had enough to obtain a search warrant for his barracks room and his car, even though I was not that confident that I had the evidence to support it. I had to convince him that honesty was his best defense and that by providing much-needed information would be essential for his benefit as well. Once he stopped to think about what I had told him, he probably would realize that I did not have anything on him. But my tactics were meant more to entice him to want to talk about what he knew.

He began to loosen up and became more talkative about hypothetical scenarios about soldiers involved with dealing hashish and what would happen to them if they were caught. I had to be careful with my responses to what he said and with what I told him, because I did not want him to clam up and refuse to talk to me any further. I had to convince him that I had his interest and welfare in mind when I talked to him about his suspected hashish dealings. I focused on honesty, integrity, and trust in attempting to get him to talk more specifically about his connections and involvement with the drug trafficking in his unit.

My efforts paid off, because he started talking to me about his German sources and other soldiers within his unit that were involved with hashish trafficking. His admissions without any supporting evidence to back up his information would not go well if, in the remote possibility, SJA would try to court-martial him. Therefore, short of him confessing that he currently had any hashish hidden in his room, his car, or elsewhere, I planned to use the information against others that he talked about. I confronted him with the request that he volunteer to work for the Schweinfurt DST. He agreed.

At the end of our conversation, interview, interrogation, or whatever you want to call it, I registered him as a confidential informant, and he turned out to be one of the most successful sources the Schweinfurt DST used during my tenure as chief. The interview that I thought would not amount to anything resulted in a proliferation of drug investigations for the next few months.

The year 1981 was good for the Schweinfurt DST. The efforts by all members made a considerable dent into the interdictions and disruption of illegal drugs to the troops of the area. I attended DST conferences with all the district and DST chiefs throughout Europe, where I discussed our DST efforts and talked about the targeting system that I initiated during my tenure as the Schweinfurt DST chief. My DST briefings with other units within Europe were well received, but many chiefs thought that it involved unnecessary extra work. I disagreed with them and steadfastly supported my operation methods and tactics, as did Second Region and Würzburg District.

Based on the attention the Schweinfurt DST targeting system received throughout Europe, the Second Region commander, Colonel David H. Stem, paid a visit to the Schweinfurt resident agency to discuss my drug investigations. After a briefing on the targeting system, he appeared satisfied with what we were doing. Colonel Stem requested I make a training video on how our targeting methods worked so that other DSTs throughout Europe could consider it as a tool for their investigations. Another purpose was that the investigative targeting methods could possibly be used at the CID basic course at the United States Army Military Police School (USAMPS) at Fort McClellan, Alabama. I made a thirty-minute video and submitted it through channels for distribution, but I never received any feedback on whether it was used for training purposes.

Later, in November 1981, Colonel Stem directed that the Würzburg District initiate a special drug operation for the period December 1, 1981, to January 31, 1982. The difference between our previous drug operation, Operation Spring Cleaning, conducted earlier in 1981, was that the new effort would not only involve the Schweinfurt DST area of operations but all the Würzburg District offices: Würzburg, Aschaffenburg, Kitzingen, Bad Kissingen, as well as Schweinfurt. The name given this fresh drug suppression effort was called Operation Snowplow, and the objective was to significantly intensify the identification and apprehension of midlevel and street-level illicit drug traffickers.

Operation Snowplow was a two-pronged approach; the first involved gathering and evaluating criminal intelligence at each resident agency in the cities of Würzburg, Aschaffenburg, Kitzingen, Schweinfurt, and Bad Kissingen. Each office would aggressively pursue potential drug trafficking targets within their own area of responsibilities, and progress was to be monitored by daily reporting requirements to the district. Secondly, during the operation, special three-member teams would be formed and stationed on a temporary duty basis for five-day periods at each CID office. These team members would consist of one special agent and two MPIs from other offices working covertly to augment the affected office's area of responsibility.

Before we even started Operation Snowplow, the CID and the entire European theater was thrown into a chaotic, frantic situation when on December 17, 1981, Brigadier General James L. Dozier, deputy chief of staff for logistics and administration for LANDSOUTH headquarters in Verona, Italy, was kidnapped.

The investigation into his kidnapping disclosed that his captors, two men, broke into his apartment in Verona and overpowered him and his wife, Judy. The men, posing as plumbers, entered the apartment on a ruse to check for water leaks in the pipes. Once inside, BG Dozier was struck in the head with the butt of a gun used by one of the kidnappers, which momentarily dazed him. To assist in their getaway, they tied his wife to the kitchen stove, put BG Dozier inside a suitcase-type box, and carried him to a waiting van.

He was held for forty-two days before being rescued by an elite Italian SWAT team. The investigation was being controlled by the Italians, but the army CID was conducting their own inquiry into the matter.[89] Although the Schweinfurt DST was not directly affected by the kidnapping of BG Dozier, the incident was on every special agent's mind, and we were directed to be extremely vigilant and report any information that could lead to his whereabouts.

Dozier was taken to a Padua, Italy, apartment and chained to a pole under a camping tent. During his captivity, he was barred from exercise and forced to listen to loud rock music so he would not hear what the terrorists were saying.

The kidnapping put pressure on the Italian government to clamp down on the Red Brigades, who had kidnapped and murdered several Italian politicians and senior officials since being formed in the 1970s.

Italian authorities began what *Time* magazine called the largest manhunt in Italian history. Their investigation tracked the terrorists to a Padua flat. On the morning of January 28, ten agents in Italy's Central Operative Security Nucleus (COSN) raided the apartment, subdued several Red Brigade members, and found Red Brigade member Antonio Savasta holding a gun to Dozier's head.

"Before Savasta could pull the trigger, however, a commando hit him from behind with the butt of his machine gun and knocked him to the floor," wrote *Time* magazine.

Within ninety seconds of entering the apartment, the COSN agents had captured all six Red Brigade members without firing a shot. Dozier, who appeared unkempt but generally unharmed, was unchained and taken to safety.[90] Years later I met BG Dozier at a Sun City Center, FL Military Officers Association of America (MOAA) luncheon where he discussed his ordeal in Italy.

During phase one of Operation Snowplow, we were directed to gather criminal intelligence from reviewing the subjects of simple possession for the previous year. If that person was still assigned to the unit, we were required to recruit him or her as a source. The DST was required to interview the leaders of any company-size unit, mainly the company commanders and 1SGs, to determine if they had any knowledge or suspicions of unit members being involved with illicit drugs and to put them in contact with CID for interviews. Phase one was required to be completed no later than December 21, 1981.

Phase two was to begin the covert operation part of Operation Snowplow. Efforts to identify reliable sources who could introduce us to the targeted drug dealers was our goal. If the suspected drug dealer would not sell the illicit drug to strangers, then DSTs could use the sources for the controlled buy. During this phase, the temporary covert teams were to converge in the designated cities for five days to investigative the dealers targeted.

Phase three of the operation was set for February 1–16, 1982, to apprehend and interrogate the drug dealers that we had made purchases of illicit drugs from. During this period, about 80 percent of the offenders confessed to their crimes and were tried for various degrees of sale, possession, and distribution of illegal drugs.

Operation Snowplow was considered an overwhelming success. The DSTs identified and apprehended 145 drug offenders, of which 126 were US forces, 4 Americans (1 dependent son of a soldier, 2 US Army civilian employees, and 1 expatriate), 13 German nationals, and 1 third-country national, from six military communities. Operation Snowplow resulted in the seizure of various illegal drugs, such as heroin, hashish, marijuana, and LSD, having a street value of $247,967, and various drug-contaminated paraphernalia. It took several months before all the courts-martial, German trials, and one US Army administrative action on the dependent son of the US soldier were completed. The effort and hard work by the drug investigators paid off because our conviction rate was more than 90 percent.

One case I personally initiated during Operation Snowplow involved the identification and apprehension of an American expatriate, Lawrence Carter,[91] who had been living in Germany for a few years. He was a former US infantry soldier who'd decided to stay in Germany after his discharge and obtain a job working for Kugelfischer GmbH, a German ball bearing factory in Schweinfurt, Germany. Kugelfischer was bombed heavily fifteen times between the summer of 1943 and spring 1945 by American and Allied air force planes during WWII. Thus, 85 percent of the plant was destroyed. However, the company steadily recovered and rebuilt its infrastructure to where it was one of Germany's largest employers.

I considered the Carter investigation a unique drug investigation, because of his misfortune. He was planning on returning to the United States only days before he was arrested by the German *polizei*. I called his investigation the Case of an American Expatriate Drug Dealer:

## THE CASE OF AN AMERICAN EXPATRIATE DRUG DEALER
Investigative cooperation is essential between law enforcement agencies

Around 6:00 p.m. on December 21, 1981, a chilly Monday during the ongoing Operation Snowplow, I was at my desk in the Schweinfurt CID office working on reports when the phone rang. It was the source that I had duped into talking about his hashish dealing. He had become one of my most reliable CIs and had some information about an American civilian, Larry Carter, living in a house in Sennfeld, a small town just outside the city of Schweinfurt.

"He is known to sell LSD," he excitedly reported.[92]

"I am not in the mood for uncorroborated information," I told the CI.

"This is good information—top notch," he stressed. "I was at a guy's house the other night, and the man himself said he could get me as much LSD as I wanted. I also have been told by two different soldiers in the unit that he is the man to go to for a quick high. We had better act fast, because he is getting ready to go back to the States in a week or so." With a sound of urgency in his voice, the CI said, "I have already told him that I have a couple of guys who want some of his LSD."

Not wanting to make a long night out of the developing activities but desiring more details from the source, I agreed to hear more from him.

"Meet me in front of the Schweinfurt Theater on Richard Wagner Strasse in about twenty minutes," I told the CI. I grabbed MPI Moore, who was working at his desk, for backup and briefed him as we left the office.

I drove to the predesignated meeting place, out of the city of Niederwerrn, turned right on Niederwerrner Strasse, drove past the community commander's quarters, the local American elementary school, and Ledward Barracks, and turned right at Richard Wagner Strasse. About a block down, Richard Wagner, Moore, and I simultaneously spotted the CI sitting on a bench near the front of the Schweinfurt Theater. I slowed the car to a crawl, the CI got in, and we continued driving east toward the main river.

As we were driving, I asked the CI a series of questions. "Did Carter act suspicious about you knowing a guy who wanted to get ahold of some LSD?" I asked.

"No. As a matter of fact, he told me that he has a bunch of the stuff at his house and wants to get rid of it as quick as he can, because he is getting ready to go back to the States," the CI said.

"Well, this is interesting, to say the least," I told the CI. "How soon can you set up a meeting with Carter?"

"I suspect he would be willing to meet with you anytime this week," the CI said.

"Do you know if Carter sells LSD from his house in Sennfeld?" I asked.

"I am sure he does," said the CI.

"Good. Set up the meeting for Wednesday night," I told him.

About 11:00 a.m. on December 22, 1981, the CI called me and reported that he had just talked to Carter, who'd agreed to meet with me at his house in Sennfeld at 6:00 p.m. that evening. Since I had about seven hours before the meeting, I asked the CI if he could get off work so he could go with me to show me where Carter lived.

"I'll have to check and call you back," he said.

"Okay, but hurry. We are now on the clock," I emphasized.

About thirty minutes later, the CI called and said he could take off about 2:00. That still gave us about four hours before the meeting. To give the CI enough time to get to the location where I could pick him up, I told him to meet me at 2:30.

Immediately after getting off the phone with the CI, I contacted Walter Schmidt, Schweinfurt Kriminalpolizei, and briefed him on my conversations with my CI about Carter. Walter said he was interested and agreed to come to my office to discuss where we would go on the case from here. About thirty minutes later, Schmidt showed up at my office. A professional investigator, Walter was always in a good mood and carried himself well, and I liked working with him; most importantly, he spoke and understood English. After hearing my plan about meeting with Carter to purchase LSD, Walter told me he liked the arrangement but was concerned about my safety.

With a worried look, Walter queried, "Is there any way that you could arrange for me to go in with you as a co-buyer? I can have a team outside Carter's house before we go in. Once inside, we can immediately be at his doorstep, and they can rush in when you come out," he said.

"Walter, I understand your concern for safety, but the CI has set up the meeting with me only. The CI didn't mention a German friend, and you going in with me and my source will undoubtedly raise suspicions with Carter," I emphasized. "Besides, there is no information on whether Carter has a gun or might become violent in any way."

"In operations of this nature, we must always consider the risks involved," Walter added.

"I know, but nevertheless, I am confident things will go as planned." I told him.

I told Walter that my cover when meeting with Carter was of a dependent husband of a wife who worked in the post exchange (PX). I figured that Carter, not being on active duty, probably did not have access to the PXs at Ledward and Conn Barracks, so it would be highly unlikely that he had any knowledge of people that worked there. Walter stood in silence for a moment, staring at me.

Reluctantly, he acquiesced and said, "Okay. You meet Carter yourself." But citing legal concerns associated with German and US agreements on legal jurisdiction, he told me, "You will be acting as my CI and not as a special agent with the CID."

I informed Walter that I had a scheduled meeting with the source at 2:30, and he was going to show me where Carter lived.

"If Carter offers me the LSD at this meeting, I will purchase a small amount, maybe twenty tabs or so," I told Walter.

"That sounds like a good amount," he responded. "Let's meet after your meeting with the CI."

"Okay, after I drop off the CI, I'll meet you at 3:30 in the Panorama Hotel parking lot. That is near your office and on the way to Carter's house," I told him.

He agreed, and we terminated our meeting.

MPI Eric Moore went with me to pick up the source. We arrived on time, and the source was there waiting on us. We drove directly to Carter's house, about ten minutes away. His residence was one of many row houses on a short dead-end street about a block long in the small town of Sennfeld, just across the main river from Schweinfurt. The neighborhood looked to be populated with older Germans mixed in with a few American families, based on the number of US-plated vehicles parked on the street. We drove by the building where he lived and turned around at the dead end and went back to the street we had entered and parked around the corner from Carter's residence. The three of us walked about halfway down the block when the CI stopped and pointed to a typical multilevel German family residence and said that was where Carter lived.

The CI told MPI Moore and me that Carter's apartment was on the second floor of the building and the entrance was at the side of the house. The source did not know any of the other residents in the building, but he thought Carter was the only American and he lived alone.

I walked up to the front door and tried to open it, but it was locked. I had wanted to get a look inside the stairway leading to Carter's apartment, but I guessed that would not be possible. Maybe the Germans could help with this when Walter and I reexamined the area.

It was 3:15 when MPI Moore and I dropped the CI off near the front gate to Ledward Barracks. I told him to meet us at 4:45 sharp at our predesignated location on Richard Wagner Strasse. MPI Moore and I then rushed to make our meeting with Walter at 3:30 p.m. Walter was waiting for us when we arrived; he was alone, indicating he had a team of other investigators scheduled to accompany him later when we kicked off the operation. On the drive to Carter's building in Sennfeld, I told Walter about my earlier examination of Carter's residence.

"I tried to see the inside entrance to Carter's residence, to check if there was any room to hide a couple of officers in the foyer leading to his door, but the door was locked."

Nodding, Walter said, "That should not be much of a problem. We'll figure it out."

We did a 360 around the house and found a couple of places on the side of the door to Carter's building where officers could conceal themselves while I was inside negotiating. I looked at my watch and saw that it was almost 4:30 p.m., nearly time to pick up the CI. The time we spent inspecting Carter's building got away from us, so we had to speed up the pace.

"We need to get the show on the road," MPI Moore advised Walter and me. "We are supposed to meet Carter at 6:00 p.m. and do not know what time he comes home, so we had better get going."

Walter and I both acknowledged our situation, and the three of us headed for our car. It took us about ten minutes to get Walter back to his car at the Panorama Hotel parking lot. Walter and I agreed to meet at the intersection just before turning onto the street where Carter lived.

At precisely 4:45 p.m., MPI Moore and I picked up the CI. He got into the backseat of the CID car, and we headed for Carter's neighborhood. The first thing I questioned him about was whether he had been in touch with Carter since we'd dropped him off.

"No," he said.

"Then we're still on for 6:00 p.m.?" I asked.

Shrugging, the source replied, "Yes."

It took us about ten minutes to reach the meeting location with the German Kriminalpolizei. They had not yet arrived.

I did not want to be parked on the street in case Carter drove by. Seeing more people together than just the source and I would undoubtedly spook him and eliminate the possibility of any type of controlled buy. To prevent this from happening, I drove out of the area for a few blocks.

It was just a little after 5:00 p.m., so I asked the CI, "Can you get ahold of Carter to see if he is at home?"

"Yes. Just get me to a phone," he said.

We pulled into an Esso gas station just across the main river from Sennfeld. The source left the car, with me following him to a telephone booth. He made the call to Carter's home and received an immediate answer, giving me a thumbs-up that it was Carter. I heard the CI ask Carter if the meeting was still on, and I saw another thumbs-up.

The CI hung up and told me, "He is at home waiting for us as I speak."

I thought, *this is good. Now we need to marry up with the Germans.*

As we headed down the street toward the turn for Carter's house, I saw Walter and three other German Kriminalpolizei investigators standing on the street. I hoped that Carter did not see them as he passed by going to his house.

I turned to the CI and asked, "When you talked to Carter on the phone at the Esso station, did he tell you how long he had been home?"

"No, he did not bring it up, and I did not ask him."

*Well, it's water under the bridge now*, I thought. Besides, even if Carter had seen them, it probably did not matter; the source and I would be the only ones that would go into the meeting with Carter.

We all got out of the car, and I introduced the CI to Walter and the other members of his team. It was now about 5:30 p.m., thirty minutes before we were scheduled to meet with Carter. Walter went over some last-minute details of what his team would do. He briefed us as a group, and everyone knew what their roles would be. MPI Moore would join Walter's team outside when the source and I entered the house. Walter and I decided that the negotiations with Carter should not be more than a few minutes, and if I was in the apartment longer than fifteen minutes, the Kriminalpolizei would enter the apartment and take appropriate action.

The plan was verbalized by Walter. Once the CI and I left the house and I gave a predesignated signal of rubbing my forehead with my right hand, the buy went down as planned, and Walter and his team would enter the house and make the arrest. The CI and I would join MPI Moore near a growth of hedges a short distance from Carter's apartment building door. Walter directed me to stay with MPI Moore and the CI until he gave the all clear to reenter the house.

If the buy did not go down, then the plan had me walking out the door and heading for my car up the street. The Germans would continue to conceal themselves for a while longer and then join me at the car within fifteen minutes. All plans were made with the knowledge that once implemented have the potential for change.

At 5:45 p.m. the German Kriminalpolizei with MPI Moore took up positions near the hedgerow where they could watch the door to Carter's building. One German Kriminalpolizei was positioned in the back of the building to ensure that, if Carter ran, we would have the advantage in catching him. The CI and I waited another five minutes and walked to Carter's building, where we rang the bell from an intercom system at the door. It took Carter a few seconds to answer, and when the CI identified himself, Carter activated the door release.

We entered the building, and I immediately noticed a little alcove to the right. *A good place to position an officer*, I thought. I was still holding the door, so I turned and motioned for Walter, who had a visual on me. It took him a second to reach me standing at the door. I pointed to the alcove, and he understood what

I was thinking. He told me to continue to Carter's apartment upstairs. As I walked away, I softly asked if the predesignated signal was the same. He said yes. Walter had a radio, so I expected he would communicate with his team to tell them his location. Walter being inside the house would prevent his team from having to smash in the door when they rushed into the house to get to Carter's second-floor apartment with no added warning sounds. I felt somewhat more comfortable with Walter being inside on the ground floor in case things went south.

The CI and I made it to Carter's apartment door. The CI knocked, and a second or two later, Carter opened the door and stared at us for another second or so before letting us inside his apartment. Dressed neatly in a plaid shirt and jeans, Carter, a white male, was small statured, about five feet eight inches tall, 160–170 pounds, with hair hanging about two inches below his ear and balding on top, with narrow, dark eyes that appeared to focus only on me. He was not so much intimidating as he was silent, stiff, and awkward for a few seconds before he asked us into his small living room. Providing us with no pleasantries even to sit down and the CI not talking at all, I felt compelled to break the ice.

"I understand that you have been in Germany a long time. What on earth caused you to want to stay here?" I started.

I was surprised when he answered right away. "I originally came to Germany as a soldier with the US Army. When they discharged me, I just stayed over here," he said.

His actions did not make me think that he was nervous or preoccupied with anything, but none of our conversation involved discussions of illegal drugs, especially LSD.

With all three of us standing in the middle of his cramped living room, I took note of how clean his apartment appeared. The living room was neat and had good-looking, up-to-date furniture and an expensive stereo unit, which sat in the corner. From my view of the kitchen where we were standing, I could see no dishes in the sink, and the counters and tabletop were clear of any clutter. The room had no unusual odors, and it looked like Carter took care of himself and the place where he lived. As a matter of fact, one might think that our friend Carter might be a man of means, indicating money in the bank.

My concentration was suddenly broken when Carter commented to the source, "Are you guys still interested in scoring some LSD?"

"Sure. Do you have any?" I fired back.

"Wait here. I'll be right back," he told us. He momentarily left the room and returned with something in his hand. He reached out and handed me a small envelope containing a long sheet of paper perforated into about thirty small squares.

"Each square has a small dosage unit of LSD on it," explained Carter.

If what he told me was true, I had about thirty dosage units of LSD in my hand. "How much do you want for the acid?" I asked.

"I'll be satisfied with a hundred [meaning US dollars]," he said.

"Okay. It's a deal," I told him. I placed the purported LSD on the table near his sofa and pulled out my wallet and gave Carter five twenty-dollar bills. He took the money and placed it into his front pocket. I immediately grabbed the envelope from the coffee table and put it inside my jacket pocket.

Since my business was over, I didn't want to hang around the apartment discussing sports, politics, or anything else, for that matter, with Carter. It was time to get out of there. I motioned with a slant of my head to the CI, who'd practically had nothing to say the entire time we were in Carter's apartment, that it was time to go. Carter also took the hint and walked over to the door and opened it for us. The CI and I bid Carter farewell and left the apartment, hearing the door shut behind us as we went down the stairs. The entire operation took about ten minutes, five minutes less than what Walter had given me before he said he would have entered the apartment if I hadn't come out.

As the CI and I approached the front door to leave the building, I looked over to my left and saw Walter. I gave him the prearranged signal by rubbing my forehead with my right hand as I passed him. Since Walter, the CI, and I were the only ones in the hallway, I whispered to Walter that I had bought about thirty dosage units of what Carter claimed to be LSD.

"That's great," Walter said in a low, heavily German-accented voice.

I opened the door with Walter directly behind me waving for his team to follow him into the building to make the arrest. When the CI and I were outside the building, Walter told me to wait for his signal before reentering the building. As the CI and I walked toward MPI Moore a few feet away, the Kriminalpolizei team ran past us into the building.

They whizzed by us like the wind. You could feel it, but could not see it, all moving in one singular motion like synchronizing swimmers, handguns drawn, not saying a word, but everyone knew exactly what their jobs were as they quickly and quietly made their way to Carter's apartment. It took me only a couple of minutes to brief MPI Moore as to what happened before one of the Kriminalpolizei team members opened the door to the building and motioned for us to return. As I entered the apartment, Carter immediately saw me, and his knees buckled, causing him to almost fall to the floor. His face turned pale, and his eyes focused downward. He knew he had been had.

The Kriminalpolizei team was quick but meticulous and precise in their search of his apartment. Their efforts paid off when they located another several envelopes of suspected LSD inside a drawer of a nightstand in the bedroom and a small amount of hashish and smoking paraphernalia in a box lying on a shelf in the kitchen cabinet. When the Kriminalpolizei team finished, Carter was escorted from the apartment to a waiting Polizei sedan that had been moved to the front of the building. As two members of the Kriminalpolizei drove Carter to the Schweinfurt *polizei* station, Walter thanked me for our part in the operation and said he would get with me in the next couple of days to shore up any details of the case. MPI Moore, the CI, and I then departed.

As we were driving the CI to our predesignated drop-off location, I thought, *What an operation!* The Germans executed the operation effortlessly and without much commotion. The others living in the building either did not know what was going on or chose to ignore it.

Walter called me two days later and informed me that they had confiscated another six hundred dosage units of suspected LSD, having a street value of about $3,000.

"The stuff has been sent to the lab, but we will not receive the results for another week or so. I will call you when that information is available," said Walter.

About a week or so after the Carter investigation, I was working late in the office doing catch-up paperwork when I received a phone call from the Schweinfurt duty agent, Special Agent Ronald Glunt, who advised me he was currently investigating a traffic accident involving a fatality of an artillery soldier from Conn Barracks.

"The reason I called, Dick, was that a passenger, who received a broken leg in the accident, was getting ready to be transported to the Würzburg hospital for treatment, asked for you by name."

"Who is it?" I asked.

"SP4 Jonathan Trumwell from the Third Battalion, Seventh ADA, at Conn," Special Agent Glunt said.

I wasn't shocked but disappointed to hear that PFC Trumwell was involved in yet another car crash where the driver was DWI. "How long before they transport him to Würzburg?" I asked SA Glunt.

"Probably in the next thirty minutes or so," he provided.

"Is SP4 Trumwell able to talk?"

"Sure. He has a stress fracture of his left leg," Glunt indicated.

"Tell him that I will be at the clinic in fifteen minutes."

As I drove to the clinic, I had no idea what I was going to tell SP4 Trumwell that would make any difference. He apparently did not listen to me before. If he did, he surely had not paid any attention to our conversation at Williamson's trial. I still had the urge to see SP4 Trumwell and at least hear what he wanted to tell me. Just maybe, talking to him again might do some good later. However, by the time I arrived at the Schweinfurt clinic, SP4 Trumwell had already left for Würzburg. I made a mental note to myself to talk to him when he got out of the hospital. I did not know it at the time, but that chance would never come. One good thing out of the information Special Agent Glunt told me: SP4 Trumwell must have gotten himself promoted, because he was a PFC when I first met him.

The year 1981 was not only one of the busy and most successful years I worked uncover narcotics, it also brought an enhancement to my social life. After meeting Elda, we became an item, were getting serious, and were talking about marriage. With her help, I began to enjoy my off time more than ever. Before I met her, I was working 24-7, but after I met her, my Schweinfurt workday was drastically reduced to about 15-6, still a considerably busy work schedule. With her understanding and support, I continued to devote a substantial amount of time to my CID duties and the profession I'd come to love and revere. Since meeting on my birthday, October 25, 1980, Elda, who loved to tour Europe, also got me hooked on traveling.

During the spring of 1982, Elda went about planning the details of our wedding. We had decided the date for our marriage would be on April 20, 1982. Elda has always been very resourceful. If she sees something she wants, she is persistent—but not in a bad way—until she gets it. She did her research and found that we could get married in the historical city of Basel, Switzerland. Basel is the home of the oldest university in Switzerland, has forty museums, and is a city of culture for enthusiasts of the arts and humanities. Basel has the highest concentration of museums in the country of Switzerland. It is a beautiful old town with modern architecture and the Rhine, an inviting spot to vacation. So, armed with this information, Elda contacted the clerk of the city hall in Basel and arranged our marriage.[93] In preparation for our wedding, I shaved off my beard that I had grown when I'd started working undercover.

On April 19, 1982, we drove to Basel, Switzerland, and found a small hotel in the city about two blocks from city hall. We checked in with the Swiss government officials at city hall to ensure all appropriate preparations were completed for our scheduled marriage at 9:00 a.m. on the April 20. That evening, we had a candlelight dinner at a small, quaint, old-fashioned restaurant about a block from our hotel.

The wedding went off without a hitch. Acting as our best man and maid of honor were two other Americans, a helicopter pilot and his schoolteacher bride from another military community in Germany, whom we had never met before nor have we seen since. We left Basel and spent our honeymoon in the city of Lucerne, Switzerland, and Heidelberg, Germany, on our way back to Schweinfurt.

Once we'd started dating, I knew I had found the love of my life. I had not felt this way with any other women I had dated. Before we left Germany in 1989 for the last time, we had been to every country in Europe at least once, and some twice or more, as well as Britain. Who would have known that a chance meeting at the Keller Bar on my thirty-fourth birthday in 1980 would start a romance that has been ongoing for more than thirty-five years?

It was business as usual when we returned from our wedding, with the exception that I felt calmer and was relaxed and more focused than ever before. Being married to Elda had put real meaning and purpose in my life.

About two weeks after I returned from Basel, I received a call from Walter Schmidt, who told me that the trial of Carter had been scheduled for the end of May 1982 and that I was the principle witness for the prosecution.

"Will I be called by the prosecution before I have to testify?" I asked.

"Probably not. You will be questioned by the judges in the case," Walter said.

*Wow. Interesting*, I thought.

"I'll get back with you when they have confirmed the date of the trial," Walter advised.

"Okay, I'll be waiting on your call," I told him.

One week later, on May 5, 1982, Walter contacted me and related that Carter's trial was scheduled for May 10, 1982, at the Schweinfurt Amtsgerichte (local courts that rule on cases where the sentences range from one to no more than four years). Walter indicated that Carter, if convicted, was looking at two or more years in prison.

"On the day of court, I'll drive you there," he said.

I continued to work and manage the Schweinfurt DST, and our investigations returned to more of a routine but still quite busy pace. SAC Boatwright called me into his office one day out of the blue and asked me to sit down. He began by telling me he was having a very hard time with the commanding general, BG Robert Wagner. BG Wagner, who had replaced BG Johnson, was anti-CID. BG Wagner did not like to be briefed by CID and would often refuse to meet with SAC Boatwright when he had a rather high-profile case to brief. SAC Boatwright indicated to me that since he was having this issue with the man that ran the community, he'd elevated the problem to Würzburg District level, who discussed the issue with the Third Infantry Division commander, MG Fred K. Mahaffey.

For some reason, SAC Boatwright had to be the one to move on. SAC Boatwright related that to defuse the issue, he was being asked to leave Schweinfurt and would temporarily take over the Aschaffenburg CID office until a permanent replacement could be identified at that office for the SAC who had recently been reassigned to the States.

"So," I asked SAC Boatwright, "who will be replacing you here in Schweinfurt?"

"You will, Dick," he blurted out.

I was flabbergasted, to say the least.

"Your appointment as SAC has been vetted all the way from the region commander, Colonel Stem, to the Würzburg District Ops and commander."

"Do we have a time line as to when that will take place?" I asked SAC Boatwright.

"Probably within the week," he said.

On May 10, 1982, the Schweinfurt Amtsgerichte called me to testify before a panel of three judges on the Carter case. As I sat down in the witness chair, Carter was looking straight at me with a sort of forlorn expression on his face from his chair at the defense table. He looked like he had lost some weight, and he did not look too happy to be in court.

The German judges have a more expanded role than those in American courts. In some cases, such as the one at which I was testifying, the judges ask most questions in open court. I recalled one of the judges asking me how I'd met Carter. I told them I was introduced to him by a friend at his house on the night of the drug buy. A second judge asked me if I used to have a full-grown beard at the time I'd purchased the LSD from Carter; I acknowledged in the affirmative. The third judge asked me why I had shaved it off, and I told him that I was finishing up with undercover work and being reassigned. I elaborated to the judges that I had grown the beard to alter my appearance, which enabled me to blend in with the local German and American civilian population who were suspected drug dealers.

They asked me several more questions about how my conversation with Carter had gone the night of the controlled buy, and I answered them honestly. One thing I noticed that was much different from American courts that I have testified in was that some of the questions the German judges asked me were not open ended. The German judge's questions lacked emphasis on "just the facts, ma'am," like the type asked in American courts. It was more like providing unsubstantial hearsay evidence instead of facts. I would never have gotten away with providing so much information about what I'd thought Carter was up to, as well as details on my actions leading up to and during the controlled buy of hashish, in the American court system.

My testimony had done the deed, and Carter was found guilty and sentenced to German prison for three years.

At the time, I left the DST, our sources were all functioning at full steam, and we had achieved great success in the interruption and interdiction of the flow of illegal drugs into the Schweinfurt military community. As I was making the transition from DST team chief to SAC, I took account of all the accomplishments we had success with in the fight against illegal drugs. I provided this information to SAC Boatwright to use when he wrote my officer evaluation report prior to him leaving the Schweinfurt CID office. I knew I would miss working undercover, but the job can eat up your personal life. With success come certain bumps and roadblocks that sort of balance out achievements along the way.

Under my tenure, the Schweinfurt DST was mostly successful, but there were a couple of investigations that fell apart through no real fault of any of my investigators or sources. MP investigators generally are hardworking, honest, trustworthy, and highly motivated. There are several things that can go wrong in a drug investigation that are no one's fault. In retrospect, I like to think of these cases with humor, but at the time, the hurdles were too high to jump over. I often think of the man-hours involved in working the cases, with the end results being unproductive. The end results of the investigations were very frustrating, to say the least.

Everyone has heard of Murphy's law. Well, the following two investigations had elements that if something could wrong, it would. The first investigation involved a source-assisted buy of hashish that occurred only a block from the Schweinfurt CID office in Niederwerrn. I call this caper the Case of the Dead Battery:

## THE CASE OF THE DEAD BATTERY
Once you coordinate a signal that a deal went down as planned, ensure that the signal works

It was a beautiful early spring day in 1982, and I had the window in my office open to enjoy a steady, cool breeze as I worked. It was around 10:00 a.m., and I had just finished a meeting with MPIs Moore and Punzalan about a source that I wanted them to contact and interview about a dealer we were targeting. They had just left the office when our secretary's voice rang through the office intercom that the source I wanted interviewed requested to see me.

"Is he here now?" I asked.

"Yes. He's upstairs and says it's important that he tells you something," she added.

"Show him to my office," I told her.

The source stepped into my office, and I offered him a seat. Once he settled into the chair I had pointed out to him, I asked, "What's the important information that you need to talk to me about?"

"I know a German national who has a significant amount of hashish that he is willing to sell. He does not deal with anyone he doesn't know," the source said.

"You mean that an introduction will be out of the question?" I asked the source.

"Probably."

"How reliable is this guy?" I asked.

"Very," the source said.

For a few seconds, I pondered what he had said and considered the fact that I had used his services only one other time, but he'd come through with no real problem. I asked the source, "Will he sell hash to you?"

"Probably, if I ask him."

Looking directly at the source with an expression of concern, I asked, "Have you ever bought hashish or any other illegal drug from this German?"

"No, never. I met him at a party a few days ago, and thought you would be interested in identifying who his dealer is. When I talked to him at the party, he indicated he often sells hashish to US soldiers, and that is the type of information you told me you wanted me to report to you about," the source said, obviously feeling somewhat offended at what I had asked him but still defending the information he was reporting.

"Okay, I had to ask the question!" I shot back.

If anything, the source could establish a rapport with the German dealer, and we could push for a controlled buy later. One of my first considerations was to alert the German Kriminalpolizei on the information. I would call my colleague at the Kriminalpolizei and chief of the Schweinfurt narcotics investigation team, Helmut Deutscher, and see if I could solicit him to allow Walter Schmidt from the Carter case to help us. I told the source to call me the next day for further advice on the German national. He agreed.

That afternoon, I called Chief Deutscher and provided him a briefing on what the source had informed me earlier. Chief Deutscher requested to come to my office for a rundown on how to target the German dealer. We arranged a meeting for 4:00 p.m. that afternoon.

Chief Deutscher arrived at my office on time.

"Do you care for a cup of coffee?" I asked.

"No. Had too much already today." Without any preliminary conversation, Chief Deutscher broke directly into the matter of the German hash dealer. "Tell me about your source."

"Well, I have used him one time before, and everything went down as planned on the case," I said. "I have no reason to doubt his sincerity this time."

We sat around for about an hour, brainstorming how we would arrange a controlled buy from the German national to make a case.

Pausing for a moment during our conversation, I said, "There is something I must tell you, Herr Deutscher. The German will not sell to anyone he does not know. This precludes us from attempting to introduce him to either one of my guys or yours."

"Yes, that is right," Chief Deutscher said, nodding.

We both knew we had to use my source for any meeting with the German.

I was anxious to tell Chief Deutscher about the plan that I worked over in my mind. Chief Deutscher listened intently as I went through the scenario.

"I'll have my source reach out to the German and ask for a meeting in the parking lot at Italo's pizzeria down the street from the CID office. I will have my source sitting in a CID sedan, and when the German dealer arrives for the meeting, I will instruct the source to invite him into the vehicle. When the German produces the hashish, the source will gently press the brake pedal, activating the taillights. Once we see the taillights illuminate, this will give us the go-ahead signal to rush in and make the arrest. I will tell the source to ask for a about ten pieces of hashish," I told Deutscher. "The price of a chunk of hashish runs about a hundred dollars."

Chief Deutscher agreed. The amount of hashish sold would determine the seriousness of the charges against the German when charges were filed, as well as how involved he was in the trafficking of hashish.

"I know the owner of the *Backerei* [bakery] across the street from Italo's. He will let us use his business to conceal ourselves while we observe the deal go down," Chief Deutscher said.

"Great. You arrange with the *Backerei* owner, and I will contact my source to set it up. When do you want to do this?" I asked Chief Deutscher.

He was silent for a few seconds, as if pondering the best time so not to interfere with anything he already had going on. "Tomorrow night at 8:00 p.m., if possible," Chief Deutscher said.

"Consider it a plan. Can I contact you in the early afternoon tomorrow to update you on what my source was able to set up?" I requested.

"That sounds good. Talk to you then."

After Chief Deutscher left my office, I contacted the source by phone; he answered on the first ring.

"I talked to the Kriminalpolizei about your German friend. Can you contact him and request a meeting for tomorrow night at 8:00 p.m. at Italo's pizzeria?" I asked.

"I think I can get ahold of him and set it up."

"Good. I want you to ask the German if he can get you a plate of hashish."

"Don't you want more?" the source inquired.

"No. Our goal here is to see where he gets his stuff."

"Okay, I'll call you after I find out if the German can meet," the source said and hung up.

I figured it would take a couple of hours before hearing from him; however, it was hardly fifteen minutes when I received a call back. The source had good news. The German agreed to the meeting the following night at 8:00 p.m. in the parking lot of Italo's pizzeria. I couldn't believe our luck; the German agreed to everything. I requested the source meet me at my office the next day at 6:00 p.m. so I could go over details of what he needed to do at the meeting.

The next morning, the weather was perfect, the sky was painted blue, and it was sunny—not bad for an early spring day. The first thing on my agenda was to call Chief Deutscher. I knew we had agreed to talk in the early afternoon, but I did not expect the source to set up the meeting with the German so quickly. Even though I'd contacted him early in the day, he sounded appreciative of my call and, when briefed, asked the appropriate questions about the upcoming planned controlled buy from the German. The source did not know his name, so we had no way of doing any type of criminal checks for addresses, cars he drove, or what type of background he had. In other words, we were going into the operation blind, and for the time being, he was being called *the German*.

Chief Deutscher told me he had arranged with the *Backerei* owner to use a second-floor window to observe our source meeting the German. I briefed him on what I had instructed the source to do during the meeting and that it would go down inside the CID sedan parked at Italo's parking lot. I told Chief Deutscher that the source was to meet us at the CID office at 6:00 p.m. We went over the entire operation by phone, and Chief Deutscher ended our conversation by indicating he would be at the scheduled meeting with the source.

At 6:00 p.m. sharp, the source arrived at the CID office. Chief Deutscher had arrived moments before with a team of four Kriminalpolizei officers. I had three DST members—MPIs Eric Moore, Ray Punzalan, and David Hanks, who was a new member. We all gathered in my office in the basement of the CID building and went over the planned operation. It was agreed that MPIs Moore, Punzalan, and Hanks would act as patrons of Italo's, along with two of Chief Deutscher's team. The group would sit at a table that had a good advantage point, enabling them to have the CID sedan in sight. Chief Deutscher and I would be observing from the window on the second floor of the *Backerei*. The two remaining team members of Chief Deutscher's squad would be positioned in a German *polizei* vehicle just out of sight of the CID sedan, but ready to rush in for the arrest once the signal had been given that the deal had gone down.

Members of both the American and German teams were introduced to the source to ensure that they all could recognize him during the operation. I personally conducted a thorough search of the source before we left for the meeting with the German. It was good I found nothing on the source, and we were ready to implement the planned operation. Since Americans and Germans were involved with the operation, both Chief Deutscher and I gave a safety briefing to the group and ensured that all team members knew or could recognize each other as the operation unfolded.

At 7:45 p.m., we all left the CID office. I gave the source last-minute instructions before he proceeded to Italo's parking lot. Since the CID office was just a block from Italo's, I instructed the source to enter the parking lot from the opposite direction to avoid any suspicion by the dealer if he was already in the parking lot and saw the source drive from the vicinity of the CID office. Utilizing a key given to him earlier in the day by the owner, Chief Deutscher and I entered the *Backerei* from a side door and took up our positions on the second floor.

Just minutes after setting up our surveillance, we observed the source drive up and park in the predesignated space. Our wait for our German suspect was short. Within five minutes, a German-plated vehicle pulled up and parked next to our source.

Chief Deutscher and I observed a man get out of the vehicle and walk to the driver's side of our vehicle to speak to the source. Since the window that we were observing from was closed, we could not hear any of their conversation, but we could see everything they were doing. A minute or two had passed when we observed the German man walk back around the source's vehicle to the passenger side, open the door, and get in. Another five minutes went by, and all we could see was movement of heads of the two inside the vehicle, but no taillights came on. Another few minutes went by, and we were getting a little uncomfortable with the dealer staying in the car with the source without any indication from the source that a deal had taken place. Customers at Italo's were starting to leave, and a couple was heading toward the parking lot near where our source and the dealer were located. With the customers getting closer to the car, it created a dangerous situation for them if a confrontation with the dealer occurred. Luckily, the couple walked right by the source's car without the taillights coming on.

Suddenly, I observed the source frantically waving his left arm outside the car and pointing his hand to the roof of the car. Still no lights. Finally, I thought I understood the reason for the source's actions; he was trying to signal us that the car's taillights were apparently not working. Because of the radical movement of the source's arm outside the vehicle, I got the impression that a deal was imminent and he was trying to communicate with us by motioning his arm outside the window. I turned to Chief Deutscher and told him that I thought the deal was taking place but that the source, for some reason, was having trouble signaling us with the car's taillights. Chief Deutscher did not want to take the chance and made the decision to give the source more time to activate the taillights if the deal went down.

Uneasy, I continued to watch for any further signs from the source, but none came. Then, not to my surprise, Chief Deutscher and I observed the German exit the vehicle get into his car, and within a second, he drove quickly drove away. What I saw next confirmed my suspicions; the source got out of the vehicle facing the window where Chief Deutscher and I were, and he shrugged as if to say, "What happened to you guys?"

Both Chief Deutscher and I left the *Backerei* and joined the source where he was standing next to the car. In a complaining tone, the source said, "I pressed the brake pedal several times, but the taillights never came on." A bit agitated, he continued, "I saw the hashish in his hand."

Chief Deutscher and I were observing the car from the second-floor window and saw the source frantically waving his arms. I didn't want to tell Chief Deutscher, "I told you so," when I suggested that I thought the deal was going down. Instead, I kept my composure intact as much as possible.

Chief Deutscher, obviously perturbed and disappointed, looked at me and said, "How could this happen?"

No one felt worse than I did. The CID car, an old German VW bug, had been around for a while, but the DST had never experienced any trouble with the lights before. *Why did this happen at this exact moment in time?* I thought. Could the German have had a guardian angel? Who knows? Well, we did not get any hashish that night, but the German was not out of the woods just yet.

About two weeks later, Chief Deutscher came to my office with a big smile on his face. Greeting him kindly, I said, "To what can I attribute the pleasure of your visit, Herr Deutscher?"

"The night we planned the drug operation with the German in the car was not all lost. The two Kriminalpolizei officers conducting the surveillance in the car that night ran the plates on the car the German was driving and identified him as Aldo Brauer,[94] who lives in Schweinfurt. He has a criminal record connecting him with illegal hashish and heroin," Deutscher explained. He elaborated further, "We conducted a raid on his house and found almost a kilo of hashish and the names of some of the people he sells drugs to."

"Were there any US servicemen's names on the list?" I asked.

"No. All were German," he noted.

The Brauer investigation turned out to be a big catch. As frustrating as it was for the CID, at least Brauer suffered the consequences of his dastardly deeds in the German courts. The Brauer investigation was also personally very frustrating for me and the Schweinfurt DST, but the case was not the most annoying one we had.

An investigation that topped the Brauer case made it to military court-martial and a conviction obtained. But the rest of the story still haunts me to this day. My reflection of the investigation is covered in the following narrative in the caper I call the Case of the Teflon Staff Sergeant Who Got Away with It:

## THE CASE OF THE TEFLON STAFF SERGEANT WHO GOT AWAY WITH IT
It's never over until it's over

This investigation started out like many other controlled purchases we made during the 1980s involving US soldiers who sold illegal drugs. It all started early one morning in 1982 when I got a call from the Schweinfurt MP desk sergeant, who reported that a command-directed health-and-welfare inspection was conducted at a medical detachment. Most of the assigned US Army personnel in this unit supported the local medical clinic (dispensary) on Ledward Barracks. The inspection of the barracks revealed several grams of hashish found in a wall locker.

The locker was later identified as belonging to SP4 Thomas J. MacGreaver,[95] a well-liked young soldier who was a good performer and got along well with his supervisors. His NCOIC was shocked to find that MacGreaver had been found in possession of several grams of hashish. The NCOIC informed interviewers that he had never had any disciplinary problems with the young man. Because of his predicament, MacGreaver told his NCOIC that he wanted to identify his source of the hashish in exchange for leniency in his case. I requested that the NCOIC arrange to have Specialist MacGreaver sent to the CID office for an interview that afternoon.

About 1:30 p.m., Specialist MacGreaver arrived at my office. The young, black specialist was neatly dressed in army fatigues, had a trim build, and appeared to be physically fit. When I introduced myself to him, he responded with a hearty handshake, and his overall personality overflowed with confidence. I offered him a chair in front of my desk. I was not used to interviewing soldiers that looked as sharp, confident, and mature as Specialist MacGreaver. Most of the soldiers I dealt with, especially those involved with illegal drugs, were somewhat on the dubious side. Many of them were frowsy looking and did not act with any assertiveness.

I started my interview with Specialist MacGreaver by letting him know that whatever he told me, it had to be valuable information that would help the US Army's war on drugs. Then, if I was to help him on his case, he had to be totally up front, direct, and straightforward with me.

"I'll be straight with you, Mr. Miller," he said.

"Well, we are off to a good start. Now, what do you have to tell me?"

Looking me straight in the eye, exuding the confidence of a person with no worries in the world, he said, "To start with, Mr. Miller, I am not a heavy user of hashish or marijuana."

Immediately, I interrupted him. "Listen to me, Specialist MacGreaver. I told you I want you to be up front with me; I don't need to hear excuses that you think might diminish your involvement in the possession of hashish. You can't help your case that way. You need to be forthcoming with me and tell me something of value, or this interview is over," I harshly admonished. "Now, tell me something I want to hear," I stressed.

"Would it help me if I told you who sold me the hash that was found in my wall locker?"

"Absolutely!" I said, encouraging him to follow through with the name.

"My source of the hash was SSG Graham Piketon,[96] who is assigned to the Schweinfurt medical detachment."

"Does he know you are down here talking to CID?"

"No. He is on leave this week, but our jobs bring us into contact almost daily at the clinic."

"Does he reside in the medical detachment barracks?"

"Oh no. He's married and has a couple of kids. He lives in Askren Manor."

"Do you know anyone else that Piketon has sold hashish to?"

"I don't know specifically, but he has a reputation of being one of the main sources to go to for hashish."

"How long have you known about SSG Piketon's illegal drug activities?"

"For well over a year."

"Would it be possible to make an introduction of someone to SSG Piketon for making a buy of hashish from him?"

"He is pretty careful, and there have been times that if he doesn't know someone, he will not sell to them," Specialist MacGreaver pointed out.

"Where did you score your hashish from SSG Piketon?"

"He sold it to me at his quarters in Askren Manor."

"Now, be totally honest with me. How many times have you bought hashish or any other type of illegal drug from SSG Piketon?" I asked.

"Over the past year, maybe four or five times," he said.

"Specialist MacGreaver, please excuse me. I'll be right back."

I found MPI Moore, who had just returned to the office and was sitting at his desk doing paperwork on a case he had worked on the night before. I explained to him that I was interviewing Specialist MacGreaver and what he had told me about SSG Piketon.

"I want you to conduct name checks on SSG Piketon. You need to also find any local personnel records on him so we can get a feel for where he has been assigned and if he has had any trouble in the US Army."

"I'll get right on it," MPI Moore assured me.

I then returned to my office to continue my interview with Specialist Mac-Greaver.

The interview lasted for another thirty or so minutes without much more information. Specialist MacGreaver denied that he had purchased illegal drugs, including hashish, from any other US soldier, but he did admit that when he first arrived in Germany, he had purchased a couple of pieces of hashish from a German national at Maggie's, a known bar that catered mainly to US soldiers.

"Can you identify the German national who sold you hashish?" I asked.

"No. I have not seen him since the night I bought two pieces of hashish from him," he said.

The final question I asked Specialist MacGreaver involved his services to the Schweinfurt DST. "Can you make a controlled purchase of hashish from SSG Piketon under CID direction?"

He hesitated a few seconds before replying, "Yes, I would be willing to help you guys, if I can get some kind of payback."

"I'll talk to your commander and SJA about your case; maybe we can work out a deal for you." I knew fully well that he was still facing, at a minimum, punishment under Article 15, UCMJ. Since his case only involved possession, he would probably face court-martial if he chose that route over an Article 15.

I told Specialist MacGreaver that I wanted him to reach out to SSG Piketon and tactfully arrange a deal for at least ten grams of hashish. I advised him that once he had SSG Piketon's cooperation and agreement that he would sell him hashish, I needed a couple of days to shore up any details to develop the case against SSG Piketon. I advised him not to push SSG Piketon, for fear that it would make him suspicious of what CID was planning. Specialist MacGreaver agreed, and we terminated the interview.

I had given Specialist MacGreaver two days to get with SSG Piketon to arrange a deal for at least ten grams of hashish. I advised him not to return to the CID office but to call when and if he could set up a deal. In the back of my mind, I wondered how much SSG Piketon knew about Specialist MacGreaver getting caught with hashish in his wall locker.

The day after the interview with Specialist MacGreaver, MPI Moore came into my office and reported that there were no hits on SSG Piketon; apparently, he was clean.

"I found a personnel file on SSG Piketon at the medical detachment headquarters in Würzburg. I have scheduled a meeting with the personnel NCOIC to review it this afternoon," MPI Moore said.

"Get it done quickly, and make sure no one in the personnel office knows why we are reviewing his file," I directed. "Thanks."

Later that day, MPI Moore came back from Würzburg, which is about forty kilometers from Schweinfurt, and reported what he had found in the file. The file disclosed a history of assignments and the most recent enlisted evaluation report (EER) on SSG Piketon, which showed him to be the perfect NCO that did nothing wrong. The EER depicted his character as infallible and his performance superb, and he had been recently selected for warrant officer and attendance at the physician's assistant program (PA) in San Antonio, Texas.

Two days had passed, and still no word from Specialist MacGreaver. My major concern was that SSG Piketon knew about Specialist MacGreaver's situation and was running scared. If this was the situation, then SSG Piketon more than likely had stopped selling hashish until things blew over. I hoped this was not the case, but time would only tell if there would be any chance to initiate a case against SSG Piketon.

Finally, Specialist MacGreaver called about 4:00 p.m. in the afternoon and told me that SSG Piketon had agreed to sell him ten pieces of hashish for a hundred dollars. The only glitch? The deal was to go down that night at SSG Piketon's quarters in Askren Manor at 6:00 p.m. That meant that I had only two hours to organize a team, meet with Specialist MacGreaver, and get everything ready.

"Can you postpone the deal until tomorrow?" I asked Specialist MacGreaver.

"It would be hard, because SSG Piketon is still on leave, and he has less than a week before he reports to warrant officer training."

*Damn, we do have to work fast*, I thought. "All right, how fast can you get to the CID office?" I asked.

"About fifteen minutes," Specialist MacGreaver replied.

"I'll be waiting for you," I told him. "Hurry."

I got ahold of MPIs Moore and Hanks and advised them of what was about to go down at Askren Manor. I requested they conduct a drive-by of SSG Piketon's quarters to ascertain if there would be any obstacles in the way of setting up a fixed surveillance near his residence. They had not been gone but a few minutes when Specialist MacGreaver arrived at the CID office. It was now 4:45 p.m., about an hour and a quarter before Specialist MacGreaver was to meet with SSG Piketon. I had Specialist MacGreaver stay in the waiting room while I went upstairs to the agents' office area. I found Special Agent Ownby at his desk working on cases. As I entered his office, he raised his head and looked at me with a stare of uncertainty.

"What can I do for you, Miller?" he asked.

"I need your help," I said.

"What do you need?" he replied.

"Can you help us with a drug surveillance in Askren Manor?" I asked.

"Sure. When do you need me?" he responded.

"Now," I said.

"That is quick."

"We have a short-fused deal going down at 6:00 p.m. and need another man for surveillance," I explained.

"Well, let's get started."

"Thanks. Meet me in my office in about ten minutes."

"See you there."

Help is one of the best traits of CID special agents. At the drop of a hat, most agents are willing to stop what they are doing and pitch in whenever needed on an investigation. I have seen this happen over and over, to include many late nights where I needed the assistance of a fellow agent, and he got out of a warm bed to come to my aid.

It was now 5:15 p.m. MPIs Moore and Hanks had returned to the CID office. I called Special Agent Ownby on the office intercom and grabbed Specialist MacGreaver from the waiting room. We all gathered in my office, and I went over the plan.

I directed Special Agent Ownby to set up a fixed surveillance in the basement stairwell of SSG Piketon's quarters. Specialist MacGreaver had informed me earlier that SSG Piketon's quarters were on the first floor of a three-floor housing unit. Staging Special Agent Ownby in the stairwell would enable him to observe Specialist MacGreaver as he knocked on SSG Piketon's door. It would be possible to hear their conversation at the doorway, but it was expected SSG Piketon would invite Specialist MacGreaver into his quarters to make the actual transaction. Special Agent Ownby could also be responsible for observing Specialist MacGreaver as he entered the building and walked to the door of SSG Piketon's quarters.

MPIs Moore and Hanks would set up a roving surveillance in the parking lot outside SSG Piketon's quarters to ensure the safety of anyone in the vicinity. Hopefully, no one would be in the area at the time the planned buy was to go down. I would fix my position just outside the main door to observe Specialist MacGreaver entering the building. I would conduct a search of his person to ensure he had no contraband in his possession and keep him in my sight from the time he left my sedan to the time he entered SSG Piketon's building. I then provided Specialist MacGreaver with five twenty-dollar bills, the serial numbers of which were recorded earlier for identification later.

The plan, as implemented, did not include the apprehension of SSG Piketon. The apprehension phase of the operation was planned for the following day, out of sight of his family. A ruse would be used to contact SSG Piketon at his quarters the following morning and have him come to the unit for an aspect of his departure for warrant school.

It was now 5:45 p.m. Specialist MacGreaver had been searched, and the other had departed for their surveillance positions. It took us ten minutes to reach the parking lot of SSG Piketon's quarters. I parked in a space designated for visitors. From my position, I could observe Specialist MacGreaver walk from my car to the main door to SSG Piketon's building. It was now 5:55 p.m. I gave Specialist MacGreaver last-minute instructions to not pressure SSG Piketon into making the deal, but to tactfully negotiate the transaction. I emphasized that he should act normal and not rush any aspect of the deal.

"I understand what you need," he said.

Contact by radio from MPI Moore assured no activity was taking place from his position to the building where Specialist MacGreaver was to enter. Special Agent Ownby turned his radio off to prevent any traffic from being overheard in the stairwell.

"Go," I directed Specialist MacGreaver.

Specialist MacGreaver had been briefed on where to go after the transaction went down. As soon as I saw Specialist MacGreaver leave the building, Special Agent Ownby was to follow him to the predesignated location around the corner to the other side of the building, where I would pick them up. Thus, Specialist MacGreaver would be in one or our sights the entire time of the operation except for when he would be inside of SSG Piketon's quarters.

I observed Specialist MacGreaver enter SSG Piketon's building. If everything went as planned, Special Agent Ownby would pick up the surveillance of Specialist MacGreaver once he entered the building and watch him walk up the stairs to SSG Piketon's quarters.

I waited in my car, continuously observing the door to SSG Piketon's building. About ten minutes later, I saw Specialist MacGreaver exit the building, followed by Special Agent Ownby. I moved my car to their location, they got inside, and we drove to the CID office.

When we arrived at the CID office, Specialist MacGreaver pulled out of his right front pocket a clear plastic baggie containing ten pieces of suspected hashish wrapped in aluminum foil. During the debriefing, Specialist MacGreaver indicated that when he knocked, SSG Piketon answered the door and invited him inside.

"His wife and two small children were in the living room when I entered the quarters. Once inside, SSG Piketon started talking about work and the hard day he had. About five minutes of this small talk took place, and then he asked me if I still wanted the hashish. I told him yes, and I saw him go to a small metal box on a bookshelf in the living room and open it, and he came back with a baggie of the hashish that I gave you. I gave him the money you provided me, thanked him, and left the quarters and walked to where you picked me up," explained Specialist MacGreaver.

I took a statement from Specialist MacGreaver and directed him not to talk about the deal.

After Specialist MacGreaver left the CID office, I field-tested a piece of the suspected hashish, which proved positive, secured the stuff in the temporary evidence locker, and called it a night. The next morning, I contacted the officer in charge (OIC) of SSG Piketon at the Schweinfurt medical clinic, and without revealing anything about the case against SSG Piketon, I scheduled a meeting at his office for 10:00 a.m. I took MPI Moore with me to the clinic for backup. When we arrived at the OIC's office, a captain in the medical corps invited us into his office and asked, "What is it that you need to talk to me about?"

I jumped right into the mix about what I needed. "One of your NCOs here in the clinic has been identified as a dealer of hashish," I informed him.

"Who is it?" he asked.

"SSG Piketon," I told him.

"What? SSG Piketon is one of the best NCOs in the US Army. Where's your proof?" he inquired.

I ran down the sanitized version of what had happened the evening before at SSG Piketon's quarters.

"I can't believe it. SSG Piketon is getting ready to leave Germany for warrant officer school and then on to Army Medical Command in San Antonio for physician's assistant school. This will ruin his career! Where do we go from here?" he said.

I needed to take SSG Piketon into custody and bring SJA up to speed on where we were on our investigation. I did not go into a lot of detail with the OIC about what still needed to be done, such as getting an official analysis conducted by the USACIL at Frankfurt or how long it would take to bring the matter to trial. I requested from the OIC to get ahold of SSG Piketon and request he report to the clinic so the OIC could talk to him about something about his scheduled training.

"I don't care what you tell him—just get him into your office so we can take him into custody."

He reluctantly complied and called SSG Piketon's home. SSG Piketon answered on the first ring. The OIC did well on the phone, because SSG Piketon told him he would be right in.

About fifteen minutes later, SSG Piketon arrived at the OIC's office. He was a tall, slender, well-built, good-looking individual who walked with a purpose.

"What do you need, sir?" SSG Piketon said as he walked into the room.

MPI Moore and I were sitting on a couch, staring at him. The OIC, obviously dismayed by what he had just been told, said, "These gentlemen want to have a word with you."

Without any explanation to SSG Piketon, the OIC departed the room, leaving the three of us alone.

"I am Special Agent Dick Miller with the army CID. This is MPI Eric Moore. We are placing you under apprehension for the sale and possession of hashish."

As he heard my words, SSG Piketon's facial expression froze. His eyes were wide open, lower jaw dropped, and his response was hardly audible. "What are you talking about?"

He was very cooperative when I searched him as part of his apprehension. Unfortunately, I did not find any of the twenty-dollar bills used in the purchase of the suspected hashish. I put hand irons on his wrists and escorted him from the building.

We got SSG Piketon to the CID office, where I wasted no time in advising him of his rights, which he declined to waive and requested a lawyer. I told him that the he had to be processed through the MP station prior to being released to his unit commander.

"How long will this mess take before I can be on my way?" he inquired.

"Look, SSG Piketon, I don't think you are aware of the severity of your situation. You are more than likely going to be charged with the sale and possession of hashish, a controlled substance, a felony. At a minimum, you are facing a bad conduct discharge or, worse, maybe a general, which in either case will probably result in jail time, so I would forget about warrant and physician's assistant training and plan your defense."

He looked devastated and bowed his head. As I walked out of the interview room, I thought I heard a whimper. I thought, *What a waste of talent.*

It took more than two weeks to get the lab report from USACIL, which indicated the substance purchased from SSG Piketon was in fact hashish, and another almost thirty days to finish his Article 32 hearing then on to his court-martial. The Article 32 hearing found there was enough evidence to go to trial. In its infamous wisdom, the US Army decided to try him by special court-martial. He faced a stiff fine, jail time of six months, and a bad conduct discharge. Jail time is significantly less than if tried by a general court-martial. Three jurors—one, a commissioned officer—were selected for his trial. In any event, if found guilty, it would have destroyed his career.

I testified as to what my actions were during the controlled buy. I explained to the court what my actions were with Specialist MacGreaver, including the fact that he was thoroughly searched before being allowed to enter SSG Piketon's quarters and that his movements were monitored by the Schweinfurt DST during the entire operation, except for when he was inside SSG Piketon's quarters, and that he was under constant surveillance. Specialist MacGreaver and Special Agent Ownby also testified as to what their involvement was. About 4:00 p.m., all the testimony was heard, and the jurors convened to rule on the evidence. About an hour later, they had reached a verdict. SSG Piketon was found guilty of the sale and possession of hashish.

Just before I left the SJA office building, I thanked Captain James Burel, the trial counselor (prosecutor), for his efforts. After finishing up some paperwork on the trial, Captain Burel was planning to join the Schweinfurt DST members for a drink at one of our favorite watering holes to cap the lid on another successful drug investigation.

I recalled feeling extremely pleased about the guilty verdict, thinking about all the good work done by the team and Captain Burel, especially because SSG Piketon was an extremely well-liked and influential member of his unit. He even had several high-ranking officers within his chain of command testify in his behalf as to his excellent character and performance. I never imagined that our celebration over the guilty verdict would be cut short. However, I was soon to find out just how the legal system can play havoc on an investigator's professionalism in the pursuit of true justice.

I went directly from the SJA building to a local *Gasthaus*, where members of the Schweinfurt DST had gathered and were just beginning to relax with a German beer. Almost immediately after sitting down at their table, the owner approached me and told me I had a phone call. I excused myself and went to answer it.

Captain Burel was on the line, and his immediate words were, "Things went to hell in a handbasket after you left."

"What do you mean?" I replied.

"Well, in a nutshell, one of the jurors went to the judge and asked if he could change his mind on his verdict, and the judge ruled that he could," Captain Burel explained.

"What are you trying to say?" I questioned.

"Since the juror changed his mind for a not-guilty verdict, it means he joined another juror who had originally voted not guilty, thus changing the balance of the jury from a third to a two-thirds vote to find SSG Piketon not guilty. Unlike civilian courts, the verdict in a court-martial does not have to be unanimous; only two-thirds can decide guilt or not guilty," Captain Burel lamented.

"This is crazy," I protested.

"He walked out of the courtroom a free man," Captain Burel added.

I didn't have the heart to immediately tell the guys what Captain Burel had told me over the phone. I let them enjoy themselves some more. Eventually, the evening was cut short when I felt compelled to let them know we'd lost the verdict in the SSG Piketon case. Later, I talked to Captain Burel about the investigation and asked if he knew why the juror changed his mind about his original verdict. Captain Burel explained that the juror had some reasonable doubt about SSG Piketon's guilt because of the character of Specialist MacGreaver.

Although nothing came out in trial that Specialist MacGreaver had any grind to settle with SSG Piketon, I am sure that his incentive to work with CID to help himself weighed on the jurors' minds. The juror reasoned that since SSG Piketon was so popular and well-liked by his chain of command, it would be a better deal for Specialist MacGreaver to go after him than anyone else. Also, Captain Burel went on to explain, the juror felt there was an opportunity for Specialist MacGreaver to have staged some hashish in the circuit box on the wall of the stairwell leading to SSG Piketon's quarters.

"That thought is nonsense, because Special Agent Ownby was watching Specialist MacGreaver from the time he entered the building to the time he knocked on SSG Piketon's door, and not once was Specialist MacGreaver observed stopping on the stairs," I staunchly defended our team's efforts to Captain Burel. "And his thinking that Specialist MacGreaver used SSG Piketon as a ghost target to help his cause is purely speculation."

Captain Burel told me, "It all boils down to not being able to convince the juror that SSG Piketon was cable of doing what he was accused of doing."

*What a miscarriage of justice*, I thought. What a finish to my drug investigation career, having a case like SSG Piketon's end the way it did.

From the spring of 1978 to summer of 1982, I had worked drug investigations in Korea, the United States, and Germany. Even with the hiccups and bumps along the way, I felt a sense of accomplishment with what I had done. The experience was tremendous, beneficial, and rewarding for me to have been involved with these types of investigations, but it was time to move on. I will forever be indebted to those that worked with me along the way, including the DST members, trial counselors, commanders, ISGs, and all the administrative staff that made it possible.

Privately, life as a married man was agreeing with me. Elda was solely responsible for a change in my lifestyle. She loved to travel and visit places that she had only heard about while growing up in southern Texas. In the spring of 1982, we took a road trip to the French Rivera and toured the east coast of Spain and then on to the Normandy beach where the Allied landing took place in June 1944. We stayed in a nice, small hotel in the coastal city of Le Havre, France, before returning to Schweinfurt.

Later in our tour, Elda and I and another couple, Pat and Lynn Gould, traveled by car through East Germany to visit the city of Berlin. The city was still divided into sections controlled by the British and Americans, another by the French, and another zone by the Russians. Berlin was the center of focus during the Cold War and where most of the tension between democracy and communism was and the primary reason we had so many troops located in Germany.

We could use our privately-owned vehicles to travel through East Germany to the city of Berlin. We had to go through the American Checkpoint Bravo at Helmstedt, Germany. Once through Bravo, we had to pass through a Russian checkpoint before entering the highway into East Germany to take us to the city. We were given a time to travel from the border to the city of Berlin. If you did not make it during the allocated time, search teams were sent out to find your location and determine the reason why you were late. We had to enter another checkpoint to get inside the city and yet another, the famous Checkpoint Charlie, to cross from West to East Berlin.

Since it was a requirement for the military to wear their uniforms while in the east, it was one of the few times I donned mine. At Checkpoint Bravo, I was chosen by the group to take the passports and my US Army ID card to the booths for the Russians to inspect. This task was extremely tense. Once the Russian soldiers stopped our vehicle, only one person could exit the car and bring the personal identification documents for inspection.

As I got out of our car, a young Russian soldier, without saying a word, motioned with his machine gun for me to approach the building nearby, which had a window like a movie theater ticket booth, except this window was painted over so you could not see who was on the other side.

I walked up to the booth and looked around for instructions on what to do, but there were none. I stood in front of the booth for a few seconds, not knowing what to do. Behind me was the young Russian soldier with a machine gun, and there was no one present to tell me where to go or what to do with the documents. Then, suddenly, I saw a hand appear from underneath the opening in the booth window. Without being provided any instructions from the man—well, a person I believed to be a man, though I could not see him—I laid the three passports and my military ID card into the hand. As if being swallowed by an animal, the documents disappeared into the small space at the bottom of the window.

I continued to stand facing the window without saying a word. Not knowing what to do, but hesitating to look behind me, for I did not want to bring any unnecessary attention of my machine-gun-toting Russian soldier, I just stood there waiting patiently for the next step in the process. It seemed like an eternity, but finally, I saw the hand holding the identification documents appear again. Since no voice came with instructions of any type, I presumed the hand wanted me to take the documents. I delicately relieved the hand of the documents and robotically turned around and walked slowly to the car and got in. I told Pat, "Let's get the hell out of here."

The drive through East Germany was enough to make one realize how lucky he or she was living in the West. The East German countryside was sparse, gloomy, and barren. Nothing was new, and the older farm implements hardly looked like they could keep up with cultivating the fields we passed on the way to Berlin. The houses, farmland, and landscape made you feel that you had been thrown back into the 1930s and 1940s. It was unbelievable what we saw once in East Berlin. Everyone walked around like they were carrying the whole world on their shoulders. No one smiled or spoke as they robotically moved around the city. The department stores had little merchandise on display. The experience in Berlin gave me a firsthand look at why we were fighting a cold war. The difference between West Germany and East Germany was like day and night, a cloudy and rainy day versus a bright and sunny one.

Schweinfurt RA hosting a party for our German counterparts from the Schweinfurt polizei. Note me talking to SAC Boatwright, circa 1981.

A tired bunch of special agents waiting at the Cairo, Egypt, airport for flights back to Germany after being depolyed on a protective service detail for Secretary of Defense Caspar Weinburger. From left, SA Bowland, Würzburg RA; SA Larry Meyers, Schweinfurt RA; SA Tom Wilkin, Würzburg District; SA Jeffrey Kuffman, Kitzingen RA. Yours truly took the photograph.

'Yes', it's me during my undercover days—circa 1981–1983.

My beauiful wife, Elda, circa early 1980s, taken while we were in Schweinfurt, Germany.

# 10

## From Team Lead to Senior Investigative Manager

### Schweinfurt, Germany

*A period of emergence and refinement of management and supervisory skills*

*M*y new role as SAC was going to be totally different from the few times I temporarily sat in as SAC Boatwright's replacement when he took leave or was on short TDY assignments. The immediate future would open the door much wider, but I was looking forward to the new responsibility.

In late 1982, SAC Boatwright transferred to Aschaffenburg, and I temporarily took his place as SAC of Schweinfurt. The transition was smooth, and all the Schweinfurt special agents were on board with the move. Although the assignment was considered temporary, everyone, including me, knew it was going to be permanent. I had a lot to learn, so I wasted no time in getting started. SAC Boatwright was a very popular SAC, and I did not want to give anyone the impression that I questioned his policies, supervision, and management style in any way. However, certain changes are inevitable with new leadership. Since I was a student in training on the job, I did not want to make major changes all at once. I had, to a certain degree, developed a management style while running the various DSTs and honed in organizational skills required at that level, but overseeing a resident agency was a grade above what I was used to working.

Before I changed anything, I wanted to conduct an inventory of all open criminal cases in the Schweinfurt resident agency. I had all agents bring their assigned cases into my office, and I matched them with the tags SAC Boatwright had on the case tracking board. The case files presented by the agents matched the number of tags on the case tracking board. I learned that Schweinfurt had eighty-five open cases dispersed between six agents, including myself. This represented about fifteen cases per agent. I retained the open drug investigations, pending the appointment of my replacement as chief of DST.

With a few months under my belt as the acting SAC, I got some very disturbing news that has stuck with me to this day. Late one evening, I received a call at home from the duty agent, Special Agent Glunt, who informed me that he had just been called to investigate a possible pedestrian fatality that occurred just outside the Conn Barracks main gate. The dead person, apparently highly intoxicated, attempted to cross Niederwerrner Strasse and was struck by a German taxi.

The time was 9:00 p.m., and Special Agent Glunt requested assistance with the fatality because he was already tied up on another crime scene when the call came in.

It was a policy of mine to have my agents call me on all death investigations. This requirement would eventually become region-wide.

Special Agent Glunt told me, "The MP desk sergeant has more details on the dead soldier. Do you want me to interrupt the case I am on and assume the death investigation?"

"Since your current case involves an aggravated assault on a young soldier, I want you to continue with that investigation, and I will get someone to handle the death investigation."

I hung up and immediately called the MP desk sergeant. I jotted down the preliminary information the MP desk sergeant told me.

"What is the soldier's name?" I asked. When the MP desk sergeant mentioned the soldier's name, I momentarily froze. "Could you repeat the name?" With a sickening, nauseated feeling in my stomach, I asked hesitantly.

"Specialist Johnathan Trumwell," the MP desk sergeant reiterated.

*Damn, the poor kid finally did it—he used up all his lives.* I must have been mumbling to myself because the MP desk sergeant's voice seemed to be fading, barely audible in the distance. Then I was brought out of my trance when I heard, "Agent Miller, are you still there?"

"Oh, yes, yes, I am sorry. I am here!" I answered, probably sounding as if I were coming from a deep sleep. My mind was reeling with heartache over Trumwell's senseless death. "Where's the body?" I asked.

"It is at the Schweinfurt medical clinic," he stated.

"Thanks," I said.

I felt compelled to go to the Schweinfurt medical clinic and positively identify Specialist Trumwell's body. I informed Angelica, the office secretary, that I was going to the Schweinfurt medical clinic and would be back in about an hour. I was still in shock as I drove to the clinic. I thought of the two times I had seen Specialist Trumwell. The first time was during an interview with him during the PFC McNeal death investigation, and the second time was at PFC Williamson's involuntary manslaughter trial for negligently killing PFC McNeal by crashing his car while drunk. Both times I talked to Specialist Trumwell about good judgment and the right life choices. Each time, he seemed genuinely sincere about changing his lifestyle, but each time I saw him or heard about him, he had been involved with incidents associated with drinking. At Williamson's trial, he assured me that he was going to change his life and cut down on his drinking; apparently, the alcohol had already overpowered him and he was helpless, without intervention, to change his habits. His unit leadership should have recognized his plight and helped him in some way, but now it was too late.

It took me ten minutes to reach the Schweinfurt medical clinic. I entered the door and approached a neatly dressed and very polite middle-aged woman at the reception desk. After I showed her my CID credentials and told her the purpose of my visit, she turned her head, pointed without looking back at me, and said, "The body is in room 5, down the hallway to the left."

I reached room 5 and slowly opened the door. There, on an examining table, was a body covered by a bloody white sheet. I walked over and pulled back the sheet at the head. Instantly, nausea washed over me when I saw the face, eyes open, staring at the ceiling. Momentarily unable to move or think, I just stood there, looking at the face of the dead body, with the sheet in my hand. A few seconds later, after regaining my composure, I lowered the sheet to where I could observe the entire body.

The body, dressed in a civilian jacket, long-sleeved shirt, slacks, black shoes, and wool socks, was contorted. The right femur bone was sticking through his slacks, exposed and protruding from the skin. His other leg was twisted, as were both arms. Massive lacerations, contusions, and abrasions were noted on the face and hands. The left foot was partially severed from the ankle. From the condition of Specialist Trumwell's remains, it was my opinion that the cause of death was massive trauma to the body, and by knowing he got hit by a car, the manner of death was an accident. Even with the extensive injuries, swelling, and disfigurement of the face, I could still positively identify who the person used to be. It was Specialist Johnathan L. Trumwell. Standing motionless as I observed the body, I thought, *I sure hope Specialist Trumwell is in a better place. His actions led him directly to where he is now—dead.*

Thinking of Specialist Trumwell and the encounters I had with him reminded me somehow of other deceased people I had investigated over the years. Their purpose or reason for being on earth no longer existed, their demise ugly and meaningless. I thought, *why are some deaths caused by another person's senseless, impulses, or uncontrolled carelessness or violent actions?* Death can also be the result of an unforeseen accident or by one who takes his or her own life or just by natural causes. However different, all deaths have one thing in common: they are permanent and forever, and they leave those who knew the dead person with a feeling of helplessness or bewilderment. Trumwell's death shook me hard. To this day, I still see his damaged body on that slab in room 5 of the Schweinfurt clinic. The image is constant and permanent; I think of him often. What he could have become in life if only he had made a few wiser choices.

In June 1982, Elda and I went home on leave so we could meet the other's relatives. We first visited my relatives in Indiana, where Elda was introduced to Chris, Mom, June, Charlie, and the family. She blended right in with everyone she met and had no trouble being accepted as a new member of the Miller clan.

I fared just as well with Elda's family in Texas. Her family appeared to like me, especially her dad, which was mandatory for the family to accept me. While in Indiana, I asked June if she would entertain the thought of visiting Elda and me in Germany later in the year. I requested she bring Chris, Charlie, and Mom with her. She agreed. On our trip to Freer, Texas, I met Elda's parents, four brothers, two sisters, and numerous aunts, uncles, cousins, and a few friends. My original thought on her family was that she must have been related to everyone in the small town of Freer, because everyone I met had some connection to her family.

Elda's mother, Fabianita, was nice, polite, and very much a homemaker. Her typical day was spent at home doing things for the family. She catered to Elda's father as if he were a king. Her father, Abel, was a bona fide war hero from World War II. At seventeen, his father accompanied him to the recruiting station to sign for him to enter the US Army. He was sent to Belgium in 1944 as a medic. His first day in battle started with a five-mile march, and then the shooting began. His job involved collecting the wounded and ensuring they got to field hospitals set up along the way. After each battle occurred and they had cleared the injured from the field, they were sent back to tend to the dead soldiers. Her father and I had many conversations over the years, and he told me that, once, they had so many dead bodies after a day of battle that a backhoe came in and dug a huge trench. The medics were told to lay everyone in the trench face up, and they were all buried together.

I am not sure why I survived and so many others died; I suppose it was God's will. I used to say, "*La Provencia y Dios no ha de ayudar*" (Surely Providence and God will help us).[97] Abel told me that the American government would return to the site later and dig up the bodies and rebury them in marked graves. Abel, however, was not so sure if they did this or not.

The trip to Freer was a good one. I met a lot of Elda's family, and they all were cordial and engaging.

After our return from visiting the relatives in the States, I dug into my duties and responsibilities with an enthusiasm like I had not known before. Elda had several weeks before she had to return to school, so she traveled the countryside with her friend and fellow schoolteacher, Karen Rose, and other close friends. I kept busy reading US Army and CID regulations to gain knowledge of how things worked. You might say I took a crash course in everything you wanted to know about the US Army and CID but were afraid to ask.

I honed the duties and responsibilities of being the best SAC possible. One of the most significant duties was learning how to be a good mentor. I wasn't always successful, but that did not stop me from trying. I learned very quickly that SACs do not have all the answers and it is best to listen to their special agents on how to proceed with investigative activities. Better yet, SACs should let the special agents run their own investigations. If SACs see they are venturing down the wrong path, then give them a slight shove in the right direction.

You must instill in your special agents the ability to think on their feet and explain the rationale on why it is okay to ask questions or seek advice when stuck. Above most everything else, instill in them that not everything is black or white; most of the time it is gray. I have been associated with a lot of special agents who were technically smart but used no common sense. Their technical proficiencies should be complemented with a good dose of understanding that each situation is different and should be handled on its own individual merits. I often had to redirect agents' actions because they were leaning in the wrong direction. Some special agents work harder, others worked smarter, but without a doubt, 99 percent of the agents in the US Army CID are mature and trustworthy and take responsibility for their own actions. All CID special agents volunteered for the position. All of them were vetted through a rigorous investigative background process to get to where they are. In my opinion, if the vetting process placed them in an elite group, then this was where the evaluation started, from the top down.

In August 1982, I was selected for attendance at a CID-sponsored course in advanced investigative management at Erding Air Base located northeast of central Munich. The course focused on many aspects of the criminal investigation, including managing a criminal case from initiation to completion, how to properly use assets, determine the legality of evidence … much more than just the investigative steps. But primarily, the course centered around how to interview suspects of crime, how to read their body movements under interrogations, and to basically learn techniques on how to detect whether they were being deceptive when answering your questions. The instruction emphasized how to use methods to keep the investigator on track during the investigation and reeling them in when following a dead-end lead. In summary, the course training provided insights into getting the case legally processed so the prosecutors could try the case in court. The course taught me a lot of basic legal procedural methods and how to tackle the hard interviews.

During the latter part of 1982, the Schweinfurt resident agency experienced some assignment changes. Special Agents Meyers, Roy Black, and Bruce Maxium departed the office. Replacements coming into the office were Special Agents David Thomas, Jeffrey Stevens—whom I served with in Korea—Barnard Cassagnol, Richard Basile, and Jerry Williams. A new LNCI, Jake Berthel, was added to assist LNCI Luckhardt. These people were totally dedicated to the job, knew how to interact with others, and were welcomed assets.

As I plowed into my new duties as SAC, I found that my focus or the purpose of my job was different from that of a narcotics or general investigator. I now had the job of managing several special agents and their investigative activities. Learning along the way, I noticed that I started viewing the criminal investigations in more totality. Not to say that I had not been doing this all along, but a review of the agents' case files brought all phases of the investigation to the forefront.

As SAC, my responsibilities grew tremendously. Now, I not only had to concern myself with investigations, I had to ensure the cases met the CID three *T* standards of *thoroughness, timeliness in investigtations,* and *timeliness in reporting.* I further had to deal with personnel, administrative, logistics, and unit organizational issues. Further, I was responsible for two local national criminal investigators (LNCI) and the hiring and supervision of civilians. In addition, I continued to testify at various illegal drug trials with the local SJA and had to travel to outlying SJA offices for cases involving soldiers we had initiated narcotics investigations on that had come to Schweinfurt for temporary periods.

One of those long-distance trials took me to Bad Kreuznach, Germany, close to 150 miles from Schweinfurt, a drive of about two hours and thirty-five minutes. The soldier that we identified selling drugs while he was temporarily assigned to Schweinfurt was assigned to an engineer battalion at Bad Kreuznach, Germany. I will call the soldier Sergeant Frank Williams.[98] In midsummer 1982, Williams traveled on a TDY assignment from Bad Kreuznach to Schweinfurt to work on an engineer project for a few months. Sergeant Williams spent most of his evenings at local bars in Schweinfurt, where he eventually hooked up with a few known illegal drug dealers. Our investigation disclosed that he became known to us through a female source. The following narrative depicts his story and the subsequent CID investigation into his drug dealing that I call the Case of the Mortified Drug Dealer:

## THE CASE OF THE MORTIFIED DRUG DEALER
Some soldiers rub salt into their own wounds

During the summer months of 1982, the Schweinfurt DST initiated a significant number of drug investigations based on source targeting. There was a tremendous amount of hard work that went into an illegal drug operation. Many of the investigative activities involved the gathering of preliminary information that associated our soldier suspects with the illegal drug culture. Once the DST developed enough data to indicate a certain target was selling illegal drugs, we acted upon that evidence as soon as possible. Sergeant Frank Williams came to Schweinfurt from Bad Kreuznach with a platoon of combat engineers to work on a project for several weeks. It was Sergeant Williams's misfortune one night to have fallen into the hands of one of Schweinfurt DST's best female sources, none other than Petra Adler.

After work one Monday night, Sergeant Williams and a couple of his buddies went to a popular downtown Schweinfurt nightspot called Tivoli, a club catering to the black soldiers. Sergeant Williams had been active while at Schweinfurt. Shortly after his arrival in the city, he met and befriended a German national drug dealer who sold hashish and other illegal drugs to local soldiers at Ledward and Conn Barracks. On this night, the Schweinfurt DST had placed their top-notch female source in Tivoli's nightclub, known as an establishment where German and American drug dealers congregated.

About 10:30 p.m., after consuming several beers, Williams noticed our female source sitting at a table, talking to two other soldiers. He kept his eye on her for a while until our female source moved to another part of the nightclub. See her standing near a post with a drink in her hand, he excused himself from his friends and walked over and initiated a conversation with her. As a part of her training, she subtly started asking questions to find out how much information she could obtain about his personal life and whether he might be involved with illegal drugs. In her approach, she opened with some general inquires: "Do you come here often?" Our source was taught not to immediately push for names and to take it slow when talking about illegal drugs. If they were into the illegal drug culture, it might take several meetings with an individual before he or she felt comfortable talking about the trade.

"This is my first time at Tivoli's," he responded.

"I come here just to unwind after a hard day at my job," our female source countered.

"What do you do? Williams inquired.

"I work at the ball bearing factory here in Schweinfurt." She had been set up with a cover as a general worker at the ball bearing factory because it seemed to be a place that soldiers would have a hard time pinning her down on or verifying details about her fictional job.

She was trained to look for certain signs, like facial expressions, how much the individual was drinking, the person's coherency, the topics of his conversations, and anything personal, such as name, rank, and unit—and of course, anything associated with illegal drugs. Our source would later relay that information to her Schweinfurt DST contact. After talking to Williams for about thirty minutes, she introduced herself. Petra went silent, waiting to see if Williams reciprocated with a name; he did.

"My name is Frank Williams."

The next bit of information Petra was trained to get was the unit of assignment. She was told to be patient in her attempts to get that information. Typically, most soldiers will initially attempt to conceal their units of assignment or want to keep their identities secret because they do not expect to see the person they meet in a bar again or due to the training they receive about methods that spies use to get information about troop strength and movements. After getting to know the individual, they more than likely will provide their unit assignments. Petra had been around the block numerous times, and she was fully aware that the primary interest on a soldier's mind when he was talking to a female at a bar, even though he might be involved with illegal drugs, was sex.

The two talked for another half hour or so, and Williams still had not brought up the subject of illegal drugs. Petra had been trained not to pursue soldiers if she suspected that their motive for conversation would not lead to drugs. Of course, the Schweinfurt DST had no control over Petra's personal life. The reason she was a source was because she was associated with criminal elements. If she started out talking to a young soldier at a bar with the goal of developing information on potential illegal drug involvement and later found that she was interested in the person, it was her business.

As the night wore on, Williams did bring up the subject of hashish to Petra. She pursued the matter with Williams, and he eventually felt comfortable enough to talk to her about his ability to get her some. Our female source indicated to Williams that she would buy some hashish from him but she had more important things on her mind now. In her conversation with Williams that night, she felt a strong attraction to him, and they ended up going to her apartment and having sex. This information was not revealed to any Schweinfurt DST members until much later in this case.

It was close to midnight, and their tête-à-tête conversation revealed that Williams was a sergeant in a combat engineer battalion working at Conn Barracks. Petra felt that if she tried to pump him for more, he would become suspicious of her motives. Petra, noticing the late hour, near midnight, made the excuse that she anticipated a rough day at work the following morning and encouraged Sergeant Williams to leave. They agreed to see each other again at Tivoli's on Thursday. Sergeant Williams promised that he would have some hashish when they met again. After Williams departed, Petra called the Schweinfurt DST office. I picked up the phone on the first ring.

"It's Petra. Sorry to catch you so late, but I wanted to let you know what I found out tonight."

I listened to her for the next several minutes talking about meeting a Sergeant Frank Williams, who was assigned to a combat engineer battalion at Conn Barracks, and that he was going to have some hashish with him when they saw each other on Thursday night at Tivoli's.

"Can you be in my office at 10:00 tomorrow morning?" I asked.

"Shouldn't be a problem," Petra responded. As I was hanging up the phone, I heard her say, "See you then," and then there was silence.

I got into the office about 8:00 the next morning, a good two hours before my scheduled meeting with Petra. I called MPI Moore in and briefed him on what information Petra ascertained from a soldier named Sergeant Frank Williams. I directed MPI Moore to check Williams's background, determine what unit he was in, and discreetly inquire with any sources in the area about his reputation. "I need this information by 10:00 a.m.," I told MPI Moore.

"That's a quick order," said MPI Moore, frowning.

Petra showed up about 10:15 a.m.; she was late as usual, and I had not yet heard from MPI Moore, who was not in his office. *The day is going to hell in a handbasket*, I thought. I debriefed Petra on what actions we would take on Sergeant Williams. I instructed her to follow through on her planned meeting with him and to shore up any new business on the deal. I told her I wanted to see her at 7:00 p.m. on the night she and Sergeant Williams were supposed to meet.

Just before Petra and I were finished, there was a knock on my office door.

"Come in," I bellowed.

It was MPI Moore, who provided me with a handwritten note that said, "I found no information about Sergeant Frank Williams being assigned at Conn Barracks; however, there was a SP4 Frank Williams assigned to a combat engineering unit in Bad Kreuznach."

MPI Moore had taken the initiative to check USAEUR-wide name check for Williams. The three of us continued to discuss the pending investigation on just who Sergeant Frank Williams was.

"Petra, I want you to meet as planned with this guy and attempt to find out what he is doing here in Schweinfurt. Let's not go through with any attempted buy of hashish until we are sure he is using his right name and find out what unit he is assigned to," I instructed.

At 7:00 on Thursday night, Petra showed up at my office. As she walked in, the smell of her perfume almost knocked me sideways, and she was dressed more elegantly than usual. Her appearance made me think that she had more on her mind than making a drug deal for the Schweinfurt DST.

I couldn't resist telling her, "You look like you're going on a date."

"I have to look like I want to see him, don't you think?"

MPI Moore, Petra, and I spent about an hour discussing all possible scenarios that might go down when she met Williams at Tivoli's. They had agreed to meet in about an hour, around 9:00 p.m., so we had to speed up the activity to set up at Tivoli's nightclub. I finished briefing Petra and had her sign for the hundred dollars to make the buy of hashish from Williams. I then drove MPI Moore and Petra to Tivoli's to begin the operation. We all agreed to give the operation an hour and a half if nothing went down before terminating the activities and heading to a predesignated location for an exit briefing.

The drive to Tivoli's took about fifteen minutes. I dropped MPI Moore about a half a block from the entrance to Tivoli's. The plan was for MPI Moore to go inside Tivoli's first and find a table where he could observe Petra once she entered. At 9:25 p.m., I temporarily parked the car to observe MPI Moore go inside Tivoli's. Because the nightclub catered primarily to black soldiers, I would stick out like a sore thumb if I went inside. MPI Moore, being black, fit right in.

Once inside the nightclub, MPI Moore sat at a table with a good vantage point to pick up Petra as she walked in. Once MPI Moore entered the club, Petra knew her role. She got out of the car, and I watched her walk directly to Tivoli's and go inside. MPI Moore, already in the club, observed her entering the establishment and meeting with a young, black male who was standing at the bar.

To avoid any suspicions on the part of the customers inside the club, MPI Moore had purchased a beer to blend into the crowd that was starting to form. When she approached the young, black male, Petra gave him a peck on the cheek, and they started talking. MPI Moore was too far away to hear what they were talking about, but he could observe them. Standing next to each other talking for several minutes, they then took a table closer to where MPI Moore was sitting but still too far for him to hear their conversation.

About an hour later, MPI Moore observed Petra leaving the table with the young male who was believed to be Sergeant Williams and head for the ladies' room, the door of which was hidden from view of the table where Petra had been. Since the men's room was close by and hidden from the main drinking and dining area, MPI Moore left his table on the pretense of going to the men's room. MPI Moore timed his arrival at the men's room door exactly right. Petra had stalled a second or two, hoping he would join her so she could update him on information she had.

"He has the hashish on him, but I have not seen it yet," she told MPI Moore.

"Have you discussed the deal with him?" MPI Moore asked.

"No, but he brought up the subject that he has the hashish on him and that he would give it to me later."

*The ideal situation would be to observe the transaction taking place, but this may not be possible if Williams wants to do it later*, MPI Moore thought. "Were you able to find out what unit he is assigned to?" Moore asked.

"Yes. Williams told me he was here TDY from Bad Kreuznach, and oh, oh, he told me that he had just gotten promoted to sergeant about a month before coming to Schweinfurt."

"Oh, by the way, the best scenario would be to make the deal inside the bar," MPI Moore added.

For fear of being seen together, MPI Moore cut their conversation short to avoid compromising their identity and continued into the men's room. A short time later, as he walked back to his table, he observed Petra had already returned to her table.

A couple of hours later, there was still no indication from Petra that anything was or had gone down. The operation had called for one buy/walk situation and to set up a second deal with Sergeant Williams for the takedown. Since radios could not be used inside the bar, I had no idea what was happening, so I continued to sit in my car, pending any word from MPI Moore.

Finally, from my surveillance position in my car, I saw a crowd of people leaving Tivoli's. MPI Moore was among them. Ensuring that no one was watching, he jumped into my car and told me to get moving. As I drove away, I bombarded him with several questions in a row without allowing him to answer. "Where's Petra? Did any transaction take place? What's happening?"

"Well, I don't think any deal went down. Petra and I could speak with each other briefly, and she told me he had the hashish on him, but she hadn't seen it. When the club started closing, and as I walked out the door, I saw Petra engrossed in conversation with Sergeant Williams, and I am not sure she is going to join us."

We hovered near Tivoli's for the next fifteen minutes or so, but we did not see Petra, assuming she left with Sergeant Williams. *Damn! She still has the money I gave her.*

We finally headed for the CID office. I looked at MPI Moore, and he seemed to have the same thought as I did: maybe Petra had a change of heart after meeting Sergeant Williams and decided not to go through with the deal as planned.

Still burning from what had occurred the night before, I was in my office when Angelica popped in and informed me Petra was outside in the waiting room and wanted to see me. I told Angelica to have her wait and that I would be with her when I could. I knew I could not make her wait forever, but I was pissed that she'd left MPI Moore and me hanging without attempting to let us know what and where she was going. Oh, well, in this business, one should not show anger but compassion and be understanding to all. I went and got Petra and brought her back to my office, where I commenced to read her the riot act. She knew I would be hot under the collar, so to speak, angry as hell, but then again, what for? I lowered the temperature a little and calmed down.

"What the hell happened last night?" I asked.

"Dick"—as Petra always called me— "Williams was not showing me the hashish that he said he had. I thought that if I got him out of the club, then he would be more at ease, and I was right. After we left the club, we went back to my apartment, where he gave me this." To my surprise, she pulled a clear plastic bag out of her purse that contained ten pieces of suspected hashish and handed it to me. "I used the money you gave me yesterday to buy the stuff from Williams," she proudly stated.

"If this is hashish, I don't know how I am going to get this evidence into court, Petra!" I halfway screamed. "Petra, you have violated my trust, the protocol of evidence, and created a basketful of legitimate arguments for the defense attorney!"

"Once he showed the hashish to me, I just could not ignore it, could I?" She bowed her head and threw up her arms in apparent frustration, obviously distraught over what she had done.

"Look, Petra, we will overcome this, but you cannot ever do this sort of thing again. You always have to be supervised for these investigations," I said, scolding her.

After taking a statement from Petra on the details of her purchase of hashish from Sergeant Williams, I released her. A small portion of the substance Sergeant Williams sold Petra tested positive for THC. I subsequently packaged the evidence up and forwarded it to the crime lab at Frankfurt. It took about three weeks before the crime lab report came back, proving that the substance submitted was hashish. I wanted to do a second buy from Sergeant Williams to shore up any issues on the first transaction, but circumstances did not allow it. Sergeant Williams returned to his duty station at Bad Kreuznach. If a second buy was to be accomplished, it would have to be attempted at Bad Kreuznach. A call to the CID at Bad Kreuznach disclosed that they had no criminal information or intelligence on Sergeant Williams. A request to have their DST attempt to initiate an investigation on Sergeant Williams was considered but was not submitted because it would not necessarily have helped our case in Schweinfurt.

So, we were now at the stage in the investigation where we had to bring Sergeant Williams in and advise him of his rights for wrongful possession and distribution of hashish. A decision was made to conduct the interview in Bad Kreuznach. The requirement would cause me to have to travel to Bad Kreuznach to conduct the interview. More than likely, any court-martial would be convened there instead of Schweinfurt.

Faith was on our side, however. While attempting to arrange the interview on Sergeant Williams, it was revealed that he had been returned to Schweinfurt for another period of TDY on the same project he was originally working on. This was a stroke of good luck for us, especially diminishing the difficult logistics to get the interview completed. A fleeting idea to attempt a second buy from Sergeant Williams was considered, but Petra was sent to another area within Würzburg District to help on a drug operation and was not readily available to assist Schweinfurt.

Williams was finally brought in for questioning. After I advised him of his Miranda rights, he declined to waive them and asked to speak with an attorney. We were now at the stage where we had to prepare for an Article 32 hearing and hopefully a court-martial.

To my surprise, SJA decided to hold the Article 32 at Bad Kreuznach instead of Schweinfurt. This posed a logistics problem in that each time I would be called to testify, I would have to drive to Bad Kreuznach, about a 150-mile trip. Each day of testimony would take an entire day away from my duties at Schweinfurt. I had no control over the SJA decision. Maybe I would get lucky in the case and Sergeant Williams would plead guilty to the charges.

About three weeks passed before I was notified that the Article 32 session was scheduled for the SJA building in Bad Kreuznach and that Petra and I were the star prosecution witnesses. The immediate problem, if the Article 32 hearing was scheduled for early morning, was that it would require Petra and me to stay overnight because of the distance. I did not relish the thought of having to babysit Petra the evening before we testified. Further, the trip would have to be repeated during the actual trial. I thought that I could drag MPI Moore or another DST member with me, but then I am not sure the TDY expense would have been approved.

In any event, luck was on my side for the trip to testify at Sergeant Williams's Article 32 hearing, because we were not scheduled to give our testimony until after lunch and had plenty of time to drive the 150-mile distance from Schweinfurt to Bad Kreuznach. We were successful during the hearing in that there was enough evidence to go to court-martial.

Sergeant Williams's special bad conduct court-martial was scheduled for late October 1982. Luck, this time, avoided me. The trial was scheduled to begin in Bad Kreuznach at 8:00 a.m., so, to avoid any possibility of being late, we had to make the drive the evening before, which meant we had to secure lodging for the night. To avoid any improprieties or innuendos about spending an evening with Petra, I brought Elda.

The trial counsel at Bad Kreuznach briefed me that the defense was going to build their case for acquittal by attempting to prove entrapment. Petra had testified during the Article 32 hearing that she had slept with Sergeant Williams at her apartment after he sold her the hashish. I had been told by Petra that she had slept with Sergeant Williams after her testimony during the hearing. Also, while on the stand at the hearing, I was asked by the defense if Petra was a "professional." I knew where he was going with this line of questioning, and I provided the best answer possible: "She is a professional informant." This was an honest answer. The defense did not pursue any further questions in this area. However, in open court, if the defense asked this same question, it could detrimentally influence the jury's decision on Petra's character.

The trial started as scheduled, and Petra was called to testify first. Since I had not yet testified, I was not allowed in the courtroom, so I waited outside in the hallway. About thirty minutes into her testimony, I heard a loud roar coming from inside the courtroom that sounded like laughter. Suddenly, Petra came bouncing out of the courtroom.

"What the hell happened?" I asked Petra.

"They asked me if I had sexual relations with Sergeant Williams, and I told them yes," she said.

"That's good. So, what is the problem?" I asked.

"The defense lawyer asked me why I had never invited him back to my apartment after he sold the hashish to me. I told him that Sergeant Williams was not a very good lay. Then everyone started laughing, so the judge ordered a recess."

I never did have to testify that day, and apparently, the judge took mercy on both the prosecution and defense. After Petra's testimony, the trial lawyers went head-to-head for a couple of more hours.

The trial counsel came out and said, "It's up to the jury; now we wait."

After confirming with the lawyers that we were no longer needed, Petra, and I did not wait for the verdict and started the long trip back to Schweinfurt. The next day, I phoned the trial counsel at Bad Kreuznach, who advised me that the jury did find Sergeant Williams guilty of the sale of hashish, and the judge ordered Sergeant Williams to forfeit two-thirds of his pay for six months and reduced him to PV1 and directed he receive a bad conduct discharge from the US Army. But he showed some leniency by not giving him any jail time. Sounded like a good day for the CID.

A debrief of Petra resulted in a strong admonishment of her actions and advisement that if she wanted to continue as a CID source, she had to abide by all the rules set in place for sources. Petra said she would comply with the rules and continued as a CID source for the Schweinfurt DST and many more DSTs in the Würzburg District for many years into the future.

In October 1982, my first crisis as SAC came while I was still an acting SAC. It occurred when I received a call from Captain David Frank, trial counsel from the local SJA office. Captain Frank wanted the CID's report on an aggravated assault that had occurred in the barracks of the Second Battalion, Sixty-Fourth Armor. Captain Frank went on to explain that they were getting ready to go to trial and needed the CID investigative report to support their case.

"I do not recall ever having an investigation of aggravated assault from the Two Sixty-Fourth," I told Captain Frank.

"This is the case that occurred about a month earlier, where a soldier struck another solider with a chair in their barracks room," he further explained.

"I'll look, but I am almost positive that we do not have a case on the incident," I said. "I will call you back in a few minutes."

I spent about thirty minutes checking the office's consolidated case management logbook and talking to the agents in the office but found no information about the investigation. I called Captain Frank back and informed him that I could find nothing about the case ever being reported to our office.

Sounding somewhat perplexed, he said, "I want you to initiate an investigation on the matter as quickly as possible, to include getting statements from the people involved."

"I'll get right on it," I told Captain Frank.

Though I didn't realize it at the time, this case would be the catalyst that started a huge investigation into the way the provost marshal was handling the reporting of crime in Schweinfurt. I started the ball rolling by assigning one of my agents to initiate an investigation into the apparent aggravated assault. I assigned one of the agents to conduct the victim interview and then talk to the suspect. Some of the details on what was to happen on the aggravated assault are recounted in the following detailed narrative of the investigation I call the Case of the General Who Wanted Crime to Go Away:

## THE CASE OF THE GENERAL WHO WANTED CRIME TO GO AWAY

Don't be so trustworthy with professionals, regardless of how close you are to them

While the agent was initiating the process to get the interviews done, I called the Schweinfurt provost marshal operations sergeant, SFC George Collins,[99] who had the best institutional knowledge about what was going on in the Schweinfurt military community to inquire as to why CID was not notified of the aggravated assault. SFC Collins, an easygoing, low-key noncommissioned officer whom I thought I could trust, came on the phone.

"Yeah, what's up?" he asked.

"I just received a call from Captain Frank at SJA wanting my report on an aggravated assault that occurred in the barracks at the Second Battalion, Sixty-Fourth Armor, on Conn Barracks, but we were never contacted about the case. Do you have anything on the case?" I asked.

A moment of silence was interrupted by SFC Collins's voice. "I'll do some checking and get back with you."

Pushing him with my sense of urgency, I said, "Sure, but could you make it fast? I've got to get some answers to SJA."

Later that afternoon about 3:00, I had not yet heard from SFC Collins, when the agent I assigned to conduct the interviews came into my office.

"Chief, there was an aggravated assault in the barracks at the Two Sixty-Fourth," he said. "Apparently, a PFC Ronald J. Cloud and PFC Gerald L.

Larsen[100] got into a fight over what they were going to watch on TV in their room. The ruckus got out of hand when PFC Cloud struck PFC Larsen with a chair. PFC Larsen received some contusions on his back and a laceration on his shoulder requiring three stiches at the clinic."

"This occurred when?" I asked.

"On September 12," the agent reported.

*"Damn! More than a month.* I thought.

"Larsen told me that he did talk to an MP who wrote down some notes but did not require him to give a written statement," the agent explained.

"Did Cloud talk to you, or did he want a lawyer?" I inquired.

"No, he waived his rights and gave me a written statement that he struck PFC Larsen, but his actions were in retaliation for PFC Cloud striking him in the face with his fist."

I thanked the agent and told him to provide SJA with the written statements and follow up with any investigation needed.

I called SFC Collins to see what he had found out about the incident but was told by his assistant that he had gone home for the day. I thought this was strange, in that SFC Collins usually got back with me one way or another on his findings when I requested his assistance. Almost immediately after hanging up the phone on my attempt to reach SFC Collins, I received a call from Special Agent Michael D. Alsip from Würzburg District, informing me that CID had initiated an investigation on the Schweinfurt provost marshal for failing to report a crime in the blotter.

"This is very coincidental to what happened here today. I received a call from SJA about wanting a report from my office on an aggravated assault that occurred over a month ago, that my office never received."

Special Agent Alsip informed me that to remove any conflict of interest, Würzburg would be conducting the investigation into the provost marshal's actions. I was informed that several agents from Würzburg were going to confiscate the files from the provost marshal's office the next morning. I swore to secrecy in the matter.

Sure enough, about 8:30 the next morning, I received a frantic call from Captain Josh Madison,[101] the Schweinfurt provost marshal, telling me that CID agents were in his office and were dragging filing cabinets out on dollies. Captain Madison and I had a good working relationship, and I felt bad for him, but I told him, "I can't talk to you about the matter, sir. Just cooperate with them."

During the investigation, Captain Madison waived his rights and provided a written statement as to why he failed to report certain crimes in the MP blotter or notify CID. Captain Madison stated he had had been placed under tremendous pressure by BG Wagner to "make crime go away." He told his CID interviewers that by not reporting some incidents in the blotter, they could still be handled appropriately through command channels. However, the captain did not consider how CID would be notified on those cases that his actions violated military law and regulations.

The investigation into the failure to properly report crime took on a life of its own. I was never privy to how the investigation came to the surface, but apparently, it had something to do with SAC Boatwright's inability to coordinate the many cases being investigated by CID. BG Wagner's frustration was related to the extent of crime that was occurring in the Schweinfurt military community. The situation apparently began to fester to the point where the balloon was ready to burst in several places. Unfortunately, the investigation also included the requirement to interview BG Wagner. If general officers are involved in a crime, additional vetting at higher levels is required. In BG Wagner's interview, a list of questions had to be prepared for his view before the actual interview took place. BG Wagner admitted that he wanted crime to go away but denied any wrongdoing on his part and placed the blame entirely on the young Captain Madison.

The CID's investigation identified a third participant in the manipulation of crime data. It was none other than my old pal SFC Collins. The investigation disclosed that one young solider had been caught with a small amount of marijuana in his possession during a traffic stop by an MP. The marijuana was released by the MP to SFC Collins, who wrongfully disposed of the evidence. SFC Collins admitted in his interview that there was an unwritten policy to be lenient on "insignificant" crimes. His actions violated the trust imposed in him by his duties.

The investigation uncovered ten felony crimes, ranging from aggravated assault to larceny, that were not reported to CID. Also found was a systemic failure of those responsible to properly document reported crime, setting in motion the foundation that crime was on the decline in Schweinfurt. Because of his involvement, SFC Collins received an Article 15 and was fined and relieved from his duties as the acting MP operations officer. Captain Madison also received an Article 15, fined $500 for two months, and was reassigned to another MP unit in Frankfurt, Germany. It was obvious that Captain Madison's career was over after his punishment. It was never proven that BG Wagner overtly ordered, directed, or insinuated that Captain Madison not report the incidents that occurred. His directions to Captain Madison to "make crime go away" were taken totally out of context and was more of a comment to Captain Madison that he should place the emphasis on good law enforcement to reduce the incidence of crime as much as possible. It was up to Captain Madison to decide how to go about this task.

BG Wagner's comments had merit, but they apparently did not influence the US Army in any way. When he departed Schweinfurt on a regular rotation, BG Wagner was given his own command. It was not an infantry unit but as commander of the Sixth ROTC Command in Washington State. This assignment was his final assignment before retiring. The assignment was not seen as a move that would have helped him to achieve higher rank.

This investigation tentatively placed me, as SAC of the Schweinfurt resident agency, in a precarious predicament. It was my job to brief the Schweinfurt military community staff on crime in their area. I also needed the community's undivided support in allowing me to conduct criminal investigations authorized by US Army regulations with impunity. Up to this point, I had no substantive interaction with BG Wagner or his deputy. The next logical person to be briefed would be the provost marshal, but in this case, he was key in the CID's criminal probe of the Schweinfurt military community's manipulation of crime data. So, for several weeks, while the investigation of BG Wagner and Captain Madison was ongoing, briefings on the circumstances and status of each criminal case were limited to the unit commanders and SJA and, of course, the CID chain of command.

This investigation tied in with former SAC Boatwright's difficulties briefing the Schweinfurt military community on CID investigations. SAC Boatwright was just trying to do his job, which he did well, but the foot-dragging on the part of the community staff caused the problem. After the provost marshal investigation, I was not sure how the CID and community relations would unfold. One of the first initiatives that I started as SAC was to identify a method to brief criminal cases that would be acceptable to the community and one that I used in future assignments as SAC.

I received a push in this direction when Deputy Community Commander LTC John Palmer[102] called and invited me to attend the community staff meetings every Monday morning. I parlayed this into arranging an early morning meeting each Monday with the deputy community commander. I also developed a CID version of the daily blotter like the MP blotter. The only difference was that it was focused on briefing the status of ongoing CID criminal investigations as opposed to the MP blotter detailing the details of a reported crime.

As part of the impetus to draw CID into the loop with the Schweinfurt military community, I was appointed to the advisory board of the Family Advocacy Crisis Management Team (FACMT). This review board discussed cases of child and domestic abuse. This position created a situation where one of the most hideous crimes I ever investigated was exposed. This investigation is annotated in a narrative later in this chapter.

I was notified through the Würzburg District that Region Commander Colonel Stem had developed a three-day SAC training/orientation seminar on how to conduct yourself as SAC. For three days in late spring 1982, several new

SACs, including myself, attended the program. The training was solid, and I came away with a better understanding on how to deal with non-investigative manners, such as personnel, the community, and logistics. The time spent at the seminar was well worth the time.

For the rest of 1982 until his stateside reassignment, I kept in touch with SAC Boatwright and used him as a sounding board for many things I had yet to master. He was an excellent listener and an a very talented and wise man whose advice was welcomed and, earlier on, surely needed.

In early 1983, once SAC Boatwright left, CID tapped Special Agent Mac-Neely from the Bad Kissingen office to replace him at Aschaffenburg.

"Congratulations and good luck," I told Special Agent MacNeely over the phone after he took over the job in Aschaffenburg.

"I'll need it, I am sure," he replied.

MacNeely finished up his short tenure at Aschaffenburg and left for the States. He tragically died at the age of fifty from cancer. With Special Agent Mac-Neely reassigned, that left only Special Agent Forbes to conduct criminal investigations in Bad Kissingen. On occasion, I would send an agent from the Schweinfurt resident agency to Bad Kissingen to work so he could take a day off.

In February 1983, I was officially appointed on orders as the SAC of the Schweinfurt resident agency. There was no fanfare or ceremony, just another day at the office. New cases kept coming in, and the "old dogs" never went away. I had spent a lot of effort conducting liaison to shore up good relationships with the community, local commanders, and the German police. It seemed to be paying off and well prepared the office for an upcoming scheduled staff assistance visit (SAV) from Second Region headquarters.

In April 1983, a couple of months into my job as the SAC, the office had a SAV inspection from Region headquarters. The SAVs were just like its name suggests; the visits were intended to be of assistance to the offices inspected. Chief Raymond Kangas from Region and SAC Thomas Whitrock from the New Ulm resident agency was two of the inspectors who reviewed programs and investigative cases files at my office. Second Region's SAV program was designed to allow headquarters staff and SACs from other CID offices in Europe to inspect sister offices. The program worked well, and because of the SAV to my office, I learned a lot from the more experienced agents, especially SAC Whitrock.

I am not sure if SAC Whitrock realized it or not, but he introduced me to a rather unique management tool I ended up calling Three-Ring-Binder Management or TRBM. TRBM was used by me for the rest of my career. It involved using three-ring binders to store specific subject matter material of a topic in one binder. I would use a different binder for each subject; for instance, all policy guidance, regulations, newsletters, and related materials associated with .0015 funds (confidential funds) would be filed in the same binder. All information about homicide investigations in another, source information in yet another, and so on.

I identified each as "Book I," "Book II," "Book III," and so on, along with the name of the subject matter (i.e., Book II was titled "CID Operations"; Book III was "Criminal Intelligence"; and so on). Depending on the amount of information accumulated on a subject, I would use a second binder and title it by the subject's name—Book II, Volume II. Book I was a list of contents of all the referenced subject materials per book. This arrangement greatly enhanced my retrieval abilities for the information in a quick and proficient manner. This system prevented me from having to conduct a search in several places to find bits and pieces of the same information sought.

Throughout 1983, Schweinfurt had a commitment to send at least one special agent on a long-lasting TDY assignment to the fraud investigative unit (FIU) at CID command headquarters. The assignments usually lasted for ninety-day periods. With the heavy caseload, this became a temporary burden on the office. All the agents in the office had no trouble pitching extra innings to get the job done. The morale was high, and we had no slackers. During this period, the Würzburg District commander, Major Markalee D. Brannen Jr.—an excellent commander who usually stayed out of his SAC's way—was replaced by Major Judith A. Browning, an equally competent commander.

During the summer of 1983, the office remained very busy, with each special agent carrying a moderate to heavy caseload. That summer, we saw an increase in incidents of DUI fatalities, date rapes, and larcenies. Each agent was pulling his share of investigations, but there was one continuing systemic problem that most offices have: the perpetual issue of special agents required to perform duties as the unit evidence custodian. Traditionally, the special agent that is selected to manage the evidence depository is also required to pull duty agent for a twenty-four-hour period and maintain a caseload. In offices with a heavy caseload, such as Schweinfurt had in those days, performing duties as the evidence custodian pretty much doubled the agent's work if he must also pull duty agent and maintain a caseload.

I had one agent that was in this situation who persistently complained about having to pull duty, maintain a caseload, and run the evidence room. Every week, he would write in his agent activity summary (AAS) that he was unable to work on his cases because he had to perform evidence custodian duties. My heart went out to him, but I had taken the action to reduce the amount of cases assigned to him to compensate for the added duties. I toyed with the idea of taking him off the requirement to perform twenty-four-hour duty as the other agents but dismissed the notion. Eventually, this situation corrected itself when the young agent rotated back to the States when his tour in Germany was over. His replacement had no management issues in pulling duty agent, maintaining a reduced caseload, and managing the unit evidence depository.

In late July 1983, June, Mom, Chris, and Charlie came to Germany for a two-week visit. It would be their only trip to Germany, and Elda and I intended for them to thoroughly enjoy themselves during the visit. It was Mom's wish to see a real windmill, so Elda took her to Holland to see the windmills. Mom's health prevented her from traveling extensively, but we could take her to Heidelberg and a few places, which she enjoyed. June was thrilled to see the German mountains, valleys, and cities. Chris and Charlie, who were both eleven at the time, took in the sites but were less excited. Mom, Chris, June, and Charlie returned to the States with a lot of good memories because of their visit. Chris would return to spend more time with Elda and me a few years later.

During late summer of 1983, a company experienced a rash of stolen US Treasury checks from the APO system. In 1983, the US Army had not yet enforced the 100 percent requirement for all US Army service members to receive their paychecks via electronic deposit to their banks. Some were still being paid with paper checks. Special Agent Ownby, the agent of record, had one such case where several US Treasury checks totaling several thousand dollars were stolen from the same APO facility in the company of an infantry battalion. Special Agent Ownby had interviewed all the APO workers and others who may have been had the opportunity to handle the checks. He took handwriting samples (exemplars) from the suspects identified and had them analyzed at the army crime lab in Frankfurt. None of the handwriting samples matched the forged signatures on the US Treasury checks that he had obtained from the US Treasury. We were at a loss as to where to go next. Then we started thinking out of the box, so to speak, about who we could focus on that was taking and cashing the checks. This investigation was unusual and worthy of mention because of the unexpected turn of events that occurred. I call this investigation the Case of the Soldier and the Fake Traffic Ticket:

## THE CASE OF THE SOLIDER AND THE FAKE TRAFFIC TICKET
Never, ever lie to your wife, because she will always find out the truth

Special Agent Ownby and I discussed the case of the stolen US Treasury checks after I had reviewed the case file. He had put a lot of hard work into the investigation, and running down every possible lead and vetting them to the fullest, but we still had no solid suspects. We brainstormed the case for a half an hour or so and came up with the plan to expand our investigation to those that supervised the flow of mail once it got into the APO system. The method used to get the mail to the troops at that time had probably not changed for several years. The mail came into Germany at a general distribution point in Frankfurt and disseminated from there to the military communities. Envelopes containing US Treasury checks were easy to identify, I thought.

"Let's expand the interviews to include those that may have had access to the mail. Doesn't the mail go through many mail handlers before it reaches its designation?" I said.

Agreeing it was a fresh start, Special Agent Ownby said, "I'll start snooping on those that normally would not routinely handle the mail but whose jobs would allow them to have access to the mail if they needed it—like supervisors."

A few days later, he informed me, "I have a couple of more suspects in the US Treasury check investigation."

"Great. Did you get handwriting exemplars from them?" I asked.

"Sure did, and they both volunteered to give them to me under right advisement. I'll get them off to the lab ASAP," he reassured me.

About three weeks later, we received the crime lab report on their analysis of the handwriting exemplars submitted. We'd hit the jackpot; the lab gave a high probability that one of the two, SFC Randy Hunter,[103] likely signed the US Treasury checks. Of course, during the interview with SFC Hunter, he denied any involvement with the larceny of the checks. SFC Hunter was brought back in for a follow-up interview, but he continued to deny that he'd forged the checks and stolen the money. The final report was submitted to SJA, and they decided to take the case to court. SFC Hunter was recommended for a general court-martial.

About a month later, SFC Hunter appeared as scheduled for his court-martial, and after a trial that lasted a day, he was found guilty of forgery and larceny, reduced in rank, fined, and sentenced to Fort Leavenworth for seven years. Everyone thought that the sentence was rather harsh for the crime. SFC Hunter was totally devastated on hearing his sentencing. He thought the legal proceedings would be minor and he would be home that evening. "Can't wait to get to trial over," he'd commented to his defense lawyer moments before the he went into the courtroom. Apparently, SFC Hunter did not listen to his lawyer during the preparation for his defense, because if he had, he would have known he was facing a lengthy jail sentence. SFC Hunter was so convinced that he would be home that evening that he'd told his wife a made-up story that he would be a little late because he had to stop and pay a traffic ticket.

After the guilty verdict was read by the military judge, SFC Hunter was ordered to be incarcerated immediately at the military confinement facility in Mannheim, Germany, to further be processed for transfer to Fort Leavenworth, Kansas, to start serving his sentence. After the judge's announcement of his sentence, he was escorted to his defense lawyer's office to complete the processing for his transfer to Mannheim. His defense lawyer momentarily stepped out of his office to speak to another lawyer about the case, and when he returned, SFC Hunter was gone. The defense lawyer looked across the room and noticed that a window was open. Knowing there was no other way for SFC Hunter to get out of the office without being seen, he rushed over to look out. The SJA office was on the second floor of the building, and for SFC Hunter to have gone through the window in an escape attempt, he would have had to have jumped to the ground, which was at least fifteen feet below. The defense lawyer immediately saw SFC Hunter lying on the ground, and he appeared to be in a great deal of pain. He yelled at him, but SFC Hunter did not answer. The defense lawyer then summoned help. Several more people came running in, and they, too, saw SFC Hunter lying on the ground.

The defense lawyer, followed by several others who had been gathered in an outer office, ran down the hall, making their way outside of the building where SFC Hunter landed after he'd jumped from the second-floor window. When the group of people got to his location, none of them could believe what they saw. SFC Hunter, obviously in a lot of pain, lying on the ground, had suffered major trauma to his feet when he landed. Both of SFC Hunter's feet had almost been severed at the ankles; they were hanging on only by the skin. A short time later, a medical team arrived in an ambulance and transported him to the US Army hospital in Würzburg. Reports came down a few days later that SFC Hunter had lost both his feet at the ankles. SFC Hunter could get out of his sentence to Fort Leavenworth due to humanitarian reasons, a tragic end to some avoidable sets of circumstances. SFC Hunter was correct about one thing, he was late getting home that day.

The rest of 1983 was spent honing my management and leadership skills and dealing with personnel issues involving a CID office with six special agents at the Schweinfurt resident agency, two at the Bad Kissingen branch office, two word-processing people, one German administrative assistant, and two LNCIs. I could not have asked for a better group of people to run the CID operations in Schweinfurt. They all had the ability to work on their own, but they would not hesitate to seek advice and guidance.

Meanwhile, in other hot spots things were not going as smoothly as in Schweinfurt. In October 1983, the American military was jolted once again, when a suicide bomber drove a bomb laden truck into a US Marine barracks in Beirut. A Defense Department report, "The force of the explosion ripped the building from its foundation… Almost all the occupants were crushed or trapped inside the wreckage." Numbers told an even more devastating story. The bomb, which had produced the largest nonnuclear blast on record, exploded with the force of twelve thousand pounds of TNT and killed 241 marines. Reagan's placement of the marines as peacekeepers of a tenuous cease-fire between Christians and Muslims in Lebanon had been conflict-ridden from the start.[104]

On October 25, 1983, my birthday, six days after Prime Minister Maurice Bishop was executed by an opponent, Bernard Coard, the United States invaded the small island of Grenada, located about one hundred miles north of Venezuela. Reagan was made aware of possible trouble in Grenada earlier when Deputy Prime Minister Bernard Coard, a Communist hard-liner backed by the Grenadian army, had overthrown Prime Minister Maurice Bishop and established military rule. Bishop, a socialist with ties to Cuba, had been taking his time making Grenada wholly socialist; he had encouraged private-sector development to make the island a popular tourist destination. With the Communist Coard in power, Reagan grew more concerned.[105] The invasion was masked by the reported anxiety Reagan had for the safety of eight hundred medical students attending Saint George's University School of Medicine. The results led to the freedom of all eight hundred medical students, but at a cost of 19 American military killed and 119 wounded.

With the two incidents occurring close together, it created a heightened alert for the military but ended up not directly affecting the Schweinfurt CID office operation. We continued to function routinely doing what we did best: investigating crime in the US Army. Cases kept coming in; most agents had a moderate to heavy load of criminal investigations that each worked vigorously to resolve.

I had taken the steps to make the Schweinfurt resident agency's physical training program a legitimate part of our overall operational routine. With the average age of our agents being almost thirty-five, most of them needed to be pushed to stay in shape. Over a period of several weeks, our group of agents and military support people gradually benefited from our fitness program. However, it was not pretty at the start. I recall the first time we gathered as a group to run; there were two or three guys that fell out and started coughing and moaning about why they had to go through the pain. It did not take long, however, for them to get with the program and catch up with the others. Before I left Schweinfurt, everyone, including newcomers, could not wait for Mondays, Wednesdays, or Fridays (PT days) to fall out for a three-mile run. Each time there was a staff visit from the district and or CID headquarters inspector general (IG) team, the agents at Schweinfurt challenged them to run. No one ever took us up on the offer, but we were prepared to prove our worth just the same.

In mid-1984, the Schweinfurt resident agency was visited by the CID headquarters IG team. They spent two days reviewing selected cases, talking to the community commander, the provost, and SJA people. They all provided laudatory comments on our office and the agents' professionalism and effectiveness as investigators.

Other initiatives during late 1983 and early 1984 caused improvements in the overall criminal source, economic crimes, and collection of criminal intelligence programs. I made it my number-one goal to ensure the Schweinfurt office did its best to conduct its investigations in a thorough and timely manner. All this effort paid off, and thus, the CID IG gave the entire office good ratings on all the areas inspected, to include strong and effective management from the special agent in charge.

After the IG inspection, I was selected for a five-day SECDEF protection mission to Cairo, Egypt. The detail was sort of a reward for doing so well on the IG inspection. I was one of five agents picked to support a team from PSA that was already in Cairo. We took a Lufthansa flight from Frankfurt, Germany, to Cairo, Egypt, and joined the team at the selected hotel where the SECDEF, Caspar W. Weinberger, was going to be staying during his trip. A typical overnight or multi-night stay for the SECDEF required agents to set up a control room near the SECDEF's room. The control room, which was in operation 24-7 while the SECDEF was in the area, was the center of all activity, ensuring that constant communication between the staff to the embassies, Washington, and foreign counterparts were established and maintained. The Cairo trip went well and without any major glitches. Just like the other protection detail I supported in Chicago back in 1976, the Cairo trip got me to thinking what it would be like to do a tour at PSU. This thought kept resurfacing from time to time. I believed that at this point in my career, I had seen just about everything there was to see. Boy, was I wrong.

After the I Want Crime to Go Away case, I worked extra hard to enhance our rapport with the new local provost marshal. Schweinfurt also had a change of command at the community level. BG Wagner left and was replaced by BG Thomas H. Tait, who was a strong supporter of CID operations during his tenure at Schweinfurt. His replacement, BG Nicholas Krawciw, a Ukrainian, West Point class of 1959. Krawciw was an equally strong supporter of CID operations as well, and both were extremely approachable. With BGs Tait and Krawciw, the working environment greatly improved. I recall that BG Tait at one point asked me directly what I thought the most effective components of a successful drug suppression operation were, and I responded to him by saying, "It's not what the CID does in drug suppression efforts that is the most effective; it is the US Army's urinalysis program that has a far more positive impact in suppressing the interdiction of drugs into the US Army." When army pacesetters strengthened the urinalysis program, soldiers throughout the US Army became fearful that if they were caught in possession of illegal drugs, their careers would be ruined.

I learned a lot during the Schweinfurt years; not only did I hone my investigative techniques and how to supervise, guide, and direct agents on the progress of their investigations, but I learned how to detect any off-kilter behavioral traits as well. When agents showed tendencies of transgression, lack of initiative, depression, or other characteristics that affected their performance, I wanted to get to the root of the cause and find out the best way to handle their situations. When I could not find ways to identify the main reasons for their actions, I would tactfully talk to them to ascertain the catalysts causing the problem. Establishing a straightforward dialogue with them usually brought about answers for their behaviors.

One special agent was having difficulty in fitting in with the others. He was still a probationary agent (less than a year as a CID agent) and was not mastering good, sound investigative techniques. He showed signs of depression, was hesitant to talk with fellow agents, and took much longer than most to achieve the simplest of investigative tasks. His training agent brought his actions to my attention but offered only that the special agent was not progressing as expected. I brought him in and confronted him with the situation. I talked to him for about thirty minutes, and he very reluctantly talked about not being able to grasp the investigative concepts of CID work.

I then took a different approach to try to identify what his problem was. Initially, I thought that building up his confidence would be a good method of teaching the special agent the investigative techniques. If he gained confidence in the job, he would do better. But as I got more in depth with learning about his personality, he convinced me that he was not interested in investigative work and only chose it to prove to his father and grandfather, both very influential people in his life, that he could do something very difficult and important. I asked him more about his father and grandfather. He told me his father was a retired US Army colonel and his grandfather a retired brigadier general. The agent told me he was constantly having to prove to the two that he could do well in life, but everything he tried appeared to be not enough for them. Eventually, the agent informed me he did not want to be a special agent with the CID and felt he would not ever accomplish enough confidence to do the job. I arranged and had it approved that he be transferred to the local SJA office at Schweinfurt, where he did very well. We continually stayed in contact with each other for several years, and the last I heard of him, he was doing well as a civilian working for the US government. This agent was not a bad person but someone who was in the wrong job.

A couple of agents in the office were always down and never upbeat, but generally both did a good job. Then one day, one of the special agents failed to transmit a serious and sensitive incident (SSI) report to headquarters. When confronted with the mistake, he got irate and walked out of the morning meeting that we always had and stormed upstairs to his office. After the morning meeting was over, I called for him to come to my office to talk about what had occurred. That meeting transformed me into a marriage counselor. As it turned out, the special agent was having marital problems. There was no infidelity, only discord over feelings for each other. My talk with the special agent apparently did some good, for he did not let his marital discord get in the way of his CID duties for the rest of his tour. The last I heard of this special agent was that he is retired from the US Army, still with his wife, and living in a Southern state and has retired from civilian job as well.

The second special agent was having a different marital problem in that he had his eyes set on another girl. I also had a heart-to-heart talk with this special agent, and he admitted that he had fallen out of love with his wife and wanted a divorce. I told him that getting involved with another woman while he was married was a career stopper, which he knew. This situation came to a peak one Friday night when the office staff met at a German *Gasthaus*.

The special agent's woman of interest and the woman's husband were in attendance. At one point during our dinner that night, it became obvious that when both the woman and the special agent got up on a pretense to use the facilities at the same time, it did not go unnoticed by the husband of the woman. Once the two went into an adjoining room leading to the facilities, the husband, following them, opened the door a few seconds later and caught the two in a clutching embrace. Obviously embarrassed and shocked, the two separated, and the woman submissively returned to the dinner table with her husband, while the special agent hid out in the most appropriate place he could think of—the men's room.

When the husband returned with his wife to the table, he told her to sit down. "We're leaving shortly," he said. He then motioned for me to join him at the bar where we could talk without the others overhearing what he had to tell me. He confided with me that he had suspected his wife had a thing for the special agent, because she always talked about him when they were at home. He told me that he was extremely upset because he had just seen his wife and the special agent embracing each other outside the restrooms. "I am taking my wife home, and I am going to try to patch up any difference that we have, and I hope that you talk to the special agent about his indiscretions, as well," he said.

It could have gone unsaid. He did not have to tell me what I needed to do; I was fully aware of my obligations. I had a decision to make: either handle it officially by bringing the incident to a full investigation or attempt to deal with it discreetly. First, I had to talk to the special agent about the incident. The special agent returned to our dinner table after the husband and woman left.

"I think you should go home and report to my office at 9:00 a.m.," I told the wandering special agent.

The following morning, a Saturday, at 9:00 sharp, the special agent reported to my office as directed. Shortly into our conversation, I just let him talk to me about what had occurred the previous night. Nothing criminal had occurred the previous evening, and hopefully no crime or military violation had taken place prior to that. I decided to let him start by telling me about what led up to his feelings for the woman whose husband caught them embracing the previous night—whether they caught up in the moment with their actions fueled by alcohol or had they had been carrying on an affair.

"I apologize for what I did last night; I just got caught up in the emotions of the evening," he told me.

"You know that you almost stepped over the line last night," I emphasized to him.

"Yes, I know it. Once I left last night, I immediately went home and told my wife [his wife was not with him the previous night] what had happened. I told her that I was sorry and would not do it again."

I decided at that time not to make the incident a formal inquiry, but I ordered him to stay away from the woman. From that time forward, no further known incidents of them being together came to my attention. I hoped to had put the situation to rest.

Throughout 1984, the Schweinfurt CID office continued to investigate numerous high-profile type cases, such as DUI fatalities, SIDS cases, rapes, and a couple of attempted murders. These cases involved enlisted soldiers. But when an officer or a member of the officer's family is involved as a suspect in an investigation, the "class culture rule," as I call it, applies. One case that we conducted at Schweinfurt stands out as being an example of just how the military class system works. The US Army and other services share in this "class culture" when shown, however subtlety, that commissioned officers and their families are treated with airs of upper-crust mentality. I call this investigation the Case of the Lonely Homesick Officer's Wife:

## THE CASE OF THE LONELY HOMESICK OFFICER'S WIFE
Just because they are expected to be truthful doesn't necessarily make them truthful

It was a clear, unusually warm day in early fall of 1984, and Special Agent Ronald Glunt had just arrived at work for the day. On this day, he was the designated duty agent for the next twenty-four hours. He'd barely had time to settle into his work routine when he received his first call of the day.

"Ron, the MP desk on line one," our secretary, Angelica, softly said into the intercom.

"I never get a break on my duty day from the time I get in until the following morning; the cases keep pouring in," he bemoaned with his usual mannerisms as he answered the phone.

The Schweinfurt MP desk had called and reported that a twenty-three-year-old wife of a 1LT assigned to the Second Battalion, Thirtieth Infantry Regiment, had been sexually assaulted. Special Agent Glunt responded by firing off a barrage of the usual questions. "Where is the girl now? What kind of injuries does she have? What time and where did it occur? Have we any suspects identified?"

The MP desk clerk answered the questions as fast as he could before more questions shot out. "She walked into the MP station to report the incident and is still here," he blurted out. "Since we knew it was going to be referred to CID, no one asked her any more questions but called you instead."

"Can an MP patrol bring her to the CID office as soon as possible?" Special Agent Glunt asked.

"Yes, we'll get her down there as fast as we can," the MP clerk answered.

Special Agent Glunt called me on the intercom and briefed me on what he had just received from the MP desk.

"Let me know if you need any help with any interviews or conducting the crime scene," I told him.

The MP patrol had the 1LT's wife at the CID office within fifteen minutes. As she was led to the waiting room, which was located adjacent to my office, I could see that she was a pretty redhead that had a nice figure. She was dressed in blue jeans and a blue blouse, and she was wearing a short, light leather jacket. Before Angelica could reach Special Agent Glunt through the intercom, I got ahold of him and told him the 1LT's wife was in the waiting room.

Special Agent Glunt brought the pretty, young girl into his office and invited her to sit in the chair next to his desk. He had the same thought as I'd had before beginning the process of talking to her—that she did not look like she had recently been sexually assaulted. After introducing himself to the girl and explaining to her what to expect, which included a rape examination, the first thing that Special Agent Glunt asked was her name.

"Roberta Payne,"[106] she replied. "I need my husband here," she blurted out.

"What is your husband's name?"

"Jeffrey Payne,"[107] she said.

"Where is he?" asked Special Agent Glunt.

"He's in the field."

Special Agent Glunt told her that he knew her husband was assigned to Second Battalion, Thirtieth Infantry, from the MP notification of her crime, but he needed his company.

"He is the executive officer of B Company," she responded.

"Do you have a phone number where he can be reached?"

"No. They do not give us phone numbers when they go to the field," she said.

Special Agent Glunt excused himself from his office, telling her he would quickly return. He went to the next office, where three of our agents shared desks. Special Agent Dave Thomas was the only one there at the time, so he requested help from Special Agent Thomas in contacting Second Battalion, Thirtieth Infantry, to arrange for 1LT Payne to be returned to Schweinfurt.

Back in his office and after ensuring Roberta that all efforts to contact her husband were currently being attempted, Special Agent Glunt started in earnest to question her about the sexual assault. "The assault occurred where?"

"About 4:30 yesterday afternoon."

"Have you showered since the attack?"

"Yes."

"What did you do with the clothes that you were wearing when the assault took place?"

"I washed them."

"Did you tell anyone, such as a neighbor or friend, about the assault?"

"No. I was very upset, so I just wanted to be left alone after the person attacked me."

"Can you describe the individual that assaulted you?"

As he asked Roberta these questions, Special Agent Glunt noticed that she was becoming very uncomfortable. She kept crossing and uncrossing her legs, folding her arms across her chest, and staring at the floor.

"Roberta, can you describe the person who assaulted you?"

"He was a black male," she answered without elaborating any further.

"Can you provide any other description of this individual? How tall was he?"

"About my height."

"Did he talk to you during the assault?"

"No. I do not recall him saying anything."

"Did he come up behind you and wrestle you to the ground?" He received no immediate response from her. "Did he penetrate your vagina during the assault?"

Either to get her bearings or because she was too overwhelmed at Special Agent Glunt's rapid-fire questions, she hesitated a few seconds before answering. "I want my husband here, please."

Purposely not focusing on her response about wanting her husband present, he asked, "Could you go over the location where this assault took place?

"To the commissary to get some groceries."

"Why didn't you report the incident last evening?"

"As I said before, I was very upset and did not want to talk to anyone."

Getting somewhat tired of the abbreviated, short, incomplete answers from Roberta, Special Agent Glunt decided to give her a rest.

He then went to my office let me know he thought that Roberta Payne might not be telling the truth about being sexually assaulted. I advised Special Agent Glunt that we had to make sure. I also told him that a motive as to why she was lying would help. I advised him that, even though she said she had taken a shower, she needed to be examined by medical officials and a rape kit taken. Based on her incomplete or lack of responses to some of the key questions, we were not sure the perp had penetrated her during the attack. We also needed the clothes she was wearing when assaulted for analysis at the lab and to examine the crime scene. Also, we needed an identikit composite of the perp. Other investigative steps would be conducted as needed, but first, we needed to get her to the clinic, so she could be examined and a rape kit processed. Then, afterward, we needed to take her home and retrieve the clothes she was wearing when attacked. Just as Special Agent Glunt was leaving my office, I mentioned to him the possibility of a polygraph to determine if she was telling us the truth.

Special Agent Glunt returned to his office and explained to Roberta that he needed to take her to the Schweinfurt clinic for a rape examination and that we needed to retrieve the clothes she was wearing when attacked. Special Agent Glunt also informed her that we needed to prepare an identikit composite of her assailant to pass around the community to assist in identifying him. And lastly, she needed to provide a sworn statement to what she had reported.

The first thing out of her month when she was told we had to accomplish was, "I just can't do anything until I see my husband."

"You mean you won't consent to a rape reexamination, give us the clothes you were wearing, assist with an identikit composite, and provide a sworn statement?" Special Agent Glunt asked.

"I would rather have my husband here first," she said.

Special Agent Glunt stopped and stared Roberta Payne in the eye and asked her if she would be willing to take a polygraph test to verify the veracity of her allegations of rape.

Roberta Payne, without responding to the specific question, started crying and said, "I want my husband home."

Special Agent Glunt detected the unusual comment from Roberta—that she wanted her husband *home* instead of *here*. Her answer was indicative of a motive. She wanted her husband home from the field, and she would do anything to make this happen, even drum up a story about being sexually assaulted.

Special Agent Glunt realized that if a crime of rape did occur, the more time that elapsed from the alleged rape incident to the rape examination would mean that valuable evidence would probably be lost. Also, even though he was convinced her story was falling apart and that the probability was that the rape did not occur, he needed to pursue the investigation to the end. She deserved the proper due diligence in investigating her case. Here we had a female victim alleging that she was raped, and she was not forthcoming in helping with the gathering of potential evidence.

Her husband was found at the US Army training center in Grafenwöhr, Germany. His command had been notified about what his wife had reported, and he was being pulled out of the field and would return about noon the following day.

1LT Jeffrey Payne reported to the CID office with his wife, Roberta. While Roberta was escorted into the waiting room, Special Agent Glunt invited him to his office. After spending about fifteen minutes briefing 1LT Payne on the investigation of the reported rape, Special Agent Glunt brought up the possibility that the rape did not occur.

1LT Payne, a tall, extremely well-built young military officer, became somewhat irritated, looked at Special Agent Glunt, and fired back, "If she said it happened, then I believe her, and you guys need to do something about the incident. There is a rapist running around, and if you don't catch him, I have some friends that will help me do the job. When I first saw her last night when I got home from the field, she told me you guys brow-punched her to the point that she did not want to talk about the rape any further."

"I did not get that impression from her when she left here last evening," Special Agent Glunt told him.

Special Agent Glunt was successful in calming 1LT Payne down somewhat and told him that we still needed more information from her. "She had promised to bring in the clothes she wore during the assault. It has been two days since the alleged assault, so, we also need her to be examined by medical personnel for any possible evidence. She did not give me a complete description of her assailant, and she still has not given me a statement covering the details of the assault. So, can you see why we are having a rough time investigating this incident? Without her help, we cannot do anything else," Special Agent Glunt pointedly made his argument to 1LT Payne.

You could see the tension eased from 1LT Payne's body as he sat back in the chair next to Special Agent Glunt's desk. "I can now understand where you guys are coming from. I will get her to fully cooperate in your investigation. I still think that CID had been too rough on her the previous day, and that's the reason she did not thoroughly answer all the questions," he added.

"Can we start by taking her home and retrieving the clothes she was wearing the night of the assault?"

"Yes. Give me thirty minutes, and I'll have the clothes here," 1LT Payne replied.

As he and Roberta left the office, hopefully to bring back the clothes, Special Agent Glunt thought, *there will be no evidential value found on the underwear; I am just going through the motions.*

About an hour later, both 1LT Payne and his wife showed up at the CID office. Roberta had a bag that contained blue jeans and a blouse. As Special Agent Glunt pulled the clothing items from the bag, he noticed there were no panties or bra, which she should have had on at the time of the assault. The panties and bra were more important than her blue jeans and blouse.

"Where are the panties and bra you were wearing when you were attacked?" Special Agent Glunt asked.

"After I washed them the other night, I placed the panties and bra inside the drawer where I keep all my underwear," she explained.

Biting his lip to keep from yelling at her, which he knew he couldn't, he asked, "Couldn't you identify the panties and bra and bring them to me?"

"I have several panties and bras in my drawer, and I can't tell them apart," she responded, incredulous at even being asked the question.

Special Agent Glunt knew he had lost the evidence, if there was ever any to begin with. Even if she would have brought in a pair of panties and bra, any smart defense attorney could tear the chain of custody apart and argue that the underwear could not positively be verified as the same as she had on that day. That was, of course, if the investigation identified the offender and the case went to trial. In addition to those points, it was improbable that the CID crime lab would be able to get any evidence, such as blood, semen, or hair samples, from them.

Special Agent Glunt did not want to spend an additional inordinate amount of time trying to pull information from her, but he knew without her truthful cooperation, we would be wasting our time on any further investigation. He needed an admission from her that the incident did not occur as reported. Hopefully, in his efforts to ascertain this, he might be able to identify a motive for her false report. The best method to get an admission was using a logical cognitive approach that would make her understand that what she had reported just could not have happened the way she described. It was around this time that Special Agent Glunt asked Roberta Payne to show him where the alleged crime occurred. Prior to their departure from the CID office, he briefed me on what he had ascertained. I was not shocked when he told me that she had not brought in all the clothing that she'd worn the day of the assault. The extent of her cooperation throughout the case was indicative that the crime did not occur as reported.

I told Special Agent Glunt that maybe once he inspected the crime scene, he would have a better perspective of what to ask her when taking her statement. Maybe if we gave the Paynes the weekend to think things over, 1LT Payne might come to his senses and realize that the incident, as reported, did not occur. If any information was found at the scene, it could either support Roberta Payne's allegations that an incident did occur or help CID's position to show the crime did not.

About 3:00 p.m. that Friday, Special Agent Glunt and the Paynes left for the crime scene. Special Agent Glunt followed their car in a CID sedan to an area near where they lived. After parking the cars, Roberta Payne led 1LT Payne, who had not been told by his wife where the assault took place, and Special Agent Glunt to a walking path that ran from behind their quarters in US housing area at Askren Manor to the commissary. Special Agent Glunt's initial observation disclosed that if Roberta Payne were walking toward the commissary as she'd indicated at the time she'd indicated, there would have been so many kids getting out of school and walking home that they could not have avoided seeing the assault.

"Were there a lot of people walking around when you headed to the commissary?" Special Agent Glunt asked.

"No. There was no one in the area where I was walking," she indicated.

Special Agent Glunt noticed that 1LT Payne also looked confused. "Can you show me the exact location along the route where you were assaulted?" Special Agent Glunt asked.

Roberta Payne's body started shaking. She froze and then suddenly reached out her arms for 1LT Payne and asked him to hold her. When he hugged her, she began to cry, became hysterical, and started pounding on his chest, shouting, "Why did you bring me here? Why did you bring me here?"

1LT Payne looked over his wife's shoulder at Special Agent Glunt and gave that sort of acquiescent glare that he now knew she had been lying.

Roberta Payne then extracted herself from her husband's hold and turned to Special Agent Glunt. "I suppose I owe you an explanation of why I have been acting this way. It is very simple: I did not want my husband to go to the field. I feel so alone here in Germany and very homesick. I know it's his job, but I just broke down. I have been here only a short time, and it is so lonely without him." She then looked directly at 1LT Payne. "I am so sorry, Jeff."

Looking at both, Special Agent Glunt said, "I think we need to put this matter to rest. Can you come back to the CID office and provide a statement as to what you just told us?"

"Can I have some time with my husband first?" she asked.

Not wanting to sway her flow of emotions that might cause her to change her mind, Special Agent Glunt told her, "I think we can hold off on the statement until Monday morning." Special Agent Glunt requested both to report to his office at 9:00 a.m. so he could get her statement. He didn't know if he'd done the right thing by delaying taking the statement until Monday, but he thought it was the best decision at the time.

After the Paynes assured him that they would be in his office at 9:00 a.m. the following Monday, he left them and returned to the CID office. I was still in my office when he got there, so he briefed me on the case and said once he got Roberta Payne's statement, he was going to unfound the investigation. I concurred.

During my weekly 8:00 a.m. briefing with the assistant community commander, Colonel Kenneth Wahl, I discussed this case and what direction we were taking. Colonel Wahl almost exploded when I told him it appeared that Mrs. Payne was lying to us and that no rape had occurred.

Obviously upset, he said, "How can you determine she is lying when you don't have all the evidence yet?"

I explained to Colonel Wahl that the motive for her reporting she had been assaulted was that she wanted her husband home instead of in the field. Colonel Wahl argued that CID must provide Mrs. Payne all due process and that if there was a rapist running free, he needed to be caught. I told him that I was convinced that there had been no rapist running around the community and the case would be completed within the next few days. As I left Colonel Wahl's office that morning, I could not shake the feeling that the perceptions that US Army commissioned officers had caused them to be class conscious or think they were in an elite or privileged group compared to others.

On Monday morning at 9:00 sharp, Roberta Payne and her husband showed up for the meeting with Special Agent Glunt. He could obtain a statement from Roberta that admitted she had fabricated the story about her being sexually assaulted because she wanted her husband, 1LT Jeffrey Payne, at home with her instead of being in the field on a training exercise. Her actions were an attempt to reveal her true feelings about being in Germany away from her family. Instead of waiting for our next scheduled meeting, I called and briefed Colonel Wahl about the Payne investigation and that she did provide a statement admitting that she had lied about being sexually assaulted.

But there was one final case I had conducted at Schweinfurt where I was the case agent. It is unique and stood above all others as being one of the most hideous crimes of my career. The case involved a single father who raped his twelve-year-old daughter and impregnated her. I called this investigation the Case of the Sinful Father.

One chilly fall day in late 1984, I was attending a meeting of the Family Advocacy Crisis Management Team (FACMT) at Ledward Barracks, when the director brought up information that a twelve-year-old girl from Schweinfurt had been brought into the emergency room of the Würzburg US Army hospital with severe stomach pain. To the surprise of the medical staff that treated the young girl, her stomach pain was relieved when she gave birth to a nine-pound baby boy. From the receipt of this information, it did not appear that anyone in the chain of command caught the seriousness of this situation: the girl was only twelve years old and had a baby:

## THE CASE OF THE SINFUL FATHER
There is nothing more depraved than the crime of incest between a father and daughter

There was no sense of urgency in the director's voice when he told the story to the members of FACMT that day about a twelve-year-old girl who had delivered a baby boy. I immediately asked the director if he was told who the father was. The director, a tall, athletic, handsome individual, had no clue as to why I wanted to know this information. His major concern was for the girl's well-being, and he did not stop for one minute to think that her pregnancy could have been a crime. He had not even considered reporting the incident to me as a representative of the local CID office, and who knows when I would have found out about if it had not been for my attendance at the FACMT meeting that morning.

It was possible that the twelve-year-old girl's boyfriend may have gotten her pregnant, but I had issues with her statement and felt her story did not hold water. The issues needed to be resolved before the young girl's pregnancy became only a socially awkward situation versus a criminal offense. The director of FACMT claimed not to have known the name of the twelve-year-old girl.

About 10:30 a.m., I departed the meeting before it adjourned and returned to my office in Niederwerrn to initiate an inquiry into who the father of the baby might be. I made preliminary calls to Operations Officer Chief Davis at Würzburg and to Captain Christopher Holiday, who had recently arrived as the new provost marshal for Schweinfurt. Neither had heard anything about the twelve-year-old girl giving birth at the Würzburg US Army hospital. I thought that the lack of notification meant that no one who had knowledge of the birth was considering the incident to be a crime—and that, I thought, was very odd. Up until this time, the identity of the twelve-year-old was not even known to law enforcement.

At around 11:45 a.m., I eventually got ahold of the hospital commander, a colonel, and explained to him what I needed and why I needed it. About thirty minutes later, I received a call from a person on the hospital staff who provided me with the girl's name, her address, and her father's name and unit. Her name was Barbara Sanders, and her father was SFC Johnathan L. Sanders[108] of Company D, 703rd Maintenance Battalion, located on Conn Barracks. I followed up with a call to the director of FACMT to see if he had any more details related to the birth.

"I heard that the twelve-year-old girl's boyfriend had gotten her pregnant," the director told me.

"What's the boy's name? I asked.

"I do not know," answered the director.

*Boy, we're getting nowhere fast on this case,* I thought.

I then called Company D, 703rd Maintenance Battalion, and was surprised when SFC Sanders answered the phone. He identified himself as "Acting First Sergeant," having apparently been given the job as top sergeant because he was on the promotion list for E8. For a nanosecond, I thought about how I should start the conversation, because I did not have any idea how much or how little SFC Sanders was involved with finding out who'd gotten his twelve-year-old daughter pregnant.

I took the direct approach. I politely introduced myself to SFC Sanders and advised, "CID is initiating an investigation into your daughter's pregnancy, and I need to talk to you in person."

I listened carefully to his response to detect any anger in his emotions. Again, I was surprised that his response did not appear to be angry, concerned, or anxious in any way. In fact, the tone in his voice was very low, almost inaudible (my poor hearing didn't help) and uninterested.

"Can you come to my office so we can talk about your daughter?"

A moment of silence went by, and then SFC Sanders said into the phone, "I'll be there as soon as I can make it."

"I'll be expecting you," I told him, and I hung up. I was extremely curious as to why he sounded so calm over the phone. I'd expected there would be more anger in his reaction to his daughter getting pregnant—or worse, that the anger was not vented at the boy who got her pregnant. I made a last-minute call to the Schweinfurt SJA office and spoke to Major David Spencer, the chief lawyer in charge of the Third Infantry Division SJA Detachment at Conn Barracks. I informed him the initiation of an investigation to determine who had gotten the Sanders girl pregnant.

"Please keep me posted," he said.

About 12:45 p.m., SFC Sanders arrived at my office. He was a small person, only about five foot six or so, slim build, timid, and introverted. I shook his hand and immediately invited him into my office and directed him to a chair a short distance from my desk. I asked him if he needed anything.

"No, I am okay," he responded.

I began the interview by asking him some background information questions about his daughter—her full name, her age, what type of personality she had, and any information he could provide on her activities and what her general temperament and behavior was like.

"She is a good student, usually stays at home, is good to her brother, and is kind and respectful to me," he responded.

I immediately detected no reference to his wife, so I asked, "How does she get along with her mother?"

"Her mother left us about two years ago, and I have been raising her and her brother ever since," he proudly said.

"How was your daughter's relationship with her mother when she was at home?" I asked.

"They seemed to get along okay, but her mother was not the affectionate type," he indicated.

"Who do you think is the father of your daughter's baby?" I questioned.

"I have no clue," he said.

"Does your daughter ever talk about any boys she likes?"

"No. That is just it; I don't ever recall her dating," he indicated.

*Boy, that is strange—the father does not have a clue as to who her daughter knows.* Added to the information that she stayed at home all the time and only went to school narrowed any potential list of who she might have had a sexual relationship with. I thought, *could it be a classmate, schoolteacher, or possibly her father?*

My curiosity caused me to start focusing in on the father, SFC Sanders. Three factors led me to this conclusion. One: the lack of a mother presence. Two: information that SFC Sanders's daughter never went anywhere. Three: no information about a boyfriend.

I followed up with a series of questions about his social life to get any information on whether he dated or was seeing anyone. Another question caused me to concentrate on his sexual habits, if any. "When was the last time you had a date?" I asked.

"I don't date—do not have time," he responded.

*Bingo, add a fourth reason: he does not date.*

"Who takes care of your son and daughter when you have to go to the field?" I inquired.

"I am lucky; so far since I have been in Germany, I have not been required to go to the field," he told me.

At no time during the interview did SFC Sanders show anger, sorrow, or other emotion to indicate he was upset in any way that his daughter had gotten pregnant. My suspicions that maybe SFC Sanders knew more about her pregnancy than he let on was stronger than ever by this point.

I continued with a series of questions concerning the time line on when he discovered his daughter was pregnant. "When did you first find out your daughter was pregnant?" I asked.

"That's just it—it wasn't until the day I took her to the emergency room at the clinic."

Another indicator that SFC Sanders might be guilty of the most hideous of crimes.

"She told me she had a pain in her stomach, and when she was examined by a doctor at the hospital, they told me she was pregnant," he said.

*How in the world would a father not notice his daughter's pregnancy?* I thought. Nine months was a very long time not to notice such an obvious physical condition. Living with his daughter, who constantly stayed home, would allow him plenty of chances to notice her pregnancy. He, however, stuck to his guns and claimed not to have observed or recalled any signs that his daughter was pregnant during her whole term. Throughout the interview, SFC Sanders was displaying classic signs of defensive protection by holding his arms in front of his chest and continually crossing and uncrossing his legs.

Another thing that struck me as odd or unusual was that no schoolteacher or official, friends, or others that she would have had daily contact with had come forth to report her condition. I had SFC Sanders in my office for about three hours now and still had no concrete evidence that proved he was the culprit. All my information was based on circumstantial evidence, but that was soon to change.

It was now 3:45 p.m., and my secretary, Angelica Muelhmeyer, poked her head into my office and said, "I need to talk to you."

I got up and left the office, shutting the door behind me. I joined her in Sergeant Alan Ladd's office. "SFC Sanders's two kids are in the waiting room," she informed me.

"Keep them occupied until I can talk to the daughter. I'll want you to sit in on the interview with her. Can you take them into your office so I can get SFC Sanders moved to the waiting room?" I directed. As I walked back to my office, I turned and told Mrs. Muelhmeyer, "Give the kids a drink and try to keep them calm."

"Okay," she responded.

SFC Sanders recoiled in his chair when I walked back into my office. I explained to him that we needed to take a break, and I led him to the waiting room. Mrs. Muelhmeyer had already taken SFC Sanders's two kids to her office and shut the door to prevent them from seeing their dad as he walked to the waiting room. Once back in my office, I called Mrs. Muelhmeyer and told her to bring Barbara Sanders into my office. We settled her into a comfortable chair, and for the first time, I noticed that she was a tall girl with an extremely large frame, who appeared to be older than her age. She was very mature physically and wore loose clothing to cover her large size. By looking at Barbara, one could tell it would not be hard to hide her pregnancy by wearing the type of clothing she had on—an oversized blouse with ill-fitting slacks. Before starting her interview, I informed her that since she was only twelve years old, CID was investigating her pregnancy, and I asked her if she understood what was going on.

She responded with a degree of maturity that I was not expecting. "Yes, I understand what is happening."

"I guess we should start by asking you who got you pregnant."

"It was a neighbor boy who has since moved," she spontaneously blurted out.

"What is the boy's name?" I asked?

She hesitated before talking and bowed her head into her hands and started crying. "It was a boy from school, but I didn't know him well," she mumbled as she continued to cry.

"Where did he live?" I asked.

"Down the street from our house," she said.

"If I took you to your neighborhood, could you show me the house the boy lived in?" I asked.

She did not respond, but kept on crying as she held her head in her hands.

"When did you realize, you were pregnant?" I asked her.

"About two months," she said.

"Two months from the time you had sex with the boy down the street?" I asked.

"Yes," she said.

"Does the boy go to the same school as you?" I inquired.

"No. He moved to Aschaffenburg with his parents," she said in a barely audible voice.

Not getting anywhere during the interview, I decided to take a more direct approach and simply and bluntly ask her a very hard question. "Did your father get you pregnant?"

Other than crying, nothing came out of her mouth.

"Barbara, I know this is very difficult for you, but we need to get to the truth of who did this to you." I asked again, "Did your father get you pregnant?"

With tears streaming down her cheeks, she gained enough strength and composure to raise her head and to make eye contact with me. A relaxed expression spread over her face, and she appeared to be at peace with herself. Letting go of her pent-up emotions, Barbara finally surrendered and just sort of caved in and said, "Yes. He did this to me." Immediately after admitting to me it was her father that got her pregnant, Barbara then bowed her head and started crying again. Mrs. Muelhmeyer put her arms around Barbara to console her, and that is where I left them. What a situation this young girl was in. Her father got her pregnant, and her life had been forever changed.

Now I had to figure the best possible technique to use in interrogating SFC Sanders for incest, rape, and any other crimes I could conjure up. This man did not deserve the right to be a father to his daughter or the grandfather to his daughter's baby. As far as I was concerned, he'd forfeited any rights as a parent. It made me sick to think of how Barbara's and her brother's lives were going to play out. SFC Sanders's disgusting, revolting, and inexcusable crime had ruined his life and the lives of his children and the daughter's baby's as well. This sickening, despicable act would undoubtedly create very difficult emotional and psychological complications for everyone involved or associated with it for the rest of their lives.

I arranged for transportation of the two children to a social worker at Ledward Barracks who had previously brought the two to the CID office. The social worker had been brought into the situation earlier in the day and thoroughly briefed by the FACMT director. Arrangements were being made for the two to be placed in foster care, pending a final resolution as to where they would be sent to live.

I went up to the office of Jack Hurley, an agent at Schweinfurt that had been assigned to the office, and requested he join me for the interview of SFC Sanders. I briefed Jack on the details of the case thus far and indicated SFC Sanders was sitting in the waiting room. After I briefed Jack, I called Major Spenser at the SJA office and gave him an update on what we knew so far. I informed him that I was ready to bring SFC Sanders in for an interrogatory interview.

"Keep me up to date on your progress," he responded before hanging up.

I just stood up and remained silent for a good minute or two before asking Jack to bring SFC Sanders into the office. I had prepared a rights warning certificate with the listed offenses of rape and incest and laid the document in the middle of my desk. When SFC Sanders entered my office, he headed for the easy chair near the window, where he had been sitting previously.

"No, I don't want you to sit in that chair," I said as I pointed to a straight-back chair directly in front of my desk. Without saying a word, SFC Sanders sat down in the chair. I was sitting down when he returned to my office. I did not get up to greet him.

With no small talk, I went directly for the jugular vein and gave him his Miranda rights. As I was articulating each right, SFC Sanders's body slumped to the point he almost fell from his chair. Fortunately, he regained his balance as I ran through the rights. "You have the right to remain silent. You have the right to have a lawyer present with you during questioning. That lawyer can be either US Army appointed at no cost or a civilian lawyer of your choice that you pay for. Do you understand these rights as I have explained them to you?" I asked. "Do you understand your rights as read to you?"

"Yes," he answered.

"Do you want a lawyer now?"

"No," he responded.

"You have the right to stop answering my questions at any time and/or to make a make any further statements. Do you understand this right?"

"Yes."

"Will you consent to answer my questions without an attorney being present, and will you be willing to make a statement?" I pointedly asked.

"Yes," he replied.

After I'd completed the advisement of SFC Sanders's rights, his face became flushed. His eyes stopped moving, his jaw dropped, his mouth opened, and he could barely be heard saying, "I knew I was doing wrong. I knew I was doing wrong."

"Did you have sexual intercourse with your daughter?"

"Yes, I did!"

Every question I asked him pertaining to his illegal sexual behavior toward his daughter was answered again, again, and again with, "Yes… yes… yes."

SFC Sanders provided me with a two-page statement admitting to having sex with his daughter over a two-year period, even after finding out she was pregnant. He admitted that he'd told his daughter that when the baby came, she was to say it was a boy from the neighborhood that had since moved from the area.

After obtaining his statement, I had Jack watch him in the waiting room until I briefed SJA Major Spenser, SFC Sanders's brigade commander, MPs, and the provost marshal. I then escorted him to the Schweinfurt MP station and went to meet with Major Spenser at his office. The entire investigation from the time of notice at the FACMT meeting to the completion of SFC Sanders's confession and the subsequent required briefings took from about 10:00 a.m. to 5:45 p.m. By the next day, SFC Sanders was headed to jail at the US Army correctional facility at Mannheim.

The next day, Major Spenser called me to advise that he was pushing for the maximum time in prison, which would be likened to life imprisonment for SFC Sanders, due to his age being thirty-five.

To get the sentence mentioned, Major Spenser said, "I know we got a confession from the pervert, but I want to convict him on the maximum possible evidence. I want to prove the case without a doubt by getting a blood test to positively identify SFC Sanders as the man."

"I will contact our lab to determine if they have the capability," I told him.

"This case needs to be tried as fast as possible, so please find out how long it will take the army lab to run the test."

Well, for reasons that cannot be recalled, USACIL was not used for the blood test. Somewhere along the way, Major Spenser commented that SJA will pay for the outside test. A German serologist in Würzburg, Germany, ran a test using the blood drawn from Barbara Sanders and her baby and compared it to SFC Sanders's blood.

It took about two weeks before the results of the blood analysis came in from the Würzburg serologist. The examination showed that there was a 77 percent probability that SFC Sanders impregnated his daughter. Apparently, the 77 percent probability was not good enough for Major Spenser, who was trying the case himself. He wanted more certainty that SFC Sanders was the person responsible for getting his daughter pregnant. I recall getting into a spat with Major Spenser about what we had compared to his desire to get further evidence.

"We have SFC Sanders's confession and a blood test that proves there is a 77 percent probability that he got his daughter pregnant. What else do you need?" I said to him.

"I want to get this guy for what he did. I don't want anything to fall through the cracks!"

"I'll see what I can do," I informed him.

LNCI Jake Betheral, one of the best German criminal investigators assigned to the CID, was instrumental in locating the Würzburg serologist used for the first analysis of blood on the case who could coordinate with the same authority to get a second test conducted. It took about two additional weeks to get the results of the second test completed. The results of the second test of blood samples presented for analysis indicated that there was a 99 percent probability that SFC Sanders had gotten his daughter pregnant. With these results in, Major Spenser was satisfied and proceeded to trial. SFC Sanders, feeling humiliated, shameful, and shattered, became overwhelmed at what he had done. Seeing the evidence against him, he waived all legal proceedings, to include the Article 32 hearing (equivalent to a grand jury), and pleaded guilty in a general court-martial to the offenses of rape and incest. He was sentenced to forty-five years in Leavenworth and reduction to PV1, and he was dishonorably discharged from the US Army. For what he did, the man—if you could call him one—should have received life without parole. The infamous jurisdictional gap did not apply to this case, in that SFC Sanders committed the crime in the US housing area and his daughter, Barbara—a civilian not subject to the UCMJ—was the victim. If the case involved a civilian father, the jurisdictional gap would have applied, and no charges would have been brought against him.

One might think that once the investigation was completed, and entered in the history books, it was over. But, for me, it was not over by a long shot. About a month after the trial, I received a call from Captain Gregory Evans, the Würzburg District executive officer, who informed me that I was possibly facing criminal charges for wrongfully making expenditures of more than $4,000—the cost of the two blood tests conducted in SFC Sanders's case.

"What?" I yelled into the telephone.

"Yeah, the CID received a letter from the Würzburg US Army Contracting Office that indicated you spent the money without being authorized," Captain Evans noted.

"Wow. SJA told me they were going to foot the bill for that cost," I told him.

"Well, they apparently didn't," Captain Evans said.

"Give me a little time to discuss this with Major Spenser at the local SJA office."

"Okay, but get back with me as soon as possible," Captain Evans added before hanging up.

I immediately called Major Spenser's office and got him on the first ring. "Major Spenser, I had just been notified that the US Army wants me to reimburse them $4,000 that was spent on SFC Sanders's case. I thought your office was going to take care of that expense; what happened?" I asked.

"Oh, I contacted our Würzburg headquarters, and they told me they would consider it. I assumed that they had already taken care of the matter," Major Spenser said.

"Well, apparently, they did not consider this matter as thoroughly as they implied, sir," I suggested to him. "Can you get back with your people and let me know?"

I called Captain Evans and let him know where I stood with Major Spenser, and he told me he needed an answer as soon as I could get one.

Two or three days later, Major Spenser called me back to let me know I was pretty much into the mud with the issue, because SJA was not going to obligate any funds for a case that was already closed.

I had been hoodwinked by Major Spenser, because I would have inquired through CID channels on how to get the money if he had not practically promised me to get the money. I surely did not want to pay the $4,000 from my own pocket for the blood tests that I had ordered, which proved without a doubt that SFC Sanders had committed one of the most contemptible of all crimes—incest. This matter was not immediately cleared up. Captain Evans, who worked very diligently on the problem, tried to get the CID headquarters to pay for the blood test from .0015 funds (confidential funds), but they would not allow it.

Then he looked at the annual budget from the Würzburg CID office, but they had no wiggle room to move money. Then, through hard work and tenacity on the part of Captain Evans, some sort of agreement was worked out between the contracting office and the CID at Würzburg to pay the debt. I think that the motivating factor that influenced the Würzburg contracting office's decision was made because of the reason for the expenditure. This situation created one of my life's rules. Rule Nine: *Don't place absolute trust in anyone or anything without ensuring absolute trust in return.*

During the last several months at Schweinfurt, a new operations officer, CW4 James Davis, replaced CW4 Matt Moriarty, who was reassigned to Fort Knox. Major George Kinoshita took over from Major (P) Browning, who left for the European Drug Suppression Operation Center (DSOC) at Mannheim, Germany. I got to know these leaders well, and we all had a mutual respect.

My assignment at the Schweinfurt resident agency lasted four years and six months—the longest tour of my career. Professionally, I was at the zenith of my career. Since my assignment to Schweinfurt, I had evolved from a good investigator with a solid reputation to an individual that was highly regarded as someone who was thought of in the highest regard—a senior investigative manager and on the road to becoming an operations officer.

Personally, events in Schweinfurt propelled my life into a sort of new happier beginning. I met and married Elda and continued to grow professionally, and at the time of my departure, my career seemed to be destined for greater success. Schweinfurt turned out to be the fourth good CID assignment in a row Schweinfurt was indeed a pivotal career assignment and led to greater roles as a leader that transformed me from being a special agent in the field to becoming a senior investigative manager in charge of the resident agency. Also, I had just received word from CID headquarters that I had been picked up for my third warrant bar (CW3). The promotion in rank was scheduled for July 30, 1985. If there was anything I could have changed while at Schweinfurt, it would have been my choice of a follow-along assignment.

About three months before my scheduled departure date (February 1985), CW4 Michael Elbert—the CID assignment officer at the Hoffman Building in Alexandria, Virginia—called. He advised that I had tentatively been picked for an assignment to Fort Campbell, Kentucky. Soon thereafter, I received a sponsor letter from CW3 Sam Brown, who was welcoming me to the Fort Campbell District. However, in its mythical way, anything in CID can change. For example, my original assignments to Fort Sheridan and Second Region were both changed through circumstances already noted in previous chapters of this book. Well, the inevitable did occur on this assignment.

I received a second call from Alexandria. Mike said, "I have been talking to Merl Kuhlman at Fort Carson. We were talking about who to send to Fitzsimons as the SAC. When I mentioned the names of who were pending assignments but not yet on orders, your name came up as a candidate for the job. Kuhlman was wondering if you would consider the Fitzsimons position. This would be an ideal assignment for a short time until we could get you back to Germany. I'll get you back to Germany in one year."

In our first conversation, I had expressed to Mike that I would prefer to stay in Germany, and if he could not find a slot, I would like to get an assignment in the States that would allow the quickest turn around.

I struggled with the assignment situation for a few days and discussed it at length with Elda. She was in favor of any stateside assignment that would allow me to quickly return to Germany. Elda had traveled to Germany to see Europe, and she felt there was still a lot that she had not seen. We had discussed her staying in Germany while I was in the States. An assignment that would allow me to return in one year was in fact ideal, so our decision that I conveyed to Mike was that I would take the Fitzsimons assignment. I had a scheduled report date of March 3, 1985.

CID assignments are never etched in stone. About two weeks after relaying my desire to be reassigned to Fitzsimons, I received another call from Mike, who was trying to find a CW2 (P) for Fort Bragg, probably the busiest assignment in the whole CID command. Although I was flattered to have been considered, I turned the assignment down.

On February 5, 1985, Elda took me to Frankfurt so I could catch my flight to Houston to pick up my car, which had been shipped three weeks earlier. June, who had been transferred to Houston by her employer a couple of years earlier because the business closed its Terre Haute facility, was waiting for me at the airport. I stayed with June and Charlie for a few days before picking up my car. It was a good visit; we got caught up on our lives and had many good meals before I left for Indiana to spend a couple of days with Mom before going west to Fitzsimons, near Denver, Colorado.

My time with Mom in Terre Haute went well. I found Mom in reasonably good health; although we never spoke about her nasty smoking habit, it concerned me about what it was doing to her health. She did have her small group of friends for support and appeared to be getting along well without June being close by. I had yet to establish myself in Colorado, so I could not take her with me, and June had a small two-bedroom apartment in Houston, a place not well suited for a third occupant. But Mom seemed happy and content living in Terre Haute and would not have consented to move for any reason. Even though I found her well and without any real needs, this did not stop me from worrying about her.

I could not believe how much Chris had grown since his visit to Germany. He was thirteen years old and as tall as I was. He had grown into a striking, handsome young man who was respectful to others. The first time I sat down with him, I could tell he was maturing. I still had to engage him, because he was quiet and reserved, but he was pleasant when talking. Even though his cousin Charlie was in Houston, they were still very close. We spent a lot of time together when I was home, and it was the first time that I got to know him as a young man. I inquired how his mother was getting along, and he told me, "She is still working at nights and sleeping during the day." I saw that nothing much had changed with her.

Chris loved sports, and it was a big portion of what we talked about. At the time, I was visiting Terre Haute, it was too early for baseball, so I could not take him to Saint Louis to see the Cardinals, but I promised him we would go when time allowed. Since school was still in session during the time of my visit, I only saw him in the evenings.

Although I was not around as much as I would have liked and his mother was not the most empathic person to deal with, I could still see that Chris had developed into a solid, decent, good kid. I never knew him to get into any trouble, and he was always doing things within the mainstream, not going off the deep end to isolate himself from others. He was quiet and reserved, but still approachable. Over the few days we had with each other on this visit, I saw Chris as a person that was troubled with confrontation, but one that I was extremely proud of, to say the least.

Members of the Schweinfurt resident agency. First row from left to right: Special Agent David Ownby, SAC Dick Miller, SAC Bad Kissingen BO Larry Meyers, and Special Agent Lynn Muelhmeyer. Second row from left to right: Special Agents Richard Basile, Fred Oliver from Bad Kissingen, and Special Agent Ronald Glunt. Third row from left to right: Special Agents Jack Hurley and David Thomas and Sergeant Alan Ladd, the military clerk, circa 1983.

# Taking a Break from the Hassle

Fitzsimons US Army Hospital

Aurora, Colorado

*A different pace for the same endeavor*

$\mathcal{M}$y drive in late February 1985 to Fitzsimons from Indiana took two days. I stayed overnight in Manhattan, Kansas, located just outside Fort Riley, where I had been stationed before my assignment to Germany. The next day, I decided to go straight to Fort Carson instead of Fitzsimons so I could meet with the operations officer, Merl Kuhlman. The day I met with Chief Kuhlman, he took me to lunch. I noticed that he had not changed since our Fort Riley days in the late 1970s. Chief Kuhlman had an assignment as the federal liaison officer (FLO) at CID headquarters between his tour at Fort Riley and Fort Carson. In the FLO assignment, he had the opportunity to travel with the deputy CID commander on trips abroad. One of those trips took him to my office in Schweinfurt, where I could brief him on the accomplishments and achievements of the unit and catch up on what we had been doing since Fort Riley.

During lunch, I asked for any information he could give me about the overall operation at the Fitzsimons branch office; he knew of no specific problems with the office or its operation. He told me I would be taking the place of CW2 Lee Farrell, who was being reassigned. We would have only a week or two of overlap before his departure, which would be plenty of time to get a handle of any issues. I left our meeting feeling good about the assignment, but I still had an uneasy thought lingering in the back of my mind about whether I should have taken the SAC job at such a small installation as Fitzsimons. *Water under the bridge*, I thought. I did accept it, and whatever the outcome, I was stuck with it.

Late on the afternoon of February 27, 1985, I arrived in Aurora, Colorado, checked into a hotel room, and called the Fitzsimons CID office. Special Agent Roy Jeffries answered the phone, and we agreed to meet the following morning for breakfast at my hotel. I spent the evening eating a leisurely dinner at the hotel restaurant and turned in early. As scheduled, Special Agent Jeffries met me for breakfast.

When we shook hands, I observed that he was taller than I, possibly over six feet in height, lean, had a full crop of black hair; and a good-looking sort of fellow. He had a pleasant manner about him, looked good in eyeglasses, and was immaculately dressed in plaid sports coat and brown slacks. He was polite and soft-spoken and did not try to hold back when talking. Immediately, I could tell he was curious and anxious to find out what type of person I was.

"Where is Farrell?" I asked.

Immediately after asking the question, I realized that Chief Kuhlman and I never discussed Farrell when we met for lunch the day before.

"He is on leave and will not be back for few days," Jeffries replied.

"How long have you been assigned to Fitzsimons?" I asked.

"Over a year," he responded.

"What is the caseload at Fitzsimons?"

"It is not bad; I have six cases I am working on now. I don't know how many cases Farrell has," he added.

"What type of cases are you working on?"

"Just about everything from larcenies, fraud, to theft of hospital equipment. However, we just got through investigating the suicide of the daughter of a CW2 medical officer. She shot herself in her bedroom a few months-ago."

Knowing that Fitzsimons's area of responsibility covered all northern Colorado and the entire states of Wyoming and Montana, I asked Special Agent Jeffries, "How much traveling are you doing?"

"A few leads in Colorado, but I have not had to go anywhere else yet," he said.

Finishing my breakfast, I said, "Let's go see where I am going to be working."

Fitzsimons Army Medical Center was founded by the US Army during World War I arising from the need to treat the large number of casualties from chemical weapons in Europe. Denver's reputation as a prime location for the treatment of tuberculosis led local citizens to lobby the Army on behalf of Denver as the site for the new hospital. Army Hospital 21, as it was first called, was formally dedicated in the autumn of 1918 in Aurora, which at the time had a population of less than 1,000. In July 1920, the facility was formally renamed the Fitzsimons Army Hospital after LT. William T. Fitzsimons, the first American medical officer killed in World War I. A new main building, known as Building 500, was built in 1941. At the time, it was the largest structure in Colorado.[109]

Special Agent Jeffries gave me a tour of our office. The CID suite of offices was comprised of three rooms at the end of a two-story wooden structure, dating possibility back to the 1940s. One room was designated for the SAC and one for an agent. The middle room was used for a waiting area. The rest of the first floor housed the MP station, manned mostly by Department of Defense police officers, a force of four civilian MPIs. The offices of the provost marshal, Major Michael Pierce,[110] and his staff occupied most of the second floor with two Defense Criminal Investigative Service (DCIS) special agents occupying a small office just above our suite of offices at the end of the building. The building was located down the street from the main US Army hospital at Fitzsimons. This hospital served, at the time, all active duty and retirees for an eight-state area. Fort Carson, located about seventy-five miles down I-25, had a clinic, but no hospital.

I spent a couple of hours learning the layout of the buildings at Fitzsimons. The base was unique in that it was entirely fenced in. There were three gates—the main gate just off East Colfax Avenue, a second one on the west side near Stapleton International Airport, and a third gate on the east side of the installation.

My first day at work was spent reviewing four case files that Special Agent Farrell was currently investigating. There was nothing unusual about any of them, and they all looked pretty much overcooked and were ready to be closed. I dug into the closed case files that had not yet been sent to Fort Carson to get a feel for what the office had been involved with. One thing I noticed was that there were no crime prevention surveys that had been conducted in the last year. I considered this an area that needed further attention.

The people responsible for typing our investigative reports were located at Fort Carson. Once a case was initiated, the agent picking up the case would call in the information to the chief word-processing specialist, usually Mrs. Brickley, who had been with the CID for many years. At the time of my arrival, there were two special agents assigned to the CID branch office at Fitzsimons—Farrell and Jeffries. Farrell left only a couple of weeks after my arrival, leaving only Special Agent Jeffries and me.

On April 1, 1985, a few weeks after taking over as special agent in charge of the Fitzsimons branch office, I was promoted to CW3. I was in an office with only two authorized special agent slots and no administrative support. In my previous assignment, I was a CW2 and at times I had up to ten special agents, three military clerks, two German criminal investigators, and several MPs were working for me. This was the US Army, however.

The caseload was low during my tenure at Fitzsimons. I never had more than six or seven investigations ongoing at any one time. I knew a week into my assignment that I had made a bad choice in coming to Fitzsimons. The assignment was better suited for someone who was ready to retire. If I had it all to do over again, I would have chosen Fort Bragg, where I could have continued developing my investigative skills and had more chances to hone my management techniques for preparation to become an operations officer.

The cases at Fitzsimons were usually routine: thefts, larcenies, and missing property, all related to Fitzsimons US Army hospital property. There were virtually no assaults or violent crimes, although there were a couple of incidents of that nature during my tenure. But, the first investigation I recall at Fitzsimons was a crime prevention survey that I initiated involving the compliance of performance by a janitorial company hired by the Directorate of Industrial Operations (DIO). As I recalled, the crime prevention survey was part of a schedule to check out several of the contracts being administered at that time by the DIO. I had obtained a list of current cleaning contracts and decided that the one costing Fitzsimons the most money would be the one I should look at first. I called my investigation the Case of the Shortcut Janitor. The circumstances surrounding this investigation are covered in the following narrative:

## THE CASE OF THE SHORTCUT JANITOR
There is nothing more unethical than taking money not earned

Early in April 1985, I initiated a crime prevention survey on a janitorial company from Denver, Colorado. One of the most frustrating aspects of being a US Army special agent back in the 1980s was conducting a comprehensive crime prevention survey where the findings revealed several indicators or actions by contracting companies wherein they received pay without question for incomplete work. The checks and balances were in place, but the US Army at that time just did not pursue action against fraud, waste, and abuse—and we had plenty of that in the day. I selected the Ajax Janitorial Services of Denver,[111] not for any real suspicions that the company might be doing something contrary to the contract but because it was one of the highest-cost cleaning contracts to Fitzsimons. The Fitzsimons DIO was paying almost one million dollars per year for routine cleaning of a series of buildings on the installation.

My survey into the performance standards of the cleaning contract disclosed that the company was supposed to vacuum the carpets and wash the windows once a week and empty the wastebaskets daily in seven World War II–era type wooden buildings. I found that these tasks were not being completed by the Ajax Janitorial Services. My information came from interviews with the occupants of the buildings. When interviewed, some told me that, at the end of the day, they had to empty their own wastebaskets and that they had never seen the company clean the windows or vacuum the floors. My investigation found that most of the floors in the buildings did not even have carpeting. A lot of the windows had so much dirt and so many smudges on them that you could not see out the windows. Each task not completed had a price value written into the contract, the cost of nonperformance of work (larceny of services) by the subject company was estimated to be more than $100,000.

When I presented my completed report to the DIO chief, a US Army colonel, he took about five minutes to review it and then said it was "hogwash."

"How can you say that, sir?" I said incredulously.

"Well, for starters, it would take so much time to do all of the work that we [meaning the US Army] would pay much more money than needed."

"Then why put the price-per-job description into the written contract?" I fired back.

"We needed a basis of work for Ajax to do the job."

Confused at what the colonel was trying to tell me, I asked him to clarify his comment.

"The contract is a standard service contract that if the service is not performed, we do not pay them," he said.

I had to remind him that my investigation disclosed that the janitorial company invoiced for the services that were never performed.

"It all balances out in the end," the colonel barked.

I departed the meeting with the DIO colonel without assurances from him that he was going to do anything about it.

There was another case that may have been time wasted because of inaction by the proper people to do something about a problem that was clearly brought to their attention.

Although the work at Fitzsimons was low-key and slow paced, we did have a variety of very unusually weird investigations. I recall a few of the particularly interesting investigations—one involving a psychiatric patient hopping a ride with a woman that was leaving the hospital building at Fitzsimons. I called this incident the Case of the Crazy and Bored Soldier:

## THE CASE OF THE CRAZY AND BORED SOLDIER
People who are receiving psychiatric and psychological counseling should be treated with caution

It was a warm, breezy day in April 1985 at about 2:00 p.m., and I had just returned from a late lunch at one of the off-post restaurants in the area and had just worked up enough energy to motivate myself to write a long-overdue case that had been sitting around for way too long, when I received a call from the Fitzsimons MP desk reporting that a patient had escaped from the psych ward.

The man, Frederick L. Swan,[112] from a unit at Fort Carson, had been sent to the Fitzsimons US Army hospital for a psych evaluation about two days prior. He was last seen about noon, two hours earlier, by an orderly who had brought lunch to his room. I asked the MP desk sergeant for the essential details on Swan, but no one knew the real reason why he was being held in the psych ward. I gathered a notepad and headed for the psych ward to talk with the head nurse.

The Fitzsimons psych ward was located a short distance from the CID office on the same block. I parked the CID sedan, walked the short distance across the parking lot to the reception area, and found the chief psychiatric nurse—a heavyset, middle-aged civilian woman—manning the phones. As I stood almost directly in front of her, she did not bother to look up when I showed her my CID credentials. Other nurses and hospital employees were scurrying around the floor as if they were getting ready for a VIP to show up, which obviously was not me. I stood there for another five minutes before she hung up the phone and acknowledged my presence.

"What do you want?" she said.

"I am Special Agent Dick Miller. I received a call that one of your patients is missing."

"That's right; his name is Frederick Swan, and he was here for a psych evaluation, sent up from Fort Carson," she said.

"What rank is Swan?" I asked.

"Our record shows he is SP4."

"What was he sent here to be evaluated for?" I inquired.

"He had some disciplinary problems and would not follow orders."

*That doesn't sound like much of a psychiatric problem as much as a pure military disciplinary issue*, I thought. "When was the last time you or any of your staff saw him?" I asked.

"One of the orderlies gave him his food tray." She momentarily looked at her wristwatch and then back to me. "It was around noon today," she said.

"Was Swan prone to be violent in any way?" I asked.

The chief nurse nodded and said, "He could be, but he did not display any violent temper while he has been here."

"How long has he been a patient here?"

"Two days, and he was sent to us from Fort Carson, like I said earlier."

Digging deeper and trying to get details of Swan's overall character, I asked, "How restricted were his movements in the psych ward?"

"He was housed in his room, for the most part, but allowed to mingle with the general patient population in the dayroom under supervision of medical staff," she said.

"Had anyone visited him since he has been a patient?"

"Not to my recollection."

"Is there anyone else I can talk to on your staff that had more frequent contact with Swan?"

"Yes. The orderlies."

"Can I have a little bit of their time?" I asked.

"Yes." Then, using the intercom system behind the reception desk, she asked for Ed Blakely.[113]

A stout-looking man in his late thirties with a full head of brown hair, a full beard, a mustache, and a wide smile approached me where I was standing near the reception desk. He was obviously a civilian employee. "Hi, I am Blakely. They told me you wanted to see me."

"Can we go somewhere where it is not so crowded?" I asked.

"Sure. Follow me." He immediately started walking down a hallway until he came to an isolated office, and then he ushered me inside and shut the door. There were two metal straight-back chairs; Blakely took one and motioned for me to take the other.

I started out showing him my credentials and summarizing the reason for my visit and launched directly into questions about how much he knew about Swan. "How frequently did you have contact with Swan?"

"He was what you would call a minimum-risk patient, but still restricted to the floor where his room was located," Blakely said.

He hadn't answered my question, so I asked him again. "How much was your interaction with Swan in the two days he has been here?"

"Well, I am responsible for bringing him his food three times a day on my shift and ensuring he takes his meds. I also escorted him to and from meetings with his doctor and made sure he was in his room."

"How many meetings with the doctor did he attend in the two days he has been here?" I asked.

"I believe twice—once a day; the meetings are usually in the mornings," Blakely said.

"When was the last time you saw Swan?"

"It was around noon, when I brought him his lunch meal."

"Was he locked in his room when not supervised?"

"As I said before, he was considered a low-risk patient, so his room was not required to be routinely locked."

"Do you often have patients leaving the building without permission?"

"No. Most of our active-duty patients are here for a psych eval prior to getting discharged. Others, the older ones—usually retirees and some veterans—are suffering for dementia or Alzheimer's," he explained, adding, "I have been here for more than five years, and I recall only a few real nutcases where we had to confine them, and they were mostly older people."

"Mr. Blakely, did Swan have any visitors while here, and are you aware if he had a car or access to other transportation?"

"No, I believe he was brought here after seeing an intake person over at the main hospital."

"So, is it possible that he drove up here from Fort Carson?"

"I don't think so, because his commander directed he get a psych eval, but then again, he may have had a car, but it is not in the parking lot."

"Okay, thanks for your time. Can you direct me to the doctor that he was seeing while here?"

"Yes, Dr. Lynn;" said Mr. Blakely.

I followed him down another hallway, and we stopped at an office door, which was closed. The name on the door was Dr. Ralph Lynn.[114] Dr. Lynn was apparently busy with a patient, so I left a message at the desk for him to call me at his earliest convenience.

I was unsure just how much I was going to get involved with locating the missing patient. I felt it was more of an MP or unit issue than a CID case—unless, of course Swan committed a crime. Then what the incident involved would determine if CID became involved or not.

I went back to my office and briefed the PMO, Major Pierce, on the missing patient, and I informed him that I did not think the matter fell into CID purview. I also advised Pierce that the preview might lie with his unit. I told Pierce that all of it was contingent upon whether Swan committed a crime while roaming throughout the community.

This incident came to a successful close when a female employee walked into the psych ward accompanied by SP4 Swan. The story that she told explained SP4 Swan's disappearance. Apparently, he was anxious to leave the psych ward, so after he ate his lunch, he left his room and wandered the hallways. Since no one was paying attention to him, he walked outside and saw the windows on a car were rolled down. He let himself into the car and lay down on the floorboard of the backseat of the female employee's car. About three that afternoon, the female employee's shift ended, and she got into her car, apparently not seeing SP4 Swan, to drive home.

As she was traveling down Highway 225 outside of Denver, SP4 Swan rose from his crouched position behind her seat and asked her where she was going.

Startled, the female employee slowed down and pulled off to the side of the road. "What are you doing in my car?" She calmly asked SP4 Swan.

He told her he was a patient at the psych ward and was bored and wanted to go back to Fort Carson.

"Well, I am not going that far, but I will take you back to the hospital," she told SP4 Swan.

SP4 Swan made no attempt to restrain or prevent her from turning around and taking him back to the hospital. It was a good thing that SP4 Swan was not violent. Still, I'll bet the female employee's degree of fear was running high when she discovered SP4 Swan in the backseat. Factors playing a favorable role in the successful conclusion of this incident were that SP4 Swan was not delusional or suffering from a severe mental illness, combined with the female employee's own calm and cool reaction at finding him in her car. This resulted in her ability to get him back to the psych ward without incident.

I interviewed SP4 Swan a short time after he was returned to the psych ward and asked him what his intentions were when he got into the female employee's car.

"I was bored with doing nothing in the hospital and wanted a quick way to get back to Fort Carson. I knew the woman was probably not going all the way to Carson, but when I tapped her on her shoulder, I was letting her know that I wanted out of the car. I was going to hitch a ride the rest of the way. I had no intent of harming her," he said.

I ran the incident by Colonel Toucher, SJA, who indicated there was no real crime that had been committed. After I got some assurance from SP4 Swan that he was not going to jump in any more cars, I released him to the hospital, and there were no other incidents.

Another off-kilter incident, involving the wife of a retired former US Army colonel SJA officer (deceased), was initiated. I considered this case one of the most memorable investigations while at Fitzsimons. The following narrative details the circumstances surrounding the wife's allegations about the CIA. I called this matter the Case of the Snake Egg Torture of a Woman by the CIA:

## THE CASE OF THE SNAKE EGG TORTURE OF A WOMAN BY THE CIA
People will report just about anything, truth or fiction

I was in my office writing a report one day in early April 1985 when I got a most unusual phone call from the wife of a deceased retired US Army SJA colonel. The woman's voice was calm, and she spoke deliberately, sounding very normal and not rushed. She politely introduced herself as Sally Wallace.[115] The following story she related was anything but normal. She initially made small talk about her ties with the US Army and how she enjoyed traveling with her husband, a colonel and former SJA officer who had died a few years earlier. Not wanting to make her angry or to cut her short, I asked, "What do you need, Mrs. Wallace?"

She indicated she'd called me to report some happenings that had occurred in the last few weeks that I should investigate. She started her story by telling me she had met a group of people at a party about six months earlier. They were all nice people, she said, and she enjoyed repeated visits with them. She indicated that about a month earlier, she'd started waking up with bad headaches and a funny sensation in her head.

"I get these headaches and feelings in my head after I meet with the group of people," she said. The headaches always occurred when she woke up on the morning after the get-togethers.

"Mrs. Wallace, why are you calling me about your situation? It sounds like you need to go see a doctor about you condition," I told her.

"That is what I am trying to tell you," she said. "I can't go see a doctor, because they would find out about it. They told me that I could not tell anyone about my condition," she said.

"Mrs. Wallace, you are not making any sense. Can you please be more specific about why you are calling me?" I urged.

She responded by saying, "The group of people have told me they work for a very secret organization and they monitor people."

"What do you mean by monitoring people?" I asked.

Rambling on, she said, "They check them out to ensure they don't talk about the secret organization they are involved in."

"What do this secret organization and your headaches have in common?" I asked.

"Well, the group of people told me that one night shortly after I met them, they gave me a sedative that put me to sleep. While asleep, they implanted snake eggs inside my head, and every time I tell a lie, one of the eggs hatches, and tiny little creatures eat away at my brain."

"They what?" I asked.

"The snake eggs hatch inside my head. That is what has been causing me to have headaches when I wake up. The sensation I am feeling is the little baby snakes coming from the eggs crawling around inside of me."

I did not know what to do at this point, but it became obvious to me that Mrs. Wallace was delusional and paranoid. "Mrs. Wallace, would you do me a favor and go see a doctor about your headaches? Tell the doctor what you think is causing your pain, okay?"

"I can't, because the group of people will find out. I think they work for the CIA, and I am not the only one they have implanted snake eggs into."

"What makes you think that I can help you in any way?" I asked.

"You guys always helped my husband when he needed it; I thought that your office would be the best place to contact. Besides, don't the CID have special investigators to coordinate these types of investigations?"

"I'll tell you, Mrs. Wallace, before we can investigate your situation, I need you to be checked out by a doctor first, to verify your condition. Can you help me by doing that?" I asked her. "As soon as the doctor checks your condition and gives you a report, you can call me back, and we'll see where we go from there, okay?"

"All right, I will do as you ask, but I hope the group of people that did this to me does not find out," she said.

"I'll talk to you later, Mrs. Wallace."

After wishing her the best and encouraging her to be careful, I hung up. I figured that if Mrs. Wallace did what I'd suggested, then the doctor would obviously see that she was delusional and probably a little paranoid as well. The doctor would know what to do with her.

Since Mrs. Wallace claimed to have been the wife of a former SJA officer, I decided to follow up with a little investigation of her to see if I could verify anything about her background. My first step was to check with Colonel Patrick Toucher, the Fitzsimons SJA, and determine if he had heard of Mrs. Wallace or at least if he knew something about her husband. I called Colonel Toucher and made an appointment with him for the following morning.

I met with Colonel Toucher, who had done a little research after he received my phone call the previous afternoon. "Dick, I found out that several years ago, Colonel Samuel Wallace[116] was the SJA here at Fitzsimons. I called a couple of my associates within the SJA and found that Colonel Wallace died in 1980 of cancer. His wife never got over his death and was thought to have been in failing health the last few years. That is about all the information I could muster up for you."

"That is plenty, sir," I told him.

We left it that way.

My call from Mrs. Wallace was received in April 1985. I left Fitzsimons on October 6, 1986, and I never heard from her again. Hopefully, she did see a doctor and told him the story she had related to me. This obviously would give the doctor a clue that not everything was right about Mrs. Wallace. I hoped that the doctor could get her some treatment that rid her of the snakes and snake eggs from her head.

In April 1985, Fort Carson was hit hard with several TDY assignments, and it did not take long for the leadership to start focusing their search for qualified individuals to fill the ranks at Fitzsimons. In April 1985, I received a phone call from Fort Carson advising me that I had been selected for a four-day TDY trip to Orange County, California, to support an overnight stay of Secretary of the Army John O. Marsh and his wife. The trip required me to depart on a Monday morning from Denver so I could arrive in Los Angeles about noon. Since the notification of the mission was received on Thursday afternoon, that left only Friday to make all the arrangements. Although I did not know it, I would keep the travel office lady at the post finance office extremely busy for the months of April and May 1985. Arrangements for the flight went off without a glitch.

I spent the weekend before the trip catching up on paperwork and talking to newly arrived Special Agent Christopher Capshaw who had replaced Dewald. Dewald had been appointed to warrant office and reassigned because the Fitzsimons CID office did not have an authorization for two warrants. Capshaw, who was an exceptionally talented special agent and his lovely wife, Becky, became two very close friends during our assignments at Fitzsimons. He assured me that he would keep everything under control and advised me to forget about Fitzsimons while on the trip.

I caught a Southwest flight out of Stapleton International Airport for a two-hour flight to Los Angeles. I obtained a rental car at the Los Angeles International Airport and drove to the hotel in Newport Beach, California, where I met the other special agents working on the mission.

We were briefed by the agent in charge from PSA in Washington, DC. She was the only permanently assigned special agent from PSA, and the remaining four were support agents like I was. She informed us that on the evening of Wednesday at about 7:00 p.m., Secretary of the Army John O. Marsh and his wife were due to land at Marine Corps Air Station El Toro. Our job would be to escort the secretary and his wife to their hotel, where they would stay the night. The secretary had a scheduled speech the following morning to a group of people who were involved in the President's Council on Physical Fitness and Sports. Once the speech was over, we were responsible for getting him back to Marine Corps Air Station El Toro for a flight to Japan. A simple overnighter, you would think; however, things do not always go as planned.

With the special agent in charge and five support agents in tow, one of whom grew up in the local area of Newport Beach, California, we set out to recon the best route from Marine Corps Air Station El Toro to the Meridian. We spent about two hours advancing the site of arrival to the hotel. The distance between the base and Newport Beach was approximately thirteen miles with a drive time of about twenty minutes in light traffic. Since it would be early evening when the party arrived, that would mean lighter traffic, which would make our trip faster. After our two-hour recon, the decision was made to take the secretary from Marine Corps Air Station El Toro to Interstate 5 and then turn right onto Interstate 405 to Newport Boulevard, and then turn left to downtown Newport Beach, ultimately arriving at the Meridian Hotel within thirty minutes. I had a concern that we needed more time to ensure that everyone knew the route, and we had two days before the secretary was due to arrive, but no further route recon was considered. The driver chosen for the secretary's car was the special agent who grew up in the area, so this lessened the concern that no further route recons were needed. Events of that momentous night are covered in the following narrative that I call the Incident at El Toro That Altered the Way CID Protects the Secretary of the Army:

## THE INCIDENT AT EL TORO
## THAT ALTERED THE WAY CID PROTECTS THE
## SECRETARY OF THE ARMY
Being too confident can lead to incompetence

Murphy's law catches you every time. We all assembled at Marine Corps Air Station El Toro on the tarmac thirty minutes prior to Secretary Marsh's arrival. The hometown special agent was driving the secretary's car, and I was assigned the position as driver of the chase car, with one other agent in the front seat, while another agent used his car to haul the baggage.

The secretary's C-20A Gulfstream, landed at El Toro at 7:00 p.m., precisely on time, a characteristic trait for US Air Force pilots. Secretary and Mrs. Marsh, followed by military assistants, exited the Gulfstream. The secretary and Mrs. Marsh walked directly to the car provided for them, and the two military aides hopped in the backseat of the chase car. The two cars immediately began the thirty-minute drive to the Hotel, while a third car secured the party's baggage. The small motorcade was traveling smoothly up until the secretary's car sped past the turn onto Interstate 405. I recall that the agent riding in the front seat with me commented in a low, almost inaudible voice, "We missed our turn."

The secretary's aides in the backseat of my car heard the comment, however. "Hey, you guys should have prevented the motorcade from missing the turn back there," the LTC said, concerned.

"We are not directing the motorcade; something must have changed that caused us to go past the turn," I said.

Seconds later, my comment proved pointless. Radio communication was almost immediately received from the personal security officer riding in the front seat of the secretary's car. "Is there another road that we can turn onto to get back to Interstate 405?" the agent pleaded with a sense of urgency.

"Unknown!" responded the agent in the chase car. Then a short distance past the turn, the secretary's car pulled off onto the shoulder and stopped. For a few seconds, the secretary's car rocked from one side to the next, and then suddenly the secretary exited the car, obviously not in a good mood. The agent riding in the front seat of the secretary's car also got out of the vehicle, and words were exchanged between the two. Then the two military aides left the chase car to join the secretary, who was apparently extremely upset that the driver of his car had missed the turn. I overheard the secretary yell to the two aides, "You are in charge!" A couple of tense minutes passed, when I suggested that we just turn the motorcade around and return to the turn that we missed. Everyone stopped in their tracks and realized that was the right thing to do at this point. Everyone got back in their respective cars, and the motorcade turned around. This time, we were successful in making the correct turn, and we arrived at the Meridian Hotel about five minutes later than planned, without further incident.

About thirty minutes after getting the secretary, his wife, and aides settled in their rooms, the PSA team met in the control room that had been set up and maintained by the fifth agent. The lead agent from PSA informed us that she had already contracted Special Agent Gene Hicks, chief of PSA, and briefed him on the incident. She did not elaborate on what he had advised her, but the issue was more than likely addressed at that level. The PSA agent did confide in us that as she was riding up the elevator with the secretary and his wife to escort them to their room, a comment was made by the secretary's wife to suggest that actions like the one that occurred could lead to someone losing his or her job. There was nothing more said about the incident on our mission.

The next morning, the speech after breakfast by the secretary and the trip back to Marine Corps Air Station El Toro went off without a hitch.

A few weeks later, after I had returned to Fitzsimons and things had settled down, a message was received from CID headquarters informing all offices in the command that a new policy had been implemented concerning all future trips by the secretary of the army. The secretary had been assigned his own PSA special agent. In retrospect, I considered the incident at El Toro a minor glitch in an otherwise overwhelmingly routine, successful mission traditionally handled by the men and women of CID in protecting senior Pentagon officials.

On April 17, 1985, I was notified that I had been selected for attendance at a specialized school in hostage negotiations, given by the Federal Bureau of Investigation. I had little time to prepare, because the training commenced on April 22, 1985, and ran through April 26, 1985. I could get a flight from Denver to Washington, DC, to attend the weeklong course. The training was well worth the time.

Shortly after returning from the hostage negotiations school, I got permission to take a weekend off to fly to Houston to attend June's wedding. After I returned from that trip, it seemed that all I was doing was traveling and not getting any work done. I thought that my travel outside the office was finally finished and I could finally get back to work, but I again underestimated the workings of CID.

In May 1985, I was notified by Chief Kuhlman that I had been selected along with him to attend a weeklong conference in San Francisco on economic crimes. Again, the notice was very short, two days, but I arranged everything in time to catch a flight from Denver to San Francisco. As it ended up, Chief Kuhlman and I took the same flight. The weeklong conference was very good, and I brought some fresh information into my economic crime program that I retained and used for years to come. The months of April and May 1985 were, to say the least, very busy outside of the office.

It was early June 1985, and I had been back to work for only a week or two when I received a call from Mary Bryant,[117] the wife of a science professor at the University of Colorado at Boulder. Mary wanted to report that she suspected her husband was spying for a foreign country. She wanted to meet with me to provide details of her suspicions. I agreed to meet with Mary the following Wednesday at 10:00 a.m. Since she did not want to come to my office at the Fitzsimons US Army base, I let her choose the location. She decided that we would meet at an outdoor shopping area in downtown Boulder in front of an old bookstore. We exchanged enough information to be able to recognize one another. She told me she would be wearing a red scarf around her neck and a brown coat. I told her that I would be wearing a blue suit with a reddish tie. I called this incident the Case of the Wife Who Thought Her Husband Was a Spy:

## THE CASE OF THE WIFE WHO THOUGHT HER HUSBAND WAS A SPY
Don't believe everything you are told

About 8:45 a.m. on a Wednesday, I drove to Boulder, about forty miles north of Denver, to meet with Mary Bryant. She had called two days before to report she suspected that her husband was a spy for a foreign country. The drive took me about an hour on Highway 36, through the small cities of Westminster and Broomfield, Colorado. I arrived about fifteen minutes prior to our scheduled meeting at 10:00 a.m. I parked my car and walked about a block to the location Mary Bryant chose. I had no trouble recognizing a woman with a red scarf and brown coat sitting at an outside table close to a coffee shop next to a bookstore specializing in older books. She had already purchased herself a cup of coffee.

When I approached, she asked, "Are you Mr. Miller from the army CID?"

"Yes, I am."

She invited me to sit down. Knowing that if this woman had real information that could lead to an investigation into espionage, any information she provided would have to be turned over the military intelligence (MI) folks because it was their jurisdiction, unless there was a crime within the purview of CID identified. Then both agencies would have to sort out who would take the lead or whether the subsequent investigation would be conducted jointly, which I highly doubted, because of the rivalry between the two units.

I sat down and showed her my CID credentials, and she extended her right hand to shake mine to formerly introduce herself as Mary Bryant. Bryant stated she first suspected her husband, whom she identified as Kral Bryant,[118] a mathematician and scientist at the University of Colorado at Boulder, of spying when he returned from a business trip about three months earlier. Her suspicions were fueled by his story that he had traveled to New York City to meet with some fellow academics. However, following his almost weeklong trip, she helped him unpack and discovered a notepad in his jacket pocket that had directions to the Russian consulate.

"This does not necessarily mean your husband is spying," I responded to Mrs. Bryant.

"But he told me he was seeing some of his colleagues, and I am sure that none of them are Russians," she pointed out.

"Is your husband conducting any classified research for the university?" I asked.

"I suspect that he had or is doing some classified stuff, but I don't actually know because he never talks with me about what he does," she explained. "Since that first visit to New York, he has gone on two other trips," she informed me. "He has been taking trips more, and I halfway expect that he might be seeing another woman, but he has denied it."

I suspected that the good old professor might be seeing another woman, but then again, if he was, that would be none of the military's business. I took her information down and told her someone would check back with her later. Seeing that there was no clear-cut CID jurisdiction in this matter, I had already made my mind to let the military intelligence at Fort Carson to look at her story. I thanked her and returned to the CID office at Fitzsimons. Once I got back to the office, I looked over my notes and did a background check on Kral Bryant but found no record. I prepared a report and drove it down to Fort Carson the next day. I briefed Chief Kuhlman, and he concurred that what we had required no further involvement with the CID and to refer the matter to military intelligence. I accomplished the motto "do what needs to be done."

Time was going fast for me at Fitzsimons. I could not wait to get back to Germany to be with Elda. More imminent was anticipating her arrival for a month in early June 1985. I thought I would coordinate a trip for Chris to come out also and be with us for that month. I set the plan into motion and obtained Melitta's permission. It would be a good month for us.

I kept myself busy during the rest of May 1985 with the many various criminal investigations that came into the office. I got a taste of the road travel required while at Fitzsimons due to the enormous size of the area of responsibility for the office. Our jurisdiction covered northern Colorado and all of Montana and Wyoming. There were several leads from other CID offices around the country that I had to investigate. I divided them between Dale and me, and we accomplished some together. There were a few theft cases that fell into CID's purview that occurred at Fitzsimons, most of which we solved.

On June 1, 1985, Elda flew in from Germany; a few days prior, I had taken a three-day weekend to drive to Terre Haute to pick up Chris and bring him back to Colorado for a month. Chris, Elda, and I spent time sightseeing in the Rocky Mountains and the surrounding cities of Idaho Springs, Silver City, and Evergreen, and sites like Pikes Peak and Mount Evans. These cities and sites are some of the most beautiful areas in the United States. It was hard to say good-bye to them at the end of June. I noticed that Chris, who was now thirteen years old, had turned into a handsome young man, was quiet but polite, kind, and considerate to others. I hoped to arrange for him to stay in Germany with Elda and me when I returned soon.

When there are only two agents assigned to an office, a relationship between a special agent in charge and his or her sole subordinate becomes closer and more personal than in a larger office where you have many agents. You get to know each other better and tend to socialize a lot more. When two special agents work closely together, there is only one personality to deal with. This situation can also be detrimental, if one or even both agents do not get along well with each other. Later in my tour at Fitzsimons, I would experience the latter when a third agent was temporarily assigned; and from ground zero, he became a problem.

Special Agent Capshaw had the ability to work on his own; he always took the initiative and was a superlative interviewer. I wish our professional and personal contacts went beyond Fitzsimons, but I never saw him after I left. There was one memorable case that Chris initiated that led to the civilian arrest of two young criminals that stole money from an elderly, retired sergeant. I called the investigation the Case of Two Young Stupid Crooks Taking an Old Man's Money:

## THE CASE OF THE TWO STUPID CROOKS TAKING AN OLD MAN'S MONEY
Being young, selfish, and thoughtless never leads to a productive life

At the end of August 1985, Special Agent Chris Capshaw came into my office and briefed me on an interview he had just completed with an elderly retired sergeant. The matter involved an elderly retired sergeant we'll call James Goodwin.[119] Sergeant Goodwin, a citizen of Denver, called the CID office the previous day and talked to Chris about his problem. Apparently, two young thugs who resided in the same neighborhood as Sergeant Goodwin had been bullying him and stealing money from him each month when he cashed his retirement check. Sergeant Goodwin had a habit of cashing his US Army retirement check on the day that he received it at the Fitzsimons Credit Union. The two thugs found out about this practice and forced their presence on Sergeant Goodwin to hand over a portion of his retirement money.

Sergeant Goodwin informed Chris that this situation has been going on for the last six months. When asked by Chris why he had not reported the matter to police, Goodwin answered that he was afraid that the two would harm him in some way.

"They have been taking at least a third of his paycheck, sometimes upward of $400 a month," Chris advised.

"Damn, we need to do something about this and fast," I told Chris.

"It's already at the end of August, and he will receive his next retirement check in a couple of days," Chris said.

"This doesn't give us much time to coordinate and set up surveillance of Sergeant Goodwin. Could you talk to him and set up a time of day that he will bring his check to the credit union? By knowing the time, it will help us plan the operation," I told Chris.

As Chris started to leave my office to talk to Sergeant Goodwin, I stopped him. "You know, we have to set this thing up to go down on Fitzsimons so we can get the feds involved. When you set up a time for him to cash his check, measures must also be in place for the thugs to take his money while they are still at the credit union so we can catch them in the act on a federal reservation," I told Chris.

Chris got Sergeant Goodwin to agree to ensure that he would arrive at the Fitzsimons Credit Union at 11:30 a.m. on September 1, 1985, to cash his check. Chris advised Sergeant Goodwin to call him once his retirement check arrived to ensure that the planned operation would go down as planned. Sergeant Goodwin told Chris that the thugs would more than likely ride in his car to Fitzsimons, so they would have no trouble getting into the installation, because he had a retired military ID card.

"For this thing to work, we must witness the transaction, so as soon as the check is cashed, give them the amount they asked for," Chris told Sergeant Goodwin.

After Chris was convinced that Sergeant Goodwin understood what was needed, he drove him home. On their short car ride, Sergeant Goodwin pointed out to Chris the house where the thugs lived.

When Chris returned to the office, he briefed me on what Sergeant Goodwin had said and told me he could get the address of where the thugs resided. I instructed Chris to call Special Agent Jon Lipsky, Denver FBI, who was the liaison to Fitzsimons. Chris coordinated with FBI Special Agent Lipsky, who indicated it would not be a priority case for his office, but if it went down as planned, he would assume the case, take the two thugs into custody, and present the circumstances to the United States Attorney for consideration to prosecute. After Chris, had briefed me on his conversation with Lipsky, it got me to thinking about my past dealings with the FBI while assigned to Fort Sheridan. It was somewhat different, but still, their assistance was always welcome in any case involving civilians who committed crimes on an army base.

The day before the operation was to be set in motion, Chris coordinated with the president of the Fitzsimons Credit Union and provided him with enough details of what was suspected to happen the following day, September 1, 1985. Chris advised the president that once the operation commenced, his tellers must hide behind the counter, and any loan officers or other credit union employees, including himself, should shut their office doors. He agreed to fully cooperate. The president was advised that at 11:20 a.m., Chris and I would be set up inside, playing the roles of customers when Sergeant Goodwin walked in with the two young thugs. He was told that his staff was not to react to anything until Sergeant Goodwin received the money from his retirement check and the actual apprehension of the two began.

After Chris left the credit union, I joined him, and we briefed the Department of Defense (DOD) police on the operation. A DOD police detention team would be standing by to serve as a backup and to take custody of the two thugs once the apprehension was completed.

About 8:00 a.m. on September 1, 1985, Chris received a call from Sergeant Goodwin relating that he did receive his retirement check and would be at the Fitzsimons Credit Union at 11:30 a.m. as planned. About 11:00 a.m., Chris and I arrived at the lobby of the Fitzsimons Credit Union and went over last-minute details of the operation with the employees. About 11:20 a.m., all the employees assumed their positions as normal, and Chris and I pretended to be preparing documents for banking transactions.

At precisely 11:30 a.m., Sergeant Goodwin entered the Fitzsimons Credit Union accompanied by two scruffy-looking Hispanic young men and walked up to one of the tellers. Fortunately, except for Chris and me, who were standing at opposite sides of a counter in the middle of the lobby, there were no customers. Sergeant Goodwin signed his check in front of the teller and handed it to her. She counted out his money, thanked him, and wished him a good day. The two scruffy-looking characters were standing motionless behind Sergeant Goodwin.

Sergeant Goodwin turned and started walking toward the door and suddenly stopped. One of the youths got in front of Sergeant Goodwin, while the other remained to his rear. Sergeant Goodwin counted out some of the cash he'd received and handed it to the man standing in front. Immediately, Chris approached the man in front, and I hurriedly walked up to the man standing behind Sergeant Goodwin. Each was simultaneously apprehended and cuffed without incident. We walked the two outside into the arms of the waiting DOD detention team. The moment we walked out the door, I recognized a member of the Fitzsimons Public Affairs Office with a camera standing on the steps of the adjacent building.

*Damn, how did these guys find out what was happening?* I thought.

The offenders were released to the DOD detention team and taken to the MP station, pending the arrival of the FBI to take them into custody. Chris and I thanked the employees of the Fitzsimons Credit Union and went to debrief the DOD police. The offenders were later identified as two small-time crooks with misdemeanor records for petty theft, shoplifting, and simple assault. Hopefully, the US Attorney would see fit to prosecute the two on more serious charges of extortion and a variety of other related crimes. When I left Fitzsimons in October 1986, the US Attorney's Office in Denver had not yet brought the case to trial.

When I first arrived at Fitzsimons, I had rented a one-bedroom apartment not far from the installation. The lodging was considered adequate for what I needed. However, I now thought it was time to look at purchasing a house. I found a small, two-bedroom townhome on the Denver-Aurora border that was being built. I liked it, so when Elda visited in the summer of 1985, we decided to get the townhome. There were reasons for our decision to buy the townhome. In August 1985, there was a bill introduced in Congress that would constrain spending and balance the federal budget. Talk within the US Army circles disclosed that the bill, known as the Gramm-Rudman-Hollings Balanced Budget and Emergency Deficit Control Act of 1985, named for the US senators who sponsored the legislation, would delay all routine reassignments for up to a year. This meant that I faced the possibility that I would be at Fitzsimons for an additional year.

I moved into the new townhome in September 1985. I immediately noticed that the house was way too big to live in alone, so I did what most sensible people in my situation do: I got a dog. No, it was not a small dog but a large—very large—one. In late September 1985, I welcomed an Old English sheepdog, named Dog, to the family. She was to be a roommate for the foreseeable future. The next time Elda visited me in December 1985, Dog, although not very welcoming at the beginning, warmed up to her. Their friendship lasted for more than eleven years, and Dog became my loyal companion in

Elda's absence. After getting settled into the townhome and learning a routine with Dog, the work at Fitzsimons continued.

Another matter that my office tangled with involved a request for assistance from the Fort Hood CID office. It was October 1985; Fitzsimons was cold and snowy most of the month. Most of our work during that period involved requests for assistance from other offices. One of those requests for assistance came from Fort Hood, Texas. I called this investigation the Contractor That Gave CID Everything, but We Found Nothing:

## THE CASE OF THE CONTRACTOR THAT GAVE CID EVERYTHING, BUT WE FOUND NOTHING
You need legitimate, thoroughly detailed, and complete information for a lead

The agent from Fort Hood wanted my office to travel from Denver to Grand Junction, around 245 miles, a four-hour trip one way, to locate and search a civilian subcontractor's business and interview the owner, who was the main suspect in the larceny of thousands of dollars' worth of tools and equipment. The Fort Hood CID office did provide a list of stolen tools, equipment, and serial numbers and other identifying data, but I saw this as not being enough to accomplish what they wanted Fitzsimons to achieve.

To start with, the prime suspect was a civilian, we had no search warrant, and we had no real jurisdiction. And to top this off, we would not have any element of surprise to pull off the requested investigative activity. So, what did I do? I called the lead special agent to discuss the validity of such a lead. My call to the lead agent was not intended to mean I refused to honor the request for assistance but to strategize just what efforts we could come up with to make the investigation more practical. I terminated the call with the agent by asking him if he could come up with some more ideas on how we might proceed on the case, and he told me he would get back with me.

Well, he surely did get back with me by way of his operations officer calling my operations officer at Fort Carson to complain that I refused to conduct the lead as requested.

"Do you know you have really pissed off Fort Hood because of your refusal to conduct their lead?" Interim operations officer Hans Klossner said when he called and told me a couple of days after I had called the lead agent to discuss strategy.

In my defense, I tried, without much success, to explain that I had not rebuffed the Fort Hood agent but attempted to make the lead more practical. So, I was forced to proceed with the lead without further infusion from Fort Hood.

I came up with the best plan I could to call the Grand Junction Police Department and request their assistance—specifically, to find out if the subcontractor was still in business and if they had any record on the owner and suspect of the Fort Hood case.

My call yielded some information; the owner was still in business and running his business from home. He had a warehouse on his property, where tools, equipment, and other construction-related materials were stored. The Grand Junction Police Department had no criminal record on the owner and would offer logistics support once I got to town in the form of an interview room. But what they couldn't help me with was to tell me when the owner/contractor would be home. My thought process was simple; I did not want to drive four-plus hours and find out that the man was not available for an interview. If I called him before I left, he would have plenty of time to hide any stolen property if he had it. Boy, what a kneejerk case this was going to be.

On October 10, 1985, I gassed up the good old Plymouth CID sedan and headed out for Grand Junction. The weather was pretty—dark blue skies, sunny with no clouds, somewhat chilly with a temperature in the low sixties. The weather remained sunny with blue skies until I drove through the Eisenhower Tunnel, about fifty-seven miles from Denver. On the other side of the tunnel, the weather took a turn for the worse. The temperature fell dramatically, it started snowing, and the driving conditions became icy and dangerous. I had no choice but to turn around and head back to the CID office. If I would have continued driving, I would have slid off the road. So, I found a hotel for the night. The subcontractor investigation would have to wait another day.

My duties and responsibilities at the Fitzsimons CID office became more intense in October and early November 1985 due to an increase in criminal investigations. It was the usual bunch of routine matters, such as thefts, break-ins, and one report of doctor mistreatment. The doctor mistreatment was unfounded, but my time was spent cleaning up the rest of the investigations. Efforts to plan the trip to Grand Junction to complete the Fort Hood lead fell on the back burner. Because of the increase in investigations, I decided to send Special Agent Chris Capshaw to Grand Junction. Chris did not want to spend a whole day on the road for an effort that probably would not result in anything worthwhile. Unfortunately, the lead had to be completed, and the quicker the better.

Chris decided to tackle the lead on a Thursday, so if he ran into any problems, he would have another day to complete any unexpected investigation before the weekend. The morning of October 24, 1985, Chris took off down the road toward Grand Junction. I received a call from him at about 8:00 that evening at my home to report he was back and the lead accomplished.

"How did it go?" I asked.

"Well, about the way you said it would," he said.

"Give me the details tomorrow," I told him before hanging up. I knew Chris was at home and wanted to wind down after the long and arduous trip he had just finished.

Chris and I both arrived about the same time the following morning. It was 8:00 a.m., and I had beaten him in by only a few minutes. I had not yet gotten my first cup of coffee when he came into my office.

"The trip to Grand Junction was a waste of time. I did meet with the owner of the firm that contractor who worked on a job at Fort Hood". Capshaw related. He consented to be interviewed and provided absolutely no information that would suggest he had taken any tools, equipment, or other property back to Grand Junction with him when he finished the job at Fort Hood. He also consented to let me search the warehouse located next to his home. I did not find any property that I could match to the list of serial numbers Fort Hood provided us," he explained.

"Wrap up your report and get it off to Fort Hood, and let's say good-bye to that baby," I told him.

In December 1985, I had to go to Cheyenne, Wyoming, to conduct an interview. Linda Crawford,[120] aged eighteen, who had recently moved there from Fort Lewis, was a victim of a sexual assault by her stepfather, SFC James L. Malloy.[121] The interview had been requested by the Fort Lewis, Washington, CID, who had initiated a case based on a complaint made by Crawford's mother and the wife of SFC Malloy. Crawford had left Fort Lewis to get away from SFC Malloy before the complaint was made. She was now living with her boyfriend, a former soldier at the installation, who had been discharged and returned to his home in Cheyenne. I called this investigation the Case of the Newlywed Victim of Sexual Assault. This investigation was not memorable for what had happened, but it took three days to complete because of bad weather. The Colorado and Wyoming weather can be intimidating. In the winter, you can wake up to sunny blue skies, and by afternoon, a blizzard is covering the ground. To the best of my recall, the details of that trip and interview are described in the following narrative:

## THE CASE OF THE NEWLYWED VICTIM OF SEXUAL ASSAULT
A girl should not have to suffer for her mother's choice of men

I received a request for assistance from the Fort Lewis CID office to locate and interview Linda Crawford as a victim of sexual assault. Her mother reported to the Fort Lewis CID office that her husband, SFC James L. Malloy, assigned to a support unit at the installation, was suspected of sexually assaulting Linda when she was a teenager living with the family at Fort Lewis. Crawford left Fort Lewis before she could be interviewed and joined her boyfriend, who had been a soldier there, in Cheyenne. The lead provided a phone number and address, but when I repeatedly called, no one answered. So, the next step was for me to drive to Cheyenne and attempt to locate her at the address.

About 8:00 one morning about five days after receiving the lead from Fort Lewis, I gassed up the CID sedan and headed for Cheyenne, about ninety miles away. The weather on this day was overcast, and the clouds were dark and ominous looking. This was in the days before GPS, so I had to depend on the good old ADC maps. The drive took me about an hour and a half up Interstate 25. This was my first trip to Cheyenne, and I took in a wonderful view of the area of northern Colorado, where you could observe snowcapped mountains and the attractive countryside far off in the distance. The weather diminished the view somewhat, but the scenery was still some of the best in the United States. I found the address provided in the lead request; the residence, tucked away on a cul-de-sac, was a well-maintained and neat two-story apartment building. Not surprisingly, I received no answer when I knocked on the door. I walked a short distance to a neighboring apartment and knocked. A young girl, maybe in her twenties, answered and in a very polite voice asked what I wanted.

"I'm looking for Linda Crawford, who is supposed to live next door. Do you know where I may reach her?" I asked.

"She moved about two weeks ago; I did not know her well, so I can't tell you where she now lives," the girl said.

Thanking her, I left and tried the apartment on the other side of where Linda was reported to be living. My luck changed; no one answered the door. My next step was to find the apartment manager and see if I could obtain a forwarding address for Linda Crawford.

The office was in a corner-unit first-floor apartment. A middle-aged lady was sitting at a desk when I walked in. She looked up and politely said, "You don't look like someone who needs an apartment; I am guessing you're the police."

"Well, you're sort of right. My name is Dick Miller; I am a special agent with the US Army CID and wanted to know if I could get an address of a former tenant named Linda Crawford."

"I don't see why not. Who is it?" she responded.

She walked over to a filing cabinet and starting searching the files. I heard her mumbling under her breath as she worked to retrieve the information I requested.

She then suddenly slammed the file drawer shut and commented, "I have no record of anyone by that name."

I then opened my notebook and provided her with the address I had just checked, thinking it was obviously in her boyfriend's name. I was in luck; a recheck using the address disclosed her boyfriend's name and a forwarding address located across town. The manager wrote down the address on a small notepad and gave it to me.

It took me about forty-five minutes to find the new address, a single-family house in an established neighborhood about five miles from the apartment complex. It had been snowing for the last hour or so, and when I got out of the CID sedan in front of the house, I noticed the ground had started accumulating a dusting of white stuff. This time when I knocked on the door, a young girl in her late teens or early twenties answered immediately. To my shock, the girl was wearing a wedding dress.

"Yes? What do you want?" the girl asked.

I introduced myself and told her I was looking for a Linda Crawford, who had once lived on Fort Lewis. The girl's expression of concern and puzzlement said a thousand words; then she said, "You're here about what happened at Fort Lewis, aren't you?"

"Are you Linda Crawford?" I asked.

"Yes, but we can't talk about this now. I am getting married in a few minutes," she said.

"Oh, I am sorry for intruding on your wedding. Are you going to be around the area after your wedding, where we might talk about this another day?" I inquired.

"Yes. We are not going on any type of honeymoon, so I guess we could do it tomorrow," she said.

Feeling relieved that I would not have to wait longer, I agreed, and we made an appointment for 10:00 a.m. the next day.

The snowstorm was picking up pace, and the roads were getting slippery and more hazardous to drive on. Based on the developing snowy weather conditions, I made a command decision to find a hotel for the evening. I found a Holiday Inn on the outskirts of Cheyenne and checked in. When I got settled, I called Fort Carson and requested to be put on TDY status until after I completed the interview with Crawford. Once I got that out of the way, I ate a nice dinner at the hotel restaurant and got some rest.

At 6:00 a.m., I got up and checked on the weather outside. There had to be at least eight or more inches of snow on the ground. I turned on the TV, and the weather was the primary news; my calculations on the amount of snow were a little off. The news was reporting that Colorado and Wyoming had been buried with up to twenty-five inches of snow, schools were closed, flights had been either delayed or canceled at Denver and Cheyenne airports, and local officials were shutting down Wyoming's state government in Cheyenne. A blizzard warning was in effect for the south-central Wyoming, much of which was covered by ten to twenty-five inches of snow. Gusty winds of up to fifty miles per hour reduced visibility to near zero and created snowdrifts of up to six feet. The news forecast for Cheyenne warned that the storm was a dangerous one and advised residents to "take all survival travel precautions." Boy, did I make a wise decision the previous evening to stay at a hotel.

It would be impossible to drive the few miles to Linda Crawford's house to conduct the interview, let alone attempt the long trip back to Denver. I waited for another two hours and then called her and asked if we could reschedule the interview for another day, hopefully the next day; she agreed. Now, I had to find something to do for the day. My options were limited to only watching TV and making telephone calls back to the office to check on things. Fortunately, the hotel had food and a TV, the two most common necessities of life. If I'd had to travel to eat, I would have starved for the day, because driving was out of the question due to the amount of snow on the ground.

I got through the day, but I had to cancel my interview with Crawford a second time due to road conditions. On the third day, the roads were clear enough to travel, so I made another appointment to meet with Crawford at 1:00 p.m., just after lunch. There were streets where the snowplow had barely cleared. It took about forty minutes to get to Crawford's house, but she answered the door when I got there. Once we sat down at her kitchen table, she commented that the snowstorm had been the worst she had ever been in. Crawford, who now went by her married name of Johnston, was open about being a victim of sexual assaults she'd faced at Fort Lewis.

Crawford-Johnston started her story when her mother married SFC James Malloy in 1980, when Crawford-Johnston was thirteen years old. Her mother had met and married Malloy when they were at Fort Hamilton, New York.

"My mother had been married to my biological father, who was also in the US Army, and he was assigned to Fort Hamilton. While there, Mother divorced, but stayed at Fort Hamilton. She met and married Malloy less than a year after the divorce. In June 1983, Malloy received a transfer to Fort Lewis, Washington, where the molestation began," she related.

"When was the first time it occurred?" I asked.

"Well, it first occurred about a month after we arrived at Fort Lewis in 1983. One evening when my mother was at work. Jim, as I call him, sat down next to me on the couch when we were watching TV. Without saying anything to me, he reached over and placed his hands on my breast. I guess I was afraid to tell him to remove his hand, and he just held it there for a minute or two. Nothing else happened that night, but he continually got more aggressive each time we were alone together, usually when Mom was at work. About two months after the first time he put his hands on my breast, he placed his hands between my legs."

I noticed that Crawford-Johnston started getting emotional and was having a hard time maintaining her composure, so I gave her a break. I departed from specific questions about molestation and focused on her relationship with her mother. She indicated to me that, except for the normal spats, they got along. Crawford-Johnston told me that her mother did not believe her when she first told her about her stepfather, Malloy, molesting her.

Then one night, again when they were home alone, Malloy raped her, and she was visibly upset when her mother got home that night. She informed her mother as to what happened, and her mother in turn confronted Malloy. Crawford-Johnston told me that based on Malloy's reactions when her mother asked him if he had ever inappropriately touched her, she could tell he was lying to her when he said no" Crawford-Johnston related that she had enough money given to her by her boyfriend, now husband, to buy a plane ticket for Cheyenne. She left a few days after she was raped. She had talked to her mother, who knew where she was. Her mother reported the incident to the MPs at Fort Lewis after she left.

I took a written statement from Crawford-Johnston using a dated Royal portable typewriter from the office and had her sign it. As I left her apartment, I felt sorry for Crawford-Johnston for what she had gone through, but I had to ask her one more question. "Would you be willing to testify under oath at a military court-martial?" I asked her.

She seemed genuinely hurt by what had occurred to her, but I felt compelled to find out if she would openly talk about her ordeal.

"I want to get on with my life and forget about what happened at Fort Lewis," she said.

"I am sure that if Malloy goes to trial over this, your testimony will be required," I pointed out to her.

"I'm not sure I can face him or my mother again," she responded.

"Would you at least consider it?" I rebounded.

"Maybe," she commented as I walked out the door.

I know she will never truly get over what Malloy did to her, but I just hope that the traumatic experience will not dominate her emotional life.

I finally made it back to the CID office the following morning; it had taken me three nights to complete a two-hour interview.

In the early morning hours of December 12, 1985, shortly after the Cheyenne trip, tragedy struck the US Army and the CID command in the form of a devastating and terrible airplane crash in Gander, Newfoundland. The plane, a McDonnell Douglas DC-8, was carrying US troops from Cairo, Egypt, to their home base at Fort Campbell, Kentucky, via Cologne, West Germany, and Gander, Newfoundland. The news reported that shortly after takeoff from Gander, the aircraft stalled, crashed, and burned about half a mile from the runway, killing all 248 passengers and 8 crew members on board. Of the 248 servicemen, all but 12 were members of 101st Airborne Division (Air Assault), most of whom were from the Third Battalion, 502nd Infantry. Eleven were from other Forces Command units, and one was an agent from the Fort Campbell CID office. Shortly after the crash, a Shiite Muslim extremist group claimed it had destroyed the plane to prove its ability to strike at the Americans anywhere. A subsequent investigation by the Pentagon and Canadian government officials rejected the claim, made by an anonymous caller to a French news agency in Beirut.[122]

Special Agent Dirk Miller from the Fort Campbell CID office was killed after a six-month deployment to the Sinai, where he had served in the Multinational Force & Observers peacekeeping mission. In August 1986, the Fort Campbell CID office building was named Miller Hall in his honor.[123]

Under the dark cloud of the Gander plane crash and the death of a fellow CID special agent, Christmas 1985 was celebrated in Indiana with family. Elda had flown to Denver on December 20, 1985, from Germany, and we traveled by car to Indiana, stopping along the way to buy gifts and wrapping them in our hotel room. That year started a tradition of having Christmas dinners in Clinton, Indiana, at Rachel's, my half-sister and Dad's youngest daughter by his second marriage to Anna Strahle. Those Christmas dinners were a feast and were held annually for over ten years before times changed and other family members took over the chore. During the Christmas dinners, Chris, Mom, June, and her son, Charlie, would be there, and we thoroughly enjoyed their company. My brother, John, and sister Nora would show up after dinner, and they had time for the many desserts prepared.

The trip in 1985 found Chris in good shape. He was still growing into a handsome young man, and I thoroughly enjoyed our conversations and catching up on his life.

We had only one glitch on our trip. When I turned on the ignition to my Nissan 300Z to begin our trip to Clinton for the family gathering, it sounded like it was on its last leg, but the engine was running. Thinking it was the extremely cold weather causing the engine to run roughly, I decided to go ahead and drive to Rachel's. We were able make the entire trip to Rachel's and back to the hotel without incident. The next morning, I found a Nissan dealer open and had the car towed there. It took them the better part of a day to evaluate the problem. A couple of valves had gone bad, possibly collapsing due to the cold weather. The bad news for Elda and I was that we had to rent a car to drive back to Denver so she could catch her plane back to Germany that weekend. The trip ended well, but it took the Nissan dealer four months, until April 1986, to completely replace the engine. The good news for me was that Nissan identified that the engine was defective at the factory and paid for the entire work and the four-month car rental as well.

After we got back to Denver, Elda returned to Germany the next day. It was good to see her, and she made the holidays great. Christmas of 1985 went down as one of the more memorable Christmases ever.

January 1986 found the work at Fitzsimons picking up where it was before the holidays. One incident during the month of January 1986 was unique in that it involved a member of our own, the MP supply sergeant, whom I'll call SSG Richard D. Franklin.[124] Details of this case are covered in the Case of the Missing M16 Rifle That Was Stolen:

## THE CASE OF THE MISSING M16 RIFLE THAT WAS STOLEN
Trust is unique and special; some have it and others do not

It was a cold morning on January 28, 1986, when space shuttle *Challenger* was supposed to fly into space. Temperatures dipped below freezing in Florida. There were certain people at NASA and among contractors that worried about the integrity of the seals on the solid rocket boosters in cold weather. *Challenger* launched at 11:38 a.m. Eastern time in front of more media attention than usual, as it was carrying the first teacher to go in space—Christa McAuliffe, who was planning to give lessons while in orbit. She and the rest of the crew never made it. *Challenger* broke up seventy-three seconds after launch in front of the television cameras and millions of people who were watching. "Obviously, there was a major malfunction," the NASA launch commentator said as pieces of the shuttle fell from the sky into the Atlantic.[125]

At approximately the time the *Challenger* exploded, I was investigating an incident involving a missing M16 rifle from the Fitzsimons MP arms room. The M16 was discovered missing in a routine scheduled inventory check of the arms room. The armorer, SSG Richard D. Franklin, was a person of interest in the matter. About 10:00 a.m., I was called by the PMO, Major Pierce, who requested a CID investigation.

My first step was to inspect the MP arms room to determine if any physical evidence could be developed. The arms room was located on the second floor of the MP station about three rooms down from Major Pierce's office. Upon inspection, the door to the arms room did not appear to have been tampered with. Additional security measures had been installed to the inside the room. On the back wall was the only window, which had iron bars on the inside. The iron bars were solidly stabilized with no signs of compromise. The window was intact; as a matter of fact, years of paint on the window seal prevented it from being opened.

The next step of my investigation was to check the inventory sheet to determine if there were any discrepancies in the inventory conducted that identifies the missing M16 as missing. I exposed photographs at various angles and directions of the entire arms room. A review of the inventory report did not reveal anything significant.

I then briefed Major Pierce on the investigation, which was essentially that an M16 rifle was missing. The only logical suspect in the case was SSG Franklin, the supply sergeant. "Is there any possibility that the missing M16 was sent out for higher-echelon maintenance?" I asked Major Pierce.

"No. We have ten M16s in inventory, and they are counted each month by me or the operations officer, Bill Biebe, but I have conducted the inventory the last several months. Last month, there were ten in the arms room; this morning when I conducted the inventory, there were only nine. Other weapons, such as the .45 cals, two shotguns, and ammunition, were all accounted for," Major Pierce reported.

"When was the last time you conducted an inventory of the arms room and all M16s were there?"

Looking down at the inventory sheet, Major Pierce said, "It was December 29, 1985. I also remember I conducted the inventory on that date, because it was SSG Franklin's first day back from his Christmas holiday leave. I usually conduct the inventory a few days before the first of the month, to get it out of the way."

My next logical step in the investigation was to interview SSG Franklin.

I had SSG Franklin escorted to my office and directed him to a chair in front of my desk. I tried to assess his attitude, weaknesses, and overall character during the few minutes he sat in the chair while I was finishing the preparation to interview him. This time was, however, way too short to get a feel for what type of individual he was and how he would respond to my questions. Would he be responsive, or would he want a lawyer? I had to advise him of his rights, because he was a person of interest in either taking the M16 rifle or somehow, through his careless handling of the weapon, losing it. He did not look anxious; as a matter of fact, he appeared to be calm and composed. Although we'd both worked in the same building for slightly less than a year since my arrival at Fitzsimons, I did not know him; I only saw him walking in and out of the MP station from time to time and had never spoken to him.

I began the interview by advising him of his Miranda rights for Article 108. This article under the Uniform Code of Military Justice (UCMJ) states that someone who has control of US property who either sells, loses, damages, destroys, or wrongfully disposes of government property has violated this article and can receive up to ten years' confinement.[126] To my surprise, he waived his rights and consented to talk.

"SSG Franklin, did you take that M16 rifle from the MP arms room?" I asked.

To my shock, he freely answered my question without hesitation. "Yes. I removed it from the MP arms room and took it home. It was never my intent to steal the M16, but only to take it home where I could practice tearing it down and putting in back together. I had taken the M16 apart and put the pieces into a carrying case to better conceal the weapon when I walked past the MP desk as I left the building. It took me three trips to get all the pieces of the M16 to my house."

Further questioning attempted to determine where the M16 rifle was and if it could be returned. "Where is the M16 rifle now?" I asked.

My heart sank when I heard his answer. "I have no idea," he responded.

"You said you took it. What did you do with it?"

"I took it to my house in Aurora."

"Well, then, why can't we go get it?"

Putting his face in his hands, he mumbled, "We can't!"

"Why not?" I said incredulously.

"Someone stole it from my house," he said.

That answer threw me for a loop. Attempting to clarify his answer, I asked, "You mean that someone unknown took the M16 from your house?"

"Yes, but I have no idea who may have entered my house to steal it."

"How did they get into your house?" I asked.

"They broke one of the windows in our back door, reached in, and unlocked the door," he explained.

"What day was it when you got all the pieces of the M16 to your house?"

"It was the evening of January 10," he said.

"Were you planning to return the weapon to the arms room?"

"Since I had to carry it back to the arms room in pieces, I had planned to have all the pieces returned by January 22. But when we came home from dinner on the evening of January 17, I discovered that someone had entered our house and taken the M16," he said.

Attempting to clarify what SSG Franklin was telling me, I asked, "So you say that the M16 was taken from your house by someone you don't know on the evening of January 17?"

"Yes!"

"Was there anything else taken from you home that night?"

"No, there was not," he responded. "I had hoped to have it back in the arms room before the next inventory, which usually occurs a couple of days before the first of the month."

"Have you had anyone over to your house, or have you told anyone about the M16?"

"No," SSG Franklin said.

"What about any of your neighbors?"

"No. I don't know any of them and never spoke to any of them, and to my knowledge, none have ever been in my house."

"Did you report the break-in to the Aurora Police Department?" I inquired.

"No. I couldn't tell them someone broke into my house and stole an M16 rifle that I had taken from the MP arms room."

"Will you give me permission to search your house?" I asked.

Sitting back in his chair and crossing his arms, he said, "Sure, why not? You ain't going to find anything."

Not wanting him to have time to change his mind, I interrupted the interview for what I thought would be a temporary period and come back after the search of his house. However, the best-laid-out plans come home to roost in a different shed sometimes.

Not wanting to show up at his house and find someone there, I asked, "Is there anyone at your house now?"

"No. My wife is at work and won't be home until this evening."

Special Agent Capshaw was out of the office working on another case, so I grabbed MPI John Doyle from the PMO and asked him to accompany me and SSG Franklin to Franklin's house.

I drove the short distance to SSG Franklin's house, located near Stapleton International Airport. The first thing I inspected was the back door to determine if there was any evidence to indicate someone had broken a windowpane to enter the house. I did notice that the door had six small windowpanes in the upper portion of the back door. One of those panes was broken, but when I looked for broken glass on the inside of the door, I found none. "If a windowpane in your back door was broken by someone who entered your house, why can't I find any broken glass on the floor?"

"Oh, I cleaned it up so no one would be cut by walking on the glass," SSG Franklin said.

For the next two hours, while MPI Doyle kept an eye on SSG Franklin, I searched the house. Exhausted, but confident that I had thoroughly searched the one-story house for the M16 and for any parts of the M16 or evidence to indicate it had been in the house, we left without finding the rifle.

Back at the CID office, I got ready to continue the interview with SSG Franklin when I received another surprise. While in the process of reminding SSG Franklin that he still had the right to stop answering my questions and seek the advice of a lawyer, he invoked his rights and decline to continue the interview. I released him to the MP station and back briefed Major Pierce, advising him that I felt we needed to be cautious about proper supervision because SSG Franklin might attempt to go AWOL. Major Pierce informed me that he would consider requesting SSG Franklin be transported to the unit headquarters at Fort Carson for restricted movement.

The next morning, I contacted SSG Franklin's wife, SP4 Patricia Franklin,[127] who was a medic at Fitzsimons, and requested she come in for an interview. I was hoping that she would provide some much-needed information on her husband and on who may have allegedly broken into their home and taken the missing M16 taken by SSG Franklin.

She showed up at the CID office on schedule, and I invited her into my office. I detected a degree of arrogance in her actions and voice and suspected it was going to be difficult to get anything incriminating out of her about her husband.

I had no reason to advise her of her Miranda rights, because there was no evidence to indicate she was involved with her husband in removing the M16 from the arms room. But I did not want her to think she was off the hook entirely, and by her being a military service member, she had an obligation to tell us what she knew. I informed her that if she knew information about the case and did not tell us, she could be charged with accessory to the offenses by not speaking up. After telling her what she may face, I began questioning her.

"I brought you in to ask if there was any information you could provide that would bring light to the case against your husband," I began.

"I did not even know he was involved with any wrongdoing until he came home last night and told me he had been questioned by CID about a missing M16."

"Have you ever seen your husband with an M16 outside the MP station?"

"No!"

"Does your husband enjoy working on guns?"

"He knows a lot about guns, but to my knowledge, he does not have any personal guns," she indicated.

"Has your husband ever brought home any MP guns or any other military equipment, such as ammunition to show you or to work on them?"

"No!"

I did not detect any signs in her body movements or facial expressions that made me suspect she was attempting any deception. She kept eye contact with me and did not move her arms or legs in any way, but her lack of classical display of body language made me consider the possibility that she may have been controlling her emotional reactions to the questions asked in the interview.

I refocused the questioning of SP4 Franklin. I directed my questions now to the break-in at her house on the evening of January 17, mentioned by SSG Franklin. Something she'd said earlier made me think questions of that nature might trip her up.

"What day did the break-in to your house occur?" I asked.

"That was the night when we were returning home from dinner. I believe it was January 17," she said.

*Nothing there*, I thought. "Did you or SSG Franklin report the break-in to the Aurora Police Department?"

"No. Since there was nothing taken, we decided it would be too much of a hassle," she said.

"Are you sure that was the reason you did not report the break-in?" I emphasized.

"Well, I know now that he is being suspected of removing an M16 rifle from the MP arms room, but the night of the break-in to our house, I did not know any of that information. We looked in every room of the house that night and found nothing missing," she said.

"What happened to the glass from the broken windowpane to your back door?" I asked.

"My husband swept it up," she said.

She had all the right answers and did not incriminate herself. I had no evidence she was involved or had any information about the missing M16, only suspicions.

No attempts were ever made to restrict or confine SSG Franklin to the Fort Carson MP company. SSG Franklin was only directed to stay in the unit area at Fitzsimons while on duty. The only exceptions to that directive were when he ate lunch or was at home during his off time. It was only inevitable that five days after the interview of SSG Franklin and SP4 Franklin, both went AWOL, and their whereabouts were still unknown on the date I departed Fitzsimons in October 1986. In retrospect, the Franklins stories are at best suspect, because the M16 is still missing. This case was different in that the missing M16 rifle was stolen from the perp that took it. Until additional evidence surfaces, that is what the report will reflect.

Throughout the spring of 1986, Fitzsimons cases came in at a steady pace. For the size of CID office at Fitzsimons, we did not have a heavy caseload, just consistent. Although the caseload was very manageable with two assigned special agents, the Fitzsimons branch office saw an increase in agent strength in the early part of 1986. A newly accepted probationary agent, Edward Christenson,[128] assigned to my office until his scheduled CID basic course started in March 1986, came from the US Army detachment at Lowry Air Force Base in Denver. A second, seasoned special agent, George Snider,[129] was temporarily assigned from Second Region due to the illness of his father. His father, suffering from brain cancer, was being treated in nearby Littleton, Colorado. The CID command sent him to Fitzsimons to be near his father during treatment. A third special agent, John Mims, came to the office as a probationary agent for training from the Fort Carson District. I guess the higher-ups had confidence in my abilities to manage the extra manpower, because I know the office did not need any increase in agents to handle the caseload. With the added agent strength, LTC Nichols and Chief Busha, from my Korean days, who recently replaced Interim Chief Klossner, were not timid about taking away from the office either.

Special Agent Snider, a tall, lanky, wisecracking sort of fellow who spoke with a Southern drawl and was from Charleston, West Virginia, had been temporarily assigned to the Fort Carson CID office from Second Region headquarters as the chief of investigative support (CIS) with the level-one drug team. His temporary assignment to Fitzsimons was undetermined. He had been given thirty days to be with his dad and was prepared to play it by ear for more time. He had a sister in the Denver area who resided a short distance from Fitzsimons that he was staying with while his father was being treated. Special Agent Snider was also married to a US Army soldier stationed at Fort Carson. They were reportedly estranged at the time and were pending a divorce.

John Mims, a good-natured, friendly person, had just finished the CID special agents course at Fort McClellan, Alabama, and was assigned to Fort Carson but was sent to Fitzsimons to receive one-on-one training as a probationary special agent. His stay at Fitzsimons was also undetermined.

SP4 Edward Christenson, a young sergeant who had been assigned to the US Army detachment at Lowry Air Force Base at the time he was selected for the CID program, had about a month before he was due to report to Fort McClellan for training. He was very amenable to supervision, guidance, and instructions. Although at Fitzsimons for a very short time, he would prove invaluable based on his work performance.

I had a one-on-one meeting with each of these individuals and related my management philosophies. I assured them that I would keep them fully employed during their tenure at Fitzsimons despite the size of the office. Sergeant Christenson, whose tenure would be very short, was told that he would get a good introduction to what CID special agents do and how they do it but that his training would be limited to time and resource restraints.

I socialized with the agents, and we frequently had lunch together. One day in late April 1986, Special Agent Snider and I ate lunch at a local restaurant not far from the Fitzsimons CID office. After lunch, as we traveled toward the office on Potomac Street, Snider asked if we could stop at a gun store so he could see what they had to offer. The gun store had a wide variety of pistols, revolvers, and long rifles for sale. We spent about fifteen minutes in the store, with Snider doing most of the looking.

When we got back in the car for the short ride to the CID office, I thought, *what in the world does Snider want a gun?* Curiosity got the best of me, so I asked him, "Why do you want a gun?"

With no hesitation and with a sincere-sounding voice, he straightforwardly said, "I may want to kill my wife!"

That comment surprised me, but at the time, I did not take him seriously and shoved the comment out of my mind.

A few days later, Special Agent Snider came to me and asked for a three-day weekend. I had no reason to refuse him, so I approved it. He then confided with me that since he was only temporarily assigned to Fitzsimons, he had additional expenses living with his father in Littleton and needed cash. He convinced me that a loan of $1,000 would greatly improve his plight while still being able to cover expenses to see his relatives in West Virginia. It was against my better judgment, but being a compassionate person, I offered to front him the money with the terms that he could pay me back with no interest as much as possible each month until the debt was paid. Snider had never given me a reason to distrust him in any way, and I wanted to help him through his rough time. I did not see or even feel like there was anything smoldering in Snider's future that might run afoul.

April 26, 1986, a windy, overcast Saturday morning in Denver, started out as any normal weekend. I did not go to the office that morning but instead slept in. Around 10:30 a.m. while in the process of making breakfast and randomly watching CNN, the newscaster blurted out that there was a breaking news story unfolding. There had been an explosion at a nuclear power plant in the Ukraine near a small town called Chernobyl.

As more details about the explosion were disclosed, it was apparent that this was no small event and had ramifications around the world. At the time, I did not think much about the incident, but I later realized that the effects of the radioactive fallout on people living nearby were life threatening. Over time, the Chernobyl incident was the worst nuclear explosions in history and affected Europeans, to include American armed forces personnel assigned to the region, for many years. The US military started getting all their produce from the United States instead of local areas. A US soldier and husband of a coworker of Elda's had been fishing in Finland shortly after the explosion and later developed leukemia and died within months after the explosion. It was strongly believed that he was exposed to radiation from the Chernobyl Nuclear Power Plant. One only wonders just how incidents on this nature affect the world in ways the average person never hears about.[130]

In CID, when everything is running smoothly and it appears that no major issues or problems are brewing or in the way—*smack!*—everything falls through a hole in your bucket. With double the authorized billets at the office, I thought I could get a bunch of needed projects done that under normal circumstances would have to be set aside or ignored. Yet with the new strength in the office, I had the manpower to tackle these projects.

It was still late April when I started the push to get the extra projects started. Feeling upbeat and certain that time would be on my side before I lost the extra men at the office, I was excited about beginning the work. Then it happened: on the day that I had scheduled a meeting with everyone to talk about their roles in the work I was planning, I received a call from Chief Klossner.

"Are you sitting down?" the chief asked.

"Yes! I am at my desk, getting ready to start a meeting." With a twinge of concern shooting through my stomach, I asked, "What is it that you are about to tell me?"

"Well, we are spread pretty thin here at Fort Carson, so Commander Nichols has made a decision to send you TDY to Washington, DC."

A brief silence fell into the exchange between the two of us before I broke it. "Washington, DC? What the hell for?" I asked.

"The PSA [Protective Services Unit] needs extra agents to help with their operation in and around Washington, DC, and you are the only possible candidate that we can give them now."

"When do I have to be there?"

"The first of May," he said.

If I had to be in Washington on May 1, I had two days to pack and get orders and a ticket. I would have never been selected for this deployment if I had not been assigned to Fitzsimons. If I had chosen a larger base with a good deal more crime, I wouldn't have been considered for the temporary assignment. I hung up the phone and called the men in for the scheduled meeting as planned. The tone of the meeting, of course, had changed. Instead of detailing what I wanted to accomplish and dishing out orders for their assignments, I told them that I would be gone for at least thirty days and that the start of the projects I had envisioned would have to be either altered or modified due to my absence.

I had another issue pending: Who could I get to take care of Dog while I was gone? I considered putting her in a kennel for the time I was gone, but I ended up opting to get a dog sitter. I couldn't impose on Special Agent Capshaw and his wife, Becky, for that length of time; I had to get someone whose lifestyle would not be altered that much. It came down to Special Agent Snider.

I had not actually chosen him for the job, but the day before I left, he heard about my dilemma and approached me with the idea. During the time, I was pondering the decision, I was doing everything needed to get things done before hopping on the plane for Washington. Then I realized that there was no time left, and I was forced to select Special Agent Snider for the job of dog sitter while I was gone.

"Please walk the dog three times a day. Lock the house when you are not there, and don't have any wild parties. You can have visitors, but don't upset the neighbors—you know, the usual things," I instructed him.

"You've got my word," he said.

With everything arranged, I was off. Special Agent Snider dropped me off at Stapleton International Airport for the three-plus-hour flight to Washington.

In 1986, the US Army's Protective Services Unit was an *activity* (PSA), not a unit, that consisted of about twenty or so special agents from the CID who were permanently assigned the mission to protect the Pentagon leaders, including the secretary and deputy secretary of defense. The other leaders at the time were the US Army secretary, chairman of the Joint Chiefs of Staff, the vice chief of staff, the US Army chief of staff, and any foreign dignitaries equivalent of those positions when they visited the United States. Other service branches have their own protection details for their leaders, but the US Army PSA is unique in that it controls the security of the defense and deputy defense secretaries as well as US Army leaders. The US Army's CID PSA found its origin in the late 1960s during the Vietnam War, when the Pentagon formed a protection detail for the then secretary of defense, Robert McNamara. The original unit was considered only as a detail (PSD); later it became an activity (PSA) and commanded by a chief warrant officer. Ultimately, PSA became a unit (PSU) under the leadership of a commissioned officer.

The original assistant to the secretary of defense for security and the conduit between the US Army and the Defense Department was former commander of the Fort Myer CID office, LTC Joe Sace (phonetically). To assist him in the newly formed protection detail was a US Air Force service member named Bill Brown. (Bill is believed to have retired from active duty with the air force and remained in the position of Sace's deputy as a civilian.) Brown replaced Sace in the late 1980s when Sace retired. Those two were with the Defense Department and conduits between the US Army CID. They were responsible for orchestrating the various and wide-ranging security details using primarily US Army CID special agents.

My plane landed in Washington at 2:00 p.m. I took a taxi to the Best Western Hotel in Tysons Corner near McLean, Virginia, about thirty minutes away.

As I walked to my room after checking in, I noticed a young man sporting a heavy black mustache and a full head of hair, sitting in a chair, and wearing a gray suit with a red tie. I introduced myself.

"Hi. My name is Dick Miller. Would you by any chance be a special agent with the US Army CID?"

"Yes, I am. My name is Tim Steenbergen."

You can always recognize a fellow CID special agent.

We discovered that both of us were sent TDY to Washington to work on the PSA detail. Special Agent Steenbergen came from Fort Leonard Wood, Missouri.

"I have already checked in, and while I was in my room, I received a call from a special agent named Bobby Leggett, who said he was headed to the hotel to pick us up and take us to the Pentagon," he added.

"I'd better get these bags to my room. I'll be right back," I informed Special Agent Steenbergen.

By the time, I dropped my bags off in my room and rejoined Special Agent Steenbergen. Special Agent Leggett had arrived and was there waiting on me. We all hopped into a CID sedan—a late-model, navy-blue, four-door Chevy Caprice—and sped out of the hotel parking lot, the car's emergency lights oscillating as we charged ahead.

As we sped down the highway, I asked Special Agent Leggett, "Are we running late?"

When he did not answer, I just kept quiet and settled in for the ride. The total trip of fifteen miles took us about thirty minutes in heavy traffic, but we arrived safety at the River Entrance to the Pentagon.

As I set my sights on the Pentagon for the first time in person, and my impression was how big the building appeared. We parked our late-model sedan in a space provided to us at the River Entrance to the Pentagon. The PSA office was located almost immediately after entering the building near the security checkpoint that was manned by DOD officers. The secretary of Defense at the time was Caspar Weinberger.

There were three or four other special agents in the small office when we arrived. They were all waiting for the SECDEF's next movement. Special Agent Steenbergen and I made our introductions, and we were welcomed to the unit. I glanced at my wristwatch; it was 4:15 p.m. There were five of us inside the small office provided for the CID security detail, but there were enough seats for all of us. We all sat around until 5:30 p.m., when a call came from Secretary Weinberger's office that he was coming down the elevator, heading to his car. The two agents that were there when we arrived left. Not being familiar with the procedures, I wondered what our role was supposed to be. I soon found out; seconds after the two agents departed, Special Agent Leggett asked, "Are you guys ready to go to your hotel rooms?"

"Uh, sure," I responded.

Little to no conversation took place on the way to our hotel. As Special Agent Leggett dropped us off at the front door to the Best Western Tysons Westpark Hotel, he rolled down the window and told us to be ready for pickup at 6:00 the following morning, and then he immediately drove off. That was it: my first day as a Protective Services agent on the secretary of defense security detail. I had been to the Pentagon and had settled into my hotel room and told that I would be picked up at 6:00 the following morning. I had no clue, nor did Special Agent Steenbergen, of what to expect the next day. I did not even know who was picking us up. I was sure we would find out.

Special Agent Steenbergen joined me for dinner at the hotel restaurant that evening, and we both turned in early to get some much-needed rest.

At 5:45 a.m., I met Special Agent Steenbergen in the hotel lobby as we'd agreed the evening before. Neither of us knew who was going to pick us up, so we waited. About 6:20 a.m., we observed a car pull up outside the front door to the hotel. It looked like the car we were in the day before, so we walked outside and spoke to the driver, who did not get out of the car. Fortunately for us, he was the CID special agent that was assigned to pick us up. The driver, who was a permanently assigned PSA special agent, drove us to 5611 Columbia Pike in Arlington, Virginia, where the CID headquarters was housed at that time. The PSA office occupied one large room on the same floor as CID headquarters in the Nassif Building, as it was called in those days. There was a supply room, an admin office, and a small room utilized by the SAC. At the time, we were TDY in 1986, and the amount of permanently assigned special agents totaled only about twenty. We received a short briefing from the SAC, Special Agent Hicks, who advised Special Agent Steenbergen and me that we were assigned to the secretary's in-town security detail and would be working for the designated personnel security officer (PSO) special agent, which changed each day. The next task was for us to rent a vehicle and report back to PSA at 1:00 p.m.

Having our marching orders, Special Agent Steenbergen and I rented a vehicle and returned to the Nassif Building with time to grab a light lunch at the Hot Shoppe on the main floor of the building.[131]

After lunch, we gathered with the permanently assigned in-town detail agents and went over our responsibilities. Our PSO for the day was Special Agent Gregory Lee, a youngish-looking fellow whose personality exuded a sense of authority, which was good in this job. After our short briefing from Special Agent Lee, we headed for the Pentagon. Special Agent Steenbergen and I were assigned as chase car drivers, responsible for following behind the secretary's car each time he moved in and around Washington, DC.

Several support agents were brought to PSA during the months of April and May 1986, because of the developing crisis with Libya. Libyan terrorists had bombed the La Belle nightclub, a favorite spot for American service members in Berlin, Germany, that killed one US service member and injured seventy-nine others; one other US service member died of injuries a day later. Over two hundred other victims were injured during the aftermath of the bombing that was attributed to Libyan agents. The United States launched a series of air attacks on Libya in an action named Operation El Dorado Canyon. It was considered the first US military action whose official primary justification was the fight against international terrorism and its sponsors.[132] Based on the terrorism time line, one might say that the official period runs from 1986 to present.

Special Agent Steenbergen and I took turns driving the chase car. On average, Secretary Weinberger moved around Washington, DC, in a motorcade about four times a day. Within a few days, we settled into a routine of twelve- to fifteen-hour days with no real scheduled days off.

I did not stay in touch with the Fitzsimons CID office for various reasons. One, there was nothing I could do from Washington to assist on cases. Two, Special Agent Capshaw had the ability to run with each open investigation the office had at the time I went TDY. And third, he had plenty of help with Special Agents Snider and Mims as well as the wannabe agent waiting for school. Any action on my part would be imposing undue grief on Special Agent Capshaw's professional abilities. I figured that if there was anything going south, then Special Agent Capshaw would let me know.

One morning, our routine was interrupted when the permanently assigned PSO failed to show for our movement to the secretary's house for his daily pickup. At precisely 6:15 a.m., the secretary's car always arrives at Secretary Weinberger's house with the PSO; This morning the PSO was not in the car. The secretary routinely left at precisely 6:30 a.m.

Special Agent Steenbergen and I had to make a quick decision on who was to walk the short distance from our car to the secretary's car to ride into the Pentagon with him. It took us about five minutes before it was decided I would act as the PSO for that morning. By the time, I had reached the car in driveway, Secretary Weinberger was leaving his house and walking toward the car. Speaking distinctly and with purpose, I greeted him with a hearty "Good morning, Mr. Secretary" as I opened the door and let him in. My actions that morning was so smooth and in sync that Secretary Weinberger was never aware of anything being awry. After ensuring that Secretary Weinberger was secured in the backseat, I got into the front passenger seat. His driver looked over at me with a large smile and mumbled, "Where did you come from?"

"Let's get to the Pentagon," I said.

Once we had Secretary Weinberger safely in his office at the Pentagon, I rushed to the PSA office a floor below and called PSA headquarters. I got ahold of Special Agent Gregory Lee, who said he'd just gotten home late the previous evening from a trip and did not realize he was assigned to perform the PSO duties that day. I briefed him on what had occurred, and he appeared to be relieved that nothing went wrong on the trip into the Pentagon.

The rest of my TDY to PSA was uneventful; our moves all ran without a glitch, and we kept the secretary safe, never putting him in a position where he was embarrassed and of course ensured he arrived on time for his meetings with President Reagan and other leaders in Washington, DC. The TDY time I spent on the secretary of defense security detail was a rewarding one. I planned to pursue more activity with the PSA in the future.

On Monday at noon, May 26, 1986, my last week in Washington, the PSA team, with Special Agent Steenbergen and me in the chase vehicle, took Secretary Weinberger from the Pentagon to Fort Myer for a Memorial Day service. President Reagan was the main speaker. We worked well with the Secret Service presidential detail, but there are no doubts about it: when the secretary of defense is on the same move as the president, the Secret Service is in charge. They do not take over our responsibilities but control our movements to a certain degree.

The memorial service had just ended, and Secretary Weinberger was walking with one of our CID agents nearby with President Reagan, the Secret Service security team surrounding them all. You could hear the cheers and excitement of the small gathering of people as President Reagan exited the building for the short walk to his car. The two stopped next to the open door to President Reagan's car, where they exchanged a few more words before bidding their farewells. Seconds later, the president's very elaborate motorcade zoomed off, presumably to the White House. As Secretary Weinberger headed for his car, escorted by the CID agent, I received a call on the brick cell phone that weighted a ton from Special Agent Chris Capshaw.

"Chief, are you sitting down?" he asked.

"No, I am getting ready to take the secretary somewhere." You never want to reveal over an unsecured line any information about the secretary's movements or his whereabouts. "What's the problem?" I asked.

"Your house in Aurora is a crime scene," he blurted out.

"A what?"

"Special Agent Snider's wife was shot in the chest in your home earlier this morning," he explained.

"What the hell!" My mind immediately brought back the memory of the day Snider and I had stopped at a gun store on Potomac Street in Aurora to look at guns and I'd asked him why he wanted to buy a gun. He'd told me he was looking for a gun to kill his wife. I had not talked to anyone about what Snider had told me that day, but without even knowing the circumstances of the shooting of his wife, I could not help but think, *the son of a bitch went through with it.* "Chris, have they charged Special Agent Snider with murder?" I asked.

"Not yet. The Aurora Police Department took the lead in the investigation into her death," he told me.

"Have Commander Nichols and Chief Klossner been notified?" I asked.

"Yes, and the commander is cooperating with the Aurora Police Department in their investigation."

"Do we know any details about what happened?" I asked.

"All I can tell you at this point is that Special Agent Snider left the office earlier today, and the next thing I know, he is calling for help on the CID car radio to respond to your house because his wife had been shot. You know the irony of this is that we all were supposed to be off today because of the Memorial Day holiday. However, because we knew you were coming home later in the week, we wanted to catch up on paperwork and clean of the office before you got here," he said.

As I was talking to Special Agent Capshaw, I noticed that the secretary's car was moving. "Chris, I'll call you later today, probably in about an hour; I've got to run now."

"Okay, I will keep you informed on as much as I can."

"Thanks, Chris."

As we followed Secretary Weinberger back to the Pentagon, I felt stunned at what had happened. Upon my departure from Fitzsimons, it never occurred to me that Special Agent Snider would bring his wife to my house while I was gone. I was under the impression that they were estranged from each other and were pending a divorce. I would later find out that she had been living with Special Agent Snider at my house the entire time that I was in Washington.

Once we got settled into the Pentagon, I checked the schedule and saw no more moves for the day. I called Colonel Nichols at Fort Carson, and he briefed me on what he had learned from the Aurora Police Department about the incident. After Colonel Nichols's briefing, I realized that not only was I a bona fide victim in the shooting death of Snider's wife and a potential witness, but I was about to become one of the lead investigators as well. Since the shooting took place inside my personal residence, some might see this situation as a conflict of interest, but I welcomed the chance to do what I could to successfully resolve the matter.

My flight left on time and arrived at Denver in three and a half hours. Because of the time difference, I arrived about the time I'd left Washington. Special Agent Capshaw picked me up, and we headed directly to the Fitzsimons CID office. On the trip to the office, he told me he did not know much more than what he and LTC Nichols had previously told me. Chris updated me on what he did know. Special Agent Capshaw told me that a neighbor had taken Dog. *Thank God for that*, I thought. When we got to the CID office and notified LTC Nichols that I was back, he updated me on what was happening on the case. He informed me that Snider was given a polygraph by the Aurora police, and the results were inconclusive. Inconclusive? Uh, *that doesn't mean he did it*, I thought. LTC Nichols told me he was going to be at the Aurora Police Department at 9:00 a.m. tomorrow to monitor Special Agent Snider's second polygraph, and he wanted me there. I informed him that I would be there. There are a bunch of pieces to the puzzle that we haven't put together yet, When I got off the phone from speaking with LTC Nichols, I walked outside and saw that Special Mims, SP4 Christenson, and Special Agent Snider were all in the office. *Great. The whole gang is here.* I called Special Agent Capshaw into my office and shut the door.

"Chris, let's talk about normal business first. Have there been any sensitive cases you have opened since I have been in Washington?" I asked.

"No. The run-of-the-mill larcenies is all," he responded.

"Good. I'll want you to work the investigations until we resolve the shooting death of Snider's wife," I told him.

"Okay, Chief. Consider it done. Good luck," he told me.

"Has Snider talked about the shooting to you?"

"Not really, other than calling to say he needed an ambulance and the police sent to your house."

"How was he acting during the time I was in Washington?"

"Well, he was gone for a few days to see his family in West Virginia, but otherwise, he was willing to pitch in and do some investigation on our open cases," Chris said. *Hum, I wonder who was caring for Dog during this time, I bet it was his estranged wife Sue,* I thought.

"Has any of the Fitzsimons command called to inquire about the shooting?"

"Well, I know that the PMO, Major Pierce, and the MPs are aware of the shooting, but I am not sure if the installation leaders know about it."

"Thanks, Chris. We'll get through this as quickly as possible." I thought, *If Major Pierce knows about the shooting, then the Fitzsimons staff know about it.* I told Chris that I wanted to see Special Agent Snider.

When Special Agent Snider walked into my office, I told him to shut the door and have a seat. Before I could tell him what I needed to get off my chest, Snider said, "We will try to pay back the money you lent me as soon as we can."

"Well, let's not worry about that now; we need to resolve the more serious issues concerning your wife's death." I dropped the topic of the money he owed me and went directly into what I intended to tell him. "Special Agent Snider, I was called back to Fitzsimons a few days early because of the shooting death of your wife. Although I want to find out the exact details of what happened in my home, I think it would be prudent that while the Aurora police and CID are investigating your wife's death, we not talk directly about the subject to each other," I explained to him.

"All right. That is okay with me."

Establishing eye contact with him, I added, "You know I am required to talk to the Aurora police about that day we stopped at the gun store and you told me you were looking for a gun because you might want to kill your wife."

Staring off in the distance as if he were in deep thought, Special Agent Snider said, "Yes, I understand."

"You've got a busy day ahead of you tomorrow, so why don't you take off so you will be fresh for tomorrow morning?"

As he got up from his chair and headed to the door, I reminded him that people might need to talk to him before the next day and that he should be near a phone.

Hoping to catch Chris in his office, I called. He picked up on the first ring and blared into the phone answered in an authoritative, louder-than-normal voice, "Special Agent Capshaw. Can I help you?"

"Chris, this is me. I sent Special Agent Snider home for the day; tell the others that they should take off too. If you want to get out of here, that's okay. I will be in my office for a while, and then, since my house is a crime scene, I'll try to get a room at the Holiday Inn across the street." I hung up before he could give me a response.

After hanging up, I sat at my desk in silence for a few moments. What did Special Agent Snider mean when he'd said, "'*We* will try to pay the money back as soon as *we* can'? Who was he talking about? I'd loaned *him* the money; there was no *we*. I shook the fog from my head and went to find a hotel room. I decided to wait a couple of days before I collected Dog from the neighbor's house. In fact, I would have to wait until the Aurora police released my house. I got a room at the Holiday Inn and ate a small dinner that night at the hotel restaurant before having a beer at the hotel bar. I then went directly to bed and slept until 5:30 a.m.

The narrative below depicts the rest of my involvement and what our investigation disclosed. The shooting incident occupied my time for the next two weeks. I called the investigation the Case of the Dead CID Agent's Wife; Was It Suicide or Murder?

## THE CASE OF THE DEAD CID AGENT'S WIFE; WAS IT SUICIDE OR MURDER?
Regardless how trivial information appears, an investigator must use his instincts

Preliminary findings disclosed that Special Agent Snider received a call from his estranged wife, Sue Snider,[133] at about 10:00 a.m., and an argument ensued over the phone about something. Sue Snider became so enraged with Special Agent Snider that she told him she was going to shoot herself. Special Agent Snider believed that she would, so he rushed to my townhome and found her in an upstairs bedroom pointing a gun toward her chest with both hands around the hand grip with her finger on the trigger. It is at this juncture that the Aurora police have trouble with Special Agent Snider's explanation of what happened next. Special Agent Snider told Aurora that he slowly reached for the gun in Sue's hands to try to take it away from her. When he got a good grip on the gun handle and pulled, it fired, shooting her in the chest, killing her instantly. There are a bunch of pieces to the puzzle that we haven't put together yet, the direction of the investigation took a turn based on developments in the case.

After getting ready for the day, I went directly to the CID office. I wanted to review the open cases before I joined LTC Nichols at the Aurora Police Department for Snider's second polygraph. I had been in my office for about thirty minutes when the phone rang. *Who can that be this early in the morning?* I wondered. I was surprised when I answered to hear an agent from Second Region calling from Germany. He wanted me to run down a lead for them that involved Special Agent George Snider. I thought, *this is getting interesting.*

"What do you need?" I asked.

The agent from Europe provided me with information for the basis of their case on Snider. He said that Second Region had opened an inquiry on Snider for writing insufficient-fund checks in Europe. During the inquiry, we'd interviewed Snider, who'd denied writing bogus checks. When we confronted him with the evidence, he told us that he had sold a Ford Bronco to his sister for $500, and she was supposed to send him the money. Special Agent Snider told them that once he received the money, he was going to deposit it into his checking account. The agent went on to explain their investigation failed to find any deposits for $500. The agent said that they were sure Snider was lying; however, they wanted to give him the benefit of the doubt and verify if the Ford Bronco was sold to his sister. If it wasn't, then Special Agent Snider would be guilty of an additional offense of falsifying an official document. I asked the Second Region agent why they allowed Special Agent Snider to leave Europe and return to the United States while the investigation was pending on him there. The agent indicated that the case only came to the attention of the Second Region CID after he'd left on emergency leave to spend some time with his father. The agent requested I try to confirm if the Ford Bronco was parked in his sister's driveway on Lansing Street. After jotting down enough information on what Second Region needed, I hung up the phone and prepared to leave for the Aurora Police Department for Special Agent Snider's second polygraph.

It took me about fifteen minutes to drive from the CID office to the Aurora Police Department. LTC Nichols was already there. I briefed him on the information about the case against Special Agent Snider that the Second Region CID was conducting. LTC Nichols did not seem to be surprised by the ongoing investigation of Special Agent Snider in Europe.

As LTC Nichols and I were standing in the hallway outside the Aurora Police Department squad room, several of their officers were reporting for work. Detective Sergeant Ruth Blackman[134] of the Aurora Police Department, who oversaw the investigation into the shooting death of Sue Snider, was one of them. She greeted us and explained that the polygrapher would begin at the scheduled time of 9:00 a.m. The polygrapher, was a former Office of Special Investigations (OSI) agent who was now a member of the Aurora Police Department. It was good that he had military as well as civilian police experience, because I felt that background would help him during the interview with Snider.

I grabbed a minute with Detective Sergeant Blackman before she stepped in to talk to the polygrapher. I wanted both the polygrapher and her to know what Special Agent Snider had told me outside the gun store that day when he and I were returning to the CID office after lunch.

"Excuse me, Detective Sergeant Blackman, but I need to talk to you about some information that may or may not be useful in your investigation on Special Agent Snider," I informed her. She stopped and looked at me with an annoyed expression on her face as if to say, "What do you want now?"

I thought, *Hell, this is not going over well. We are supposed to be colleagues in the business of criminal investigations, not adversaries.* I could not understand that she had not even requested an interview with me to this point. "I just wanted to let you know of a comment that Special Agent Snider said to me shortly before I left for Washington, DC," I told her.

"What was the comment?" she curtly fired back.

*Damn! Did I catch her after she got up on the wrong side of the bed or what?*

She acted withdrawn and distant toward me, as if she could not care less about what I was about to tell her.

"Well, one day, Special Agent Snider and I were returning to the Fitzsimons CID office after lunch, and he asked me to stop at this gun store on Potomac Street. After spending about fifteen or so minutes looking at guns, without buying any, we returned to the car, and just as we were getting in for the ride back to the office, I looked over the roof of the car and asked him, "Why do you want to buy a gun?" His response to me was, "I may want to kill my wife.""

I went silent for a few seconds to see what kind of reaction she would have, but none came.

She did tell me, "I think our case is contingent upon what comes out of this polygraph; cross your fingers." She then continued through the door to the polygrapher's office.

The exam started as scheduled, and LTC Nichols and I observed through a one-way mirror. The procedure took about an hour, and the polygrapher completed his questioning and brought the charts to Detective Sergeant Blackman. We were invited into the room to hear the polygrapher tell us his interruption of the charts.

"He's telling the truth that he did not shoot his wife."

LTC Nichols and I looked at each other in silence.

"Where do we go from here?" I asked LTC Nichols.

"I think we've still got some ammunition to use," he said.

As we left the Aurora Police Department, LTC Nichols decided to head south to the Fort Carson District. "I'll let Chief Klossner know what I find out."

I had no feeling for what direction Detective Sergeant Blackman was taking on the Snider case. If they depended entirely on the polygraph to decide not to pursue the investigation further, then I felt, because there were still some very significant issues yet to be resolved, that they would be closing an incomplete case. *Time will tell*, I thought. I radioed the MP station and requested that the desk sergeant inform Special Agent Capshaw that I would be handling a lead on one of our cases and that I would be back in the office in an hour.

I drove from the Aurora Police Department to the address given to me by Second Region. It took me about ten minutes to reach the residence. As I drove by, I did not see the Ford Bronco. I figured that if the Bronco did exist, then the sister or one of her family members probably drove the vehicle to work, or the sister maybe went shopping. I decided to check once again later in the evening.

It was noon when I arrived back at the Fitzsimons CID office. I immediately checked in with Chris to see what was going on.

"The usual things," he said, indicating to me not to worry—that he had everything covered.

Special Agents Mims and Snider were also there. SP4 Christenson was out to lunch. Snider's presence confirmed that the Aurora police had not arrested him for the shooting death of his wife, Sue. I went to my office and called Chief Klossner at Fort Carson to see if he had anything pending he needed to tell me.

"Everything is as well as it can be, considering what is going on with Snider."

"Chief, don't you think it would be better for Snider to spend time at Fort Carson while he is waiting for the completion of the investigation?"

"We thought about that, but his emergency TDY orders direct that he be at Fitzsimons, pending a resolution of what they are going to do with his father."

"Boy, that could take forever. Do they have any time to where they will pull his TDY or make a decision to reassign him?"

When I hung up from talking to the chief, the *we* issue popped back into my mind. I asked myself again, *who is "we"?*

About 6:00 p.m., I was the last one to leave the office. I took another drive by the house of Snider's sister to see if the Ford Bronco was in the driveway, but I did not see it. I did not like the idea of Special Agent Snider hanging around the office waiting on the completion of the Aurora Police Department and CID investigations. I'd keep pushing the argument for Special Agent Snider to relocate to Fort Carson.

Nothing significant occurred for the next two days, and then on the third day back from Washington, I got the go-ahead to remove the crime scene tape from the door to my townhome and received permission from the Aurora police that I could move back in. I called the neighbor who had Dog and told her I would be by to see her but that I first wanted to look at the inside of my house before making the decision to bring her back. The neighbor told me that she would keep Dog longer if I needed.

I stayed in the office the rest of that day, using part of the time to update Major Pierce on the Snider case.

"I'll make sure that the general and his staff are briefed. To get you off the hook, I will let them know you are tied up with the case and will brief them when you find the time," he advised me.

I thanked him and returned to the CID office about 3:00 p.m.

As soon as I walked into the lobby of the CID office, SP4 Christenson asked to see me. "Come on in, Ed," I told him. "What is it you need?"

"I just got the word that the CID wants me to report to Fort McClellan next weekend."

"Ed, that is great! Glad to see that it is all coming through for you. I suppose you will need next week to clear Lowery. Well, you got it," I told him.

I saw SP4 Christenson as a very promising young guy who would go far within the CID and wished him the best of luck before he left my office.

I informed Chris that I was picking up my dog and that I would probably be in over the weekend.

"Okay, Chief. I'll take care of all the calls this weekend."

I thanked him and headed for the neighbor for the first time since I'd returned from Washington. I decided not to check out of the Holiday Inn yet, leaving that decision after seeing the inside of my house.

As I drove up to the townhome, I noticed crime scene tape on the front door. I raised the garage door with the automatic door opener and saw nothing awry. Just in case I was not able to stay, I kept the car outside and walked through the garage to the kitchen door. I walked in, and the downstairs area did not look bad. You could tell that a large group of people, probably the medical personnel and police, had been in the house. I was not concerned about the first floor; it was the second level of the house I was worried about. After taking my time surveying the living room and kitchen and finding no real damage, I turned toward the basement door, wanting to check out that part of the house next. I was in no big hurry to go upstairs.

I slowly walked down the basement steps, anticipating the worst once I got to the bottom. I turned at the base of the steps and took my time looking around the room, I was relieved that there was nothing that required my immediate attention. Now, as I ventured back up the steps to the first floor to the landing at the bottom of the stairs and then to the second floor, butterflies swam around in my stomach, causing a sensation of churning fullness. As I walked up the thirteen steps and stood on the landing, I could see into both bedrooms. I decided to check out the guest room first, leaving the master bedroom, the scene of the crime, for last.

I used the guest bedroom for a study area. I had an assortment of books and reference materials on shelves against one wall. As I walked into this room, I noticed that the desk had been hastily but thoroughly gone through. On one pedestal, the top two drawers had been left open, and there was a binder that I used to record my daily jogging stats—time to run two miles, times and days of the week, and that sort of thing—was not there. For some reason, the police apparently took it to be evaluated for evidence. The room in general was not too bad and did not need any major repairs or work. A good cleaning would do the trick and it would be back to normal. The master bedroom was the area I was most concerned with. It was time to go check it out.

As I turned my attention to the doorway of the master bedroom, I noticed some floor carpet had been cut, but I did not see the extent of the damage until I walked into the room. Where Special Agent Snider's wife had fallen after being shot, there was an outline of her body cut out of the carpet and taken as evidence. It is normal for the police examinations to take a portion of the carpeting during their crime scene investigation to determine if there is any trace evidence, like hair, fibers, or other material that can be associated with a suspect or victim.

I looked inside the master bath, but there were little remnants of a crime scene. I backed out of the bath and turned my inspection to the floor where the body had been lying after being shot. I immediately saw that I had to replace a large portion of the carpet that had been cut out. There were signs of fingerprint powder in various areas on top of the chest of drawers and nightstand, but other than that, it was not as bad as I had anticipated.

Having seen everything, I felt that I wanted to get the place cleaned up before moving back in. This meant that I had to let my neighbor know to continue keeping Dog until I could get the job done, as she'd offered earlier; if she couldn't, I would put Dog in a kennel. I had to contact a carpet store and hire a cleaning crew to come in and go over the entire house. That might take a week or so, which made me think that Dog would be better off in a kennel until the work was completed.

The first step I took was to reach out to the neighbor down the street that was looking after Dog. The second was to get a carpet repairman to replace the portion of the carpet torn out by the crime scene people, and third step was to identify a cleaning company to do the house. Since it was almost 6:00 p.m., I decided to wait until the next day to find a carpet store and janitorial service to clean the house. I never considered asking for any help from the Aurora Police Department for assistance in this matter, because I probably wouldn't have gotten it anyway. I took the financial burden upon myself.

I left the house through the garage and stepped over to the main entrance of the townhome. I ripped the crime scene tape off the door and made sure the house was secured. I lowered the garage door with the electronic switch. I then walked two doors down to talk to the neighbor who was dog sitting. She was a nice lady, very friendly, and did not ask a bunch of questions, which I liked.

After some pleasantries with Dog, I graciously thanked the neighbor for the much-needed help. I told her that I needed probably another week or so to get the house in order before I moved back in.

I told her, "I could put Dog in a kennel for this period." But just as I finished the sentence, she vehemently reiterated that she would take care of Dog for however long was needed.

The meeting with the neighbor lady went well, and I thanked her again for the help she was giving me. It was a done deal; she would continue caring for Dog until I could move back into the house. As I drove away from the neighborhood, I thought, *Good neighbors like her are extremely hard to find.*

Because Elda was visiting from Germany in late June, I had to get the house in order. I had called and talked to her a few days after the shooting incident occurred in our house. It took almost two weeks to repair the upstairs carpet and to get the entire house cleaned. I eventually retrieved Dog from the neighbor, and things were getting back to some sense of normalcy at home.

It was entirely the opposite at work. One day in mid-June while sitting in my office doing paperwork, I answered an incoming call from a female claiming to be Special Agent Snider's wife, who lived in West Virginia.

"Who are you?" I asked the female on the phone again.

"My name is Connie Snider.[135] I would like to speak to my husband. Is he there?"

Feeling surprised and dumbfounded, I replied, "Why, no, he is currently at Fort Carson." *If his wife was shot dead in my house, then who is this other female calling herself Snider's wife?*

Tactfully, I engaged in small talk with her as a ruse to get her to talk more about her alleged marriage to Snider. "I'll bet you miss George while he is out here, don't you?" I asked her.

"Yeah, I sure do. I haven't seen him since the weekend we got married almost two months- ago. We got married on May 10, and he had to quickly return to his job in the army."

As a bonus, she told me that she wanted to tell Snider she had some time off and wanted to come out to see him. *Boy,* I thought, *the Snider case is getting weirder by the week.* "Look, I'll contact George and tell him to call you. Does he have your number?" I asked her.

She gave me a West Virginia number, and before I hung up, I told her he should be calling her in a couple of hours. I needed to get either the chief or LTC Nichols on the phone and let them know about Special Agent Snider's second wife.

Wow, I could not believe what I'd heard. I now knew what Special Agent Snider was insinuating when he'd indicated, "*We* will try to repay you"! Since Snider's first wife was alive on May 10, 1986, the date he was believed to have married his second wife, Connie, then he was guilty of bigamy. CID may not get Snider for murdering his wife, but we had him for writing worthless checks, falsifying official documents, having an unregistered firearm, and any other crime we could prove. Now, we potentially had him committing bigamy with a side charge of adultery.

I'd told Connie, Special Agent Snider's wife, one truth: that he was at Fort Carson. I finally won the battle of having him relocated there, pending the resolution of his legal situation.

I contacted Fort Carson and advised them of the revelations about a potential second wife. Subsequent investigations into this matter resulted in verification that Special Agent Snider was in fact married to two different women on May 26, 1986, the date that his first wife died in a shooting incident. A decision was made to interview Special Agent Snider at Fort Carson about the offense of bigamy.

This decision posed a major problem. Even if they interviewed Snider at Fort Carson within the next hour or so, Connie was still waiting on my call to let her how to get ahold of Snider. So, I let the special agent who was assigned to conduct the interview know that it should take place immediately because of the pending call. We hastily put together a scheme to immediately interview Snider about the double marriage; then I would have Connie call him at Fort Carson shortly after the interview. If he confessed to the crime of bigamy, it would not be an issue, but if he denied the new marriage, his reaction at the phone call would be priceless. I hung up and waited for the results of the interview.

About forty-five minutes later, I received a call from Fort Carson indicating that Snider had confessed to bigamy. I then discussed strategy with the Fort Carson agent about how to handle future contact with Connie. Now that we had a confession, there was no real advantage one way or another about her contacting

Snider. I eventually contacted Connie at the phone number she had provided me and passed on Snider's phone number to her. The added charges of bigamy and adultery were enough to court-martial Snider, and if he were found guilty of those offenses in addition to writing worthless checks, it could mean a considerable amount of time in prison.

The most serious offense of murder was off the books, however, because the Aurora police did not pursue the case after Snider passed a second polygraph, and the US Army's decision not to mess with a highly-publicized court-martial knocked the wind right out of the case. Instead, the US Army proceeded with a general discharge under the provisions of Chapter 10, AR 635-200, in lieu of general court-martial.

The decision to administer Special Agent Snider a general discharge was a compromise between CID and him. He chose this punishment rather than face a general court-martial because he was facing numerous felony charges. Snider's decision allowed him to get out of the US Army with what little grace he could.

For several weeks after he was discharged, I received numerous inquiries for a recommendation for a position from employers who were checking his background. I responded to each with an honest reply that his trustworthiness and responsibilities could be questioned at times. I have never heard from him directly again, and I have not received any money from him as payback for the loan— money he'd used to finance his trip to go home and marry a girl while still married to his wife that died under questionable circumstances. It was my opinion, based on facts of the case, that his wife Sue's death by shooting was not accidental or suicidal. The Aurora police and US Army CID did not fully consider all the elements that should have been explored. I provided an explanation on my thoughts to both the Aurora Police Department and CID, but neither agency acted upon it. The facts reported in both final reports of the Aurora police and CID investigation were essentially the same.

The most probable scenario that played out in the master bedroom of my home the day of the shooting was the result of a purely diabolically clever scheme orchestrated by none other than Special Agent Snider.

It was a well-known fact that Sue had some emotional issues. She had been in the US Army for several years when she married Snider. From all accounts, people that knew the couple were aware of Sue's highly emotional bouts of anger and over-the-top behavior that caused their marriage to become strained. Often, Sue would show up at the Fort Carson CID office and be heard pacing up and down the main hallway of the building, yelling for Snider, possibly thinking he was trying to avoid her or was in a location of the building that she did not have access to.

Moving forward to the day I stopped at the gun store on Potomac Avenue in Aurora so Snider could look at some guns, it all makes sense to me now. After spending several minutes in the store viewing the various types of guns available, we left without him buying any. Once we got to the car, I asked him why would he want to buy a gun. Responding without hesitation, Snider said, "I may want to kill my wife." I did not take him seriously at the time, but now that all the elements were in place, I feel he was methodically planning and scheming, over a period of a few weeks, to create the perfect scenario for his wife do herself harm.

He was never interviewed about his comment to me that he may want to kill his wife and that this was the reason he wanted to buy a gun. Another issue not explored was that Special Agent Snider knew that his wife suffered from emotional stability issues and that she acted irrationally at times. He needed to fuel this emotion whenever he could. By purchasing the gun and having it lying around, unlocked, loaded, and accessible, he purposely set the stage for her to act on her frustrations.

A third issue not explored was that though his story of the events that occurred the day he went to my house and found his wife holding a gun to her chest was unconvincing and his actions afterward were suspect. Special Agent Snider said he grabbed the grip of the gun with both hands and tried to pull it away from his wife. He said that as he pulled the gun closer to him, the gun suddenly fired, causing the bullet to enter his wife's chest, killing her instantly. The autopsy verified the bullet entered the body from the gun that was fired at a short distance of maybe less than a foot. The bullet caused massive trauma to the heart and other vital organs in the chest but remained in the body until extracted by the pathologist.

A fourth issue not explored was that Special Agent Snider's wife was allegedly holding the gun to her chest. People planning to commit suicide by shooting themselves most commonly point the gun to the side of their head.

There were several other factors that were never fully explored or considered. For one, why did Special Agent Snider buy bullets for the gun? He never mentioned any plans to use the gun for target shooting. For two, why did he get married to another woman before he divorced his first wife? For three, why wasn't his second wife interviewed in detail by CID? What role, if any, did she play in the investigation? Another element of the entire investigation on Special Agent Snider was that his wife was also a military service member, which supported a military connection to the case.

The above unresolved issues were solid investigative leads that were never pursued, but only went away by him being discharged. It was a fact that the shooting of Sue was investigated by the civilian police department, but a lateral investigation by CID should have been considered. The investigation of Special Agent Snider will forever be embedded into my mind, because it occurred in my home. I wish it would go away, but it never will.

In late June 1986, Elda came for a visit so we could spend quality time together for the rest of the summer. She was not required to return to Germany until the end of August 1986. I took leave, and we took a trip to Indiana to visit Chris, family, and friends. In all, it was a good summer, but the time went way too fast. One good thing after Elda departed was that it brought me closer to the time I would be moving back to Germany.

In late August, I received a phone call from the CID assignment officer, CW4 Michael Elbert from the Hoffman Building in Alexandria, Virginia. Michael advised me that I had been tentatively selected for assignment as the special agent in charge of the Stuttgart resident agency in Stuttgart, Germany. I accepted the assignment without reservations. I was given a reporting date of October 13, 1986. This allowed me about two months to clean up things at Fitzsimons and make the move.

Mike gave me a brief rundown and makeup of the office. There were eight special agents assigned to the Stuttgart resident agency, with several support personnel, and two more special agents at the branch office in Böblingen, Germany, about twenty kilometers away. The Stuttgart CID office had two more special agents than Schweinfurt, but otherwise, the offices were similar.

"I don't know what you are getting into over there," he said, a comment that puzzled me somewhat.

Once I was alerted to my deployment to Stuttgart, I contacted Elda and informed her of where I was going to be stationed for the next three years. We agreed that she should work on getting a transfer in her DoDDS school system and get everything ready for the move from Schweinfurt to Stuttgart as soon as possible. Also, since she was already in Germany, she could start working on housing for us in Stuttgart.

In the meantime, while awaiting my departure date, I continued to work the usual felony crimes, involving thefts, a few housebreakings and larcenies, and a bunch of leads from other offices around the United States, to have people interviewed on one of their investigations.

One case I recalled for its unique side component that was not part of the investigation. The investigation involved an eleven-year-old girl who had been sexually assaulted by a US Army soldier at the Presidio of San Francisco. The girl and her family moved to Denver after the incident, and Presidio requested she be interviewed. In this case, I went from the interviewer to the interviewee because of the death of her father. The father had retired from the US Army several years earlier and stayed at the Presidio of San Francisco working as a Department of the Army civilian employee. (DAC). He originally grew up in the Denver area and decided to return to the area for full retirement. They were in the process of moving when the incident took place, and they left before their daughter could be interviewed. I called this investigation the Case of the Overweight Father Whose Luck Ran Out:

## THE CASE OF THE OVERWEIGHT FATHER WHOSE LUCK RAN OUT
Investigative inquiries can eliminate involvement in the same fashion to prove guilt

It was in the waning days of my assignment at Fitzsimons when I received an RFA from the Presidio of San Francisco field office to interview Sally Ramsey,[136] an eleven-year-old girl who had reportedly been sexually assaulted by a US soldier. The incident occurred at the Presidio of San Francisco about two weeks before the Ramsey family moved from that location to Denver. The lead involved a request to interview Sally. Apparently, most of the arrangements were set forth by the case agent at Presidio, and all I had to do was to pick a date for the interview of Sally, with her father Frederick Ramsey.[137] Mr. Ramsey agreed that the interview would take place on a Monday, the first workday of the following week. Mr. Ramsey requested and was granted permission to sit in on the interview with his daughter, Sally.

The two of them show up at precisely 10:00 a.m. on Monday as scheduled. As we shook hands, my first impression of Frederick Ramsey was that he liked food. He was obese and looked untidy in an ill-fitting plaid sports jacket with black pants that were one or maybe two sizes too small, making him appear very uncomfortable. His tie was wrinkled, and his shoes—which were dirty, scuffed, and scratched—did not match his clothes. He spoke softly, using choppy sentences, and did not make eye contact.

Without touching her, he said, "This is my daughter, Sally."

After the initial introductions, I invited them to sit in chairs that I had arranged prior to their arrival.

When Mr. Ramsey sat down, with no small talk or preliminary discussion as to why they were there, he opened a book he had been carrying with him when he walked into the CID office and started reading it. Sally, a beautiful eleven-year-old little girl and obviously very nervous, dutifully sat in her chair with her hands folded in her lap, staring downward.

I was still spinning and somewhat puzzled from the cold, robotic actions of Mr. Ramsey. I had to take a moment before getting into the interview. The way his actions were playing out, I did not want to just jump right into asking questions. I also thought *it very strange that Mr. Ramsey did not insist on setting some ground rules for the interview of his daughter.* Maybe he was using the book as a crutch of some sort to divert his attention from the painful situation involving his daughter. I did not want to bring him into the interview, but I at least expected him to say a few words before we got started. On a pretense of checking on one last thing before we got started, I excused myself and left the two alone in my office. I spent the moment outside the office telling Chris to ensure we were not interrupted. I returned to my desk, sat down, and shuffled some papers before speaking. I was waiting for Mr. Ramsey to say something, but I heard no words coming from his mouth.

To break the silence, I started. "Mr. Ramsey, I want to thank you for bringing you daughter in so we can get her version of what happened at Presidio of San Francisco. I cannot imagine what you and your family are going through at this moment. You have my sympathies," I told him. I included the word *we* to make him understand that it was all right to let me know if my questions presented to his daughter entered any areas he felt were unnecessary or uneasy. I then realized that I never offered him to chance to speak to me without his daughter being present. "Would you feel more comfortable talking with me first, before we talk to Sally?" I asked.

"No, that is not necessary; let's get on with the interview," he said.

*Well, he does speak*, I thought. "Okay, let's get started." Turning to Sally, I asked, "Sally, do you know who I am and why you are here?"

"Yes. You are a policeman," she responded.

"Do you know why you are here?"

"Yes! It is because of what the soldier did to me."

"We are here with your father to get the details of what happened. Is it okay for me to ask you some questions about what happened?"

"Yes."

"Sally, can you tell me what the soldier did to you?" I asked.

She hesitated a moment, but in a very clear and calm manner, she told me the following story. "The soldier who touched me lived across the hall from us. He would often come over and talk with Dad about things and stay for long periods of time. One night, I stayed at his house, because my father and mother stayed out late for dinner. His kids, who are much younger than I am, were put to bed, and I stayed up watching TV with the soldier. Mrs. Daily went to visit another neighbor in the building, leaving me along with Mr. Daily."

After each question, I would look over at Mr. Ramsey to see if he wanted to comment, but he appeared to be more interested in his book and remained silent.

"What did Mr. Daily do when Mrs. Daily left to see the neighbor?"

"He moved from a chair to the couch and sat next to me," she said.

"What did Mr. Daily do to you then?"

"He moved his hand and placed it between my legs and started rubbing my private area."

"How long did Mr. Daily do this to you?"

"A few minutes."

"Has he ever tried to take your clothes off at any time?" I asked.

"He started taking my pants off, but he quit when Mrs. Daily came back home."

"Was this the only time he did this to you?"

"He has hugged me real tight sometimes, but nothing else."

"Did Mr. Daily do anything else to you?"

"No!" she said. "No, he didn't."

"Could you go have a seat in the other room, Sally? I would like to talk to your father, okay?"

As she obediently got up and went to the outer room, I made sure she found a chair. I went into the MPI office and asked their secretary to sit with her while I talked to her father. She agreed.

I went back to my desk and asked Mr. Ramsey several follow-up questions. I hoped that he would see fit to take himself away from his book long enough to hear what his daughter told me. I began with a couple of clarifying questions. "What is Mr. Daily's first name?"

"I believe it is Ronald."[138]

"Where exactly did Ronald Daily and his family live?"

"Directly across the hallway from our apartment, a few blocks from the Presidio," he said.

"Had you noticed or suspected any indications of Ronald Daily's actions toward your daughter?"

"He had been to our house; in fact, we have exchanged visits for dinner and evenings on several occasions, and there was never any indication he would do such a thing."

"How did you find out about the incident your daughter described to us a short while ago?"

"She actually came home that evening and told my wife, who called the MPs."

"Did the San Francisco police get involved?"

"Yes. They came to our house one evening about two days before we left and talked to us about it."

"What actions did the MPs take once it was reported to them?"

"They requested I bring Sally to the MP station, which I did, and they interviewed her. It was at the MP station that the CID got involved."

"Why wasn't Sally interviewed at Presidio?"

"I told them that my family and I were moving, and they indicated they would get a statement from her later."

I thought it was rather unusual to wait, knowing that the victim was moving out of state. I told Mr. Ramsey that I wanted to take a written statement from

Sally, and he agreed. We brought Sally back into the office, took a statement from her, and I then released the two. I saw the interview as pretty much cut and dried and would finish writing up my report the following day. Nothing happens the way you expect or anticipate.

About 3:00 p.m. the following afternoon, as I was writing my report to be sent to the Presidio of San Francisco, I received a call from Special Agent David Sage, Sixth Region, USACIDC. Dave wanted to know what I'd said to Mr. Ramsey in the interview the previous day, because they (apparently, CID) had some concerns. Thinking this was unusual, I told him that nothing out of the ordinary occurred during the interview with his daughter and that Mr. Ramsey sat through the entire interview without showing concerns or making any complaints. Then Dave threw me the bombshell.

"Are you aware that Fred Ramsey died this morning at a Denver hospital from an apparent heart attack?"

I was startled but not surprised, recalling how Mr. Ramsey appeared physically when he was in my office. Dave started questioning me about how I had treated Ramsey and if I possibly had been too rough on him or his daughter during the interview. I assured Dave that the interview went without incident and that Mr. Ramsey had no unresolved issues when he'd left my office.

"How did you guys find out so fast that Ramsey had died?" I asked Dave.

"His wife called us this morning and reported he had died at a Denver hospital earlier."

"Did she complain about anything related to my interview of her daughter, Sally?" I inquired.

"Not really. We just want to be prepared in case any issues come up."

"In the meantime, what am I supposed to do?" I asked.

Without much reassurance, Dave told me that if he did not hear anything in the next few days that there probably would not be a formal inquiry into the death of Ramsey. I thought, *I have nothing to worry about; I did everything possible not to pressure Ramsey and his daughter during their interview the previous day.*

After Dave hung up, I did worry that I might be implicated and a formal inquiry initiated. This incident is a good example of how nothing becomes something. Fortunately for me, I left Fitzsimons about a month and a half later without hearing anything more, but it still did not stop me from worrying about possible CID actions into the matter.

Regardless of the Ramsey and Snider deaths and the Gramm-Rudman-Hollings Balanced Budget and Emergency Deficit Control Act of 1985 and some follow-up legislation causing my tenure at Fitzsimons to be extended for ten months, I considered the assignment to be an overwhelming success. The Fitzsimons staff offered me a medal for my services while assigned there, but I declined, assuring Colonel Meyers, chief of operations of Fitzsimons, that USACIDC would take care of me in that department; they never did.

Shortly before I left Fitzsimons, CW4 James Busha took over as the new operations officer at Fort Carson. I knew Jim from Korea and was confident that he would do a good job. He chose Fort Carson as his retirement assignment.

I learned a great deal from my experiences at Fitzsimons. In retrospect, however, I should have taken the assignment to Fort Campbell, Kentucky. Campbell, being a large installation, would have obviously led to greater challenges and more opportunities within CID. Fitzsimons was my fifth CID assignment in a row where I seemed to excel in every facet of CID investigations. My luck would forever change, however, in my new assignment and upcoming role as the special agent in charge of the Stuttgart resident agency in Germany. Those changes that I never anticipated would alter my perspectives on personnel, CID leadership, operations, and liaison with local German Kriminalpolizei (KRIPO) for the rest of my career.

With old Dog by my side, I left Fitzsimons on October 6, 1986, with a good feeling. I spent a few days in Terre Haute with Chris, Mom, family, and friends and then drove to New York City and dropped off Dog at JFK and my car at a transfer company for shipment to Germany. I caught the seven-hour red-eye flight out of JFK to Stuttgart Airport. Elda was waiting for me as I got off the plane. She anticipated the worst with Dog. She just knew that the carrying cage would be messy from Dog's business, but when we picked Dog up, we got the surprise of our lives.

**Author getting promoted to CW3 by Fort Carson District Commander March 1985.**

12

# Changes on the Horizon

Humanity, Tolerance, and Perseverance

Stuttgart, Germany

*Greater efforts for greater excellence*

On October 10, 1986, at 8:00 a.m. I landed at Stuttgart Airport. It was a bright, warm, sunny day; I was happy to see Elda, who was waiting for me at the gate. She was acting somewhat nervous, so I asked her, "What's the problem?"

Nervously, with lips quivering, she blurted out, "Dog is the problem! I just know her carrying cage will be messy from being cooped up during the long flight," she said.

Her worries were soon forgotten when we saw Dog on the conveyor belt coming toward us. To Elda's relief, Dog's carrying cage was as clean as a whistle.

On the drive from the Stuttgart Airport, Elda revealed to me she was successful in obtaining US military housing within walking distance of the Stuttgart resident agency office.

*Fantastic*, I thought, *don't need a car.*

Elda had brought her clothes from Schweinfurt, and I had most of what I needed. I was technically still on leave from Fitzsimons, so I figured we would get the rest of our personal belongings in the next few days. I was anxious to visit the Stuttgart resident agency office to meet as many of the special agents and support staff as possible.

> USAREUR has named Stuttgart an enduring location ... nestled in the beautiful Swabian region of Southwest Germany, Stuttgart is the state capital of Baden-Württemberg. The city of 593,639 residents boast highly successful industries (Mercedes and Porsche automobiles are made there), a cosmopolitan downtown, modern shopping malls, an active culture calendar, and abundant woods, parks and gardens. USAG Stuttgart provides support services at four primary installations; Panzer Kaserne, Patch Barracks, Kelley Barracks, and Robinson Barracks, and maintains a presence at the Stuttgart Army Airfield.[139]

The US Army has had an established presence in Stuttgart since the end of World War II. I was amazed at the number of smaller US Army installations (*Kaserne*) that made up the Stuttgart US military community. Each individual *Kaserne* had its own commander and staff. The smaller *Kaserne* of course, had less elaborate management units, and the "commanders" were junior in rank. I could not find anyone in the CID office, including any support personnel, who understood just how each *Kaserne* fit into the overall operations of the Stuttgart military community. It would take me a few weeks before I had a working understanding of the vast responsibilities each *Kaserne* had.

The Stuttgart resident agency office was just out the back door of the military housing unit Elda had signed for. It was a short walk across a field to the building co-located with the MP station. I found as I walked into the building that the MP desk was located to the right and the local MPI section was to the left. The Stuttgart resident agency occupied the entire third floor. The second floor had various other offices associated with supporting the local military community. There was no elevator in the building, so to gain access to the CID office, one had to walk up three flights of stairs. I thought as I trekked up the stairs, *Wow, we've got our own physical training program already in place.* I would be wrong there; I soon found out that the office had a good, solid physical training program in place that was directed by Special Agent Jim Boysen.

I walked into the administration office and introduced myself to a military clerk. The admin office had three military clerks assigned. All three were female soldiers; each stopped her activities long enough to greet me and then immediately went back to her tasks. The first clerk I met introduced me to Special Agent Richard (Dick) Smith, the office's chief of investigative support. Dick stood about five foot nine, had a full head of grayish hair, and talked with a very distinct mid-western accent. We greeted each other, and he immediately commenced to talk about the operations of the office.

I interrupted him before he got too involved with his briefing to explain that I was still on leave and wanted to use the time to move my personal belongings from Schweinfurt, where I was at one time stationed there with Elda, my wife. I told Dick that Elda had stayed in Schweinfurt while I'd spent almost two years in Denver before being assigned to Stuttgart. I politely asked that he give me the briefing once I was on board and ready to work.

I advised Dick that I wanted him to set up times and dates so I could meet one-on-one with each special agent and support personnel. As we were finishing up, word had already gotten out that I had arrived. Several people walked into the office where Dick and I were. I noticed one special agent carrying several case files into the office and without explanation placed them in what would become my in-box. I shook hands with them all: Jim Boysen, Wayne Lee, Lee Wong, Ester

Harwell, Dan Cates, Dennis Green, Carl Hoecker, and a few more. I briefly explained to them that I was still on leave but wanted to drop in to meet as many people as I could before I started moving to Stuttgart.

Before I begin my move, I stopped by the Stuttgart District, which was only a short distance down the road, where I met with Chief Frank Conley and LTC Markalee Brannen, both of whom I knew from previous assignments and with whom I had good mutual working relationships. LTC Brannen had been my commander at the Würzburg field office for a little while, and Chief Conley had inspected my office at Schweinfurt when the office temporarily fell under the Southern District (provisional). I left the office feeling that the people I had meet at the resident agency and district were good people, and I looked forward to working with them.

Elda and I took the next week to move our personal belongings from Schweinfurt to Stuttgart and to settle into military housing on Robinson Barracks. Robinson Barracks was our first and only experience with living in post housing. We made good friends during our stay there; to this day, we continue to associate with some people we met in Germany. If it wasn't for a snafu caused by Melitta, Chris would have traveled with me to Germany, but instead, it was the middle of December 1986 before he got there.

I spent the first week in the Stuttgart CID office getting to know everyone. I had one-on-one meetings with all the people, including the two-local national criminal investigators (LNCIs), Wolfgang Haupt and Hans Hoffman, both long-time US Army employees. It did not take long before I noticed there were at least five areas of concern I would have to address early in my tenure as special agent in charge of Stuttgart.

One, I got the impression that our LNCIs appeared to be more loyal to the German Kriminalpolizei than the American CID. Whether this was a real issue or a perceived one, time would let me know. I felt I needed a better understanding of the way our LNCIs worked—a situation that I told myself I would have to monitor.

The second concern I became aware of was from talks with several special agents. They indicated that there was a problem with the German prosecutor, Herr Bechstein. Bechstein became too involved with US Army investigations, especially if the crime occurred outside the installations. When I learned of this problem, I thought that the status of forces agreement (SOFA)[140] should protect us from a lot of the interference from the German. However, I soon found out how wrong I was. I was told that Herr Bechstein reportedly went beyond SOFA and took over investigations until the last minute. I interpreted this statement to mean that Bechstein oversaw the Kriminalpolizei, and he wanted them to run with the investigations until they were completed and then give them to the US Army.

A third matter cropped up when I had a one-on-one talk with one of the special agents. He advised me that he would work for me during the day, but after 5:00 p.m., it was his time, and he spent it with his family. I couldn't believe him when he told me this. I immediately asked him about what his statement meant when he was pulling duty.

"I'll pull duty, but that will be the only exception," he said.

I dropped the subject during our one-on-one meeting, but I knew that this issue would more than likely need to be addressed.

A fourth matter concerned other problematic issues or situations I would have to tackle head-on. This matter involved developing a complete understanding of just how the forty-nine identified *Kasernes* supporting the Stuttgart military community worked.

And a fifth matter troubling me during the first weeks of my tenure was that of special agents in the office not working with each other effectively. My work was cut out for me to say the least. It was a big order, and to be successful in our overall support to the community and CID command, changes in management philosophy that were compatible with everyone would be required.

The former SAC had reassigned team chief positions with each team in the office right before he left the office, and this undercut my management and control of the office. It was almost like the entire leadership of the office was brand new.

To top off my incoming tasks, I arranged and held meetings with Herr Bechstein and the Stuttgart Kriminalpolizei liaison officer, T. K. Hoffmann. The first meeting with T. K., a tall, well-built man in his early forties, was held in my office. He spoke fluent English, and we could speak without an interpreter, but I asked LNCI Haupt to sit in just in case. Hoffmann gave a quick briefing about his department, what they expected in cooperation from the US Army CID, and how they handled cases. Nothing seemed out of the ordinary, and I had a fleeting thought that maybe some of the special agents had gotten the wrong impression of the Germans and how they work. Time would tell. We thanked each other and shook hands. As he left the office, I thought he was a nice man and it was probably going to be good working with him.

The meeting with Bechstein was also held in my office. Herr Bechstein, a small, stout-looking individual in his fifties, arrived on time. We shook hands, and I invited him to sit on the sofa directly against the wall facing my desk. LNCI Haupt was also invited to the meeting. Bechstein immediately produced a type-written note that said in part, "Glad to have you on board. Looking forward to restoring good reputation between our two offices. If there is ever anything you need, let me know…" Bechstein talked with a very thick German accent and was hard to understand at times. On occasion, LNCI Haupt would interpret what he said. He was not one for small talk and started right in on US Army German *polizei* cooperation. He brought up working together on serious crime within the Stuttgart area. I asked him what we (the US Army CID) needed to do to improve our relationships. Bechstein stated that anything involving a German victim, suspect, or subject should be the responsibility of the German police.

I agreed, but I countered with a question about incidents where the perpetrator was unknown.

"Simple, any crime committed off the US Army *Kasernes* without a known suspect or subject will be the responsibility of the Germans. We have had problems in the past about who was take the lead in an investigation," he added. He alluded that this problem was in the past and he was looking forward to better cooperation with the US Army CID. Analyzing what he meant, I thought, was *the problem with my predecessor?*

"What about the same type of scenario, but the crime is on a US Army *Kaserne*?" I asked.

"It's yours; we just want to be notified," he added. "We want to work well with the Americans, and we should be able to iron out any problems that come along," Herr Bechstein pointed out.

I thought, t*his fits with the SOFA; I don't know what the special agents are talking about.* The man seemed fair and earnest in wanting to work with us on crime. We ended the meeting on a positive note when Bechstein suggested he might attend the US Army Christmas holiday party. *Good*, I thought. *This will go a long way with restoring or at least shoring up relations with the Germans.*

I had been told that Herr Bechstein's main claim to fame was his ability to reach a legal resolution between the Germans and US Army concerning an inspection of all brake systems on our vehicles and on the two-and-a-half-ton truck. Apparently, several years back, there had been a serious collision involving a US Army soldier driving a deuce and a half truck and a German car and the German was killed. The subsequent investigation revealed that the primary cause of the accident was the failure of the truck's brakes.

Even with the good feeling about the meetings with both Bechstein and Hoffmann, most of my objectives to correct the management of the office, personnel, German relations, and working cooperation with special agents would be sidetracked for one reason or another, but mainly because of two factors: the Stuttgart resident agency would become a hot potato within Second Region due to the higher rate of violent crimes involving mostly murder and the lack of cooperation from the Germans.

The increase in complex investigations kept every special agent in the office extremely busy. I gave them all credit for the hard work, dedication, and never-give-up determination when dealing with their cases, but I knew that we would have to work better, not harder.

The storm hit the week I started working. I sat down at my desk as the special agent in charge of the office on October 13, 1986, and the tide of death investigations and issues with German liaisons was continuous and did not seem to slow down until late 1987. Then, once the flow of cases reached its peak, internal conflicts among several special agents started boiling over. As I was struggling aggressively to address this problem and all other issues, there were multiple operations officer changes at Stuttgart District. The new and various management styles that they brought with them created different and often arbitrary policy changes.

In late October 1986, the trend in death investigations began. A nineteen-year-old soldier committed suicide. Other deaths included a dependent wife, an American schoolteacher, a tourist, and an elderly grandfather staying with a soldier. These deaths were not murder cases, but the investigations still required our special agents' complete attention—attending the autopsy of the nineteen-year-old soldier and conducting full field investigations on the other people to eliminate any possibility of foul play.

Other death investigations conducted during late 1986 and early 1987 by our office involved a former US Army soldier who had stayed in Germany after being discharged. He died while working at his place of employment, the auto craft shop in Stuttgart. Then there was the SFC who died in his sleep, and the autopsy did not reveal the cause of death. We were having so many deaths in the community that we couldn't keep track of them all without reviewing the case files. I recall one incident where Special Agent Lee was returning from a death investigation and I asked him what his thoughts were on the death of the person, who had been found in his bed.

"Chief, you were there," Lee said. "The man didn't die in his bed—he was at work."

We then realized that we were talking about two different death cases.

It was early evening on October 31, 1986, Halloween, and I was sitting at my desk in the Stuttgart resident agency finishing up the review of criminal investigative case files. I had hoped to complete the reviews so I could go to a Halloween party hosted by Special Agent Michael Blades. It was quiet, and I felt good that I was getting somewhere with reviewing the many open criminal investigations. That quite ended soon when one of the agents walked in and started making small talk. I felt the agent had something on her mind and was waiting for me to ask what she wanted to talk about.

The agent finally spoke up and commenced to tell me that I had been too rough on another agent, when I kicked back his investigative report on an assault for having too many mistakes. I recalled the case that I had reviewed the day before. The report had many misspellings and poor grammar, and some information that was not thoroughly covered.

"What do you mean I was too rough?" I asked.

"We are not used to having our cases kicked back. Generally, what we turned in was acceptable to the former SAC."

"Okay, you've got to understand that that policy was in the past, and now we are in a new era in the office. I don't think it would be prudent to turn in a case that has many things wrong with it. The cases, depending on their nature, can be reviewed up the chain, to include the Department of the US Army leaders and even members of Congress. So, I don't think it is being too rough when I kick a case back for mistakes as simple as grammar and misspellings, as well as not being thorough. And another thing: I don't think that one agent should come into my office and question me about a review I conducted of another agent's work. Matter closed," I said.

I don't think I was too rough on the agent who had submitted his report and my review found several issues with it, and I felt I was equally justified in reminding the other agent that it was not proper to question my decisions without thoroughly knowing why I made them. I had an inkling that my confrontation with this agent was only the beginning of things to come.

After the unpleasant conversation with the special agent I went back to reviewing the cases on my desk. The cases I reviewed made me think of how busy the office was becoming. I did not have to wait long before that thought became reality. My reviews were quickly interrupted by a call from the CID duty agent. The case he wanted to brief me on involved a possible SIDS death of a three-month-old baby boy who was found dead in his crib by his mother. The case was unique in that it was not only the tip of the iceberg, but was the type of investigations that started flowing into our office. The case also revealed how grief can take hold of parents who lose a child, especially from unknown natural causes. I called this investigation the Case of the Baby Who Never Had the Chance to Grow Up:

## THE CASE OF THE BABY WHO NEVER HAD THE CHANCE TO GROW UP
It is hard for good parents to understand that the death of an infant son is not their fault

The CID duty agent reported he was at the scene of a possible SIDS death that looked straightforward with no unusual signs indicating that the baby had met with foul play. The CID duty agent did request assistance, however, so I located two other special agents and directed them to back him up. After ascertaining the name and address of the parents, Sergeant Jake and Lorain Collings,[141] Second Region policy required SACs to go to all death scenes, regardless of the suspected cause of death. So, following through on that policy, I obtained the keys to a CID sedan, found the car in the parking lot, and drove to the quarters in the Pattonville housing area near Ludwigsburg, Germany, where the baby had died.

As I walked in, I immediately was greeted by the CID duty agent, who briefed me on the investigation thus far. He told me, "The mother stays home with their infant son during the day while a seven-year-old daughter goes to the Pattonville Elementary School nearby. The father is a sergeant assigned to a support services company."

As the duty agent led me into the room where the dead infant lay in his crib, he said, "This is how we found the baby." The infant was on his side with his mouth touching the sheet covering the mattress.

*An unusual position for the baby to be lying in*, I thought. There was a blueish tone to the skin of the baby's face and fingers. However, the infant did appear to be healthy, with no markings or signs of abuse on its body.

"Have you had time to talk in detail with the parents?" I asked the duty agent.

"Yes. The mother came in to check on the baby about 6:30 p.m. She noticed that the baby's face around his mouth was blueish in color. She picked him up and discovered he was not breathing. She panicked, laid the baby back in the crib on its stomach, and immediately called her husband at work, and he came directly home."

*This would explain the unusual position in which the baby was lying in the crib*, I thought. The duty agent continued, "An ambulance was not called until the father, SGT Collins, came home and made the call." The duty agent explained that all the information he had ascertained came from Sergeant Collings or his wife, Lorain.

I looked around the house, and it was neat and clean, had modern furniture, and looked well kept. The baby did not look like it was undernourished, and the parents showed genuine grief for their loss. Still, seeing a dead three-month-old baby is a horrible, ugly sight that no one, especially the baby's parents or seven-year-old sister, should ever have to endure. The seven-year-old joined her parents in the living room; all were visibly upset. I thought that the death was probably going to be determined to be unknown, but I believed it to be from natural causes.

The subsequent investigation into the infant's demise eliminated any evidence of foul play as a cause, and the death was ruled to be SIDS. When the parents were formally interviewed at CID, they both expressed shame and felt inadequate at being parents and wished they would have taken better care of their infant son. The special agent who interview them tried to emphasize that fault should not fall to them for the death of their infant son. He pointed out to them that they were raising a beautiful, vibrant young girl as evidence that they were good and capable parents.

The tragedy in this case is that there is no more devastating loss than the death of a child. Sudden death is a contradiction to everything that is known to be true in life. Losing a child to sudden death is a disruption in the natural law and order of life. It is a heartbreak like no other. Parental grief is different from other losses—it is intensified, exaggerated, and lengthened.

> Children are not supposed to die... Parents expect to see their children grow and mature. Ultimately, parents expect to die and leave their children behind... This is the natural course of life events, the life cycle continuing as it should. The loss of a child is the loss of innocence, the death of the most vulnerable and dependent. The death of a child signifies the loss of the future, of hopes and dreams, of new strength, and of perfection.[142]

After a child's death, parents embark on a long, sad journey that can be very frightening and extremely lonely—a journey that never ends. The hope and desire that healing will come eventually is an intense and persistent one for grieving parents.

> The child who died is considered a gift to the parents and family, and they are forced to give up that gift. Yet, as parents, they also strive to let their child's life, no matter how short, be a gift to others. These parents seek to find ways to continue to love, honor, and value the lives of their children and continue to make the child's presence known and felt in the lives of family and friends. Bereaved parents often try to live their lives more fully and generously because of this painful experience.[143]

No one that has not experienced a loss of a child, especially an infant, can ever imagine what parents go through when dealing with grief. I never made it to Blades's Halloween party that night.

It was one thing to require us to spend an inordinate amount of time investigating these natural death cases, but then a new phase of deaths investigations came in. The new phase changed the deaths that piled up to victims of murder.

Throughout my tenure at Stuttgart, there were several SIDS cases, but each had to be vetted to the fullest to determine if the death was natural, neglect, or outright murder. One case involved another baby death that was originally reported as a SIDS that turned out to be murder by a parent. That circumstances of this case are recounted in the following narrative.

A week or so later, in late 1986, coming on the tail end of the Collings SIDS investigation, was a particularly grisly, horrific, and unnecessary baby death with a completely different set of circumstances. There is nothing good about investigating deaths, but when it comes to a three-month-old infant, it gets worse. I call this the Case of the Overly Callous Disciplinarian Mother:

## THE CASE OF THE OVERLY CALLOUS DISCIPLINARIAN MOTHER
A mother's love for her newborn does not always match her behavior toward the infant

I recalled that I was working in my office one afternoon in late 1986 when I received a phone call from my duty agent indicating that he was at the scene of another baby death with suspicious circumstances. He requested I come to the scene to get a firsthand view of the situation. Per my usual routine, I grabbed a CID sedan and headed to the scene, which was in the same housing area near Ludwigsburg as the Collings infant's death. Once I arrived, I noticed two MP cars and a CID sedan driven to the scene by the duty agent parked outside the quarters. As I walked inside, I saw a small baby being held by a woman I assumed to be its mother. There was a staff sergeant sitting next to her on the living room couch. I also assumed that the baby was dead.

The duty agent, who was standing in the doorway to the baby's room, motioned for me to join him. There were two MPs, one standing beside and one behind the woman holding the baby. I walked over to the duty agent, and he escorted me inside the baby's room. There was a small stand-alone baby crib and clothes lying on the floor, but no chest of drawers or other furniture. The bed linen was soiled and did not appear to have been washed for some time. The room was shaping up to be like others I had seen during the investigation of baby deaths. To me, if the room where the death occurs is dirty, messy, and in need of cleaning, as was the case of the one we were in, then the risk factor goes up exponentially for the safety and well-being of a baby.

As we were standing near the crib, I asked, "What are the parents' names?"

"SSG Tyrone and Simone Compton,"[144] an MP replied.

"Have you talked to them yet?"

"No. The mother won't talk, and the father is pretty quiet too."

The duty agent pointed out to me something very unusual he had found lying inside the baby's crib—several strips of duct tape. "What in the hell was it being used for?" the duty agent asked.

"I'm not sure, but I'll bet it was used to secure the baby's diapers," I informed him.

"You're kidding!"

"Nope. What else do you think the duct tape would be used for?"

In moving the bed linen around in the crib, both the duty agent and I simultaneously noticed a small hairbrush protruding from between the crib railing and the mattress.

"I wonder why that is in here," I murmured, not intending for the comment to be directed to anyone. "We had better bag the hairbrush," I told the duty agent.

We both were thinking; *do we have SIDS or something else here?*

"I think we need to start with the father! Let's bring him in here and talk to him without his wife being present," I informed the duty agent, at the same time motioning for him to get the father. The duty agent placed the brush into a plastic bag and laid it down on top of the crime scene kit case and then went to get SSG Compton.

With the father inside the room, I asked him, "What did your wife tell you about your son?"

"She called me at work and told me that our son was not breathing. I asked what happened and she told me to come home."

"What did you do when you first got home?"

"I saw my wife holding our son in her arms, and she continuously mumbled, 'Our poor baby. Our poor baby.'"

Pointing down at the duct tape inside the crib, I asked SSG Compton, "Why is the duct tape in the crib?"

"My wife uses it to hold the baby's diapers in place."

"You mean she uses duct tape instead of safety pins or disposal diapers?"

"Yes. It saves us money," he indicated.

"Does your wife ever discipline your infant son for, let's say, crying?" I asked him.

"She is home with him all day, and she has told me that he gets on her nerves by crying a lot. But I have never seen her strike him in any inappropriate way," SSG Compton explained.

"Do you think your wife would release your son to you without too much fuss?"

"I'll try," he said.

We walked to the door of the baby's room and watched as SSG Compton approached his wife and asked for the baby. Without getting up from the couch, she reluctantly gave the lifeless body to SSG Compton. As she released the infant to SSG Compton, we unexpectedly heard her mumble, "I didn't mean to hit him; all I wanted was for him to stop crying."

*Damn! She did kill the baby!* I thought.

SSG Compton, while holding his dead baby, asked his wife, "Why?"

"He just kept crying, and I hit him on top of his head with a brush."

An examination of the infant while it was held by SSG Compton did revealed a laceration on top of the center of the head. Torn tissue filled with blood and swelling was observed that could be indicative of blunt force trauma with an object. It looked like Mrs. Compton had a lot of explaining to do to the German *polizei* about what occurred when she was home alone with her infant son. Unfortunately, this case went unprosecuted due to the infamous jurisdictional gap.

After the admission from Mrs. Compton, we brought the Kriminalpolizei into the investigation. The Kriminalpolizei became the primary agency for the investigation, because Mrs. Compton was a civilian, not subject to the UCMJ. The maximum punishment for murder under German law is fifteen years, but if the circumstances of the death are grave or hideous in nature, then an order by a judge can keep the offender in jail for more than fifteen years. However, in Mrs. Compton's case, even though she killed her infant son, the circumstances were less severe than a cold-blooded killing. The Germans chose not to prosecute Mrs. Compton and allowed her to return to the States without punishment. I have seen it go both ways with the Germans; sometimes they prosecute, and other incidents they do not. This case tore me up emotionally. The Compton baby never had a chance at life.

December of 1986 put Elda and me in the Christmas spirit. Chris flew over to be with us for a year. It was good to see him, and I was very proud that, at fourteen years of age, he came by himself on the plane to Germany; he was growing up. When I picked him up at Stuttgart Airport, he was a couple of inches taller than I was. The holiday season during Christmas in Stuttgart was a special time to introduce Chris to the German culture.

The center of Stuttgart is transformed into a magical winter wonderland during Christmas. There were uniquely charming and lavishly decorated Christmas stands tempting visitors from all over the world. Christmas concerts on the steps of the town hall and in the inner courtyard of the Old Castle drew people into their path with their festive ambience. The children especially love the nativity scenes, the giant nutcracker, and the many other attractions in Weihnachtswunderland, where they can paint and bake to their hearts' content. Stuttgart's famous Hutzelbrot, with its many fruits, is a real treat. More unusual delicacies from the Christmas village were grilled salmon, reindeer slices in sauce, and Glögi—a mulled berry wine, which Elda and I thoroughly enjoy. If you're feeling cold, warm up in the pavilion next to a log fire crackling away in a brazier. You can always find a special gift in the market on Karlsplatz.

Things were extremely busy at Stuttgart during the first part of 1987. I started realizing that the heavy caseload was adding to the difficulty in management personnel. Special agents, support personnel, and coordination with the German Kriminalpolizei were tremendously challenging. With Herr Bechstein's influence, the Stuttgart CID office virtually had its hands tied when trying to investigate an incident off the many installations covered by the CID, even when the case clearly had a US Army interest. I would soon find out that influence overflowed onto the US military installations as well. Just when things couldn't seem to get any worse, the US Army Criminal Investigation Command and the Military Police Corps were dealt with a tragedy of overwhelming proportions.

On January 20, 1987, Brigadier General David H. Stem was killed in a plane crash in Missouri. The tragic accident occurred when the U-21 Beechcraft US Army plane piloted by a US Army major collided with a Piper Navaho craft about seven thousand feet over Independence, Missouri.[145] Many saw Brigadier General Stem as an innovator of MP/CID programs and a potential future commander of the CID command. He was also a very personable and well-liked universal leader within the MP Corps and CID command. His death created a loss to the CID and MP Corps of such magnitude it would be years before anyone realized just how great his impact had on our organizations.

Death investigations did not cease but rather increased during the early part of 1987. Many of the death investigations were murders, usually where the perps and victims knew each other. There were several incidents where a US Army soldier husband killed his wife. We had no shortage of wives who were also soldiers and victims themselves.

One murder investigation that I recall did not fit the usual pattern, involved a US Army female victim, and took CID over five months to solve. The circumstances surrounding the murder turned out to be an assignment-defining case for me and a career-defining investigation for Special Agent Mike Blades. Aspects of the investigation amplified already festering liaison problems with the German Kriminalpolizei and CID at Stuttgart. The victim, an attractive twenty-four-year-old female soldier, was TDY to the European Command (EUCOM) from Fort Hood, Texas. I called this investigation the Case of the Fort Hood Female Soldier's TDY That Became Permanent:

## THE CASE OF THE FEMALE SOLDIER'S TDY THAT BECAME PERMA-NENT

Youth has its challenges, but you never think they're insurmountable, unless death intercedes

It was a Monday, February 9, 1987, a cool winter day in Stuttgart. I had arranged to come into work late that day so that Chris and I could see a doctor at the clinic. I had a regularly scheduled checkup, and Chris was suffering from a head cold and needed some medicine. It was around 8:45 a.m. when I received a call on one of the clinic phones from Special Agent Mike Blades from the Böblingen branch office near Patch Barracks.

Without identifying himself and cutting to the chase, Mike blurted, "We have a murder at Patch Barracks."

"You were notified when?" I asked.

"About an hour ago; Runion and I have been here about twenty minutes or so," he said.

"Who was murdered?" I inquired.

"SP4 Waleska Marrero."

"She was killed where?"

"In her barracks room."

"I'll call the Stuttgart CID office to get you more help and will see you out there as soon as possible," I told Blades.

I returned to the doctor and informed him that I had been called out on a case. I informed Chris, who was talking to him when I answered the phone, that he should find his own way to school. As I departed the clinic, I heard Chris say, "Okay."

I hurried to the Stuttgart CID office, a short distance from the medical clinic, briefed two other agents who were in the office that a female soldier had been murdered in her dormitory room at Patch Barracks, and told them I wanted them to accompany me to the scene. Prior to leaving the office, I put in a call to Chief Conley at the Stuttgart District and advised him of the incident and told him and a couple of more agents were joining Special Agent Blades and me at the scene. Before we hung up, Chief Conley told me to keep him updated.

At the crime scene, we located Mike, who was working at identifying evidence. Once inside the dormitory room, I observed two beds separated by wall lockers. To the left, there was a lifeless female body lying on top of a bare mattress, her head covered by a pillow. If one did not consider we were in the middle of a death investigation, the female body gave the impression of a young women in a deep, serene sleep. An inspection of the body disclosed that rigor mortis had set in, giving a preliminary indication that death occurred less than twelve hours earlier, possibly nine to ten hours based on the stiffness of her limbs.

Mike briefed me on what he had ascertained thus far, which wasn't much. It appeared that the victim had been hit over the head with a bottle or some other hard object. I took a closer look and saw that she had a large laceration just above her forehead on the right side.

"You think that is what killed her?" I asked.

"Probably not, because she has bruising around her neck, which might have been caused by someone placing their hands around her throat," Mike explained.

"So, you are saying that she may have been strangled?" I asked.

"That's the way it looks," he responded.

Mike did advise me that the roommate of the deceased female soldier was outside waiting for us to talk to her. "Let's let the other agents continue to process the crime scene, and you and I will talk to the roommate."

We let the other agents know where we were going to be and told them to continue processing the scene.

Mike and I found a room where we could talk to the roommate. While other agents continued to process the crime scene, Mike invited her into the room and asked her to be seated. Mike and I decided to wait before deciding to read the roommate her Miranda rights, because we had no real evidence or even suspicions that she might be involved in her roommate's death.

Mike began the questioning by asking her what her name was.

"Christine Coe," she replied.

We noticed that she was dressed in a US Air Force uniform with the rank of airman first class (A1C).

"Can you tell us your roommate's name?" Mike started.

"Her name is Waleska Marrero."

"What can you tell us about your roommate's death?" Mike asked her.

"Well, we went out for dinner to a German *Gasthaus* and returned to our room about 10:30 p.m. We both turned in shortly after, and I heard some commotion on her side of the room about 3:00 this morning. I heard Waleska talking to a man, but I couldn't hear what they were talking about."

"Did you know the man who was with her?" Mike asked.

"No, but the guy's voice had an accent like he was from the South."

"Meaning the Southern states in the United States?" I asked.

"Yes, like a black or Puerto Rican person from a Southern state," she explained.

I interrupted Mike and asked him to join me outside the room.

Once outside the door, I asked Mike, "Do you find it disturbing that Coe was inside the room at the same time a man, probably the killer, was talking to our victim? Do you also find it hard to believe that she could be inside the room and not be concerned that something was going on with her roommate that early in the morning? I think we need to take Coe down to the office and interrogate her. She may know more than what she is trying to make us believe."

Mike arranged for the MPs to watch Coe, and we rejoined the other special agents who were working the crime scene.

We had not been inside the crime scene room more than five minutes talking to others about what they had uncovered when suddenly Herr Bechstein, T. K. Hoffman, and a group of KRIPO officers barged into the room.

T. K. Hoffman was the first to speak. In a controlling voice, he said, "We received communication that a murder had occurred at Patch Barracks and the offender was not known." He indicated to us that the Germans needed to be involved with the investigation until a determination on the identity of the offender was made. Herr Bechstein almost immediately begin directing the KRIPO officers to process certain aspects of the scene. Herr Bechstein appeared not to be concerned with what CID had done before the Germans arrived.

"Herr Hoffman, please understand that I think this is very unusual, to say the least," I protested. Maybe I should not have been so augmentative with him, but I just wanted to express my concern over the Germans commandeering the crime scene. I understood that they had a right to jointly investigate the case with the US Army CID to determine who the perp was, but not to shove my agents out of the way on our own turf and take over the scene. To emphasize my point, I told T. K. that what they were doing was the same as if a group of US Army CID special agents converged onto a scene in their jurisdiction and took over because of the possibility that a US soldier might be involved. T. K. stood still without commenting and then turned his attention to Herr Bechstein.

I thought I had made a good point to T. K. and that he was conversing with Herr Bechstein about what I had told him, but I was wrong. They were speaking in German, and I couldn't catch everything they were talking about. I got enough to understand they were upset that I had brought up jurisdictional matters on the case. I was able to get T. K.'s attention and asked if he and Herr Bechstein could come with me so that maybe we could discuss the issue away from the crime scene. They both agreed, and we walked out of the room and commandeered the company commander's office. As we scooted him out, I shut the door and attempted one more time to present my argument that the case should be jointly investigated and not unilaterally by the Germans. Neither T. K. nor Herr Bechstein was going for it. I then asked them to please wait while I called the Seventh Corps SJA to get a legal determination. Murphy's law shoots you in the foot every time. All SJA members that could answer my question were attending a joint conference in Heidelberg and were not available. I never received an answer from the SJA on this issue.

Realizing that the Germans were not going to relinquish the crime scene back to us, I suggested to Mike that he escort A1C Coe to the CID office before Herr Bechstein got wind that she was a person of interest in the murder of SP4 Marrero. If he found out, he would have demanded that the Germans be allowed to interview her without the US Army CID present. At the CID office, A1C Coe could be interviewed by CID without interruptions by the Germans. The goal by the end of the day was to either eliminate her as a suspect or prove she was our murderer.

As the day progressed, none of the US Army CID special agents were processing the crime scene, and by 5:00 p.m., Herr Bechstein, T. K. Hoffman and other KRIPO officers had completely taken it over and were still gathering potential evidence without cooperating with the CID. Time was becoming a concern to the unit leaders, because it was time that the troops were returning to the barracks after a hard day's work.

The Patch Barracks installation commander, a US Army colonel, kept pressuring me to have Marrero's body removed and the room sealed off. I told him that Herr Bechstein was in control of the crime scene and I could not make the decision on when the Germans would be finished.

Standing just outside the crime scene room, the colonel, in a louder-than-usual voice, initially asked Herr Bechstein when he would be finished, but there was no response. Then, about ten minutes later, the colonel made a demand that Herr Bechstein finish his investigation as quickly as possible so the unit could let their troops return to the building. Herr Bechstein still did not answer, and this nonresponse further infuriated the installation commander, who made another plea with the Germans to finish as soon as possible and leave the barracks.

As much as I was angry with Herr Bechstein for taking over the crime scene, I disagreed with the installation commander when he told Herr Bechstein to wrap things up and leave the barracks. I know that if I were still processing the murder scene, I would not have left without ensuring that everything was completed.

It was 6:00 p.m. when Herr Bechstein, T. K. Hoffman, and the group of KRIPO officers started packing up their equipment and gathering the bags of evidence. Soon after, they left the barracks with evidence in hand—satisfied, I am sure, that they had finished a very productive but busy day. Prior to the Germans leaving the crime scene, Herr Bechstein gave permission for the US Army ambulance team to remove Marrero's body and transport it to the Fifth General Hospital, Bad Cannstatt, Germany, for an autopsy. *What a day this has been*, I thought.

We finally allowed for medical personnel to remove the body for transport to the Fifth General Hospital. The Germans had retained the bed linen and clothing worn by SP4 Marrero for evidence. To ensure continued access to the crime scene, I ordered the room sealed, pending further developments that would warrant our reinspection. I briefed the unit commander on what we had ascertained during the day and told him we would follow up with updates as needed.

By the time, I had arrived at the CID office, Mike and a couple of other agents obtained some significant background information on A1C Coe before she was interviewed by Special Agents Blades and Ester Harwell, a female agent who was considered an excellent interrogator. I joined a couple of other agents who were observing the interview from a side room through a one-way mirror.

It appeared that they had not gotten far with A1C Coe, who was still claiming her innocence. A1C Coe was sticking with her story that she'd heard SP4 Marrero arguing with an unidentified man, whose voice sounded like a black or Puerto Rican from the South (United States). A1C Coe claimed not to have known SP4 Marrero to have a boyfriend in the two weeks she had been residing in the barracks. The only information she added from what she had told Mike and me earlier in the day was that she and SP4 Marrero had gone to a German restaurant for dinner and both had returned to the barracks for the evening about 10:30 p.m. They were not close friends, and their common ground was being roommates.

When Special Agent Harwell started coming down hard on A1C Coe's story as being unbelievable, A1C Coe started crying and shutting down. Our goal was to see if A1C Coe would change her story to something a little more plausible. If she was not involved in the murder of SP4 Marrero, then we needed something to hang our hats on to help her prove it.

The interrogation was intense, which pressured A1C Coe to stop freely answering any further questions by the agents. When we all heard, her utter an investigator's most reviled cluster of words— "I want a lawyer!"—all of us groaned our frustrations. Her wanting a lawyer put a new spin on our efforts to get anything out of her now. We obviously were done with her for the day, so we released her back to her unit. I still wanted the chance to see if she would consent to a polygraph. I instructed all agents involved in the case to return to their offices and prepare their agent investigative reports (AIR) and have them on my desk by 6:00 the next morning.

Anticipating a rash of phone calls on the Marrero murder case, I got to the office at 6:00 the next morning. Since the military clerks had not arrived yet, I had no messages waiting for me. I could not make my first cup of coffee before the phones started to ring. The first call was from Chief Conley, who wanted an update on what our investigation had found out thus far. I updated him on the crime scene fiasco with the Germans, the interview with A1C Coe, and informed him that Mike Blades had prepared a serious and sensitive incident (SSI) report on the Marrero murder case and, upon review, it would be going out today.

"Second Region is already asking questions," Chief Conley said before hanging up.

Other lines in the office started ringing while I talked to him, but I made no attempt to answer them. I answered two or three other calls, none of which were very significant, and it was not until about 7:30 a.m. that I first heard people reporting for work.

My plan for work that day was that I had no plan. I knew that the entire day was going to be consumed by the Marrero murder, mainly working the phones and keeping everyone updated and getting briefed by what the special agents found. I was not wrong; one of the military clerks called me on the intercom and advised me that Herr Bechstein and T. K. Hoffman and another person had just entered the office and wanted to talk with me. *Wow, totally unexpected, but now, at least I get to communicate with Herr Bechstein.* I went to the military clerks' office, greeted the group, and directed them to my office. I asked them if they wanted a cup of coffee; all declined. I excused myself and went to get one of our LNCIs, Wolfgang Haupt, so he could translate for me during the meeting.

Herr Bechstein spoke first by wanting to know why there was such confusion at the Marrero crime scene. He spoke mainly in German, and Herr Haupt had to translate most of what he asked.

"The SOFA gave the US Army CID primary jurisdiction on the US military installations on crime scenes. There should be a joint effort by both the Americans and Germans and not a unilateral independent investigation by only one agency. You guys did not do anything jointly; you took over the crime scene and pushed the CID out of the picture," I stated.

Herr Haupt said, "Bechstein supported his decision by indicating that a suspect who had not been identified may be a German citizen, subject to only German law."

"Yes, but shouldn't it be a team effort and not to have pushed the CID out the door of their own house?" I said.

Herr Bechstein had no time to answer before Special Agent Harwell knocked on the door to my office and peeked inside. "I thought it was necessary to interrupt, because of your visitor outside—it is the Stuttgart community commander," she said.

When I got up to greet the one star, an imposing sort of guy stood just outside the door to my office. I escorted him inside, where he acknowledged Herr Bechstein from previous meetings on community matters.

"I just dropped by to let you know that VII Corps SJA has provided CID with a full-time use of a lawyer to assist you in your murder case," said the commander.

I offered him a seat, which he refused, and he said he had to attend a meeting at VII Corps headquarters at Kelley Barracks. When we got back to the meeting, Herr Bechstein advised that he had to get back to his office and cut the meeting off. I wanted to resolve this issue, but not to the point where it would interfere with everything CID did that might involve the Germans. This attitude established life Rule Ten: *Stand firm and be resolute in your principles.*

After Herr Bechstein departed the CID office, I asked LNCI Haupt if he thought we gained any ground because of talking with Herr Bechstein.

"I don't think so. Bechstein has always wanted to take control of criminal investigations until he is absolutely sure no Germans are involved," he said.

We still had an unsolved murder at Patch Barracks, and we had no real evidence from the scene. *This is bad*, I thought. I did not know how bad it was going to be until Special Agent Dick Smith approached me in the hall just outside my office.

"Chief, some very bad news."

"What now?" I asked Dick.

"The Germans just dropped off the evidence they took away from the Marrero crime scene."

"That's good, isn't it?" I said, excitedly.

"Under normal circumstances, it might be, but in this case, it is not. Before they returned the evidence, the Germans stuffed everything into one large bag."

"Damn! This means that all the evidence is useless because it is now all contaminated and compromised. None of the evidence can ever be used by any suspect that we might find in the future."

The rest of the day did not go any better. Most of my time was spent briefing Region, the district, and the assistant community commander.

Both Second Region and Stuttgart District wanted to give us direct help in identifying the offender of the murder of Marrero. They offered one person each to supplement Special Agent Mike Blades's investigation. I learned later that the cry for help would not generate any real assistance, even though two additional agents, one from Region and the other from Stuttgart District, were temporarily assigned to help on the murder case.

The morning after the murder of Marrero, LTC Brannen came to my office for a briefing, and I updated him on the investigation. While I conducting the briefing, the phone rang. Since most of the special agents were out conducting leads on the Marrero investigation, I momentarily interrupted my briefing with LTC Brannen and answered the phone.

The caller identified himself as a medic assigned to the Fifth General Hospital. I hurriedly wrote down his name as SSG Ronald Johnson.[146] I asked him why he'd called, and he told me, "A Sergeant Sanchez was just in the hospital inquiring if a female soldier had been recently brought in to the hospital with any injuries. Since I was aware that they'd brought a dead female soldier into the morgue yesterday evening that had been strangled, I figured this was who Sergeant Sanchez was inquiring about. I did not tell him any specific information."

Hoping that somehow, we could keep the soldier there until one of my agents could get to the hospital to talk to him, I asked, "Is he still there?"

"No. I could not think of any way to keep him here."

"Where can you be found in the hospital?"

"I am on the first floor at the reception counter," he said.

"Stay there; an agent from the CID should be at the hospital in less than thirty minutes."

After I hung up, I excused myself from LTC Brannen and hurriedly went down the hall, looking for the first agent I could find. Special Agent Robert Vaughn drew the lucky straw. I caught him just as he was coming out of his office.

"Bob, drop everything you are doing; I need you to get over to the Fifth General Hospital and locate a medic named SSG Ronald Johnson, who should be at the reception desk waiting for you. I just got off the phone from talking with him, and he said that a sergeant he believed was named Sanchez, because of the name tag on his uniform, approached him at the hospital and asked about the condition of a female soldier who was brought in last evening. This may be our perp," I told Bob.

Bob obtained a set of car keys to a CID sedan, grabbed his notepad, and was rushing down the stairs before I could rejoin LTC Brannen.

I returned to the office where I'd left LTC Brannen and briefed him on the phone call I had received from SSG Johnson.

"This is good news," LTC Brannen said.

I spent a few more minutes talking to LTC Brannen about what direction we were taking with the Marrero murder case, when a man in his mid- to late thirties, wearing a blue suit and red tie, showed up at the CID office.

"Can I help you, sir?" I asked.

Immediately, he reached inside his suit jacket and brought out a set of Office of Special Investigations credentials and answered, "I am Special Agent Paul Scott,[147] the commander of the local OSI." After we shook hands, he immediately launched into the reason he'd come to my office. "Since one of your main suspects is a female airman, I need to be briefed on the murder investigation that you guys are working on that occurred at Patch Barracks yesterday."

Sounding somewhat confused, because he caught me off guard, I responded, "Oh, all right. I can do that!"

I invited him into my office down the hall. Prior to leaving the room, I looked over at LTC Brannen and asked, "Do you want to sit in on the briefing?"

"No, but keep me posted on the progress of the Marrero investigation," he said as he left the CID office.

I showed OSI Special Agent Scott to a chair. He declined a cup of coffee, so I sat down behind my desk. Thinking that the Stuttgart OSI did not have a criminal investigative mission, but primarily an intelligence presence, I assumed (which is something that most investigators should never do) that the agency having the primary investigative jurisdiction was the Stuttgart CID. I apologized to Special Agent Scott for not reaching out to him before. He looked at me and stated, "Since it occurred in my jurisdiction [meaning his OSI area of responsibility] and the primary suspect is a female airman, I need to brief my headquarters," he said.

"I understand that." I commenced to bring him up to date on what we had found out. "A1C Christine Coe was the only roommate of our victim, and she might have been in the room at the time of the murder. She told us that she left for work at 3:30 the morning of the murder but returned about 7:00 a.m. to retrieve a hat to give to one of her colleagues to wear. When she entered the room, she noticed that the victim had yet to get up for work. Thinking she had overslept, Coe went over to the victim's bed to wake her and then realized something wasn't right. Fearing the worst, Coe ran out of her room and reported to the CQ that the victim was not responsive." I also informed him that A1C Coe had requested a lawyer, but CID was still pushing her to take a polygraph.

When Special Agent Scott got up to leave, I brought up the idea that if Coe remained our main suspect, it might not be a bad idea to have the services of an OSI special agent helping with the investigation.

Without saying a word, Special Agent Scott reached out his hand, and I shook it. He thanked me for the briefing and left the office. Our meeting was cordial, but I sensed something wasn't right when he left. Well, at least I'd gotten the AF OSI briefed. A lot was completed on the Marrero murder case in the next two days.

The next day, Marrero's autopsy was conducted by pathologists at the Fifth General Hospital, which verified our suspicions at the crime scene: her cause of death was asphyxia due to manual strangulation, the manner being homicide. The doctors determined that the murder occurred sometime between 1:00 a.m. and 4:00 a.m. A1C Coe could be placed in the room for most of that time—from 1:00 a.m. to 3:30 a.m., when she departed for work. A1C Coe, through her lawyer, consented to be polygraphed by a CID polygrapher. The results were inconclusive. There seemed to be nothing we could do to help this young girl out of trouble. Fortunately, for A1C Coe's sake, the results of her polygraph could not be used against her. Within a week or so, A1C Coe slipped from CID's hold and fell into the grasp of AF OSI. OSI ran her on two additional polygraphs; the second one again came up inconclusive, but the last one showed no deception on Coe's part, and she was eliminated as a suspect in the Marrero murder.

Special Agent Vaughn had met with SSG Johnson, who provided him with a description of the man known only as Sergeant Sanchez, who had come into the hospital inquiring about the condition of a female soldier brought in with injuries. Bob arranged for SSG Johnson to come to the CID office to view a photographic lineup to identify the right Sanchez. It took Bob several days to identify several soldiers by the name of Sanchez. He found six soldiers named Sanchez, all assigned to MP companies and other units near Patch Barracks. SSG Johnson viewed the photographs but could not identify the man that had talked to him at the hospital.

The Marrero murder started to go cold in late February. Initially, there were plenty of leads generated, including searches for the elusive Sergeant Sanchez, but we were back to ground zero. The additional help was sent back to their units, and Special Agent Blades kept plugging away at leads he generated from energy and persistence. As often as operations allowed, I assigned an agent to help Mike with the leads. Not much information came into the office concerning the Marrero murder case. Investigative leads were becoming few and far between. I do not recall seeing any other agent work as hard as Mike did on this case.

In June 1987, Second Region zoomed into the district offices for their annual staff assistant visits (SAV). Stuttgart resident agency did not fare well with inspectors. Several improvements were cited in our DST operations, timeliness in cases, and the criminal informant programs. The agents worked hard over the last few months, but their time was mostly dedicated to working the many death and homicide investigations instead of working on programs in the Stuttgart CID office. All in all, none of our programs were in such poor shape that they were not supporting the office, but improvements were nevertheless necessary in each of them. We provided time for the inspectors even though we were all running around the community trying to find answers on the Marrero murder case as well as other ongoing death investigations.

Later in the month of June 1987, Second Region got hit with several requests for support agents for Protective Services missions around Europe; Oslo, Norway, was one of those locations. The secretary of defense, Caspar Weinberger, was planning to meet with Norwegian government leaders in early July 1987. As a reward for getting through the Second Region SAV, the Stuttgart District SACs were chosen to support the mission.

In early July 1987, four SACs, including me, caught a Lufthansa flight to Oslo, Norway, and married up with the Protective Services agents from

Washington that were already on the ground. The mission was scheduled to last five days, including the day of arrival and departure. We had scheduled our flight to Oslo so we were on the ground two days out before Secretary Weinberger's arrival. We arrived around 1:00 p.m. Norwegian time, had no problems getting through customs, and were checked in at a downtown Oslo hotel by 3:00 p.m. We had one and a half days to coordinate the travel routes and to confirm the scheduled meetings and social functions with the Norwegian leaders.

I was assigned to the control room to monitor all phone calls from Washington and to secure the secretary's room. We had two advance agents whose responsibilities were to travel to each location ahead of the main party and to ensure that the area was clear and there was no danger to Secretary Weinberger upon his arrival.

Secretary Weinberger arrived on time, and the mission went off without any glitches. We had to run a control room for the length of time the secretary was on the ground. We left Oslo with a good feeling that the mission was successful.

Special Agent James Hatcher picked me and the other agents up at the Stuttgart airport. On the drive to the CID office, he told me, "LTC Brannen has requested to see you the first thing in the morning concerning the Marrero murder case."

That meant I had to talk to Mike Blades to get an update on the case before I met with the commander.

It was about 3:30 p.m. when we arrived at the CID office, and I immediately went to my office to check messages and see what was waiting for me in the in-box. I greeted the admin staff and a couple of agents in the hallway before reaching my office. I was not surprised to see my in-box overflowing with case files and other documents requiring my review. I saw several yellow sheets of paper containing messages I suspected that would be waiting for me.

I went through the messages, mostly from commanders and 1SGs wanting updates on criminal cases. I could never understand why they could not contact the agent conducting the investigation. I set aside all but two of the messages that I thought needed my attention most. They both were associated with the Marrero murder case. One was a VII Corps SJA who wanted to talk about the status of the case, but the second was from Marrero's mother in Texas. I knew she wanted an update on whether we'd identified the killer of her daughter. Over the weeks since Marrero's death, I'd talked to her mother on several occasions. Each time, the main question and primary focus was if we'd caught the killer and when we were going to trial.

Before I talked with Marrero's mother, I wanted to talk with Mike to see what he'd come up with while I'd been gone. Talking with Mike would also allow us to prepare for the meeting with LTC Brannen.

I caught Mike at his office, and we discussed the Marrero murder investigation at length. "We have no solid leads to focus on, and our investigation is expanding all over the world," he said.

By saying the investigation was expanding all over the world, Mike was referring to the leads sent out to try to find the mysterious Sergeant Sanchez, who had gone to the Fifth General Hospital to check on the status of an injured female soldier. The leads were to identify all the soldiers named Sanchez that had departed Stuttgart since Marrero was killed. Mike indicated the leads that were coming back had no real information. As a matter of fact, the CID offices that were conducting the leads were going beyond what was requested. Most were interviewing and fingerprinting soldiers with the name Sanchez that had arrived at their installations after the murder. We had leads coming in that interviewed and fingerprinted soldiers named Sanchez who were not even in Germany before arriving at their current assignments. Mike updated me on what he had completed since I'd left on the Protective Services mission and what new leads were to be pursued.

Using this information, I called Marrero's mother in Texas and talked to her for a few minutes. I'd become familiar with her daily routine. I updated her on some of the details I felt she should know and kept other information from her that had nothing to do with her primary concern—namely, who'd killed her daughter. I feel bad each time our conversations ended, because I was unable to tell her we had identified the person who'd murdered her daughter. She always ended the phone call by saying, "Please call me when you find the person who did this to my daughter." I realized that she always said "*when* you find the person," not "*if* you find the person." At this point, all I wanted to do was to put forth all the effort we could muster to find the perp who killed her daughter.

About 8:00 the next morning, I received a call from LTC Brannen.

"I'll come to your office for the briefing," he told me.

We agreed on 9:00 a.m. for the meeting. The agents in the office were extremely busy with running down leads on the Marrero murder as well as other cases that they had. We had two more death investigations since Marrero was murdered. Fortunately, foul play had been ruled out on both deaths, and natural causes were the culprit.

Before LTC Brannen arrived for the meeting, Mike received a call that someone needed to talk to him about the Marrero case, and he had to excuse himself from the scheduled meeting.

The meeting with LTC Brannan began on time. We spent about forty-five minutes discussing the Marrero murder case; our focus was on operations and manpower. It was not a matter of how many agents were needed to assist on the investigation but how to employ them. Second Region had provided their input, but except for one temporary agent on the ground—who went away very quickly— and several senior operational advisors on the case, their assistance was minimal.

As we discussed the investigative options on the case, a call came in from the Second Region commander, Colonel Alfred Simpson.

"Are you sure Colonel Simpson is calling for me and not LTC Brannen?" I asked.

"Nope, it is you he is asking for," the female clerk answered.

As I thanked the military clerk, I placed my hand over the mouthpiece and told LTC Brannen, "Colonel Simpson is calling to speak to me." I noticed the look LTC Brannen gave me as I removed my hand and said hello to Colonel Simpson.

There was no gap in silence when Colonel Simpson immediately begin the conversation by asking me, "Did you kick a special agent from the OSI out of your office a while back?"

Shocked and bewildered by what he was asking, I knew he was referring to my meeting with Special Agent Paul Scott, the SAC of Stuttgart OSI. "No, sir, I did not kick him out of my office; I briefed him on the Marrero murder case. When he left, we shook hands, and he did not appear to be upset or annoyed by anything I had told him. As a matter of fact, I asked the OSI agent if he could lend us one of his agents to assist in our investigation, because the primary suspect at the time was the roommate of Marrero and a US Air Force A1C."

"I received information that the US Air Force OSI is not very happy with CID not briefing them," Colonel Simpson added.

"Sir, the OSI detachment in Stuttgart does not have a criminal investigative mission; their mission here is intelligence. CID has the primary investigative jurisdiction for the US military here in Stuttgart."

During our phone conversation, LTC Brannen gave me the evil eye but did not interrupt.

"I guess that will about do it," Colonel Simpson said.

"LTC Brannen is here in my office; would you like to speak to him, sir?"

"No. I just wanted to talk with you about what I had heard from the OSI commander, Colonel Law."

"Sorry, sir, but I did not do anything that I would consider bad treatment or imply in any way that he should leave."

"Okay, Dick. Just wanted to hear your side of the story."

When I got off the phone with Colonel Simpson, I immediately briefed LTC Brannen on our conversation. LTC Brannen reassured me that he and the district had my back on this one.

"It does seem that every time Stuttgart CID makes a move on this case, we are criticized on this investigation," I lamented.

"Keep pushing; you will come to a successful conclusion," LTC Brannen said.

The rest of the week was spent reviewing the many case files left in my inbox and coordinating investigative activities with other cases being pursued by agents in the office.

The Marrero murder case got colder by the day, and the pressure to solve it became hotter by the week. Many leads were pursued, but none panned out. Mike analyzed details of other cases, both German and CID, involving murder in the Stuttgart area. One came to his attention that had some merit, but CID was not working that case. It involved a German national from the Stuttgart area. On July 1, 1987, a thirty-year-old German girl named Gerda Rakoezy was stabbed to death on a suburban Böblingen street not far from Patch Barracks. Rakoezy's body had been found nude in some bushes near a sidewalk. Because of Special Agent Blades's tenacity in pursuing all leads, his efforts paid off. Mike expanded his investigation to cover the Rakoezy case. While pursing leads, he worked the streets and his sources in hopes that someone would come forth with any information on either case. His efforts paid off when one of his sources provided him the name of Carlos Rodriguez, a former MP who had been discharged from the US Army and returned to Germany for a visit. Rodriguez told the source he'd killed a female soldier at Patch Barracks a few months earlier. Mike dug into this information and not only identified Rodriguez as a suspect in the Marrero murder but linked him to the Rakoezy case as well.

On July 29, 1987, his source, an MP named James J. Husemann from Patch Barracks, told Mike that while he was on duty in a Patch Barracks guardhouse, Rodriguez approached him and expressed an interest in Husemann's Bible study group. While they were talking about the Bible study group, their conversation turned to the Rakoezy murder. Husemann told Mike that Rodriguez had mentioned in their conversation that one night he had killed a female that he had run into who was walking down the street. Husemann told Mike that Rodriguez went up to the woman and demanded money. She started crying and yelled, "Rape!" Husemann indicated that Rodriguez said he became scared that others would hear the girl's screams, so he grabbed her and dragged her into some nearby bushes and removed her clothes to have sex with her. When she would not stop crying and screaming, which only intensified his fears that people nearby would hear her, Rodriguez said he pulled out his knife and stabbed the girl to keep her quiet. Mike could not believe the story and was glad that the German girl's murder may have been solved.

After Husemann's incredible story, Mike located Rodriguez, who was at Patch Barracks, and apprehended him without incident; Rodriguez was very calm and showed almost no emotion as if expecting to be caught. Subsequent investigation by

Mike also linked Rodriguez, who was now a civilian and no longer subject to the UCMJ, to Marrero's murder. Mike arranged for Rodriguez to be detained by the MPs until the German Kriminalpolizei came to the Böblingen MP station. When they arrived, Mike informed them that, based on the information known about the Rakoezy case, Rodriguez was a lead suspect in that case and that his investigation also linked Rodriguez to the Marrero murder that occurred in February 1987.

On the day that Mike apprehended Rodriguez, I was sitting at my desk reviewing reports when he called with the good news that the perp who'd killed Marrero had been tentatively identified as Rodriguez. When Mike related the news that he had gotten two for one, I asked, "What do you mean?"

"Rodriguez is also the prime suspect for the Rakoezy murder that happened in suburban Böblingen in early July 1987."

Additional investigation revealed that Rodriguez was assigned to the 385th MP Battalion. A short time after the Marrero murder on February 9, 1987, he was honorably discharged from the US Army and traveled back to the United States. While there, he joined a reserve unit and returned to Stuttgart, Germany, for a personal visit. It was while he was in Germany as a civilian that he committed the Rakoezy murder, for which he was later tried in German court along with the Marrero murder.

Rodriguez's German trial lasted several months, from late 1987 to early 1988. The delay and length of trial was caused by the many witnesses who had to be located and brought back to Germany, many of whom were former MPs who had been discharged from the US Army and several of which had returned to their homes in the United States. The German state court spent several hundred thousand deutsche marks to pay for the trip to Germany by those witnesses who had left. Rodriguez was convicted on two murder counts, one for Marrero and the other for Rakoezy. He received two life sentences, to run consecutively, for his crimes, to be served in a German prison. The conviction of Rodriguez for Marrero's murder was based primarily on testimonial evidence. The physical evidence that CID obtained from the crime scene had been contaminated when all the items gathered were placed in one bag by the Kriminalpolizei.

The mysterious person named Sanchez who'd gone to Bad Cannstatt was ultimately identified as one of the people Special Agent Vaughn had interviewed, and his photograph was shown to SSG Johnson. A short time after Sanchez was brought in for the interview by Special Agent Vaughn, he was reassigned to Fort Hood, Texas. He was brought back to Germany for the trial but was not prosecuted by the US Army for his involvement. If circumstances surrounding this investigation would have only involved the Marrero murder, Rodriguez's discharge would not have prevented the US Army from trying him anyway in a military court. The UCMJ allows former military personnel who have been discharged to be recalled to active duty for trial on murder cases.

The Stuttgart CID office took a sigh of relief once the Marrero murder investigation had been solved. The office got down to a more routine work schedule. The caseload kept up its usual heavy pace with each agent having enough to do. Since the pressure or radar was turned off due to the successful resolution, I spent more time with personnel issues I thought were not so much insurmountable but rather had workable solutions. Some of the issues I dealt with could have been avoided if the instigator would have stepped back and taken a more thorough look.

I dealt with one agent who became so angry and outraged with me because he had heard that another agent's wife had spoken unkindly about his wife at a social function he and his wife did not attend. The angry agent wanted me to call the agent's wife that allegedly said the unkind things about his wife into the office and counsel her for making the remarks. I refused, telling the agent who demanded this that, for one, I had neither the authority nor desire to counsel an agent's wife for supposedly making a comment during a private conversation. I explained to the agent that my wife and I were also in the group that night and overheard the wife's comments and that the remarks were not derogatory or defamatory in nature; therefore, it was inappropriate to pursue the matter further. The agent making the complaint stopped discussing cases with me and would not participate in any social activities for the rest of his tenure at Stuttgart.

The LNCIs in the office balked at translating information in letter format to Herr Bechstein, the German prosecutor. I had written a letter to Herr Bechstein on one occasion that defined my responsibilities as the SAC of the office to respond to all death investigations by Second Region direction. The letter had no information that argued SOFA jurisdiction between the American CID and the German Kriminalpolizei. I had put a sentence in the letter that provided information that I was to be called on all death investigations by the duty agent. The notification was to be made regardless of whether there were suspicions of foul play or by natural causes. I could not convince the LNCIs that I was not somehow trying to shortchange Herr Bechstein so that the CID could act on the cases before his arrival at crime scenes.

My management style did not sit well with many of the special agents in the Stuttgart office. This was a major problem throughout my tenure as a special agent in charge that impacted heavily on my efficiency as a senior investigative manager. I had not experienced such a situation at any other assignment. The problem was not merely as simple as saying it was bad management skills or bad agents who failed to follow orders. I had a fine record of previous assignments where—as a field investigator, supervisory special agent, or special agent in charge—the offices ran smoothly and received excellent evaluations for operational effectiveness, and there was a steady flow of kudos during inspections by the region, district, and CID command headquarters staff. Also, there were many excellent, professional, and dedicated special agents who knew how to investigate and did it well, but as a group, something did not jell at their level of professionalism. I knew proper management techniques, but for some reason, I was not able to implement them into our operation, and I lost credibility with some of the special agents.

There was a uniqueness in the office that, in my opinion, fell into an area I would call a perfect storm—failure of special agents to work effectively together, LNCIs working too independently, ineffective management, and a higher-than-normal rate of homicide and death investigations. With all the internal operational snafus going on within the office, we still had a mission and for the most part did get it accomplished. The solve rate was high, and we let little fall through the cracks. We met our goal to "do what needs to be done."

During early June 1987, Elda and I took Chris on several short excursions in and around Stuttgart, and in early July—a quiet lull in activity—we took a short trip to London, England, to enjoy several world-renowned sites, such as Piccadilly Square, London Bridge, Portobello Road Market, and many more areas of interest. Chris made a hilarious comment once we left. I asked him, "Well, is London a place you would like to visit again?"

He replied, "Yes, because they all speak American [sic]."

Elda and I got a kick out of that one.

About two weeks later, we took a weekend trip to Rome, Italy. Chris spent most of the trip reading a Stephen King novel as we went through the beautiful northern mountain ranges of Italy. Occasionally, at either Elda's or my suggestion, he would look out the car widow to see a sight. He even snapped a few pictures with the camera he brought from the States, but when they were developed, the car window post was right in the middle of most of them. What a time he had. We had time for only two nights in Rome before I had to get back to work, but it was very memorable, to say the least. We had decided to eat at a small restaurant in the center of Rome. Chris ordered a plain pizza, thinking it was going to be just like the one he has eaten at Pizza Huts around Indiana. Well, he got the surprise of his life when out the waiter brought a plain Italian pizza: red sauce on a piece of baked bread. Boy, what experiences we had with him and traveling in England and Europe.

The travel with Chris was worth the time and effort, but all good things must come to an end. After the Rome trip, Elda took Chris back to the States, and I had to get back to work.

The office experienced a leadership change when Chief Conley departed as the Stuttgart operations officer and was replaced by CW4 Richard Shook, a special agent I had originally met while we were both assigned to the Yongsan District, Seoul, Korea, in the late 1970s. Chief Shook was a good solid leader and manager who allowed his SACs to work independently if they did the job. I felt his presence as chief of operations would benefit the office, and I looked forward to working for him.

With 1987 being one of the busiest years of my tenure at Stuttgart, the office continued to investigate some of the most highly visible criminal cases in Europe. During the summer of 1987, two investigations locked into my memory as being most memorable cases. The first one I called the Case of the Cheating Wife Who Should Not Have Gone Home:

## THE CASE OF THE CHEATING WIFE WHO SHOULD NOT HAVE GONE HOME
If you don't like your husband, don't go find another one until you get rid of the first one

The duty agent received a call about 7:00 p.m. on June 28, 1987, from the MP that a female soldier had been murdered in her off post apartment. The duty agent notified me, and we went to the scene along with two other special agents. Prior to leaving, we loaded the car with the crime scene kit and other evidence-gathering materials and items to assist us in processing the scene. I had received word from the MP desk sergeant that Herr Bechstein was already at the scene. I wondered just how much he would allow us to accomplish with his presence. On the drive to the scene, I reflected about the last time I'd encountered Herr Bechstein at a crime scene; that meeting did not go well. The situation was now reversed; the CID was going to a Kriminalpolizei crime scene instead of the Germans coming to an American crime scene.

Upon arrival at the apartment complex, I observed several German *polizei* cars in the parking lot. I told my crew that before we started processing anything at the crime scene, I needed to talk to Herr Bechstein to get a status of what CID's role will be. Immediately upon entering the foyer of the building, I saw Herr Bechstein talking to a couple of Kriminalpolizei officers. He instantly acknowledged me and came over and shook my hand; considering the last time I'd spoken to him in person, I thought this was a good gesture. We exchanged a moment of pleasantries, and he escorted me inside the apartment of the dead female solider. Once inside the apartment, I got an eerie feeling, knowing someone had just been murdered.

Bechstein showed me where the murder had taken place. "When the Kriminalpolizei got to the scene, they observed the woman, lying dead in a pool of blood between the couch and the coffee table. The knife blade used to kill the woman was still in her body, and the handle, apparently broken off during the attack, was lying next to her," he said.

I was shocked at what he said next.

"Herr Miller, this is CID's crime scene. I have obtained preliminary information that the main suspect in the murder is the husband of the victim, who is also in the US Army. For some reason, her husband jumped, naked, from the apartment's fourth-floor balcony. The body of the woman and her seriously injured husband have been taken to the US Army Hospital at Bad Cannstatt," Herr Bechstein explained. "We have kept the crime scene as we found it. Because of the time, the only thing I asked is that you may want to consider keeping a guard on the door to the apartment for the rest of the night and complete the crime scene examination tomorrow."

I looked at my wristwatch and noticed it was already 9:00 p.m. and dark outside.

The German *polizei* had done a good job of controlling the crime scene prior to the CID's arrival, but Herr Bechstein did not want the CID to disturb other residents in the apartment building by CID processing the crime scene. Since the crime scene was in the city of Stuttgart, to conciliate CIDs relationship with Herr Bechstein and the German Kriminalpolizei, I decided to honor his request and directed an MP to stand guard until the following morning.

Prior to leaving the apartment, CID identified the dead female soldier as Sergeant Cindy Lou Davis-Newsome, age twenty-five, and her husband as Sergeant Jock Newsome, age twenty-nine, a licensed practical nurse, assigned to the Bad Cannstatt Fifth General Hospital. CID went to Bad Cannstatt Hospital to obtain the status of Sergeant Newsome's condition, who had been admitted for treatment of his injuries sustained when he jumped off the fourth-floor balcony. CID ascertained from medical personnel at the hospital that the only injuries suffered by Sergeant Newsome after he jumped was that the air had been knocked out of his lungs. Unfortunately for Sergeant Newsome, this meant that his fate would be soon be in the hands of the US Army legal system. Since he was in no condition to be interviewed, an MP guard was assigned to guard Sergeant Newsome's room until his condition allowed us to interview him.

CID special agents returned to the scene the next morning and relieved the MP who was standing guard. Based on CID's crime scene examination, information ascertained from the Kriminalpolizei and the autopsy, the following scenario of what most likely occurred was pieced together.

Sergeant Davis-Newsome returned home after spending the day with a male coworker that she was having an affair with. Her husband, Sergeant Newsome, having knowledge, confronted her about the affair, and a verbal argument ensued between the two. During the initial phase of the verbal confrontation, Sergeant Davis-Newsome obtained a knife from somewhere and cut Sergeant Newsome in the neck, causing non-life-threatening, superficial lacerations.

Sometime after being cut by Sergeant Davis-Newsome, Sergeant Newsome went into the kitchen and returned with an eight-inch butcher knife. Catching her off guard and apparently with her back to him, he thrust the knife into her back with such force that the handle broke off, leaving the blade still lodged in her body, as she fell, bleeding profusely, to the floor between the living room sofa and the coffee table.

To make her death look like a suicide, he picked up the knife that she had used to cut him and slashed her wrists. Seeing his wife's dead body lying on the floor in a pool of blood with the blade still embedded into her back, he realized the implications of what he had just done and panicked. He went into the bathroom, removed his clothes, and tried to wash his wife's blood off him. Then, noticing that there was blood smeared on the bathroom floor, tub, and sink where he'd unsuccessfully tried to wash the blood from his clothes, he grew anxious. Then, in an apparent suicide attempt, he jumped, naked, from the fourth-floor balcony to the ground. Unfortunately for Sergeant Newsome, he did not die, nor was he seriously injured. He would fully recover and be healthy enough to stand trial for the murder of his wife.

After Sergeant Newsome's release from the hospital and just prior to being sent to the US military regional confinement facility in Mannheim, Germany, he was advised of his Miranda rights by CID, which he declined to waive. With no testimonial information to use, the entire case hinged on the physical evidence gathered at the crime scene.

The blood patterns and splatters were plenty incriminating, and Sergeant Newsome's fingerprints were found on the handle of the knife used to kill his wife. The autopsy showed that Sergeant Davis-Newsome died almost immediately from the wound inflicted by the eight-inch knife. SJA took two months to prepare for the one-day trial at the Stuttgart Law Center. All the hard work by CID at Stuttgart and the Frankfurt crime lab paid off, because on November 12, 1987, Sergeant Newsome pleaded guilty to unpremeditated murder as part of a pretrial agreement. He was originally charged with premeditated murder but was found guilty of the low-degree murder. The judge who ruled over the general court-martial proceedings sentenced Sergeant Newsome to a thirty-year prison term to be served at the US Disciplinary Barracks at Fort Leavenworth, Kansas. Sergeant Newsome was also dishonorably discharged from the US Army, ordered to forfeit all pay and allowances, and reduced to PV1.[148]

It's tragic that Sergeant Newsome chose murder over divorce. He and Sergeant Davis-Newsome had begun divorce proceedings a few months prior to her death, but Sergeant Newsome had moved back in with his wife in an attempt at reconciliation; it did not work. Based on a fit of uncontrollable anger, Sergeant Newsome's act ruined the lives of so many people, including his.

The second case that comes to mind involved a dishonest and uncompromising postal clerk who wanted to rip off his own post office to get instant money for himself. He was a careless, freewheeling sort of joe who had few friends and was a loner. I called this investigation the Case of the Postal Worker Caught Before He Could Do the Crime:

## THE CASE OF THE POSTAL WORKER CAUGHT BEFORE HE COULD DO THE CRIME
If you plan a crime, but tell someone before committing it, you can still be punished

In August 1987, one of the special agents in the office came to me and reported he had developed an informant who'd informed him that one of the postal workers at the 139th Postal Company in Stuttgart was planning on robbing a mail truck as it drove from Stuttgart to Frankfurt, Germany. The special agent informed me that Sergeant Joseph LaSelle had confided in him that he wanted to rob a mail truck as it was delivering mail from Stuttgart to Frankfurt. LaSelle's plan was to stop the truck along the Autobahn and force the driver to get out. Then he and the informant, whom he'd invited to join him in the caper would divide the loot fifty-fifty. Then they would move the vehicle to a predetermined site, where they could conceal it. The driver was to be told to walk from the truck, and it was Sergeant LaSelle's intent not to harm him. The informant did not tell the special agent the location of where they would park the truck, nor was he told when and where the heist was to take place. The informant related that Sergeant LaSelle had already attempted to stop a mail truck as it traveled from Stuttgart to Frankfurt but apparently was unsuccessful because the driver refused to stop.

I was not totally convinced that Sergeant LaSelle had tried to rob the mail truck, because there was nothing ever reported to the MPs. Sergeant LaSelle's plan on the surface sounded elaborate and ambitious, to say the least. But hell, Sergeant LaSelle had purportedly tried it once before, so it might work with the help of another man. I did not even know if it would be possible under German law to thwart a crime of this nature on the open roads. We immediately considered involving the Kriminalpolizei since it might take place on the German Autobahn. I contacted T. K. Hoffman and requested a meeting to discuss our operational plan.

T. K. Hoffman arrived for the meeting within the hour. Even though there was some tension in the air stemming from the Marrero murder investigation, he was polite and courteous. I invited him to sit down in my office and offered him a cup of coffee, which he declined. I did not waste any time briefing him on the information that the special agent's source provided.

T. K. said that any attempt by the US Army to stop a crime in process off US installations would be illegal under German law.

"T. K., our dilemma here is that if we bring the suspect in and interrogate him on his intentions, we may not be able to prove a crime because it would be our source against our suspect," I emphasized to him.

"The Germans have separate jurisdictions at each *Kreis* [county district], which have individual police departments. We are not allowed to enter into any other jurisdiction without permission and lengthy coordination," T. K. said.

*Well, that puts the brake on this operation*, I thought. However, it was understood that CID would have to redirect our investigative activity. I thanked T. K. for his time and help and wished him the best. Unfortunately for CID, T. K. not only told me that the moving surveillance to try to catch Sergeant LaSelle in the act could not be done, he also did not encourage any alternative methods or offer any further Kriminalpolizei assistance on the case.

The next step I took was to advise the special agent that the only way we would be able to catch Sergeant LaSelle was to interrogate him and hope that he copped to the plan. We would more than likely reveal the identity of our informant if the case went to trial.

A few days passed, and the special agent called the informant back in to see if any other people had been brought into the plan to rob the mail truck. The informant told the special agent that Sergeant LaSelle was still planning the job, but the informant was unaware of anyone else being brought in.

"How serious do you think Sergeant LaSelle is about trying the pull off this heist again?" I asked.

"Real serious," the informant replied.

Without any other direction to pursue, we were forced to bring in Sergeant LaSelle and press him with what we had. Sergeant LaSelle was brought in a few days later and advised of his rights for attempted robbery and solicitation for the plan for a second attempt with the source. As expected, Sergeant LaSelle declined to waive his rights and requested the assistance of a lawyer. We were at a crossroad in the investigation, and now we knew our entire case would have to be built on testimonial evidence.

It took weeks for SJA to prepare the case for trial, which could very well end up in an acquittal because there was no physical evidence. During the preparation of the case, SJA and the local command never authorized pre-confinement for LaSelle while waiting to go to trial. This situation set the stage where our informant constantly faced reprisal for his assistance to CID. Fortunately, there were no efforts by LaSelle or any of his friends to harm our informant before the trial, which was held in March 1988. The good angel must have been on CID's side during the legal battle in this matter.

After a two-day trial, a general court-martial convicted Sergeant LaSelle of trying to rob a mail truck in August of 1987 and solicitation of another soldier's help for a second robbery attempt. Sergeant LaSelle was sentenced to seven years' confinement at hard labor to be served at the US Disciplinary Barracks, Fort Leavenworth, Kansas, received a dishonorable discharge, was ordered to forfeit all pay and allowances, and was reduced to PV1. Kudos for the primary prosecutor, Captain Mark Romaneski, who argued during the trial that our source's testimony was more creditable because he had informed the CID immediately after he found about what LaSelle was planning. Captain Romaneski gave additional kudos to the Stuttgart CID for putting together a very difficult case. CID's brilliant investigation meant the difference in finding Sergeant LaSelle guilty instead of innocent.[149]

During late 1987, on top of being extremely busy with a heavy caseload, the Stuttgart District was struck by a bombshell. During a medical exam, the doctors found that Chief Shook had cancer. His luck was riding with him because the medical treatment caught the cancer and put it to rest. Chief Shook chose to return to the United States to receive further treatment, and his absence created a void in the senior leadership at Stuttgart District. Once the decision was made by Chief Shook to leave, a search began for another operations officer. First, there were attempts to locate candidates already in Europe. This search, however, was unsuccessful.

The next step was to find a suitable replacement through CID HQ Command. Efforts paid off when CW3 Thomas J. Whitrock was chosen for the job. I had originally met him when he inspected my office at Schweinfurt back in the early 1980s. Chief Whitrock was an extremely competent and capable professional whose selection as the Stuttgart operations officer was considered by all as an excellent choice. Chief Whitrock had a stellar reputation within the CID command, and I looked forward to working for him.

Chief Whitrock was a more hands-on type of leader who sought perfection in everything he directed. It was my opinion that because of our similar traits, we had run-ins with each other over how to handle some operational matters. I still considered Chief Whitrock as one of the most capable and talented CID leaders I ever encountered; I just had a hard time in expressing this opinion or showing it during our association with each other. I felt bad that I did not present a more positive attitude, but so many other aspects of the assignment at Stuttgart were overshadowing the picture. I earnestly took his advice and attempted to implement many of his agendas into the mainstream of the Stuttgart resident agency operations.

A couple of his procedures were when Chief Whitrock told me he wanted me to review agents' criminal cases without them present. I had been reviewing case files with the case agents present my entire career, and the method seemed to work. This system allowed me to engage in discussions on what the agents had done and where they were taking the investigation and make recommendations on further investigative steps to take. Chief Whitrock insisted in placing all the duty agent gear into storage bins precisely as other offices did within the Stuttgart District. I thought this procedure was good. It organized the equipment and made it easier for the duty agent to grab what he needed on his way out to a crime scene. Another positive management procedure, but could just as easily been handled directly by the resident agency was the scheduling of duty during the Christmas holiday period. He wanted to standardize each district office on the way duty was performed. For years, I had devised a scheduling plan for the holiday period with great success and saw no reason why it should be changed.

Just like reviewing cases without the agent present and organizing the duty agent equipment, this to me meant that he was taking the responsibilities to manage the resident agencies away from the SACs. I guess, in retrospect, I let these matters get to me far more than I should have at the time.

Despite our differences, I would have to say that Chief Whitrock was an excellent operations officer, who was considered an outstanding senior investigative manager, and I would rate him at the top of those I have worked for. One thing that Chief Whitrock did not do, which I respected him for, was interfere with the special agents' investigations. On inspection visits, he would review the case files and make suggestions on investigative steps, but never once did he take control of any special agent's case.

Regardless of how overmanaged I felt the office was, highly sensitive incidents kept coming in and were investigated by CID. Our mission did not falter, and the Stuttgart special agents all worked hard and were committed to doing the job at hand: finding the bad guys and proving they committed the crimes.

Two of the most highly visible cases that we initiated and successfully resolved in early 1988 involved a unique rape and sexual assault case and a drug investigation that expanded into other charges for the young man involved. The first investigation I called the Case of the Meticulous Rapist who thought he could get away with it:

## THE CASE OF THE METICULOUS RAPIST WHO THOUGHT HE COULD GET AWAY WITH IT
A man who seeks to do wrong will inevitably be judged unfavorably

In December 1987, SP4 Kevin D. Thomas, a young supply clerk from Minneapolis assigned to headquarters detachment, Thirtieth Medical Group at

Coffey Barracks in Ludwigsburg, was on top of the world. He had what he thought was a perfect system to seek out young female soldiers for his own pleasure. Young SP4 Thomas would frequent local bars and nightclubs near Coffey Barracks and watch for young, newly assigned female soldiers who got drunk. SP4 Thomas would then follow them back to their barracks and wait, sometimes as late as midnight, and then break into their rooms, rape, and assault them.

SP4 Thomas's luck ran out in in early March 1988 when a female soldier assigned to the Thirtieth Medical Group reported to the MPs she had been raped by Thomas. Once reported, the Stuttgart CID was notified, and a duty agent picked up the case. The duty agent thoroughly interviewed the victim, who related that in early February 1987, she had just arrived in country. About a week later, she and a group of friends went to a local bar. She admitted that she'd probably had too much to drink that evening. She and her friends returned to their barracks at around 11:00 p.m., and she eventually went to bed. She told the CID duty agent that later that night, she was awakened by a male lying on top of her, groping her groin area. He eventually forcibly removed her nightclothes and then his clothes and raped her on her bed. The male then got up, took his time putting his clothes back on, and told her if she knew what was good for her, she would not report the incident to anyone.

Once the male left her room, the victim said she got up and threw up in the bathroom sink. She did not report the incident until several days later after she had confided with a couple of friends from her unit about what had happened. She told them that several days later, she was walking to the unit dining hall when she saw the male who had attacked her in her room, although she did not know him by name. She made some inquires and found out his name was Kevin D. Thomas, a SP4 who worked in the unit supply room. Even with the encouragement of her friends, she still did not report the incident until a couple of weeks later when she found out through the company grapevine that SP4 Thomas had assaulted at least two other female soldiers. In her interview with CID, she identified the two other female soldiers who had been attacked by SP4 Thomas. The two other female soldiers were called into the Stuttgart CID, where they both admitted to being attacked by SP4 Thomas. Both females said they were newly assigned to the Thirtieth Medical Group and, the night of their attack, had been drinking at a local bar near Coffey Barracks. After they returned to the barracks and were settled into bed, a man forcibly entered their room and assaulted them. The two attacks occurred three days apart in the same barracks building.

Armed with the information the victims provided, agents from the Stuttgart CID interviewed SP4 Thomas, but he declined to talk and requested the advice of a lawyer. He was processed and released back to his unit.

The investigation identified three other females who provided similar stories as to how they were newly assigned to the Thirtieth Medical Group, had gone out drinking, and returned to their rooms where they were attacked. A total of six female soldiers said they had either been raped or assaulted by SP4 Thomas. Each positively identified him as their assailant during a physical lineup.

During a two-day trial from May 12 to May 14, 1988, Thomas was found guilty by a military judge for the offenses of rape, assault and battery, indecent assault, two counts of burglary, and two counts of unlawful entry. The judge, LTC Robert D. Newberry, sentenced Thomas to twenty-five years' confinement at Fort Leavenworth, Kansas, a dishonorable discharge, reduction in rank to private, and forfeiture of all pay and allowances. During the sentencing, Judge Newberry said that "the evidence has shown the accused has cold-bloodedly calculated these offenses," adding that Thomas's methods became increasingly brazen with each crime. The prosecutor, Captain Paul D. Kerian, had recommended a twenty-year sentence, and Thomas's defense counsel recommended only five years.[150]

This investigation was another example where good hard work from special agents of the Stuttgart CID made the difference. The evidence was based on testimony rather than physical evidence because it was weeks before the victims were identified. If it weren't for the CID's persistence in connecting even the smallest or most innocuous details, the case would have been hard-pressed to prove. PV1 Thomas will have a long time to think about what he did to the six female soldiers.

The second case that I recall that was most visible in the spring of 1988 involved a twenty-two-year-old soldier by the name of PV2 Patrick Thurmond, who was a minor drug dealer, mainly selling marijuana and LSD in and around his unit, Forty-Fifth Medical Company, 421st Evacuation Battalion, Seventh Medical Command, Stuttgart. The Stuttgart DST had targeted PV2 Thurmond for a small amount of marijuana. I called this investigation the case of the Man Who Wanted the Source Dead.

## THE CASE OF THE MAN WHO WANTED THE SOURCE DEAD
A person who ignores the rule of justice can expect to be ruled by justice

One of the Stuttgart DST members, Investigator Abdul Rahman Tofi Adada (phonetic spelling), who came to the Stuttgart CID via an aviation unit because his MOS involving maintenance of helicopters was being eliminated, developed the case. I interviewed Adada, accepted him, and assigned him to the Stuttgart CID DST. Adada caught on to investigative work quickly, was a hard worker, and became a good friend.[151] During this investigation, Thurmond was pending punishment by his commander for possession of a small amount of marijuana. Another member of his unit informed on him to the command about his dealing in marijuana.

Adada, working undercover as a drug buyer, began targeting Thurmond based on the same source's information. Adada was successful in gaining Thurmond's trust after a meeting. The case took a unique turn when, in conversation with Adada one night, Thurman told Adada about wanting to eliminate the source who was scheduled to testify against him. Thurmond, having a loose lip, confided in Adada that he knew of a Lebanese individual who could hook Adada up with any amount of marijuana he wanted. Thurmond also told Adada that this Lebanese individual was also willing to kill the source for a price.

Based on this information, Adada arranged for a meeting with the Lebanese drug dealer. He briefed the team chief of the Stuttgart DST, Special Agent Sam Conklin, who briefed me. The plan was to meet with the Lebanese on Robinson Barracks and discuss a deal for a small amount of marijuana. During the meeting, the Lebanese individual did verify with Investigator Adada that he would be willing to kill the source who was going to testify against Thurmond. The Lebanese man agreed to provide Thurmond with some marijuana and LSD so he could in turn sell the substances to Investigator Adada.

When Investigator Adada met with Thurmond, the DST was waiting in the shadows to swoop in and apprehend him once it was certain he had the marijuana and LSD in his possession. On a warm evening, several days after Investigator Adada met with the Lebanese man, the meeting between Investigator Adada and PV2 Thurmond took place at the predesignated location on Robinson Barracks. The signal was given to indicate PV2 Thurmond had the marijuana and LSD on him. The DST apprehended him without incident.

I was not very optimistic about our chances in getting a conviction for solicitation to commit murder in the PV2 Thurmond case. I thought we had a shot with intent to distribute and transfer of marijuana and LSD, however. SJA told us it would take the better part of the summer before that case went to trial.

In mid-June 1988, Chris flew in from the States and joined Elda and me for his summer visit. We had planned several trips to Brussels, the Netherlands, and if time permitted, back to London. At the end of June 1988, Elda and I took Chris to Brussels. The trip was short, but we made the best of it. We toured the city for two days and then returned to Stuttgart. With incoming cases not slowing down, the other summer trips were kept on hold.

Then a final obstacle preventing us from going on any of the planned trips came one evening when June called in early July 1988 to advise Elda and me that Mom was in the hospital with terminal lung cancer.

"I think it would be a good idea to return to the States to see Mom as quick as you can," June said. June then provided me with the phone number to Mom's hospital room. I briefly talked to her on the phone; she sounded like she was sedated, and our conversation was extremely short. I told her I would be by her side in a few days; she then hung up.

The next morning, I called Chief Whitrock and requested leave to go to the States to see Mom and if necessary to take care of her estate. He agreed, and I submitted the necessary form to the district clerks and got it approved that day. It was a foregone conclusion that Chris was returning to the States with me, but Elda and I agreed that she would stay in Stuttgart unless Mom passed, and if so, she would join me in Terre Haute. I arranged a flight from Stuttgart via New York to Indianapolis. I would pick up a car rental at Indianapolis International Airport for the trip to Terre Haute. Chris and I were scheduled to leave in two days.

On the day before I was to depart for the States, Chief Whitrock called and requested lunch. We met at the German restaurant on Robinson Barracks. Over lunch, we spoke about things going on in the Stuttgart CID and talked a little about my trip to the States.

"If I were you, I would go home, check on your mother, and return as soon as possible," Chief Whitrock said. "Depending on how serious she is, I feel a need to ensure that her private affairs are taken care of before returning," I told him. I explained to Chief Whitrock that she had no one nearby that could assist her if she needed full-time care. "If I must put her in a nursing home, I need time to do this," I explained to him.

We also discussed my future with Stuttgart District. Chief Whitrock felt it was time to consider joining the Stuttgart District as a staff officer. This did not actually catch me by surprise, because LTC Brannen and I had discussed this a couple of months earlier during the middle of the Marrero murder investigation.

"We can further talk about the district staff job after my return from home leave to visit Mom," I said.

I thought about what he was saying and concurred that this may be a good idea. We both kind of made a loose end agreement that this was to take place sometime after I returned.

Chris and I made it to Terre Haute on July 11, 1988, and went directly to the hospital to see Mom. She did not look good, and it appeared to me that she was fading fast. She was weak, but lucid. We stayed with her only a few minutes, and before leaving her, I spoke with her doctor. He informed me that she had a cancerous tumor the size of a golf ball on her right lung, and he thought it was too late to operate because of her declining health.

I dropped Chris off at his mother's house and checked into a hotel for a week. I spent the next few hours contacting relatives and informing them of

Mom's condition. Fortunately, Nora Mae and Hubert were visiting Mom daily. On the day before I got to Terre Haute, June had returned to her home in Houston because she had to get back to work. After notifying everyone, I thought that it was time to make prearrangements for her funeral. I contacted the Wampler funeral home in Bicknell, the town where she'd met Dad and I'd grown up, and completed the arrangements. Everything was pretty much status quo until July 14, 1988, when Mom took a turn for the worse and the doctor put her on a morphine drip.

On Monday, July 18, 1988, Mom died. I spent about a week clearing up Mom's personal affairs and emptying her house on South Third Street, Terre Haute, where she had moved only a few weeks before she'd entered the hospital.

With the time spent on the funeral arrangements and handling her estate, it was already July 29, 1988, and my leave ran through August 8, 1988, so I decided to visit Elda's parents before returning to Stuttgart. We spent a week in Freer, Texas, before flying back to Stuttgart from Houston.

Once back in Stuttgart, I spent the first day notifying everyone that I was back in the saddle. Chief Whitrock did not have a warm and fuzzy feeling about me taking the entire thirty-day leave, but when I explained to him the sequence of events that occurred while on leave, we never discussed it again. Cases were still coming into the office on a consistent basis. I called Investigator Adada into my office and asked about the Thurmond case. He informed me, "They threw the book at him." I congratulated Investigator Adada for a job well done.

I contacted the SJA at the Stuttgart Law Center and ascertained that PV2 Thurmond's trial was held on August 1, 1988. Thurmond was convicted of solicitation to commit murder, obstruction of justice, possession of marijuana with intent to distribute, and transfer of LSD. He received ten years at Leavenworth, a dishonorable discharge, forfeiture of all pay and allowances, and reduction to PV1.[152]

Over the next few weeks, Chief Whitrock and I continued our discussions on the transfer from the Stuttgart resident agency to the Stuttgart District headquarters. This idea was looking better and better to me. I had become increasingly melancholy about the job as a criminal investigator; the job was becoming way too political. The mechanics of the profession had become too intense, the excitement gone. What I had experienced in the last twenty years had taken a toll on my psyche and broken my spirit. My thoughts turned to images of the many deaths and victims of murder, especially the sight of dead babies, the constant stress involving personnel problems, endless battles with CID staff, and most recently the clashes with the German prosecutor and Kriminalpolizei, which had dampened my enthusiasm for the job. I knew I had to do something to survive until retirement, so a staff job might be the right remedy if I wanted to keep my self-esteem.

In September 1988, I applied and was accepted for a year's extension on my current tour at Stuttgart District. With almost a year left on my current assignment, this added almost two years and allowed time to make the job at the Stuttgart District more meaningful. My transition to the district was a foregone conclusion, but snags kept delaying my transfer. The initial obstacle was getting a replacement for me at the Stuttgart resident agency. A search to identify a suitable replacement found a very capable, able-bodied candidate in Special Agent Robert "Bobby" Lyons. The glitch was that he was not due until early 1989. Originally, the plan was to keep me in my current job until Special Agent Lyons reported in, but another hurdle popped up that no one expected. The SAC at the Vicenza CID office in Italy, Special Agent Wayne T. Nardolillo, had received an assignment to the Protective Services unit with a reporting date sometime in December 1988. The Italy office had no one qualified to take over an interim SAC.

In November 1988, Chief Whitrock brought me into his office and informed me that I had been selected to take Special Agent Nardolillo's place as an interim SAC until his replacement, Special Agent Timothy Crabtree, finished the defense language institute at Monterey, California, in July 1989. I was to go to Italy as the interim SAC in a TDY status. *Damn*, I thought. *December 1988 to July 1989—more than seven months.* Not that I was given a choice in the matter; unfortunately for me, it was a deployment. Well, so much for a change from operations to a staff position.

Shortly after being told that I was to take over the Italy CID office for a six-month tour, I came down with one of the worst pains in my back I had ever experienced, which made it unbearable to sleep or walk. I had been experiencing back pain for a few months, but I'd ignored it. However, when it flared up this time, the pain became so severe, I went to the clinic and they ran some tests and took x-rays. The test revealed that I had gallstones affecting my gallbladder to the point the doctor said it had to come out. I wondered if this medical condition would cause the Italy trip to either be put on hold or terminated altogether. The diseased gallbladder diagnosis came on the tail end of another medical issue I was taking care of involving my eyes. I had been seeing an ophthalmologist concerning my eyes, and he, too, suggested surgery to fix the problem.

On November 18, 1988, I had my gallbladder removed and had eye surgery on the same day at the Fifth General Hospital in Bad Cannstatt. An eerie feeling came over me in knowing that I'd just had surgery at the same hospital where I had inspected many dead bodies and attended a couple of their autopsies. I stayed in the hospital for about three days and finished recuperating at home and the office.

During the same period, I had the surgeries, the Stuttgart District offices, including the Stuttgart resident agency, were undergoing staff assistant visits from Second Region. The day after I got out of the hospital following gallbladder and eye surgery, I went to the office and met with the inspection team and conducted the general office briefing. I suffered in pain the whole day but did not take any medication, for fear I would not be coherent enough to answer questions to the inspecting team.

A few days after the Stuttgart CID offices were inspected, Chief Whitrock had scheduled a district-wide SAC conference for the first week in December 1988. Special Agent Nardolillo drove up from Italy. Chief Whitrock advised me that he wanted me to travel to Italy with Special Agent Nardolillo after the SAC conference was completed on December 9, 1988. I did leave Stuttgart with the satisfaction of knowing that our primary goal of investigative quality had been met. But there were other aspects that needed attention to allow for a more proficient operation of the office. From day one, there were missteps after missteps, and I was slow to recognize them. The primary issues that never seemed to improve or get resolved were problems with people, liaising with the German police, dealings with the district staff, and my own miscues with management techniques.

The biggest mistake I made as SAC of the Stuttgart resident agency was my failure to get to know the special agents' abilities as investigators and individually as people. I committed the cardinal sin in management: that of attempting to be friends with everyone. Subordinates do not look for their boss to be friends; they want them to be there to make the difficult decisions, give advice, and be there for them when they may have strayed down the wrong path. I violated this rule during the early part of my assignment to Stuttgart. This situation created a tremendous dearth in confidence that in effect caused me to lose credibility with the special agents. Regardless of what had occurred, that was the past, and I could do nothing to change it; I only wanted to look forward.

Chris and me sitting in the courtyard of our hotel in Rome, late 1980s, on one of our road trips.

Chris and me in Venice, Italy, in the late 1980s.

My in-laws Abel and Fabianita Guajardo, a good couple who welcomed me in their family with open arms.

Chris and me in Paris, France, standing in front of the Eiffel Tower, circa late 1980s.

To the left is Elda with our Old English sheepdog named Dog.

Having fun at the MP ball are Stuttgart resident agency Special Agents Dick Miller, Robert Vaughn, and Dan Cates.

Author enjoying conversations with two other Stuttgart alumni, Executive Officer Captain Carl Hunt and Special Agent Larry Marshal. Hunt would retire as a colonel and was the first commander of the CID's Computer Forensics Unit.

# 13

# Fresh Restart

## Status Quo

## Vicenza, Italy

*A rehabilitation assignment*

$\mathcal{W}$e started out early on Saturday morning for the eight hour trip to Vicenza. I was prepared but not excited about starting a new assignment. Wayne, a superlative briefer whose talking style is legendary, introduced me to each person by describing his or her character, effectiveness, abilities, and so on, and he did not skip a detail on anyone. It was late on the afternoon of December 10, 1988, when Wayne dropped me off at the Viest Hotel, a short distance from Caserma Ederle, where he had a room reserved for me. We scheduled a meeting at the Vicenza CID office at 8:00 Monday morning

The area where Caserma Ederle sits is beautifully positioned at the foothills of the Dolomites in northern Italy. Vicenza is the capital of the Vicenza province in the Veneto region and lies midway between Venice and Verona. The six-month assignment looked to be a welcome sight after just over two years at the Stuttgart CID office.

The following morning, I had a light breakfast at the hotel café and waited for Wayne to pick me up; he was on time. It took us only minutes to drive into Caserma Ederle from the hotel. The office was in the same building as the community provost marshal's office. All the MP and CID operations were run out of the building.

The Vicenza CID office was in a suite of offices on the east side of the building. As you walked into the area, there were two offices to the left; the first housed the administration, one civilian secretary, and one Italian word-processing operator. The next office was occupied by the Italian interpreter / criminal investigator, Paolo Corradi, and a second office where an MP and Special Agent Brian Beville worked. The last office down the line housed the SACs. On the other side of the hallway was the office's evidence custodian, Special Agent Moran, and the evidence room. Right outside to the right of the SACs office was another door leading to the outside.

The working environment was good, and for a small office, everyone appeared to have enough room. Having given me the grand tour, Wayne and I called it a day. There was virtually no overlap between my beginning tenure in the office and Wayne's departure. He and his family flew out only a couple of days later, but it would not be the last time I had contact with him or his family.

When I met everyone in the office for the first time. I recognized each one of them due to the excellent briefing by Wayne on the trip down. There was another special agent that I would meet later, Craig A. Ganster, who oversaw the Livorno CID branch office.

The first thing I did as SAC of the Vicenza CID office was to review all the open case files. My assessment of the investigative effort by the special agents was good. The special agents' attention to detail and timeliness on each case file were well within the standards set by CID. The investigative quality of the cases was a direct reflection on just how detailed Wayne was in his overall management of the Vicenza CID office. The case type was typical of other CID offices, but light.

The second step I took was to call everyone in for a meeting so that I could brief them on my philosophy on operational and management style. The main point I wanted the special agents and support personnel to bring away from the meeting was that, based on my brief review of case files, case flow, and overall operations, there were not going to be any major changes from the way Wayne ran the office. This decision was based on the adage that "you don't fix something that isn't broken." Wayne had been an excellent SAC that did not let much, if anything, fall through the cracks.

The next step in my orientation at the Vicenza resident agency was to liaise with the Italian police, called Carabinieri. With the help of Paolo Corradi, we requested a meeting that was convened at the Caserma Ederle CID office. I did not want the same thing to happen here in Italy that had occurred with the Stuttgart *polizei*. I wanted to have good working relationship with them. The meeting went well, and in the months that I was assigned to Vicenza, the cooperation with the Carabinieri was first rate. We worked well with joint investigations, and their assistance was invaluable during my tenure in Italy.

There were two provost marshals at Caserma Ederle—one being with the community and chief of the garrison MPs and the second with the SETAF (Southern European Task Force). SETAF's primary mission was to help our Italian allies with major logistics support in time of need. SETAF's commander, MG Lincoln Jones III, a no-nonsense type of person was very approachable for scheduling meetings or briefings on short notice by CID. I also arranged for a weekly briefing with his chief of staff, a US Army colonel, to discuss ongoing criminal investigations. Another weekly briefing was set up with the community commander, a US Army colonel.

The first week or so went smoothly at Vicenza; I saw that the agents and support personnel worked well together. I had no areas of real concern about how the office was functioning. Each person knew his or her job and was motivated in doing it; Vicenza pretty much ran itself.

On occasions, I received calls from a special agent from Stuttgart who wanted advice on a case. Tim informed me on one call that the death investigations had continued at an alarming rate.

"Hang in there, buddy," I told him.

In mid-December, I returned to Stuttgart for the Christmas holidays, and Elda and I were looking forward to a festive and enjoyable time. I planned to spend time in Germany and return to Italy the day after Christmas. Unfortunately, a new tragedy was about to happen that would dampen our spirits and good cheer and that would reverberate around the world.

On a Wednesday, December 21, 1988, after taking off from London's Heathrow Airport, Pan Am Flight 103 was still gaining altitude at thirty-one thousand feet over Lockerbie, Scotland, when it exploded, killing all 259 people on board and 11 people on the ground. A subsequent investigation disclosed that two Libyan terrorists were responsible for planting a bomb inside a suitcase and somehow smuggled it onto the plane. Most military units were placed on a heightened alert.

My time spent in Stuttgart was short and quick. Special Agent Timothy Graham, a very capable special agent and manager, was acting SAC until my replacement, Special Agent Bobby Lyons, came in. While back at Stuttgart CID, I saw Special Agent Graham sitting at his desk, looking haggard as he worked the phone in between reviewing case files.

"Tim, you look worn down," I told him.

"Sure. You ought to be glad you left this behind."

"Tim, different office, same old thing," I told him. "How are things in the office since I left?"

"Well, the politics are the same, maybe worse, but the agents appear to be able to handle themselves."

As I left Tim that day to begin my trip back to Vicenza, I did find myself fortunate for only one reason: I had spent my time in one of the busiest CID offices in Europe—an accomplishment. As a matter of fact, when I entered his office to say good-bye, Tim was reviewing the latest murder that had come into the Stuttgart CID office. The murder had some quirky aspects to it. I could not let this book be published without providing the reader with a narrative of the Soldier Who Got Something Different from What He'd Bargained For:

THE CASE OF THE SOLDIER WHO GOT SOMETHING DIFFERENT

# FROM WHAT HE'D BARGAINED FOR
## You can never tell a book by its cover

We'll start our story on January 30, 1989, a Monday morning, when PFC Thomas E. Fell, a twenty-one-year-old soldier from Hamilton, New Jersey, went to work on a routine day just like any other weekday at his job as a signal communications specialist for Company A, Fifty-First Signal Battalion, Ninety-Third Signal Brigade on Krabbenloch Kaserne in Ludwigsburg, Germany. He had no idea that his actions after work that evening would change his life forever. Here was a young soldier more than likely involved in sports and enjoying his life at that age in Hamilton, but he was seeking an escape from his hometown. So, he did what many his age have done in the past and will do in the future: he joined the military. Eventually, he ended up in Germany.

PFC Fell spent his entire day at his job doing what he normally did each day. However, on this day, whether he'd had a hard day or just wanted some relaxation, he decided later that night to go find some beer. He didn't want just any beer; he wanted a strong German lager. So, in the early morning hours of January 31, 1989, he started walking to a German establishment not far from Krabbenloch Kaserne that sold the brew.

PFC Fell purchased several bottles of his lager and started walking back to his barracks, where he could drink the stuff. As he was walking alongside the road, a car slowed, and the driver, a female, rolled down the passenger-side window and asked if he wanted a ride. He gave her the once-over and—based on his condition at that time, probably having had several beers that evening—thought, *here is a woman who stopped to pick up a soldier who is not even hitchhiking*. It was obvious what she wanted.

"Yes, I would like a ride," he probably responded and then got into the car. There was not much talk between the two, because both knew what they wanted.

The driver, obviously familiar with the area, did not hesitate to turn off the main street onto a dirt road near the US Army's Pattonville housing area, where they parked in a secluded location to begin their tryst. The woman, who looked strange, moved closer to him, and they started to kiss. Kissing led to more intimacy, which turned into the itch for sexual intercourse. At some point, they decided to get into the backseat to consummate their relationship. When PFC Fell reached for the private area of the woman, he got the shock of his life; he found out that the woman was not a woman at all but a man who was dressed up as a woman.

Shock turned into infuriation, and PFC Fell probably started to have feelings of disgust at his actions. PFC Fell's temper suddenly flared, and he became enraged to the point of violence. At some point, a fray between the two swelled, and he struck the man in the head hard enough to stun him and then began to strangle him. Afterward, PFC Fell got off the person and climbed out of the car and stood, perhaps trying to regain his composure. PFC Fell then obtained a beer from the car and started drinking it as he listened to the man, dying and gurgling in blood. PFC Fell was possibly thinking that what he had just done was serious, and if caught, he knew he would go to prison. So why not help himself to the man's watch, ring, and bracelet? PFC Fell then left the man in the backseat of his car and returned to his barracks.

In the early morning hours of January 31, 1989, the man was found dead in his car where PFC Fell had left him. The Kriminalpolizei coordinated the case with the Stuttgart CID, and there was enough circumstantial evidence that the perp was a US soldier. The ensuing investigation opened criminal investigations on the incident, and on February 14, 1989, PFC Fell was identified as the primary suspect in the case. Special Agent Tim Graham interviewed him at the Stuttgart CID office. After a proper advisement of his rights, PFC Fell admitted to the murder of Richard Bode, a seventy-four-year-old German, who was identified as the murder victim by the Kriminalpolizei. PFC Fell told Special Agent Graham that he felt bad about what he'd done, but he admitted he'd killed Bode because when they were preparing to have sex and he'd found out that Bode was a man and not a woman, he just went berserk. The Kriminalpolizei mentioned that Bode, had a life long history of being a transvestite.

The subsequent general court-martial was held on June 7, 1989, at the Stuttgart Law Center found Fell guilty of murder, attempted sodomy, and larceny. PFC Fell was sentenced to life in prison, reduction to PV1, forfeiture of all pay and allowances, and a dishonorable discharge. His sentenced was served at the USMDB, Fort Leavenworth, Kansas. An endnote to this case: PFC Fell was released from the USMDB on October 19, 2004, and is believed to be living in the Hamilton, New Jersey, area.[153]

Back in Vicenza, the first major crisis I had at Caserma Ederle started for me after the entire office was ordered to attend training for a week at the district headquarters in Stuttgart, Germany. Since I was TDY to Vicenza, Chief Whitrock and LTC James Crockett, who replaced LTC Brannen as commander, decided to allow me to stay in Italy while the training was ongoing. Fortunately, there were few duty calls while they were gone.

However, about 10:00 on the morning that the special agents left for Stuttgart, I received a very strange call from MG Jones's military secretary, who, in an almost rude, demanding voice, requested that I provide her with the phone number to my boss in Germany.

"Can I be of help to you?" I asked.

"No. I need you to provide me with your command phone number in Germany."

Somewhat concerned, I asked her again, "Is there anything I can help you with?"

She repeated in a tough-sounding voice, "No. I need the number in Germany."

Hesitating for a second, I asked her, "Do you want my district or Region phone number?" thinking it might be a general question someone on the SETAF has for CID.

"Region, thank you."

I provided her with Second Region's duty officer number, and before I could say another word, she had hung up. I sat in my office and tried to think of why she'd wanted Region's phone number.

It puzzled me that not only did she want Region's phone number, but that she'd asked for it in such a condescending tone, and I started thinking I might have some trouble brewing that I didn't know about. It bothered me to the point that I called MG Jones's chief of staff to see if he knew why one of his staff members needed the CID headquarters phone; however, he was traveling. He was out of the office for a few days on a trip, but his secretary gave me a tentative date and time of Thursday at 10:00 a.m. to meet with the colonel, a three-day wait. Well, that put me in a quandary about what to do next. I put this situation in the back of my mind and went back to work. As Paul Harvey used to say on his radio program, "Now, this is the rest of the story."

The following morning about 8:00, Chief Whitrock called, telling me that I had one angry general in Italy.

Confused and uncertain as to what was going on, I asked, "What are you talking about?"

"I was told that the Caserma Ederle principal at the elementary school called the general and complained that CID would not brief him on a case concerning the indecent assault on several of the children by one of their teachers," Chief Whitrock said.

I informed Chief Whitrock that I had no knowledge about the principal not being briefed. I also commented that the case he was referring to was assigned to Special Agent Beville. For me to get to the bottom of this, I had to speak with him, and he was in training in Stuttgart. Chief Whitrock arranged for him to call me. Before Chief Whitrock hung up, he directed me to provide a status report on the case to the principal by the next day.

As soon as Chief Whitrock hung up, I retrieved the case in question. I recall reviewing it a couple of days after taking over the office and thinking that the investigation was on track. Apparently, Chief Whitrock had the same thought, because the file showed that he'd reviewed the case on his last inspection to the office two weeks before.

Within fifteen minutes, the phone rang; it was Special Agent Beville.

"I am in a little trouble down here; do you know what is happening?" I asked.

"What are you talking about?" Beville replied.

"Apparently, the principal of the local elementary school called the SETAF general and complained about not being briefed on the sexual assault case you have open."

"Okay, I know what happened. The principal called me yesterday morning right before we took off for Stuttgart, demanding a briefing on the case. I told him I did not have the time to brief him on the details of the case. He has been calling almost daily to asked what the status is, but I haven't gotten all the kids interviewed yet."

"Jesus! How many kids are you talking about?"

"There are eleven victims," he responded.

"Brian, I might be calling you from time to time throughout the day, because I have been directed by Chief Whitrock to get a status report to the principal by tomorrow," I told him.

Immediately after Brian and I finished our call, I reviewed the case file for the second time in a week and then called the principal of the elementary school. I introduced myself to him and apologized that my agent did not update him on the investigation, and I requested to meet with him to discuss the case. I went to the principal's office, located just a few short blocks from the Vicenza CID office, and met with him and the vice principal. I thoroughly briefed them on the investigation. I told them that the Italian authorities were interested in the case and were anxious for our report.

"What is the status of the suspect?" I asked the principal.

"He has been placed on paid leave, pending the results of the CID investigation," the principal advised me.

I informed the principal that the case had become the highest-priority case CID had and gave him an estimate of about two weeks before it could be wrapped up. The principal said he was satisfied with the progress of the investigation and was happy that I had provided the update to him. As I got up to leave his office, the principal thanked me again and told me that if he had known I was at the office, he would have called me instead of the SETAF general. I assured him that he could call me anytime if he needed any more information. I left his office, feeling relieved that I had made a friend that day, but the CID was not out of hot water yet. I had to make amends with the SETAF staff as well, but that had to wait; I had to concentrate on managing the office.

Italy was not immune from death investigations, but they just did not have as many as Stuttgart. Vicenza's first death investigation while I was SAC involved a soldier who had family and financial problems. I called the case involving the Suicide of a Fashion Producer:

THE CASE INVOLVING THE SUICIDE OF A FASHION PRODUCER
You should learn to handle stress in a productive way

On April 18, 1989, Special Agent Brian Beville came into my office and advised me he had just received notice from the Vicenza MP desk that a soldier had been found dead in a field not far from the apartment where he lived. "Information we had was that his death appears to be a suicide. There is evidence that he killed himself by inhaling carbon monoxide fumes from the exhaust of his car," Special Agent Beville said.

"Get the crime scene kit ready; I'll go to the scene with you," I told him.

It took us about fifteen minutes to find the scene.

As we pulled up in the CID sedan, I noticed there were two Carabinieri officers on the scene. Neither Special Agent Beville nor I spoke or understood Italian, so we showed them our CID credentials and greeted them by shaking their hands and acknowledging their presence in English and hand signals. They both were extremely helpful and courteous, and we were relieved to find that one of the Italians spoke fluent English. This made our crime scene examination much easier.

The Carabinieri officer who spoke English commenced to brief us on their findings. "A passerby notified our station that there was a man sitting in a parked car in a field a short distance off the road with the motor running. The passerby became suspicious that something might be wrong, so he called us. When we got to the scene, the car engine was running, and we saw the soldier inside. We opened the car door and turned off the motor. We checked the soldier for any signs of life and found none. We identified him through his driver's licenses, as Sergeant Ronald Hill," The Carabinieri officer said. He then gave me a key they found on Sergeant Hill. The key appeared to be to an apartment door.

Both Special Agent Beville and I then turned our attention to the scene. We saw a hose hooked up to the car's exhaust pipe at one end, and the other end was placed inside the back with the window nearly closed. We observed the body in the driver-side front seat, leaning to the right. The body was a thirty something black male dressed neatly in a shirt, slacks, and a light jacket. I bent over to get a closer look at the body. The face and hands had a bright red shade to them. Further inspection of the body found no external injuries; however, an autopsy would be required to determine the exact cause of death. The body's reddish skin was indicative of someone who had inhaled too much carbon monoxide. The inside of the car was clean of debris. A search of the glove box disclosed documents consistent with Hill being owner of the vehicle.

It took us about two hours to finish processing the scene and gathering evidence. Special Agent Beville arranged to have Sergeant Hill's car towed to the US Army salvage lot near Caserma Ederle. We supervised the removing of the body from the car, and with the approval of the Carabinieri, it was transported to the hospital, pending an autopsy.

Special Agent Beville and I left the scene for the short drive to Sergeant Hill's apartment to conduct a search for any evidence to explain his likely suicide. Special Agent Beville, who was driving, parked the car in front of a small, two-story building that we suspected to be Hill's residence. We walked up the stairs leading to a small porch with a stoop. I pulled the key that the Italians had given us from my pocket. Looking at Special Agent Beville, I said, "I hope it works. I hope it works." I inserted the key and turned the lock; it worked. We entered Hill's apartment and found it to be tidy and clean, and everything seemed to be in its place. There were no signs of anyone besides Hill living in the apartment. The bed was made, and the laundry room had no dirty clothes waiting to be washed. I instructed Special Agent Beville to search the bedrooms and bathrooms while I took the living room.

I almost immediately observed a folded, yellow, lined sheet of paper on a table beside a reading chair. I unfolded the paper and discovered that it was probably intended to be a suicide letter left by Sergeant Hill. The letter addressed to Hill's wife and two children started off by saying how sorry he was for spoiling their lives, and he asked for forgiveness. He explained in the letter that he saw death as the only way out of a life of misery he had caused them so that his wife and kids could get on with their lives. This was an interesting development in our investigation, indicating that Hill's wife and kids had apparently moved out and more than likely gone back to the States. The last portion of the letter spoke of a fashion show sponsored by Sergeant Hill wherein he'd spent over $5,000 to bring it off. I thought this was very strange.

We spent another hour looking for anything else that could be linked to his likely suicide and found nothing. We secured the apartment, locked the front door, and returned to the CID office to complete paperwork on the case.

Further investigation by Special Agent Beville revealed that Sergeant Hill was assigned to headquarters and Headquarters Company, Third Battalion, 325th Infantry Regiment at Caserma Ederle. Sergeant Hill had been in Italy since September 1987, and his wife and two kids were at one time command sponsored. On April 24, 1989, the autopsy was performed on Sergeant Hill, and his death was attributed to carbon monoxide poisoning. All the evidence that CID accumulated in the case was consistent with suicide—a failed marriage and a life that went off center where he saw no way out. Sergeant Hill was living a life that he saw as worthless and nonfunctioning—a tragedy of mistakes that, if caught, might have altered Sergeant Hill's fate.

A second death investigation I covered in Italy was that of a reported crib death. Based on our investigation of the incident, the circumstances and evidence all led toward a SIDS case that I called the Family That Lost a Loved One:

THE CASE OF THE FAMILY THAT LOST A LOVED ONE
Life is full of unknowns—some good, some bad; be prepared for whatever life brings you

On a Sunday morning in late May 1989, I got a call from Special Agent Beville, who said, "We have a crib death in Verona."

"Any signs of foul play?" I asked Beville.

"Don't know. You want to go with me to the quarters where the baby was found?"

"Sure. My hotel is on the way. Stop and pick me up; I will be waiting on you," I told him.

On the drive to Verona, Special Agent Beville briefed me on what he had been told by the MPs. The father of the deceased baby was LTC John L. Donaldson,[154] a marine, was assigned to the NATO element in Verona and reported he'd found his five-month-old son dead in his crib. Since it was on a Sunday morning with virtually no traffic on the autostrada, our drive took us a little less than an hour.

LTC Donaldson met us at the doorway to his US military–leased apartment in the city of Verona. The marine had two other children, ages eight and ten, who were in a room with their mother. We were led through the quarters, and my initial observation of the apartment was that it was clean, neat, and fully furnished. The interior of the apartment was homey and tasteful. I got a glance at the two children with their mother, and all three of them were well dressed.

As we passed the mother and two children, the youngest, a boy, asked his father, "Dad, where is Johnny?"

LTC Donaldson, trying to be brave for his family and in control, said, "He is gone, son."

When we entered the baby's room, it was well stocked with diapers, linens, swabs, blankets, and other materials that one would have to care for a new baby. Our inspection of the crib showed clean linen, with a spinning toy hanging from the ceiling. Special Agent Beville filmed the area. We were both confident that the death appeared to be SIDS related; however, we wanted to view the infant's body first. There was absolutely no evidence of child abuse or foul play. We asked LTC Donaldson to accompany us to the CID office for an interview to gather details concerning the time of death and to shore up other aspects. He consented.

At the CID office, LTC Donaldson freely provided answers to all our questions. Neither Special Agent Beville nor I felt it was necessary to interrogate LTC Donaldson, because based on everything we knew, we did not think he was guilty of any wrongdoing.

The next morning, Special Agent Beville examined the infant's body. He reported back to me that there were no visible injuries to the body. Special Agent Beville commented, "The infant was well developed for five months and showed no signs of malnutrition or neglect."

The full investigation on the baby's death, to include toxicology results and a full examination by medical authorities, did not disclose any evidence of foul play. In such a tragedy as seen in SIDS deaths, parents often blame themselves. I hoped that this did not happen to LTC Donaldson and his wife. They appeared to be good parents and close to their two surviving children. The case was closed as a SIDS death, and no formal charges were brought against either LTC Donaldson or his wife, nor should there have been.

Another investigation that was noteworthy during my tenure at the Vicenza CID office was a request for assistance from the FBI to CID headquarters, which wanted help in conducting the background on a US Army captain who was one of the victims from Pan Am Flight 103, which was brought down by two Libyan terrorists. I called this investigation the Case of the Army Captain That Did Not Make It Home:

## THE CASE OF THE ARMY CAPTAIN THAT DID NOT MAKE IT HOME
Fate determines your destiny

The case involved a check of the US Army captain who'd left his unit in Italy for Frankfurt to catch the plane to the United States; he was unlucky to be scheduled on Pan Am Flight 103 that crashed over Lockerbie, Scotland. The Vicenza CID was responsible for verification of as much information as we could find on who the captain saw in his final days in Italy, who packed his bags, and what his travel itinerary was. Our investigation was successful in verifying most of the information sought. There was no evidence found during our investigation that connected the captain to anything suspicious

The young captain had no earthly idea what his fate was going to be that day he purchased a plane ticket to return to the United States to be reunited with his family and friends. If the young captain had decided to leave Italy a day or two before or after he'd purchased his plane ticket, his future would probably have resulted in an uneventful trip back home. Who would have known that the actions of two terrorist thugs, days before the crash, would change thousands of lives of family, friends, and many more people, as well as the passengers of the ill-fated flight? It is an eerie feeling to know that any stranger can predetermine how one dies.

In late July, my time in Italy ended. The assignment was unique, and I'd enjoyed the Italian food; they never stop eating in the country. Elda and I enjoyed the trips through Brenner Pass in the Alps along the border between Italy and Austria. We found a small Austrian *Gasthaus* just off the A13 highway near Innsbruck, where we'd stayed many times. The trip usually meant that Elda was coming from Stuttgart, Germany, and I was driving up from Vicenza, Italy, and we would meet at the *Gasthaus*. We liked the place because Dog, our Old English sheepdog, became very good friends with the *Gasthaus* owner's sheepdog. Ah, the good old memories of the area were everlasting.

One day, I received a phone call from Wayne Nardolillo from PSU in Washington, DC. He wanted to check on how the office was and catch up on the people and so forth. I updated him on the events and activities and some of the cases that were still open that he was involved in when he was SAC at Vicenza. He brought me up to date about his assignment at PSU and what was happening with him and his family. Our conversation turned toward my future in CID and where I might want to be assigned when I left Germany.

I posed a question to him about any possibilities of an assignment to PSU. I had spent a month in Washington working on the Weinberger security detail and was a support agent for several Protective Services missions in my career. I had also considered for many years that I would like an assignment to PSU for a change of pace, but I'd never acted on the thought. The stress of criminal investigations, especially the death cases and constant pressure to resolve every case, was overwhelming.

"I'll do some checking; expect to hear from me shortly," he said.

The next day, I received a second call from Wayne, who advised me that he had arranged an assignment to PSU with two schools at Fort McClellan—one for counterterrorism protection and the other for the PSU school. After thanking Wayne for his efforts on my behalf, I immediately got Chief Whitrock on the phone and informed him that I had been approved for an assignment to PSU, and of course I would be pulling my extension for a year at Stuttgart. I am not sure what his reaction was, because he only acknowledged what I had told him without making any further comments.

Two days before my departure from the Vicenza CID office, I took the two-hour trip to pick up Special Agent Crabtree from the US Air Force Base in Aviano, Italy. I briefed him on the status of cases and personnel of the office on the trip back to Vicenza. Tim, a good-looking lad in his early thirties at the time, was anxious to start working. Tina, our civilian secretary, had made all the arrangements for Special Agent Crabtree to meet with the leaders of the Vicenza military community and SETAF headquarters. Having given my best to sustain the Italy CID office, I departed Italy for Stuttgart on a warm, sunny day in late July 1989.

Back in Stuttgart, I spent the rest of my tour processing out and wishing everyone Godspeed. In looking back at my time as the special agent in charge of the Stuttgart resident agency, I felt the assignment was an extremely tough one. My management techniques and style never took hold. There was a tremendous number of talented special agents in the office, but some strange influence surrounding the operation prevented the organization from working smoothly. The glitches were not contributed to any one person or a singular aspect of our mission; it seemed to be associated with several problematic factors simultaneously. I rated my assignment at Stuttgart as marginal at best, but even through all the fog and uncertainties, the office could successfully resolve most the assigned investigations.

## 14

# New Beginning to the End

Pentagon

Washington, DC

*Secretary of defense security detail*

On August 19, 1989, Elda and I flew from Stuttgart to Washington, DC, via New York City. When we arrived at Reagan International Airport, we got a rude awakening at the terminal. As I was completing the process to rent a car at one of the rental agencies, I carelessly left my briefcase open for all to see. I was momentarily distracted, and person(s) unknown stole it. To add salt into the wound, so to speak, along with various personal items, such as a watch, calculator, and assignment orders, I had $2,500 worth of unsigned travelers' checks. Elda had been after me the entire trip to sign the travelers checks, and I kept telling her I would, but I never did. *Payback time*, I thought. We had succumbed to being an easy target. Here we were, both of us, with two baggage carts, carry-on suitcases wrapped around our shoulders, and our loyal, good Old English sheepdog in tow, making us the ultimate mark for a theft. The only thing we could do was make a report for the insurance company and chalk the experience up to a lesson learned.

We settled into a hotel nearby the CID headquarters at 5611 Columbia Pike, Arlington, Virginia, had a good dinner, and went to bed early. The next morning, Elda and I checked in with Wayne at his desk. He was expecting us but still acted surprised when we walked into his office on the fourth floor of the building near the CID command group.

Wayne gave me a brief rundown on the office but reserved operational details for a later time when I was ready to go to work. When we left Wayne's office, I ran into Tim Steenbergen, my good friend from our time on Secretary Weinberger's security detail back in 1986. Tim had been a member of PSU for about a year. We spoke briefly agreed to get caught up on things when I next saw him.

Elda and I found a nice townhome in Burke, Virginia, rented by John Miller (no relation), a retired marine colonel. We were lucky that our hold baggage arrived within a couple of days after we moved in. Our furniture came sometime later.

Having most of the moving part over, I reported to work on a hot, sunny day in late August 1989 and was assigned a desk just outside Wayne's office. The office layout at PSU when I checked in was tight. All special agents had their own desk, but the space was very cramped. At the time of my arrival, there were about forty special agents assigned to the unit. This was an increase from when I was TDY in 1986. After extensive negotiations between branches of the service over PSU strength, it was decided the additional billets would come from the US Air Force.

It was a practice when I arrived that all newly assigned special agents assigned were to spend time on the in-town SECDEF security detail to get experience before venturing to other locations around the world; I was no exception.

The PSU was responsible for the personal protection for most the senior leadership at the Pentagon. This included the SECDEF and deputy SECDEF, secretary of the US Army, chairman and vice chairman of the Joint Chiefs of Staff, the US Army chief of staff, and vice chief of staff of the US Army, and any foreign counterparts that visited the United States. The PSU duties and responsibilities were an extremely extensive and complex operation that functioned 24-7 and was worldwide.

Special Agent Kathy Klug was the agent in charge of the in-town security detail. Kathy, a small-statured young woman who knew her job, was well liked and carried herself in a very professional manner. We kept busy, working most days from 6:00 a.m. or earlier to late in the evening, depending on the number of moves each protectee had. I went directly to the SECDEF security detail, which included Dick Cheney and Donald Atwood. The team was called the Office of the Secretary of Defense (OSD) Security Team, and the team chief position carried a second title of distinction of being the number-two person in charge of the entire unit. I would spend all my time as a CID special agent personal security protection for these two individuals.

Richard B. "Dick" Cheney was a well-known congressman when President George H. W. Bush nominated him to become secretary of defense on March 13, 1989, after the failed attempt to give the job to Congressman John Towers. Secretary Cheney took the oath of office on March 20, 1989. Secretary Cheney came to the job with a varied background in politics. He was the youngest presidential chief of staff in history under Ford and served six consecutive terms as the lone congressman from Wyoming 1978 to 1988.[155]

Donald J. Atwood became the deputy secretary of defense on April 24, 1989. He was formerly the vice chairman of the board of General Motors and president of Delco Electronics Corporation and GM Hughes Electronics.

Most of our activities on the in-town security detail involved trips to the White House, Capitol Hill, and locations where the SECDEF or his deputy would have meetings or give a speech and on occasions when the two were dining out with friends and family. I stayed on the in-town security detail for about two months. During this period, I learned a tremendous amount of knowledge on Protective Services; the methods and tactics employed on the job were invaluable for the rest of my tour.

On days that I did not provide protection to the SECDEF and deputy SECDEF, I worked in the office. I spent time learning the internal and external operations of PSU. Wayne did a superb job in managing the overall operation of PSU. He designed and implemented the use of forms and documents used in each movement and overseas missions. I was impressed by the way PSU operations worked now compared to when I'd worked at the unit in 1986. Wayne created uniformity and continuity of effort on missions. Each special agent assigned missions was required to prepare reports on the notification, identify the number of support agents required, and document post-mission activities.

To assist special agents with the cost of trips, both in the United States and worldwide, the Department of Defense and US Army both provided advance monetary compensation for their travels. This policy benefited the lower-grade enlistment members of the unit, especially those with families to care for. Each year, the director of Travel Division DOD/WHS would issue annual blanket travel orders to those authorized to travel on Protective Services missions. Those orders were general in nature but specific enough to cover any trip worldwide. The authorized the use of both commercial and government modes of transportation. The itinerary authorized variation and allowed travel from "Washington, DC, to such places at such times and in such frequency, as may be necessary in the performance of our official duties, either within or outside the continental limits of the United States, and return to Washington, DC. Clearance requirements of DOD Directive 5000.7 must be observed."[156] Needless to say, for accuracy, a detailed oversight review of all TDY vouchers was mandatory.

The special agents mostly flew by commercial aircraft when traveling on missions out of town and overseas. However, on occasion, the SAC of the mission or a special agent that was to assist on the missions, such as handling the security of personal bags, would be assigned a seat on one of the 707s maintained by the Eighty-Ninth Air Wing at Andrews Air Force Base. "Some of these planes had been used as Air Force One by Presidents Kennedy, Johnson, and Nixon. One of them, tail number 26000, was the plane that flew President Kennedy to Dallas on November 22, 1963, and returned his body back to Andrews Air Force Base on that tragic day."[157] I flew numerous times on 707, tail number 26000.

Another plane, a 707 with the tail number 27000, was also used to fly the secretary and deputy secretary to locations outside Washington, DC. There was one spooky ghost story flowing around when I was in PSU. When you were flying on the former Air Force One, tail number 26000, late at night to an overseas country, President Kennedy's voice could be heard coming from the back of the plane in the area where the security and strap hangers always rode.

One of the first tasks I had while assigned to PSU was to attend the two-week Protective Services course at Fort McClellan, Alabama, and a follow-along course in counterterrorism. I spent approximately a month in training at Fort McClellan, where the lectures, practical exercises, and hands-on scenarios were excellent avenues to learn the material needed in my current job assignment. I returned to Washington armed with a wealth of ideas, methodology, and skills to put into action.

My assignment to PSU was during a time of historic change in the world. The USSR was losing its grip on Eastern Europe, the Warsaw Pact was disintegrating, and the Berlin Wall fell. Because of these monumental political changes, the United States government wanted to strengthen our relationships with countries that were previously under the influence of the USSR. During my tenure at PSU, I was involved with many security details, both as a supervisor and as a personal security officer for Secretary Cheney and Deputy Secretary Atwood when we traveled to Eastern Europe.

One very significant event that occurred in November 1989 was when the wall dividing West and East Germany came tumbling down. Everyone in the East and West were jubilant. The news shook the world, and the event ended up on every news program on television. It gave a feeling of triumph to people in military circles, especially people like Elda and I, who had served in Germany for so many years, that we had accomplished something. The wall coming down was symbolic that the Cold War was in fact over, even though it was many months before the Eastern Bloc countries could squeeze out of the clutches of the USSR.

My first missions out of town were in October and November 1989 to Los Angeles, California; Los Alamos, New Mexico; and Helena, Montana, to provide protection for Secretary Cheney. He went to Los Angeles for a meeting with the editor of the *Los Angeles Times* and then traveled to Los Alamos National Laboratory for meetings with scientists and Siegfried S. Hecker, the director. The third mission was to set up security for the secretary while he took a couple of days off to go fly-fishing on the Snake River. They all went without incident.

In December, our nation's first significant military crisis since Grenada was the invasion of Panama. My initial involvement was to escort Secretary Cheney and General Colin Powell, the chairman of the Joint Chiefs of Staff, to a meeting with President Bush at the White House to discuss the war plan to invade Panama, at that time called Operation Blue Spoon, though it later became known to be Operation Just Cause.[158] I recalled that afternoon vividly; it was a chilly Sunday morning, December 17, 1989, and the sky was dark blue. We could see the Christmas decorations hanging on lampposts as we drove from the Pentagon to the White House. Our car pulled into the White House Southeast Gate and stopped at the west entrance. Both Secretary Cheney and General Powell climbed out of the car, holding rolled-up charts and briefing materials, and headed for the briefing with President Bush. The subsequent invasion of Panama was an overwhelming military success and met its intended goal of removing General Manuel Noriega from and inserting the legitimate elected president, Guillermo Endara.

My first and most tense overseas trip was to Manila in February 1990. In November and early December 1989, Filipino rebels opposing President Corazon Aquino's rule had seized some military bases in an attempted coup. The coup was quickly put down with help from the United States Air Force, who, using F-4 Phantom jets stationed at Clark Air Base, buzzed the air bases taken over by the rebels. Orders were to fire in front of any T-28 attempting to take off and to shoot any down if they did take off.[159]

The PSU team—consisting of mission SAC Steve Holcomb and fellow special agents Tim Steenbergen, James Vandoli, and myself, who went to Manila in advance to set up security for the mission—was stressed a little. After the coup attempt, tensions between the Filipino government and the United States escalated over US criticism of Aquino's administration as being "too soft" on coup plotters. The Aquino administration was also upset with the United States for slashing $96 million from the $481 million that Washington had pledged in compensation for use of Clark Air Base and Naval Base Subic Bay.[160] Because of the reduction of funding, to protest, President Aquino snubbed Secretary Cheney by not seeing him while he was in Manila. The visit was for naught, because about six months later, both Clark Air Base and Subic Bay Naval Station received catastrophic damage because of the eruption of Mount Pinatubo, and the bases were abandoned by the United States government.

Upon our arrival after reporting into the US Embassy in Manila, we learned that demonstrators stormed the US Embassy compound in Manila. Police fired tear gas to hold them back during the fracas. Police officers were injured by flying wood from the exploding mailbox.

At Clark Air Base, 50 miles north of Manila, hundreds of young people hurled rocks at club-wielding police who stopped them from tearing down barbed-wire barricades at the entrance to the US base. Several protesters suffered cuts and bruises.[161]

One morning while sleeping in my hotel room, a sound of voices woke me up. It wasn't just a few voices—it was many, like you would hear in a large crowd at a football game. I got out of bed and looked out my tenth-floor window, and to my surprise, I saw hundreds or more people in the front of the hotel, just milling around. I suspected the worst: that protesters—or, even worse, rioters—were ready to storm the lobby of the hotel and wreak havoc as they went. I reached for the telephone and called each member of the team. I had a fleeting thought that we could all converge with our Uzi machine guns and service revolvers in my hotel room, because it was at the end of a hallway on the tenth floor and harder to get to. But before I called any of the team members, I dialed the hotel receptionist and quickly asked him, "Do you know why all the people are outside the hotel?"

"They are getting ready for a marathon run down Magsaysay Boulevard," he said.

To say the least, I was relieved to hear what he had told me. I looked out my hotel window again and saw that everyone had dispersed. What was initially thought to be a crisis turned out to be something funny.

When Cheney arrived in Manila, the Filipino military of 169,000 was on high alert amid rumors of another imminent coup. There were anti-American slogans on Magsaysay Boulevard with signs saying, *Cheney Go Home* and *Bases Out*. Outside Camp Aguinaldo, the military headquarters equivalent to the Pentagon, where Cheney met with Ramos, demonstrators burned Cheney in effigy and shouted, "Yankees, go home!" "Cheney, warmonger!" and "White monkey, go home with your bases." The whole purpose of Secretary Cheney's visit was to shore up cooperation with our Filipino allies.

Special Agent Vandoli and I were to organize the security for Secretary Cheney's stop to meet with the minister of defense, Fidel V. Ramos, at Aguinaldo. We visited the main building at the compound and saw actual damage caused by the last coup in November and December 1989, where machine-gun fire struck the walls of the building outside. Inside on a stairwell wall, there were still bullets holes, not yet repaired, that shattered the glass on picture frames covering the photographs of previous ministers of defense hanging on a wall. One caught my attention—that of Ferdinand E. Marcos, who was also a former president of the Philippines whose wife, Imelda Marcos, had a reputation for expensive shopping trips and buying thousands of shoes.

Special Agent Vandoli and I argued with the Filipino leadership at Aguinaldo to change arrangements already made to drive Secretary Cheney and Minister of Defense Ramos in an open-aired Jeepney to review the troops. Reviewing the troops is a tradition when leaders of one country visit another country. After some very tense negotiations, it was decided that a hard car would be used to transport the two in reviewing the troops. Under normal circumstances, the two dignitaries would walk in front of the troops, but due to the heightened alert and ongoing protest, it was felt caution was the better part of valor in this case. The review went without incident, and the meeting was safely held in Ramos's office. The Manila mission was an experience of a lifetime. It enabled me to understand the workings of a security mission overseas. I would have plenty more foreign trips and many stateside missions, but I will always remember this one first.

I routinely assisted Wayne in the overall operation of the unit; I honesty felt that this is what he primarily wanted me to do. About four months into my tour at PSU, I was elevated to the team chief position of the Office of the Secretary of Defense (OSD). This initially involved the management and supervision of all security activities of the secretary and deputy secretary of defense. It was a large order with many aspects involving both in-town and travel teams conducting OSD missions. There were many other missions throughout the spring and summer of 1990, both stateside and overseas. I traveled to New York, NY; New Haven, CT; Indianapolis, IN; Wright-Patterson Air Force Base, OH; Detroit, MI; Bern, Switzerland; Moscow, Russia; Paris, France and a few more places that I cannot recall.

In the summer of 1990, I was tapped as the personal security officer to travel with Deputy Secretary Donald J. Atwood to London and Paris. He met British leaders in London and attended the fiftieth anniversary of the invasion of Paris, France, by Germany. While in Paris, a very bizarre sight caught my attention. The powers that be at the time of Germany's invasion of were General Charles de Gaulle and General Dwight "Ike" Eisenhower. During one of the days' activities, I observed Eisenhower's son, John, talking to de Gaulle's son. De Gaulle was dressed in his father's era military French uniform, and Eisenhower's son was dressed in a regular business suit. Each of these individuals were the mirror images of their fathers. The scene was surreal in that it made me feel as if I were back in time. I also noticed several people looking at these two gentlemen, and they were probably thinking the same thing as I was.

The missions went without incident, and I got the deputy secretary of defense safely back to Washington.

During early August 1990, I had escorted Deputy Secretary Donald Atwood to Colorado Springs, Colorado, for visits to NORAD/Cheyenne Mountain and Peterson Air Force Base. On August 2, 1989, while we were driving from Cheyenne Mountain back to our hotel, the news came by phone from the Pentagon that Iraqi leader Saddam Hussein had crossed into Kuwait.

Sitting in the backseat, Deputy Secretary Atwood told his military aide, "He was not going to cross the border," and then asked me, "How much longer will it be before we get to our hotel?"

"About ten minutes," I informed him while motioning with my hands for the driver to speed up.

We arrived back at our hotel in about ten minutes; the rest of mission was cut short, and the following morning, Deputy Secretary Atwood flew back to Washington to focus on the situation. Thus, our country began the planning of what would turn out to be Operation Desert Shield.

After I got back to Washington, the next few days were a fury at PSU headquarters. There were rumors going around that many of the protectees were planning trips to various places, so we had to plan for contingencies on which special agents would go where. On August 4, it came down from the Pentagon that Secretary Cheney was headed to Saudi Arabia to brief them on the size of our forces that would be needed to push Saddam out of Kuwait and for them to allow our combat troops into their country.

Although I had never been to Saudi Arabia, I knew I wanted to go, and I expressed my feelings to Wayne. After a meaningful discussion, he convinced me that the best person to take the mission to oversee security was Special Agent Jim Hatcher. It was agreed that my services would best be served in assisting with supervision and management of the unit.

Secretary Cheney and Special Agent Hatcher left on August 5. They spent a day in Saudi Arabia, where Secretary Cheney briefed the king and his staff. Once that meeting was over, Special Agent Hatcher and his team were required to make a stop in Egypt for a day, where the secretary briefed President Mubarak on what the Saudis had agreed to. Then, on the way back to Andrews, they had to make an unscheduled stop in Morocco to brief King Hassan.

On August 8, 1990, the mission over, Hatcher and his team landed back at Andrews Air Force Base. Special Agent Hatcher, with little sleep over the previous several days, was one tired-out special agent.

The United States spent the next several months deploying our troops to Saudi Arabia in preparation for a showdown with Iraq.

In October 1990, we deployed another series of overseas security details missions to London and Russia; I was assigned the Russian portion of the trip. Three of us—Special Agents Kathy Klug, Dennis Burdette, and I—flew from Washington via Frankfurt to Moscow. On Sunday, October 14, 1990, at 7:00 p.m., after a grueling fifteen-hour flight, we landed at Sheremetyevo International Airport. We exited the American Delta plane and headed for the terminal. We were herded into a large open room where people from multiple planes were prepared to get their baggage and go through Russian customs. First, we were directed by airport personnel to complete the customs declaration form. The first question on the form asked if you were carrying any guns. I thought. *All three of us have guns. Hell, we're on a security mission.*

I then started looking for the embassy expediter; he was nowhere to be found. I then told Klug and Burdette to follow me. We could not get through the

Russian customs without an expediter, I thought. With all our weapons, communications equipment, and other security apparatus, without an expediter, we would go to jail for sure. I looked around the room and saw a lone Russian soldier standing in front of a black curtain, holding a machine gun across his chest. I moved toward him, holding up my black diplomatic passport, thinking that just maybe someone on the other side of the curtain, possibly a custom official, could speak English; I was wrong.

As I approached the Russian soldier with Klug and Burdette walking behind me, I was about to say something to him when he stepped aside, opened the curtain, and motioned for me to go through. Feeling sort of anxious, I followed his instructions and walked through the open curtain and found myself in the main terminal. No customs, police, or military present, just passengers scurrying around to try to find their transportation to take them to their destinations. I looked back at Klug and Burdette, and we all grinned at each other and sighed with relief.

"Now, we've got to get transportation to the embassy," I said.

There was also a small snafu about the taxi service. There were three of us, but as we found out, our large, hard carrying cases would not fit inside the trunks of the taxis. We ended up taking two taxis to the embassy. I rode in one, and Klug and Burdette rode in the other, with hard cases extending out of the trunk. We made the trip in about thirty minutes and off-loaded our equipment on the street in front of the marine guard post at the side of the embassy. When I went to pay my driver with Russian rubles, he refused to take it. He demanded American cigarettes as payment, and when I told him I did not smoke, he sped off, the rubles still in my hand.

When we tried to enter the embassy, we were stopped by a marine guard who asked, "Who are you guys, and what is your reason for being at the embassy?"

"We are the advance security detail for the secretary of defense trip to Moscow," I told him.

"I have no authorization to let any security detail in the embassy," he told us.

"How do we resolve this?" I asked the marine.

The marine contacted the embassy regional security officer (RSO), who sent a representative down to our location, and after several moments of confusion, he cleared us to enter the embassy. The RSO representative informed us that the embassy had not received any message traffic from our unit that we were coming. I informed him that I personally sent a message containing specific details on the number of special agents, to include support personnel, our time of arrival, what flight we were taking, and request for reservations for my group and the support special agents coming in later.

"There was obviously a misconnect by someone. We'll settle this issue in the morning," the embassy representative said.

Our next hurdle was in the evening after most essential personnel had left the embassy for the day. We could secure our hard cases containing our weapons, communication equipment, and other security items in a vault near the RSO's office.

"Do you have any reservations for us to stay anywhere?" I asked him.

"I'll have to check; give me a few minutes."

He left us in small waiting room, where we remained until his return. The three of us sat on a bench for about fifteen minutes when the embassy representative returned and told us, "The embassy had booked three rooms at the Hotel Ukraina, just across the Moskva River from the US Embassy."

He provided us ground transportation to the hotel. I thought, *if they had made reservations for the three of us, then they must have received my message traffic before our arrival.*

On the short ride across the Moskva River, past the Russian parliament building to the Hotel Ukraina, I was too tried to worry about the embassy's efforts on our part. Checking into the hotel was yet another simple task made more difficult by our host than what it should have been. All three of us had to relinquish our diplomatic passports and received in return a green card made of paper that we were instructed to carry around with us while in Moscow.

Early the next morning, Special Agent Burdette and I jogged along the Moskva River for a couple of miles, and I got the eerie feeling that we were being watched. Our run was uneventful, and we returned to the hotel to get ready for the day. It was a cold October day in Moscow, and I started my trip to Russia by wearing an overcoat. While in Russia, one of the buttons of the overcoat had come loose, so I pulled it off and placed it in a pocket. I had forgotten about the button until one morning I put on my coat for the short walk to the US Embassy. Realizing the coat without the button would look tacky, I left it in the hotel room.

When I returned to the hotel room that evening, I noticed that someone had sewed the button back on the overcoat. I immediately thought it was one of the two ladies that we had to relinquish our green cards to when we'd left the hotel. Wanting to thank them for their effort and kindness, I grabbed my overcoat from the hanger, left my hotel room, and walked to the floor lobby to find which lady had sewn on the button. When I approached the two ladies, who were sitting on a sofa watching Russian TV, they eyed me worriedly. I asked them in English, "Which one of you sewed the button on my coat?"

Neither one spoke English, but one turned around, picked up the phone, and called someone and then handed the phone to me.

I spoke first. "Who is this?"

Speaking in perfect English, a woman answered, "This is the receptionist in the lobby. Can I help you?"

I explained to the receptionist the situation, and she then asked me to put one of the ladies on the phone. A moment later, the lady returned the phone as she commented something in Russian. I took the phone, and the receptionist informed me, "Neither of the two ladies sewed the button back on."

"Okay, thanks." I then hung up. I thanked the two ladies and went back to my room and scratched my head. I never did find out who sewed the button back on my overcoat.

For the next couple of days, the PSU security team met with the embassy staff, including the RSO and his special agents from the Bureau of Diplomatic Security, who would assist us with the routes and conduct liaison with the Russian security personnel. We also discussed the various itineraries and visits to the many facilities and meetings with the Russian leaders.

On October 16, 1990, Secretary Cheney arrived in Moscow aboard one of the United States blue-and-white 707s from the Eighty-Ninth Air Wing. Our team picked him up at the airport. His first stop was to lay a wreath at the Tomb of the Unknown Soldier and then be driven to a dacha (seasonal or year-round second home) often located in the exurbs (outside) of Moscow. The dacha was used primarily by Soviet Defense Minister Yazov. Burdette and I served as the two primary security agents for this trip. After this event, we escorted Secretary Cheney to his lodgings at the US Embassy.

The next day, Secretary Cheney and his entourage, including me, hopped aboard a Russian Mi-8 transport helicopter at a Russian military airfield near Moscow and flew to Tula, about two hundred kilometers south of Moscow, to the site of a training center for Russian special forces. The installation was like our Fort Bragg in North Carolina. Upon our arrival, Secretary Cheney met with his host, and I met with my equivalent host, a Russian aide and a Soviet Army captain who was probably assigned to watch me while I was on the installation.

The Russians went all out on this visit. The had a tent set up for a reception area that had refreshments galore, including as much Russian vodka as you wanted. Fortunately for me, I did not imbibe in the substance. This is a good example that shows the differences between their military culture and ours. They went through an exercise involving airdrops of tanks from planes and many hundreds of paratroopers. One paratrooper caught my attention as he was floating down from the airplane from which he had just jumped. The parachutist was directing his landing at the point where the secretary was standing. My left hand moved slowly toward the handgrip of my .38 revolver, and the next few seconds were very tense. No one that was viewing the event seemed concerned or worried, but I thought it was unusual that the soldier was sailing right for Secretary Cheney.

The Russian soldier finally landed and stood toe to toe with Secretary Cheney. I locked onto the soldier's hand movements as they moved toward his helmet. The soldier took off the helmet, and the prettiest head of long blonde hair poured out; the parachutist was a beautiful twentysomething woman who reminded me of a model. I eased my hand off my gun but continued to watch the woman's actions. I was convinced now that it was a staged event. The women then unzipped her jacket and pulled out a bouquet of roses and handed them to the secretary. Everyone standing around the secretary, even Defense Minister Yazov, showed approval for the show the girl put on, and some clapped. You never know what is going to happen when providing security for a dignitary.

We then observed a realistic training exercise by the Russian special forces, where they ran through an obstacle course, culminating with a hand-to-hand bout between two soldiers that both drew blood. It was very interesting action and a very historic moment that the senior leadership of the US military could see the way the Russians fight and deliver their tanks and people into battle. The Cold War was fading into the past.

Although the Cold War mentality had changed somewhat, our Russian security counterparts were still stiff and were very hesitant to be open with the American security detail. We were escorted everywhere we went. Part of this situation may have been caused by the Russian culture of historical distrust of outsiders. I would find out much later that this atmosphere did change.

From October 1990 to January 1991, I traveled little, making only one overseas trip to Warsaw, Poland, and Brussels in early December 1990. Instead, I stayed in the office, helping to get PSU ready and situated so they could conduct their security missions during wartime. We had sent Special Agent Steven Holcomb from PSU on a six-month TDY to Saudi Arabia to perform as the personal security officer (PSO) for the deputy commander in chief for military operations, Major General Calvin A. H. Waller, during the impending war with Iraq. I was selected to be the point of contact for Steve and to assist him with what he needed. This included a personal agreement between the two of us that I would call his wife to let her know how he was doing about once a week.

Our office, crowded with the normal unit members going about doing their jobs of mainly preparing for security trips and documenting post-trip mission lessons learned, had to exist with an additional two activated CID reserve units augmented to PSU prior to the war starting. This increased our unit from about forty-one to over hundred-special agents and support personnel. Our additional help was much needed to fulfill our mission, but it was a double-edged sword. The CID command never gave us any more space for operations. This meant that people were sharing desks, bumping into each other, and often had no place to even sit down. I think that Wayne did a superb job of organizing and managing the unit, which grew to three times the authorized strength as normal, allowing it to be effective throughout the war.

During the buildup of the PSU just before the start of the Persian Gulf War, it was considered a time of heightened security awareness for our team. The unit rented a townhome for use as a security control center near Secretary Cheney's residence in McLean, Virginia. The security control center was manned 24-7 by two special agents performing twelve-hour shifts. The center had the most up-to-date CCTV and radio communication equipment that the US Army had at the time. Without the augmentation of additional CID special agents, security requirements would have been difficult.

Late in the afternoon of January 16, 1991, several special agents had gathered around my desk to watch CNN. I got a sick, nervous feeling in my stomach when the news broke that the start of the air war with Iraq had begun. The breaking news showed relentless, intense bombing of Baghdad; we were at war. The air campaign had started in earnest and would last until February 24, 1991. It took just another four days, one hundred hours of ground fighting, before the United States and coalition forces defeated Saddam and his army. I believed that the short length of the war surprised our military leaders; the Iraqis soon surrendered.

One of my new duties during the period leading up to the war kept me extremely busy. The newly opened security control center near the secretary's townhome was now in full operation and kept several of our special agents busy. I set up a mandatory training class for all newly assigned special agents. Every special agent that worked in the security control center attended the class, and I thought everyone was on track with what their duties and responsibilities were while working the center. One very specific item I put out in the training class was that if anything suspicious occurred on their watch, such as an unauthorized or suspicious person seen loitering outside the secretary's townhome, either in person or on CCTV, they were to detain the individual and determine why they were in the neighborhood. If they could not give a good reason why they were in the area, one CID special agent was to watch the person while the other was to call the Fairfax County Police Department (FCPD). Special Agent Steenbergen had already conducted liaison with the FCPD, and they were ready to assist when called.

One night while monitoring the CCTV, two on-duty special agents observed a person climbing over Secretary Cheney's backyard fence. The agents failed to call the FCPD and allowed the unidentified person to enter the backyard and nose around. It was our good fortune that the secretary and his family were not at home and the townhome was secured. The individual, realizing that he could not get into the secured residence, left in the same manner he had entered the backyard—by climbing back over the fence and disappearing into the night.

The two-special agents who were lacking in their duties did call and reported the incident to PSU. I directed replacements for both and ordered the two to report to my office. Wayne and I discussed the strategy as to how we were going to handle the situation. Major Charles Alvarez, the newly assigned PSU commander, directed me to conduct a formal investigation and have my report on his desk by that afternoon. CID command was anxious to get to the bottom of the issue, because it was a foregone conclusion that Secretary Cheney would be informed about what had happened.

I started by interviewing the two-special agents. Since there was, at a minimum, the offense of failing to follow orders, I read them their rights; both declined to say anything. I wrote a report about what they had reported and the fact that they'd declined to be interviewed and submitted it to Major Alvarez. He was not satisfied with my report and wanted more information about training and what their requirements were while in the security control center.

Wayne and I continued working the investigation, and I had to explain to Major Alvarez that the report would not possibly be completed by the afternoon. Wayne and I spent the next couple of days identifying every aspect of what we knew, and a second report was submitted to Major Alvarez for his review. Accepting it, the only action left was for Secretary Cheney to be informed. Wayne took it upon himself to do this task.

The secretary was briefed on the incident when he returned from a trip. The special agent who was a reservist requested to terminate his active duty status and return home, which was granted. The second special agent remained on duty with no further action. Wayne and I spent the next several days developing a training program that was more in depth. I was later told by a source that the one PSU special agent who was not on my team did not attempt to detain the unidentified man because he was not sure if CID command would have supported him if the incident had escalated into a physical altercation—or worse, maybe a shooting. This one embarrassed PSU.

On December 4, 1990, Tuesday, the SECDEF's 707 landed at Warsaw Chopin Airport for a two-day visit to Warsaw, Poland. Secretary Cheney was the first United States defense secretary to ever visit Poland. His trip was also seen as an attempt to strengthen ties with former Eastern Bloc countries that had recently recovered their independence from the USSR. We had several locations to visit in the short time we were in Warsaw, and the schedule for the secretary was hectic, requiring unexpected changes throughout the trip. I was assigned as the personal security officer when Secretary Cheney met with Lech Wałęsa, the solidarity leader who would become Poland's first president in only five days. He next met with the Polish defense minister, Vice Admiral Piotr Kołodziejczyk. Their talks involved the economic plight of Poland and the potential sale of weapons to Eastern Bloc countries.[162] The security of the mission ran without major issues.

On December 7, 1990, we flew from Warsaw to Brussels for the biannual North Atlantic Treaty Organization (NATO). Our liaison with the Brussels Gendarmerie (police) was excellent. The two agencies worked extremely well with each other. I suspect that the ease with which the Gendarmerie and CID special agents of PSU worked together came from years of routine planning for the annual meetings. The Gendarmerie were spread thinly due to their agency having to provide aid and security for all the foreign defense secretaries and ministers each time they came to Brussels. Our security teams in Brussels had the advantage of repeating the trip many times, therefore, ensuring that the proper plans went in effect from a great deal of experience with meetings with the NATO defense ministers and NATO's secretary general, Manfred Wörner. The meetings came at the same time the United States was continuing the troop buildup in Saudi Arabia because of the crisis in Kuwait. I liked to be associated with the security trips to Brussels, because we were always treated fairly and professionally by the local Gendarmerie.

Back in the United States, the US Army still had its eyes on my career potential development. I was selected for and attended the warrant senior course at Fort McClellan. The cadre of CID special agents at the United States Army Military Police School (USAMPS) was excellent. The course taught some very good managing and leadership principles that were used for the rest of my career. The course also made me eligible for promotion to CW4 and the promotion board at the Hoffman Building in Alexandria, Virginia, selected me for that grade in mid-1991.

On May 12, 1991, I flew out to Colorado Springs to set up security for Secretary Cheney's visit to Colorado College to deliver its commencement speech. This was a special trip for Secretary Cheney because his youngest daughter, Mary, was in the graduating class. I had met Mary on a few trips in my tenure as the team chief of Secretary Cheney's security detail and found her to be courteous, gracious, and sincere.

My first meeting on this mission was with the Colorado Springs Police Department (CSPD). Because of the Persian Gulf War, their department had provided a sort of informal security presence for Mary that had been arranged by Special Agent Tim Steenbergen and I with one of their detective lieutenants, who we'd met when he was attending a law enforcement conference in Washington, DC, in late 1990, just before the war started.

The Colorado Springs detectives brought me up to date on security of the area. They had met with the Cheney family on a few occasions throughout this period. Their intelligence had picked up on some unsubstantiated information that there were a few students reportedly preparing to throw HIV-contaminated blood onto Secretary Cheney as he walked down the aisle with the president and other prominent people of Colorado College, including the famous primatologist Jane Goodall, a commencement speaker.

One of the four Colorado Springs detectives I met accompanied me to the Colorado College security office, where we could coordinate the security aspects of the commencement exercise. However, on our way, he drove to Mary's off-campus apartment. When I told the officer, I had no reason to see her, he said, "It is our daily routine to at least drive by her apartment to check on her."

"Okay," I said.

She was at home and told us she had no immediate needs or concerns but was anxious for her commencement to be over. After the visit to Mary's apartment, we then drove to the campus security office.

Based on the information the CSPD had revealed in our meeting, a decision was made to have Secretary Cheney join the VIP party as they gathered on the stage. It was planned to have the secretary exit a door directly behind the group and fall in line with them as if he had also walked down the aisle. This maneuver, if it worked, would seamlessly position the secretary into the group without any interruption or distraction.

Later that day, Secretary Cheney's plane came on time at Peterson Air Force Base, Colorado Springs, Colorado. I had the motorcade waiting on the tarmac. I greeted the secretary, Dr. Cheney, and the secretary's parents. As our motorcade sped away to their lodgings, I briefed Secretary Cheney as to how the events of his trip would play out. The next day after breakfast and last-minute telephone calls, I escorted Secretary Cheney and his wife to Colorado College and enroute explained what our plan was.

"Sounds good to me," the secretary responded.

Once at the college, I secured Secretary Cheney in a room near the doorway where he was going to exit when the party walked up on the stage. With time being critical, I acted.

"Mr. Secretary, it's time," I announced.

He followed me to the door behind the stage, and when the time came, he was whisked outside and joined the VIP party as planned without anyone noticing. With the secretary speaking after the famous anthropologist Jane Goodall and the diplomas given out, only one small incident occurring was good, all things considered. It was planned that the students would shake hands with the speakers as they walked by them on the way to receive their diplomas by the presenters. As one female student approached Secretary Cheney, she attempted to secretly give him a piece of paper by inserting it in his hand as she shook it. The president of the college saw what she was trying to do, so he grabbed the note before Secretary Cheney took it.

After the graduation ceremony, I escorted the secretary and his family to a small gathering, and then the motorcade took him and Mrs. Cheney to the plane for their trip back to Washington.

After I got the Cheneys on the plane, I met with several Colorado Springs police officers at their headquarters to thank them for a job well done. Mary Cheney attended my briefing. I passed out several takeaways in the form of ink pens, small paperweights, tie clips, and other mementos.

On May 29, 1991, I flew on the SECDEF's 707 to Tel Aviv for a two-day visit to meet with the leaders of Israel. The visit was arranged so that Secretary Cheney could thank Israel for its restraint during the Persian Gulf War. Talks also included the United States' Middle East arms race proposals and that the United States would give Israel $65 million worth of US fighter planes and underwrite most of a new Israeli missile system. There was tension in the air, and although helpful, I considered the Israeli security detail to be arrogant and patronizing to the United States security team. Since I would be escorting Secretary Cheney to each meeting in and around Tel Aviv and Jerusalem, the SAC of the Israeli security team handed me a skullcap (*kippah* or yarmulke or *yarmulka*) and demanded that if any shooting broke out that I put it on and hit the dirt. Israel was one of the counties that allowed us to bring in weapons, but officials there were very reluctant to let us use them if needed. To our good fortune, the mission went off without any incidents.

On June 10, 1991, New York had a ticker-tape parade starting at Battery Park in Lower Manhattan, within sight of the Statue of Liberty, and made its way through Manhattan's Canyon of Heroes; that lasted over four hours and was attended by an estimated 4.7 million people. It was reported to be the biggest parade ever and cost over $5 million, paid for by private donations. The parade was led by Secretary of Defense Dick Cheney, chairman of the Joint Chiefs of Staff General Colin Power, and Persian Gulf War Commander General H. Norman Schwarzkopf. Many thanks go out to Special Agent Nick Padilla, who headed up the security arrangements with the New York Police Department (NYPD). Nick found three period Cadillacs—colored red, white, and blue—to symbolize our American flag, one each transporting Secretary Cheney and Generals Power and Schwarzkopf and their wives, respectively. Wayne, the PSU chief, also ensured that every special agent assigned to the PSU participated in the parade. The day culminated in several months of national postwar celebrations.

On August 18, 1991, an attempted coup against Mikhail Gorbachev was initiated, led by communist hard-liners of the Soviet government and military.

The attempt was poorly planned, and when the leaders of the coup, seeing that most of the Soviet military did not support their actions, called it off, the coup collapsed on August 21. The coup elevated the security in the United States military to a higher level and changed the way we dealt with the fading Soviet Union. Although Gorbachev could stay in power, his days were numbered, and he eventually resigned on December 21, 1991, and the world saw the end of the USSR. Boris Yeltsin eventually took over leadership of Russia[163] and replaced Gorbachev as the popular leader of the region.

Shortly after the coup, I was selected to lead a security team for Deputy Secretary of Defense Donald Atwood to Moscow. Deputy Secretary of Defense Atwood was scheduled to stop in Kiev after leaving Moscow. The trip was multifaceted and was to cover aspects of business, a tour of factory conversions from war materials to domestic items, and to reassure Gorbachev that the United States still supported him. I started preparing the requirements for support agents and operational equipment needed. I sent off message traffic to the embassy so that they knew we were coming. I did not want a repeat of my last Russian trip where the RSO at the US Embassy did not arrange to pick up our support agents on arrival and he had questions on why we were bringing in so many agents to support the mission. Having been told via message traffic that the security for our trip had been accepted by the Russian Embassy, I was ready for the mission.

In early November 1991, I accompanied Deputy Secretary Atwood on his plane to Moscow. He had two scheduled stops—one in Moscow and the second in Kiev. I was his personal security officer for the entire Moscow portion of the trip. We visited some factories that were converted from production of war materials to domestic items. The visit also involved meeting some of the Soviet leaders, including Mikhail Gorbachev in the Kremlin. My security team worked jointly with the Russians to ensure the safety of protectees. The highlight of Deputy Secretary Atwood's visit to Moscow was his visit with Gorbachev. I escorted him into the foyer of Gorbachev's office, and he entered the actual office for talks with the Soviet leader. Once their meeting was over, our security team escorted Deputy Secretary Atwood back to his hotel. While driving back to the hotel, Deputy Secretary Atwood told his senior military aide, BG John Rhoads, that before their meeting, Gorbachev admitted that he had not heard of Deputy Secretary Atwood.

The Moscow trip lasted three days, and then Deputy Secretary Atwood left for Kiev for four days of visits with business and community leaders in that city. While the security to Kiev was provided by other members of the team, I stayed in Moscow until the deputy secretary's party returned to Moscow prior to the flight home. On our flight home, Deputy Secretary Atwood came back to my seat on the plane and personally thanked me for "a splendid job well done."

I told him the Soviet security folks deserved a large portion of that thanks, because they really did go out of their way to ensure our mission went well.

After the Russian mission, I made it home to spend Thanksgiving with Elda in Virginia.

On December 5, 1991, I landed with Secretary Cheney in Honolulu, Hawaii, via Travis Air Force Base in California for the fiftieth anniversary of the Japanese attack on Pearl Harbor. The two-day trip involved speeches by President Bush along with Secretary Cheney at the USS *Arizona* Memorial. After the official activities, Secretary Cheney was interviewed aboard the USS *Missouri* by news media person Harry Smith for a later broadcast on a morning TV show. We departed Honolulu enroute to Budapest, Hungary, on December 7, 1991, with a refueling stop at Elmendorf Air Force Base, just outside Anchorage, Alaska. While at Elmendorf, due to the long flight and the remaining portion of the trip to Budapest, Secretary and Mrs. Cheney wanted to take a relaxing walk.

When we landed, I commandeered three parkas from the air force, one each for the secretary and Mrs. Cheney and the third for myself. As the huge 707 was being refueled, the three of us left the plane for a walk down the edge of the tarmac. Sometimes, the best-laid-out plans go awry. What we did not count on was the foot of snow we had to wade through. The secretary and Mrs. Cheney handled it like real troopers. We had walked about a half mile when an air force pickup truck approached, and the driver leaning out the window was none other than the local provost marshal, who was a LTC.

The Cheneys, a little in front of me, turned toward the truck, and the driver asked, "Mr. Secretary, are you all right?"

The secretary then turned around and asked me, "Dick, are you all right?"

"Yes, sir," I responded.

"Well, then, I guess we are all okay, thanks," the secretary said as he kept walking. Secretary Cheney's concerned was not only for himself and Mrs. Cheney; he had me in mind as well. This made me feel extremely proud to be working for a man with such empathy for his security special agents. He showed me this good trait time and time again, even at a farewell gathering when he left office and during Christmas holidays.

Within the hour, we had returned to the plane and gotten ready for takeoff to Budapest.

Taking on a full tank of fuel added weight to the plane affected its lift on takeoff. The fuel was needed due to the distance the 707 had to travel. To counter this situation, everyone in the front of the plane, except the pilots, communicators, and the secretary and Mrs. Cheney, went to the back of the plane where lower-level strap hangers and security agents were seated and took theirs place in available seating for the takeoff. By doing this, it allowed the 707 greater lift capacity on takeoff. Once we leveled off at cruising altitude, the people moved back to their regular assigned seats. During takeoff, Rear Admiral Joseph Lopez, Secretary Cheney's senior military aide, sat next to me. During this time, the two of us had a meaningful conversation about crime in the military. He expressed his views as a senior leader in the US Navy, and I provided mine on a personal experience level.

About 2:45 p.m. on December 8, 1991, we landed at Budapest Ferihegy International Airport. After a short welcome by the Hungarian minister of defense (MOD), Colonel Laszlo Botz, we departed via motorcade to our lodging about forty minutes from the airport. I escorted Secretary Cheney and Mrs. Cheney to dinner that evening hosted by MOD Botz.

The following day, I escorted Secretary Cheney to meetings with Hungarian MOD officials and a wreath-laying ceremony at the Hungarian Tomb of the Unknown Soldier and then to their parliament. On the third day in Budapest, additional meetings were held with Hungarian government officials. I found that the Hungarian security people were extremely cooperative and gave my security team a lot of leeway in allowing us to perform our close-in protection for the secretary. Our security mission teams worked well with each other. We departed at noon for a one-hour flight to Prague, Czechoslovakia.

On Tuesday, a cold, cloudy day at 1:00 p.m. on December 10, 1991, the SECDEF's 707 landed at the airport in Prague and was met by Czechoslovakian government officials and Ambassador Shirley Temple (the famous child movie star), a very pleasant and friendly person. I escorted the secretary to meetings with the Czechoslovakian leaders and with the Czech president, Václav Havel. Dick Cheney was the first American defense secretary to visit Czechoslovakia. The visit lasted two days and was intended to strengthen ties between the two countries and to address security concerns now that the Czechoslovakians had rid themselves of the hold by the weakened USSR. The trip went without incident, and the cooperation with our host security people was very cordial.

After the Czechoslovakia mission, Elda and I spent the holidays in Indiana visiting with family and friends. We had a grand old time seeing some family members for the first time in a year or two. My sister Rachel had lost her husband, Bob Lamberth, earlier in the year, and it was good to see she was getting on with her life. We found Chris to be well and getting along with studies at Indiana State University in Terre Haute. We attended the annual holiday party in Linton with my niece Marsha and her husband, John Richards, with June, Nora and Hubert, and the Miller clan. We were sad to leave, but we had to get back to work, as the year 1992 was shaping up to be a very busy and productive year for both Elda and me.

January 1992 was a busy month for the special agents at PSU. Secretary Cheney was scheduled to visit Great Britain and Germany, and he had many stateside trips planned for the end of January. Wayne gave me a break during this time, and we sent other OSD team special agents to arrange security for the secretary's trips overseas. It was decided, however, that I would supervise Secretary Cheney's overnight trip to Madison, Wisconsin, for late January where the mission would involve Cheney giving a political speech on the evening of January 28, 1992, to the Wisconsin Manufacturers & Commerce leaders with Governor Tommy G. Thompson in attendance. He would attend a brief meet-and-greet reception at the hotel the following morning and then motorcade back to the Madison airport for the flight back to Washington.

My second in charge on the Madison mission would be Mark Launde, a very capable and knowledgeable special agent who knew his stuff. He was the unit's technical craftsman and the go-to guy for any communications hookups or CCTV installations. If I were to ever need any muscle to assist with rowdy people, well, then, Special Agent Launde would also be that person.

On January 26, 1992, I grabbed a two-hour commercial Delta flight to Madison and made the initial liaison with police and hotel people; Special Agent Launde was to follow the next day. I worked from the time I arrived in Madison until just before the arrival of Secretary Cheney in the evening on my second day to set up security routes. The Madison police were very cooperative and provided anything I asked for.

On that evening, I was enjoying a tasty dinner at the hotel's restaurant, when I kept sensing someone was watching me. I looked over at the bar and noticed a young person, maybe in his late twenties or early thirties, wearing a red baseball cap with no markings and staring at me. I initially disregarded his stare, thinking that my imagination was playing tricks on me. When I finished my meal, I headed for the elevator to go up to my room on the sixth floor.

As I waited for the elevator door to open, I felt the presence of someone standing directly behind me. When the door opened, I turned around and motioned for the person to enter the elevator first, which he did. To my shock, it was the young man with the red baseball cap. I followed him in without any attempt to make a conversation. Immediately after the elevator door shut and we started to rise, the man turned his head toward me and started swearing and calling me a warmonger and a killer, and accusing me of being part of the military-industrial complex.

I just stood there and tried to absorb what he was trying to say. I was not sure I should respond to his tirade. As the door opened to my floor, I looked at him and said, "I am not sure what you are telling me, but you're off base."

He continued to stand without trying to walk out the door of the elevator as it closed. As I walked down the hall to my room, I thought, *Damn! Am I back in the 1960s?* I had done nothing to attract this young man's attention. I finally made it to the door to my room, and I checked to see if the lock or the door itself had been tampered with. Finding the door secure, I opened it, took a panoramic view of the inside, and saw nothing out of the ordinary. Five minutes later, I had prepared for bed, lay down, and turned on CNN. I found myself dozing, but as I fell asleep, I kept thinking about the man in the red baseball cap.

The next morning, I was startled out of a sound sleep by a ringing phone. I picked up the receiver, and Tim Steenbergen was on the other end.

"Did I wake you up?" he asked.

"Well, it all depends on what you want," I told him.

"I heard that you are scheduled to be promoted to CW4 on February 1, 1992."

"Yes, that is correct," I told him.

"How would you like to be promoted by Secretary Cheney at the Pentagon?"

"Well, I haven't thought much about it," I responded to him.

"We have been talking back here in Washington and felt that we can have your promotion arranged by the time you get back from your current trip," he explained.

"If there is no fuss, make it happen, Tim," I told him.

After the phone call, I was no longer sleepy and had to get up anyway. I enjoyed a good breakfast, ensuring first that my friend with the baseball cap was not waiting in the shadows for me. The day started out well; the young man was nowhere to be seen, and the breakfast was decent.

The first day of my time in Madison, I had completed a lot of the work in getting the routes and security arranged. One of my first meetings that morning was with my Madison Police Department contact.

After some small talk, I asked my Madison police sergeant contact, "Does the city of Madison still have a lot of protestors?"

He told me that the city had always had trouble with protestors of many types. "The governor could mention something that people don't like—it could be raising taxes or laying off workers at a plant or something—and the protesters come out of the woodwork. Then he realized that I probably had a reason for asking him about protesters, and he asked, "Why do you ask? Are you worried about protesters because of Secretary Cheney's visit?"

I hadn't even thought about it until last night. I then told him the story about the young man in the red baseball cap.

"Oh yeah. We are all familiar with the man you described. He is part of the protest culture in the city. No one really knows where he is from; he just showed up one day at a protest rally, and he has been identified with that group ever since."

"Are we expecting any protest because of Secretary Cheney's visit to Madison?" I asked the sergeant.

"None of our intelligence has picked up on anything of this nature," the sergeant reported.

The police sergeant told me a funny story about one incident that happened at an Air National Guard base just outside Madison. The story went that one very obese lady who was well known to the Madison police as a regular protestor had somehow come into possession of a set of police handcuffs and used them to lock herself to the chain-link fence that secured the gate to the Air National Guard base, apparently not knowing that most police-style handcuffs have a universal key maintained by all police officers and any Madison police officer could have unlocked her from the fence at any time.

On this day, the small group of protesters who were parading in front of the same gate were arrested, leaving the lady locked to the fence. Thinking that being handcuffed to the fence at the gate prevented the police from taking her, she just smiled and beamed with satisfaction that she was in control. What she did not realize, the sergeant said, was that the police knew that eventually she would have to relieve herself. Knowing this, the sergeant directed one of the officers to remain with her for safety. About two hours into her ordeal, she begged the police officer to let her go because she had to use the bathroom. He was directed by the sergeant telling me the story to not release the women for a half hour after she indicated she needed to go.

What the Madison police officer did not take into consideration that there were no facilities near the gate for the women to use. When it was time to release her, the officer put the female protestor in the back of his patrol car and raced for the Madison police station several miles away through moderate to heavy downtown traffic. The officer made it about halfway before the woman could not hold it any longer, and she relieved herself in the backseat of his patrol car. The young officer had to spend some extra time after his shift to clean the patrol car.

"It looks like the women still won a psychological battle between the protesters and the police," I told the sergeant.

Without saying a word, he nodded, indicating he agreed with my statement.

The University of Wisconsin was one of the most radicalized schools in America during the Vietnam War, culminating in the killing of a researcher inside the university's physics building. The intended target of the criminals—who called themselves the New Year's Gang—was the US Army Mathematics Research Center located adjacent to the physics building.[164] The protests in Madison, regardless of cause, continued throughout the '70s, '80s, and '90s. During our trip to Madison, there were no exceptions; the potential for protestors coming out for the secretary's visit were reminiscent of the hippies in the '60s.

I made another check of where Secretary Cheney was having dinner with Governor Thompson and was satisfied that there were enough police and hotel security personnel to monitor the doors and the event area. By the time, I picked up Special Agent Laude at the airport late on the morning on January 27, 1992, I had completed a great number of the security arrangements. I briefed him on the young man in the red baseball cap, what the Madison police had told me, and the security arrangements coordinated thus far.

Special Agent Launde and I, along with a couple of support agents and one Madison police officer driver, picked up Secretary Cheney at the Madison airport as scheduled. We motorcaded to the hotel in downtown Madison with no incidents. There were no signs of protesters near the hotel as our motorcade pulled up. Our security team got Secretary Cheney to the dinner on time and without incident. There were several hundred-people attending the dinner but still no signs of protesters. As I positioned myself near where the secretary was talking to the audience, I saw one middle-aged man stand up and started shouting disparaging comments about the secretary's speech.

As the man was shouting as loudly as he could, the secretary said, "Is he one of yours, Tommy?"

As two Madison police officers grabbed the protestor's arms and were escorting him out of the room, I overheard the heckler asking the officers, "How much time will I get? Do you think five, ten, fifteen years or what?" He was escorted by the Madison police from the room. The Madison police officers did a fine job by removing the gentleman from the area without further disruption.

After the dinner, Special Agent Launde and I got Secretary Cheney to his overnight accommodations without incident.

The next morning, and I escorted Secretary Cheney to the scheduled reception area, where he met and socialized for about thirty minutes. As this was going on, the police sergeant assigned to assist me approached me and said, "There are about fifty to sixty protestors milling around outside the hotel garage entrance, some with antimilitary signs, ready to pounce on us as we start our motorcade to the airport."

*Ah, this is our unexpected group of people*, I thought. "How would you describe the tone of the protest?" I asked.

"There is no way we can tell. They are chanting antimilitary-type stuff," the sergeant told me.

Special Agent Launde and I discussed the best route to get away from the hotel. I looked outside and saw that there were more protesters in front of the hotel than on the side. I went back inside and informed Special Agent Launde, who was designated to ride with the secretary to the airport, that we should arrange for the departure to come from the side entrance of the underground garage. He agreed.

When it was time, the small motorcade, which was made up of two cars, started moving from the garage onto the street. A few of the protesters raised their voices and chanted more antimilitary comments as the motorcade came out of the underground garage, but due to the excellent blockage by the Madison police patrol cars, Secretary Cheney was escorted out of the area without real incident. With the excellent help from Madison police and hotel security staff, the mission was a success.

Several days after the Madison mission, I was promoted to CW4 by Secretary Dick Cheney in his office. Elda, Chris, June, and Charlie, as well as several invited guests from the PSU—including Wayne, my outstanding boss—were present. Others in attendance were my commander and representative from CID command, Major Alvarez. I felt proud that the US Army recognized my performance throughout a career that has lasted for over twenty-two years. If it were not for Elda's persistence, I would have left the US Army at ten years and sought a professional career in the civilian world. Elda talked me into staying for at least twenty years; she understood far better than I that the grass is not necessarily greener on the other side of the hill.

My promotion to CW4 did not change the fact that I had started looking at retirement after the Persian Gulf War, however. Before the war, the US Army planned a massive drawdown of troops, and to make my decision easier, the Department of Defense reinitiated the reduction in force after the war.

After the war, a larger-than-ever reduction in troop strength for all the branches of service was to be initiated. So, at the same time of my promotion to CW4, the US Army was already in the process of reducing the number of armed forces personnel.

Having gotten promoted gave me more time to make up my mind about retirement. I now turned my focus back to the job at hand. I wanted to help Wayne where my services could be best served. Wayne was one of the best managers I had ever worked for, and I wanted to do my best to see that he kept that excellent reputation. So, I decided to delay retirement for the next few months. However, in providing my assistance, Wayne sometimes made my efforts difficult in that he managed the unit so well that he essentially did not relish or need the help. Thus, I eventually stayed on the road during the first half of 1992. One of the jobs I did assist Wayne on was to take his place as the acting SAC in his absence when he took leave for a few days in February 1992.

The first several days during his absence went smoothly with no major managerial decisions required. On his last day of his leave, Friday, February 14, 1992, was an exception. After work, several special agents in the office, including me, took our wives to dinner; after all, it was Valentine's Day. We all decided on Italian food; therefore, we gathered at the local Olive Garden in Dale City, Virginia, for a semi-romantic night of food and drink. We all sat at the same table and were well into devouring our food. Everyone was enjoying themselves, and we male special agents had made our wives very happy, when suddenly my cell phone rang.

Special Agent Jim Hatcher called me from Jamaica to report that the chairman of the Joint Chiefs had been in a helicopter crash with his wife, Alma, earlier in the day. My jaw dropped, my heart started pounding, and the juices from the Italian food started churning in my stomach.

"He what?" I nervously asked.

"We were taking a helicopter across the bay to Norman Manley International Airport when the helicopter's rotor blades jammed up and the craft started falling into the water, but the pilots were able to nurse it to the beach, where it landed hard, and everyone jumped out and ran as fast as they could."

"Was General Powell or his wife injured?" I inquired.

"No. No one was injured, and we got another helicopter to finish our trip."

I felt relieved that no one was hurt. Special Agent Hatcher informed me that as the helicopter was whirling toward the water, he covered Mrs. Powell to protect her and lessen her injuries if the craft did crash.

Special Agent Hatcher said, "The general did not want to make a big deal out of the incident, but I called you to cover my bases."

I got the feeling that Special Agent Hatcher reported the incident to me, but he did not want me to elevate the information further up the CID chain of command. "I really don't have a choice, Jim," I told him.

"You do what you think is right," he said.

I thanked him for the information and disconnected our call. I knew I had to brief our chain of command, because if I didn't, I would be battered with whys over the weekend or on Monday at work. I called the CID duty officer and briefed him on what Special Agent Hatcher had reported to me. I spent the better part of the rest of the evening answering follow-up calls from CID command about the incident, and I finally put the matter to rest about 1:00 the following morning. By the time, I left the restaurant that evening, my dinner was ancient history.[165]

In mid-February 1992, Wayne drew on me to accompany the secretary on trips to Guatemala and then to Howard Air Force Base in Panama, as well as to Chile, Argentina, and Brazil. The trip to these countries would end up being one of my last major trips overseas. The trip to Guatemala, a short overnight stay, allowed Secretary Cheney to meet with the Guatemalan government officials. Security was tight on this stop, but everything went off without incident. Our next stop was Howard Air Force Base in Panama, where Secretary Cheney thanked the troops for a job well done during Just Cause in a hangar on the base. Afterward, we boarded his plane and took off for Santiago, Chile.

On the stop to Santiago, the party stayed one night, and then Secretary Cheney took a side trip to an area outside Punta Arenas, Chile, for a brief fishing trip, escorted by Special Agent Dennis Burdette. Others on the trip stayed in the city of Punta Arenas for a couple of nights. Punta Arenas is located at the bottom of Chile, near its border with Argentina. The area has some of the highest mountain ranges in the Southern Hemisphere. One day on the trip, I escorted Mrs. Cheney on a trip to a mountain resort area. The beauty of the snowcapped mountains was breathtaking. Our party was flown by a DHC-4 Caribou transporter and landed on the side of the mountain. As we came in for the landing, I kept watching for the airstrip; however, the transporter, known for its short takeoff and landing (STOL) capability, set down on a grassy field where llamas were grazing. The Caribou came to a stop, and then the Chilean pilot turned the plane around on a dime, where it was positioned on a downhill slope for takeoff. What an experience. As Mrs. Cheney and I walked to our waiting motorcade, we both commented on how windy it was. The pilot had done a fantastic job landing the plane despite the high winds.

When we returned to Punta Arenas, I turned over the security responsibilities for Mrs. Cheney to another special agent assigned to our protection team and then flew back to Santiago with a couple of communicators on the secretary's plane, where I arranged security for the traveling party

After the Santiago trip, we all boarded the secretary's plane for a two-and-a-half-hour flight to Buenos Aires, Argentina. Our plane landed at Jorge Newbery Airfield, where Secretary Cheney was met by Minister of Defense González. Then our security team escorted Secretary Cheney to his scheduled meetings with the Argentinean leaders, including Acting President Menem, the brother of President Menem. There were no glitches in the overnight stay in security for our route or personnel, and the trip went off without incident.

Our next stop took us two hours and fifty minutes to Brasília, Brazil. In arranging security for this portion of the trip, the Brazilians required all PSU security special agents to obtain a concealed carrying permit for their assigned service handguns. These permits, good for thirty days, were obtained from the Brazilian Embassy in Washington prior to our trip. Secretary Cheney was escorted to meetings with Brazilian leaders and American embassy officials. This trip had its hiccups and bumps; however, generally, the stop was completed without any significant issues involving Secretary Cheney. After a whirlwind tour of Central and South America, I was very glad to be back in Washington. This mission would end up being my longest while assigned to PSU.

In May 1992, I was assigned a unit mission to set up security at the Citadel, a military college in Charleston, South Carolina. Secretary Cheney had accepted an invitation to speak at the commencement. After prepping for the mission and arranging for the assistance of the US Air Force Office of Special Investigations (OSI) liaison, I got two OSI special agents to support the mission. I reported two days before the secretary's arrival. My first stop was to meet my support agents at the local OSI on Charleston Air Force Base. I obtained a rental car and headed out to the base.

I met with Special Agent in Charge Terry Boatwright, a pleasant and unassuming sort of guy who had a hearty handshake and polite disposition. When I walked into his office, he was sitting at his desk on the phone and motioned for me to sit down. While he was talking on the phone, I noticed his nameplate with the last name of Boatwright. When he hung up, I asked him, "Do you know of a John Boatwright from the US Army CID?"

"I believe he is my cousin," he said.

"I used to work for him in Schweinfurt, Germany," I told him. "It sure is a small world." This broke the ice between us.

The US Air Force OSI has its own methods of providing protection to dignitaries, which differs a little from the US Army CID.

"I have been notified by OSI headquarters at Andrews to provide you with two special agents to help with you mission. I have arranged for a small office for you to work in while you are in Charleston. When do you need them?" he asked.

"Well, if I can have about thirty minutes to make some phone calls and set up a short briefing, let's say have them meet with me in about forty-five minutes."

"Okay, consider it done." SAC Boatwright then got up and walked me to my temporary office.

I made two phone calls—one to the Pentagon public affairs gal that was at the Sheraton Inn in Charleston. We planned to meet the folks at the Citadel after I finished my briefing with the OSI. I then placed a call back to the PSU office and spoke to Special Agent Launde, my assistant on the mission, and informed him of what I had accomplished. We agreed that when he flew the next day, he would rent a car and meet me at the Sheraton Inn. I then wrote down the requirements for the motorcade and security for getting Secretary Cheney from the Charleston airport to the Citadel campus for his speech and back to his plane.

I had just completed the briefing notes when three men, all dressed in well-fitting suits and ties, entered the small office. I acknowledged them and asked them to sit down. I was well into my briefing and talking about how many special agents we needed on the mission, two of which would drive cars in the motorcade. As I moved forward with my briefing, I was suddenly interrupted by one of the OSI special agents.

"OSI agents do not drive cars in protection details," he rudely commented.

The young, cocky OSI special agent's unsolicited input momentarily threw me off track, but I finished without further interruptions.

After the briefing, I released the special agents and sat down at the desk provided to me and started working the motorcade assignments and realized that if the OSI would not drive any of the vehicles, I did not have enough special agents to work the mission.

Then, unexpectedly, SAC Boatwright walked into the office and without prompting said without explanation, "I can't give you another agent—don't have any to give you."

Without mentioning the agent by name, but knowing he was talking about the one that had shot off his mouth during my briefing and thus maybe was not acceptable for the job, I replied, "Well, I need two drivers, two advance agents, and a personal security officer to ride with the secretary. I'll try to work around this glitch, but I want to tell you that without using two special agents from OSI to drive the cars to and from the airport, I can't do the job without impacting the safety of the secretary."

"I understand," he said.

I thanked SAC Boatwright for his candid comment concerning one of his special agents as he left the office.

My options were to possibly find an additional two agents from the Charleston Naval Investigative Service (NIS) or to have another one sent down from PSU. Regardless of what my decision was, I had little time to fix the problem. It was too late to work the phone because of the meeting I had with the Citadel people. I called Mark at PSU and asked him to see if any other agents could be identified to come to Charleston.

"I'll work on it," he said.

I then reached the SAC at the local NIS office.

"My men have just returned from an extensive training exercise, and most are off a couple of days, and I barely have enough agents to work cases this week, so please don't go to headquarters to request any from my office." The NIS SAC was not nasty about his situation, but firm in his reply.

I told him that I understood where he was coming from; I had been in the same predicament myself. It was up to Mark now. I received a cell phone call from Mark as I was just reaching the main gate of the Citadel.

"Can't do—can't find any agent that is not committed for the next couple of days," Mark said.

I thanked him and told him I would see him the next day.

Once on campus, I met with the Citadel's chief of security, a fiftyish, white-haired, retired US Air Force LTC who wore a Citadel uniform and carried around a Motorola radio everywhere he went. He then took me to the Citadel's provost and dean of the college's office, where the Pentagon public affairs person was present. We discussed the logistics and movement route the secretary was going to make the next day leading up to his commencement speech. Everyone was in sync with the security and protocol of the mission, and the meeting broke up.

As I walked out of the provost's office, I asked the chief of security if he knew of anyone that I could use to drive two cars in our motorcade from the airport to the Citadel and return.

"I think I do! Would you like to have two Charleston police officers for the job?" he asked.

"Wow, that would be great! We need them tomorrow morning," I told him.

"Can do."

That evening, plugging the two Charleston police officers into the motorcade as drivers, I could now field each required position on the security detail.

The next morning, Mark met up with me shortly after he flew into Charleston. We then went to the US Air Force OSI, where I introduced Mark to the two OSI special agents who would be working with me. I scheduled a second briefing on the mission for 1:00 p.m., and Mark and I headed to the chief of security's office at the Citadel. The chief was waiting for us in his office when we got there. I noticed two young men dressed in police uniforms and assumed they were the two that were going to help us. We shook hands, and I was pleasantly pleased with their appearances; both were muscular, good-looking young officers who looked like they could handle themselves in a dangerous situation. I was further pleased to find that both young Charleston police officers were graduates of Citadel, but instead of pursuing careers in the military, they'd chosen law enforcement.

I took about an hour to brief them on their duties the following day, and both were extremely receptive to the assignment. They both agreed to meet at the US Air Force OSI at 1:00 p.m.

Our meeting at the OSI started as scheduled. We shored up final details on the mission, ensured each special agent knew what was accepted of him, and identified the routes and location involved with each movement. Finally, we took two hours to practice running the routes and practice where they were to position themselves at each location the secretary would be. I worked the detail until I felt comfortable they knew every aspect of the mission. I encouraged questions from those that might need clarification. The two Charleston police officers had a couple of good questions that I had answers for, but I did not hear a peep from either of the OSI special agents. I told the detail that Secretary Cheney was due to land at 10:00 a.m. the next day and that we would assemble the team at 8:00 a.m. for any last-minute questions before heading to the airport. Special Agent Laude and I had an early dinner and turned in.

As always, the night before the mission kicks off, there is a certain level of anxiety or nervous feeling in your stomach caused by the lingering thought, *have we done everything we need to?*

At 8:00 a.m. sharp, the team met at the OSI office. We went over everyone's assignments and their duties and responsibilities one last time and then headed for the airport. We arrived at the Charleston airport at 9:30 a.m., a full thirty minutes prior to the scheduled arrival of the secretary. The motorcade was positioned, ready and waiting to pick up Secretary Cheney as he got off the plane. Mark and the two OSI special agents took up their positions at the Citadel. Radio contact established that everyone was where they were supposed to be.

At 9:50 a.m., the secretary's blue-and-white Gulfstream came into view on its approach for landing. It landed and taxied up to the tarmac at precisely 10:00 a.m. as scheduled. We rolled the motorcade up to the plane just as the secretary exited the aircraft. As he entered the car, he said, "Hi, Dick. How are things going?"

"Okay, Mr. Secretary," I replied.

It took us about twenty minutes to drive the eleven miles to the Citadel. We drove up to the building where the secretary was greeted by the Citadel president, the provost, and a few other dignitaries. The commencement speech was on schedule, and there were no disturbances or interruptions. The entire event took approximately one and a half hours, and we got the secretary back to his plane about thirty minutes later. The mission was a success, but it further emphasized the importance of each of the branches of the armed forces getting along and understanding how the others function if they are to continue working Protective Services missions.

It was after this mission that I finally decided to retire from the US Army. I submitted the required documentation and received the approval in about thirty days. It was final; my retirement date was set for March 31, 1993. Until then, I would continue to manage, supervise, and execute security missions.

In June 1992, Special Agent Dennis Burdette and I set up security arrangements for Secretary Cheney's annual trip to Beaver Creek, Colorado, to attend the American Enterprise Institute (AEI) annual event. The area has some of the most beautiful scenery in the United States, and in the wintertime, Vail is one of the most popular skiing resorts in the country.

The Cheneys were scheduled to stay at former president Gerald R. and Betty Ford's residence. The Fords were hosts to Secretary and Mrs. Cheney during their annual trip to Beaver Creek, Colorado. We worked extensively with the Secret Service detail who were assigned to protect the Fords in setting up security for the mission. There were several movements during this mission—to Aspen and Vail and to dinners at a resort in the mountains around Beaver Creek. Special Agent Burdette and I played the role of cowboys when we escorted the Cheneys on a mountain trail horseback ride outside Beaver Creek. The Fords were very cordial to special agents Burdette and me.

The Cheneys were invited by Rupert Murdoch, the media mogul, for a one-day series of meetings on the freedom of expression in the media. There were two areas of concern Dennis and I had on this side trip. One involved the transportation for the Cheneys to get to this event. We had arranged for a helicopter from a unit of the Colorado Air National Guard to transport the Cheneys to the event from Beaver Creek to Aspen. Our coordination with Rupert Murdoch did not alter or change any of our security plans; despite his insistence that he provide the helicopter for the Cheneys ride to the event, we won that battle. We won the argument about who was to furnish transportation, but Murdoch then asked if he could pay for the fuel. I explained to him that the flight was considered training hours for the Air National Guard unit, and the cost was in their budget. That answer must have satisfied him, because he never mentioned it again.

The second issue involved one of Murdoch's production managers for the event attended by the Cheneys, who took it upon himself to present an extreme example of freedom of expression by allowing a male stripper to perform in front of the panel that included the Cheneys. We stopped his performance and escorted him out of the building. During his very brief performance, Mrs. Cheney maintained her poise through the incident by turning her back to him as he did his thing. This mission would go down as one of my most unforgettable trips while in PSU.

In late August 1992, I was assigned to a team that traveled to the Astrodome in Houston, Texas, to help set up security for the secretary and Mrs. Cheney, who were scheduled to speak at the Republican National Convention. After the security team's arrival, we were all identified and provided access authorization tags by the Secret Service to wear around our necks while inside the Astrodome. The Astrodome was a huge place that had several security details with various political, celebrities, and well-positioned private and government officials. It was hard to keep up with them all, but the groups of security rarely had a miscue with each other.

A side note occurred when two highly visible people—Secretary Cheney and Arnold Schwarzenegger—ended up in the same holding area together. I had just escorted Secretary Cheney into a canvased area where he could hold a private conversation without being bothered by the many state delegates aimlessly walking around. Secretary Cheney had just entered the holding area, and I had positioned myself at the entrance. I was looking very much the security agent, with a suit and dark glasses and my hands interlocked in front of me, watching everyone that walked by.

As I stood there for several minutes, Mr. Schwarzenegger and his entourage approached and entered the holding area to join the several other dignitaries inside. As I closed the curtain to the holding area, a young lady who was probably in her early thirties came running up, and I immediately stopped her from entering. She tried to sway me with every trick she could think of to convince me to let her into the holding area, looking seductively with big, beautiful brown eyes and asking me in a very low and sexy voice, "Please let me in so I can get their autographs, especially Arnold's."

"Ma'am, I just cannot let you in; the people inside want privacy," I told her.

When she found out I would not let her in with her current tactic, then her actions turned more aggressive by getting very close to me and angrily raising her voice to tell me I could not violate her rights to see the politicians and movie actors inside the curtain!

Just when I thought I would have to radio for backup, two of Houston's finest came strolling by and heard our conversation.

"Need any help, sir?" asked one of the officers.

"Yes. The lady just does not understand that she is not allowed inside this curtain," I told them.

The two Houston police officers then approached the lady, and each grabbed an arm and briskly escorted her away, hopefully just to get her out of the area and not to arrest her. Despite a few dozen members of La Resistencia (a pro-immigration group) demonstration outside the Astrodome,[166] security for the 1992 Republican National Convention went without major incident.

My last overseas mission included a trip to set up security for Secretary Cheney on a visit to Singapore in the fall of 1992. The two-day visit was scheduled as part of a multi-country trip to create greater cooperation between the United States and its Asian allies. Special Agent Roland Jackson and I had a couple of days to get the mission ready for Secretary Cheney before his arrival. We coordinated with the local leaders on movements and lodging for the party. This mission went off without any incidents, and the secretary seemed pleased with our security efforts.

In December 1992, my last mission while assigned to PSU was to set up security for the secretary and Mrs. Cheney when they flew to Jackson Hole, Wyoming, to look for a new home after he left the job of secretary of defense. Special Agent Dennis Burdette and I flew on a commercial flight from Washington, DC, to Denver and then caught a turboprop to Jackson Hole to work on security for the mission. The weather was clear, but snow was in the forecast. Our job on this mission was to keep a low profile so the secretary and his wife could spend their time looking for their new home.

Dennis and I booked rooms in the old Wort Hotel in Jackson Hole. By the time, we picked up our rental vehicles and drove from the local airport to our hotel to check in, the county sheriff was waiting for us in the lobby. He recognized us as we walked into the hotel. I guess that wasn't hard, since the two of us were the only ones within miles wearing suits and ties. A tall, lanky-looking man in his forties and dressed like a cowboy, the sheriff casually extended his hand to shake ours. He was cordial, unassuming, but confident in his demeanor.

"How you boys doing?" he asked.

"Okay," I said without the enthusiasm of the sheriff.

"I heard you boys were coming to town with Dick Cheney, and I want you to know that if there is anything you need, I'll try to provide it for you," he offered.

I informed the sheriff that we would be in Jackson Hole for three or four days and the secretary and his wife would be here for two of those days.

"Don't worry; I know the Cheneys well and have met them before. They are always welcome here, and that goes for anyone that travels with them, like the two of you," he told us.

I went over with the sheriff what our tentative schedule would be but emphasized that the Cheneys were coming for personal reasons, and the secretary had no formal speeches or meetings with anyone.

"I figured that," the sheriff said.

We wrapped up our impromptu meeting, and tilting his hat, the sheriff left.

Dennis and I checked in and immediately ran recon on the routes based on information the Pentagon had given us. There was one scheduled dinner at a resort on top of a nearby mountain; otherwise, all the time the secretary and his wife had left would be free. We decided to search out the local eating establishments and places where we knew they liked to go when they had free time.

The first night in Jackson Hole was uneventful, but after a long plane trip, both of us were bushed and turned in early.

The next day was spent familiarizing ourselves with the routes to all the known locations the Cheneys would be going. As dark approached, we ran the routes at nighttime to ensure that there would be no surprises. The day was long, but we were satisfied that we had done all we could to be ready for the secretary and his wife, who were scheduled to arrive early the next day. The next morning, Dennis and I both knew the routes inside and out, and we were prepared for any contingencies.

The secretary's plane came in on time, and the pickup was without incident. Dennis and I escorted the Cheneys to their lodging, where they wanted some downtime. That evening, we took them to a mountain resort for dinner with local dignitaries and back to their lodging.

The next day, early in the morning, I escorted the Cheneys on a morning walk, and they ended up in downtown Jackson Hole at a local restaurant. The first thing they wanted was a local paper to read while they were eating breakfast; however, Murphy's law was not far away. Mrs. Cheney put some coins in the newspaper stand that was located directly outside the restaurant, and the door would not open. The Cheneys were short of change, so I produced another quarter for them to insert into the newspaper stand. The additional quarter still did not produce a newspaper. They gave up and decided to eat breakfast without reading.

As is our practice in providing security at restaurants, especially when enjoying private time, our principal and his companion(s) sit alone, and members of the security detail find a table close by to provide unobtrusive surveillance. I got them settled into a nice corner table and selected one for myself. I then immediately got on my cell and called Dennis in his hotel room. I instantly knew I had awakened him from a sound sleep, because he sounded sluggish and drowsy as he mumbled into the phone, "What is it?"

I barked into the phone, "I need two newspapers ASAP!" I told him where to bring them before hanging up. Five minutes later, Dennis walked into the restaurant with two newspapers in hand. Without even a mere acknowledgment to me, he walked straight to the Cheneys' table and handed each a newspaper. As Dennis turned and made his way to my table, I saw grins appearing on the Cheneys' faces. As he sat down, I said, "You did well, my friend."

He stayed with me until the Cheneys moved, and we trailed them back to their hotel room.

At the end of this trip, the Cheneys became familiar with the area and probably decided on a home for the future. At Jackson Hole Airport as the Cheneys were getting onto their plane to return to Washington, they both stopped and, knowing I was getting ready to retire, thanked me for all my efforts and gave me their best.

There were more trips and incidents throughout my tenure at PSU, but too many to detail in this book. All the trips were noteworthy in that I was extremely proud to have been a part of the excellent team of protective security special agents who put their hearts and souls into the job, never thinking about themselves and always maintaining the security environment that allows protectees to have the peace of mind and freedom to concentrate on the defense of our nation. In my opinion, the special agents I worked with were always low-key and unassuming people who kept their protectees from embarrassment and harm and provided them with the safest possible environment.

I recall traveling to many more countries and locations in the States where the secretary had business interests. I either managed, supervised, or conducted security missions to Norway, Denmark, Sweden, Finland, Egypt, and Switzerland. During these missions, I either assisted or directly coordinated with host governments to ensure that the trips were the safest possible. However, regardless of how arduous your work, there is always something, like Murphy's law, that prevents everything from going smoothly.

We had snafus in motorcade alignments and miscues in protocol—and you always had to expect the unexpected. At the end of a mission in Egypt, the secretary's motorcade was enroute to the plane with a portion of the traveling party. Our security team had arranged for the Egyptian government to use their K-9 dogs trained to sniff out explosives to check our baggage before putting in on the plane. We had lined up the passengers' suitcases on the tarmac next to the plane. It was hot and humid, and I was the only security agent at the plane waiting on the arrival of the secretary and others. Some had boarded the plane—the crew, communications specialists, and a few passengers. We were approximately thirty minutes from take-off time and still no K-9s, so I improvised, using a universal key for suitcases to inspect each bag and getting them in the underbelly of the plane just as the secretary's motorcade arrived.

Another incident occurred in Bodø, Norway, when we exited our helicopters and headed for the waiting ten-car motorcade. We had just finished an hour-and-a-half-long helicopter ride from Oslo to visit the Norwegian defense minister's vacation home in Bodø. Each car obviously had a driver, but the problem was that, except for the secretary and Norwegian defense minister, no one knew which car they were assigned to. It took about ten minutes to fix the problem, and off we went.

Another incident occurred when one of our special agents had escorted Secretary Cheney to the Capitol Building to appear in front of a committee. Our driver and I waited outside while the agent and Secretary Cheney went inside. About forty-five minutes later, I saw Secretary Cheney walking from the Capitol Building toward our car without his security agent. By the time, Secretary Cheney arrived at the car, it was obvious that the glitch had occurred inside the building, where the two got separated. I asked Secretary Cheney if he wanted us to get him back to the Pentagon without waiting on the other agent.

Secretary Cheney looked at me, and a wide smile broke out on his face. He told me, "No. We can wait on him."

I radioed the missing agent, who responded by saying, "The meeting in the house has adjourned, and I am waiting for the secretary to come out."

I informed the agent that the secretary was already at the car and we were all waiting for him.

While we were waiting for the agent, Secretary Cheney talked to people who were walking on the grounds. He took everything in stride; he was calm and showed no signs of anger or frustration.

There was yet another incident that occurred while in a car leaving the underground garage of the Pentagon carrying General Powell and the secretary to a meeting with President Bush at the White House. The car had stopped suddenly at an automatic barrier that the Pentagon guard was slow in lowering. Our chase car, being close behind as required, tapped the bumper of the secretary's car. General Powell looked over at Secretary Cheney and said, "Why do we do this to ourselves?"

The secretary responded, "It's tradition."[167]Despite these embarrassing episodes, the agents at PSU are overwhelmingly thorough in adhering to the highly skilled standards of protection details and employ the best techniques possible in ensuring the safety of their principals.

In January 1993, Secretary Cheney came by the PSU to bid farewell and to say thanks to the special agents of PSU. Some of the special agents' wives attended the function. The visit was made more special knowing that the secretary had taken the time out of his busy schedule to make the effort to show his appreciation in person.

By being a part of the PSU, it allowed me to see how our government works from all sides of the spectrum. I saw the highest ranks in our military working in their environment. One thing I now realize is that regardless of your rank, whether it is secretary of defense, chairman of the Joint Chiefs, a commander of corps, divisions, brigades, battalions, companies, platoons, or squads, they all have one thing in common: leaders want to do the job right. When you are at the bottom, it may get a little cloudy looking up, and when you are on top, it is not always clear, but decisions are made in the best interest of our mission.

PSU was my second-longest assignment in the US Army at three years, seven months, and ten days. I considered the assignment as a change from the nerve-racking job of criminal investigations. The assignment provided me with exactly what I was looking for at the time: a change of pace. When it came down to the final inning, I was at bat with two strikes, there was one runner aboard, and they pitched me a curveball. The US Army did not make it easy for me to leave.

It was early on a Friday morning when CID assignment officer Special Agent Edward Boyer came to see me at my office in the PSU headquarters on Fort Belvoir. Since I wasn't expecting him, I was surprised to see him, but I put aside my work and invited him to have a seat.

"What brings you to see me today, Ed?" I asked.

"I want to run something by you, if you don't mind," he said.

"Okay, what is it?"

He then very calmly opened his portfolio and took out a document and ripped it into several pieces in front of me. "This is what we think about your retirement, Dick!" He then placed the torn strips of paper on my desk.

I looked down and examined the paper to find it was a copy of my retirement orders. "What are you trying to tell me, Ed?"

"We don't want you to retire and would like you to take over the Panama CID office!"

I stared at him for a few seconds and asked him to repeat what he had just told me.

"We don't want you to retire and would like you to take over the Panama CID office! What do you say?" he added.

"Well, I don't know what to say. When do you need an answer?"

"Better soon than later," he said.

"I am very grateful for the offer, but I cannot give you an answer before I discuss it with my wife."

"We want you to give the offer serious consideration and assure you the job is waiting for you if you decide to take it."

"Fair enough. I will call you Monday morning."

That weekend, Elda and I discussed the pros and cons of taking the job in Panama. We went over all the possibilities of how it would impact our eventual mutual retirements. It obviously would be rewarding for me to oversee another CID office, but I kept thinking, especially one that located in a country that had recently been in the middle of an invasion by the United States to take out its leader. The repercussions such a decision would have on Elda's plan to retire from the Fairfax County Public Schools was another issue. By Sunday, we had made up our minds: I would follow through with my impending retirement from the US Army and allow Elda to continue her work with Fairfax. We thought that, under the circumstances, the decision was best for us at the time.

First thing Monday morning, I called Ed at his office in the Hoffman Building and told him of our decision. I expressed my sincere gratitude for considering me for the position, and we hung up. That was it: I would leave the US Army within a few days and see what my options were on the "outside."

Although I felt that my US Army career was a success, there were several decisions that shaped it that I should not have made. I should have accepted assignments to larger installations instead of smaller ones. I should have taken Chief Whitrock's offer to serve as a staff officer in Stuttgart. Although I found my assignment to PSU very rewarding and interesting, after Stuttgart, I may have been better off asking for an operations officer's job somewhere in the States. In retrospect, I would have dealt with personnel complaints, problems, and personal situations a lot differently.

Author sitting in middle of front row, holding class sign of the graduating personal protection course conducted at Fort McClellan, Alabama, October 1989. Some of the special agents who attended the course were David Thomas, D. Patrick, Wayne Runion, and Richard Deguise. Others attending are military police investigators.

Trip to Russia for meetings with Russian leaders and inspection of training bases south of Moscow. Notice author behind and to the left of Secretary Cheney, circa 1990. Photograph courtesy of the Pentagon.

Special Agents Wayne Nardolillo, Kathy Klug, and yours truly standing outside a
meeting with Secretary Dick Cheney at the Russian Ministry of Defense in Moscow,
circa 1990. Photograph courtesy of the Pentagon.

The author escorting Secretary of Defense Cheney and the Egyptian defense minister to a meeting in Cairo, Egypt, circa early 1990s. Photograph courtesy of the Pentagon.

Author with Secretary Cheney in Czechoslovakia for meetings with their leaders. Note: Author is directly behind US ambassor to Czechoslovakia Shirley Temple, the former child movie star, circa early 1990s. Photograph courtesy of the Pentagon.

Christmas get-together for his CID security protection detail hosted by Secretary of Defense Dick Cheney at the Pentagon, 1990. Front row: In-town driver Bill Brown; Special Agents Tom J. Colson, Clarence L. Jorif, and Michael Dixon; Secretary Cheney; OSD team chief Special Agent Dick Miller; and Robert "Tim" Steenbergen. Second row: Special Agent Mary A. Wolfe, Operations Officer Wayne T. Nardolillo. Special Agents Paul Perez and Eugene Hicks' faces are hidden. Photograph courtesy of the Pentagon.

Secretary Cheney talking to me right before promoting me to CW4 in his office. Photogrtaph courtesy of the Pentagon, January 31, 1992.

CID staff attending my CW4 promotion ceremony at the Pentagon: From left To right: Special Agent Alan Welch, Operations Officer Wayne T. Nardolillo, Special Agent James A. Vandoli, LTC Isom from CID command, Special Agent Kathy Klug, Special Assistant to Secretary for Security Thomas Higgins, and Special Agent James H. Hatcher.

Author escorting the secretary to the USS Arizona Memorial at Pearl Harbor in Hawaii for the fiftieth anniversary in 1991. President Bush also spoke at the annual function. Photograph provided by me from personal collection received from the Pentagon.

An Israeli crew chief and the Author flying high over Tel Aviv on a protection detail for Secretary Cheney in a portion of a Middle Eastern trip that included not only Israel but also Egypt, the Gaza Strip, and Lebanon, circa early 1990s.

I have the secretary's airplane all to myself, so to speak. Only four or five passengers were flown from Punta Arenas to Santiago to get ready for visits with Chilean leaders. From my personal collection of Pentagon photographs, given to me by Pentagon photographers during my tour with PSU.

Secretary Cheney pinning on my CW4 bars,
January 1992.

I am in the middle. looking up at the
Welcome Home parade for troops
who served in Dessert Storm, June
10, 1991, in New York City. Note:
provding security protection for
Secretary Cheney druing the parade.
An estimated four million people
attended the ceremonies—one of
America greatest moments and one
of the largest parades ever. Photograph among my personal collection
from my tour at the Pentagon.

Getting ready to board the secretary's plane. Note
Secretary Cheney and Dr. Lynne Cheney saying
farewell to the Norwegian ambassador with the
author in the background ensuring everyone is on
the plane while keeping an eye on the secretary.
Photograph from personal collection provided by
Pentagon photographers while on assignment with
the secretary, circa 1991.

In Punta Arenas, Chile, escorting Dr. Lynne
Cheney to a function high in the mountains,
circa 1990s. Photographs from personal
collection while working for the secretary
protection detail.

The author introducing his sister June to Secretary Cheney at my promotion ceremony, January 31, 1992.

Secretary Cheney came to the PSU at Fort
Belvoir, Virginia, to bid farewell to his
CID proection detail. From left to right:
Yours truly, Secretary Cheney, Special
Agent James A. Vandoli, and Operations
Officer Wayne T. Nardolillo,
circa January 1993.

# Epilogue

*W*ayne Nardolillo and Major Robert Jones, who replaced Major Alvarez as the commander of the Protective Services Unit (now Battalion), sent me off in royal fashion at a well-organized retirement event. Most special agents who were not traveling were in attendance with their wives. I said good-bye to all the good folks by telling them that my career had been good and I'd enjoyed every aspect of it. After thanking Major Jones and Wayne for their counsel and leadership, I advised the special agents to pursue their goals and aspirations, but along the way, they should never ignore the individuality of the people that work for them. I left them with a thought that being a leader requires one to be honest, inspiring, empathic, and to always be conscious of their own character. Also, people should not do anything that taints or destroys their creditability, for if they do, they lose their effectiveness as leaders.

As a special agent in the US Army CID for almost twenty years, I experienced many directional changes in the command mission, structure, and vision. Our basic mission of catching the bad guys remained intact, but new techniques, better equipment, and advances in forensic science have led to improved methods in the way we go about that job. The CID has taken steps toward bringing the CID back into the US Army. When I joined the CID command, it was structured like the FBI. We had branch offices, resident agencies, field offices, and district offices, but shortly after I retired, those organizational identities were changed to US Army unit names. Most of the CID units are now designated by unit numbers. For instance, Sixth Region became known as the Sixth Group, and Third Region is now Third Group. Districts were changed to battalions, and the Protective Services Unit had several changes but is currently called the Protective Services Battalion and is considered the largest battalion in the CID command [sic].

The US Army CID has also gotten smaller in terms of offices and personnel. Because of smaller budgets and mission responsibilities, several of the offices I served with are now deactivated. The FAMC branch office, Fort Sheridan field office, and Schweinfurt and Stuttgart resident agencies are now closed. Fort Riley District has been changed to the Seventy-Eighth Military Police Detachment (CID). A few years ago, the CID was deactivated as a major command and reactivated as a direct reporting agency (DRA) to the US Army chief of staff.

I am surprised that no one has ever asked if the US Army won the war on illegal drugs in the 1980s. In my opinion, that answer is not so simple. Today, maybe, just maybe, the soldiers of the US Army are healthier, leaner, more physically fit, and are focused on careers instead of getting high, but neither the US Army CID nor MPs had much to do with this development. Sure, in 1970s and 1980s we may have temporarily hindered the drug users and dealers with our efforts. However, it is my opinion that the reason for positive change in the US Army concerning the use of illegal drugs has been based on internal attitudes and cultural changes over the years. Most people who enter our armed forces today want to make it a career, and the use of illegal drugs is not compatible with this goal. Are there exceptions? Yes, but the wide consensus of the population of the US Army has changed for the better in the last thirty years. I like to think that in a small way, I had something to do with this the positive changes.

What I learned in a long and industrious investigative career is that you must be detailed in every aspect of a case. You cannot go forward without knowing all the facts and options on how to get there. This trait includes pursuits in your personal life as well as professional career. It has been over forty years since I first entered the US Army. I would never have imagined that I would have a college degree and a great career as a special agent in one of the best law enforcement organizations in the nation, the US Army CID. It was not always easygoing, but with persistence, determination, and consistency, I molded a professional life that bridged into personal achievements and accomplishments as well. The things I learned professionally led to a second career as a security investigator, analyst, and consultant. The résumé that I built allowed me to work for several US federal intelligence and law enforcement agencies. Then the world changed!

On September 11, 2001, terrorists attacked the United States by slamming two hijacked commercial jets into the World Trade Center and one into the Pentagon, killing nearly three thousand innocent people. That same day, a fourth hijacked commercial jet, headed for another target believed to be either the White House or the Capitol, crashed in the countryside near Shanksville, Pennsylvania, killing another forty-two-innocent people. It is widely speculated that several passengers on the flight that crashed in Shanksville played a role in preventing that plane from reaching its intended target.

Immediately, this horrible crime completely altered Americans' way of life as we knew it. Politicians are consumed with it; everyday citizens are affected by it. Everything that occurs on a public transportation bus, train, or airport terminal involves it. The terrorist attacks, historically known as 9/11, have also created new US federal agencies and departments—most notable are the Department of Homeland Security, US Immigration and Customs Enforcement, and the Transportation Security Agency (TSA). Other, older US government agencies and departments were consolidated into the Department of Homeland Security. It seemed that everything generated by the US government since 9/11 has been classified. To staff the massive new departments and agencies and to handle the increase in classified information, thousands of US government jobs have been created.

For several years after 9/11, the US government contracted with major corporations like Lockheed Martin, CACI, Science Application International Corporation (SAIC), Booz Allen Hamilton (BAH), DynCorp, and countless other companies, small and large, as well as individual consultants, to staff the many employment opportunities created. With the increase in jobs, the US government determined that the people filling these positions needed a full security background investigation before allowing them to come to work. To conduct the millions of security background investigations for these positions, an influx of former special agents with federal law enforcement and intelligence agencies and Department of Defense (DOD) military investigative agencies were sought for their expertise in investigations. There was an unlimited supply of talent, and the budgets of US agencies were bulging with money to hire these individuals.

At the time of 9/11, I had developed a good reputation as a security investigator for several US government law enforcement and intelligence agencies. Then I was recruited by a major private corporation that brought me inside to manage the security background investigations it was contracted to conduct by the US government. This initial integration into the corporate security field led to additional responsibilities in management and leadership positions with private and later with a well-known US government federal law enforcement and intelligence agency. During the time, I worked as a security manager, I had an eye-opening experience in how the US government vetted a person's background and witnessed the overall quality of these investigations diminish over the years. The cost to the US government to process, investigate, and monitor the people receiving security clearances ranged into the millions. Quality assurance programs identified only a fraction of those background investigations that were deficient, and the deficiencies continue.

Then, in 2005, I was hired by a US government law enforcement and intelligence agency as an investigative analyst to work on security matters. I completed my tenure with that agency in 2011. My last security project was spent writing a training manual for the organization's security section. The manual brought together the many aspects needed to conduct security background investigations into one book that previously were found in multiple sources. It made the job of vetting the individuals needing top-level security clearances easier, and the processing time was reduced tremendously.

In 2011, I fully retired from US government work. In the five years since my retirement, I hope that the system has been improved. I am now enjoying retirement at its fullest in Florida with Elda, my wife of over thirty-five years, who continues to be my best friend and companion. We visit Indiana once a year to see Chris and his family and attend the family reunions.

Chris obtained a degree from Indiana State University, my alma mater, and works for the Indiana State Department of Health. He and his wife, Nichole, have two beautiful daughters, Sydny Marie and Lauryn Raye, who are active in school programs and extracurricular activities. Life could not be better for them.

Robert, Melitta's son from her first marriage, graduated from Purdue University in West Layette, Indiana, with a degree in aeronautical engineering and works for a major US government contractor in Sunnyvale, California.

I now spend my time reading the many books I have accumulated over the years and traveling with Elda. You can say I have come a long way from the small southwestern town of Bicknell, Indiana. I have been associated with additional security and analytical positions in my post–US Army CID career, and there has been a lot that would be interesting to the public, but then again, it is too much information for this book and possibly will be contained in a future book.

# My Personal List of CID Heroes

*M*y list of CID heroes is not based on individual heroic actions or achievement but on the positive influence they had on my career. The individuals are not ranked but are listed to relate where they were assigned when they had the greatest impacted on my career.

1.  MG David H. Stem, Second Region commander and commandant of the United States MP Corps, was a leader that inspired, motivated, and challenged me to achieve the most from my career. If it were not for his untimely death in an airplane crash over Fort Leavenworth, Kansas, he could have become commander of the CID command.

2.  LTC Henry S. Matlosz, executive officer, Fort Knox, Kentucky, acting commander, Fort Sheridan, Illinois and operations officer, Second Region, instilled and reinforced confidence in me to perform as a CID special agent.

3.  CW5 John K. Boatwright, my first SAC, allowed me flexibility in performance and was extremely tolerant of my investigative methods, that got results.

4.  CW3 Ronald Gann, special agent, Fort Sheridan, taught me how to use attention to detail in everything I did in CID.

5.  Matthew E. Moriarty, an operations officer who never lost sight of my abilities to work undercover narcotics and a stanch supporter of my investigative programs.

6.  Colonel Markalee D. Brannen, who was my district commander at Würzburg and Stuttgart, always supported me and showed his appreciation for my investigative work.

7.  CW3 Donald M. Shanley, acting operations officer and team chief, Fort Riley, was a very knowledgeable leader, problem solver, and mentor.

8.  SP4 Gary Kral, special agent, Fort Sheridan, was probably the most energetic CID special agent I knew who enjoyed the work but failed

to understand CID leadership and chose to leave the US Army CID and pursue a civilian career.

9.  CW3 Robert T. Steenbergen, Protective Services Unit, SAC, Fort Huachuca, Arizona, and staff officer, Sixth Group, Fort Lewis, Washington, was my best all-around partner.

10. Jose Chavez, special agent, Fort Riley, Kansas, was the least pretentious all-around special agent that I worked with.

11. CW4 Thomas J. Whitrock, operations officer, Stuttgart District, was the best senior investigative manager who was an exceptional organizational planner and leader that taught me good management principles.

# Miller's Rules

Rule One: Focus and timeliness are the best components to success on a job.

Rule Two: Trust is the most valuable component when dealing with people.

Rule Three: You must find ways to accomplish even the most challenging tasks.

Rule Four: When venturing into the unknown, ensure everyone required is briefed.

Rule Five: If you are in a new job where your duties and responsibilities are not clearly defined, you should expeditiously concentrate on identifying the goals, objectives, and needs of your personnel; then set forth procedures to organize steps to achieve those goals and objectives and help your personnel.

Rule Six: Do not rush into investigations with a mind-set that what was reported is always factual.

Rule Seven: Report facts, not what someone reports as facts.

Rule Eight: When doing something for the first time, ensure all steps are taken before executing action.

Rule Nine: Don't place absolute trust in anyone or anything without ensuring absolute trust in return.

Rule Ten: Stand firm and be resolute in your principles.

# Notes

Chapter 1

1. FCMHSA Source: http://arlweb.msha.gov/MSHAINFO/MSHAINF2.HTM
2. History of Bicknell, Indiana; source: http://www.bicknell.in.gov/our-history/.
3. Source: 2010 Census Bureau.
4. Dizzy Dean Statistics; source: www.baseball-reference.com.
5. Interview with Hubert McAtee.
6. Chris Bishop, ed., *Vietnam War Diary* (New York: Chartwell, 2003), p.12.
7. Harry G. Summers, *Historical Atlas of the Vietnam War* (New York: Swanston, 1995), p. 94–98.

Chapter 2: The Awakening Years

8. Source: www.yourmilitary.com.
9. Bishop, *Vietnam War Diary*, p. 22–30.
10. Source: www.bragg.army.mil.
11. US occupation of the Dominican Republic; source: www.Wikipedia.org.
12. In the 1960s, the morning reports were prepared on DA Form 1 by typewriter and tracked the daily personnel status and whereabouts of every soldier in the unit, whether they were on leave, hospitalized, AWOL, TDY, or at a service school. The US Army stopped using DA Form 1 in 1974, when they initiated the use of mark-sense cards to transfer data to computers.
13. Source: www.secondrangerinfantrycompany.com.

Chapter 3: Years of Responsible Decision Making

14. In February 1965, thousands of US military personnel and tons of supplies and materials were arriving daily at the port of Qui Nhon during the huge buildup. The beach and adjacent land area were experiencing constant infrastructure growth of facilities, buildings, and roadways on a level unimaginable.
15. US Army Transportation Museum; source: www.transchool.lee.army.army.
16. The Republic of Korea (ROK) Tiger Division protected the area around Qui Nhon.
17. Back in the 1960s, the US Army had no formalized counseling programs to tackle the issue of suicidal tendencies.
18. Source: www.webmd.com.

19. History on the Quy Hoa Leprosarium was obtained from their website. On June 25, 1976, the

Franciscans handed over the Quy Hoa Hospital to the Vietnamese Ministry of Health. Source: www.guyhoandh.org.

20. Source: www.illyria.com/evacs.

21. Information was paraphrased from the history of the Da Nang airport at this website:

www.danangonline.com.

22. A wall made of plywood was used to divide the tent into two rooms: one for work, which was further divided into two small rooms, and the other for sleeping.

23. The 344th Transportation Company was subordinate to the Tenth Battalion at Cam Ranh Bay.

24. Occasionally, LARCs were fitted with .50-caliber machine guns and used to patrol the waterways in and around Cam Ranh Bay, Vung Ro Bay, Nha Trang, and Vung Tau. The mission gradually transformed from hauling supplies from ships to gunboats patrolling the bays and many waterways in those areas. In October 1967, the 344th Transportation Company was deactivated, and a lot of the members were transferred to the 458th Transportation Company; the unit was designated as the only US Army Patrol Boat River Unit (PBR) in Vietnam.

25. DeLong piers were the title of deep-water ports that could hold large cargo and passenger ships. Once the DeLong piers were developed, there was no further use for the LARC-Vs. The DeLong floating pier expedited port construction. Patented by the DeLong Corporation, the piers were sectional and were fabricated outside of the theater in a variety of sizes and configurations. They were then towed to a site and quickly emplaced. The DeLong piers made it possible to develop additional deep-draft ports and berths at Qui Nhon, Vung Tau, Cam Ranh Bay, Vung Ro Bay, and Da Nang in record time. The first DeLong pier was towed to Cam Ranh Bay from the eastern United States in a trip that took two months. The 497th Port Construction Company installed it. The pier was essentially a ninety- by three-hundred-foot barge supported by eighteen tubular steel caissons six feet in diameter and fifty feet long, driven into the harbor bottom. The first DeLong pier, completed in mid-December 1965, doubled the capacity of the Cam Ranh Bay port. Work started on a third pier in 1966 that was ninety feet wide by six hundred feet long. Source: www.transchool.lee.army.mil.

26. [i]Information about Penang, Malaysia, obtained from this website: www.Wikipedia.org.

27. [ii]Marvin Wilson is a pseudonym.

28. On February 16, 1965, Vung Ro Bay was an area where a North Vietnamese naval trawler was observed by a US Army helicopter pilot loading supplies. The trawler was attacked by the Vietnamese navy, and soon afterward, the US Army

moved transportation units into Vung Ro Bay and made it a port area for supply ships that lasted throughout the rest of the war, from late 1965 to 1970. Source: www.worldhistoryproject.org.

29. The ROK White Horse Division protected the area around Vung Ro Bay.

30. SSG Michaels, Sergeant Allen, Wilson, Fisher, and Collins are pseudonyms.

31. Allied troop levels 1960–73; source: www.americanwarlibrary.com.

32. James F. Dunnigan and Albert A. Nofi, *Dirty Little Secrets of the Vietnam War* (New York: Thomas Dunne

Books, 1999), p. 244.

33. Ibid., p. 136.


Chapter 4: The Learning Years


34. I recalled that the name given to me of the MP who killed a fellow MP at Fort Gordon was Billy Jean King (not the tennis player), and the information that King hacked up the other MP's body and ate some of his parts was not substantiated beyond talk with active-duty MPs who told me the story. In writing this book, I have attempted to independently confirm this information, but I have not been able to do so. At the time, I was at Fort Leavenworth, King was pending transfer to the federal prison system to finish out his life sentence, because he was incarcerated without the possibility of parole.

35. Information on the history of Madison, Wisconsin was found at www.wikipedia.org

36. 1970 census bureau statistic.


Chapter 5: Focusing on a Career


37. Ruth Berta, Donna Paterson and Carl Matthews are pseudonyms.

38. David Crawford is a pseudonym.

39. Otis Johnson is a pseudonym.

40. Information on the history of Fort Gordon; source: www.wikipedia.org.

41. Information about PFC Brems was obtained from this source: www.hon-oredmps.org/brems-patrick.

42. The US Army spells *marijuana* with an *h* (*marihuana*) instead of *j*, which is the more common spelling.

43. An Article 32 hearing like a grand jury that is held to determine if there is enough evidence to proceed with a trial.

44. My CID application was submitted in June 1973.

Chapter 6: Career Path Interrupted

45. Ray Kangas became the first CW5 in the CID.

46. CID basic investigations training has improved and been greatly enhanced in the forty years since I attended the course. The greatest innovations have been in forensic science. A former deputy director of the security division of the FBI confided with me one time that CID training was on a level with FBI.

47. Cabrini-Green housing project was constructed 1942–1962 and was demolished 1995–2011. The housing project was bordered by the apex of Clybourn Avenue and Halsted Street (north), North Larrabee Street (east), Chicago Avenue (south), Halsted Street (west). It contained 586 apartments that housed an estimated fifteen thousand. Source: www.wWikipedia.org.

48. Some of the wording used in this paragraph was extracted from CID Regulation 195-5, dated August 19, 1977.

49. Ralph P. Swanson is a pseudonym.

50. The seven-plus million and an additional almost two million in northern Indiana were 1974 figures.

51. The addresses 302 and 304 South Yates Street were fictitious, used for the convenience of the story and reader.

52. Steven Blackburn is a pseudonym

53. Jane Henning is a pseudonym.

54. Source of information on Yongsan was obtained from the World Cultural Heritage *Kyosu Sinmun* (*Professors' Newspaper*), September 10, 2013, and from personal knowledge of the garrison from being assigned there in 1977/78.

Chapter 7: Career Back on Track

55. "Often twitching of fingers and movements of the foot are noted in small joints after death. These movements, sometimes referred to as postmortem spasms, occasionally cause distress in the grieving Family leading to allegations of premature burial or wrongful certification of death. ATP is required to reuptake calcium into the sarcomere's sarcoplasmic reticulum (SR). When a muscle is relaxed, the myosin heads are returned to their 'high energy' position, ready and waiting for a binding site on the actin filament to become available. Because there are no ATP available, previously released calcium ions cannot return to the SR. These leftover calcium ions move around inside the sarcomere and may eventually find their way to a binding site on the thin filament's regulatory protein. Since the myosin head is already ready to bind, no additional ATP expenditure is required and the sarcomere contracts. When this process occurs on a larger scale,

the disturbing twitches of post-mortem spasms, leading to gruesome postures associated with rigor mortis can occur. These movements have been repeatedly described in medical history; ranging from mild movements in small joints to grimacing, occasional jerks, tears in eyes etc. However, respiration-like movements that represent coordinated simultaneous contractions of different muscle groups are UNLIKELY. Therefore, the absence of breathing is an indicator of post-mortem spasm instead of misdiagnosed death. Just an odd occurrence, but is perfectly normal and explainable by science and medicine." Source: http://emergencywebnotes.blogspot.com/2008/12/post-mortem-spasms.html.

56. At the time, I was in Korea, the drug teams were known as Joint Drug Suppression Teams (JDST). They were considered joint teams, because they were operated with a combination of CID special agents and MPs attached to augment the teams, thus suggesting a joint team concept. In later years, the word *joint* was removed from the drug team's designation, because the CID/MP combination did not qualify as a joint operation under the written polices of the US Army's definition of a joint operation. The word *joint* can only be used when, as an example, a joint task of multiple branches or law enforcement agencies is assembled to run a certain operation. Nowadays, the US Army has many joint operations in war, and CID special agents are also members of FBI Joint Terrorism Task Forces (JTTF).

57. Daniel Apaqya is a pseudonym.

58. James Andrews is a pseudonym.

59. Keith D. Wilson, *Cause of Death* (Cincinnati, OH: Writer's Digest Books, 1992), p.116-117.

60. Samuel Jennings is a pseudonym.

Chapter 8: Career Going Forward

61. Source of information on MG Bennett C. Riley came from www.wikipedia.org.

62. In the late 1970s, CID still had the policy to mail agents' service weapons to their next duty stations. This changed in the early to mid-1980s, when the agent took responsibility either carry his or her weapon to the next assignment or mail it.

63. Information on ROTC program was obtained from www.todaysmilitary.com.

64. Ronald Murphy is a pseudonym.

65. Contingency funds of the secretary of the army are made available to the commanding general (CG) of the US Army Criminal Investigation Command (USACIDC) for emergency and unusual expenditures incurred during investigations

and crime prevention. Source: Army Regulation 195-4, paragraph 1-1, p. 1-1, published April 15, 1983.

66. *The Posse Comitatus Act and Related Matters: The Use of the Military to Execute Civilian Law, Congressional Research Service (CRS) Report for Congress*, August 16, 2012; source: www.crs.gov.

67. In the 1970s, Camp Forsyth had a lot of abandoned World War II–era buildings where I could conduct almost undetected surveillance. This is the reason I had chosen the site for the heroin transfer.

68. David Henderson is a pseudonym.

69. Randy E. Olsen and Daniel L. Bo'nes are pseudonyms.

70. William Smith is the assumed name of the Fort Riley assistant provost marshal who contacted me on that day in 1980. It is known that his last name was Smith, but his first name of William is uncertain. Incidentally, Smith took over as the Fort Riley CID commander sometime after I departed for Germany in August 1980.

71. Bridle is part of the tack, or harness, of a horse, consisting usually of a headstall, bit, and reins; source: www.dictionary.com.

72. Carol Henderson is a pseudonym.

73. PV2 James Wilmore is a pseudonym.


Chapter 9: Pivotal Career Assignment


74. US Army Garrison Schweinfurt and the Third Reich in Ruins contain a general history of Ledward and Conn Barracks; sources: www.en.wikipedia.org and www.thirdreichruins.com.

75. History of Daley Barracks; sources: www.eaglehorse.org and www.skylighters.org.

76. Jonathan L. Trumwell is a pseudonym

77. Stephen M. Williamson is a pseudonym.

78. PFC George L. McNeal is a pseudonym.

79. John Albert is a pseudonym.

80. Petra Adler is a pseudonym.

81. Johnny Parker is a pseudonym.

82. Information on the Sergeant Seeloff murder investigation was obtained from various references; sources: www.kbfdradio.tripod.com/murder and *Stars and Stripes*, October 15, 1980.

27 March 3, 1981, records of the Federal Bureau of Prisons, and from personal involvement and memory of the investigation.

83. Reagan's Assassination Attempt source: www.history1900s.about.com/od/1980s/qt/Reagan-Assassination.

84. Personal Interview with LTC Barry McCaffrey

85. Information about the apprehension numbers and Schweinfurt DST drug operation source: Personal archives, notes and memory.

86. Walter Kohler is a pseudonym.

87. Jason McGuire is a pseudonym.

88. Body observation techniques; source: Dr. Murlene E. McKinnon, "A Guide to Nonverbal Deception Indicators," *Law and Order* 30, no. 1 (January 1982): p. 53–54.

89. Information on the kidnapping of BG James L. Dozier was obtained from personal memory and from source European *Stars and Stripes*, December 19, 1981, p. 1, 27.

90. "Librarian of the Internet," Finding Dulcinea; source: www.findingdulcinea.com/dozier.

91. Lawrence Carter is a pseudonym.

92. LSD (lysergic acid diethylamide); source: *Narcotics Investigator's Manual*, United States Dement of Justice, Drug Enforcement Administration, Bureau of Operations and Research Internal Association of Chiefs of Police (publication date unknown).

93. Information on the City of Basel, Switzerland, was obtained from the city's website; source: www.myswitzerland.com.

94. Aldo Brauer is a pseudonym.

95. Thomas J. MacGreaver is a pseudonym.

96. Graham Piketon is a pseudonym.

Chapter 10: From Team Lead to Senior Investigative Manager

97. This information was obtained from the *Freer Press*, Wednesday, June 26, 2002, an article titled, "Guajardo Served in Germany: Veteran Recalls Years in Military Service," front page and 3A; personal interview with Abel Guajardo.

98. Frank Williams is a pseudonym.

99. George Collins is a pseudonym.

100. Ronald J. Cloud and Gerald L. Larsen are pseudonyms.

101. Captain Josh Madison is a pseudonym.

102. LTC John Palmer is a pseudonym.

103. SFC Randy Hunter is a pseudonym.

104. Information for the Beirut Bombing—*American Experience: Reagan* from source: www.pbs.org.

105. Information for the invasion of Grenada—*American Experience: Reagan* from source: www.pbs.org.

106. Roberta Payne is a pseudonym.

107. Jeffrey Payne is a pseudonym.

108. SFC Sanders and Barbara Sanders are pseudonyms.

## Chapter 11: Taking a Break from the Hassle

109. The history of Fitzsimons US Army Hospital; source: www.wikipedia.org.

110. Major Michael Pierce is a pseudonym.

111. Ajax Janitorial Services of Denver is a pseudonym.

112. Frederick L. Swan is a pseudonym.

113. Ed Blakely is a pseudonym.

114. Doctor Ralph Lynn is a pseudonym.

115. Sally Wallace is a pseudonym.

116. Samuel Wallace is a pseudonym.

117. Mary Bryant is a pseudonym.

118. Kral Bryant is a pseudonym.

119. James Goodwin is a pseudonym.

120. Linda Crawford is a pseudonym.

121. James L. Malloy is a pseudonym.

122. Information on the Newfoundland crash was taken from this source: Terrence J. Gough, "Tragedy at Gander," *Department of the Army Historical Summary Fiscal Year 1986* (Washington, DC: United States Army Center of Military History, 1995), p. 101.

123. Information obtained from source www.honoredmps.org.

124. Richard D. Franklin is a pseudonym.

125. Information about the space shuttle *Challenger* disaster; source: www.space.com.

126. Exact wording on offenses under Article 108 were obtained from *The Manual for Courts-Martial, United States* (1984).

127. Patricia Franklin is a pseudonym.

128. Edward Christenson is a pseudonym.

129. George Snider is a pseudonym.

130. Information about Chernobyl and the aftereffects was partially derived from an article in *Live Science* and from a conversation with my wife about her coworker's husband.

131. The US Army CID headquarters moved to its current location in 2005 to the new MILDEP campus at Quantico as part of the base realignment and closure (BRAC) action as well as in an initiative to improve collaboration: Naval Criminal Investigative Service (NCIS)—743 personnel; Air Force Office of Special Investigations (OSI)—506 personnel; Defense Intelligence Agency/ Counterintelligence (DIA/HUMINT) and its Counterintelligence Field Activity CIFA) group—745 personnel; US Army Criminal Investigation Command

(CID)—291 personnel; Defense Security Service (DSS) and its DSS academy—774 personnel.

132. Libya bombings of 1986; source: www.britannica.com.

133. Sue Snider is a pseudonym.

134. Detective Sergeant Ruth Blackman is a pseudonym.

135. Connie Snider is a pseudonym.

136. Sally Ramsey is a pseudonym.

137. Frederick Ramsey is a pseudonym.

138. Ronald Daily is a pseudonym.

139. Stuttgart background provided by source www.gettingaround.net/usareur-stuttgart.

Chapter 12: Changes of the Horizon

140. "A status of forces agreement (SOFA) is an agreement between a host country and a foreign nation stationing military forces in that country. SOFAs are often included, along with other types of military agreements, as part of a comprehensive security arrangement. A SOFA does not constitute a security arrangement; it establishes the rights and privileges of foreign personnel present in a host country in support of the larger security arrangement"; source: "Status of forces agreement," https://en.wikipedia.org.

141. Jake and Lorain Collings are pseudonyms.

142. Joan Hagan Arnold and Penelope Buschman Gemma, *A Child Dies: A Portrait of Family Grief* (Philadelphia: Charles Press, 1994), pp. iv, 9, 39.

143. Department of Health and Human Services, Heath Resources and Services Administration, National SIDS / Death Resource Center (NSIDRC), *The Death of a Child: The Grief of the Parents: A Lifetime Journey* (2005).

144. Tyrone and Simone Compton are pseudonyms.

145. Information concerning BG David H. Stem's death was obtained from this source: www.honoredmps.org.

146. SSG Ronald Johnson is a pseudonym.

147. Paul Scott is a pseudonym.

148. Details of the Sergeant Newsome murder case are based on personal memory and *Stars and Stripes*, Friday, November 13, 1987, p. 28.

149. Details of the LaSelle investigation were derived from personal memory and *Stars and Stripes*, Wednesday, March 23, 1988, p. 28.

150. Details of the Kevin D. Thomas investigation were derived partially from memory and *Stars and Stripes*, Saturday, May 14, 1988, p. 2.

151. Adada came to the Stuttgart CID via an aviation unit because his MOS was being eliminated. I interviewed, accepted, and assigned him to the Stuttgart CID

DST. He caught on to investigative work quickly, was a hard worker, and eventually became a CID special agent and was assigned to Fort Benning. He went to the Gulf War and due to his Farsi and Arabic language skills was used as both an investigator and interpreter. He left the service and became a special agent with the US Customs Office.

152. Details concerning the PV2 Thurmond investigation were derived partially from memory and *Stars and Stripes*, Tuesday, August 2, 1988, p. 2.

Chapter 13: Fresh Restart

153. Information for the PFC Thomas E. Fell case was derived from the following sources: *Stars and Stripes*, February 14, 1989, p. 2; *Stars and Stripes*, June 23, 1989, p. 2; personal memory; and records of the Bureau of Prisons (www.bop.gov).

154. John L. Donaldson is a pseudonym.

155. Information on Secretary Cheney was obtained from a PSU Profile.

156. The information on blanket travel orders was obtained from an actual copy of one of my annual DD Form 1610, Jun 67 forms, issued to me in September 1992.

157. Information of the Eighty-Ninth Air Wing fleet of 707s, especially the one with tail number 26000, was mentioned in Dick Cheney's book *In My Time* (New York: Simon & Schuster, 2011; p. 189) and from personal memory.

158. The original code name for the invasion of Panama was Blue Spoon, but the powers at the time did not think this seemed right—a little too frivolous. So, in a meeting between General Thomas Kelley and Rear Admiral Joseph Lopez, Secretary Cheney's eventual senior military aide, they discussed the name and that it needed to be changed. Lopez said, "How about Just Cause?" So, they decided the code name should be changed to Operation Just Cause." Source: Cheney, *In My Time*, p. 175.

159. Information on orders to fire upon the Filipino aircraft was obtained in part from General Colin Powell's autobiography, *My American Journey* (New York: Random House, 1995; p. 443).

160. Information about US Congress slashing money from the amount they had pledged to the Filipino government and being too soft on the coup plotters was obtained in part from the *Chicago Tribune* article "Cheney Visit Riles Filipinos," February 20, 1990.

161. Ibid.

162. Information on the nature of Secretary Cheney's visit to Warsaw, Poland, was partially derived from memory and an article in the *Los Angeles Times*, December 6, 1990.

163. Information in part on the coup in Russia derived in part from the website www.history.com.

164. Information obtained through a review of www.solidarity-us.org.

165. In General Colin Powell's book *My American Journey* (pp. 4, 5), he does not mention Special Agent Hatcher's involvement, nor does he refer to security being on the helicopter with him on February 14, 1992.

166. Information on the La Resistencia was obtained from a review of republican Convention Protests at source: www.republican-convention.org/protest.

167. Comments by General Powell and Secretary Cheney after our PSU car bumped their car when they were leaving the Pentagon were confirmed by the PSO who was riding with them.

CPSIA information can be obtained
at www.ICGtesting.com
Printed in the USA
BVHW06*0917270418
514526BV00007B/190/P

9 781457 561580